Apollo's Struggle

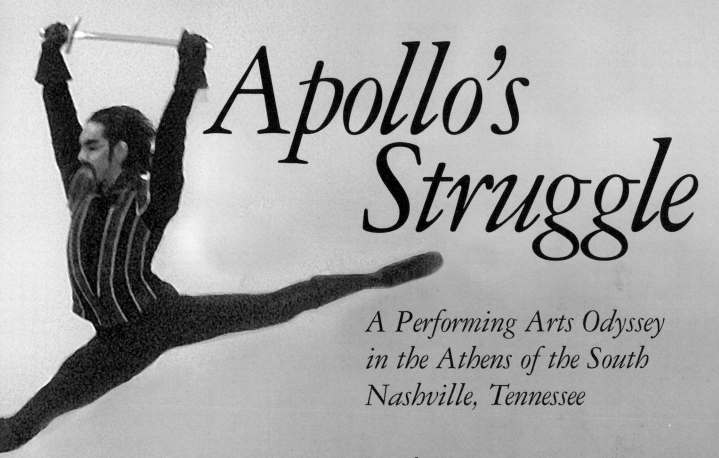

Apollo's Struggle

A Performing Arts Odyssey in the Athens of the South Nashville, Tennessee

Martha Rivers Ingram
with D. B. Kellogg

Hillsboro Press
PROVIDENCE PUBLISHING CORPORATION
FRANKLIN, TENNESSEE

TENNESSEE HERITAGE LIBRARY

Printed in the United States of America

Library of Congress Control Number: 2004104746

ISBN: 1-57736-310-8

Cover design: Susan Hulme

*Front cover photo and art courtesy of The Parthenon, Nashville, Tennessee. Back
cover artwork provided by Earl Swensson Associates; design by David M.
Schwarz/Architectural Services. Inc.*

Title page photo of the Nashville Ballet's production of
Robin Hood *by Marianne Leach. Used by permission.*

*Photo opposite table of contents of Kenneth Schermerhorn and the
Nashville Symphony, Harry Butler, Nashville. Used by permission.*

*Acknowledgments photo of the Nashville Opera's production
of* Turandot *by Marianne Leach. Used by permission.*

Preface photo of Mockingbird Theatre's production of The Glass Menagerie,
*directed by René Copeland in January 2003,
featured Cinda McCain as Amanda and Erin Whited as Laura. Photo by Joe
Hardwick. Used by permission.*

HILLSBORO PRESS
an imprint of
Providence Publishing Corporation
238 Seaboard Lane • Franklin, Tennessee 37067
www.providence-publishing.com
800-321-5692

To
artists, patrons, and audiences,
past and present,
who have participated in
this odyssey and struggle
that today allows Nashville
to justify its claim as
the Athens of the South.
It is my hope that future
artists, patrons, and ever-growing audiences
will sustain this heritage.

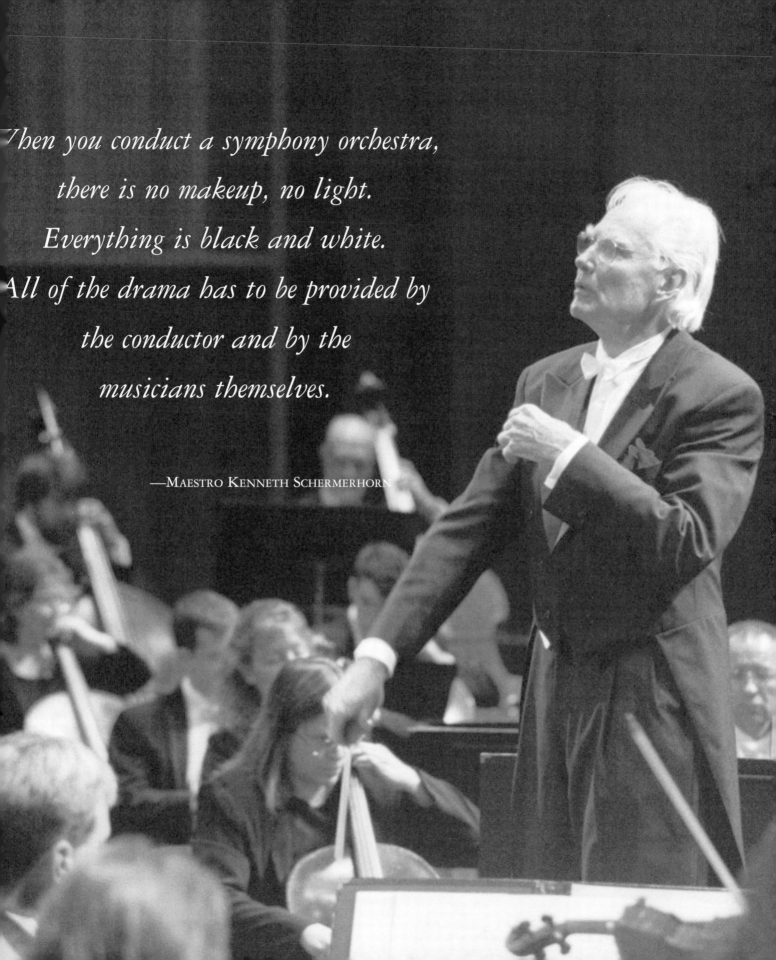

*When you conduct a symphony orchestra,
there is no makeup, no light.
Everything is black and white.
All of the drama has to be provided by
the conductor and by the
musicians themselves.*

—Maestro Kenneth Schermerhorn

We're the fun art form. —CAROL PENTERMAN

ACKNOWLEDGMENTS

COUNTLESS PEOPLE have participated in the creation of this book, and it is impossible to name everyone who has offered input on the topic of the performing arts in Nashville. Many Nashvillians—natives and newcomers—enthusiastically volunteered their experiences and insights, historical and personal. Businessmen and businesswomen, medical doctors, educators, presidents and administrators of universities, philanthropists, writers, musicians, actors, directors, dancers, vocalists, architects, governmental representatives, historians, and staff members of arts organizations—all have shaped this work. Comments from more than sixty formal interviews, conducted by D. B. Kellogg, have been included throughout this work and the interviewees are named and their positions identified, yet it was often an informal remark in a casual conversation with a theatergoer, an actor, or a musician that led to a new avenue of research or a perspective worthy of further exploration.

D. B. Kellogg also helped me by digging through archives, newspapers, and histories and tracking down relevant stories that would shed light on more than two hundred years of Nashville's performing arts history, by bringing order to the massive amount of materials that resulted from the research, and by finding illustrations and photographs. In fact it is quite correct to say that this book would never have known completion without D. B. Kellogg!

Early in the process of developing this topic, Don Doyle, Bill Ivey, John Bridges, John Egerton, and Carroll Van West contributed historical viewpoints, and Larry Adams identified performing artists and groups in recent history. Ridley Wills II helped by pointing out stories and sources, permitting the use of illustrations from his personal collection, and reviewing the manuscript.

The staffs of the Tennessee Performing Arts Center, Nashville Symphony, Nashville Ballet, Nashville Opera, Tennessee Repertory Theatre, and Vanderbilt's Blair School of Music supplied photos, records, and other useful materials. Mercedes Jones, owner's representative and project manager for Schermerhorn Symphony Center, kept me apprised of details about the building and the site.

The librarians throughout the city deserve a round of applause for their help: everyone at the Nashville Room, Nashville Public Library, but especially Carol Kaplan, who reviewed the manuscript; Kathy Smith and Strawberry Luck at Special Collections, the Jean and Alexander Heard Library, Vanderbilt University; Beth Howse and Jessie Carney Smith at the Franklin Library, Fisk University; Darla Brock and Susan Gordon at the Manuscript Division, Tennessee State Library and Archives; Jane Thomas at the Lila D. Bunch Library, Belmont University; and Sharon Hull Smith at Special Collections, Brown-Daniel Library, Tennessee State University.

James Hoobler provided a tour of the Tennessee State Museum's artifacts related to the performing arts. Harold Bradley and others in the Nashville Association of Musicians shared stories, histories, and a rare photo of the early Nashville Symphony. David Grapes of the Tennessee Repertory Theatre permitted the use of actors' photographs from his personal collection.

Frank Sutherland and the *Tennessean* provided several photos from the newspaper's archives free of charge as part of the *Tennessean*'s continuing support of the performing arts.

Special recognition must go to Louis Nicholas, who granted multiple interviews. His personal history extends across most of the twentieth century, and he knew, worked with, or performed with significant people in Nashville's music scene for almost forty years, such as William Strickland, Walter Sharp, Thor Johnson, Charles Bryan, Kenneth Rose, John Lewis, and Joseph Macpherson. Born in 1910 in West Tennessee, Mr. Nicholas moved to Nashville in 1944. He became a vocal teacher at Peabody College, a vocalist, a conductor of church choirs, the president of the National Association of Teachers of Music, and the music editor and critic of the *Tennessean* (1951–75). Mr. Nicholas succeeded Alvin Wiggers, who spent thirty years as an arts reviewer for the *Tennessean*. Before his death at age eighty-seven in 1961, Wiggers had passed on stories of the performing arts to Mr. Nicholas; for example, Wiggers saw the production of *Tannhäuser* in Nashville in 1895. A woman who, as a child, had been in the congregation in 1887 at McKendree Methodist Church told Mr. Nicholas about Emma Abbott and the reverend. In the 1930s Mr. Nicholas heard Rachmaninoff, Paderewski, Jascha Heifetz, and Grace Moore, and he saw Maude Adams in the *Merchant of Venice*. Thank you, Mr. Nicholas, for keeping alive the stories and handing them down to us.

Andrew B. Miller and his staff at Providence Publishing Corporation added their professional touch to give the manuscript its printed form.

Apollo and the Performing Arts

Know thyself. —INSCRIPTION ON THE ORACLE OF APOLLO, DELPHI

GREEK MYTHOLOGY portrayed the multi-faceted Apollo as the leader of the Muses; the patron of the arts; the representation of order, reason, and harmony; the god of light and the god of truth; and the father of Asclepius, god of medicine. People throughout the ages have sought to uphold the ideals represented by the figure of Apollo.

Nashvillians, too, have embraced these ideals. In the medical field the city of Nashville has made a name for itself from its early days, and architecture, education, and government in this Athens of the South reflect the pursuit of excellence. Apollo has not had an easy time of it in regard to the performing arts in Nashville, however. Any positive achievement was hard won, and arts organizers often had to travel torturous paths and endure a multitude of ordeals on their journey. A healthy balance of the arts with other elements in the city is only now coming closer to being a reality as established professional organizations inspire and uplift citizens of all ages and all races.

Nashvillians owe a sincere debt of gratitude to the individuals and the organizations throughout the decades that have attempted to animate the Apollo of the arts, no matter how briefly. A primary reason for this book is to highlight many of the successful arts ventures and identify many of the gifted, talented, hardworking, sometimes hard-headed individuals who have refused to give up in spite of seemingly overwhelming obstacles on the road to success. Please note that I said *many* ventures and people; if I named all

of the artistic high points and notable people, much less explored them in depth, you would be holding a five-pound book in your hands. Instead of using an encyclopedic approach, Mrs. Kellogg and I have selected representative examples of events and individuals after doing extensive research and conducting in-depth interviews with people who are or have been directly involved in the performing arts in Nashville. (Notes, referenced by article titles, are placed in the back of the book.)

The focus of this study is the live performing arts of classical music concerts, theater, opera, and dance from the early 1800s to the present. I have chosen this foursome because they are art forms to which I have devoted personal time, effort, and financial support for more than thirty years and because they are traditional forms that have received less emphasis than popular culture in studies of Nashville. Nevertheless, other artistic endeavors appear briefly in these pages because they are often intertwined with one or more of these four areas.

My hope is that you will come away from your reading of this work with a better understanding of what has happened in the history of the performing arts in Nashville, what it takes to create and maintain a healthy arts environment, and why the performing arts are important to the human spirit. Recognizing that Apollo's struggle will never be at an end in this imperfect world, we can ever aspire to ease that struggle. "Know thyself" is a timeless injunction, just as necessary to us today as it was to the Athenians centuries ago.

*I always thought the performing arts
are for everybody.*

—DAVID ALFORD

PREFACE

Coming from the wilderness, where we had been leading a rather rude life for some time, Nashville, with its airy, salubrious position and its active, bustling population, is quite what an oasis in the desert would be.

—Diary of Mr. Featherstonehaugh,
an early visitor to Nashville

WHEN I ARRIVED at Vassar College back in September 1953, it was a very proud moment. I was a freshman at a college considered one of the best in the nation, yet one that I had never visited until that day. I was wearing a new blue-and-gray tweed suit—my Sunday best—with a matching tulip-shaped hat, high heels, purse, and gloves.

I managed alone the train ride from my hometown of Charleston, South Carolina, in my own roomette and crossed New York City from Pennsylvania Station to Grand Central Station in a taxi, footlocker trunk in tow. Then there was the two-hour train ride on the New York Central to Poughkeepsie with many glimpses of the shimmering Hudson River. At last I took a taxi to the campus to a dormitory called Davison, my new home away from home.

Awaiting me and other arriving freshmen were many helpful upper-classmen, already in knee socks and Bermuda shorts, the style of the day at Vassar. They welcomed me in my traveling outfit without ridicule, as did my assigned roommate, Cinda, from Wyzata, Minnesota. That was the first time I realized that the *r* in the middle of my first name was not silent, and Cinda pronounced one on the end of my name that was not even there! I went from being called "Ma-tha" to "Mar-thar," but I did not mind a bit. It was just wonderful to finally be at Vassar.

I soon shed my suit and hat (which never appeared again that I can recall), donned newly purchased Bermuda shorts and knee socks, and hopped on a bike, the transportation of choice on campus since cars were not allowed. I had never been happier.

There were so many things to get used to, such as dining in a new friend's dorm across the quadrangle. Sheila, the first one to ask me for dinner, was from Boston, and we met in freshman English. She wanted me to see her room, which I soon learned was the customary thing to do before dinner, and she wanted to share with me her large classical record collection. Talk was not about hairstyles, boys, and fingernail polish colors, but about classical composers. Although I had taken piano lessons in Charleston for seven or eight years, I felt stumped when asked to choose my favorite composer. I think I finally stammered out "Johann Strauss," and I began to marvel to myself about the difference between this conversation and the ones to which I was accustomed back home.

I should not have been so surprised, for I had chosen Vassar for this very reason. A handsome Princetonian, Ben, several years older than I, had told me on the beach one summer when I was about sixteen that he would like to ask me out but first I needed to go to a fine college in the Northeast, such as Vassar, where I would become more sophisticated. He said that I should learn about opera, such as *La Traviata* and *La Bohème*. I immediately rushed out to Seigling's Music Store to buy these vinyl discs with my modest allowance. Next I withdrew my application to Sweet Briar in Virginia and applied to Vassar. The head of admissions interviewed me while at a meeting in Williamsburg, and I was accepted. I am certain that geographical distribution worked in my favor, but I continue to be deeply grateful to this day that Vassar took a chance on me. (Incidentally my Princeton friend, Ben, and I never had a date. He married a girl from Sweet Briar, but by then I was so enthralled with Vassar that I hardly gave it a thought.)

My new friends, mostly from metropolitan areas north of the Mason-Dixon line, made me realize by their conversation how little I knew about the exciting world of the arts. I have spent the rest of my adult life indulging this passion and helping to bring the joy of the arts to the various communities in which I have lived—Charleston, New Orleans, but mostly Nashville.

My personal history is not unique for a southern woman. I was brought up to have what were called the social graces. Young women were expected to know how to play the piano in addition to getting the basics in education. I took piano from Hester B. Finger, and somehow I never saw the humor in her name until years later. She was a maiden lady, quite serious about her teaching, and she instructed me to play serious things—Chopin, Bach, Beethoven sonatas—and taught me music terminology. She had recitals every year, which were my first exposure to getting up on the stage by myself and having to play something before an audience— mostly parents, I might tell you.

An outstanding memory of those recitals was my sincere hope that I would not forget what I was supposed to play. Several years I won a couple of the awards. Finally I was getting to a level where I was expected to be rather good, and someone beat me out and got the award because she was considered more improved than I was, even though her recital was not as good as mine. That defeat took the wind out of my sails, and I think I decided, *Well, perhaps this is for somebody else, not for me.*

My parents pushed me to avail myself of other opportunities, so I took ballet. I never could understand why one held one's feet in those funny positions because, you see, I never had seen a full performance of a ballet. This was before the days of TV or videos. I did have some Victrola records of things like *Peter and the Wolf* and *Alice in Wonderland* but no visuals. I think I lasted only a year, but again I learned some of the jargon—*plié, chassé, sauter.*

The summer before entering college, I went on a student tour to Europe with people from around the country. I had been to stage productions in New York with the family because my father, being in the broadcasting business, took us there probably more times than would have been usual for other families from South Carolina. We enjoyed *South Pacific* and *Annie Get Your Gun* and

Harvey. But it was not until the European tour that I saw opera or ballet, and the group went to some symphonies as well. The first opera I saw was *Aida* in the baths of Caracalla in Rome. Talk about starting at the top! That little taste of the arts on the tour only made me want more.

Then at Vassar, after taking Music 140 and Art 105, among numerous other arts-related courses, I came away thinking, *Everybody in the world should be exposed to these things because they are so beautiful, so thrilling, so moving. There must be some way that I can encourage my friends back in Charleston to share my newly found enthusiasm for the arts.* By then I knew that I wanted my life to make a difference, having internalized the admonition of my maternal grandmother, Ola Craig Robinson, to me as a child: that we should strive to make the world a better place by the end of our lives than it was at the beginning.

When I went back to Charleston after graduation from Vassar and started trying to figure out my next step, my father, John Rivers, suggested that I work for him in his broadcasting business, which included WCSC-AM, WCSC-FM, and WCSC-TV, the first television station in South Carolina. If I were any good at it, I might become his successor. (I was the oldest child of three.) He said, "Just show up and start typing in my office because that is the best way for you to learn my business." He had forced me to take a typing course in the summer between my junior and senior years in high school, even though I wanted to be at the beach waterskiing with friends. I was pretty good at typing, at least able to work with the Dictaphone machine, although I never mastered shorthand. I did learn a lot about the broadcasting business from doing that and reading through my father's mail and trade magazines.

The typing job was not very fulfilling, however. I did not feel as though I was doing what I had hoped to do—help bring my friends in Charleston into this whole pleasure palace of arts activities. I asked my father if I could take the FM part of the radio station and program it at night, separately from the AM part. He said, "How would you do this?" I told him I had just read—this was in 1957—that some stations were beginning to separate their AM and FM bands and offer different programming on each. The FM audience would be very small because not many FM receivers were in homes yet. He said, "If you can make it work, if you can find some advertisers, you can do whatever you damn well please. But I think it might be appropriate for you to use a different name because of my being well known in the community and you would be more convincing if you had another name."

Elizabeth Crawford became my broadcast name, after a great-grandmother whom I had never met. I lowered my voice, and I spoke slowly and distinctly (well, at least I thought I was speaking distinctly). I set about creating a program that was to be from seven to eleven, seven nights a week. The first segment, "Candlelight and Wine," went through the dinner hour. It was mostly light, Montavani-type music. Then "Music from the Masters" played. I gave a little information about each performance, and I played full symphonies. I taped the commentary during the daytime and timed it in with the recording because I wanted to go out at night and have dates; I did not want to work twelve hours a day. An engineer spliced my remarks into the music. Some nights were devoted to Beethoven; other nights the feature was the Romantic period, for which I might play Tchaikovsky or some others of the same period. Every Sunday an opera played from eight o'clock until it finished.

That all went rather well until one day my father came to me, pointed to a letter in his hand, and said, "I've got a little of your fan mail here. How strong do you feel?" I said, "I feel okay." He said, "I want to read it to you." I said, "Well, go ahead." He read it: "Dear Mr. Rivers: Why don't you fire that announcer you have on Sunday nights? Her German is so bad when she is introducing the operas that she needs to go!" I absorbed that before asking him, "Oh, dear. I did not know my accent was that bad. What are you going to do?" My father replied, "I want you to take this letter down." It basically stated, "I cannot fire her. She is my daughter, and I am trying to teach her the business."

My career had a few lumps and bumps in it. For about a year and a half, I worked at the combination of being my father's secretary and doing my messianic bit to spread the gospel of classical music. It is a little embarrassing to me now, thinking back on it and how fatuous I was to think I knew enough to teach anyone anything. Yet I thought I did, and I went about the task enthusiastically. The sponsors for the program were mostly banks where I knew the presidents, insurance companies, and at least one real estate company. They were all local people, and the charges to advertise on an FM station were minimal. Then, so were the audiences! We did cross-promote the program from the AM radio station, and we promoted it a little on the television station.

The audiences developed over time. My German improved because I got coaching, but I mostly stayed away from any works involving that language. I did more French and Italian opera because I could bluff my way through those. It was a great experience, and it was my first serious effort to make things better. My engagement and subsequent marriage to Bronson Ingram in October 1958 put an end to my radio project.

Bronson had spent most of his growing-up years in Nashville and had a job in his father's business there. I did not do anything right away except write thank-you notes for wedding presents. We had hardly established our home before we were moved to New Orleans, where I became very involved with the Junior League and the children's theater. I also spent a lot of time with the symphony, but few others from the Junior League or people I had met socially were interested in the symphony. It was very much a repeat of what I had found in Charleston in regard to the arts there. I thought it strange compared to the enthusiasm that my schoolmates at Vassar had shown and their easy conversation about the arts. Because I was young and had a lot of other things going on, including starting a family, I did not really think about it long.

When we moved back to Nashville after almost three years in New Orleans, I discovered that the Nashville Symphony was only modestly supported, yet the Symphony was the primary organization in the performing arts at that time. Even among educated people, the arts were incidental attractions. Again I wondered why.

Now that I have researched the history of the performing arts in Nashville, I have learned about what a rich cultural heritage it has had from its earliest days. It is just that much of it was forgotten, overlooked, or pushed into the background throughout segments of the city's history.

Many factors have come into play in this complex issue, and the following list is not presented in any specific order, other than the first factor. More than a few of these factors can apply to other cities in the South and even across the United States; some are unique to Nashville; all indicate how tightly the cultural life is interwoven into the fabric of a society.

Economics. The number one factor in the vitality of the performing arts is money. That sounds rather basic, but professional artists and support personnel have to be paid, venues have to be built and maintained, costumes or musical instruments have to be available, and audiences need funds to attend performances. The music may not stop completely, the show may go on in some form, but a professional arts organization cannot flourish without a healthy economic structure. Making the huge leap from an amateur to a professional organization, with full-time performing artists, is difficult in any situation, but financial panics, depressions, stock market crashes, or economic slowdowns complicate the process and sometimes bring about the demise of the organization before it can attain professional status. Even in booming financial times there is no guarantee that audiences will spend their dollars on the performing arts.

Diversity of businesses. Nashville has maintained a broad base of major businesses. Agriculture has not dominated the economic scene since the nineteenth century. Even then there were few plantations, and cotton was not king in Middle Tennessee, although today one can see farm land in Davidson and surrounding counties. Education, medicine, wholesale and retail firms, publishing, music, insurance, and banking have provided a healthy mix since 1900.

Attitudes. Nashvillians have inherited dual traditions: a desire for the arts and a suspicion of the arts because they are not "useful" enterprises; the suspicion has too often counterbalanced the desire. In conservative Nashville there has been resistance to the new or the unknown. Whenever an arts organization achieved a certain comfort level, moving it up to the next tier of professionalism has sometimes been perceived as a threat to "the way we have always done things" and to the current group in control of the organization. Consequently there has been a reluctance to push forward to a more professional status. Anti-intellectualism rears its head again and again. The misperception that the performing arts are only for the elite or the rich or the educated class may be tied to a fear of embarrassment about proper attire or proper protocol at a performance. Granted, at one time the *grandes dames* tried to perpetuate the idea that the performing arts

were the exclusive domain of the elite, but that has not been the case in Nashville for decades. Arts groups are working very hard to overcome that persistent attitude.

Education and educational institutions. Nashville was called the Athens of the West and then the Athens of the South as the frontier moved farther west. The early presence of educational institutions—even for young women—earned the city this name. Yet education was not available to all in the city, and public schools were slow to gain acceptance for all youngsters, certainly for African-Americans. Even when schools were in place, illiteracy remained a problem, and ignorance of what the arts can do for human uplift is a part of this illiteracy. Historically education in the arts has had little consistent support, but thank goodness, I can report that that is changing. Nevertheless, Fisk University, Tennessee State University, Peabody College, Ward-Belmont, and the short-lived Nashville Conservatory of Music, among others, have produced notable performing artists. Many people who received an education at local institutions remained in the city because they found it so appealing, and many instructors have been an inspired stabilizing force in the performing arts.

Politics. As the capital, Nashville has a central role in the political life of the state of Tennessee. Beyond that, Nashville has sent presidents, influential senators and congressmen, and others to the national political stage. During political campaigns, especially in presidential election years, money, time, and efforts that might have gone toward the performing arts have been contributed to politics. In the early years of the state almost everything but politics came to a halt in election seasons. Politics in Nashville has been theater.

Geographic location and transportation. From its beginning Nashville *was* the frontier. Its position on the Cumberland River worked to its benefit to permit people and goods to be transported to the town, despite being on the edge of civilization. Performing artists made Nashville part of their circuit because of the river access. Not being on the seacoast or on a major river such as the Mississippi limited its development on the scale of that of New Orleans or Charleston, however. The introduction of railroads made the city a more accessible stop and contributed to its growth. Today 50 percent of the U.S. population is within a 650-mile radius of the city, and Nashville has a convergence of interstate highways and an international airport. Not only do performing artists readily come to Nashville, but many live here and take advantage of the location to travel to other cities for performances.

Family heritage. Lucky was the family that had among its members someone who appreciated the performing arts or was actually a performer and passed on that love to his or her children or grandchildren, who in turn passed it on. A wonderful turn of events now is that children who have had arts education are encouraging their parents to become participants in the arts.

The Nashville Association of Musicians. Local 257 of the American Federation of Musicians, which celebrated its one hundredth anniversary in 2002, has provided continuity for musicians and support to help them gain living wages, pensions, and fair contracts. Talented people who might otherwise have left the community have been able to remain here and contribute to the community in many ways beyond their professions.

Social issues. The attempts to ban alcohol and to gain the right to vote for women literally consumed the waking hours of supporters and opponents. It is a wonder that anything else was accomplished in the city when those lengthy campaigns were under way.

Governments. Sometimes ordinances and laws had a direct impact on the performing arts, but just as often they had unintended consequences.

War taxes and, at least at one point, an entertainment tax on nonprofits really hit them hard. (The Metropolitan Opera in New York City almost went under because of this tax, so you can imagine what happened in arts groups in smaller cities.) Politicians' support could mean the difference between the failure or the success of a performing arts venture. Two success stories are found in the unique cooperation between the private and the public sectors in the creation of the Tennessee Performing Arts Center in the 1970s, and in the development of Schermerhorn Symphony Center, which will be completed in 2006. The last two mayors of Nashville—Phil Bredesen and Bill Purcell—have been arts proponents who have recognized that the city is about more than sewers and streets, important as structural improvements are to a city's well-being.

Work ethic. Primarily men were allowed in the workforce for many years, leaving arts development to women. Arts were approved for exhibition purposes only (that is, your daughter could play the piano or sing for family and friends, but you did not want her to become a professional artist or your son to become an actor). There has always been an emphasis on making money as a sign of having "arrived," and choosing the arts as a career path was far from compatible with that. Yet professional performing artists who dance in the Ballet or who play in the Symphony do have a "real" job—one for which they have trained and practiced countless hours and to which they have devoted their talents and gifts.

Leadership. Performing arts organizations are strong when a strong leader, such as a managing director, artistic director, or executive director, is in place. A board of directors composed of dedicated, savvy members is essential.

Vision. Having the vision is not enough; it has to be supported with work, money, and boosterism to make the public accept the vision and go along with it. Actually Nashville has been long on vision—just short on many other essential components to make that vision a reality. The tedious journey to build the Municipal Auditorium is one example, and it still did not meet the needs of the classical performing arts.

Technology. Technological advances have enabled people even in rural areas to hear—and later see—performers. With the introduction of Victrolas, Americans played recordings of singers and musicians. Radio introduced many people to classical music, although WSM carried country music and often sermons or Sunday school lessons between classical music performances. Movies were available almost nightly whereas other performing arts were not available except during the "season." Then television shows such as *The Bell Telephone Hour* presented ballet dancers and opera singers, *Playhouse 90* broadcast dramas, and *Voice of Firestone* featured classical and semiclassical music. Videos, CDs, and DVDs permit people to have high-quality recordings in their own homes, and now with CD burners people make their own recordings. Nashvillians (and people in other communities) have yet to see the full extent to which the Internet will affect the performing arts.

Personal relationships. Who knows how many personal relationships have been responsible for bringing performing artists to Nashville? Many of those conversations are not recorded anywhere. I can say with certainty that having Francis Robinson in New York City at the Metropolitan Opera enabled Lula Naff to bring all kinds of performances to the Ryman Auditorium that might not have happened otherwise. Francis was able to put in a word to major stars with whom he was acquainted. Two young women, Sarah Jeter and Louise Smith, were friends of Ruth St. Denis and Ted Shawn. They brought modern dance to a city that has chosen to have little to do with dance. Musicians in the past and the present have

had a network often reaching to international boundaries and have been able to recommend (or in some cases to veto) the appointment of a teacher to a position or the appearance of a particular performer.

Wars. The Civil War was pivotal in Nashville's history, as it was in the history of other southern cities. Nashville was an occupied town for most of the war. There was a cost in lives but also in real dollars and a general deflation of spirit. People's aspirations seemed to evaporate, and self-image was badly damaged. As local young men were called into the service during World Wars I and II, the town's attention turned to the support of war efforts. Many young servicemen had the opportunity to join a military band or chorus or a Special Services orchestra and gain valuable experience that they brought home with them.

The GI Bill. Following World War II, many young men went to college for the first time and others gained advanced degrees in music or drama, thanks to the GI Bill. Peabody College's music department drew aspiring musicians, some of whom remained in Nashville to teach or to perform.

Newspapers. The various newspapers throughout the city's history advertised upcoming events and often reviewed them. Sometimes previews of the events had an educational purpose, informing citizens of what to expect and occasionally explaining how they should behave at a performance. Even an individual who was unable to attend—but could read or could have someone read the paper to him—would have an understanding of what he missed, from the glorious clothing of the audience or performers to the misbehavior of a few uncouth bumpkins to the wondrous sounds of an Emma Abbott or the elocution of an Edwin Booth.

Health issues. Epidemics of cholera, yellow fever, and smallpox halted gatherings of all kinds. Many people who had the financial means fled the city, either permanently or briefly, until the threat passed. Performing artists would not come to town during an epidemic, even if they had been scheduled to do so. Better to lose a few dollars than one's life.

Slavery, segregation, and desegregation. The practice of slavery diminished both the African-American and the white populations of Nashville. The city's early policies directed toward African-Americans were quite progressive. A noted early tavern was called Black Bob's, owned by Bob Renfro (who gained his freedom *after* he started running the tavern); free African-American men could vote until the 1830s. After the Civil War, the city's recovery was complicated by the building of two school systems: one for whites and the other for African-Americans. By restricting access of various kinds, slavery and segregation hampered the development of individuals' gifts—whether in the arts or in other areas. Desegregation orders continue to affect the city's school system. Although the civil rights movement did not have a smooth, easy path in Nashville, the community escaped most of the horrific experiences of southern cities such as Birmingham and Little Rock.

Religious beliefs and houses of worship. Yesterday, fiery sermons against the theater and dance were fairly commonplace; today, some houses of worship offer dramas and dance in their services. People who could not afford to attend the theater or who had convictions against entering a theater—even to hear a musical group or an opera singer—could bask in the music in their houses of worship, and there are an abundance of them throughout the city. The building of local churches and synagogues and the funding of missions—at home and abroad—at different periods have called upon people to dig very deep into their pockets and their sources of energy. The presence of denominational publishing houses and associated boards has meant that local people have had a role in shaping what the nation was reading in authorized religious materials.

Venues. Entrepreneurs and civic-minded people have provided venues for the performing arts that would appeal to the artists and the audiences. Whereas some cities were lucky to have a little hall or a school auditorium, Nashville has had the Adelphi and the Vendome and the Ryman and the Bijou and the War Memorial Auditorium and the Grand Ole Opry House and the Tennessee Performing Arts Center—and soon the new Schermerhorn Symphony Center.

Population makeup and density. The core population of Nashville has historically been of Scotch-Irish or English descent. African-Americans were on the scene early, as free blacks and slaves. Only small numbers of Germans and other Europeans settled in the city. Today Nashville is more ethnically diverse than it has ever been, with Latinos, Kurds, Bosnians, Vietnamese, Koreans, Chinese, and more. The growth of the city has been steady, not explosive, in numbers.

Climate. Nashville has a rather moderate climate, rarely exceeding 100 degrees or going below zero. But it is still hot and humid in the summertime, often feeling hotter than the thermometer would indicate. Weather affected the season of the performing arts in earlier times, extending through early fall to early spring. During the summer, indoor performances were rare—the heat was bad enough, but because of having the windows open, the noise from outside the venue made it almost impossible to enjoy what was happening. Outdoor performances were held, but a downpour of rain or extreme heat could cancel them. (The bugs and the mosquitoes were other unwelcome attractions.) The next factor is closely tied to this one.

Air-conditioning. Oh, what a marvelous invention! No one who grew up, as I did, before the days of air-conditioning can truly appreciate how hot a summer night can be. The *Long Hot Summer* meant more to us than the title of a film. This invention did more to change the South than perhaps any other. It has affected population growth, new or expanded businesses, architecture, and family and social life.

Sports. Hunting, fishing, foot racing, horse racing, baseball, golf, tennis, boating, football, basketball, stock car racing, ice hockey—the list is long. Nashvillians have often been so enthralled by sports that other endeavors have been neglected, yet balance is the key to a well-rounded citizenry.

The great outdoors. The allure of a city park may overpower the allure of the Tennessee Performing Arts Center on occasion, and people just will not go indoors on a beautiful evening. City parks have been the sites of performances of the Nashville Symphony and other musical groups, and the Parthenon has been the backdrop for outdoor dramas and dance ensembles.

Enlightened philanthropists. Being willing to donate funds to an organization is commendable, but it is my position that one should also contribute time and personal energy. Just throwing money at something does not give a person the satisfaction of really having made a contribution—nor is it any assurance that one's dollars will be well spent. Within my family we have chosen to support organizations about which we have passionate feelings, and we want to see our funds used wisely. The number of people in Nashville with substantial means has grown exponentially within the past fifteen to twenty years, and they have made a difference in the financial health of many performing arts groups. Yet the category of enlightened philanthropists certainly includes people with lesser means who understand the importance of participation as well as monetary support.

The star syndrome. From the time of Jenny Lind's appearance (1851) a performing artist who has been labeled a star has almost always been able to fill theaters in Nashville, and sometimes at an exorbitant price for tickets. That is all well and good, but the syndrome has also carried with it the notion that homegrown artists have not reached the quality of stars from elsewhere—and sometimes that notion has persisted after a hometown artist has become famous in Europe or throughout the United States.

Serendipity. Things often work out in unexpected ways for the good, whether it is a child who is given a flute instead of a violin—and then goes on to become an educator and a performing artist—or a young soldier with a passion for the performing arts who meets a young conductor and convinces him to create a new symphony in town.

Human nature. Some people's love of the performing arts is never quenched while other people cannot be bribed to attend a performance of any kind, even though they have had the best education and easy access to the best performances. Sometimes audiences are fickle; despite having built up a good relationship with an audience and offering high-quality work, arts organizers can be sorely disappointed or surprised by attendance. One cannot account for human nature.

Through my work with the performing arts, I have experienced the effects of many of these factors, both positive and negative. I did not realize it while I was living through the events, but my involvement in the formation of the Tennessee Performing Arts Center was like a years-long, learn-as-you-go graduate course in this whole topic.

The Tennessee Performing Arts Center

It was something that would serve the entire state because it was the Tennessee *Performing Arts Center.*

—ANNETTE ESKIND

PUT TOGETHER a man with a vision, a luncheon of several women with strong interests in the community, and a site at Metro Center, and what do you get? The birth of a performing arts center.

Victor Johnson had gathered us for lunch in his Aladdin Industries executive dining room to make a presentation about what Metro Center was to be—a city within a city worthy of Nashville proper. Among other projected buildings was a performing arts center by the river, but he admitted he had not been having much luck with any backers among city leaders. After he finished his slide show, he asked, "Are there any questions?" I said, "Well, you remember you mentioned that you had set aside some property for a performing arts center at Metro Center and that the city fathers had turned it down." He said, "Yes, that's right." I asked, "Well, would you give the *city mothers* a shot at it?" He responded, "Why, sure." That meeting was the impetus behind what became the Tennessee Performing Arts Center, although it ended up being built downtown, not in Metro Center.

At that luncheon in 1972 I suddenly realized that somebody in Nashville could visualize a performing arts center. It was the first I had heard of anything concrete. I knew about the fiasco with the Municipal Auditorium and how that had gotten off track. Leaders at National Life had talked about having an auditorium that would be suitable for plays and small concerts right across from the War Memorial Auditorium. That had gone nowhere. Now here was a glimmer of hope, so I pursued it with several other women I knew.

Annette Eskind recalled, "You [Martha] talked to a few of us later about the performing arts center; the group was a heterogeneous group of women, embodying the black and the white communities, which was to your credit. That really had not happened before in terms of initial planning. After all, we did not want this to be a Belle Meade project. And indeed it really wasn't. If anybody thinks it is, that's his problem. It brought in the entire community."

A new group was formed, the Tennessee Performing Arts Center Advisory Board, to push the idea forward. There were no bylaws, no formal structure, because the group did not intend to last any longer than it needed to last to get the job done. The goal was to act as lobbyists. Members of the new group were united in wanting to provide more opportunities for people to participate in the performing arts—as audiences or artists—and the city needed a facility for that. The initial members were Gertrude Caldwell, Annette Eskind, Jean Heard, Clara Hieronymus, Sarah Mac Jarman, Ann Kennedy, Lillian Lawson, Alyne Massey, Sue Morris, Chippy Pirtle, Frances Preston, Ann Roos, Peggy Steine, Ann Wells, Mary Jane Werthan, Anne Wilson, and I. Through her articles in the *Tennessean*, Clara Hieronymus kept readers informed about what was happening as the weeks turned into months before the project ended—eight years later!

Our first thought was to set an appointment with Mayor Beverly Briley. Annette's involvement

TPAC, completed in the fall of 1980, is in the James K. Polk Building.

with the Metro school board gave us easy access to him. When asked to support a performing arts center, the mayor informed us in no uncertain terms that his interest was in funding the sewer system that was under construction as well as the interstate ramps that were needed to complete access to the new highway system. So much for help from the mayor's office!

With a feeling of utter rejection, Annette and I—who had made the call—licked our wounds at Candyland (now Vandyland). Over a milkshake and a sandwich, we asked ourselves, "What next?" Having been recently appointed to the advisory board of the newly opened Kennedy Center for the Performing Arts in Washington, D.C., I desperately wanted something comparable for Nashville—for my children, for my friends, for my community, for myself.

The mention of Washington midway through lunch reminded Annette of an article that she had seen describing the federal government's proposed Bicentennial celebration plans—still four years in the future (1976). Each state would receive $1 million to create its own commemorative event. Should we not appeal to the new governor to secure Tennessee's $1 million? It would be a start. (Of course, we did not know at that point that the federal money that renewed our hopes would never materialize for Tennessee or any other state.) How would we get an appointment with the newly elected governor, Winfield Dunn?

I called Anne Wilson, who had been at Victor Johnson's luncheon, and said, "The mayor has turned us down flat. Do you think Pat could get us an appointment with Winfield Dunn?" Winfield had been elected governor with much help from Anne's husband, Pat, and had begun his term in 1971. Pat was able to arrange a meeting for us.

We planned to ask Governor Dunn if he would consider pledging the expected $1 million coming to Tennessee to celebrate the Bicentennial and add more money from the state of Tennessee. It could be a showcase for the arts that were in existence and, we hoped, a beacon to encourage more professionalism in the arts. All of the people in the state would benefit more from that than from transitory fireworks displays or elaborate parades in 1976.

Anne Wilson, Annette Eskind, and I entered the state Capitol with great confidence for the meeting with Governor Dunn. I just knew that if we suggested this obviously wonderful idea of a performing arts center in Nashville, the state would take over, and we could go home and do what we normally did in our lives. How wrong I was!

We briefly stated our case, stressing that we must have culture as well as commerce in Tennessee. The governor said, "Let me call in Ted Welch." (Ted was the state's finance commissioner.) After listening to us for a few minutes, Ted asked, "It sounds like a nice idea, but what would go on in such a place?" We told him that we envisioned a replication of the Kennedy Center in Washington, D.C. They agreed to think more about it.

Many years later I learned that after we left, Governor Dunn and Commissioner Welch turned to each other and asked, "Do you think Martha has the staying power to see such a project to its conclusion?" (Anne and Annette had indicated that they had other pressing matters with which they were involved.) If I had known what I was getting into, I might have asked the same question.

At a second meeting with the governor and Commissioner Welch, I presented material to them—furnished by Victor Johnson's Metro Center consultants—about what other cities were doing; there were only five or six performing arts centers in the country at that time. Robert Lamb Hart, master planner and architect, put the whole

War Memorial Auditorium

In 1925 the city finally had a facility that was to be the home of the Nashville Symphony, under the direction of F. Arthur Henkel. Dedicated in September of that year, the War Memorial Auditorium had been approved by an act of the legislature in 1919 as a memorial for the Tennessee servicemen who fought in World War I. It cost $2.6 million ($1.2 million from the state, $1 million from the city, and $400,000 from the county; $2.6 million then, about $26.7 million today), and it seated 2,200. As part of the effort, Governor A. H. Roberts had to acquire and demolish a block of elegant houses for the site, including the governor's residence. The War Memorial Auditorium was a public building, built with public money, on a state government site, and the state government controlled the building from 1925 to 1999.

Not only the Nashville Symphony but also other orchestras and musicians took advantage of the new venue. In January 1926, for example, Henkel conducted a Sunday afternoon concert of the Nashville Symphony with Mary Cornelia Malone as soloist. The numbers included Tchaikovsky's "1812 Overture," Wagner's "Lohengrin," and the premier performance in the South of "The Call of the Plains" by Rubin Goldmark, an American composer who had studied with Dvořák. A "unique social event" was the appearance of the Minneapolis Symphony, with Henri Verbruggen conducting, on February 10, a Wednesday. The matinee was at 3:00 and the evening performance at 8:15. The matinee cost 50 cents for children and $1 for adults. Later in February, Florence Macbeth performed "Three Generations of Prima Donnas" with George Roberts as her accompanist; the music department of the Centennial Club sponsored the event. Macbeth, coloratura star of the Chicago Grand Opera Company, stopped in Nashville on her way to Chattanooga to sing the leading soprano role in *The Barber of Seville*. The Symphony led by Henkel had disappeared, however, by the 1930s.

It was not many years before the inadequacies of War Memorial precipitated a call for a new hall for the performing arts. In 1949 a meeting held at the Watkins Institute, as part of the weekly "Let's Think" discussions, featured a panel of Walter Sharp, Charles S. Mitchell, Sydney Dalton, and George Pullen Jackson. The moderator was Will R. Manier Jr. A small audience attended to hear the consensus that "the War Memorial Auditorium is too small to meet the city's musical demands, and . . . Ryman auditorium meets the requirements acoustically, but just doesn't have 'class.'" Charles Mitchell recalled the time more than twenty-five years before when Nashvillians would not sit through a symphonic program, but he added that the early endeavors developed a taste for the music. The Nashville Symphony, the one chartered in 1946, that is, continued to use War Memorial Auditorium until 1980 when TPAC was completed.

As of 1999 TPAC undertook the management of the auditorium, which had been refurbished in 1995. Further improvements were made after that to permit the removal of 775 orchestra-level seats to use flexible seating and tables on its flat surface. The venue has received new life and has had successful bookings of musical and social events.

concept together. He had, in fact, worked with Victor Johnson in developing a master plan for Metro Center. When Victor asked him what Nashville needed more than anything else, Bob said, "An arts center." So he recognized the elements of a well-balanced city. Governor Dunn expressed interest but emphasized that if the state became involved, the facility would have to be downtown in the government complex. That meant that the Metro Center site would no longer be an option. The governor also wanted to know what the private sector would contribute.

I said, "We will raise money for an endowment if the state will put up the building." The estimated amount needed for an endowment was between $3.5 and $4 million (about $15 and $17 million today). I left that meeting with a mixture of feelings. The governor had not said "no" immediately to the idea—that was exciting. I had just talked about raising millions of dollars, a huge sum at the time, and I had never done anything like that—that was a bit unnerving.

My mother-in-law, Mrs. O. H. Ingram, was a clear thinker who had an almost uncanny ability to understand finance. I could count on her to offer sound recommendations. I went by her house to tell her of this extraordinary meeting with the governor. She was not home, but I wanted to tell someone, so I went next door to Alyne and Jack Massey's house and described the highlights of the meeting. (Alyne had also been at Victor Johnson's luncheon.)

Both were supportive of the performing arts center, and both knew the necessity of having an endowment to make it succeed. Alyne noted, "Jack was adamant that we have a foundation because of what happened in Atlanta. People in Atlanta had promised a lot of money to build a performing arts center, and suddenly they all died together in an airplane crash." (In 1962 more than one hundred cultural leaders of Atlanta, returning from a tour sponsored by the Atlanta Art Association, were killed in a plane crash at Orly Field, near Paris. On that day in June, the city's cultural history was radically changed.) Others in Atlanta used their money for bricks and mortar. There was nothing left. There was no endowment. They had opened their performing arts center but had to close until they could raise operating capital. Having learned from Atlanta's experience, we determined that the state should build the building and we (the

private sector) would build the endowment. The performing arts center would use the income from the endowment to make up deficits between operating expenses and income, bring performers to the arts center and send some to other cities, and commission original works by Tennessee composers and writers.

The next person I called was Pat Wilson. Pat had been president of the Symphony board, and he and Anne loved music and loved the Symphony. They could see how this center could promote other things. I said, "Pat, this is what Winfield Dunn and Ted Welch have at least verbally tossed toward us. Do you think we could raise this amount for an endowment?" He said that we would need to present it to the Group. (The Group was composed of civic leaders who met occasionally and unofficially to cooperate on initiatives in the city; it was later known as Watauga.) With their support we would have a chance. He also told me that he and Anne would be willing to participate financially. Pat could see the vision, and I knew he could add to it, which was even more significant than his financial contribution.

Jack and Pat were behind us logistically and financially for this entity that we decided to call the Tennessee Performing Arts Center (TPAC). Being very unsure of myself in a business way, I also asked my husband, Bronson, if he would become involved. He agreed. All of us went to the meeting with the Group, and Pat explained the idea. The Group believed that it would be a boon for the city and the state but was doubtful that we could pull it off and raise the funds. Perhaps we should hire a lobbyist to help. (A young lawyer, Bill Leech from Columbia, Tennessee, was retained; he later became attorney general for Tennessee.)

We took it from there and formed the Tennessee Performing Arts Foundation, which became the fund-raising arm for TPAC. Jack

Jackson Hall, here still under construction, is the largest of the three theaters at the Tennessee Performing Arts Center.

became chairman of the board, Pat became vice president and treasurer, and I became secretary. Warner Bass, a young lawyer at the time, helped us with incorporation and other legal matters. Bronson was an advisor, not an official member. Bronson, Pat, Jack, and Bill Weaver Jr. (CEO of the National Life Insurance Co.) pledged $250,000 each to get the campaign started, and we eventually raised $5 million. At an organizational meeting in July 1973 the following people were elected directors of the foundation: Dr. Andrew D. Holt (Knoxville; president of the University of Tennessee), Scott Probasco (Chattanooga), Norfleet Turner Jr. (Memphis), William L. Barry (Lexington, Tennessee), Thomas D. Baker (Nashville), Dorothy Ritter (Nashville), Bernard Werthan (Nashville), and Athens Clay Pullias (Nashville).

We wanted people in each of Tennessee's three grand divisions—West, Middle, and East—to feel included in this effort to establish TPAC as a place for cultural exchange in the state. The foundation had a fifty-six-member women's advisory board, and each woman had a subcommittee in her community. The advisory board member was to help raise funds and lobby her legislative representative. People agreed to host teas, coffees, and parties to promote TPAC to friends and neighbors. Sarah Cannon, Dorothy Ritter (wife of Tex), and Chet Atkins were enthusiasts from Music Row.

During our negotiations with Governor Dunn and Commissioner Welch, we were asked where in the capitol complex we would like to see this performing arts center. When we suggested that we would be delighted with the site of the recently imploded Andrew Jackson Hotel, the officials informed us that the site was taken. The state government had plans for a new state office building already on the drawing board. (The Nashville Housing Authority had to grant the state permission to use the site, so the city did become involved in the project at least to this extent.)

As though a light bulb had been turned on, we suggested that the state office building be "lifted" and the performing arts center slipped in at ground level. The office workers could use the lobby space during the day, theatergoers could use the same space during the evening, and best of all, there would be no need for more real estate.

This concept was applauded by the state officials, who soon added a state museum in the building's basement. Altogether it became the James K. Polk Building with a greatly enlarged scope. It was estimated that the addition of the three-theater performing arts center increased the building's cost by $13 million—a bargain for both the state and the Tennessee taxpayer. We were off and running. I thought it was going to be a sprint, but it turned out to be an eight-year marathon.

Plans were moving forward, and I was becoming optimistic that we could actually have a performing arts center. Then a low point came at a meeting at my home of the heads of the existing arts groups throughout Nashville. I described the project and stated that I wanted them to be fully informed because I was hopeful that some of them might be eager to use the facility and that some amateur groups might turn professional.

Someone stood up and declared, "I am just so angry with you. I can't believe that anyone seeing all that we need here in Nashville would do something instead for the whole state. The local groups need that money."

I was so flabbergasted that I was speechless. I could not understand the shortsightedness of that position. Here we were going to build a beautiful new facility, and these people were performing in musty, dusty old movie theaters. I thought that they would be thrilled with the opportunity to turn professional. As it turned out, most of them had other, daytime jobs. They were not interested in professionalism at all. I realized that they wanted to have total control of the space and not have it run by a group such as the board of TPAC. Some of those people were sniping at our heels at every opportunity, but there was enough strength in our organization that we were able to proceed.

Building support for TPAC in the legislature was another challenge. Having Republican Governor Dunn on our side was not enough because legislation would have to be passed for a bond issue and Democrats controlled both the House and the Senate. Ned Ray McWherter became the new Speaker of the House in 1973; John Wilder had been Speaker of the Senate (and thus lieutenant governor) since 1971, so he, too, was fairly new in his office. I spoke to both men.

When I went to see Ned, he said, "You have to make friends with the head of the House Ways and Means Committee, Representative John Bragg." I made an appointment to see Representative Bragg in Murfreesboro because I had been advised that it was a good idea to see people in their hometown offices. After I made my case to him, John said, "I just have to ask you why you want to do this. I'm like that country boy whose wife took him to Atlanta to see the ballet. He looked up there and saw all those girls running around on their tippytoes, and he said, 'Honey, if they want those girls to look so tall, why don't they just hire taller girls in the first place?'" I said, "Well, you know, Representative Bragg, this is something that we need to do. We need to make it so that people can understand why they don't just hire taller girls." I thought, *Wow, this is going to be more difficult than I thought.* The late John

Bragg and I often laughed about this first meeting, and even after that shaky beginning, he became one of our staunch supporters throughout the legislative struggle.

Ned McWherter needed no convincing. He thought that Tennessee children should have more opportunities for exposure to the performing arts. He said in his West Tennessee style: "Honey, if you're willing to put your money into it and work for it, there must be something to it. If you'll do that, I'll support you." He was true to his word. (I found out later that his college-age children had discovered the arts in Europe because he could afford to send them there. He realized others with less wealth did not have this chance.)

To meet Lieutenant Governor John Wilder on his home turf was also important. I flew into the tiny West Tennessee town of Somerville one dreary, rainy day. My meeting with him was at his office over a cafe on the town square. Settling into his waiting room, I was most surprised to see two reproduction prints of scenes from my hometown of Charleston, South Carolina: one was of St. Philip's Episcopal Church, which my family had attended for years and where my father was still senior warden; the other was of my family's home on Church Street. I happened also to have these prints in my Nashville home, but to see them in Somerville as decorative art was quite a remarkable coincidence. Our meeting went well, and

This aerial view of TPAC taken while it was under construction gives perspective on its placement in the Tennessee State Capitol complex.

The Long-Awaited Municipal Auditorium

An official proposal to construct a municipal auditorium surfaced in October 1941. Of course, there had been talk about it long before then. The proposal for a $1.35 million city auditorium with seating for 8,000 also involved tearing down the Ryman Auditorium. From the beginning two sides formed: (1) performing arts proponents who wanted a place for concerts, plays, and lectures, and (2) others who envisioned a place for sports events and exhibitions. The attack on Pearl Harbor and the declaration of war put a halt to further action. It was 1949 before the General Assembly authorized a $5 million bond issue, subject to Nashville voters' approval, for a civic auditorium. The performing arts people worked hard, with help from the Chamber of Commerce and Trades & Labor Council, and the referendum for $5 million passed.

Then serious lobbying began. What about location? Heated discussion touched on sites of the Ryman Auditorium and lower Broadway; Church Street near the west end of the viaduct; somewhere near Centennial Park; McGavock Street; and between Fourth and Fifth Avenues North, the latter being the choice. The Centennial Park site had so much opposition that the entire project nearly ended in 1950.

The City Council voted to issue the $5 million auditorium bonds in November 1957 (about $32 million today). Three ideas for the structure were (1) a modern theater and concert hall, (2) a small auditorium with a large arena nearby, and (3) an auditorium in conjunction with a hotel. Mayor Ben West thought that having a hotel, with underground parking, plus a convention hall and theater would be a worthwhile effort, but his vision was not to be. The theater facilities were rejected; the people from the Symphony, Circle Players, and Community Concerts lost their fight, despite having Francis Robinson, a man with a longtime Nashville connection then working at the Metropolitan Opera House, come to town at least twice to speak on the importance of having an honest-to-goodness performing arts facility. (Francis even held out the possibility of bringing the Metropolitan Opera if the city had a proper hall.) Construction started in June 1960, and the auditorium was completed in October 1962, thirteen years after the referendum passed. It has never been a suitable space for the classical performing arts, *but* it does have air-conditioning.

John Wilder remained one of our supporters throughout the elongated process.

The vote came up in the House on March 19, 1974. The act passed easily, but the proposed name of the structure was changed from the John Sevier Building to the James K. Polk Building. The next day the bill was debated in the Senate. Many senators were hostile, one attacking the performing arts center as a "sop for Nashville's affluent." The vote was delayed a week.

Matt Lynch, the head of the state labor board, had encouraged Senator Avon Williams to support the bill. Matt had become a booster because his wife, Maude, was a member of our advisory committee. Avon represented one of the historically poorer districts, and before the Senate vote, he made an impassioned speech in the legislature on behalf of TPAC, saying, "There is more to life than just bread and meat. The poor people need more than bread and meat, too." Despite protests from others, the Senate bill passed 23-7 on March 27. I am convinced that Avon Williams's words carried the day.

Governor Dunn signed the following act on April 5, 1974:

An Act to authorize the State of Tennessee, acting by resolution of its Funding Board, to issue and sell its institutional and public building interest-bearing general obligation bonds and bond anticipation notes in an amount not to exceed Thirty-six ($36,000,000) million dollars for the purpose of building a state office building, including office space for state government, a general auditorium for use by state government for training, seminars, and workshops and by the general public for performing arts, educational and cultural facilities, including planning, the acquisition of real estate and equipping of facilities, and to provide for the expenditure of said funds.

The projected completion date was July 4, 1976. On July 1, 1974, we opened the office of the Tennessee Performing Arts Foundation as guests of the Third National Bank Branch (now SunTrust), 4304 Harding Road, and also held a symbolic groundbreaking ceremony downtown where the center would be located. It was symbolic because we were literally unable to break the ground; the old hotel site had become a parking lot. Political figures, including a member of President Nixon's cabinet, Secretary of Housing and Urban Development James T. Lynn, and private citizens were on hand. What a milestone!

Construction did not begin until 1976, however, and the dream of TPAC came perilously close to being only that. Ray Blanton followed Winfield Dunn as governor, assuming office in 1975. Blanton had decided to stop TPAC completely, but I did not find out about that until I was in a meeting with him in 1976. Fortunately I had asked Bronson to accompany me because Blanton had made inappropriate remarks to me earlier at a social event. Even though the hole in the ground for the building was already dug and we had raised the money that we said we would raise, Blanton said that he was going to pull out the performing arts center part of the architectural plans and put in a parking garage! That was the *lowest point* of the whole project. My heart sank when I heard him say "parking garage."

At Bronson's suggestion he and I immediately went to talk to Ned McWherter. That great, kind bear of a man hugged me and said, "Don't worry. We have committed to you, and I will see that we live up to that commitment." All of a sudden that became a *high point* because I knew I could trust Ned.

From that moment there were more lows than highs. The $36 million bond issue had been approved, but the initial bids came in at $42 million, and the state ordered a redrawing of the plans to cut $6 million out of the building costs. To accommodate that change, the architects lowered the lobby ceiling, eliminated the escalators and theater lobby elevator, and built fewer rest rooms. The initial plans had called for a conservatory-style lobby with fountains and trees, one that would let light in all day. It would have been good for state employees as well as arts patrons, but these features were tossed.

Chief architect Bruce Crabtree, of the firm Taylor and Crabtree, was distraught over the mutilation of his beautiful design, which filled 540 sheets of drawings. Bruce had traveled at his own expense to the few performing arts centers then in existence so that he could learn from their successes and failures. I remember accompanying him on the trip to the Milwaukee Performing Arts Center. We arrived in the largest performance space (Uihlein Hall) just as the Milwaukee Symphony was rehearsing Camille Saint-Saëns' Symphony No. 3 (The Organ Symphony). (The dynamic conductor on the podium happened to be Kenneth Schermerhorn, then music director of the Milwaukee Symphony. Our delegation never met him then and, of course in the early 1970s, had no way of knowing that he would become the Nashville Symphony's own music director in 1983, sparking Nashville's plans to build a world-class orchestra.) I remember the thunderous, explosive entrance of the organ that begins the last movement of this magnificent symphony. Bruce was so thrilled by the sound that he had tears in his eyes and could not speak for a time. It was there, I think, that he dedicated himself emotionally to creating the best building for the arts that he could possibly design. His devotion to this complicated project never wavered—no matter that he had to include a state museum in addition to a performing arts center, all sandwiched into the original office building that he had been hired to create in the first place. He never lost his enthusiasm despite the brutal financial cuts and difficult hurdles he encountered.

Compromises with the state had to be made all the way through the process. At least the insides of the theaters were not affected. Inflation was so severe during the year of redesign that it ate up the difference, and the cost to the state was $42 million anyway—minus all of the original refinements. (Here is some idea of what was happening: the prime interest rate in July 1972 was 5.25 percent; in March 1974 it was 8.85 percent, and it shot up to 12.00 percent by August of that year. The prime rate continued to bounce up and down throughout the project; the high in 1980 was 20.35 percent.) The design with an eighteen-story office building, theaters, and a museum complicated the engineering, causing slow progress. The bad news included a fire on the sixth-floor roof (the precise cause was never proved), a crack in the wall of the office building that had to be repaired, and a broken water main. Three severe winters in a usually mild climate brought about more delays.

Nevertheless, we kept making plans for the opening of TPAC. The Tennessee Performing Arts Foundation signed a contract with the state to create the TPAC Management Corporation, which was to operate TPAC without state interference—or the need to get three competitive prices to see who would play Hamlet. The first board members included Thomas Baker (Nashville), William L. Barry (Lexington), Marylyn Bullock (Knoxville), Sonya Butcher (Clinton), Joseph Davenport (Chattanooga), Sandra Fulton (Nashville), David Pack (Nashville), Brooks Parker (Nashville), Athens Clay Pullias (Nashville), Ken Roberts (Nashville), James W. Stewart (Nashville), Lon Varnell (Nashville), William F. Venable (Nashville), Raymond Zimmerman (Nashville), and me. We hired Warren K. Sumners in February 1979 to be the manager.

In its directory the Chamber of Commerce noted that "Nashville is currently the scene of a bold experiment, perhaps unparalleled in the often uneven history of the arts in America." That was true; TPAC was a unique cooperative effort between the public and the private sectors. It was the first performing arts center in the U.S. to be built with a public (state)/private partnership. Yet I learned that you cannot count on government to lead in this sort of endeavor for the arts. It has to be led by the private sector; at least the idea and initial funding must come from the private sector for it to have a chance to work. You cannot count on government to sustain it either; you have to count on the private sector to do that. Before TPAC was completed, we had dealt with three governors—Winfield Dunn, Ray Blanton, and Lamar Alexander—and their administrations. I have to believe that if Lamar Alexander, instead of Ray Blanton, had followed Winfield Dunn, the whole process would have gone more smoothly. Without Ned McWherter in the legislature as Speaker providing continuity and support in state government, I do not think we could have completed the project.

Finally the building was ready. Opening night was Saturday, September 6, 1980. I will long remember that thrilling date, eight years after I became a part of this effort to help create an arts oasis for the city and the state. We had scheduled a variety of performances, from pop to opera, city and state performers to Broadway performers. We just knew we had a successful week to set the tone for what would happen in this new place, and we tried to plan something appropriate for the size of each theater.

The New York Philharmonic had been scheduled years in advance, but alas! Their schedule had it down for *1981*, not 1980, and they sent their regrets because they would be in Europe in September 1980. Instead we had Joel Grey and the Cincinnati Pops Orchestra in Jackson Hall; Carlos Montoya in Polk; and the Nashville Jazz Machine in Johnson on the first evening. Other performers included Princess Grace of Monaco reading poetry, Mel Torme, the Blair Quartet, Memphis Playhouse in the Square, the Atlanta Academy Theater, the Hartford Ballet, the Johnson City Civic Chorale, the Grey Mouse Theater, the Air Force Band, Judy Collins, the Play Group of Knoxville, the Nashville Symphony Chorus and Nashville Youth Orchestra, and the Nashville Symphony with Renata Scotto and Sherrill Milnes. (We had been informed that because it was to be the *Tennessee* Performing Arts Center, it would be bad form to start off with the Nashville Symphony.)

Despite the diverse events, my wealthy friends did not come; my not-so-wealthy friends did not come; very few people came. It was really scary. Some reviews blamed the poor turnout on the costs of the events, but more often they cited audience attendance habits and lack of arts education in the schools, both public and private. Fortunately we had the endowment income, and that was growing nicely. We would be able to withstand times of drought.

John Bridges, who has been involved with the arts in Nashville for many years, from employee of the state arts commission to critic for the newspaper, offered this view: "Both the high point and the low point was the opening of TPAC. It was so wonderful to have it happen. We realized the things that were possible because it was there, but that opening week was a very, very disappointing time. The crowds were just abysmal for those fabulous things."

Once things got under way with TPAC, I had a talk with Ed Wilson, the arts reviewer at that time for the *Wall Street Journal*. He had grown up in Nashville. I said, "Oh, Ed, we have this wonderful center. When will you be reviewing it?" He basically said that he would not; he considered it a roadhouse and told me that TPAC needed to have a repertory theater, a dance company, and an opera company in addition to the Nashville Symphony and a community theater (the Circle Players) to gain credibility. I said, "Well, we will be bringing in outstanding groups from other cities." That would not do. He kept repeating the word *roadhouse*. That was certainly not the response I was hoping to hear. I took a deep breath and thought, *We have more work to do.* I will save that story for later in the book.

The seeds of cultural responsibility had been sown by men of enlightened vision, and the late 1830's saw them ripen into full flowering.

—KENNETH ROSE

Beginning Steps: 1780-1865

FROM 1780 TO 1865, Nashville evolved from an undeveloped site on the western frontier to a full-fledged city. A statement that appeared in the 1857 City Directory made a significant point about that evolution (and in many ways it still holds true today): "Its growth in wealth and population has never been rapid at any time; yet it has held an even, onward progress in such physical and moral wealth as forms the basis of permanent prosperity."

The city became known for its educational endeavors and for its politics and politicians, sending Andrew Jackson, James K. Polk, and Andrew Johnson to the presidency. As the state capital, it built a magnificent governmental structure (completed in 1859) high on a hill for all to see—just as the Greeks might have done.

First river and then rail transportation promoted trade and enabled the coming and going of visitors and citizens alike. The economy became so diverse—with wholesale dry goods, hardware, drugs, and grocery items; printing, retail, and manufacturing enterprises—that it did not depend on any one industry. Being at the crossroads of the east and the west, the north and the south, was another factor in the city's development. Actors and musicians were among those who made Nashville a stop on their circuits and sometimes stayed a while, and Nashvillians themselves pursued dramatic and musical activities.

The god Apollo had a glimmer of hope that the performing arts would be firmly established in this new place as he looked at the theaters built by entrepreneurs and heard what was happening in the musical academies and societies. He accompanied Nashvillians as they meandered past the War of 1812 and the Mexican War and financial panics and other hard times, such as epidemics, still trying to sustain the creative, artistic spirit. When music publishing got under way, his hopes rose higher, yet the interest in things artistic waxed and waned, and the Civil War dealt such a harsh blow to all facets of life that Apollo was in despair: Would the citizens be able to regain lost ground, even move farther along the pathway toward a community supportive of the performing arts? ❖

~

Early Aspirations

*It is much the fashion to speak of pioneers
and emigrants as rude and illiterate.
Whoever makes that assertion in regard to
the early inhabitants of Tennessee, will widely miss the
truth. The great body of them were men of information,
of good sense, of sound judgment, and great self-reliance;
and in all these respects were fully the equals
of those whom they had left behind.*

—WILLIAM H. STEPHENS
ADDRESSING THE ALUMNI SOCIETY OF THE
UNIVERSITY OF NASHVILLE, 1871

THE FOREFATHERS and foremothers of Nashville brought with them lofty aspirations for their new community and the determination to attain them. In his speech Stephens also mentioned why many came to the wilderness: they were "fired by ambition or the love of adventure." Yet by 1871, after the nightmare of the Civil War, he had to admit that developments were not what they should have been: "We habitually overestimate every thing distant or foreign, and underrate and disparage whatever originates at home. . . . We are encouraged to look abroad for education, for intellectual entertainment . . . to the utter neglect of our own institutions and enterprises, to the disparagement of ourselves. . . . Much of the blame for all this, lies at the door of the educated class in Tennessee."

James Robertson and John Donelson certainly did not lay the groundwork for that outcome. In 1779 Robertson led a group of men by land from Watauga (now northeastern Tennessee) to the future site of Nashville, and they reached their destination by Christmas Day. Donelson set out in late December 1779, commanding his boat *Adventure* and flatboats carrying men, women, and children on the one-thousand-mile trip from Fort Patrick Henry on the Holston River to Big Salt Lick on the Cumberland River. The weather and water conditions caused so many delays that they did not arrive until April 24, 1780.

Individuals on the trip who would become significant in Nashville's history included Charlotte Robertson, wife of James, and some of their children, and Rachel Stockley Donelson, wife of John, and their children (one of whom was Rachel, future wife of Andrew Jackson). Donelson and his company really did have an adventure as they endured fiercely cold temperatures, the death of an infant who was born on the trip, attacks by Native Americans, overturned boats, and smallpox. Despite all of that, the children on board the *Adventure* received educational instruction from Ann Johnson, the sister of James Robertson. That early commitment to education continued—no matter how imperfectly the educational system developed—and led to the identification of Nashville first as the Athens of the West and then as the Athens of the South.

The desire to have an orderly society was formalized in the Cumberland Compact, composed by Richard Henderson, just days after the landing of the Donelson party. On May 1, 1780, 250 men signed the document that provided a basic government and a means to handle land transactions. (Remember that the Revolutionary War was still in progress and some settlers did not want to choose between the Crown and the colonies. Charleston would fall to the British on May 12, 1780, and the U.S. Constitution would not be created until 1787.) An unfortunate fact is that approximately one-third of those signers were killed in clashes with Native Americans within the next few years, but the Compact remained in place until 1783 when North Carolina's legislature created Davidson County.

Two years later, in December 1785, the North Carolina legislature passed "An Act for the Promotion of Learning in Davidson County," and leading men, including the Reverend Thomas Craighead, Hugh Williamson, Daniel Smith, William Polk, Anthony Bledsoe, Lardner Clarke, Ephraim McLean, Robert Hays, and James Robertson, became trustees for Davidson Academy (renamed Cumberland College [1806]). There at Hayesboro, a small number of male students followed a curriculum based on the classics, overseen by Rev. Craighead, a graduate of the College of New Jersey (Princeton). Costs and the distance from Nashville restricted the size of the student body.

Nashville had been incorporated as a town (1806) and had grown from a small number of log structures to more than one hundred two-story brick houses, more than two dozen wholesale and retail stores, a few taverns and banks, a theater, and other structures by the time Cumberland College's new president, Philip Lindsley, arrived in 1824. Lindsley, a classical scholar who had attended the College of New Jersey, turned down offers of presidencies of other educational institutions—including the College of New Jersey—in favor of the post in Nashville. In 1825 he successfully advocated a name change to the University of Nashville and pursued a vigorous campaign to raise the school's standards to become what a first-rate university should be. It is not going too far to say that he wanted it to be a Princeton of the West, with scholars teaching everything from the classics to science to mathematics to geology. He also advocated education for all, not just the wealthy or the elite, so that all people could be better human beings. In an address delivered in 1848 Lindsley noted the changes in the prevalence of educational institutions over two decades: "When this college was revived and reorganized, at the close of 1824, there were no similar institutions in actual operation within two hundred miles of Nashville. [Enrollment was 43 in 1825, 118 in 1836, and 68 in 1848.] There were none in Alabama, Mississippi, Louisiana, Arkansas, Middle or West Tennessee.

There are now some thirty or more within that distance, and nine within fifty miles of our city."

Education for young women was a priority, too, in Nashville, although they were not being trained to take roles in public life, and the costs for training affected the numbers who could attend. In 1815 John J. Abercrombie, from France, taught French, music, dancing, and a literary course at the Belmont Domestic Academy. The Nashville Female Academy, begun in 1816, had teachers with good training, and some were European. Subjects included reading, writing, history, and geography, and the academy was a leader in musical events for the town.

City on a Hill

Looking back at the settlement of Nashville, the Reverend Leroy J. Halsey wrote in 1859:

It was precisely such a spot as the old classic Greeks and Romans would have chosen to build a city. It was a site of gently rising and continuous hills, almost as numerous and quite as elevated as the seven hills of Rome. . . .

Beautiful green cedars, once the glory of winter, have disappeared from all the hill-tops, and in their place have sprung up the marble mansions of wealth or the neat cottages of the artisan. That central summit, where in olden times dwelt the wild genii of the woods, is now surmounted with the Capitol of Tennessee,— the temple of law and justice, built of native marble, whose massive proportions, rising without an obstruction, and seen from every direction as if projected against the very sky, would have done honor to the Athenian Acropolis in the proudest days of Pericles.

Music was a part of life that gained more and more popularity and more and more significance in the town's future. Scottish ballads and traditional Irish songs, fiddles, and sometimes banjos accompanied the settlers to their new home. Slave musicians often played at dances and weddings for white families. When Rachel and Andrew Jackson entertained at the Hermitage, one of their slaves, John Fulton or Squire, was likely to have been the fiddle player for dancing. The Hermitage also had a piano, a guitar, and a flute with song books of hymns and popular music for the family's use.

That there were slaves in Nashville—and a slave trade—is an unfortunate historical reality, but there were also free African-Americans who had certain rights and privileges. (In 1801, the free African-Americans in all of Tennessee numbered 361.) Suffrage for free African-American men was abolished in 1834, however.

According to musician and musical historian Kenneth Rose, "Patriotic Song" (sung to the tune of "Indian Chief") by a "Lady of Tennessee" is the earliest known song written by a Tennessean. It appeared in the *Nashville Whig*, February 7, 1815, and commemorated the brave acts of General Jackson and others in the War of 1812. Here are two stanzas:

A *Jackson,* a *Gaines,* and a *Brown* still appear
At the head of my legions: what have I to fear?
They shall scatter the foe like the dust of the air;
Few again to their proud puny Isle shall repair.

. . . .

See the patriot mother, the sister and wife,
Give up all that is lov'd, or endearing in life—
With heart rending sighs, they yield them to go,
To drive from my shores the murderous foe.

Patriotic songs in fairly good number appeared again during the Civil War—many published in Nashville—and Nashvillians recognized other memorable or landmark events with music.

A notice in the *Nashville Whig,* April 9, 1816, describing the resolutions of the Nashville Musical Society set forth at a meeting on April 6, illustrates other musical aspirations:

Resolved, That this society deem it expedient to give concerts, the more effectually to enable them to pay the expences of said society, and to purchase music and musical instruments for the use of the same.

Resolved, That the President be, and he is hereby authorised to appoint a committee to make arrangement for a concert to be given on Thursday, 18th inst. [John B. West was president, and E. Talbot, secretary.]

Resolved, That this society solicit the aid of gentlemen, who have, and wish to cultivate a taste for music.

Resolved, That the surplus funds of this society (when created) be applied to some public good.

At the beginning of the next month, John J. Abercrombie held a "grand concert of vocal and instrumental music by ladies and gentlemen" at the Nashville Inn. The details were provided on handbills so we will have to trust that it was a "grand concert."

As you will see in the episodes included in this book, high aspirations for the city recur throughout Nashville's history—with varying degrees of success.

⁓

The Early Temples of the Muses

There certainly was no great elegance attached to the interior or exterior of this "Temple of the Muses."

—NOAH LUDLOW,
REFERRING TO THE RENOVATED SALT HOUSE OF 1817

THEATER-LOVING Nashvillians had brief satisfaction on December 4, 1807, with a double bill: the comedy *Child of Nature: or, Virtue Rewarded* and the farce *The Purse, or the Benevolent Tar.* That is the extent of what we know about this first performance in the barely organized town, and there was a lengthy wait until the next dramatic display, in 1816. Samuel Drake's company had been playing in Frankfort, Kentucky, and he decided to add Nashville to his circuit.

The following year, 1817, Noah M. Ludlow (a New York City native, born in 1795) and a troupe hired carpenters to renovate an old salt house, which came to be called the Market Street Theater. It was about six hundred feet from what Ludlow referred to as the "Branch Bank of Tennessee." The floor always looked wet because it was so saturated with salt, but Ludlow thought it at least seemed cooler, and in hot weather, that was no small benefit. A stage and simple benches "in the amphitheatre order—one raised a little above the other, from the orchestra to the back of the building," their seats covered with green baize, were the extent of the carpenters' handiwork.

Despite the rather stark furnishings, Ludlow declared, "The elite of Nashville seemed to enjoy themselves as much in it as they ever did, according to my observation, in a more ornate building. The very finest ladies of the city would sit out a long five-act comedy or tragedy on a narrow board not more than ten inches wide, without any support for their backs, and appear to be delighted with the performance." He added his explanation for their stoic behavior: "They had not been corrupted with *fast times*, sensational dramas, and easy, cushioned chairs."

The troupe had a target for opening of July 4, 1817, but it was July 10 before they gave the "*first season-performance* of a regularly organized dramatic company." Cherry's five-act comedy of *The Soldier's Daughter* was followed by the farce *Village Lawyer.* The young widow who would become Ludlow's wife, Mary Squires (née Maury) of Franklin, may have been Tennessee's

first professional actress. She acted under the name Miss Wallace in this run in Nashville.

Love of the theater and love of this woman lured Ludlow to Nashville in the first place. They had met in Louisville, Kentucky, and he was not at all interested in making the circuit to Nashville—until he was smitten. He thought it would be a good idea to meet Mary's parents and friends before their marriage in September, so the couple made the commitment to the circuit and to each other. The Ludlows attempted more than once to enliven the theatrical life in Nashville but were frustrated in the end.

During the summer of 1817, the troupe performed several plays and farces. The "orchestra" consisted of one actor/musician who came with them and two or three musicians recruited from Nashville. They closed after three weeks not because of poor attendance but because of lack of new material, and they wanted to leave the audiences wanting more. They gave the excuse of the heat, however, and that was not far from the truth since Ludlow thought Nashville was the hottest place in which he had ever been.

Ludlow and another troupe member rode horses to Cincinnati to recruit additional actors for a return engagement in the fall with a bigger cast. The company opened the season with *Speed the Plough* and *The Day After the Wedding.* They gave performances four nights a week, on Monday, Wednesday, Friday, and Saturday.

In 1818 a group of amateur actors got together as the Dramatic Club of Nashville and asked Ludlow to be the stage manager. Among them were Sam Houston (then in his mid-twenties), William Fulton, Ephraim Foster, Wilkins Tannehill, and General John H. Eaton. Andrew Jackson and Felix Grundy were honorary members. Mrs. Ludlow and Miss Macaffrey filled in parts as needed.

An episode with Sam Houston reveals something about him that is seldom, if ever, mentioned

Not only a military man and a politician, Sam Houston, pictured here at age thirty-three, was an amateur thespian in his younger years in Nashville.

in history books. Ludlow cast Houston in the farce *We Fly by Night* as a drunken porter because he saw "a rich vein of comic humor" in Houston, and Ludlow wanted to bring it to light. Houston vigorously protested the role: "Great God! my friend Ludlow, what are you thinking of? Surely you're not serious? . . . 'By the Eternal,' sir, the people will hiss me."

Ludlow was willing to take responsibility and step before the audience if that outcome occurred. Houston agreed, saying, "I will attempt the character, because I have pledged my word not to refuse any part assigned to me."

Another round of protests came from Houston on the night of the performance after they dressed him in an outlandish outfit, complete with a long-haired red wig, and painted his nose red. He "swore by all the gods he would not go on stage." He relented, however, although he raised the stakes with Ludlow: if there was hissing from the audience, he would shoot Ludlow the next day.

The minute Houston came on stage and started to say his lines, the audience applauded. By the time he staggered off in character, he heard a roar of applause. Houston misunderstood and thought they were ridiculing him: "D——n their souls! What do they mean by that?" Ludlow wrote that he had never seen the part done so well by anyone, and the newspapers gave Houston good reviews the next day. Ludlow was right in thinking that Houston had a keen "sense of the ridiculous."

The amateur theatricals did not last long, and Ludlow clearly stated why: (1) the people who had a burning desire to act satisfied it and then began "to feel a lukewarmness towards it"; (2) others used the excuse of business that did not allow time for rehearsal; and (3) still others did not intend to be active—they had become subscribers just to get the theatricals started. The "affair finally died of indifference."

William Jones, who had acted in the Park Theatre in New York City, Ludlow, and others performed in the spring of 1819 in the Market Street Theater. One entrepreneurial citizen decided it was time to have a *real* theater in Nashville and set to work. Ludlow offered his on-the-spot observations about this theater built in 1820 because he said that false information had been broadcast about it. A Frenchman living in Nashville, Mr. Terraas, built it to be a theater—and only a theater. It was in no way a barn, as some had referred to it. On the west side of Cherry Street (Fourth Avenue), north of the Public Square, it had a pit and two tiers of boxes. Although it would seat only about eight hundred patrons, it was adequate for the town. In 1825 smoking was forbidden in the theater, but the ban likely had more to do with preventing a fire than preserving patrons' health. Read very much about theatrical history, and the loss of theaters—and sometimes lives—to fire recurs too often.

In May 1820 the Nashville Thespian Society gave the first performances in the New Theatre; they were the comedy *The Poor Gentleman* and the farce *A Miss in Her Teens, or a Medley of Lovers*. Within the year, Joshua Collins and William Jones leased the theater for their dramatic company, and Ludlow performed with them for twelve nights. The company had a money-losing season, and Collins and Jones gave up their lease. Nevertheless, the *Nashville Whig,* May 2, 1821, alerted readers that the Nashville Theatre was about to open for a short season. (Almost immediately after the theater opened, the name was changed, and it remained the Nashville Theatre until 1826.) William Jones and his wife brought a company that included Mrs. Groshon and John H. Vos, "whose abilities as a Tragedian are so generally acknowledged." Drama lovers could expect "much gratification" with the talented actors.

Actors had to be tough in many ways to make their circuits. Ludlow observed that "actors were afraid of the West, and still more of the South," but opportunity beckoned some, who persisted in their craft. Getting from place to place was a constant challenge. On one arduously slow trip from New Orleans to Nashville, Ludlow and his family started on one steamboat, had to change to another, smaller one that could negotiate the Harpeth Shoals, had to stop twice for the crewmen to cut wood, and eventually had to hire oxen to pull them along on one stretch. Sometimes male passengers were required to join in the wood cutting. On overland routes, more prosperous actors had access to wagons and horses while less prosperous ones were reduced to foot power.

Ludlow joined Samuel Drake Sr. and Jr. in the summer of 1822. The run was fairly unremarkable except for the appearance of Julia Drake; she would become the mother of Julia Dean, a well-respected young actress who also graced Nashville's stage and became a hit in the area and in other towns of "the West." Families of actors were often similar to the Barrymores later in America's dramatic history.

Up-and-coming stage stars passed through Nashville, even in the early days. Edwin Forrest, an American-born actor who would achieve international fame, performed as Poins in William Shakespeare's *Henry IV* on December 4, 1825, and he came back in July 1829 as William Tell. A broadside from November 3, sometime in the 1820s, indicated that Forrest played Banquo to James H. Caldwell's Macbeth and Ludlow's Macduff, "with all the Original Music of the Witches, composed by Doctor Arne, Purcel, Handel, &c." Mrs. Noke and Miss Placide were two of the singing witches; tickets cost $1 each (about $16 today). Forrest had first acted on Nashville's stage in the summer of 1824 with Ludlow's company, but it was such a poor season financially—the heat had driven most people out of town to the cooler watering holes of the area—that it is somewhat surprising that he returned.

Sam Houston was portrayed as one of his favorite characters in Roman history, Marius, in this painting done in Nashville in 1831.

The advantage to him could have been that in Nashville and other southern towns, Forrest could hone his acting craft that enabled him to move on to bigger stages of the world.

James H. Caldwell had opened the 1823 season in July, and Ludlow was in the company, yet

A New Orleans Connection

Between New Orleans and Nashville lay twelve hundred miles of river, and in 1815, a keel boat took five months to make a round trip. With the introduction of the steamboat and later the railroad, the trip required less time and was much less arduous for traveling troupes. Yet James H. Caldwell, Noah Ludlow, and Sol Smith devoted more of their assets to business in New Orleans than in Nashville. Perhaps that had to do with their ability to realize a healthy financial return on their investments.

The twenty-seven-year-old Caldwell, who had debuted as a child actor on the stage of Manchester, England, arrived in New Orleans in 1819. Before his death in 1863, he had become a successful businessman as well as a builder of theaters and manager of actors. In fact, he founded the gas business in New Orleans, and that was related to his theater construction. When he was building the Camp Street Theatre in 1822–23, Caldwell imported a "gas machine" to provide light for the chandeliers. (It was the first American theater in New Orleans because the city was decidedly more French/Creole than American at that point in its history.) His ultimate theater, however, was the elegant and expensive St. Charles Theatre, which opened in 1835 at a cost of at least $325,000 (about $5.6 million today). Following its destruction by fire, Noah Ludlow and Sol Smith built a new St. Charles Theatre on the same site in 1843, and they operated it until they retired ten years later.

Caldwell was apparently not content just to bring actors to town. He built a theater in Nashville in 1826 that very much resembled the exterior of his Camp Street Theatre in New Orleans, but the interior was never finished "according to the original intention." It was located at the corner of Summer (Fifth) and Union Streets. (The New Nashville Theatre opened in 1863 in Odd Fellows Hall, which was erected on the site of Caldwell's theater.) To help with the expense, Caldwell borrowed money from Nashvillians, and the people who loaned him money received season tickets until the money was repaid. The tickets were considered interest payments.

A poetry competition with a silver cup as the award was part of the momentous occasion, and Caldwell read the winning entry, written by a Bostonian, on opening night, October 9, 1826. For some time afterward the populace expressed its displeasure in the newspapers over the loss of a local entrant, Isaac Clark, in favor of the out-of-towner.

You may judge for yourself which poet should have won. Here is the winning poem's first stanza:

In those proud days when polished
    Athens rose
In arts and arms superior to her foes,
When godlike courage bore her
    trusty shield
And conquered Persia at her
    footstool kneeled,
And all excess of evil and of good
Marked a great people's highest altitude,
Then was the drama's mighty sway confest
The acknowledged passion of the
    Athenian Breast:
Heroes and artists to her altars came.
Statesmen and warriors owned alik
    the flame;
Pleased with the moral scene,
    e'en cautious age

Gave the warm tribute and approved
the stage.

Here is the opening of Clark's poem:

To beauties write some lovers choose.
To favor gain but none to lose.
But one man wrote to homely one
Though of fair sex had beauty none.
My last sweetheart, Miss Nancy Flack
You homely are as Susan Black;
She is no beauty well you know,
In mirror looked—she found it so.

Six hundred witnessed Jane Placide starring in *The Soldier's Daughter,* followed by the farce *Turn Out.* Women took their places in the front of the theater; slaves and children, admitted at half price, sat in the gallery. The people so loved the actress that Mayor Wilkins Tannehill and his aldermen prepared a petition asking her to stay in town. She refused because she had an engagement in the Bowery Theatre, New York City, which was under construction. The only problem was that she had not reserved a place on the stagecoach, and she had to wait until the river rose before she could catch a boat. Since her stay lasted several weeks, she performed Sheridan's *Pizarro, Merry Wives of Windsor,* and *Richard III,* among other plays.

Caldwell's season was reasonably profitable, earning no less than $130 and $140 a night (about $2,000 and $2,200 today). His bottom line had help from the state government, too. In 1819 the General Assembly had given culture a boost by passing a bill that exempted concerts and theatrical performances from a $50 tax charged on other shows, particularly "feats of activity, slight [*sic*] of hand, or any other exhibitions, for which money is taken." The legislators must have been serious about requiring the tax because noncompliance brought with it a fine of $500.

According to M. Liston Lewis, one-time reference librarian at Nashville's Carnegie Library, "An outstanding stage fad of the Nineteenth Century was originated in Nashville, when in the summer of 1829, Caldwell played five different characters in an operatic farce entitled 'The Age of Tomorrow.'"

With the arrival in 1830 of Signor Antonio Mondelli, who was Caldwell's scenic artist from his Camp Street Theatre in New Orleans, the plain set in the Nashville theater was transformed with lighting and special effects, including real waterfalls, boats, storms, and forest settings. Yet attracting audiences was a constant problem, and Ludlow said of Nashville, "It required all classes to take an interest in any amusement that was to be made profitable."

Sol Smith and his thespians toured Tennessee in 1829, and they often stayed from one to almost two weeks at each stop. They had sizable audiences, despite the warring rhetoric between some newspapers, which praised the theatrical productions as a cultural benefit to communities, and some ministers, particularly Methodists and Presbyterians, who warned theatergoers about the "brimstone roasting" awaiting them. From 1830 to 1839 there were 700 performances of 296 plays in Nashville. The theater might have been controversial, but people were still eager to see the next production at the "Temple of the Muses."

The Rutledges

They brought a touch of old world colonial charm, dignity, and refinement into their chosen exile.

—Mary Bray Wheeler and
Genon Hickerson Neblett

TWO EARLY INHABITANTS of Nashville brought with them a heritage of cultural appreciation, love of family and country (their fathers signed the Declaration of Independence), strong belief in education, dedication to their faith, and willingness to help their fellow human beings. Born into wealthy, honorable, and politically connected families in South Carolina, they are an even more remarkable pair for coming to "the West." There was a pull to make a life of their own while there was a push to escape overbearing relatives and others' expectations for them and their future.

Arthur Middleton turned to Latin for his daughter's name—Septima Sexta Middleton—since she was the seventh child, sixth daughter. Henry Middleton Rutledge was the son of Edward Rutledge. In 1799 Septima married her first cousin, Henry, when she was sixteen and he was twenty-four.

Language, literature, and music were parts of Septima's classical education. She learned to play a golden Italian harp, and at special events or at Wednesday evening musicals in Charleston, Septima often played the harp and sang. From her mother, she learned to run a huge household, to be the perfect hostess, to care for the less fortunate.

For his education Henry attended Columbia University in New York, and later on he went to London. An integral experience for him was becoming secretary for his uncle, Charles C. Pinckney, in the American delegation to France where Henry became fluent in French, made contacts in political and social circles, and studied law. He also made time to go to the opera in Paris.

In 1816, the couple and their five children arrived in Franklin County, Tennessee, after a six-week journey from South Carolina. Henry had built a home there on the plantation they called Chilhowee. Twenty covered wagons were filled with furniture, a library of books, food, and other items to set up a household. One cart was reserved for Septima's golden Italian harp. More than fifty slaves accompanied them, and Septima tended to the slaves' physical and spiritual needs. On Sunday afternoons she held a worship service for them, and daughter Mary taught religious classes.

The artist Edward Marchant painted Septima Sexta Middleton Rutledge in 1839. The Rutledges moved from South Carolina and became an influential and philanthropic family in early Nashville.

The Rutledge boys would go to school in Baltimore. The girls had been instructed by a tutor in Charleston, but they would attend the Nashville Female Academy in Nashville. At their mother's insistence, the children spoke only French on Fridays. (More children were added to the family after the move to Tennessee.)

By 1820, the plantation in Franklin County was prospering, and the family purchased a small town house in Nashville where they lived while Henry oversaw the building of Rose Hill (a portion of the original house remains at the corner of Rutledge and Lea Streets). Their wealth and their friendships with Rachel and Andrew Jackson and other political figures placed them higher on the social scale than most newcomers to Nashville.

When Lafayette visited Nashville in May 1825, Henry Rutledge was his interpreter. The festivities included entertainment at Rose Hill, where Lafayette spent one night, and a ball at the Masonic Hall. Approximately 20,000 people crowded the town that usually held 6,000 in hopes of at least seeing the famous Frenchman.

For many years Septima spent time at both houses in Tennessee, visited relatives in Charleston, and also traveled to Philadelphia. She corresponded with relatives and others to keep up with family, social, and political news. One correspondent was Mary Helen, wife of Septima's brother Henry Middleton, who was the American ambassador to Russia (1820–29). As her ties deepened in Nashville and as she grew older, Septima spent more time in her adopted home, but she continued to keep up with family and cultural happenings elsewhere in the world.

Law and educational interests occupied Henry. He was admitted to the Davidson County bar in 1827, and a few years later he became a trustee of the University of Nashville, which had its campus near Rose Hill. Francis Fogg, a lawyer, was already a trustee and Henry's son-in-law, having married Mary Middleton Rutledge.

The whole family was involved in the founding of Christ Church Episcopal in Nashville, but the women became leaders in the Sunday school. Not tied to the church then, the early Sunday school was more like a regular school, taught on Sunday. Young Septima Fogg, granddaughter of Henry and Septima Rutledge, grew up to sing solos in church, and her grandmother accompanied her on the harp.

Septima Rutledge and her daughter Mary Fogg devoted themselves to other philanthropic efforts. Septima taught young girls at Rose Hill, and eventually, in 1837, the Nashville Protestant School of Industry for orphaned or destitute girls was formed. In 1840 Joseph Elliston donated land and built a structure for them on Vine Street (Seventh Avenue). Mrs. James K. Polk led the board of managers, and others on the board included Septima, Mary, Mrs. Thomas Maney, Mrs. A. V. Brown, Mrs. G. W. Martin, Mrs. D. McGavock, Mrs. G. W. Campbell, Mrs. James Porter, Mrs. H. H. McEwen, Mrs. Washington Barrow, Mrs. H. Kirkman, and Mrs. O. Ewing. Another institution that had Septima's and Mary's support was the Nashville Protestant Orphan Asylum.

Henry died in 1844, at age sixty-eight, of a sudden illness. An indication of the respect with which he was held is that the Tennessee legislature adjourned so that members could attend his funeral. Following her husband's death, Septima continued to work on behalf of others, and she offered assistance to soldiers during the Civil War. She died in June 1865, not long after peace was declared. Her golden harp was sold at her death because even previously prosperous families needed funds after the end of the Civil War. The harp was exhibited in a museum in Birmingham, Alabama, in 1931, but its current whereabouts remain unknown. A section of Nashville still bears the name of Rutledge Hill, and the example that the couple set for the community remains one to follow for any era.

~

The Piano

There is nothing that lends more pleasure, refinement or culture to the home than music.

—AD FOR CLAUDE P. STREET PIANO CO., 1921

MUSIC PRODUCED BY THE PIANO has been heard in Nashville almost from the city's official beginning, and at least two music dealers have had lengthy histories. Sales of the instrument worldwide did not really start to gain momentum until decades after the city's birth, but even then sales numbers were far from astronomical. By 1800 the English manufacturer

Broadwood was selling four hundred pianos per year while other manufacturers were averaging about forty per year. Until the mid-1800s the United States was primarily an importer, not a manufacturer, of pianos—and transportation across the seas had to have been hard on the instruments—yet by October 1820 J. H. Taylor had come from London and was manufacturing pianos next door to James Irwin, a hat manufacturer, in Nashville. Not many more than three thousand persons lived on this western edge of civilization, and the piano itself was then slightly more than one hundred years old.

James Aykroyd advertised pianos that had just arrived by steamboat in June 1830, and he urged patrons to come to his shop south of the Public Square, where he also sold other instruments, such as the two dozen violins he had in stock.

Musician and music historian Kenneth Rose referred to John B. West as "the dean of early Nashville music dealers." His firm was "the focal point of musical activity," wherever it was, because it did not remain at one site. He had been in business several years by June 1838, when a Nashvillian could choose from four secondhand pianos that were for sale or hire from West's store. Few details of prices appear in the early years of ads for music dealers; potential customers must have been expected to stop by and take a look—and maybe try to negotiate a bargain.

The year 1850 marks the point when more and more people were placing the piano in their homes, and schools were not far behind in offering instruction. Nevertheless in that year, fewer than 50,000 pianos were manufactured worldwide, and they were not yet mass produced. By the early 1850s, Nashville musicians could shop with James Diggons, importer and dealer in music and instruments (30 Union Street); L. Gitter and Co., piano and harp makers (14 South Vine Street [Seventh Avenue]); E. Morton, music store (33 Union); H. Reed, pianos (31 Union); or

Music in the Newspaper

The first music printed in a Nashville newspaper was "La Marseillaise," the French national anthem (*National Banner and Nashville Whig*, October 28, 1830). It appeared on the front page, and the words were in both French and English.

The next composition appeared a few weeks later in the same newspaper, and it was C. E. Horn's "The Banks of Allan Water." (C. E. stands for Charles Edward; just a few of his numerous compositions can be found at the Library of Congress: http://memory.loc.gov/ammem/mdbquery.html.)

John Wert, pianos and music (43 Union). A writer for the *Republican Banner*, May 26, 1854, noted, "We have heard the opinion expressed that there were, probably, more pianos in Nashville than in any place of its population in the United States." Although that statement is difficult to verify, there were plenty of stores from which to purchase a piano, and who knows how many from previous years' purchases continued to be in working order. In 1855 Diggons was still at his Union Street address where he had pianos for sale, for hire, or for exchange, and Bacon & Raven of New York supplied him with the "very best approved pianofortes."

Many shops disappeared during the Civil War, and others sprang up afterward. Roderic D. Dorman was a part of Dorman & Freeman's Musical Emporium in 1867. Located in the Masonic Temple at 81 Church Street, the firm was an agent for Chickering & Sons, Milles, Gabler, and other pianos. Watson F. Freeman was the other party in the firm, and based on available evidence, he lived in Philadelphia, although other Freemans in the firm W. Freeman & Co. boarded in Nashville. (W. Freeman & Co., also at the Masonic Temple, sold wallpaper, and another branch of this firm was in the Colonnade Building, 78 North Cherry Street [Fourth Avenue], selling picture frames, mirrors, window shades, etc.) The next year, 1868, Dorman's name alone was listed as a music dealer at 83 Church Street. Also on Church Street (No. 110), John Luck sold musical instruments (in 1860 he had been on Union Street, selling toys, "fancy articles," musical instruments, and sheet music).

In 1872, McClure's Temple of Music advertised its Steinways and sheet music for sale at 36 Union Street where it had been since 1868. At some point McClure's placed a Dunham piano in the parlor of the prestigious Maxwell House Hotel so that the ladies could have music while they were there. It probably was a good advertising move, too.

Jesse French founded his company in the 1870s. He started with sheet music, and an important example in 1875 was the "Centennial National Song" with music by Henri Weber. When French started building pianos, Jesse French Piano and Organ Company added its own line to that of other manufacturers.

French incorporated in 1887, and by 1890 his firm had a nationwide reputation and branches in St. Louis, Little Rock, Memphis, and Birmingham with seventy-five employees and thirty-five traveling salesmen. He constructed a five-story brick building at 240–42 North Summer Street (Fifth Avenue) in Nashville with a front of plate glass said to be the largest sheets of plate glass in town; elevators served the building, which had 15,750 square feet. At his Nashville store he usually kept in stock two hundred instruments by these makers: Hardman, Steinway & Sons, New England, Chickering & Sons, Vose and Sons pianos; Story & Clark, Jesse French, Mason & Hamlin, Packard, and other organs.

French did not confine his musical interests to his business. He organized the Orchestral Society of Nashville in 1894. It was an amateur orchestra that met on Tuesday and Friday nights with Professor William Thomas as concertmaster and Professor W. L. Eiseman as conductor. Officers were Dr. George W. F. Price, president; Dr. John T. Lacey, vice president; Jennings R. Dortch, treasurer; Austin Davis, secretary; and Binford Throne, librarian.

Henry A. French had clerked at Jesse French's company, but in 1883 launched the H. A. French Co., which sold music books and musical instruments (violins, guitars, band instruments, and so on). Its claim to business fame rested more with its music publishing, totaling more than 12,000 titles. The company was sold in the 1940s.

Although Jesse French left Nashville by 1906, the company bearing his name operated a while longer in the city, and Claude P. Street was manager for a time. In May 1908, a letter addressed to Street from Alfred E. Howell, regarded as a foremost musician and critic of the South, was reproduced in the *Banner,* and it basically praised the Steinway. (This appraisal of Howell and similar comments about other people come with a caution because laudatory descriptions were fairly common in newspaper accounts.) Howell thanked Street on "behalf of the Watauga Club" for providing a "Steinway Miniature Grand Piano" for a recital by Bruno Steindel, cellist, and Ferdinand Steindel, pianist, of the Thomas Orchestra. The recital had been held on April 21.

The peak period for U.S. piano sales was 1890 to 1928, and 1909 was an unexcelled year with sales of more than 360,000 units, more than double the amount sold in 1900. Sears, Roebuck and Co., through its catalog, participated in the sales boom by offering Beckwith pianos and organs from 1900 to 1925 and other musical instruments over the years. Someone could purchase a 1913 Beckwith Majestic Grand Organ for $52.95, and while he was at it he could order a kit house, selling for around $1,100, in which to put the instrument ($1,100 in 1913, about $20,000 today).

Prospects for the piano business looked good when, in 1914, Street opened the Claude P. Street Co., which continues ninety years later under the leadership of the third generation of Streets. Fine instruments and professional service have been hallmarks of the business.

In 1921 the O. K. Houck Piano Co. sold Steinway, McPhail, Houck, Jesse French, Pianola Player, Houck Player, Krakauer, and Duo-Art Pianos. Rounding out the stock were Victrolas and records—at easy terms if the buyer so desired. Piano rolls were available for $1.25 each (about $12.50 today). Comparable prices of other goods were twenty pounds of flour for $1.05 at the Acka Packa store and French kid walking gloves for $1.50 at D. Loveman, Bergen and Teitlebaum. Technology tapped the piano with the invention of the player piano; an owner did not have to know how to play the instrument—he just needed enough money to buy the player and new rolls. The instrument had a thirty-year or so run of popularity, from about the turn of the twentieth century to the Great Depression. Records and then radio spelled d-o-o-m for the player piano.

The headline "Nashville Spends $1.5 Million for Music Every 12 Months" appeared in the *Banner*, April 5, 1925. Although that figure also included talking machines and radios, music education, and small instruments, the biggest amount went toward pianos—acoustic and player—about $750,000 (about $7.7 million today).

At prices starting at $875, a home owner could purchase a Steinway in 1926 from O. K. Houck Piano Co., proud of its "One Price—No Commission." With the extended payment plan, someone on a modest income could have the piano with the "singing golden tone [that] gives perfect voice to the greatest music of the masters."

In 1926, a music lover could shop as late as nine o'clock in the evening at Claude P. Street's Piano Co., 168-70 Eighth Avenue North. Someone on a tighter budget could purchase a used upright for $54, but with a more expansive budget—and a larger home—one could buy a grand piano for $445. (A Steinway grand began at $695 in 1922, just four years earlier.)

During the Great Depression, piano sales were abysmal (about 27,000 in 1932 sold *nationwide*), and many piano manufacturers and dealers went bankrupt. By the early 1940s, however, the economic scene was looking brighter. In May 1941, W. R. Steinway, European general manager for Steinway piano manufacturers, stopped in

FRANCIS JOSEPH CAMPBELL

Francis Joseph Campbell, born in Franklin County, Tennessee, in 1832, was blinded in an accident at age four. He was one of the first students to attend the Tennessee School for the Blind in Nashville, and he performed so well musically (the piano was his instrument) that he became a teacher of music and an interim superintendent of the school until the early 1850s. Wanting to expand his educational horizons, he went to Massachusetts for more training, then taught piano and music at the Wisconsin Institute for the Blind. He returned briefly to Nashville to teach before literally being forced out of the city in 1856 for teaching African-Americans to read—and he came very close to being hanged for that offense. He held a teaching position at the Perkins Institute in Boston before going to Germany to study music. He is remembered primarily as a cofounder of the Royal Normal College and Academy of Music for the Blind in Upper Norwood, England, in 1872. He was knighted in 1909 by King Edward VII. Campbell died in 1914, yet his efforts lived on in his school and his students. One report stated that 90 percent of his pupils were teachers of music, organists, or tuners of musical instruments.

Nashville to talk with Claude P. Street, whose firm sold Steinways. (This was Claude P. Street, the son.) Steinway was the grandson of the founder of the House of Steinway. When asked to comment on the industry, he spoke of both American and European markets: "The entire piano industry has increased 20 per cent over 1939. One hundred and forty thousand pianos were made last year in the whole industry. I believe that this increase is due to the increased appreciation for good music among poorer families, in this country that is. In Europe, sales have increased due to the lack of motion pictures and automobiles, which keeps people in their homes." He certainly knew of the perilous conditions in Europe at that time, but there is no way that Steinway could have predicted what would happen just months away. The U.S. War Production Board ordered all piano building stopped in 1942 because of the war effort, but Steinway's firm built upright pianos to be used to entertain Allied soldiers.

When the D. H. Baldwin Co. had a store in Nashville in the 1890s, one can imagine the surprise on a shopper's face had she been told that Baldwin would become the largest piano builder in the United States and be acquired in 2001 by Gibson Guitar Corp., headquartered in Nashville. Baldwin offers acoustic pianos with Baldwin, Chickering, and Wurlitzer brand names, and with its digital instruments, technology has again tapped the piano. In the winter of 2002 the Baldwin Nashville Showcase opened at the corner of Grundy Street and Eleventh Avenue. The 24,000-square-foot building is also a site where one may receive music instruction.

The piano has found a place not only in homes and schools, but also in houses of worship, theaters, recording studios, and clubs. As long as there is music in Nashville, there will be a need for the piano.

Years of Promise

*The seeds of cultural responsibility
had been sown by men of enlightened vision,
and the late 1830's saw them ripen into full flowering.*

—KENNETH ROSE

KENNETH ROSE, violinist, music teacher, and student of pioneer music, wrote in 1943 that the decade 1830–40 was a transitional one in Nashville, which brought about a cultural lushness in the 1850s. By 1830, the town had a population of 5,566, which included 1,808 slaves and 204 free African-Americans; it ranked fiftieth in U.S. population. New Orleans had slightly more than 46,000 (ranked fifth), Charleston had more than 30,000 (ranked sixth), and Louisville had almost 11,000 (ranked twenty-second). To serve the population's physical needs in Nashville were seventy-seven retail and grocery stores; coffee cost about 18 cents a pound and salt, $5 a sack (about $3 and $85 today). To take care of thirsty individuals were sixty taverns and tippling-houses.

As for meeting cultural needs, music had already become a well-established part of life with instruction, both personal and institutional; a few traveling performers; and local musicians, many of whom had excellent training. Rose considered the city's musical awareness "an augury of better things to come," and the latter part of the 1830s was more vibrant than the first.

The Nashville Female Academy, Mr. and Mrs. Hunt's Female Academy, and Dr. and Mrs. Weller's Female Academy were only some of the places where young ladies were taught music. John D. M'Collum's singing school at the Baptist church was more suited for people interested in sacred music. Private teachers included Henri Corri, member of the Royal Academy of His Majesty's Chapel in London; Mrs. Joseph Dwyer, a singing teacher; and M. L. B. Hemmingway, offering instruction on the piano, organ, flute, violin, and clarinet. In 1836 a Mr. and Mrs. Grove brought to town a man whose name would become more important later in the city's musical history: Henri (or Henry or Heinrich) C. Weber.

Henri C. Weber

In 1855–56 the Academy of Music, 24 Vine Street (Seventh Avenue), provided instruction in instrumental and vocal music. The principals were Charles Hess and Henri (or Henry) C. Weber. The board members were Neil Brown, John Trimble, James P. Clark, Dr. John S. Young, James Walker, Alex Mackenzie, James B. Craighead, W. O. Harris, R. C. McNairy, Dr. T. O. Winston, and G. M. Fogg.

The instructional system was said to be the same as that at the Royal Academy of Paris, with several classes: primary ($20), freshman ($25), sophomore ($30), junior ($35), and senior ($40, about $775 today). The Recapitulation Department ($60) was for students who wanted to be professional musicians. All of those classes were in piano and guitar only. Harp ($45) and Italian-style vocal training ($45) were also offered. There were two sessions, and the charges cited were per session.

Henri Weber, born in Germany, composed "Blow, Bugle, Blow," "The Storm," and "The Centennial National Song," which was used in Philadelphia in 1876. An earlier composition, "Hail Washington," was published in 1842 by C. D. Benson & Bro. of Nashville. He had a daughter named Mary, who married Frederick Emerson Farrar. In 1910 they had the Farrar School of Voice and Piano on Eighth Avenue North. A composer and pianist, Frederick was born near Boston in 1864 and trained there and in Germany and Italy. He had come to Nashville in 1891.

An editorial in the *Nashville Republican and State Gazette* reveals the extent of much of the learning designed to complete a young lady before she came out in society: "At the present day a knowledge of music is considered an indispensable accomplishment in the education of a female; but so short and imperfect is the course allotted to this subject that . . . her knowledge [is] confined to a few easy and popular airs which she had practiced at school, of which she is tired of learning, and by the repetition of which her friends are sadly wearied."

Very little of interest in the musical performing arts occurred—or was reported—until after 1835, which likely had to do with the home- and school-based nature of most musical happenings. Four men assumed musical prominence in the latter part of the 1830s: William Nash, Emil Heerbruger, C. F. Schultz, and William Harmon.

The first to arrive was Nash (June 1836), and he established the Nashville Academy of Music on High Street (Sixth Avenue). Both Nash and his wife, a singer, taught at the Female Academy, and both had private students. In addition Nash had a music store, and his pianos were warranted "to stand the climate, and for tone and touch [were] equal to any in our country."

In June 1837, Nash placed a notice for his academy in the newspaper:

The usual studies will commence on Monday, the 19th inst., and it is desired that if any pupil wishes to withdraw from the school in the vacation, they will make it known before that time, as there are several who have applied for an entrance at the first vacancy. The course of study is the Elementary principles together with the Major and Minor scales, Common Chords, &c. and practice in Singing and Piano Forte Playing, founded on the unerring laws of Nature.

It is required of every pupil to attend four hours a week, and the following rules must be strictly attended to, viz. No pupil will be permitted to practice until the Elementary principles are perfectly understood. No lesson will be given on the Piano Forte except to pupils counting their own time audibly.—No second lesson will be given until the first can be done in tune and in time. . . .

Terms—$20 per quarter [almost $320 today], each quarter consisting of twelve weeks. . . .

All pupils must be entered by some responsible person.

Next to his notice was one from Mrs. King who, with her sister Miss Christian, had set up a musical academy in the house that had been occupied by Dr. Weller (Dr. and Mrs. Weller's Female Academy). Miss Christian had advertised her services a month earlier because she was to teach at two other schools, too. Having been in Nashville for at least five months, Miss Christian had already established herself with parents and pupils. The sisters were to teach singing and harp, piano, and guitar playing. Mrs. King stated that she had "studied under the most celebrated masters, being finished by Herz, Pianist to the King of France. [Heinrich Herz, a piano instructor at the Paris Conservatory, wrote several method books.] In opening this Establishment, Mrs. King feels convinced she offers to the public advantages rarely to be met with, particularly in the theory of singing, a science in general too much neglected; and she has no hesitation in stating, that Pupils receiving instruction in this academy, will after a short period be enabled to sing without the assistance of a master, with beauty of style and ease to themselves." Unlike Nash, Mrs. King did not advertise her terms. There seemed to be a competition between Nash's teaching "founded on the unerring laws of Nature" and Mrs. King's "theory of singing" that she considered a "science."

Nash soon gained a favorable reputation among the citizenry, and he was listed with such notables as Philip Lindsley and Dr. Boyd McNairy as a reference for the surgeon dentists L. T. Gunn and J. G. Mitchell. Someone felt strongly enough about his work in music education that he wrote this anonymous letter to the *Daily Republican Banner:*

Mr. Nash—What he has done, is doing, and offers to do.

The name of the gentleman at the head of this article is too well known in this community to need any preliminary remarks: It is sufficient to say he came to our city two years ago, well recommended as a gentleman and a teacher of music, and his labors among us have confirmed all that was spoken in his favor. As a teacher, Mr. Nash is unrivalled: and the late examination of his pupils, where we observed children of 7 or 8 years of age, defining every musical character, reducing the calculations of time to a perfect system, giving directions for writing all the major scales according to their signature, as far as four sharps or flats, and performing accurately, music which had been that moment for the first time placed before them on the Black Board, has led me to wonder how it is that those children do so completely understand what adults have generally considered a very abstruse science. Those who have attended the Episcopal or Presbyterian Church in the course of the last year can easily discover what has been done for the improvement of Church music by Mr. Nash; and those who attend the private or public performances of his piano forte and singing pupils will readily see the improvement making in that branch of music. Mr. Nash's style is at once elevated, particularly in vocal music; and his labors have gained him universal approbation.

Now, while we see that children can be taught the science and practice of music, both vocal and instrumental, by a gentleman who has, and is devoting his whole life to it, and in such a manner that instead of making it laborious it becomes a pleasure to children; while we see him offering every advantage for the improvement of our youth, and at the same time at such a rate as to enable whole families to attend without any great expense; (I allude to his proposition to teach our children to sing.) I say, while we see all this shall we withhold our mite, or shall we go forward with our children and at once make music a branch of Common Education?

This suggestion about adding music to the regular educational curriculum was forward looking, but no action was taken on it until decades later, long after Nash had left the city for places unknown (probably 1846). It is possible that he went to Louisiana because a W. Nash arranged the music of "I Cannot, Cannot Say Farewell," published in 1861 and written by a student leaving Centenary College, then in Jackson, Louisiana.

Emil Heerbruger and C. J. Schultz, both Germans, began offering their services in 1837. Heerbruger, a musician and composer, had been a member of the Italian Opera Company of New York. He taught music and also had a music store in Nashville, while being a guiding force in the Musical Fund Society. Heerbruger composed "Swiss Air," "Grand Grecian Military March," "Hungarian Waltz," and "Cicilian Waltz." The Houston *Morning Star* reported on the first musical concert in Houston, Texas, which occurred in May 1840 under the direction of Emil Heerbruger, and he was called "the most accomplished musician that has ever visited the country." More than likely he was just visiting in Texas then, but he was certainly no longer a Nashville resident by 1842 because he left behind debts made public that year. C. F. Schultz stated that Nashville appealed to him for "its known refined taste in music." Having studied in Berlin, he was a pianist and composer, who gave guitar, violin, and voice lessons. Schultz composed "Impromptu Waltz," "March," and "German Song," and according to Kenneth Rose, "the earliest known piece of

G. H. Burrell printed the earliest known piece of sheet music published in Nashville: C. F. Schultz's "Pas Redoublé," composed around 1838.

sheet music published in Nashville" is Schultz's "Pas Redoublé," composed around 1838 and printed by G. H. Burrell. At some point Schultz left Nashville, and his destination might have been Louisiana because the 1850 U.S. census for DeSoto Parish, Louisiana, listed a C. F. Schultz, age forty-five, a musician from Germany.

In 1838 Nashville gained another new resident, William Harmon. A Baltimore native, educated in Europe, "he was the first American born musician with foreign training to locate in Nashville, and the fact that he made his decision immediately after completing his studies suggests that he found here [in Nashville] certain advantages that other cities could not provide," observed Kenneth Rose. Harmon worked with William Nash at the Nashville Academy of Music and with other leaders of academies, and when a theatrical occasion arose, he played in the orchestra.

That 1837 was a notable year for music in the city is remarkable, given financial conditions. A financial panic, which the editor of the 1865 Nashville City Directory called "the great financial revulsion of 1837," brought with it a suspension of specie payments by banks, plunging real estate prices, and the departure of many folks for Texas. For weeks merchants ran ads similar to this one from Hicks, Ewing & Co.: "In consequence of the derangement in the monied concerns of the country, and the difficulty of sustaining the business of Manufacturing IRON and CASTINGS without obtaining more prompt payment than we have heretofore required, we have been compelled to lessen the length of our credits, and shall require for all Iron and Castings that we may sell after this date *Cash* or good notes at 4 months date, payable in Bank." Things were not good and people knew it, but reading about the "derangement in the monied concerns" in the morning paper must have had a sobering impact.

Yet Nash and Mrs. King and the other teachers had students, and a significant group, the Musical

Masonic Hall, constructed in 1818 at 422 Church Street, was the site of balls and concerts and dramatic performances. During Governor Sam Houston's tenure, the General Assembly met there.

Fund Society of Nashville, was formed in 1837 by both amateur and professional musicians. The society had "social and benevolent purposes." Emil Heerbruger was much involved in the society and was a featured performer in the first concert, December 26, 1837, at the Masonic Hall. The musicians tried to give monthly recitals and had a schedule until March 1839, after which the group seems to have disbanded. Everything from Strauss to Mozart, Rossini, Meyerbeer, and Bellini had been on the programs.

Charles Edward Horn, an Englishman who was a composer, singer, and musician, scheduled a "Soiree Musicale" on Saturday, April 15, 1837, at the City Hotel. A ticket cost $1 ($16 today) and could be purchased at the door or at three music stores. Horn had been on stages in London and New York, and Miss Marianne (or Maria) Horton, who would become his wife in 1838, was from an English family of performers. Horn "presided at the piano," and both sang. William Nash and James Diggons assisted them, and the "beauty and fashion of the city" were delighted with the evening.

The City Hotel in August 1837 was the site chosen by Mr. Pucci of Italy for his concert. Perhaps as an extra incentive to attend, a cotillion party followed his performance on Thursday, August 3. He was a much lesser known figure than Horn but no less proud of his accomplishments on the "Pedal Harp." Pucci "had the honor to perform in all the principal cities in the Union," and his "entertainment of *Vocal and Instrumental Music* [was] never equalled in the United States." He had asked the young men in the "Social Band" to be his backup musicians. Tickets could be purchased at the hotel's bar.

The Masonic Hall, which had been constructed in 1818 on the north side of Church Street (422 Church, behind what would be the site of the Maxwell House Hotel), was the location for the more fashionable musical evenings. With the help of an anonymous commentator's description, we can visualize what a performance there was like. Concertgoers entered a large room that, thanks to numerous hog lard candles, was dimly lighted and perfumed by a scent like that of fried bacon. They sat on benches in rows, facing a platform for the performer(s). Usually the concertgoers talked through the whole performance, although they were gracious with applause and the demand for encores.

Licensing Drama

In an enlightened city like Nashville,
where some of the first men in the Union exist,
I did hope no laws could be formed
that would remind me of the 13th and 14th centuries.

—JAMES WARRELL, 1837

TAXES AND LICENSING issues affected the performing arts environment even in the early nineteenth century. The need for a license to perform in Nashville fired up one theater manager, and more than one ignored the legal niceties.

James Warrell wrote an eloquent, angry letter on this subject to the publisher of the *National Banner and Nashville Whig* to explain why he petitioned the City Council to "ameliorate the license for opening the Theatre," and he gave a little history lesson in the process:

It must be well known to many of your citizens that Mr. James H. Caldwell never paid any license. If a corporation license existed at the time the Theatre was built and opened, he resisted it and never paid a cent. In Petersburg and Richmond, Virginia, the corporation required of him a license in each place; he battled with them and defeated them. In the cities of Mobile, New Orleans, Natchez, Vicksburg, Memphis, Louisville, Cincinnati, Pittsburg, Boston, New York, Philadelphia and Baltimore, and I believe St. Louis, no licenses for dramatic entertainments exist. Since the days of Thespis down to those of Oliver Cromwell, no licenses were in operation; on the contrary, the Drama was fostered. It is true that in the days of Cromwell, when a stiff-necked puritanical race had their sway, Players were regarded as vagabonds and vagrants— but since that period the drama has been fostered throughout all Europe. The Stage, the Bar and the Pulpit, are now standards for our pronunciation. The first season when I acted as agent for Russell and Rowe, the cash receipts were between 12 and $13,000 every dollar of which was left in your city, and the Theatre sustained a loss of nearly two thousand dollars. A Circus or Caravan of wild beasts visit this place, and pay from thirty to fifty dollars, and carry away two or three thousand dollars. There is no tax on Philosophical experiments. What are these Philosophical experiments? A celebrated Doctor Somebody from down east, comes along with a green bag of gas, and a magic lanthern, and he has cunning enough to trick you out of several hundred dollars—but do his experiments illume the mind? Are such experiments to compare with the sublime works of the immortal Shakspeare?

I informed your Council that I had no disposition to oppose the law—all I wanted was the indulgence to pay the license by instalments, or to appropriate one or two nights for the benefit of the Corporation. There are at least from thirty to forty tippling houses in town, and none of them pay, I believe, more than one eighth of the amount assessed or levied on the Theatre. I repeat, that I have no disposition to oppose the law, but if driven into a corner I must contend for my just rights.

Warrell and the City Council came to some kind of agreement because he presented Mr. and Mrs. A. Addams, Mr. Nickerson, and Mr. Delmon on the stage. The players' opening night in early July featured *Othello,* and the music was supplied by a local amateur band. On August 2 the evening's performance was *King Lear,* followed by the farce *Lady and Devil.*

Decades later, on October 31, 1879, J. R. McCann, county court clerk, issued the following to T. H. Fogg, trustee:

> You are hereby notified that John W. Edwards and others have been giving Theatrical Exhibitions in the building situated on North Cherry St. [Fourth Avenue] in the City of Nashville and Known as the Grand Opera House, without having first obtained a license therefor, and that any further exercise of said privilege after service of this notice will render you privy hereto and liable for the same under Sec. 556a 556b 556c etc. Code Tennessee.

Immigrants

The personality of Nashville
is compounded of many phases.
The long continuity of its citizenship is one.
There are several thousand citizens of metropolitan
Nashville who are direct descendants
of the place's founders, arriving in 1780.
And that adds a thick and tough
stratum of conservatism to the city's life.

—ALFRED LELAND CRABB, 1960

THE COUNTRIES OF ORIGIN of newcomers to Nashville and the numbers who became citizens affected the development of the performing arts. The majority of the early settlers were American born, of Scotch-Irish or English heritage. African-Americans—free and slave—were the next largest group. Later arrivals came from Germany, France, and Italy, although in limited numbers, and these immigrants had more deeply rooted classical performing arts in their native cultures than did the other groups. Tides of foreign-born individuals have not swept through Davidson County, and following the Civil War when more workers were needed and governmental efforts were made to recruit foreigners, barely a trickle materialized. The South as a region, not just Nashville, had a similar experience.

A heated debate over immigrants and their character appeared in the newspapers in January 1837 when the city had fewer than seven thousand inhabitants. What was happening in the East was alarming to some who feared similar problems with immigrants in Nashville (and other southern cities). The points raised by both sides are being repeated today, more than 150 years later.

The anti-immigrant spokesman emphasized the low character of immigrants, especially from England and Ireland, pointing to the "vice, the pauperism and the ignorance with which emigration is desolating our land." Of serious concern to him was "the necessity of placing greater restrictions upon the elective franchise . . . now so easily and so speedily enjoyed by foreigners."

He explained why immigrants were attracted to the United States: "The inquisitiveness of curiosity, the wild spirit of adventure, the thirst for acquisition, the love of change and the anticipated pleasures of a free and unshackled liberty, have all tended to widen and deepen the stream of population that has rolled from Europe." Yet he viewed the immigrants as

> most generally the refuse and the dregs of European society that have been drifted to our shores by want and impending starvation at home. . . . Debased by oppressions and goaded by famine, numbers are allured to a land reported to flow with milk and honey, and the exuberance of whose soil they idly imagine will, without toil and without culture, supply their wants. . . . Freed from the restraints by which they had been fettered, they use power that they before felt but wielded not, only to tyrannize and to oppress. Mistaking the political privilege with which the American constitution presents them for a lawless licentiousness, they are made the instruments of unhallowed passions and the fit materials for mobs. Already in the Eastern cities has their influence been felt in rapidly extending pauperism, adding to the catalogue of crimes and in increasing the frequency of mobs. We have seen them disturbing the peaceful quiet of our cities, sporting with property, and ready upon every provocation to apply the burning torch to consume our dwellings. We have seen them snatching the administration of justice from the hands of its proper officers, and involving in one common ruin the innocent and the unoffending.

He admitted that he did not want to characterize all foreign-born people in that way, and he noted that some brought wealth, talent, ability in the trades, and scientific know-how. In the laudatory category he specifically mentioned Gerard Troost, born in the Netherlands and a resident of Nashville since 1827, who was the state geologist and the science teacher at the University of Nashville. In that short period of time Troost had become a much-admired citizen. He added,

> It is not with such that we are jealous of sharing our privileges, but with that vitiated pauperism and ignorance of which parish charity and liberality are daily draining England and Ireland. To such we are unwilling to extend the elective franchise—as soon as they set foot upon our shore as though they had been purified of their vices and healed of their ignorance by a voyage across the ocean. To place in their hands the power of filling our Senate Chambers, our courts of justice and of selecting Executive officers with safety, an interest in the west of our Republic must be kindled and their minds must be sufficiently enlightened to discriminate between true ability and impudent quackery, between sincere devotion to country and a spurious and noisy patriotism.

Instead, "they must be educated and trained in the great school of our republic. They must imbibe our spirit, become identified in the prosperity of our country, and witness and study the operations of our government." If these things do not occur, "then may we reasonably anticipate . . . that these Vandal and Gothic hoards [sic], armed not with the dart, the javelin and the spear, but with their vices and the elective franchise, will destroy the fair fabric of American liberty and leave it an existence only in story or in song."

The pro-immigration spokesman (who was an immigrant) stated that opponents always pointed to vices and not virtues of immigrants. He wrote,

> The vices of the lower classes of that villified [sic] people, generally proceed from poverty,

the parent of many ills, owing to unavoidable want of employment at home, and inadequate wages when it is obtained; but as this poverty soon disappears with the cause of it, in a new, thinly peopled, yet vigorous country, its effects also then disappear; and indolence and laziness are certainly novel charges against them, when they have an opportunity of displaying the opposite qualities. America, as yet, on a view of her whole immense extent, requires hard working people more than those of any other description, and it can hardly be expected that such people will possess that superior intelligence, and delicate regard to propriety of conduct, which are too often wanting even in those who have had from infancy all the advantages that wealth, rank, education and perfect political and personal freedom can confer.

After all, the founders of the country encouraged immigration. How else could the United States have achieved "rank and population of a great nation" or have "executed the numerous public works, which perhaps, more than any thing else, have contributed to give her that character"? If permitting too many immigrants was bad, then the American people should encourage the passage of new laws to cope with the situation.

The pro-immigration spokesman agreed that Troost was an asset to the community, yet he questioned "whether, on the whole, a hardy European peasant, who is capable of ably wielding his pick and his axe, is not as great an acquisition to the country." There was more "inducement" for a "poor illiterate laborer or peasant" than for someone with Troost's qualifications to come to a new country. A laborer had a richer field of opportunity in America than in his native land.

Immigrants were no more criminally or violently inclined than native-born Americans, declared the writer. He concluded, "I exempt from these reflections common murders for the sake of spoil, for these are too frequent in every country where there are affluence and indigence.—Even in our own beautiful Nashville, which although there are so many natives of the proscribed country in it, is confessedly one of the most orderly and virtuous communities in the nation, some very gross outrages could be referred to, in which, however, none of that injured people have been implicated."

Another pro-immigration spokesman wrote,

To no class of men in our Community are Nashville and her citizens more indebted for her prosperity and flourishing appearance, than to the *Emigrants*. Look to her ware-houses, her stores, her splendid private dwellings and churches, and the variety and excellence of the goods displayed upon the shelves of her wholesale and retail Merchants, and, while we would by no means institute an invidious comparison between her native-American and Emigrant population, which is as unnecessary as it would be groundless, we fearlessly and unhesitatingly re-assert, to none is she *more* indebted than to the latter. Is any public project on foot, is internal improvement to be advocated, are fire-companies to be formed, steam-boats to be built, colleges, schools or hospitals to be advocated, or are the services of good, sturdy, faithful, hardworking laborers wanted; who are more forward than our foreign-born fellow citizens? And, *both best and least*, to whom is our humble self more indebted for a good dinner, a flowing bowl, the delights of a social hour and hearty good fellowship than to the SONS OF ST. PATRICK AND ST. ANDREW? We answer, emphatically, to *none*. Both individually and as a component part of the Nashville population, we feel grateful to them for their courtesy and for their exertions in her behalf, while we feel equally so to our native-born fellow citizens who have assisted in beautifying our town and in advancing her interests.

In her book *Nashville, 1780–1860: From Frontier to City*, Anita Shaefer Goodstein stated, "In 1850 the total foreign-born population amounted to 810 men, women, and children: Frenchmen, Italians, a lone Swede, but mostly Germans and Irishmen, in all 10 percent of the city's free population. Ten years later the foreign-born population had tripled and accounted for 20 percent of the free population." Nashville's free population in 1850 was 7,626 (total population, 10,165), and in 1860 it was 13,043 (20 percent would have been about 2,600 foreign born; total population, 16,988).

By the close of the Civil War, more Germans had decided to move to Nashville; some had learned about the city from their time in the army. Germantown had been established in the 1850s as a suburb and was home for tradesmen, craftsmen, butchers, and a few musicians. (The name has survived, yet the effects of World War I and attitudes toward Germans or German-speaking groups devastated the neighborhood that is only now beginning to recover.) A German citizen explained in a letter to the editor of the *Republican Banner* (October 14, 1867) why he thought efforts to promote immigration to Nashville had failed: "So long as our wealthy men refuse to assist public enterprise, so long will our city and State fail to come up to the flourishing condition of our [Northern] States and cities." He also pointed out an error in the legislature's approach to immigrants: "The Tennessee Legislature gave foreigners the right to vote after a residence of twelve months, and thought that was all it had to do to bring them here. . . . My German countrymen will not go to any country merely because they are offered a vote, but go where they are invited to come, and where the greatest inducements are held out to them."

Colonel A. S. Colyar, a lawyer and businessman with many interests, including the Tennessee Coal and Railway Company, began a concerted effort to encourage foreign immigration in 1871. He organized the Tennessee Immigration and Labor Association, managed by John Moffat, and set up representatives in the counties to promote real estate sales. Colyar backed a bill before the state legislature to have a state immigration officer, but it was defeated. He saw his wish granted, though, in 1875, when the legislature approved the Bureau of Immigration with John Moffat as its first commissioner. Still no great numbers of immigrants came.

In 1882, European immigrants—250,630 of them—fled to the United States to escape economic depression, but most headed to the Midwest. Thinking to entice some of them to the South, businessmen formed the Southern Immigration Association in 1883, and the proceedings of the first session of the association were held in Nashville the next year. Andrew J. McWhirter gave the speech "An Appeal to European Immigrants to Come to the South" in which he summarized problems on both sides, native and foreign-born populations, affecting immigration. He began by saying, "The cry has gone up against us that we breathe an atmosphere of death; that the vampire of infection hangs ever over us and sucks the lifeblood from the channels of industry and trade. Immigrants are imposed upon by corrupt agents representing the railway and other real estate corporations of the great and unfathomable Northwest, . . . and these agents often display maps of the United States, with the entire list of the Southern states marked in Ethiopian darkness, with here and there a skull and crossbones labeled *Yellow Fever District, Famine and Pestilence*."

He also addressed the misconception among southerners that immigrants were less-desirable types: "The honest laborer of Europe is often highly cultivated and well-prepared for any station in life, and yet for want of occupation he must remain a pauper at home or find employment in other lands where labor is in demand, and the soil more productive, and the burden of life less difficult to bear. . . .The fact that paupers and criminals were once sent over to America by the wholesale from Europe has done much to prejudice the South against immigration." He ended on a hopeful note: "Exhaustless possibilities are ours. The future is pregnant with glory, and it is a well-ordered immigration that shall pronounce the 'open sesame' to the treasures of our Southern soil."

McWhirter did not include a rather major point that had to weigh heavily on the minds and hearts of the devout citizens of Nashville. In 1853 John P. Campbell, the editor of the City Directory, had written, "No City in the South is more justly celebrated for its intelligence, morality, and courtesy to strangers. Its Sabbaths are quiet and orderly, and its Pulpits and Churches well filled." A problem with some "strangers," foreigners who might seek to live here, was that they brought continental Sunday with them, and activities of the day just might include drinking beer and dancing. How could the native-born population, adherents of the sedate "approved prayer and worship only Sunday," ever be reconciled to that situation?

Few immigrants responded to the "open sesame" invitation; perhaps they did not perceive the "treasures" as southerners did. Some likely believed that *all* southerners treated immigrant workers as slaves, as some land owners did. Others might have had their fill of rural or small-town life in their homelands and perceived that big-city life would be easier or at the very least more exciting. Having relatives or persons from one's homeland—in other words, a network of allies—already in place has a drawing power to a location that is difficult to quantify but is real nonetheless. Availability of funds to go farther than the eastern seaboard had to have been another factor.

Nashville in 1880 had 3,025 foreign-born persons and a native population of 40,325. Ten years later the native population shot up to 72,374 while the foreign-born increased modestly to 3,794. According to the annual police report of 1890, 110 Irish and 112 Germans were among the total 6,010 persons arrested, hardly a crime wave among the foreign-born group. After the turn of the new century, in 1905, the police report cited a total of 10,329 arrests: 28 Germans and 24 Russians. (There were 2 actors and 13 musicians; laborer and porter were the primary occupations of those in trouble with the law.)

A great wave of immigration into the U.S. peaked from 1900 to 1910 when eastern cities were bursting at the seams and officials were scrambling to find ways of moving some of them into the rest of the country because city services were overwhelmed. During that period, South Carolina actively recruited immigrants from Europe, and after two years of effort, the state saw limited results. In the fall of 1906, the steamship *Wittekind* of the North German Lloyd Steamship Company brought a few hundred people to Charleston. The previous little wave of immigrants into Charleston occurred just before the Civil War. Being a seaport did not mean that immigrants would arrive on a southern city's docks.

May 1907 was a time to discuss sending immigrants to the South. A dispatch from London that appeared in the *New York Times*, May 1, 1907, reported that Governor Hoke Smith of Georgia was trying to recruit immigrants to his state. The governor said he had succeeded in "removing some of the prejudices held against emigrating to the Southern States," and he had better luck in Scotland than in the other countries.

A few days later, the editor of the *New York Times* wrote that New York City had received 21,000 immigrants in one day, and he offered his advice on what to do with all of the people: "Certain enterprising steamship companies whose managers are gifted with foresight should offer special inducements to immigrants colonizing Charleston, Mobile, and Galveston.

The companies would have to launch a hundred ships to supply the unopened Southern empire, once the stream of immigrations were deflected thither."

At the end of May, Jacob H. Schiff spoke at a dinner for the Independent Order B'nai B'rith in New York City. He expressed his concern about "unordered immigration" of the United States, and he said, "Such an immigration is forced into the North Atlantic cities. The Jew should be and has been a blessing wherever he goes." Then he specifically urged sending Jewish people to Texas: "I can see no greater work than to aid this cause, to make the immigrants welcome not in the crowded towns, but in this region."

The editorial page of the *Nashville Banner,* June 21, 1907, had disturbing comments about why immigrants were not coming to the South:

The announcement made in a New York dispatch that the North German Lloyd and the Hamberg-American Steamship lines would decline to transport immigrants to America who are destined for the Southern States, for the alleged reason that the Southern people do not know how to treat immigrants justly, is an indication that there is some systematic agency at work, instituted in and directed from this country, to prejudice the minds of Europeans against the South, by disseminating false stories of peonage and ill treatment of foreigners in this section. It is believed that a bureau has been established, probably by Northern and Western railroads, which still have large grants of land to sell, to prevent a turning of immigrants to the South and to maintain the tide in the direction of the North and West. This is a matter which should call for government investigation. The South does not want the full tide of indiscriminate immigration turned this way, but it can justly complain against a counter movement based upon misrepresentation and slander.

In his December 1903 State of the Union Address, Theodore Roosevelt had weighed in on the immigration discussion: "We can not have too much immigration of the right kind, and we should have none at all of the wrong kind. The need is to devise some system by which undesirable immigrants shall be kept out entirely, while desirable immigrants are properly distributed throughout the country. At present some districts which need immigrants have none; and in others, where the population is already congested, immigrants come in such numbers as to depress the conditions of life for those already there."

Republican Senator William Paul Dillingham of Vermont had been active in the Senate as a proponent of restricting immigration, and in 1907 Senator Dillingham was appointed to form a commission to study immigration patterns. Much had been done already to restrict Chinese and Japanese immigrants, and after four years, the Dillingham Commission produced a multivolume work that recommended various exclusionary policies, including literacy tests, for all immigrants.

Laws citing immigration quotas, the Great Depression, World War II—all slowed immigration to the United States as a whole. Then changing policies of the American government and the Immigration Act of 1965 affected not only the pace of immigration but also the places from which immigrants came. Suddenly Mexico and Asia, not Europe, were the leading sources of immigrants. In 2002 the foreign-born population of the United States totaled 33.1 million, and from 2000 to 2002, 3.3 million immigrants entered the country.

The 2000 census for Nashville is broken down in this way for major groups: white: 381,783; African-American: 147,696; Latino/Hispanic: 26,091; and Asian: 13,275. Clearly the white population remains the biggest group (people of German, English, Scottish, and Irish ancestry continue to have high percentages). Given that the city's foreign-born population was about 3,000 in 1900 and about 1,500 in 1940, the designation of Nashville today as a "New Ellis Island" is remarkable.

Two researchers, Steven A. Camarota and John Keeley, have identified "New Ellis Islands" as counties in which "the number of new legal immigrants (1991–1998) was equal in size to at least 50 percent of the existing foreign-born population in 1990." The South has 131 of these counties, followed by the Midwest with 75. In the nation's one hundred largest metropolitan areas, "Nashville ranks first in the number of new immigrants (1991–1998) relative to its foreign-born population in 1990." (In Nashville the figure for 1990 is 18,012, and the 1991–98 figure is 10,330; the top three "sending" countries are Vietnam, Iraq, and India.)

It is worth mentioning that Nashville has had and continues to have a transient immigrant population associated with the institutions of higher learning. They may live in Nashville one to four years or more as they pursue advanced degrees. Some choose to make the city their new home after graduation, but the majority return to their homelands with the skills and knowledge they have acquired, perhaps as scientists, teachers, or doctors.

The changing makeup of the city's population has implications for the performing arts in what may be offered in programming to appeal to new audiences and in opportunities for newcomers to participate as donors, artists, and/or leaders. Maestro Kenneth Schermerhorn noted, "The influx of people from the West, the North, Southeast Asia, and Mexico has changed the composite of people who go to the Rep, to the Ballet, and to the Symphony. One senses an alteration of tastes." Leaders of arts organizations will be challenged to incorporate their interests, but will also be able to build on their energy.

~

"Longing for Amusements"

*In this city we must have "Stars,"
as all other attraction fails.*

—JOEL DAVIS, THEATER MANAGER, 1857

THE DECADE of the 1850s for Nashville's theatricals had an auspicious beginning with the completion of the Adelphi Theatre and its opening in July 1850, but almost immediately the buoyant mood was deflated. Citizens, actors, and most orchestra members fled the cholera epidemic. The orchestra leader, Signor Matteozzi, stayed, however, and tragically his children died of the disease. Then as now, Nashville musicians extended their sympathy and generosity by holding a benefit for one of their own in need.

By August things were somewhat back to normal, and despite the extreme heat, Julia Dean and her father, Edwin Dean, were performing. They felt an affinity for the city that might have had something to do with the experiences of their relatives. Julia's mother was the former Julia Drake and her grandfather was Samuel Drake Sr., considered the founder of drama in Kentucky; both had acted on Nashville's stage. Unfortunately the Deans made a poor choice in their production, and theatergoers laughed when they should have cried in the scenes of *Lucrèce Borgia*. Nevertheless, Nashvillians were so fond of Julia that they gave her a $150 diamond bracelet. She would return to Nashville again, but her career was short-lived—she was only thirty-eight at the time of her death.

Another popular actress was Eliza Logan. She and her father participated in a Firemen's Benevolent Association benefit on September 23, 1850. In return, two days later the house was filled with firemen in uniform, and the wealthy and fashionable in their best attire. The firemen gave Eliza a silver pitcher.

When Charlotte Cushman was to play at the Adelphi on April 28, 1851, a circus was also in town. Given the preference of many citizens for such amusements and Jenny Lind's appearance just weeks earlier with its costly tickets, no one was sure what to expect. Cushman played to a full house and the circus to an almost empty one. An American, she had already achieved star status in England and the United States.

In the fall season of 1851 *Lady of Lyons, London Assurance, Sir Giles Overreach, Hamlet,* and *Romeo and Juliet* were among the offerings. Over time, Shakespeare proved as popular as other dramatists to Nashvillians, and perhaps audiences in the early days showed a preference for his works—or it might have had something to do with the actors who chose Shakespearean roles. In the spring of 1852 the Adelphi's manager hired a scenic artist and took a turn toward the spectacular with the productions of *Cherry and Fair Star* (complete with grottos, hanging woods, moonlit vales, and serpents' dens) and of *Forty Thieves.* An excellent stock company was in place by 1854 with G. K. Dickenson, a London actor, at its head, but that excellent company must have moved on fairly soon. A six-piece orchestra was another addition to the Adelphi.

Commentary from editor T. H. Glenn of the Nashville *Daily Gazette* gives insight into the social and political environment in the mid-1850s as it was reflected in the theater. Harriet Beecher Stowe had published her novel *Uncle Tom's Cabin* in 1852, and by 1853, others had turned the story into plays. Still others in the South had created reactionary plays against *Uncle Tom,* and one of them was the subject of Glenn's articles.

The actor Mr. Jamison had performed the play of which he was the writer, *Uncle Tom as He Is,* in Memphis early in October 1855. Glenn wrote of it,

> We have always regarded theatrical representations of negro life as in bad taste, even when put forth by a regular Ethiopian corps, but more especially so when attempted by a theatrical company.—To represent negro character correctly requires a peculiar talent, and much

Arias in the Air

James Parton, born in England and reared in the northeastern United States, became a biographer of many famous people including Horace Greeley, Aaron Burr, Thomas Jefferson, and Andrew Jackson. When he was in Nashville in 1857 researching the life of Jackson, he wrote these revealing comments about the city's character:

> Pleasant Nashville! It was laid out in the good old English, Southern manner. First, a spacious square for court-house and market, lined now with stores, so solid and elegant that they would not look out of place in the business streets of New York, whose stores are palaces. . . .
>
> Pleasant Nashville! The wealth of Nashville is of the genuine, slowly-formed description that does not take to itself wings and fly away just when it is wanted most. . . . Those roomy, square brick mansions are well filled with furniture the opposite of gimcrack. . . . Where but eighty years ago the war-whoop startled mothers putting their children to bed, the stranger, strolling abroad in the evening, pauses to listen to operatic arias, fresh from Italy, sung with much of the power and more than the taste of a prima-donna. Within, mothers may be caught in the act of helping their daughters write Italian exercises or hearing them recite French verbs.

close study and observation. . . . [The actors need a thorough] acquaintance with the various traits of the slave negro South and the free negro North [to be able to give] something like a passable performance of the piece—otherwise, such hope were but a guaranty of disappointment. . . .

On this subject, we know not how better to say in a few words, all we intended, than by remarking that negro shows and the drama are two very separate and distinct things, each doing very well when kept to itself, but producing a flat and insipid effect when mixed, particularly if the mixture be badly made up. We strike against all unions that mar beauty and promote discord.

A week or so later when Jamison brought the same play to Nashville, the Adelphi was filled with citizens who saw it and another play. Glenn had more to say:

To the play of Uncle Tom, and all others of a like ilk, however well they may be rendered, we believe the majority of people have a decided aversion. In witnessing a representation of Dame Stowe's misrepresentations dramatized, at the North, a year ago, we thought that no person of cultivated taste and honorable feelings could be inspired by the nature of the play with impressions other than of disgust and were chagrined that the stage had become so prostituted as to pander to the vulgar sympathies of a vitiated taste. There is no good to be accomplished by such representations,—increased mischief and sectional prejudice rather. The elevation of the legitimate drama to a standard of excellence should be the constant object of its friends and devotees, and we believe that an enlightened public will bear us out in the position that these plays foisted upon the stage under the color of a partial and diseased public sentiment, which are depreciating in the tendency, and degrading in their character both to the stage and the public, should be ignored.

As an histrionic author, Mr. Jamison possesses much talent. There is a perspicuity as well as strength in his style, which is at once pleasing and attractive. In but one instance have we noticed any thing like tediousness in his productions. We hope he will direct his talents in channels other than the "black drama," for we feel assured he will succeed quite as well, and give more satisfaction to himself and friends and benefit to his profession.

A new manager of the Nashville Theatre (the name changed from the Adelphi Theatre at this time), Joel Davis, repainted and redecorated to prepare for the 1856 season. Apparently he would have been better advised to spend his money on talented actors instead of theater niceties. A firestorm of controversy slowly built until it engulfed and overpowered him.

Theatergoers were eager to see Jean Davenport, an acclaimed English actress, in 1856. The problems with the theater and its manager lay in the stock company, which the townspeople felt was severely deficient. They wanted excellence in each performance—whether stock company or star. Davis, for his part, was trying to do the best he could with available funds. By the time John Drew and his wife, Louisa, appeared in 1857, things were boiling over in the press.

The Drews performed in early October, and a favorite play was the *Irish Emigrant.* Drew, of course, was Irish, and many of the Irish who had immigrated to Nashville in the 1850s were in the audience. (John Drew was the father of actor John Drew [1853–1927] who worked with Maurice Barrymore in the 1870s, and of actress Georgiana Emma Drew [1856–93], who married Maurice and was the mother of actors John, Lionel, and Ethel Barrymore. The contemporary actress Drew Barrymore is the granddaughter of John Barrymore.) The Irish were the most enthusiastic of the theatergoers, and overall the performances were successful—a stark contrast to the performances of the stock company.

On Saturday, October 3, the editor of the *Republican Banner and Whig* spelled out the problems with Davis while praising the Drews:

> The most emphatic rebuke that the theatre goers could have administered to Mr. Davis . . . was in filling the house on the first appearance of Mr. and Mrs. John Drew on Thursday night and again last night. These artists, acting together in their peculiar line of character, have the ability to carry a play through with a merely nominal support. . . . There is no doubt that they have made a decided hit on both of their appearances. They are comedians of very superior ability, and whoever fails to see them will lose a very pleasant entertainment.
>
> Our theatre goers are longing for amusements, but no extent of fasting would ever force them to patronize Manager Davis' company. The gross receipts of Wednesday night amounted to the immense sum of *seven dollars and fifty cents*—on Thursday night Mr. and Mrs. Drew drew $190 [about $3,600 today]. When will our theatre manager learn that the amusement seekers of Nashville can discriminate between good acting, and such ungainly and offensive antics and murdering of the King's English, as they have had the effrontery to offer this season[?] If Mr. Davis will but add to the strength of the present company, in which we confess there is some good material, we doubt not he will receive a remunerating patronage during the winter. The city is going to be literally crowded, and he would show his good sense by providing a fine company. He deserves credit for securing at this juncture so rich an entertainment for our own people and the numerous strangers now in the city, and we trust that he will receive in the shape of full houses, an earnest of the patronage we are willing to bestow upon true merit.

Charlotte Cushman first played in Nashville at the Adelphi Theatre in 1851. When she appeared as Lady Macbeth on March 31, 1858, at Crisp's Gaiety (formerly the Adelphi), the important scene 1 in act 5 had a new—and unexpected—twist. While Cushman was carrying a lamp in her hand, her veil caught fire. Women in the audience gasped and then shrieked, but Cushman calmly took off the burning veil and put it out.

Joel Davis responded in the *Nashville Daily Gazette*, October 24:

> Messrs. Editors:—Gentlemen, with your leave, I will say one word in my own defence, since Local Rains of the Banner, thinks it but right that the public and himself particularly, should be relieved from the inflictions nightly put upon them, by the *"horrid orgies"* enacted at the *Nashville Theatre*. All I can say is what any honest merchant or trades man would say,—they

are free to visit the Theatre or stay away, although it is my greatest desire to please my fellow citizens of Nashville, and for that purpose I have gone to the extent of my own personal means and the means of others who were kind enough to befriend me, and assist me in the undertaking. For this purpose I have employed the best Stock talent to be had in the Theatrical market West or East.

Mr. R should consider that Nashville will not afford a Stock Company as complete in every instance, as Miss Laura Keene's Theatre or the Broadway, where they play no "Stars."—In this city we must have "Stars," as all other attraction fails, although by [the] Banner it appears that I alone am the guilty one, I am glad it is so. That he vents his paltry spleen at me personally, is easily accounted and little heeded on my part; that he is capable of criticizing a good Theatrical performance, I deny, he lacks the years of experience necessary to do so. No few months of newspaper scribbling will place any man on a par with Bennett, of the Herald, G. D. Prentice and others in these matters. . . . I here say, as I have always said heretofore to the public generally and Members of the Legislature, individually come and judge for yourselves and if dissatisfied, you are at liberty to demand a return of your money, and it shall be refunded.

Despite his defense, the public won the battle, and Davis closed the theater on November 14, 1857. William H. Crisp became the new manager, with a five-year lease, and changed the name of the theater to the Gaiety. (Crisp also managed a theater, Crisp's Variety, in Memphis.) Nashville was approaching a population of almost 17,000, and the county, about 47,000; the shifting numbers of traveling salesmen, visitors, and legislators added to those figures. Crisp did his utmost to provide the talent demanded. Train travel for acting companies may have helped him in his efforts (in 1858, the trip to Washington required sixty-two hours by train; in 1829, Andrew Jackson took a month to make the journey by stagecoach).

In his first season Crisp opened with James E. Murdoch in *Hamlet*, and Julia Dean, Charlotte Cushman, and Eliza Logan followed him. Yet the theater did not pay expenses. The 1857 financial panic was still having its effects.

Edwin Booth arrived in early March 1859 for two weeks, and capacity crowds applauded his *Richard III, Hamlet*, and other Shakespearean productions. Only Jenny Lind was said to play to larger crowds. His father, Junius Brutus Booth, had played in Nashville late in 1838, Edwin would return to Nashville several times in the coming years, and his brother, John Wilkes Booth, would appear during the Civil War. Edwin never lost his drawing power among the townspeople.

The summer of 1859 was devoted to improving the Gaiety with better stairways, additional seats, new scenes, and a new drop curtain. Beneath a domed ceiling painted like a blue sky, the auditorium's pale blue, violet, pink, and stone white were tinged with gold. Twenty-eight crystal chandeliers "ornamented" the front of the first tier, and twenty-eight footlights were added to the stage. A reporter for the *Republican Banner* added, "The proscenium has also been elegantly adorned and the side mirrors have been removed to give place to a prettily designed open shell, with ornamental tracings extending to the stage boxes, in front of which is suspended on each side a magnificent chandelier."

James E. Murdoch returned in the fall of 1859 for ten days, and his *Othello* was widely acclaimed. Crisp had scheduled many other worthy performances, but although he corrected the "faults" of his predecessor and satisfied the townspeople's "longing for amusement," he was still struggling as he approached a new decade. Solid financial success remained elusive.

The Glory of the Adelphi

*The building is
an ornament to the city.*

—Nashville Daily Union,
June 21, 1850

AN ACT PASSED by the Tennessee General Assembly on January 7, 1850, dealt with the construction in Nashville of "an appropriate and handsome building for the legitimate drama"; the new theater was "to elevate the character of stage representation." The Adelphi Theatre Company was authorized to purchase a suitable lot for the building, and capital of $10,000 was permitted, to be increased to $20,000. The stock's shares were to be sold for $25 each, "to be subscribed with the commissioners hereinafter named, and paid in as the directors, to be elected, may call for it; *Provided*, Said corporation pay a bonus of one-fourth of one per cent, on the capital stock, for common school purposes, annually." The board of nine directors had the task of managing the affairs of the company. Hugh Kirkman, J. P. W. Brown, E. G. Eastman, John B. Johnson, John M. Bass, and Sterling R. Cockrill were appointed commissioners to open books for the subscription of the stock.

Adolphus Heiman, a Prussian stonecutter and architect, designed the Adelphi, and he looked to the classical style in architecture and copied from the Triumphal Arches of Rome with a three-story arch on the front of the theater. A vestibule behind the arch provided access to the parquet and orchestra, and stairs at either side led to the lobbies of the dress circle. The Adelphi was a sturdy structure, with floors, seats, roof shingles, and doors made of poplar.

The dress circle was said to be "a graceful lyre bend." The proscenium was formed by "four pilasters, resting on pedestals of the chase and beautiful Ionic order of architecture, from the crown of the entablature of which springs an Eliptic arch." Paintings in frescoe adorned the ceiling. The stage was large enough that "the most intricate and difficult scenic pieces can be brought out to a great advantage." There were four traps in the stage, and two stairways led to the rear of the stage from below.

The lobbies were spacious, and the theater itself was well ventilated. A *Banner* reporter commented that "most sultry evenings can be spent pleasantly in it, and the old evil of close air be avoided."

Considered to be a "gentleman of character and credit," John Green was the lessee and manager, who wanted to make Nashville his home. Having a manager who had been an actor, who was known to the citizens, and who wanted to put down roots in the city would seem to have worked in the theater's favor, and his reputation was such that he brought an air of respectability to the enterprise.

Green supervised the scenery and decorations of the theater, which were the work of a Mr. Smith, a scenic artist. The painters used colors of sienna, yellow ochre, rose pink, brown, Paris green, Prussian blue, and Venetian red. Gold leaf was much in evidence. The upholstery was of crimson damask.

Manager Green also lined up the theatrical offerings. For July 2 he scheduled the comedy *Love Chase* to be presented with the overture of *Caliph of Baghdad* by the orchestra, and the farce *Married Rake* concluded the bill. Tickets for boxes and parquet cost 75 cents (about $16 today), and for the second circle, 50 cents. Green's plans did not last much past that date, however, because of a cholera outbreak.

Thomas Boyers, editor of the *Daily American*, wrote on July 2, 1850, the day after the theater's opening, that it was a success. Today, reading the cholera report, which appeared just above his column, of three dead and fifty in the penitentiary being treated puts a damper on the whole event, which should have been a triumph. Imagine building such a theater and holding a play in it within six months of its authorization! The truth was that the theater company was unable to meet its financial obligations. Even having Jenny Lind for two concerts could not help. By April 1851, less than a year after the opening, contractors sued for payment. The filing date was April 23, 1851, for *Gilman et al. vs. Adelphi Theatre Company.* Timothy W. Gilman of Gilman and Hughes was the chief carpenter; major stockholders named were Anthony Vanleer, J. Walker Percy, and Hugh Kirkman.

Chancellor A. O. P. Nicholson ruled that the theater was to be sold at public auction to raise money to pay its debts. Adolphus Heiman was an agent for the creditors, and he had the winning bid of $10,000. The property was to be "vested in them as tennants [*sic*] in common" with shares in proportion to the debt owed them, but Heiman failed to "execute his note." The theater again went up for sale, and W. W. Wetmore won the bid. After others were paid, architect William Strickland received $100 for his work. That was not the end of the theater, but it certainly was off to an unfortunate beginning, and the pattern would be similar for other theaters in Nashville over the upcoming years. Having the vision of a fine place to hold "legitimate drama" and executing that vision were not enough.

The Adelphi Theatre, designed by Adolphus Heiman and constructed in 1850, was the site of Jenny Lind's noted 1851 performance. It was located on the west side of North Cherry Street (Fourth Avenue) near Cedar Street (Charlotte Avenue). Note the state Capitol in the background to the right, and the broadside for Zoe on the left. This photo was taken in 1864.

Jenny Lind:
Now Singing at the Adelphi

Jenny Lind, this wonderful woman,
the very enchantress of song,
is now coming up our river and is soon to be in Nashville.

—DAILY NASHVILLE UNION, MARCH 29, 1851

STAR POWER. The flamboyant P. T. Barnum taught everyone what that concept meant when he signed Jenny Lind for a lengthy tour of the United States. The publicity campaign for the "Swedish Nightingale" brought her name into households across the country, and whether one was present at a concert or read about it in the countless newspaper articles or heard about it from an acquaintance or family member, everyone seemed to know about her tour and her talent. Tickets to her performances were auctioned, bringing unrealistically high prices for a concert of any type. Merchants sold products with her name attached to them to boost sales of gloves, hats, billiard tables, cigars, and more. People composed poems in her honor.

The two were an unlikely pair. That an entrepreneur not known for musical connections would choose to present a classical singer was an unprecedented endeavor. Barnum had opened his American Museum in New York with its "living curiosities" in 1842 (his circus days were yet to come) and had earned a reputation as a promoter and a hoaxer, but Lind was the real deal. Born in Stockholm in 1820, Lind had sung opera as a coloratura in her hometown and later in Germany. She gained such acclaim that the English wanted to see what the furor was all about. In London (1847), she sang the part of Amalia in Verdi's *I Masnadieri,* and following that, she sang throughout England with such success that Jenny Lind fever was a new ailment to which people readily succumbed. Queen Victoria noted in her diary that Lind "has a most exquisite, powerful and really quite peculiar voice."

Lind stopped performing opera in 1849, however, on the basis of religious grounds—she was displeased with the story lines and characters of some operas and with the reputations of some opera singers. Instead she chose to be a recitalist and an oratorio singer. After Barnum made her the offer of a U.S. tour and they signed a contract, he placed money with Baring Brothers to guarantee her fees. Lind must have had some sense of business or had good advisors—or both—to have negotiated the deal.

Lind arrived in New York in September 1850, and Nashville was scheduled to have her sixty-sixth and sixty-seventh concerts, March 31 (Monday) and April 2 (Wednesday), 1851. It was a good thing that her dates were no earlier because renovations had to be made to the theater. Initially she was to perform in a tobacco warehouse, but Barnum knew the almost brand-new Adelphi Theatre would be a more appropriate venue and thus contracted with the manager for the space.

The Adelphi, which could seat two thousand, had opened in July 1850 on the west side of North Cherry Street near Cedar Street (Fourth Avenue North near Charlotte Avenue). Some said that it had the second largest stage in the United States, but that point is debated. William Strickland, the architect who was at work on the Tennessee State Capitol building, was hired to add a tier to accommodate more patrons. M. Liston Lewis, reference librarian at Nashville's Carnegie Library in the 1930s, observed that "Nashville dared to express the hope that future stars theatric would point in future years to her Adelphi as one of the stepping stones to the heights of greatness they had attained." Lind was already a bona fide star by the time she stepped on the Adelphi's stage.

People from across Middle Tennessee and beyond descended on Nashville the weekend

Jenny Lind was an international star in 1851 when she appeared for two performances in Nashville; an unknown artist made this lithographic print of her in 1851.

before the performances. Lind mania had taken hold. Hotels and livery stables charged two and sometimes three times their usual rates, and people might not have gladly paid the inflated prices—but they paid them. Diners at Willard's Restaurant on Cedar Street could be seated in the Jenny Lind Room.

When the steamboat from St. Louis docked at Nashville's wharf, a huge crowd awaited Lind and her party. They landed on Saturday, March 29, the day of the auction for choice seats on Monday evening. Admission to the auction was 10 cents, and the proceeds were to go to the Orphan Asylum. The bidding started at $50 for the first ticket, and it reached $200—far from the high of $650 in Boston but still a handsome sum.

The more typical prices of tickets at the Adelphi's box office were $4 and $5, and $3 for standing room ($3 in 1851, about $66 today).

A governess later wrote that Nashville in the 1850s had "as much fashion as in New York," so the men and women entering the theater must have been stylishly dressed. The doors opened at 6:30 for the Monday evening concert, which was to begin at 8:00. Souvenir books with Lind's songs were on sale for 25 cents. A wise concertgoer would have purchased one to keep his mind off the state of the theater and perhaps the discomfort of his seat. The workmen had been unable to finish the job: there were holes in the walls and the ceiling; some seats had no cushions, and others were unfinished planks.

On Tuesday morning, there was another auction for tickets for the Wednesday evening performance. Sales were brisk, despite complaints about the theater. People wanted to hear Lind, and whether at her first or second concert, she gave them an evening they would never forget. Among other selections were "Perche non ho del vento" by Donizetti, "The Echo Song," and "Home, Sweet Home." Lind and the baritone Signor Giovanni Belletti, who had been with her from the beginning of the tour, sang a duet. Lind's musical director, Julius Benedict, had chosen a blend of pieces, classical and contemporary, that appealed to the vast majority of the audience. One naysayer was the editor of the *Nashville Daily Gazette,* John L. Marling, who criticized an aria from *Lucia di Lammermoor* sung in Italian; he found "little of that melody which alone can captivate and ravish an American ear."

One enthusiastic listener was Isaac Paul, who bought the piano that had been used in the concert and gave it to his daughter, Martha (later Mrs. Ira P. Jones). Her son traded it in to Castner-Knott on a new instrument, and in 1922 the department store gave the "Lind" piano to Ward-Belmont School. It is now in Belmont Mansion.

Before Lind left Nashville, she and Barnum and his daughter, Mrs. Lyman, visited the Hermitage. Barnum had been there before, in 1837, and met Andrew Jackson. On the estate Lind, the "Nightingale," heard mockingbirds for the first time, and she took from Nashville that memory as she set out for Louisville.

The performances in Nashville brought in $7,786.30 for the first night and $4,248.00 for the second. (Compare those figures to these: in Charleston, the earnings were $6,775.00 and $3,653.75; in Memphis, the sixtieth stop, $4,539.56.) Lind chose to end her contract with Barnum after ninety-five concerts. The entire tour grossed $712,161.34, out of which Barnum paid Lind and her expenses. Jenny Lind netted slightly more than $175,000, and over the years she gave much of that money to various charities.

Lind continued on her own in America, but never did as well without Barnum. In 1852, she married her accompanist, Otto Goldschmidt, and they eventually settled in England. She and her husband founded the Bach Choir in London, and she taught at the Royal College of Music. Although she chose to step out of the limelight, she remains a star, and we do not even have a recording of her voice.

Lind left behind memories among Nashvillians, more than 150 years after her visit. Alyne Massey said, "I remember that my grandmother told me that her mother saw Jenny Lind," and her ancestor made the trip from Columbia, Tennessee, to Nashville. For that memory to have remained in a family so many years is remarkable; perhaps that memory played a part in Alyne's love of the performing arts. Today's performing artists may have a similar effect on future generations, and great-grandchildren will remember the story that began: "I heard Dawn Upshaw in Nashville, and she was wonderful." That is the way in which traditions are built.

Camilla Urso

M'lle Urso is truly a wonder.

—Nashville Daily Gazette, May 7, 1856

"SHE RETIRED into private life in Nashville," "she withdrew from public life to Nashville"— these comments are common in sources discussing the life of the violinist Camilla Urso. A bit of a mystery surrounds her "retirement" here.

By the time Camilla came to Nashville in 1855, she had received instruction at the Paris Conservatory of Music, had given concerts throughout France, and had toured the United States in concerts with other artists. There were two remarkable points about her: (1) she was becoming famous for her expertise in playing what was then considered a "masculine" instrument, and (2) if the birth date cited in reliable sources is correct—June 13,

Camilla Urso, a gifted violinist, had her own concert company long before the turn of the nineteenth century—even though the violin was considered a man's instrument then. She spent several years in Nashville during what has been called her "quiet period" when she married and had two children.

1842, in Nantes, France—she was only thirteen.

Her mother began working at the Nashville Female Academy, and by early May 1856 Camilla (spelled Camille in the newspaper reports) joined Mrs. Macready, the "eminent actress" and "only dramatic reader before the American public," in several "dramatic and musical entertainments" in Nashville, including the Adelphi Theatre, the Lunatic Asylum, and the Odd Fellows Hall.

At the Adelphi on May 3 while Camilla was playing "The Dream" a huge rat crept onto the stage, but we do not know what happened next because the newspaper reported no more about the episode. Mrs. Macready and Camilla took turns for an hour entertaining the patients at the Lunatic Asylum, and one man stood and sang along with Camilla during a "mournful air." For the evening's performance at the Odd Fellows Hall on May 5, a Monday, the inclement weather kept many people from attending, yet "a highly respectable" number heard the duo. George M. Taylor accompanied them.

The review in the *Nashville Daily Gazette* stated, "Professor Taylor seemed to be in one of his happiest moods, judging from his brilliant execution on the Piano (one of McClure's best) for the yielding keys, obeying the impulse of his magic touch, gave back a thrilling 'concord of sweet sounds' at which those of the profession more eminent in reputation might justly have felt an inward satisfaction." It continued, "M'lle Urso is truly a wonder. She plays the violin with a skill and taste which but few of the eminent artistes of the day surpass or equal, executing the most difficult pieces with an ease which is delightful and wonderful, and with a grace and simplicity of manner."

Taylor was listed in the city's directories as G. M. Taylor and in 1853–54 was noted to be a music teacher at 27 North Cherry Street (Fourth Avenue). By the time of this performance at the Odd Fellows Hall he was teaching at the Nashville Female Academy. Perhaps he was in such a happy mood at that particular concert because Camilla had agreed to marry him. They were wed in Davidson County a few weeks later, on June 24, 1856. (Her name is spelled Camillo Urso in the Marriage Record.)

Randal McGavock had occasion to interact with Camilla before her marriage and wrote about the encounter in his journal. Her name is cited as "Camille Urn," however, and he referred to her as "a young french [*sic*] girl who performs exquisitely on the violin." McGavock was selling tickets for Mrs. Macready's May 12 performance on behalf of the Robertson Association and Camilla was also to appear, but the two females had a disagreement and Camilla refused to perform. McGavock went to the St. Cloud Hotel and was able to convince Camilla to proceed with the performance.

The spectacular sight of this bridge greeted traveling actors and musicians coming to Nashville on the river. The painting, *The Suspension Bridge, Nashville* (before 1862), was done by an unknown artist (ca. 1851–86).

Here is where the mystery enters the story. The 1860 census lists George Taylor at age forty and Camilla at age thirty; they had two children: Emily, age three, and Lindsley, age one. If the census report is correct, her birth date cited in historical sources as 1842 is incorrect because she would have been born in 1830. Perhaps she or her husband lied about her age, or possibly the canvasser recorded it incorrectly.

After the census was taken, something obviously happened in the Taylor household to shatter it—besides the outbreak of the Civil War—because by 1862 Camilla was in France and had married another man. She was soon playing in public back in the States and achieving success with orchestras and bands. She formed her own company, touring Europe and going as far away as Australia and South Africa. She settled in New York City in the mid-1890s where she taught students at the National Conservatory and also private students.

(As for George Taylor, he arranged compositions by F. Beler for piano, and at least two were published by J. A. McClure in Nashville: "Manassas Quick Step" and the "Rock City Guards Quick Step." On the sheet music his name was cited as Geo. M. Taylor. He is not listed in the city directories after the Civil War.)

Camilla came back to Nashville at least twice to perform, January 1897 at the Vendome and December 1900 at the Masonic Hall, before her death in 1902. (According to a local music teacher, Aline Blondner, who knew Camilla well, the violinist tried to play while she was dying, but she was just too weak to hold the violin.) For her December 14, 1900, appearance at the Masonic Hall, ticket prices were $1 (boxes and orchestra; $1 then, about $21.60 now), 75 cents (orchestra circle), and 50 cents (gallery). Nashvillians on the program were Mrs. W. H. Jacobus, soprano, and Mrs. W. D. Haggard and Professor C. J. Schubert, accompanists. An advertisement for the recital included a review by Mr. Kriehbiel, *New York Tribune* critic, of Camilla's playing at the New York Philharmonic Society: "Her playing is innocent of every vice, it is rich in every merit. Her perfect reposefulness begets a confidence in the mind of the listener which frees enjoyment from every concern. Her tone is firm, her taste faultless, her style chaste as Diana."

Health at the Academy

Health issues affected every aspect of life in Nashville, and educational institutions had to address them. The following announcement appeared in Nashville's 1855 Business Directory for the Nashville Female Academy, which provided musical instruction for the students and recitals enjoyed by the citizenry:

This institution has enjoyed thirty-nine years of uninterrupted prosperity.

In regard to health, it is believed to have no equal in the United States. Cholera, chills and fever, typhoid and scarlet fever, and similar fatal diseases, have never occurred here. But three deaths of boarders in thirty-nine years.

In regard to maternal influence, it claims equality with the best regulated private families, in all that relates to personal habits, and moral and mental culture.

The institution employs, almost exclusively, Southern teachers. No Southern parent who gives this institution a personal examination will, we think, find a reason for going farther North.

The Nashville Female Academy must have been doing something right in regard to student health and education. Although it was "abused for its dancing," the academy had a $25,000 profit for 1860 (about $500,000 today). Not many businesses could claim such a healthy bottom line, and not that many had been operating as long as the academy.

Camilla had come to Nashville some time before the recital and was to remain a few days afterward. Despite her fame and her status as a one-time resident of the city, the Masonic was far from full. The audience was composed primarily of musicians and families who had known her earlier. She played brilliantly and had at least two encores—"The Last Rose of Summer" and "The Lost Chord."

Mlle Urso as an artist was truly a wonder.

Drama in Real Life

The interval of the Civil War was the only period up to its time that the Nashville stage made money. The Yankee soldiers and other outsiders here in those years were responsible.

—Francis Robinson

SUNDAY MORNING, February 16, 1862, found many Nashvillians in their houses of worship, as was their custom. The Civil War, and Tennessee's participation in it, meant that they had more than usual to add to their prayer lists. Despite the Federals' attack on Fort Donelson on the twelfth, Nashvillians felt increasingly confident in a Confederate victory. The fort surrendered that morning, however, and the news blasted the calm of the day and signaled the beginning of an uncertain future. Most church services were dismissed, sending terrified Nashvillians into the streets.

Witnesses to the ensuing panic—and that was the word most often used—were unanimous in the hope that they would never see the like again. Confederate soldiers from the military hospitals were relocated to camps; the seriously injured had to remain behind. Secessionist leaders, including John Overton, Andrew Ewing, and Nathaniel Baxter, businessmen, ministers, students, and others, numbering in the hundreds, boarded the train or drove wagons or carriages or set out on foot to leave the city as soon as possible. Sarah Polk, widow of President James K. Polk, refused to budge from her home on Vine Street (Seventh Avenue).

THE SOLDIER'S DREAM

All soldiers—Union and Confederate—dreamed of home and family while caught up in the conflict between North and South. This piece was published in 1862, written by D. O. (Otto) Becker, who had been a professor of music in Nashville.

The city presented no opposition to the Federals, who took over on February 25, 1862. The visible changes to the landscape were apparent almost immediately as trees were felled, fences were torn up, and houses were damaged or demolished. Fortifications were constructed, and trenches were dug. The Confederates had already destroyed the suspension and railroad bridges before the takeover.

The deeper changes—in people's hearts—showed up in various ways, from despair to defiance. Kate Kirkman, writing in 1895, retold what she found in an old diary concerning the Civil War: "The men remaining in the city are described as gloomy and crest-fallen. The ladies, however, carry their heads haughtily and persistently look in the opposite direction when Federals pass." Men were "sullen and silent," but women and boys and girls were insolent. When

the Federals were marching down a street, a little boy said, "Hurrah for Jeff Davis!" A Federal replied, "Pshaw, hurrah for the Devil." "All right," said the boy, "you hurrah for your captain and I'll hurrah for mine." Kirkman added that "the more opulent found themselves compelled, for protection's sake, to share their houses with the Federal officers, and to secure themselves against doubtful espionage." Being able to live peaceably in one's home became a fond memory. Yet they were the lucky ones because some citizens were evicted from their homes as Federal officers—and sometimes their wives—moved in.

Theft and murder were too commonplace; citizens feared for their goods and their lives. People who lived outside the city had their crops and stock either stolen outright or commandeered by the U.S. government. Belle Meade Plantation's deer and buffalo were killed, a groom was shot, and the slave women were molested—and Mrs. W. G. Harding was supposedly under the protection of four Union soldiers.

Schools and churches were closed, most of the buildings used for hospitals. The disruptions to education and to religious life were severe. Nashvillians loyal to the Union or neutral in the conflict kept many businesses open. Some businesses shut their doors, to be reopened by Northerners who descended on the city to provide for the needs of the soldiers. New government employees, also from the North, took up residence.

The war's effect on the theater was quite unexpected: profitability became the norm. For the most part, theatergoers were not Nashvillians; local people either had no money to buy tickets or did not want to be seen in the company of Federals or Federal sympathizers. Given this order of Colonel John A. Martin, provost marshal, dated May 20, 1863, there is little surprise at the reaction of many locals: "The places of amusement in this city are patronized liberally by Union officers and soldiers, and courtesy demands that their sentiments and feelings shall be consulted in the performances. The orchestras at every place of amusement will, in future, be required to play at least three of the National airs each night." Nashvillians might have been known for their courtesy, but that was just too much to ask of them.

Before the war, in January 1860, for example, Nashvillians had the opportunity to hear Teresa Parodi's Italian Opera Company, which produced *Don Juan, Il Trovatore, Ernani, La Traviata, Lucrezia Borgia,* and *Barber of Seville.* High fashion was in evidence, with women in their silk dresses with wide hoops and men in their swallowtail suits. A special section of the theater was reserved for African-Americans.

In the Nashville Theatre (formerly the Adelphi Theatre) Manager William Crisp had abolished the saloon and prohibited the sale of liquor on the premises. Drunken patrons had proved to be too disruptive, and sometimes their excessive drinking led them to become ill in the theater—not exactly the atmosphere to appeal to theater-

Pauline Cushman, Actress Turned Spy

Spying on both sides—the Confederate and the Union—was a common practice during the Civil War, and women were active participants. A thirty-year-old actress, Pauline Cushman, came close to playing a death scene that was no act, however. Born in New Orleans, she grew up in Michigan. Recruited by the Federals in 1863 while she was in Louisville, Cushman next went to Nashville to work on her cover, still pretending to be an actress with Southern sympathies. She managed to get behind the lines of General Braxton Bragg's army and gather information, operating in the areas of Columbia and Shelbyville, Tennessee.

Cushman had been a struggling actress, and perhaps if she had been better at her craft, she could have pulled off the spy role with flying colors. But that was not to be. She was caught with secret papers, tried by a military court, and sentenced to hang. Before her sentence could be carried out, the Union army descended on the area, and the Confederate army left. The Yankees released Cushman, still locked in a Shelbyville prison, and she was able to fill in useful details for General William Rosecrans. Her spying days were over, but President Lincoln made her an honorary major. To try to support herself, she gave lectures throughout the country—except in the South—about her adventures and wrote a book about them. She had no further success as an actress, although she pursued acting for a while. At her death at age sixty, veterans of the Grand Army of the Republic buried her in the Presidio cemetery in San Francisco.

goers in silks and in swallowtail suits. Oranges, figs, raisins, candy, and flowers were still available and for sale.

The year in which war was declared, 1861, Walter Keeble leased and managed the Nashville Theatre at least for a while in the fall. A writer for the *Nashville Patriot* (October 15, 1861) asserted that Walter Keeble's Southern Company was the only company then in the South and that his theater was the "only one open now in Dixie." The writer encouraged Keeble to defy "old Abe," who could keep his "Yankee actors and stars." The company had performed *Othello,* followed by *Pocahontas,* on October 9, and then the *Hunchback,* followed by *Pocahontas,* two evenings later. On October 12 the company and Nashville had to say farewell to Miss Annie Taylor, whose last appearance was in the *Lady of Lyons.* In mid-November the Zouave French soldiers staged a "Grand Military Pantomime of the Crimean War" at the Nashville Theatre. Keeble did not remain in Nashville long thereafter, and the theater closed.

By the middle of April 1862, the Nashville Theatre was reopened for business with Harry Everett, the stage manager, doing stock plays for a few months. Traveling theater companies were not yet willing to come to town because of the wartime conditions.

A serious incident on September 5 in the theater had repercussions beyond its walls. Rowdy patrons were fairly common, but on that night some Ohio soldiers started what can best be described as a riot. When the soldiers could not find standing room in the whites' part of the theater, they went to the gallery reserved for African-Americans. As some African-Americans tried to leave, the soldiers assaulted them, and then the soldiers beat and ejected every African-American, throwing some down the stairs. The same soldiers went outside, where they beat any African-American in a Federal uniform.

When similar events occurred on other evenings, the provost marshal made the city off-limits to any soldier not on duty and instituted a nine o'clock curfew for citizens. No evening theater productions were allowed from September 19 to November 12, although matinees were permitted so that the performers could earn money. Guards and ushers were in place when the theater reopened. The theater was suspended again, from January 21 to February 2, 1863, but the reason then was no gas for lighting. Muddy streets and slippery sidewalks rounded out the dreary winter scene.

Nevertheless, the Nashville Theatre did so well that there was a need for a new theater to accommodate the growing audiences. The New Nashville Theatre, formerly known as Odd Fellows Hall, at Summer (Fifth) and Union Streets opened in May 1863 with J. R. Allen as the manager and proprietor. It tended toward lighter, more sensational plays than the classic pieces offered at the Nashville Theatre. No matter what was scheduled, though, the crowds were overflowing in both theaters.

Between the two, patrons were treated to opera (Campbell and Castle's English Opera Troupe); ballet (Jane English Ravel Ballet Troupe doing ballet, singing, and staging tableaux) and other dance (Spanish dances and songs by Signor Ximenes and W. H. Leek; Mlle Zoe, a danseuse and pantomimist); spectacles (*Seven Sisters,* which had as its main attraction the "Birth of Cupid in the Bower of Roses" and ran two weeks; equestrian shows with trained horses); comedians (John E. Owens); and drama (Maggie Mitchell in *Fanchon the Cricket;* Edwin Adams in *Hamlet* and *Macbeth;* Avonia Jones for a whole week, doing roles from Lucrezia Borgia to Leah in *Forsaken* and Lady Audley in *Lady Audley's Secret*). Attendees saw the same acts that were presented in other parts of the country. In 1864 ticket prices for the dress circle were 50 cents, and for the gallery, 25 cents (50 cents then, about $5.75 today).

Music by the Ninth Indiana and Eighth Kansas Regiments bands could be heard almost every evening, and "The Star-Spangled Banner" was always played. Before war's end, vaudeville houses, such as Poland's Variety owned by T. W. Poland and the Nashville Opera House, opened, but they had short lives.

Against this backdrop, consider what was happening in other segments of local society. So many prostitutes settled in town that venereal diseases became a serious debilitating problem for soldiers. Refugees—people coming from the country, contrabands, and camp followers—often had no shelter, no food, and inadequate clothing. The unfortunate women whose husbands were killed in battle sometimes had no means of support and no way to feed their children. Smallpox epidemics struck civilians and soldiers. Confederate prisoners were brought through town on their way to prison camps, and wounded soldiers from both sides filled the hospitals. Newspapers kept up with the war's progress and listed casualties. Daily life was far from what it had been.

Yet not rain, storms, severe weather, or threat of military attack deterred the crowds in search of entertainment. On December 9, 1864, the temperature dropped below freezing, and there was a sleet-and-ice storm. General George Thomas was poised to attack the Confederates in what would become the Battle of Nashville, but activity had to be delayed in deference to the weather. That is, all activity but the theaters and the Howes and Norton Champion Circus, which had been on Market Street (Second Avenue) near the Louisville and

During the Civil War, the New Nashville Theatre was established in Odd Fellows Hall, which had been built on the site of an early theater constructed by James Caldwell at Summer (Fifth) and Union Streets. Note the broadside at the right-hand corner of the photo for Miss Emily Thorne, *The Pet of the Military*. The photo was taken in 1864.

Adelina's Brother

Adelina Patti, who became a celebrated soprano throughout the world and demanded high fees, lived briefly in Columbia, Tennessee, before the Civil War. She sang on the stage there at Hamner's Hall on South Main Street with her brother's group, the Carlo Patti Concert Troupe. (Adelina had appeared in Nashville on November 15, 1860.) Carlo wrote the song "'Twas But a Dream," published in 1860 by J. A. McClure of Nashville and dedicated to Miss M. Shallie Kirk of Memphis; the cover notes that it was "as sung by Adelina Patti."

Mrs. Margaret McLean Dale, who had been a student at the Columbia Female Institute, recalled years later that the pianist Maurice Strakosch was with Adelina and Carlo. His wife, Amalia, was their sister, and Strakosch had helped young Adelina develop her talent. Mrs. Dale added, "We girls went to hear her [at Hamner's Hall], but no less interesting was her handsome brother Carlo Patti." Carlo joined their music class taught by Professor Hoffman, the German teacher, and Mrs. Dale even sang a duet with Carlo.

When Adelina left, Carlo Patti remained in Columbia as leader of the Grand Opera House orchestra and also as a violin teacher at the Athenaeum, a girls' school. He lived in the Franklin House. Seventeen-year-old Adelina performed at Covent Garden in London, May 1861, but her brother, Carlo, had become enamored of the Confederate cause and joined the Maury Rifles by then. Other soldiers with him commented that he played his violin when not on duty.

The singer Adelina Patti, then ten years old, joined the violinist Ole Bull in two concerts in Nashville: April 7 and 11, 1853. She returned to Nashville many times, including her first farewell concert in 1894 and the last farewell concert in 1904. Almost sixty-two in 1904, she sang only two numbers plus encores.

Besides having a famous sister, Carlo is credited with bringing the song "Dixie" to the South when he was the orchestra director at New Orleans' Varieties Theatre.

Nashville Depot since November. Benefit performances during December, in fact, raised funds to assist the poor. (Note: a benefit in the case of an actor or actress meant that the person received a share of the gate, something like a bonus.)

The battle finally commenced on December 15 and lasted through the next day. Confederate General John Bell Hood's defeat compounded the devastating losses to the Army of Tennessee at the Battle of Franklin on November 30. The

Christmas season proceeded with some cheer, however, as people held open houses and served traditional dinners because the threat of further local combat was resolved. Within four months Lee would surrender at Appomattox, on April 9, 1865. The conflict ended after Confederate General Joseph E. Johnston surrendered to Union General William T. Sherman, April 26, 1865.

Two actors who had been on Nashville's stages at separate times came together in high drama in Washington, D.C., at Ford's Theatre. Laura Keene and her company were to present *Our American Cousin*. They had performed it in Nashville on October 20, 1863, and had also featured comedies of Sheridan during their stay. John Wilkes Booth had portrayed Richard III, Hamlet, and Richelieu, among other characters, in late January and early February 1864 in Nashville. On the fateful night of April 14, 1865, Good Friday, the comedy of Keene's troupe was disrupted by the tragic real-life character of Booth as he shot President Abraham Lincoln—just as the audience was laughing loudly at a character's lines. Booth leaped down to the stage, breaking his leg, and shouted, "Revenge for the South!" before he fled the theater.

When they heard the story, Nashvillians were shocked at the news and stunned to realize that Vice President Andrew Johnson, who had been both civil and military governor of Tennessee, would become president. Theater managers responded to the national tragedy by not holding plays in Nashville during the first part of the week following Lincoln's death.

With the end of the Civil War, the city could be grateful that it was not completely devastated as Atlanta had been. Nevertheless, scars on the land and on the people remained. The loss of life and property went beyond mere numbers. Confederate total casualties were 486,000, of whom 54,000 were killed in action; the South had 900,000 serving in the army and navy from 1861 to 1865, so a Confederate soldier had about a 48 percent chance of death or dismemberment (among Union soldiers, it was closer to a 30 percent chance). Many young women would have to go without husbands, although at least thirteen Nashville women married high-ranking Union army officers who chose to remain in the city. One was Mary Florence Kirkman, daughter of Hugh Kirkman and sister of Van Leer Kirkman; she shocked Nashville's social set by marrying Union Captain James Pierre Drouillard in 1864. Estimates of direct costs of the war have been $6.6 billion, which works out to approximately $206 per person in the North and South in 1861 (the figure includes expenditures of the Union and the Confederacy, costs of conscription systems, loss of human capital, death and wounds of soldiers, and general destruction). A commission in January 1869 determined the following losses in Davidson County: $159,457,000 for property destroyed or taken by the federal government, and $69,094.16 for damage done by rebel armies and government.

The deep and long-lasting effects were evident in other ways and hard to forget. For example, Nashville artist Ann Street inherited paintings of her ancestors more than a century after the war, and she said, "The portraits of my great-great-grandmother and great-great-grandfather now in my living room—when they came to me, they still had bayonet wounds in the throats." Other families had stories about their real ancestors, not their portraits, having been bayoneted.

If you were newly impoverished, busy trying to feed and clothe your family, rebuild your home and/or your livelihood, and return to some semblance of normalcy, you were not very concerned about going to see the latest offering at the theater or replacing stringed instruments or pianos that were burned or smashed. Artistic endeavors were set aside. Repairing churches, homes, and other structures, educating the children, and figuring out how a group of people with new status—freedmen—fit into the city added to the tasks of city fathers.

It is highly gratifying and touches the state pride of every patriotic Tennessean to witness this recognition of talent from our own commonwealth and from our own South.

—TENNESSEAN, FEBRUARY 9, 1928

Big Steps: 1866-1945

FROM 1866 TO 1945 in Nashville the footsteps along the road to financial and physical recovery—for the landscape and for citizens—began haltingly. As Nashvillians gained more and more confidence, they founded universities, built a grand theater and an auditorium destined to become a famous performance hall, and celebrated a milestone in the city's history (the Nashville Centennial in 1880). The biggest step forward was the Tennessee Centennial Exposition (even though it was a year overdue, in 1897), which showed the citizens, the state, and the world what Nashvillians could do when they worked together toward a common goal. They built a replica of the Parthenon that symbolized the dreams for the city's future as the Athens of the South. Nashville became the Wall Street of the South for a while as insurance, banking, and securities firms became established. Printing gained in importance as an industry.

The *Union and American,* August 28, 1868, had a reference to Nashville as being "far-famed in the musical world for the eminent talent of its amateurs and professionals in the Apollinarian art." The city's fame as a musical center grew and spread around the world for not only music publishing and music education but also music broadcasting—despite more wars (Spanish-American War and World War I), more financial panics, more epidemics, and energy-consuming social issues such as prohibition and the suffrage movement. Opera, dance, and amateur and professional theatrical events gained a measure of prominence, too.

In the 1920s, Apollo was picking up speed on what he perceived could be the end of a marathon with established professional performing arts groups at the finish line. The city finally had a symphony of its own, with a ten-year history by 1930. A conservatory of music, sponsored by eminent citizens, provided exceptional training in voice and music. But the Great Depression brought Apollo almost to a standstill, and the coming of World War II killed the momentum. Again, Apollo wondered: Could the citizens of Nashville once again recover and rebuild what they had lost? ❖

"Pure, Elevated Drama"

*Today we have a pure, elevated drama
that appeals only to refined tastes.*

—Nashville Gazette, September 19, 1867

A WRITER for the *Nashville Gazette*, September 19, 1867, strongly urged public support of the city's two theaters, the Adelphi and the New Nashville, by stating, "'Tis a fact not to be gainsayed that in the past, we have never done justice by such institutions. During the war was the only era when they proved remunerative; and then their support came not from citizens, but from a nomadic class among us whose patronage served to drag down the stage to the verge of the brothel.

"Today we have a pure, elevated drama that appeals only to refined tastes. Let us give such support as will make it self-sustaining. Perhaps the price of admission nightly is too great a drain on us. Then let us purchase season tickets." The cost was about $50 (about $640 today) for season tickets.

Given this statement, one would have expected *Hamlet* or *Othello* or another serious drama to be the upcoming theatrical event. Beginning on October 12, the unprecedented hit at the Adelphi for almost a month was the *Black Crook*. It had opened in New York's Niblo's Garden in September of the previous year and had a stunning run there, even though moralists condemned the extravaganza—a combination of melodrama, ballet, and "leg" show.

In Nashville an estimated five hundred people were turned away at the door for the opening night. The reviewer for the *Republican Banner* was beside himself with enthusiasm for the "delicious music," the "gorgeous and very changing scenery," "the mechanical and hydraulic effects," "the intricate mazes of the dance," and of course, "the flitting forms of nimble, scantly-attired dancers." Two primary dancers were Mlle Galletti and M. Cardell, and Tony Denier was a noted pantomimist. The reviewer stated that "all the religious people will go to see it on account of the transformation and other scenes; all the rest of the population will help to crowd the house nightly, on account of the gentle and voluptuous influence it casts over the scenes." However one categorized the audience members, even women went in abundant numbers and dressed in their best finery.

The *Nashville Gazette* writer's hopes that the city could make drama self-sustaining fell flat. The Adelphi fared better than the New Nashville, however, because it survived as a theater. By 1870, the New Nashville was turned into a skating rink.

Fisk University and the Performing Arts

*Fisk University can rightly claim
that the Jubilee Singers made Nashville famous.
They made the name of this city a familiar word
in the mouths of millions of people in the United States;
and hundreds of thousands of people in Europe
who, otherwise, would not have known
even that there was a state of Tennessee,
learned through them that there was such a state
and that Nashville was its capital. . . .
But in my opinion, more far-reaching,
more vitally important [of all things]
presenting to the world the Spirituals.*

—James Weldon Johnson
Jubilee Day, October 6, 1933

THE SCHOOL bearing Fisk's name opened in 1866 in wooden barracks that had served as a hospital for Union soldiers near what is now Union Station in Nashville. The name honored

General Clinton B. Fisk of the Kentucky-Tennessee Freedmen's Bureau, who was integral in securing the site. Fisk University was chartered on August 22, 1867, and within a few years the present campus was obtained in North Nashville (formerly the location of Fort Gillem).

People in this country and around the world are familiar with the Fisk Jubilee Singers and their music. Yet the school has made other contributions to the performing arts through work on the stage and in the classroom. Dr. Carolynn Reid-Wallace, the first female and thirteenth president of the university (2001–3), stated recently, "The performing arts on this little campus brought people from Nashville to hear the Jubilee Singers every time they performed and also to other events." She recalled a photograph of students sitting on the third floor of Cravath Hall: "The room was elegant, the fireplace was burning, and James Weldon Johnson, the poet, was talking to a seminar of students. That was taken about twenty years before I came to Fisk [she attended from 1960 to 1964], but the point is that the tradition of performance was not simply on the stage; it was also in the classroom. If you were reading T. S. Eliot or Langston Hughes, your professors were bringing you into the action of that particular poem or drama." The students and the greater community have benefited from the work being done at this small liberal arts school, which had to struggle for its existence very early in its history.

The Jubilee Singers. Jubilee Day is October 6, and each year there is an observance to mark the Singers' departure as they set out hoping to raise funds to keep Fisk going. The small group, some of whom had been born into slavery, included Isaac Dickerson (bass), Greene Evans (bass), Benjamin Holmes (tenor), Jennie Jackson (soprano), Maggie Porter (soprano), Thomas Rutling (tenor), Ella Sheppard (soprano, piano, organ, and guitar), Minnie Tate (contralto), and Eliza Walker (contralto). Phebe Anderson (contralto) and George Wells (performer) participated in only part of the first tour. George L. White was their leader.

Before this specific group was organized, Memphis, Chattanooga, and Nashville heard the singing of Fisk students. In 1867, for example, White's best singers performed in Nashville a variety of songs, from "The Sultan's Polka" to "No Slave Beneath the Starry Flag" to "Are Ye Sleeping, Maggie?" and $400 (about $5,100 today) was added to the school's treasury. A major undertaking was the cantata *Esther, the Beautiful Queen* with Maggie Porter in the title role at Nashville's Masonic Hall, March 9–10, 1871. Tickets cost 50 cents; reserved seats, 75 cents. Most of the people who became Jubilee Singers were in the cast.

They were not singing what we today call spirituals—what they called sorrow songs or plantation songs. Ella Sheppard explained why: "The slave songs were never used by us then in public. They were associated with slavery and the dark past, and represented the things to be forgotten. Then, too, they were sacred to our parents, who used them in their religious worship and shouted over them." But White heard something that he felt needed to be preserved, and he began to collect them. The irony is that the singing of these songs "not for public hearing" saved the school, and as Dr. Lucius Outlaw, a Fisk graduate and now a professor of philosophy and associate provost of undergraduate education at Vanderbilt University, explained to the Singers' audience in January 2002 at the Blair School of Music, "Through their exceptional, impassioned artistry in exemplifying the spirituality that sustained and nurtured Africans-become-Negroes through centuries of dehumanizing enslavement, they were living testimony to the humanity of African peoples, to the eloquence of our artistry, to the definite reality of our capabilities and thus of our promise." The writer Ralph Ellison discussed individuals who raised the vernacular to the level of the high arts, and that is what the Jubilee Singers did.

The first group of Fisk Jubilee Singers included Minnie Tate, Greene Evans, Jennie Jackson, Ella Sheppard, Benjamin Holmes, and Eliza Walker (*seated, left to right*) and Isaac Dickerson, Maggie Porter, and Thomas Rutling (*standing, left to right*).

The Singers' tour in the fall of 1871 to the Northeast was just the beginning of their journey. The reviews ranged from the glowing (a minister in New York, William H. Goodrich, wrote, "The slaves of the South came to begin a totally new history," and their songs were "the only style of music characteristically American") to the harshly critical (the *Musical Gazette* stated that the "performance is a burlesque on music, and almost on religion"). Their first programs included "Annie Laurie," "Old Folks at Home," perhaps an English or Scottish ballad, but few spirituals. By the time they sang for the American Missionary Association, the group that sponsored the school, on March 12, 1872, a more typical program included "Keep Me from Sinking Down," "Brokenhearted, Weep No More,"

and "Didn't My Lord Deliver Daniel?" Other favorite pieces were "Steal Away to Jesus," "Go Down, Moses," and "In That Great Getting-Up Morning."

Eventually the Jubilee Singers went to Europe. They sang before Queen Victoria, William Gladstone (who heard them more than once), Samuel Clemens (who became a fan), the Prince and Princess of Wales, and Mrs. Goldschmidt (the former Jenny Lind, who caused such a stir in Nashville in 1851 but by the 1870s seldom sang in public). They sang in orphanages, churches, private homes, and famous performance halls. In London the crowds filled Charles Spurgeon's Metropolitan Tabernacle, capable of holding six thousand. Through the Singers' financial success, the school was able to remain afloat, and Jubilee

Hall, now a National Historical Landmark, was constructed.

Ella Sheppard was an original Singer who maintained strong ties to Fisk. She taught music to pupils in Nashville twice a week when she first entered Fisk, and she became the music teacher at the school (the only African-American staff member then). In his book *Dark Midnight When I Rise: The Story of the Fisk Jubilee Singers*, Andrew Ward refers to Sheppard as the matriarch of the Singers, and she was in many ways the heroine of that story. After the touring ended and she married George W. Moore, they lived away from Nashville for a while, but they returned to the house that Ella had built on Seventeenth Avenue North (it is no longer standing, but a historical marker is on the site). At Fisk she joined in the efforts of the Work family in preserving spirituals, and she helped in the training of student choirs. Her great-granddaughter, Beth Howse, is currently the Special Collections librarian at Fisk, and she assists students and scholars in their studies of the Jubilee Singers.

A huge Jubilee concert was held at the Ryman Auditorium, May 13, 1913, led by John W. Work II. The event was to help Fisk toward its endowment of $300,000, and four thousand people heard three hundred voices make "the big auditorium ring with perfect harmony." Participants were students and local alumni of Fisk, State Normal students, the Nashville Choral Society, the Fisk Glee Club, and soloists. Each selection was "more beautiful than its predecessor," wrote a reviewer. James A. Myers directed "Couldn't Hear Nobody Pray," and Mrs. C. O. Hadley led "Great Camp Meeting." There were other spirituals, remarks by Chancellor James Kirkland of Vanderbilt University, and readings of Paul L. Dunbar's work. Perhaps the most touching moment came at the end of the evening when Ella Sheppard Moore led the last number: "Swing Low, Sweet Chariot." She was then sixty-two years old, and she died the next summer.

Musical groups from Fisk had eager audiences among Nashvillians—white and African-American. The *Daily American* (August 6, 1888) reported that "no music, not even excepting Jenny Lind, 'the Swedish Nightingale,' ever attracted so much attention as the company from Fisk University." The Singers and the Glee Club often sang for the benefit of other

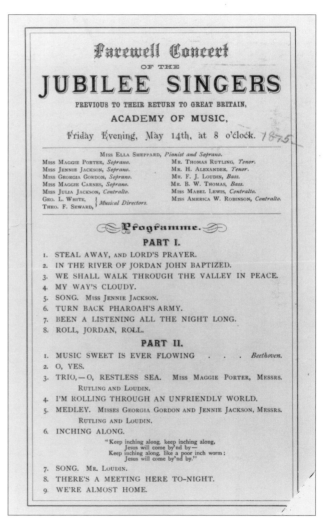

Although the Fisk Jubilee Singers began their career singing more classical numbers, this program for the Academy of Music, New York City, in 1875 lists a typical concert of that period.

groups in Nashville as well as for their own school. On March 3, 1898, at Fisk's Memorial Chapel a grand concert raised funds for First Baptist Church, and a ticket cost 25 cents. Solos were "Only a Rose" by Miss Napier and "Past and Future" by Mr. Scribner. An editorial in the *Tennessean* (1923) referred to Fisk's singing groups and their leaders as "a real civic asset." (There was not always a group of Fisk Jubilee Singers made up of mixed voices. Sometimes there was only a male group, and at one point, as Matthew

Two Noteworthy Programs

Often on the Fisk University campus students and Nashvillians were introduced to unique musical programming. Here are only two examples from the 1940s.

In February 1941, Fisk's music department featured compositions by African-Americans in a concert. Four of the composers were Samuel Coleridge-Taylor ("Life and Death"); Cecil Cohen ("Death of an Old Seaman"); Florence Price ("Canebrake Dance, No. 1"), who had been a student of George Chadwick and has been regarded as the first African-American woman in the United States to be recognized as a composer; and William Grant Still ("A Bit of Wit").

Louis Nicholas, a tenor who taught in the music department at Peabody College, presented a concert on June 29, 1945, in Livingstone Auditorium. He began with the works "Ombra Mai Fu" by Handel and "Cardellini" by Recli, but spent most of the evening singing songs by Nashville composers: "Nirvana," Cyrus Daniel; "At Dusk," Sydney Dalton; "This Little Light o' Mine," arranged by John W. Work II; "Tides," Irving Wolfe; "The Rose Family," Elmer Schoettle; and "Cold Dawn," Walter Ihrke. He finished with Rachmaninoff.

Kennedy explained, "Mrs. James A. Myers had lost the sponsorship of Fisk for the Singers; it was just too expensive, and the school couldn't afford to pay traveling expenses." She kept the group going as Jubilee Singers, not affiliated with Fisk. Then there was a vacuum for a brief time until John W. Work III started the *Fisk* Jubilee Singers again.)

Matthew Kennedy had a lengthy tenure at Fisk. As a student at Juilliard Institute, he was pursuing a diploma in piano at the same time he was completing his high school work. With the assistance of his piano teacher, Lois Adler, and her brother, Max Adler, he was able to enter Fisk as a freshman, and Mrs. Myers, then the director of the Fisk Jubilee Singers, appointed him to be the accompanist. Kennedy received his degree in piano from Fisk (service in the army during World War II interrupted his studies, but the GI Bill permitted him to return to the school) and a master's degree from Juilliard. He became a part of the Jubilee Singers led by Mrs. Myers, and then came back to Fisk as a piano instructor in the mid-1950s. He met and married Anne Gamble, also a piano instructor, there.

In 1956 the Singers had an extensive tour in Europe, and Anne was the accompanist. The grueling tour took its toll on John W. Work III, and when his health prevented him from continuing to direct the Singers, he called upon Kennedy to take over the rehearsals. Subsequently Kennedy became the director, and he said, "I was the director at the time we celebrated the Fisk Jubilee Singers Centennial. That was a really big event, and we did that at War Memorial Auditorium and charged admission. The Voice of America recorded it and used it on the overseas broadcasts." (His daughter, Nina, is a pianist, who also went to Juilliard for her master's degree, and she has performed in Europe and throughout the United States.)

Paul Kwami, who had been a Singer, is the current director of the Fisk Jubilee Singers. The group

Thomas E. Jones (president of Fisk), Roland Hayes (an alumnus and gifted singer who often helped the school raise funds), and John D. Rockefeller posed following Rockefeller's delivery of the commencement address at Fisk University, 1928.

is touring again in the United States (performing in venues including the Smithsonian Institution, the Kennedy Center, and Harlem's Apollo Theater) and Europe. The Singers have been inducted into the Gospel Music Hall of Fame, and the documentary *Jubilee Singers: Sacrifice and Glory* vividly told the story of the original Singers as part of the PBS series *The American Experience.*

An exciting recent venture is the collaboration of Fisk University, Curb Records, and Belmont University in the production of the CD *The Fisk Jubilee Singers: In Bright Mansions,* which begins

with "I'm Gonna Sing Till the Spirit Moves" and ends with "In Bright Mansions," eighteen songs in all. It was recorded at Ocean Way Studio in Nashville with Mike Curb as executive producer. He is eager to see Fisk grow and hopes to do more projects similar to this one. Dr. Bob Fisher of Belmont is equally enthusiastic about the project, and he said, "It is just stunning. When people say they sing spirituals, it *is* spiritual to be in one of their performances."

More music. "Music at Fisk is not a luxury; it is both a habit and a necessity," wrote Charles S.

Johnson, first African-American president of the university, in 1950. In 1954, Fisk became the first private African-American college accredited for its music programs by the National Association of Schools of Music.

Voice instruction began in Fisk's first year, and piano and organ were added the next year. The Department of Music was not established until 1885, but by 1892, it had 140 students (instrumental and voice).

In 1880 Adam K. Spence, professor of English, organized the Mozart Society (later called the Fisk University Choir). It was a large mixed chorus devoted to singing oratorios, such as Handel's *Messiah,* Mendelssohn's *St. Paul* and *Elijah,* and Mozart's Twelfth Mass.

In what was billed as a "Complimentary Concert" for the governor and legislature of Tennessee at Fisk's chapel, Friday, March 19, 1897, at 8:00 P.M., the Jubilee Club sang "Steal Away," the "Lord's Prayer," and "They Led My Lord Away." The Mozart Society mixed the classics with patriotism: the chorus of "Italia!"; "Dixie"; "The Star-Spangled Banner"; and "Red, White, and Blue." The Glee Club's number was "Nelly Was a Lady."

On May 14, 1899, the Mozart Society presented Rossini's *Stabat Mater* at the chapel. The reviewer commented that there was "no auditorium [in Nashville] that can be compared to this ideal music hall." Unfortunately only a small audience heard Albert Greenlaw, basso, who was noted as "musicianly in the extreme," in his solo "For His People Unrelenting."

A work by Samuel Coleridge-Taylor was performed twice in the early 1900s. Coleridge-Taylor, born in London in 1875 to a Sierra Leonean doctor father and an English mother, had written *Hiawatha*, a trilogy based upon Longfellow's poems. The Mozart Society performed parts 1 and 2 in April 1902; the cost to attend was 25 cents (about $5 today). The entire work was performed in early May 1913 with Harry T. Burleigh, an African-American baritone from New York City, singing for the first time in Nashville. Professor Richard Hill, writing a review in the *Nashville Globe,* stated that Coleridge-Taylor was "one of the ablest of modern musicians, and the greatest composer his race has produced." He added that the audience was "unexcelled in any city in the country for culture and refinement." One hundred singers participated in the event led by H. H. Wright, and Alice May Grass played the organ. In addition to Burleigh, John W. Work II, a tenor, and Misses Jones and Boulder, sopranos, sang. Even though one part was long enough for a concert, much less three, Professor Hill found it remarkable that the audience was "spell-bound."

The Fisk University Choir performed at Carnegie Hall, January 26, 1933. Ray Francis Brown, director, led the group beginning with works by Palestrina, Rachmaninoff, and Tchaikovsky, and ending with spirituals. At home in Nashville the choir presented Good Friday services at the chapel (the German Requiem by Brahms, April 7, 1939, and Fauré's Requiem, April 11, 1941). Over the years students' interest in the choir waned as other, nonclassical forms of music became popular and caught their fancy, but the choir is once again finding members.

In an address at another university in 1979, Ralph Ellison asserted, "There was a time when a Negro singer of classical music was viewed as a mere exotic, so if you're surprised that there are now so many Afro-American opera and concert singers, I'd remind you that it didn't happen accidentally. God didn't reach down and say, 'All right, Leontyne Price, Shirley Verrett, Betty Allen, Jessye Norman, Simon Estes, you may now sing opera as well as your native Negro spirituals.' No, this came about because there were agents of culture among us." Fisk has had its share of those agents of culture, notably Roland Hayes, a student and member of the Jubilee Singers.

Hayes returned to the campus several times and occasionally performed at the Ryman Auditorium when he was in the city (often in conjunction with the Singers in fund-raisers for the university). In 1932, the university conferred a doctor of music on him, the first honorary degree from Fisk, and it was said then that it was "fitting that it should go to her most famous son." For the occasion Warner Lawson and Edward Matthews, friends of Hayes, provided the music. Hayes had given a recital in late 1929 to help the school overcome its deficit, and people stood outside the chapel to listen to the tenor sing songs in Italian, French, German, and English. He had become known for his repertory of the classics *and* spirituals. When he came back in October 1961, the seventy-four-year-old was again supporting the school as it was working toward a $6 million development fund.

Francis Robinson, then in U.S. military service, took the opportunity to hear Hayes sing again at Negro Catholic University in New Orleans. In November 1943 he wrote to his friend Lula Naff, "It amazed me to find that outside the clergy we [a friend from Nashville had accompanied him] were practically the only whites there and it struck me what a liberal place Nashville is. I mean that seriously. Whenever he sang in Nashville his audience was always one-third to two-thirds white depending on whether he sang in one of our houses or theirs."

Festivals. Dr. Outlaw remembered his student days: "The high point for me in all my years at Fisk was the spring arts festival. It was such a week. Fisk had really become one of *the* nurturing and demonstrative sites of the fine arts for black folk in this city well before I got here in the early sixties." The first arts festival on the Fisk campus, held April 19–21, 1929, was a rather modest effort of dances, gymnastics, and a student recital in the chapel, but the festival became more and more ambitious in its offerings and in the artists and scholars who performed or lectured.

In 1942, there was a Latin American emphasis with Yoruba dances, the Fisk Stagecrafters presenting *Emperor Jones,* chamber music on Sunday afternoon, and Olga Coelho, a Brazilian soprano and guitarist, on Sunday evening.

Harry Belafonte and Sidney Poitier spoke on the theme "The Negro in Art and Music" in April 1966. Belafonte received Fisk's first annual Humanitarian Award for the Performing Arts, and Poitier received a similar award for the dramatic arts. For the school's centennial celebration, the opening event was to begin at 11:00 A.M. in the chapel, but when students started arriving at 7:30 A.M., the celebration was moved to the

Fisk University started holding annual music and arts festivals in 1929; for the thirtieth festival resident artist Aaron Douglas designed this program.

gym to have enough seats. There were several concerts: Belafonte singing at War Memorial Auditorium; the Fisk Choir in the chapel, accompanied by members of the Nashville Symphony and Arthur R. Croley, organist, for Bach, Brahms, Mozart, compositions by John W. Work III, and the premiere of the cantata *Personals* by T. J. Anderson of Tennessee A & I music faculty; and the Fisk Jubilee Singers. For the closing event William Dawson, an African-American composer-conductor, directed a reduced-member Nashville Symphony in a concert of works by African-American composers, including "Festive Overture" by William Grant Still, "Yenvalou Suite" by John W. Work III, and "African Suite" by Sowande, a Nigerian. A standing ovation rewarded Dawson as the last notes of his "Negro Folk Symphony" sounded.

The forty-third festival was the centennial of the Fisk Jubilee Singers (April 19–23, 1972). Quincy Jones and the Fisk Jazz Ensemble (founded and directed by Robert Holmes) had a concert, and several works commissioned for the occasion were "We Gonna Make It" by Arthur Cunningham, "We Sang Our Songs" by William Grant Still, and "Lord, We Give Thanks to Thee for These, Thy Servants," by Undine Moore.

For the seventy-fourth annual spring arts festival, there were ten days of events, ending April 6, 2003. The festival opened with dance by Orchesis; a play, a jazz performance, the Fisk Jubilee Singers, speakers, and an art exhibition rounded out the offerings.

Drama and dance. The Little Theatre, built in 1860 as a Union Army hospital, is the oldest structure on campus. It was remodeled as a theater in 1935. Dr. Reid-Wallace spoke of the impact of Dr. Lillian Welch Voorhees on her when she was a Fisk student: "She was a white woman who came from a very wealthy family. She graduated from Mount Holyoke with an undergraduate degree, and she got her Ph.D. from Columbia. She as a young woman made a decision that she didn't like what was happening in America; she didn't like that it was not legal for people of color to have the experience of going to school next to people who were not of color. She came from a peculiarly progressive family because her parents believed the same thing.

"Dr. Voorhees was chairman of speech and drama, and she was a very well-respected professor here at Fisk and was one of the most extraordinary human beings I've ever known in my life. . . . She was a wonderful director, and she was an exceedingly intelligent woman. If you were doing *Oedipus Rex*, she wouldn't simply have you know a little bit about the author. She would have you understand that Greek town in that period so that you could connect the history with the drama and the literature and poetry. Then she would juxtapose it and say, 'Now imagine that we were doing this in modern-day dress. How might it have been written by a modern-day playwright?'"

Mabel Love organized Orchesis, a dance company that gave students performance opportunities. The university now offers a minor in dance with an emphasis on performance, teaching, or composition/choreography.

Dr. Reid-Wallace discussed a Fisk student who became the lead dancer in Alvin Ailey's troupe: "I can remember vividly when Judith Jamison came here. She stood out in many ways. She was unusually tall. She wore her hair in an Afro before I ever saw an Afro. She almost glided across the lawn. She looked like a Dahomey queen to me. I can remember thinking, *She came straight from Dahomey here.* All of that grace and elegance. She danced magnificently. She had studied under a Russian ballerina in Philadelphia before coming here so she had been trained in classical ballet. Then she left Fisk after a couple of years and eventually became very, very famous.

Carolynn Reid-Wallace was the first female president of Fisk University. She is a 1964 graduate of the institution.

"I've always reminded myself that a university, and maybe any other community would fit this model, is a peculiar place. While you don't know who, you do have the certainty of knowing that some people amongst all of the people present will one day stand out. The same thing in high school—you don't know who those people are, but somebody in that group is going to become the great Pulitzer Prize winner or the great Nobel Prize winner. Judith as a performing artist—I didn't know that she would become great and famous and powerful, but I knew that there was something about her that spoke to a higher calling, an aesthetic vision, that kept refining itself. She danced in all of the recitals here. She was just very disciplined. She put in the requisite number of hours and probably more than that."

Artists series. Whenever possible, Fisk has given students (and Nashvillians often at little or no charge) exposure to artists from the greater performing world. The list here gives some idea of the variety and quality presented. The fourteen members of the Russian Cossack Chorus, directed by Sergei Socoloff, sang an entire program in Russian (December 7, 1929). Alyne Dumas Lee, an African-American soprano, performed Brahms's "Four Serious Songs" (October 23, 1953). Various chamber music groups have appeared over the years. The guitarist Andrés Segovia had the largest audience of the series the year he performed (February 13, 1954). For a $1 ticket (or 50 cents for a student), someone could hear Jean Langlais, a blind organist and composer from Ste. Clotilde, Paris (March 11, 1954). Years before her Metropolitan Opera debut (1961), Leontyne Price sang Puccini ("La Canzone di Doretta" from *La Rondine*), Handel ("Sommi Dei" from *Radamisto*), and Gluck ("Di Questa Cetra in Seno" from *Il Parnaso Confuso*), but ended the evening with spirituals; tickets were $5 and $2.50 for students (October 17, 1955; a $5 ticket then, about $33 today). Mattiwilda Dobbs, a coloratura soprano, was said by reviewer Sydney Dalton to be the "only Negro singer who has sung at La Scala [1953]" and received "acclaim at Covent Garden" and at the Metropolitan Opera House in New York City (December 11, 1956). Ragtime composer and performer Eubie Blake, then age ninety-one, played to an overflow crowd (January 28, 1974).

Hearing with different ears. Joyce Searcy, president and CEO of Bethlehem Centers in Nashville, grew up in Mississippi in a musical family of several siblings—everyone played an instrument (or two)—and she started taking piano lessons at age five. She played for local churches and organized a youth choir at her own church. She said, "On Sunday morning I had to get up and play for mass at eight o'clock in the morning, go to my own church to play for Sunday school at 9:30 and stay for church, play for the eleven o'clock service, be back there to play for BTU [Baptist Training Union] in the evenings, and then play for night church." She played other instruments and was also in the school orchestra. By the time she was ready to enter Fisk as a freshman, she planned to be a music major. Joyce recalled, "I went to the music room at Fisk and—this was before there were auditions—I did the tour before we sat down to declare a major. I don't know why that sitting at that desk I changed my mind and somehow became an English major . . . rather than a music major. It was probably because I had done so much classical all my life that I wanted to do the other kinds of music. So I changed my mind, but I was still able to pass on the music to my kids."

She passed on the music to her own children and is now seeing that the children who come to Bethlehem Centers are introduced to music of all kinds, from classical to country. She explained, "In order to provide them with choices, we have to expose them to those choices. It's not that we're trying to make choices for them; we're just trying to say, 'This is available, this is available, and this is available.' You begin to hear with different ears when you learn more about the music."

Dr. Reid-Wallace shared Joyce's opinion about the importance of choice: "I believe that the great, wonderful thing about living in a free society is the concept of choice." She continued to speak about being haunted by the thought of another Fisk student from her own student days: "The reason this woman haunts me—she was a Jubilee Singer, and she had the most magnificent voice I have ever heard in my life. Nobody could go to that chapel and hear her sing the lead in any of those songs without just feeling chills. She had such a stately presence. There were some very good performers at this school during my time who never became famous, but they touched your life. They moved you. I am possessed by this curiosity about how in this whole complex universe does one person become a Marian Anderson and another person doesn't when there may be no distinguishable difference in talent between one and the other?"

At Fisk University the students have the opportunity to explore choices in the performing arts and other areas, and the school's tradition of a nurturing environment encourages them to realize their potential, whatever that may be, so that they may come to see with different eyes and hear with different ears.

Herr Rubinstein

*Herr Rubinstein,
the world-renowned Russian pianist,
was the most important personage of the troupe.*

—Republican Banner, 1873

ANTON RUBINSTEIN toured the United States for several months in 1872–73, playing more than two hundred times and becoming a tremendous financial success. He stopped in Nashville in mid-February of 1873 for two concerts, and he brought with him three other performers: Henri Wieni-awski, violin; Mlle Louise Liebhart, soprano; and Mlle Louise Ormeny, contralto. Admission to the Masonic Hall was $2 or $2.50; general admission, $1 (about $15 today). The financial Panic of 1873 would not hit the country until later in the year, so the ticket price may not have been the sole reason for the small crowd.

Expectations about what a Russian pianist would be like may have deterred some people from coming. After the first concert, the reviewer commented, "If any one expected to see a dainty, dressy dandy shake highly oiled ambrosial locks over the keys," he was surely disappointed. The music from the Steinway greeting the ears of that "intelligent and, to a great extent, critical auditory" was "magnificent," and Rubinstein, rarely smiling, had a "slightly pragmatic method" of approaching his work. His playing elicited a "grand and sonorous harmony" as well as "the gentlest and softest of passages."

He began with a Beethoven overture, then selections from Mozart and Handel, and Mendelssohn's "Wedding March." For the second part of his program he played something by "a rather unfamiliar author" (no name cited) and then Liszt's arrangement of "Ere Konig" and a passage from Beethoven's "Ruin of Athens." Earnest applause met the last piece, and Rubinstein concluded with Chopin.

Wieniawski played three selections—the crowd's favorite was his "Airs Russes." Mlle Ormeny sang "Ah Mon Fils" in German, much to the displeasure of the reviewer who thought it should have been rendered in French to avoid some "rugged places" into which her voice was carried. Mlle Liebhart sang "Angels Ever Bright and Fair" and "Robin Adair," and rated more comments about her lovely appearance than about her singing.

The program for the second evening was as follows (not in this order): for Rubinstein, "Air and Variations" by Handel, "Rondo" by Mozart, a sonata for piano and violin by Beethoven (with Wieniawski), "Variations Serieuses" by Mendolssohn, "Nocturne" by Chopin, and "Wedding March" by Mendelssohn; for Ormeny, an aria from Bellini's *Romeo and Juliet* and "Il Segreto" by Donizetti; for Wieniawski, "Air Varie" and "Airs Russes"; and for Liebhart, "Convien Partir" by Donizetti and "Il Bacio" by Arditi.

Lydia Thompson was to present *Blue Beard* and *Kenilworth* at the Grand Opera House (formerly the Adelphi Theatre) on February 14, the day of this review, and her anticipated appearance rated many more lines of newspaper coverage over a period of days than Rubinstein's appearance. She and her troupe were to stay a week, and the reserved seats were selling out early. Her burlesque plays seemed more appealing to the Nashville audience than the music of Rubinstein and his group.

A German Peace Festival

The German members of Nashville's population held a special event on March 9, 1871, at Turner Hall on North Market Street (Second Avenue). The occasion was to honor the victory of Prussia over France in the Franco-Prussian War (1870–71), the declaration of peace, and the unification of Germany with William I of Prussia as emperor. There was no charge to attend, but expectations were high that attendees would make worthy donations to a fund for widows and orphans of soldiers killed in the conflict.

By seven o'clock a large crowd had gathered for the firing of one hundred guns for the national German salute and the shooting of rockets into the sky over the housetops. At eight o'clock in the "brilliantly illuminated and decorated hall" the music began with the 16th U.S. Infantry Band, which had volunteered its services. It was noted that the band "discoursed the music with their accustomed proficiency and skill." The program included classical music (selections from Donizetti's *Daughter of the Regiment* and Bellini's *Sonnambula*; Mendelssohn's "Wedding March" from *Midsummer Night's Dream*), a march, and a waltz. The Turner Glee Club sang patriotic German songs, J. Molengraft sang a baritone solo, and B. Meyer sang a tenor solo. General Theo. Trauernicht delivered an address that "was highly conciliatory and well conceived." He hoped that the German and French peoples would benefit from the peace, and he was enthused about having the emperor in place to unify Germany, thus conferring "lasting blessings upon Europe and upon mankind."

Following the official program, "dancing, socialities and merry-makings were kept up till a late hour." Based upon the attendance, it is likely that a nice sum was contributed to the fund.

Going for the Gold

*It will demonstrate
our capacity to sustain
a people's theater.*

—DAILY AMERICAN, OCTOBER 5, 1885

THE OLYMPIC THEATER at Union and Summer (Fifth) Streets attempted an experiment, beginning October 5, 1885. As reported in the "Dramatic Notes" of the *Daily American* that day:

> From a dramatic standpoint, the past week has been one of interest locally, if from no other fact than simultaneous entertainments at three places of amusement [the Olympic, the Masonic, and the Grand Opera House], the first time since somewhere in the sixties, when Nashville was yet unduly inflated with a riff-raff population long since extinct. Whether they will all keep open is another thing.
>
> The venture at the Olympic is an interesting one, as it will demonstrate our capacity to sustain a people's theater, as they are known in the larger cities. To do this, something more than cheap entrance is essential, for, regardless of the price of a ticket, the public insist on an expensive interior arrangement.

The entertainment for the upcoming week at the Olympic was provided by Beatty and Snyder's People's Theater Company, and the opening play was *Queen's Evidence* followed by a farce.

The experiment was short-lived, however, and it seemed the city could not support three theaters. On November 16, a reporter stated, "The Olympic has expired—for lack of gold."

Harry L. B. Sheetz was a clerk at McClure's New Temple of Music in Nashville when he wrote this "Grand March" in 1879. He later had his own music publishing business.

Emma Abbott and the Reverend

*The Theatre Vendome
has been dedicated to the histrionic muse
and the fairest product of the inventive genius
and progressive spirit of the city
wedded through architectural and mechanical skill
has at last been offered to the public gaze.*

—DAILY AMERICAN, OCTOBER 4, 1887

EMMA ABBOTT'S opera company opened on a Monday, October 3, 1887, and was to stay for the entire week. She had been to Nashville several times before and was a favorite of the citizens. In November 1885, the bill included *The Mikado, Faust, The Bohemian Girl,* and *Norma*. In March 1887, she and her company performed *La Traviata, Mignon,* and *Martha*. No one-night stands for her.

The October 1887 week was special because Abbott was to christen the Vendome Theatre. (Its drop curtain had representations of the Place Vendome in Paris.) Her choice for the opening night was *Il Trovatore*. Ticket prices ranged from $8 for a private box of four seats to $1.50 for the orchestra circle to $1 for the dress circle; the family circle cost 75 cents, and the gallery, 25 cents ($1 then, about $20 today). Abbott had a reputation for opening theaters across the country and bringing success to them, which was a most desirable outcome for the Vendome's backers.

A group of men, James Warner, Van Leer Kirkman, Augustus H. Robinson, Godfrey M. Fogg, R. F. Wilson, M. M. Gardner, Thomas Craighead, and Oliver Milsom, got together to build the theater that had an initial cost of $65,000. Wilson was the owner and lessee of the theater until his death, and W. A. Sheetz was the active manager.

Built on the south side of Church between High (Sixth) and Vine (Seventh) Streets (the site of the new downtown Nashville Public Library), the Vendome had the latest facilities. It boasted steam heat, electricity, and an elevator. It seated sixteen hundred patrons, there were sixteen private boxes, and each of the initial group owned in "perquity" a lower box. Last but certainly not least for patrons and performers, the acoustics were said to be marvelous.

People started making reservations on the Wednesday before the opening on Monday. Telegrams from Chattanooga and Memphis arrived, and Middle Tennesseans made sure to get their tickets. "It had been so long felt that Nashville, with its wealth and culture, should eclipse her sister Southern cities in their recognition of the stage, that the assurance that at last this obligation had been fulfilled, excited the pride of the community and the curriosity [*sic*] of the State to witness the evidence of the happy consummation," stated a reporter for the *Daily American*.

An hour before the doors opened, onlookers on Church Street waited to see the fashion parade of theatergoers. By 7:30 the ticket holders

There's No Place Like Home

James M. Trotter wrote in *Music and Some Highly Musical People*, published in 1878,

In those towns and cities containing a preponderance of cultivated people, theatres do not flourish to the same extent as in neighborhoods where the reverse is true. The reason is obvious: cultured people have attractive and generally musical homes, and are thus made, to a great extent, independent of the amusements afforded in public places. . . . Our firesides should be made to compete with, nay, to far surpass in attractiveness, all places of public amusement; for it is very much better that the employments and entertainments of our homes should charm and retain their members, than that these should be sought for outside their, in some respects, sacred confines. . . . Briefly, then, in the home is safety: over its members are extended the protecting wings of guardian angels; while without are often snares and danger, either in palpable forms, or in those hidden by the glittering, the alluring disguises which are so often thrown over vice.

Emma Abbott and her opera company opened the Vendome Theatre in October 1887. Here she was costumed as Violetta for *La Traviata*.

for the galleries had taken their seats, but the elites in their carriages dashed up at the last minute. The house was full by the time the curtain rose.

The reporter gushed over Abbott and her group: "In the grand aria with flute obligato at the beginning of the last act . . . Miss Abbott rose to a height that was grand. The purity of her tone, the liquidness of her trills and the brilliancy of her execution of all the little turns and roulades, combined with her talent for acting out the part, is wherein lies the strength of her hold upon the American public." The scene was then repeated in response to prolonged applause. Miss Annandale, Signor Montegriffo, and Mr. Pruette earned his praise as well. Abbott's costumes were so splendid that the reporter had to comment on them, especially a black velvet, hand embroidered in gold fuschias, with rose pink crepe panels, and a lilac satin embroidered in pearls.

Following the performance, the reporter had an interview with Abbott, who thought that the Vendome was "a perfect gem, the prettiest and finest theatre in the South. Though smaller in size it is as handsome or handsomer than the Metropolitan Theatre in New York City. And the acoustics—well, this is perfect. I and my company have been in raptures the whole evening over the fine acoustic effects.

"You know," she continued, "so many theatres are built just for show, and one's voice comes right back to them. Such a theatre is very trying. But oh! my—my benedictions rest on the man who built the theatre. He knew his business well."

The audience might have been taken with her attire, but she had her eye on them. She observed, "You can't imagine how beautiful they did look from the stage—so many full toilettes. And, do you know, I love to sing before a Nashville audience. They are so enthusiastic—so appreciative. Did you notice how they applauded my first aria? I have had in my life very cold audiences, and they are so trying."

She was to give *Ruy Blas* another evening. Having worked on it in Paris with M. Got, who had been an actor at the Comédie Française, Abbott said, "I learned from him all the great dramatic business such as has made Sarah Bernhardt famous in the role of the *Queen*. The acting is as great as the music and that is perfectly divine—soul inspiring. I am always a handsome dresser and in the part of the *Queen* I have some of the richest toilettes ever seen in this country. And, then too, I studied the vocalization under Pauline Vierdot so I consider myself as well nigh perfect in the part." Of her company, she stated, "I can cast any opera from the 'Huguenots' to the 'Chimes of Normandy' without the least exertion."

The rest of the week went relatively well for her, and the company also presented *Faust, Mignon,* and *The Bohemian Girl.* She did not consider it a "heavy one with the company; still it was not an engagement of which to complain." To many Nashvillians, it was an exceptional week for the city and its performing arts.

Abbott went to services on Sunday at Mc-Kendree Methodist Church. The Reverend Warren A. Candler was the pastor, and if Abbott was there seeking solace for her soul, she did not get it that morning. Thomas H. Malone Jr. was present, and he vividly described the events. He compared Candler to "a particularly venomous stumpy-tailed rattlesnake," literally "quivering with fury." For more than thirty minutes the reverend denounced theaters and anything and anyone associated with them.

When he stopped, a voice came from the back of the church. It was Emma Abbott, who stood and said her piece. These are the words that Malone remembered: "I, Emma Abbott, wish to denounce as false and un-christian what has just been said. I try to be a good member of the church. That is why I came here today. And when I go down on my knees in 'Mignon' or the 'Bohemian Girl,' I pray just as sincerely as if I were in church." After all, she had spent many of her growing-up years in Peoria, Illinois, where her father directed the choir of the First Baptist Church and helped her develop her voice. Churchgoing was not out of character for her.

Everyone in the congregation must have been shocked; such things just did not happen in church. And having a woman *of the theater* speak to him in such a way was apparently more than the reverend could take. Candler "turned a ghastly white" and then stated, "I shall not undertake to answer the lady, because she *is* a lady." A burst of applause followed his statement. According to Malone, the applause was for Candler, but newspaper reporters and Abbott's biographer believed the applause was for Abbott.

That was not the end of the service. Someone handed Abbott a hymnal, and she began to sing. She was into the second line before she realized that she was singing alone with an organ accompaniment. All told, that had to be one of the most unusual services that anyone there had attended. Abbott later explained to her husband that her "wrath" was aroused, and that caused her to respond as she did. (The story, circulated across the country, was misreported in that many newspapers incorrectly identified the city or the reverend or the church—sometimes all three.)

Abbott and her company returned to Nashville in November 1889, advertised as the "largest, strongest and only successful English Opera Company in America," and performed *Rose of Castile, Ernani, Romeo and Juliet,* and *Yeomen of the Guard.* She died two years later at the age of forty-one.

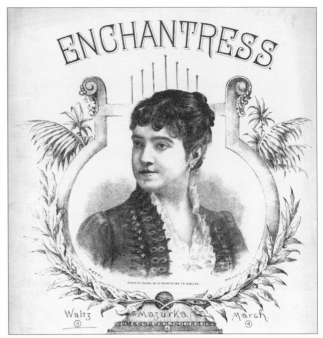

On January 18, 1883, despite inclement weather, the "whole town" was said to be at the Grand Opera House. Christine Nilsson sang "in a degree marvelous beyond description, with a caressing, clinging sweetness." Alas, she was no Patti in brilliancy, but "the fair Swede" won many hearts in her audience. She had previously appeared in Nashville in 1871 *(upper left).* Truly an enchantress, Adelina Patti was often noted to be the most famous soprano of her time, and her reign was a long one (b. 1843; d. 1919). She was also one of the most highly paid performers, then or now; this music was published in 1884 *(upper right).* Annie Pixley starred in Bret Harte's *M'liss, Child of the Sierras* at the Masonic Theater on February 4, 5, and 6, 1880. It was her second appearance in the city, and her soprano singing and "signally effective" acting brought her repeated encores. She autographed the back of this photo *(lower left and right).*

"Shall We All Go to the Theater?"

Turn away from the theater,
on account of the evils connected with it,
and seek for the good there is in it elsewhere.

—J. M. HUBBERT, 1888

FOUR DENOMINATIONS with substantial memberships in Nashville—Presbyterian, Methodist, Southern Baptist, and Church of Christ—have differed over several doctrinal aspects, but they have shared the prohibition on theatergoing. J. M. Hubbert explicitly stated the reasons for this prohibition.

Pastor Hubbert of First Cumberland Presbyterian Church in Nashville delivered a sermon with the title "Shall We All Go to the Theater?" on Sunday morning, January 22, 1888. It was later published as a forty-eight-page booklet, so one has to wonder how long it took him to deliver it to his congregation. He clearly echoed the sentiments of the Reverend Warren A. Candler, who castigated Emma Abbott and others of the theater.

At the outset Pastor Hubbert explained why he needed to ask and answer the question: "When an institution assumes the proportions of the modern theater, which is recognized as one of the most potent influences in society—some saying it is moral, and others that it is immoral—and which has so wide a patronage, both out of the Church and in it, we are certainly justified in writing books and delivering discourses concerning it."

He made a distinction between the drama and the theater (drama was in text form; theater was presented on the stage), and he did see some good in theater. Yet "none would claim that we are to encourage and patronize every good thing that has good in it." He certainly saw evil in it.

He acknowledged that the church in the Middle Ages was a patron of the arts with sacred plays of Bible events and mystery plays, and "out of these vile 'sacred plays' of the Middle Ages grew the modern theater, says Professor Henry B. Smith." Pastor Hubbert also discussed Samuel Johnson and his view of the stage's "irreligion and licentiousness."

Because an actor assumed a character not his own, he was "by profession a 'hypocrite.'" Thus, the soul was injured—a solid reason to object to the profession of acting. The pastor referred to Fanny Janauschek, "the Bohemian actress, [who advised] all girls, for their happiness, to keep off the stage."

The audience was not immune to the theater's evil influence because the artificial emotions and excitement taught "degrading and corrupting sentiments," "the imagination [was polluted] by its scenes of vice and crime," and the costumes aroused "bad passions" and were immodest. Overall, the theater ate "away the vital piety of its patrons," who then compromised their influence outside the church.

He referred to the law of Christian charity: "When we patronize the theater, we virtually tear out of our New Testaments the leaf on which Paul's law of Christian charity is printed." That is, we should avoid doing things that make our brothers and sisters stumble.

Pastor Hubbert observed that "one city after another, New Orleans, San Francisco, Cincinnati, Chicago, St. Louis, Milwaukee, San Antonio, opens the play-houses on the Sabbath." Then he added, "Who are the two great enemies of the Sabbath laws in our cities? *The saloon and the theater.*"

He quoted Edwin Booth's letter to the *Christian Union*: "If the management of theaters could be denied to speculators, and placed in the hands of actors who value their reputation and respect their calling, the stage would at least afford healthy recreation, if not, indeed, a wholesome stimulus to the exercise of noble sentiments."

What was the proper course? Pastor Hubbert stated, "Turn away from the theater, on account of the evils connected with it, and seek for the good there is in it elsewhere." No one needed the

The Vendome Theatre was located on Church Street between Sixth and Seventh Avenues. By the time of the Tennessee Centennial Exposition (1897), electric fans cooled the summertime audiences. It later became Loew's, a movie theater.

stage to interpret drama. Reading a play or going to lectures about it was adequate.

He approved the following: "Sweet music we have in parlors, concerts, and churches. As for painting and statuary, public galleries and private collections are open to us." He ended his sermon in this way: "Shall we all go to the theater? The answer is, *no*, no, NO!"

The early leaders of Vanderbilt University, which was affiliated with the Methodist Episcopal Church, South, agreed with the pastor. The young, mostly male students were required to sign a document stating that they would not attend the theater. Other prohibitions extended to horse racing, drinking, and frequenting billiard saloons. Yet signing something and abiding by it are two different things. Bishop Holland McTyeire, integral to the university's founding, was president of the Board of Trust, and there was no question where he stood on this issue. As long as he was alive, the bylaws would remain unchanged.

Nevertheless, the students were not deterred from expressing their opinions in the *Observer* and the *Hustler*. Here are only two examples that were repeated in various forms.

W. C. Cherry might have been sitting in the congregation (although he did not say so) because he composed a rebuttal of Pastor Hubbert's negative points. He noted that Reverend Small at the West End Church had given an anti-theatergoing sermon, and it is likely that Small and other pastors touched on similar points in these diatribes.

Cherry began by asking, "Is acting a God-given talent?" and followed by stating that we should use the gifts we have been given by God. He said, "It will not do to say that Emma Abbott's voice could find full scope in the doxology in the McKendree choir," and a talented actor or actress with the ability to convey emotion as a character in a play should not be denied the opportunity to exercise that gift.

When he presented *Hamlet* on February 28, 1876, Edwin Booth *(left)* played to a packed Masonic Theater, even though hard times were upon the townspeople. He wrote his daughter that the countryside still showed signs of the war, ten years after the fact, and that the police had to keep crowds back to permit his carriage to drive from the depot to his hotel. In late January 1888 Edwin Booth and Lawrence Barrett *(right)* appeared in *Othello*, *Hamlet*, and *Julius Caesar*. In an unprecedented move they gave a matinee of *Merchant of Venice* because so many people wanted to get tickets to any of their performances and had to be turned away at the door.

As to reading plays as a substitute for attending performances, he explained the problem with that proposal: "Any student of Greek history will tell you that the unequaled grandeur of Grecian education and literature is due mostly, if not nearly *entirely*, to theatrical *performances*, not to plays read." For example, "a friend told me he got more from one night at Virginius a better idea of Roman customs than five months of study of Leighton's Rome."

Cherry challenged readers with this question: "Do the immoral and the vicious so far outnumber the good and intelligent in both number and means that a city, which now supports four theaters, can not support a clean one patronized by the respectable element?" The ministers should see for themselves—in disguise if necessary—a play "considered pure by theater-goers" and then make a judgment. Listening to rumors about the theater itself, about the plays, about actors and actresses, was a wrongheaded approach.

Cherry finished with a series of questions: Why was it all right to go to the Quintette Club, and all wrong to go to a dramatic entertainment? Why was it so elevating to hear one person read a play but morally degrading to hear it by ten? What was the difference between a Christmas entertainment at church and a comic opera? His hope for the future was that drama would become a means of moral education, working as a "handmaid of religion" in the twentieth century.

"A Blow to Patriotism"

A reviewer ended a discussion of Nashville's theatrical events of the Christmas season of 1894 by reviewing the citizenry:

Felix Morris closed the week at the Grand, to audiences utterly disproportionate to the performances. CHAT is intensely locally patriotic, it will speak for Nashville, even to exaggeration, but the humiliation of greeting the most exquisite productions that have been, or will be produced here this season with a handful of people is a blow to patriotism. It raises doubts of our vaunted intelligence and culture, it answers the question so often asked, Why does Nashville have such poor attractions? The reply is, Nashville in this respect is just about four times as slow as Philadelphia; it takes three seasons for us to discover merit. We shall not see that master of comedy, Ed Sothern, in many a day because he played here twice and did not take in as much as a weinerwurst peddler would in one night. Now comes Felix Morris who eclipsed the star when he was with Rosina Vokes. Three thousand of our best people saw Vokes, and Morris had a right to expect when he gave his great plays, the only exponent of the Coquelin school in this country, the most charming artist of a most delicious art, that he should turn away hundreds. Mr. Morris' company was excellent and every way competent for their respective roles. It is to be hoped Nashville will be given just one more opportunity to redeem her reputation for theatrical taste.

Lillian Lewis played the role of Cleopatra in December 1894, and the review in *Chat* was less than glowing: "When she essays Shakespeare the poverty of her talent lies like an abyss at the foot of the mountain of her nerve. . . . She is ungraceful and to appear as the sinuous serpent of the Nile, is as preposterous as Grover Cleveland essaying the role of the living skeleton in a dime museum."

In the same issue of the *Observer*, an anonymous writer took up the subject of the detested bylaws. Even though visiting theaters "and other places of dissipation" was prohibited, students and professors were regular theatergoers and discussed the latest plays the next day. It was so common for Vanderbilt students to go to the Vendome that one section of the gallery was known as the Vanderbilt Box, and there were usually more students at the theater than at chapel the next day. The bylaws were ridiculous because they were not being enforced and should not be enforced, and even the faculty members were not in sympathy with them, he wrote. The students and professors were Roman Catholic to Methodist, and at that time, there was some division among members of the Methodist Church on the morality/immorality of theatergoing. The solution, declared the writer, was to abolish specific bylaws and appeal to each student to be a gentleman.

After Bishop McTyeire died in 1889, Chancellor Landon C. Garland recommended to the Board of Trust that bylaws prohibiting specific forms of dissipation be abolished. He made his case with these words:

> Of nothing am I more fully persuaded than of the evil consequences of retaining in the code a law which you dare not enforce, and indeed one the infraction of which you cannot fasten upon a single student, without a system of impracticable and offensive espionage, which, of itself, if practicable, would demoralize the whole body of students and maintain them in continual antagonism to all law. You cannot manage a body of young men but by dealing with them as gentlemen of truthfulness and honor, whether they be so or not. It is an elevating power to treat young men as if they actually were what you want them to be. A young man may know himself to be unworthy of the trust and confidence you put in him; but the reposing itself of such trust is the most powerful incentive to bind him to the path of duty. . . . If the student goes to a theater he sits by some of the most intelligent and refined and influential gentlemen and ladies of Nashville. More than these; he sits by the side of members of churches which prohibit attendance upon theaters. Can you dismiss that student from the University? If you do you attack the public sentiment of the whole community and immediately begin the depletion of your halls. It is no offset to this to say that we dismiss him, not for going to the theater, but for violating his written pledge of honor to obey the laws. For then we are held responsible for taking the pledge as a group not to do that which is done, possibly, by his own father and mother, and certainly by a considerable number of the most highly esteemed persons in the community and by numbers of those

It was so cold in February 1895 that not even Lily Langtry could draw a full house for her role in *A Wife's Peril.* Tickets were 25 cents to $1.50 (about $16 to $33 today) at the Vendome. Perhaps it was just as well because the reviewer said that the piece was "lacking," although Langtry was a beauty. She had earlier appeared at the Vendome (March 1888) in *As in a Looking Glass.*

who profess to be followers of Christ. (Minutes of the Board, June 16, 1890)

The Board went along with his recommendation, and Chancellor Garland announced to the students that the only rule would be that they should act as gentlemen—the position asserted all along by writers and editors in the *Observer* and the *Hustler.* James Kirkland was chancellor when the denominational ties to the Methodists ended in 1914. (The Methodist Church removed the prohibition on theater-going from its *Book of Discipline* a few years after that.)

Churches increasingly present dramas as part of their services or as special events, and church-affiliated colleges and universities now have drama departments training young people to enter the world of theater. Yet negative attitudes persist toward the theater and its participants—whether audience or performers—as individuals continue to ask, "Shall we all go to the theater?" The answer, for some, is still "NO!"

Several young people have spoken with me about this subject. They have grown up in the church and have attended denominational schools from kindergarten through college. Their pursuit of a drama major or their work in the theater as an avocation, not a vocation, has brought them grief from some members of the church. They have heard negative comments about their futures on this earth and beyond; they have been snubbed and treated as if they were nonpersons. That is a real tragedy, and I must agree with the young man who perceived acting as a gift. What could be more wonderful than for someone to discover his or her gift and pursue it passionately?

Eleven-year-old Joseph Jefferson appeared in a production in Nashville in 1840 with his father, also named Joseph Jefferson. The younger Jefferson's most famous role was to become that of Rip Van Winkle (pictured). In February 1891 he visited his cousin Jennie McKenzie, a math teacher at Ward Seminary, after a performance. He last appeared in the city in *The Rivals* at the Vendome in 1904, the year before his death.

The Prodigy and the Diva: Blind Tom and Black Patti

Her color does not prevent the best people from attending her concerts.

—CHAT, JANUARY 14, 1895

TWO DISTINCTIVE African-American performers, one male, one female, who made history in their own time visited Nashville on more than one occasion. The first was called Blind Tom (1849–1908). His real name was Thomas Greene Wiggins (sometimes referred to as Thomas Bethune, Bethune being the name of his owner), and he was born without sight, into slavery, in Georgia. His musical gifts became apparent by the age of four when he was heard playing his master's piano, yet his forty-year career was managed for the financial benefit of others. The subtitle of a book about him written by Geneva Handy Southall, *Continually Enslaved,* just about sums up his life. The soprano Sissieretta Jones ([1869–1933] known as Black Patti because of favorable comparisons to the famed Adelina Patti) achieved popularity and a measure of independence despite being an African-American woman in a historical period when women of all races were struggling for their rights, much less as performers of classical music. Musical historians have referred to her as the first African-American diva. She was the lead singer for Black Patti's Troubadours from 1896 to 1916, and she sang operatic arias while the troubadours tended toward vaudevillian numbers and antics. She, too, was managed by others but reaped some financial returns for herself.

Twelve-year-old Wiggins and his manager were in Nashville for several months in 1861 following the Battle of Manassas. In the city he heard details about the battle and composed his

"Battle of Manassas," published in 1866, which became one of his most popular works. On October 10, 1861, he appeared at the Masonic Theater at eight o'clock. Before his next appearance in Nashville, December 1877, he toured Europe and was said to earn $100,000 for his manager in the London concerts alone.

A lengthy article about Wiggins in the *Daily American,* reviewing his appearance at the Vendome on July 20, 1891, described his abilities and the depth of his program. He usually included works by the masters, from Bach to Beethoven to Liszt, some popular melodies, and his own compositions, which often were imitations of nature, such as a rain storm, or other sounds, such as a sewing machine. All of the regular seats in the theater were taken, most of the boxes were full, and several hundred people stood to hear him.

Wiggins introduced his numbers in this way: "Tom will now present. . . ." His first piece was from the opera *Rigoletto.* Next he sang in his pleasant baritone voice "Rocked in the Cradle of the Deep." A regular feature was his challenge to an audience member to play something, and he would then reproduce it. That was exactly what happened with Professor Loud, who played something he had personally written called "Dream of Youth."

Then Wiggins played a few of his own compositions before changing the pace and asking people to suggest a word for him to spell. One man called out, "Phlegmatic." Wiggins replied, "Please suggest something more odd." No one did, and the laugh was on the man who offered the word. Wiggins sat down and played "Fishers Hornpipe" with his right hand, "Yankee Doodle" with his left, and sang "Tramp, Tramp, the Boys Are Marching." Before the evening was over, he repeated a speech he had heard by Stephen A. Douglas in 1860, and he played "Battle of Manassas." After his performance, he returned to the Bailey House.

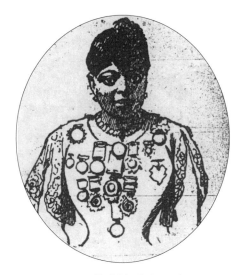

Sissieretta Jones was called Black Patti because critics compared her voice to that of the soprano Adelina Patti. In March 1893 she sang at Spruce Street Baptist Church in Nashville.

A few years later, May 16, 1895, Wiggins appeared at the Vendome, sponsored by the Ladies' Hermitage Association, and one could obtain a reserved seat for 75 cents (about $16 today). Also on that trip, he gave a concert at St. John A.M.E. Church.

In an effort to preserve Wiggins's work, John Davis released a CD in 2000, *John Davis Plays Blind Tom, the Eighth Wonder,* and it includes "Battle of Manassas," "Cyclone Galop," "Rainstorm," "Wellenklänge" (Voice of Waves), and "Reve Charmant—Nocturne."

That Mme Jones came to Nashville at all is remarkable. She preferred to remain in the northern states because of unfavorable conditions confronting African-Americans in the southern states. Yet she was scheduled to sing at the Union Gospel Tabernacle (the Ryman Auditorium) on March 29, 1893, and a chorus of African-Americans was to join her. Because only one section of the auditorium was reserved for African-Americans, the singers refused to appear at the Tabernacle, however, and the program was moved to Spruce Street Baptist Church. For the daughter of a pastor and choir director of an A.M.E. church, singing in a church was comfortable for her.

The previous year, 1892, Jones had sung at the Grand Negro Jubilee at Madison Square Garden, and she offered opera and a popular tune to several thousand in attendance. The year before her next appearance in Nashville, 1894, she joined Harry T. Burleigh, another African-American, in singing Antonin Dvorak's arrangement of "Old Folks at Home" at Madison Square Garden. In her career she would sing before presidents and the Prince of Wales, before audiences in Canada,

Ryman Auditorium

Not far off Broadway, on Fifth Avenue North, sits the Ryman Auditorium. Thanks to a riverman, Thomas G. Ryman, and a revivalist, Sam Jones, Nashville has had the red-brick auditorium since 1892. Religion and the arts have uniquely come together in this building that began its life as the Union Gospel Tabernacle, a place to hold worship services, and achieved its fame as a venue for the performing arts—and the classical performing arts long preceded the regular broadcasts of the Grand Ole Opry, which began in 1943. With the completion of the new Opry House in 1974 the Ryman is no longer the permanent home of the Opry. The Ryman remains a performance hall, however, and the Opry makes occasional stops there.

Over the years it has undergone a name change (after the death of Ryman in 1904) and alterations, including a gallery, dressing rooms, and a larger stage, to make it more usable for performances. It barely evaded the wrecking ball on more than one occasion. Now on the National Historic Register, the Ryman was given new life after the most recent owner, Gaylord Entertainment, completed extensive renovations in 1994. It still has the original pews, but audiences can sit in air-conditioned comfort with the windows closed and enjoy the performances.

Opera stars, actors, classical musicians, and ballet dancers were regular performers at the Ryman Auditorium before it became the home of the Grand Ole Opry. The new Country Music Hall of Fame is visible just down the street.

England, Europe, the West Indies, and the United States, at Carnegie Hall and music halls. A comment in a January 1895 edition of *Chat* (a local magazine), before her appearance at the Broad Street Amusement Hall in Nashville that month, rang true: "Her color does not prevent the best people from attending her concerts."

Professor Schemmel and His Conservatory

[August Schemmel] recognized in Nashville's citizenship a music loving people, and had faith in their willingness and ability to sustain an institution such as he would start if it was apparent that there was talent behind and merit in the venture.

—CHAT, MARCH 2, 1895

THE STORY of various conservatories of music in Nashville in the 1890s is a complex one, and many of the same people were involved with them. This opening commentary on the Nashville Conservatory of Music, led by Professor August Schemmel, sounded much more optimistic than was actually the case because it was not sustained and Schemmel and some of his musicians left the city. They had been drawn to Nashville by the prospect of jobs; all of the reasons for their leaving are not clear but lack of support for their work played a part. Signor de Luca's Nashville Conservatory of Music decades in the future had an all-star cast of financial backers, but these conservatories do not appear to have had that good fortune—or perhaps the business sense needed to run a profitable enterprise.

Schemmel's conservatory was registered January 7, 1893, with Schemmel, Franz Strahm (a musician), Edward Schoenpflug (co-owner of the

Commercial Hotel), Charles H. Roberts, and Warren B. Ballard (a real estate broker) signed up as charter members. The mission was the "dissemination and encouragement of a taste for music and the cultivation and promotion thereof." Practically the goal was to educate music teachers, public singers, pianists, and composers. The school was located on the corner of Cedar and Summer Streets (Charlotte and Fifth), at 331-33 North Summer, which was the old Hugh Kirkman home.

By March 1895 the *Chat* reporter could point out that the past year had been prosperous for the Nashville Conservatory of Music. Given that the financial Panic of 1893 was still having its effects on firms and institutions, it was probably miraculous that the conservatory survived that long. The reporter stated, "At first the air was rife with predictions of failure on the part of musicians and others who thought it too big an undertaking for a city the size of Nashville, but Prof. Schemmel had traveled; had been all over Europe and America, and knew a city when he saw it. . . . It is known that no Southern city can point to as large and successful conservatory of music as the one of which Prof. August Schemmel is at the head in Nashville." People thought it would compare favorably to any other in the nation, and "no one would tolerate the idea of giving it up." (Well, that must have been wishful thinking on the reporter's part.)

Schemmel gained experience on the faculty of the Royal Academy of Berlin and Vienna. He was teaching at Ward Seminary in 1891, and the next year he led the local Philharmonic Society's chorus in a Mendelssohn Memorial Concert. In 1894 he featured his own compositions at a musical soiree at the conservatory's hall, and on December 28 of that year, the conservatory held a Christmas concert.

Another charter, September 1895, was requested by August Schemmel, Gideon W. Gifford (business manager of Ward Seminary and eventually treasurer of the Tennessee Children's

In 1893 August Schemmel founded the Nashville Conservatory of Music, housed in what had been the Hugh Kirkman home at 331–33 North Summer Street (Fifth Avenue).

Home), William Bellock (a teacher), Phylonzo D. Carr (an employee of D. H. Baldwin and Co., which sold pianos and organs), and James G. Kirkpatrick (a real estate broker) for the Nashville Conservatory of Music. This group is different from that listed on the 1893 charter, and one of the previous charter members, Strahm, would fairly soon start his own music school. The conservatory was to "teach any useful profession, trade, business or Art and to give instruction in any branch of Learning, practical or theoretical (such as vocal and instrumental music, painting, etc. etc.)." This listing is so broad that we have to wonder whether the offering of music could not bring in enough pupils to pay the instructors and the bills.

The conservatory is reported to have had three hundred students, though, by 1896 when yet another change occurred. On April 27 a contract was signed between the University of Nashville and the Nashville Conservatory of Music. The conservatory became a department of the university under the name "The College of Music of the University of Nashville." The conservatory was to focus on applied music instruction, and Peabody Normal College, music instruction for teachers. (The Normal College had been established in 1875 at the University of Nashville. John E. Bailey was the instructor of music from 1876 to 1889. Mary E. Cheney followed him in 1889 and remained until 1899. Lula O. Andrews joined Cheney for one year, 1894, and they taught music education methods, the history of music, women's chorus, and piano.)

According to the 1897 University of Nashville Catalog, the teaching method was that of Berlin and Leipzig. The founder and president was Schemmel, Xaver Scharwenka was the vice president, and Chevalier Giuseppe Ferrata was listed as a coworker. The latter two signed on to give master classes, not to be on hand for daily work, and their association was quite brief with the school— an unfortunate outcome, given their qualifications.

Scharwenka, a Polish-German pianist, composer, and teacher, had founded his own conservatories in Berlin (1881) and New York City (1891). He toured in Europe and the United States, and he made several appearances in Nashville, the first in February 1892 at the Vendome. In December 1893, students from the female seminaries filled Watkins Hall and listened in rapt attention to him. In April 1895, the Wednesday Morning Musicale sponsored his appearance at Watkins Hall, and Mrs. Gates Thruston sang. Following the concert, club members and Scharwenka joined members of the German Club at Miss Elizabeth Price's for refreshments and more casual entertainment.

In his biography, Scharwenka explained his tie to Schemmel's conservatory. Schemmel asked him to enter into a relationship with the conservatory, similar to one he had with Harbin

College. After extensive negotiations, Scharwenka agreed to come to Nashville for ten days each year, but he carried out his duties only twice. Why? He said, "The city was too 'dry' for me, even though it had plenty of water."

Ferrata, member of the Royal Academy of St. Cecilia in Rome, immigrated to the States in 1892. He had studied piano with Giovanni Sgambati and Franz Liszt. He eventually obtained a position as the professor of piano and composition at Newcomb College in New Orleans (1909), and he remained there until the end of his life (1928). Not only a professor of composition, he also was a composer, and many pieces were for piano. Ferrata had purchased a few shares in Schemmel's conservatory, played a recital there and at Monteagle, and gave a master class. He spent even less time in Nashville than Scharwenka did. (A lawsuit filed against Schemmel by five former faculty members likely played some part in Ferrata's abbreviated participation.)

Other instructors in 1897 were Ivo C. Miller on violin; Rosa H. Schemmel, piano; Addine Campbell, piano and organ; Caroline C. Smith, voice; Mary S. Clements, guitar; and Mary K. Bailey, harp. Emil Winkler, from Leipzig, was also in the piano department. A woman whose name has now become a part of the vocabulary at Vanderbilt University is Myra Jackson Blair, thanks to her love of music and her family's love for her and their desire to honor her memory with the Blair School of Music; she taught piano and the theory of music at the conservatory.

Schemmel had left the city by the beginning of the 1898–99 school year. An August Schemmel began teaching music in San Antonio then and subsequently became director of music at the Virginia Institute, Bristol, Virginia, which was a boarding school for girls; it is more than likely the same man. So the founder of the conservatory that started much of this musical education effort was in Nashville less than ten years.

The 1899–1900 City Directory advertised the Conservatory of Music, College of Music, University of Nashville, as having "Unrivaled Faculty, Superior Instruction, piano, violin,

Monteagle

High on Monteagle Mountain, almost ninety miles south of Nashville, a weeks-long summer season of culture has taken place at the Monteagle Sunday School Assembly. Beginning in 1883, limited numbers of people fled the heat and disease of the lower regions of Tennessee and other southern states to participate in events typical of the Chautauqua movement: drama, lectures, music, and religious activities, including Sunday school and Sunday services.

The School of Music offered piano, violin, and voice lessons, and students and professors gave concerts. Guest orchestras were invited, and in 1905 a two-day Musical Festival was begun, featuring the Assembly Orchestra and chorus. In 1913 Mme Ernestine Schumann-Heink, who had sung at Germany's Bayreuth Festival and, from 1898 to 1903, was considered "the world's greatest contralto," agreed to perform at the Assembly. Special trains for the event brought people from Nashville, Huntsville, and Chattanooga. In 1914 the Cincinnati Symphony Orchestra and David Bispham of the Metropolitan Opera Company performed. Not long afterward the festival was canceled. Although the Music School did survive the Great Depression, the Assembly Orchestra did not last past 1931. Following a lag in the number of live performances, the Sewanee Music Center offered recitals and orchestral concerts in the latter part of the twentieth century. In the 101st season, 1983, pianist Enid Katahn of Nashville gave a concert. Monteagle is one of the few remaining Chautauquas in the country.

voice, orchestral instruments, mandolin, banjo, and guitar, elocution, art." Emil Winkler and Ivo Miller had been the directors since 1898, the time of Schemmel's departure. In 1901 Christian J. Schubert became a codirector with Miller, but Winkler was no longer at the school, which remained a part of the University of Nashville.

In January 1902, Schubert incorporated the Conservatory of Music (still at 331 North Summer) with the following people: Joseph P. Connor (a real estate broker), W. H. Metz (a bookkeeper at 311 Third Avenue North), James A. Ryan (a lawyer), and Dr. J. M. Coyle. The tie seems to have been broken with the University of Nashville. (Schubert had a big year in 1902 because he was

A friend of a local musician, Franz Strahm, Victor Herbert presented this signed photo to Mrs. M. S. Lebeck during the Tennessee Centennial Exposition. He was in town several weeks with his Twenty-second Regiment Band, the most popular of all the bands during the Exposition.

also a charter member of Local 257, the Nashville Association of Musicians.) The school advertised "All Branches of Music, Art and Elocution Taught" with an "Unexcelled Faculty." Tuition was $5 to $25 per month (about $100 to $525 today). Schubert's wife, Centia, and daughter, Cecilia, were teachers. As for Ivo Miller, he became music director at the Vendome Theatre.

More specific information is available about Franz Joseph Strahm: why he came, where he went, and why he left. Born in 1867 in Freiburg, Germany, Strahm studied piano with Franz Liszt. He left his native country in 1891 in response to an advertisement to play in the Vendome Orchestra in Nashville. He taught piano at Schemmel's Nashville Conservatory, then taught privately until he opened the Tennessee Academy of Music, which was registered June 4, 1896. Named on the charter were Strahm, who was president and musical director, R. O. Tucker (dean of the Joint Medical Department), Charles Schardt (a salesman), Phylonzo D. Carr (a piano salesman), William C. Golden, Miss Mollie F. Noell (a secretary and assistant piano teacher), and Miss Omagh Armstrong (a vocal teacher). Music—vocal and instrumental—bookkeeping, typewriting, and stenography were to be taught. The school was initially in the Wilcox Building (530 Church) but at the turn of the century moved to Strahm's residence.

Strahm was living at 1226 North Vine (Seventh) Street in what had been the Buddeke house, by then an apartment house, not a personal residence. The house was built by the grocer John H. Buddeke, who came to Nashville with his wife, Mary Jane, in the 1830s from Hanover, Germany. Oral tradition has it that Jenny Lind visited Mrs. Buddeke at that home when she was on her tour with Barnum. Having musicians entertain guests was fairly typical for the Buddekes, so the house kept up the tradition of hosting musicians. Other musicians lived there in addition to Strahm and his family.

Strahm had a son, born in 1895. You may be thinking, *Well, that's nice, but so what?* His name was *Victor Herbert* Strahm, and he became a flying ace in World War I and later a test pilot. The important point is that his father was a friend of the musician Victor Herbert, and Herbert visited Strahm more than once in North Nashville. During his extended stay in town for the Centennial Exposition (1897), Herbert wrote some of his opera *The Fortune Teller,* which debuted in 1898. Another connection to Nashville is that Herbert wrote *The Fortune Teller* specifically for Alice Nielsen and her newly formed Alice Nielsen Opera Company. Nielsen had been born in Nashville (1876?), although she grew up elsewhere, and she had debuts in Naples, Italy, and Covent Garden, London, in the early 1900s.

For a number of years Strahm directed the music at Monteagle Sunday School Assembly, and he was choir director and organist of First Lutheran Church in Nashville (at least in 1900). In 1908, he organized the Nashville Choral Society, which had a part in three spring festivals (1908, 1909, and 1910). The chorus also held other concerts, for example, one in November 1909 at Watkins Hall. Florence Hinkle of New York had been passing through, and she agreed to stay and perform with the group. By 1910, Strahm still had his school, but it was located at 240 Fifth Avenue North. A teacher there was Amy Schardt, which may tell us why Charles Schardt became a charter member of the Tennessee Academy in 1896.

Strahm was so well known for his spring concerts that they were directly responsible for his getting a new job. When Strahm wrote Dr. Hardin H. Cherry, president of Western Kentucky Normal School in Bowling Green, in July 1910, he said that he was anxious to try new ideas for teaching teachers of public school music. A letter of recommendation suggested, however, that Strahm wanted a change because he was discouraged over the financial failure of Nashville's May Festival that year. Dr. Cherry did not think twice about hiring Strahm because he was so impressed by the choral work that Strahm had done for all of the festivals, and Strahm continued to hold extremely successful music festivals in Bowling Green from the year of his hiring. Strahm became the director of Western's School of Music in 1910, after almost twenty years in Nashville, and he held that position until his death in 1941 at the age of seventy-four.

Music in Nashville

Let us hope that with our progress in civilization our advance in music may be equal to that of science and the industrial arts.

—JEANIE BASS, 1895

JEANIE BASS wrote an article on Nashville's music for the March 2, 1895, edition of *Chat.* Her opening observation was that other than a few students and teachers of music, there was "little taste for classical music in our city." She added, "Nashville is a social place, and its gaiety interferes with the thorough cultivation of fine arts."

According to her, "When Lohengrin was given in Nashville some years ago an editor's criticism of it was that 'Lohengrin does not contain one single melody.' Where was he during the singing of the Swan song and the Bridal chorus?"

She thought that population density had been a factor, saying that Nashville was not yet large enough to be a musical city. Fifteen years ago, she said, a violin teacher needed multiple sources of income (such as teaching and also conducting an orchestra at a theater). But by 1895, "the chief progress of music is due to the fact that Nashville has become an educational centre, which enables us to support a greater number of instructors and of a higher class."

She listed important points that helped more people enjoy music: (1) music and musical instruments being sold at cheaper prices, (2) Nashville students being sent away to study, in the United States and/or abroad, and (3) artists being willing to travel and perform in town. There had been a growing trend to educate boys as well as girls. She noted that only women in the United States were supporting the arts: "Men in America have not countenanced a musical man even though all our greatest compositions and attainments have been achieved by men. . . . Let us hope that with our progress in civilization our advance in music may be equal to that of science and the industrial arts."

The Tennessee Centennial and International Exposition

The Centennial Celebration, to some extent, was the defining moment in our celebration of the arts.

—BILL PURCELL, MAYOR OF NASHVILLE

CENTENNIAL PARK on West End Avenue is home to a unique structure in the world—an exact replica of the Parthenon in Athens, Greece. It has been in place for more than a hundred years now in the Athens of the South, and it owes its creation to a delayed celebration of the state's founding. In some ways the cooperation of public and private entities, men and women throughout the state, that produced the celebration foreshadowed what happened in the development of TPAC.

Beginning in 1892 in a letter to newspapers in Knoxville, Chattanooga, Nashville, Columbia, Jackson, and Memphis, Nashville businessman Douglas Anderson suggested the need for a celebration. He thought that there should be a contest among those cities as to the site and what each could offer, and that the legislature should pick the city as well as appropriate funds for the event.

He stated in the letter that Tennesseans "should celebrate the occasion because they are a progressive people; because an exposition would redound to the pecuniary benefits of the State and keep alive State pride." Other points in favor of the celebration were honoring the ancestors who founded the state and educating children about the state's history. He stirred up initial interest in the idea, but Coal Creek riots by miners, state and national elections, a legislative session, the World's Fair, and the failure of banks in Nashville (another financial panic) diverted everyone's attention.

Nevertheless, Anderson summed up why the Centennial idea eventually gained steam: "When the crisis had been reached [in 1894], and the people of Nashville realized that they would suffer from the failure to hold the Exposition after it had been advertised throughout the United States [in newspaper accounts], and after Atlanta has shown such enterprise in holding an exposition, they woke up, reorganized their forces and went to work." Tully Brown and his "scathing eloquence" at Watkins Hall gave a big push to the townspeople at a meeting that called for action.

A Centennial Association was formed in 1894, two years away from the actual anniversary of statehood (1896). The financial picture remained clouded by the 1893 depression, 1896 was an election year, and politics always dominated the scene. Yet Tennesseans were beginning to see the value in showcasing the progressive strides they had made in the New South.

Other cities had expositions—Louisville's Southern Exposition in 1884–85, Chicago's Columbian Exposition in 1893, and the World's Industrial and Cotton Centennial Exposition in

The O. K. Houck Company offered a $100 prize for the best original composition for piano in the form of a march, which would become the "Tennessee Centennial Prize March." Out of the 288 manuscripts submitted from 22 states, the winner was Maurice Bernhardt, a music teacher from Memphis.

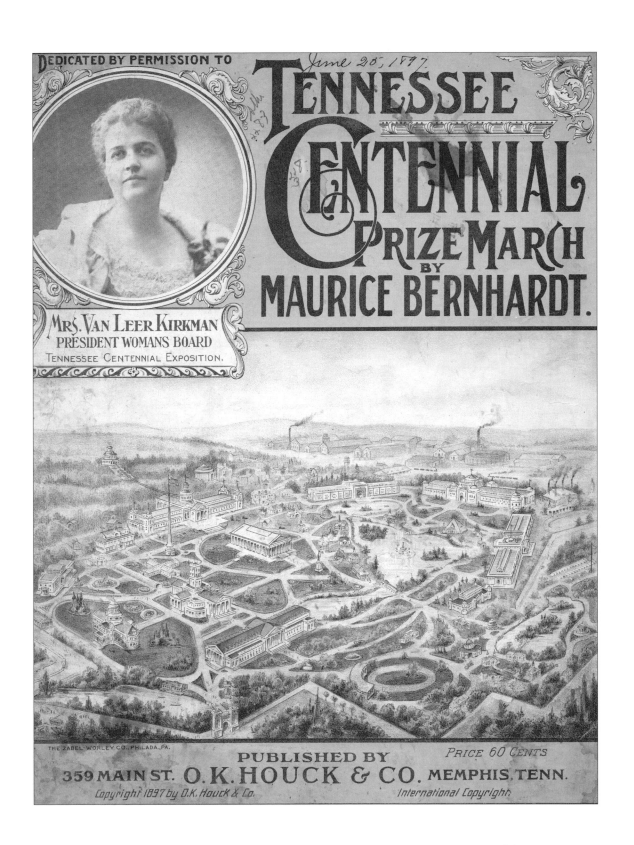

Atlanta in 1884–85, followed by Atlanta's Cotton States and International Exposition in 1895—and Nashville as the state capital was the logical place to hold the event. It was just a matter of money, organization, and hard work, and somehow everything came together by May 1, 1897, opening day of the Tennessee Centennial and International Exposition. Governor Robert Taylor said, "Some of them who saw our ruined country 30 years ago will certainly appreciate the fact that

Herman Bellstedt Jr. was not only a composer for band, orchestra, piano, violin, and cornet but also a gifted cornetist and occasionally a conductor. During the Centennial Exposition, he was in Nashville with Bellstedt & Ballenberg's Band. Roderic Dorman was the man for whom R. Dorman & Co. (pianos, organs, and music) was named.

we have wrought miracles." For an event that was a year late and that some feared would be a failure, the success exceeded all expectations, and compared to other major events in Nashville, the dillydallying was minimal.

The initial funds were broken down this way: the Exposition board had a $100,000 bond that was to run twenty years, the federal government provided $130,000, and subscriptions from the citizenry totaled $500,000 (these are rounded figures; $730,000 in 1896, about $15.8 million today). Of the $730,000, 13.7 percent came from the board, 17.8 percent from the federal government, and 68.5 percent from the private sector. Congress approved an act to assist the Exposition by providing government exhibits, and the Smithsonian Institution prepared special exhibits for the Government Building. The rest of the funds came from concessions, ticket sales, and other sources.

The L & N Railroad was a leading financial backer, contributing $25,000. The railroads also cut rates and encouraged riders to come from all parts of the United States.

Two officers of the Nashville, Chattanooga, and St. Louis Railway were John W. Thomas and Eugene C. Lewis, who became the guiding lights of the Exposition. (That railway contributed about $13,000.) Thomas was president of the Exposition, and Lewis, the director general. To Lewis is given the credit for having the idea to build the Parthenon. Other Exposition officers were Van Leer Kirkman, W. A. Henderson, and John Overton Jr. (vice presidents), W. L. Dudley (director of affairs), and A. W. Wills (commissioner general).

Once the decision was made to hold a Centennial, fund-raising events became common. Kate Kirkman, wife of Van Leer Kirkman, was known as *the* hostess of her time, and as president of the Woman's Board for the Exposition, she set the example by holding receptions and whist parties at her home, Oak Hill. Musicals were staged at

The Parthenon was the centerpiece for the Tennessee Centennial Exposition in 1897, and it housed the art exhibits. It still stands in Centennial Park as a symbol of Nashville as the Athens of the South.

Polk Place, and other social events were arranged. The women also worked on a Woman's Edition of the *Nashville American* as a fund-raiser. A comment in the official history of the Exposition paid tribute to their determination: "Insensible to the danger of defeat, indifferent to rebuff, unmindful of their own comfort, practicing the noblest self-sacrifice and self-effacement, the women stood as a wall between the Exposition and the possibility of failure."

The Centennial Club of Nashville: A History from 1905–77 noted that the women had gotten organized on November 27, 1894, and the group "was called the *State Board of the Woman's Department of the Tennessee Centennial Exposition.*" They were in charge of the Woman's Building and managed projects related to women, and their building was the first to be completed.

All kinds of exhibits were planned: education, agriculture, commerce, transportation, and more. Organizers wanted to make sure that the arts were included, and the Parthenon, constructed of plaster and wood, was to be a focal point in itself in addition to being a hall for arts exhibits. The arts had a long-lasting effect on the event, and the Parthenon had such an impact that it was not destroyed at the end of the Exposition, as were most other buildings.

In November 1895, the grandstand and stables at what was then West Side Park, a horse-racing track, had to be torn down so that the building of Centennial City could get under way. One architect was Fred Thompson, who would in the future build Luna Park at Coney Island and the Hippodrome in New York City. (Several years after the Exposition, he would marry a Nashville girl, Selene Pilcher, who owned a gown and blouse shop in New York City.) Sara Ward Conley of Nashville, who designed the Woman's Building and also served as chairman of the committee that selected artworks to be displayed at the Exposition, must have relied on much of what she learned from her study of art in Paris and Rome. The building process was not without a few trials, but all of the finished products presented a strong visual image.

The opening day was momentous, with many speeches heard by the sizable crowd. Early in May, Kate Rooney appeared in an operetta at the Vendome Theatre, followed soon afterward at that theater by Grau's Opera Company, beginning with the *Beggar Student.* (Throughout the Exposition, the Vendome offered plays and operettas.) May 17 was the day of the Music Convocation in the Woman's Building; events were to be held in the Assembly Hall there, but so many people wanted to get in that some had to stand outside on the porch or underneath the windows to hear. Attendees heard Miss Heineberg of New York play the piano and Miss Esther Wilcox, Metropolitan School of Music in Indianapolis, offer a violin concerto by Vieuxtemps. Nashvillians on the program included Mrs. Aline Blondner (piano), Mrs. G. P. Thruston (vocal), Mrs. M. S. Lebeck (vocal), and the Girls' Glee Club of Price's College for Young Ladies. Mrs. Claude Street was the piano accompanist for the afternoon. Gustav Fischer, who usually was directing an orchestra for the Exposition, led

a quartet: he was first violin, Arno Waschler, second violin; Franz Strahm, viola; and Max Froehlich, cello.

Following James C. Napier's resignation from the Executive Committee of the Negro Department, Richard Hill became chairman. Others on the committee were Rev. T. E. Crawley, Dr. F. A. Stewart, Rev. Preston Taylor, S. A. Walker, W. T. Hightower, Rev. Randall B. Vandavall, and Thomas Tyree. Mrs. J. C. Thompson was president of the Women's Board of the Negro Department

Nashville's Centennial

The celebration of the city's founding lasted from April 23 to May 29, 1880. *Music, music, music* was the word for Saturday, April 24. There was a parade of military units, state officers, and decorated wagons representing businesses. Bands from neighboring Murfreesboro, Franklin, and Clarksville were on hand in addition to St. Joseph's Total Abstinence Band of Nashville and Professor Freny's band.

Calmer events took place at the Masonic Theater with the violinist August Wilhelmj playing a concerto by Paganini and "Old Folks at Home," the pianist Max Vogrich playing a Chopin concerto, and the soprano Marie Salvotti performing an aria from *Nabucco*. Of the three, Wilhelmj was reported to be the audience's favorite.

The high point was the unveiling of Andrew Jackson's statue, created by Clark Mills, on Capitol Hill late in May. Throughout the month-long celebration, many people visited the Centennial Exposition Building at Broad and Spruce Streets (where the federal courthouse stands in 2004). It was filled with exhibitions of industry and art, and suspended inside its dome was another wonder: "a powerful electric jet which shed a light over the entire building as bright as sunshine, yet as soft as the rays of the moon." The city itself did not get electric lights until 1882.

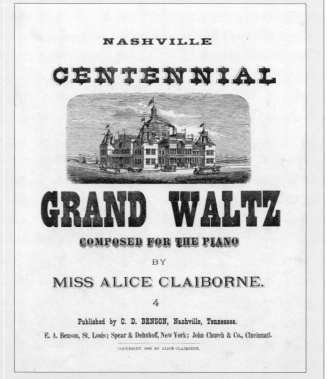

Nashvillians have celebrated all kinds of special occasions with music. Alice Claiborne composed a "Grand Waltz" for the city's Centennial in 1880. The Centennial Exposition Building, pictured here, was located at Broad and Spruce (Eighth) Streets.

Special days were designated throughout the six-month period to recognize individuals or groups. On opening day, the Fisk University Mozart Society sang in the Negro Building, and they appeared again on Negro Day, which was Saturday, June 5. African-Americans had traveled on trains from across the state to celebrate that day. Admission was reduced from the usual price of 50 cents for adults to 25 cents for adults and 10 cents for children. There was a big parade, and ironically enough the Negro State Guards played "Dixie." The Fisk Jubilee Singers took the stage on Jubilee Day, October 6. The Chickering grand piano was rarely silent in the Negro Building with all of the recitals and solos.

On June 12, Mr. Innes and the municipal band played the tune "Belle of Nashville," and local choruses were frequently heard. Gustav Fischer's Centennial Orchestra with fourteen musicians was featured on Nashville Day, September 11. (Fischer, who had been the music director of the Vendome Theatre, composed the "Centennial Exposition March.") Kate Kirkman Day, September 30, was a highlight of the Exposition.

The organ in the auditorium on the Exposition grounds amazed everyone who heard it. Its case was made of oak, and it weighed 15,000 pounds and had 1,847 pipes. Built by Hook and Hastings, the organ was twenty-one feet wide and twenty-two feet high. The bellows were operated by a Ross water motor, which automatically stopped working when the bellows were full; it started up again as the wind in the bellows was used.

Grand Opera Night was July 29, and Martha G. Miner, Rosa Linde, and Minnie Vesey sang. Marie Louise Bailey, a pianist from Nashville who had gained recognition in the United States and Europe, played with the military band the first movement of Rubinstein's Concerto in D Minor, rewritten by Victor Herbert.

Victor Herbert and his Twenty-second Regiment Band were the most popular of all the bands, and they performed for several weeks. Herbert's performances on the cello were certain crowd pleasers. (Herbert would come back with the Pittsburgh Symphony Orchestra in 1903 for a concert at the Ryman.) The composer and pianist Edward McDowell played for the first time with the Boston Orchestra at the Exposition. All in all, music was abundantly supplied.

The total cost of the Exposition was a bit more than $1 million (more than $90,000 of that was spent on music and entertainment), and there were almost 1.8 million visitors by the time the gates closed on November 1. Wonder of wonders, the Exposition made a profit, which was an almost-unheard-of outcome for such an event. It was a small profit of $39.44, but adding in the assets of $12,000 from the salvage of the buildings increased the figure.

The Exposition left behind a legacy in two parts: the invisible and the visible. The invisible included the invigorated civic spirit and the determination of the reform-minded groups, notably what became the Centennial Club, that has lasted long past the dismantling of Centennial City. The ability of women as organizers was reinforced, and they did not look back as they forged ahead to make the city a better and a more beautiful place to live. Visitors from across the country as well as around the world learned more about the city of Nashville and the state of Tennessee.

The visible reminders were the organ, the bells, the Parthenon, and the park.

Long before the Centennial Exposition took place, the Mozart Society of Fisk University was trying to raise money for a pipe organ. On December 28, 1885, Professor A. K. Spence led the group in the *Messiah* at Livingstone Hall, and after almost exactly twelve years to the day, the Grand Centennial Exposition Organ ended up at Fisk in the Memorial Chapel. In "the Great Musical Event of Christmas," 1897, George Whitefield Andrews, a professor of organ and composition at

Tennessee's Bicentennial Celebration

For Tennessee's Bicentennial, the General Assembly created 200, Inc., a nonprofit corporation, and the Assembly got to work on it ahead of time—no delays for this celebration. Governor Ned Ray McWherter established by executive order on June 1, 1992, the Tennessee Bicentennial Commission, and the governor appointed me chair of that commission, which included legislators, historians, and citizens from the three grand divisions of the state. All of Governor McWherter's appointees had loyalty to him, none to me. My great challenge was to build a team that could create an exciting plan. This was a most difficult assignment and often quite frustrating.

After months of deliberations, the commission decided on a three-pronged mission: (1) a special train that would travel across the state with historical artifacts, (2) a performing arts festival at TPAC, and (3) contributions of $10,000 each to Tennessee's ninety-five counties as seed money to help each one plan its own local activities. By the time I got on board, the Bicentennial Mall was already under way and had funding in place, but nothing else did. The Mall is one of Governor McWherter's legacies and was managed and funded through the Department of Finance and Administration. We on the Bicentennial Commission had to make our case to the legislature and to private groups for funds: the state government finally provided $4.32 million, and another $2 million came from corporate and individual donations. Unlike the Centennial Exposition in 1897, the emphasis was on Tennesseans—citizens *and* entertainers. But similar to Centennial Park, the Bicentennial Mall is a park that owes its birth to a celebration of the state's founding. Although our budget was tight, we did manage to close our books with a small surplus.

A notable structure on the Mall is the Tennessee Amphitheater, with two thousand seats, which was designed with Greek amphitheaters in mind; the Wall of History has events from the past two hundred years engraved into it; and there is a large map of Tennessee for children to play upon and several lovely fountains. Many of the Mall's paving bricks have donor names etched into them (a part of our fund-raising efforts). The nineteen acres of the park are just down the hill from the state Capitol building.

The Bicentennial Train made stops in thirty-eight cities. It had a theater and many railroad cars with displays featuring the state's advances in commerce, industry, agriculture, manufacturing, education, and research. This was the commission's way of reaching out to Tennessee citizens.

The Performing Arts Festival, the coming together part of the celebration, took place from May 2 to 25, 1996, and approximately 25,000 tickets were sold. Events were held in Nashville, the state capital, conveniently located in the center of the state, at TPAC, the Ryman, the Hermitage Hotel, and Fisk University's chapel. *A Joyful Noise*, the story of the Fisk Jubilee Singers, and *Perfect 36*, the story of women's suffrage, were commissioned for the celebration. Outstanding performers were brought in: violinist Itzak Perlman was guest soloist with the Memphis Symphony, pianist Andre Watts with the Nashville Symphony, cellist Mstislav Rostropovich with the Knoxville Symphony, and folk musician Nanci Griffith with Nashville Ballet.

More than five hundred local events were planned across Tennessee, and most charged no admission. The counties spent their grants on everything from producing plays about local history to constructing a bandstand to holding workshops related to the state's history.

The Bicentennial Celebration Day took place at the Mall on June 1, 1996, with fireworks, a laser light show, humorous political sparring between then Vice President Al Gore and Governor Don Sundquist, and performances by country music stars and the Nashville Symphony. It was another milestone in the state's history and began preparations for the Tricentennial as time capsules from each county were buried nearby.

Oberlin Conservatory of Music, held three recitals with the instrument as the star in its new home. On December 24, 25, and 27 (the twenty-sixth was a Sunday), the featured vocalists were Mrs. Walter Dake and Mrs. Kate Gillespie, and the Fisk Glee Club also participated. The cost was 25 cents, or 50 cents for a reserved seat. That organ remained there until it was replaced in October 1960.

The Tennessee Centennial Bells were purchased by what is now the Tulip Street United Methodist Church. The ten bells hang in the main tower of the church and are still played.

The Parthenon was rebuilt in more permanent materials beginning in 1920 and completed in 1925. The interior took longer to finish (1931), primarily because of financial dilemmas, and it was not until 1990 that an enormous statue of Athena by Nashville sculptor Alan LeQuire was to stand proudly inside—and it is now gilded. The building remains a symbol of the ideals of harmony, beauty, and high aspirations for humanity. The classic architectural style set by its construction has appeared and reappeared in civic buildings, churches, businesses, and homes all over Nashville.

Centennial Park is still a gathering place for many events, notably festivals, plays, and concerts, and it has been an integral part of the city's park system.

Douglas Anderson's inspired idea became a defining moment for the city, and Nashvillians continue to reap benefits from it.

∼

Organized Women

I have never found life dull,
I have not retired, am still working.

—Louise Grundy Lindsley, 1943

FOLLOWING THE CIVIL WAR, many things other than the arts demanded the attention of women. Even though Nashville was not as devastated as many southern cities, such as Atlanta, Nashville's women had to rebuild their lives, their churches, and sometimes their homes. They had to care for widows, orphans, returning soldiers with disabilities, and homeless relatives who too often moved in with them—never to leave. Before the turn of the century, they tackled other things, organizing formal societies that focused on prohibition, home and foreign missions, preservation of Confederate ideals, city beautification, pure food and drug legislation, education, preservation of historic sites, child labor and other issues relating to children, and suffrage. Women had been involved in many of these issues over the years, but they tended to remain in the background. Their work on behalf of the Centennial Exposition (1897) proved what they could accomplish when working together, *not* in the background.

This is not to say that all women jumped wholeheartedly into these endeavors. Ideology and/or indifference kept some from participating. Even after a group such as the Women's Missionary Union (WMU) was formed among Southern Baptists, men *and* women objected to women doing work outside the home in a public way, and other women simply would not join the WMU.

Fund-raising was a growing component of their work. For example, church- and denominational-related groups often set lofty fund-raising goals. First Baptist Church built a new worship center at Broadway and Vine (Seventh) that cost more than $80,000 (about $1.6 million today) and was finished by 1886; the women were responsible for bringing part of that amount. The WMU began a fund in 1888 that garnered about $3,300 to send three missionaries to China, and that fund became the Lottie Moon Christmas Offering, which has raised more than $2.2 *billion* over its lifetime (these figures reflect amounts from the whole Southern Baptist Convention, not just in Tennessee). In 1919, the Home Mission

Board of Baptists was asking for $1 million (about $10.4 million today) from the South. In the same year, the Southern Baptist Convention sought $75 million to be given over a five-year period to support its work, and more than $58 million was actually collected, much of it by women.

Cora Sutton Castle conducted a statistical study of eminent women, and she reported in 1913, of actresses, women writers, dancers, musicians, educators, travelers, physicians, politicians, martyrs, and reformers around the world, "England had the most writers, France the most actresses and politicians, Italy and Germany the most musicians, but *all* the reformers were American." A good example of a local reformer was Louise Grundy Lindsley, daughter of John Berrien and Sallie McGavock Lindsley. Born in 1858, she wrote this about herself in 1943, the year before her death:

> I have traveled far and near in this country and abroad, have seen much and accomplished much for my state. Such as assisting in the preservation of Andrew Jackson's home, founder of the Nashville Branch of the Housewives League, a national organization, worked with the U.D.C. [United Daughters of the Confederacy], have held offices in the D.A.R. [Daughters of the American Revolution], the U.S. Daughters of 1812. As President of the Woman's Division of the Southern Commercial Congress, held meetings in many of the Southern states, also meetings held in Panama. I dedicated a spot for a tablet to be placed for John Tyler Morgan of Alabama, the father of the Canal Zone idea. At the time there was no water in the canal and I had the experience of walking through the canal and seeing all the intricate working of the place.
>
> I have always been interested in everything for the promotion of my state, sanitation, education, and also politics. I'm a graduate of the University of Nashville and George Peabody

College. I'm a Presbyterian. I have never found life dull, I have not retired, am still working.

Louise also actively participated in the Tennessee Equal Suffrage Association and the Centennial Club. She was single, so she had a different set of family responsibilities and perhaps different opportunities from those available to married women. Some women had to work to support themselves or their families, which limited their free time. (In 1910, 16,705 women in Nashville were working outside the home.) Yet married or single, working or not working outside the home, white or African-American, the women of Nashville had numerous possibilities for social involvement: Colonial Dames, Ladies' Hermitage Association, St. Luke's Settlement House, the James K. Polk Association, YWCA, Democratic Club, Sunday school teaching, Vanderbilt Aid Society, home and foreign missionary societies, Colored Relief Society, Confederate Soldiers' Home, Florence Crittenden Mission Home, Hebrew Relief Society, Old Colored Woman's Home, Swiss Benevolent Society, lodges, Nashville Free Kindergarten Association, Day Home for Children, Nashville Housekeepers' Club, German-American Ladies' Society, Phillis Wheatley Club, City Federation of Colored Women's Clubs, the predecessor organization of Bethlehem Centers, Red Cross Society, Fannie Battle's Nashville Relief Society, Women's Christian Temperance Union, and suffrage groups—and this is just a partial list.

Three groups dealt with issues that had nationwide implications: the Women's Christian Temperance Union (WCTU), the United Daughters of the Confederacy (the UDC), and the suffragists. The WCTU had a moral agenda of eliminating alcoholic beverages. Although the UDC and the suffragists seemed to have opposing agendas—the UDC supported the Old South, focusing on the past, while the suffragists supported a new day for women, focusing on the future and more rights—some women belonged to both groups.

Prohibition. Historian Anastatia Sims wrote that in 1887, "John J. Vertrees, a Nashville attorney and Democratic politician who included liquor industry executives among his clients, suggested that the temperance movement harbored feminists, Republicans, and other 'fanatics bent on undermining social and political order in Tennessee.'" That year the "fanatics" of the WCTU held a national convention in Nashville. The WCTU and other temperance groups did not have a swift path to success by any means, but the women became a power for politicians to reckon with. A bill passed by the General Assembly in 1909 supposedly made Tennessee a dry state, but it took ten more years before the passage of the Eighteenth Amendment of the U.S. Constitution. The results were so far from perfect in eradicating alcoholic beverages that Prohibition was repealed in 1933, although some counties in Tennessee are still dry.

The Confederacy. Founded in 1894 with Caroline Meriwether Goodlett as its president, the UDC became the largest women's club in the South—and an influential one—and it had its start in Nashville. Goodlett also led the first chapter of the UDC, Nashville No. 1, and eventually five more chapters joined in Nashville alone. A primary function of Nashville No. 1 was to maintain the Confederate Soldiers' Home at the Hermitage. Other tasks of the UDC included organizing memorial day celebrations, keeping alive Confederate anniversaries, raising funds for public monuments (one was the Tennessee Monument to the Women of the Confederacy located on Legislative Plaza in Nashville), and screening history books and visiting classrooms to assure that the Confederate story continued to be told. The *Confederate Veteran* magazine was founded in Nashville in 1893, and Edith D. Pope became its second editor, following Sumner A. Cunningham.

The UDC helped the magazine stay afloat for many years.

Kate Litton Hickman (1847–1917), a charter member of the UDC and the first secretary of Nashville No. 1, certainly had an unforgettable story related to the Civil War. She was the daughter of Isaac Litton and the wife of John P. Hickman, who had served in the Confederate Army as a young man. Kate's mother refused to take the oath of allegiance when the Federals took over Nashville, so the family joined Mr. Litton, then working with the relief corps of the Army of Tennessee south of Nashville. Young Kate brought back the original flag of the Second Tennessee Regiment concealed in the folds of clothing around her waist when the family returned to Nashville.

During World War I, the UDC supported the war effort and the troops. Nashville No. 1 raised approximately $90,000 (about $1.08 million today) in three Liberty Bond drives, sent care packages to soldiers, and sponsored beds in French hospitals. Other UDC chapters in Nashville financed an ambulance in France and made hospital gowns. Fanny Walton was the first Nashville Daughter to be a Red Cross nurse in France. During the years of the Great Depression, the UDC raised and contributed $50,000 (about $657,000 today) as part of the costs for a dormitory for female students at George Peabody College.

Nashville No. 1 and other chapters remain active in Tennessee more than one hundred years after the founding of the UDC.

Suffrage. The fear of what would happen if women got the vote was reinforced by handbills, newspaper reports, and public meetings. Handbills proclaimed, "A Vote for Federal Suffrage Is a Vote for Organized Female Nagging Forever." An AP report out of London must have had men, particularly those in government, shaking in their boots: "The *Daily Mirror* asserts that a suffragette plot has been discovered to kidnap a cabinet minister, dress him in women's clothes and submit him to a mock trial"; suffragists in England were literally wreaking havoc by throwing "nails thrust through pieces of stiff leather bearing a suffragist inscription with the object of puncturing automobile tires" and by setting fires. One of many meetings at the Ryman Auditorium encouraged people to come "To Save the South from the Susan B. Anthony Amendment and Federal Suffrage Force Bills." There was no kidnapping or literal fire setting among Nashville suffragists, but they tried to light a figurative fire under men and women to support them. Abby Crawford Milton, who was from Chattanooga and was on the front lines of the battle, stated in an interview many years after the decisive vote in the Tennessee General Assembly that men did not want women to vote because it would interfere with their political "setups" and

The Home of the Philharmonic Society, 1899

In 1898 a split occurred among the membership of the Wednesday Morning Musicale, and a group formed the Philharmonic Society (sometimes called the Philharmonic Club). Not only a social club, the society was to actively study music, which would assist members in self-advancement and expand their cultural knowledge. By the fall of the next year, the Philharmonic Society had almost five hundred active and associate members and a new hall, the Philharmonic Hall, on the second floor of the Odd Fellows Building at the corner of Church and Sixth Streets. The president was Mrs. S. A. Champion, and the chair of the building committee was Mrs. M. S. Lebeck. Both were on hand for the inauguration of the society's winter season and the dedication of the hall in early October. Mrs. Champion was attired in a dress of black brocade, white taffeta overlaid with ivory white chiffon, and gold beading. Mrs. Lebeck's dress was French, black net over white taffeta and chiffon.

If the surroundings were any indication of the quality of the music to be performed in Philharmonic Hall, it should have been of a high caliber indeed. There were wooden floors, mahogany paneling, and satin wallpaper. The ceiling was ivory colored with garlands decorated in gold, and chandeliers of electric lights brightened the scene. The hall would seat about 450 people on high-backed mahogany chairs with rubber tips, and storm doors on the landing outside the hall could be closed to deaden the sounds from outside. The twelve windows had window seats with tapestry cushions. On the stage, which had sunken electric footlights, were a pipe organ and two new pianos made of rosewood.

It was standing room only by the time the event began. Frank Clark King, a bass, had been scheduled to appear, but he missed his train. Mrs. Genevieve Clark Wilson, a soprano from Chicago, had to provide the whole program, consisting of an "unhackneyed list" of songs: "When Celia Sings," Michaela's Aria, the Riedel Cycle from *The Trumpeter of Lakkengen* (reportedly sung in Nashville for the first time), "The Merry Maiden," and Henschel's "Spring," among others. Mrs. W. D. Haggard Jr., a member of the society, accompanied her on the piano.

John Trotwood Moore, a future state librarian and archivist, recited the poem "Philharmonia" he had written for the special occasion, and it began,

O, let me sit and listen—nay, not speak—
No unanointed sound shall enter here,
Nor uninvited guest of discord seek
To break the sweet communion.

The "sweet communion" was to continue just a few days later at the Philharmonic Society's next event—featuring the pipe organ and an orchestra led by Ivo C. Miller, a local musician and music teacher.

politics was the men's "big game." Nevertheless, some men such as Guilford Dudley, a businessman, and Luke Lea, founder and publisher of the *Tennessean*, were supportive of the suffragists.

As with the temperance movement, the suffrage movement was not able to accomplish its goal swiftly. The National Suffrage Convention was held in Nashville in November 1914, and in that year Nashville's suffrage organization had one thousand members. Anne Dallas Dudley, Catherine Talty Kenny, and Kate Burch Warner became significant standard bearers of the movement. J. Frankie Pierce, a leader in the African-American community, spoke out in favor of women's suffrage. (In February 1916, the Nashville Equal Suffrage League sponsored a production of *Aida* by the San Carlos Opera Company.) The movement achieved a victory in 1919 when the Tennessee General Assembly passed a law permitting women to vote in municipal and presidential elections. The next year a hot Nashville summer turned into a hotbed of political maneuvering as the pro-suffragists barely triumphed over the antis and Tennessee could claim to be the Perfect 36, the thirty-sixth state to ratify the Nineteenth Amendment—and one of the few southern states to do so. With that positive vote, the majority needed to amend the Constitution was achieved.

Musical Appetite at the Turn of the Century

The white heat of interest confined to so small a circle may work its own destruction.

—ROBERTA SEAWELL, 1899

ROBERTA SEAWELL was the music critic and reviewer for the *Nashville American* when she wrote about the city's musical appetite on the eve of the twentieth century. The year of 1899 had an abundance of musical offerings, both local and imported, and Seawell perceived that the abundance caused a "menace" to a segment of the population. There had been an "over-supply of musical food for those who [were] developing a healthful appetite for a moderate amount of the richness of musical seasoning in their more material diet of life." Being served with "whole dishes of such unaccustomed food, at meals and between times, in season and out, is almost enough to destroy one's musical digestion." For people who had more gradually acquired "the 'musical habit,' the present activity [was] a stimulation and a joy."

A further concern for the future was that such a small group had the "musical habit." Seawell commented that "the white heat of interest confined to so small a circle may work its own destruction, but in the process the concentrated intensity will spread and bring to life a broader, wider space." She remained confident that "the lasting qualities of any art spirit . . . lie solely and only in its sincerity. Nothing that is false or unworthy or of ill-repute can endure, and be it Nashville or elsewhere, only that man is counted worthy who is unselfishly, unceasingly, but reverently and dignifiedly working for the spread of his art, that all men may know, and knowing, love the sole and uplifting power and solace . . . of music."

According to Seawell, Nashvillians were on the verge of advancing to a third stage of musical appreciation. They had come through the first stage of thinking that popular music consisted only of "Home, Sweet Home" or "Marching Through Georgia," and the second stage of expressing a preference for the "Spring Song" or "Traumerel." The musical offerings at the Centennial Exposition over the course of six months had brought Nashvillians to a point of being ready for the symphonic stage—they just lacked a permanent orchestra to satisfy that need.

The Trouble with the Diva

While it was an appreciative audience
it could not be called an enthusiastic one.
This fact . . . can be laid at the door
of Mme. Calvé's non-appearance.

—ADA SCOTT RICE, 1901

EMMA CALVÉ was going to sing in *Carmen*! The role for which the soprano had gained such acclaim for herself was to be presented at the Union Gospel Tabernacle (now the Ryman Auditorium) in October 1901 by the Metropolitan Opera Company, managed by Maurice Grau. The event was a coup for the city and its opera lovers. The preeminent organization could not have chosen a better opera for its first visit to Nashville—although some people were not completely happy about the story line and the title character of a Gypsy woman.

It was also an opportunity to remove the debt on the Tabernacle that seemed to have a death grip on the building. Months earlier, in June, a Tabernacle Committee was formed to consider means of retiring the $9,000 debt. E. B. Stahlman, publisher of the *Banner,* was the chairman, and committee members included James B. Richardson, Joseph Frank, Firman Smith, L. Jonas, W. E. Norvell, R. W. Buttorff, A. Perry, Julian Cooley, Hamilton Parke, W. T. Hardison, M. B. Pilcher, and Thomas G. Ryman. Stahlman recommended that the Tabernacle Committee join with the women of the Philharmonic Society to bring the Metropolitan Opera Company to Nashville, and his recommendation was approved.

The Philharmonic Society had issued the invitation in the first place but soon realized the costs were too ambitious for the group and put the idea on hold. The opera company was asking $10,000

(about $216,000 today) for a two-evening engagement, so fifty men guaranteed $200 each. A stage had to be built ($750), and then there had to be money for advertising and sundry items ($1,000). The costs were steep to try to carry out a civic duty and provide the highest quality performances at the same time, but the goal of grossing $30,000 seemed attainable.

Stahlman's *Banner* held a Grand Opera Contest, which was another way to stimulate interest in the upcoming event. If the number of votes received—327,000—is any indication of interest, the contest performed its task well. People wrote the name of a deserving young person on a ballot and sent it to the *Banner* office. The winners were from the entire area, as far as Huntsville, Alabama, and across the midstate—usually one or two per county. The winners—mostly young, unmarried women—were to meet at the Tulane Hotel the day of the opera and go to the Tabernacle as a group.

Another civic-minded part of the endeavor was the raising of $500 for tickets for the 125 students at the School for the Blind. Because the Tabernacle Opera Committee had it figured down to the last square foot of floor space for standing room to bring in enough money to retire the Tabernacle debt and pay the opera company, they could not give free tickets to anyone. (Ticket prices were $5, $3, and $2; $1.50 [about $32 today] for standing room.) The front page of the *Banner* urged: "Charity could take no form more beautiful, more gentle or more considerate than this. Music is ever dearer and more precious to those whose sensibilities are shut in by constant and unceasing darkness than it can ever be to those who can behold all the loveliness of life." Contributors responded, and their names and donations were published each day, for example, Southern Turf, $10; Lebeck Bros., $5; and Percy Warner, $30, until the total amount was received.

A column on the *Banner*'s editorial page, October 19, emphasized the importance of having receipts higher than expenses. The operas were to serve a higher purpose than "rare entertainment." Getting to hear the Met's singers was an opportunity that should not be missed, but clearing the debt on the Tabernacle was a "stronger reason," which "appeals to every resident of Nashville regardless of his or her ability to appreciate opera." Nashville needed a place for events "of a respectable character." All should come, and induce others to come, to achieve the result.

The railroad offered reduced fares to operagoers, and many came from across Tennessee and surrounding states. The hotels were jammed, and people were shopping, some buying evening clothes at the last minute. Others went to Fite's Music Store to get the latest sheet music and librettos of the operas. Still others were making selections from the opera glasses at D. Lowenheim & Co. on Union and Cherry (Fourth) Streets, where cheaper ones sold for $3.50 but platinoid and finely crafted ones went for $50 and up ($50 then, about $1,100 today).

Then a serious announcement from the Maxwell House Hotel threatened to dash the high spirits and high hopes: Mme Calvé was not up to a performance. The rumors flew that she was not ill. One rumor was that she had seriously overimbibed "adult beverages." Another rumor was that the problem was her temperament, which had undergone two significant irritations. The previous stop was Louisville where the audience, for some reason, was the coldest that the famous singer could recall. She was given the "zero treatment," according to a Louisville newspaper. Calvé flew into a rage backstage after the end of one act and in subsequent scenes "was by no means particular to sing all the music allotted to her," yet still was an incomparable Carmen. Blow number one—to her ego. Then the second blow was an insult to her beloved collie, who traveled with her; the Maxwell House chef prepared overdone meat for the dog. The singer had a stand-off with the L & N Railroad over the dog because she had ordered a drawing room in a Pullman car, with the understanding that the dog would join her. The porter refused to let the dog in the car, citing railroad policy. Calvé said the dog went with her in her room or she would withdraw from the opera company. A railroad superintendent finally met her demand, and the diva set out for Nashville. The dog food incident sent Calvé over the top, and there would be no singing in Nashville.

What could the Tabernacle Committee and Mrs. W. D. Haggard Jr., president of the Philharmonic Society, do? Plans were made and people were anticipating the performance of the year, perhaps the performance of the decade. They turned to the law for help. The contract stipulated that in the case of Mme Calvé's illness, Emma Eames would perform in *Faust*—if she was available. Well, Calvé was not technically ill, but she was "physically incapacitated" and Mme Eames was on the train to Memphis.

Mrs. Haggard, members of the Tabernacle Committee, and Maurice Grau had a conversation about the situation on the evening of October 22. We do not know what was said then, but the discussion moved to the public forum the next day. Grau responded to the letter composed by Mrs. Haggard's legal counsel, demanding compliance with the contract, with his own letter, and both were published in the newspapers for all to read. Part of Grau's response dealt with Calvé's condition: "Madame Calvé is at the disposal of such physicians as you desire to send to her, to ascertain the exact condition of her throat, and I am sure they will easily convince themselves that she is absolutely incapacitated by illness from appearing in the performance for which she is announced tonight."

Also appearing in the newspaper was a doctors' certificate: "Ladies of the Philharmonic Society and gentlemen of the Tabernacle Committee: At

Emma Calvé sorely disappointed operagoers who hoped to hear her in *Carmen*, October 1901, when the Metropolitan Opera Company presented it at the Union Gospel Tabernacle (now the Ryman Auditorium). In later years, however, she made up for it with other outstanding performances; this photo was in the *Banner* for her January 1908 appearance.

your request, we have called upon Mme. Calvé and find her complaining of a bronchial irritation which she insists will incapacitate her to sing in to-night's performances. She also states positively that she will be unable to sing at Memphis or Atlanta, but hopes to be able to appear in New Orleans, October 31." It was signed by Drs. W. D. Haggard Jr., Hillard Wood, and George H. Price. That left no doubt about Calvé's plans.

Grau paid a $1,500 forfeit, added $500 to the Tabernacle fund for goodwill, and offered the services of Mme Schumann-Heink at a later date if the Nashvillians determined that they suffered a severe financial loss because of Calvé's non-appearance. The Philharmonic Society and the Tabernacle Committee refunded money to anyone who asked for it. Few people chose the refund, however, and only $1,025 in ticket sales was lost. The fund was still $900 ahead.

Musicians and music lovers, businessmen and the social elite were in the audience, which almost completely filled the Tabernacle, to hear the substituted Camille Seygard as Carmen on October 23. Boxes had been installed in front of the gallery, and a few of the box holders were Mr. and Mrs. Percy Warner, General and Mrs. G. P. Thruston, Mr. and Mrs. Leslie Warner, Mr. and Mrs. W. B. Earthman, Mrs. J. Horton Fall, Major and Mrs. E. B. Stahlman, Mr. and Mrs. John B. Ransom, Mr. and Mrs. Frank O. Fite, and Mr. and Mrs. Bruce Douglas.

The conductor was Philippe Flon. The company and Mme Seygard did a fine job, yet they heard only the barest, polite applause from the disappointed audience. After all, they had their musical taste buds set for Calvé.

The next night's performance was the *Barber of Seville,* featuring Mme Marcella Sembrich, with Armando Seppilli conducting. In an interview Mme Sembrich announced that her favorite role was that of Rosina, and her comments were recorded exactly as follows: "I am varee glad to sing it here for my first appearance. Oh, ze beautiful comedy, ze dainty coquetry of Rosina—it is charming—and ze other parts of ze opera, too, are fine." Her love of the part seems to have translated into the audience's love of her work. The entire house was filled—not one vacant seat.

Reviewing the event, Ada Scott Rice stated,

It would have been a good object lesson for Mme. Calvé, could that disappointed genius have come back from another city to witness the production of last evening. Surely she would have realized that she missed more than did her Nashville audience, in losing the inspiration of the sweeping applause which came again and again as a tribute to great Sembrich. It was more than mere transitory delight at the glorious music. It was an expression of the audience's discernment of the fact that the star was as learned humanly as she was gifted musically. The audience of the first night was cold because it felt itself aggrieved. That of last night was spontaneous with its bravos because it was returning in some measure the pure enjoyment furnished by Sembrich's seductive charm. As an object lesson it was complete in its vividness.

The Tabernacle Committee and the Philharmonic Society had reason to be satisfied with their efforts. They had brought the Metropolitan Opera to Nashville, and although the Tabernacle debt was not eliminated, it was reduced. Nashville merchants were overjoyed at the "snug sum of money" they added to their coffers. One commented about the out-of-town visitors: "They could afford to come to Nashville, pay railroad fare, hotel bills and $5 for a seat and were consequently people of good financial standing, as a rule. This being the case, many of them spent money freely. They were away above any crowd of visitors who have entered the gates of Nashville since the Centennial Exposition, when it comes to spending money in the stores."

Calvé did, in fact, give concerts in Nashville several times in the ensuing years. Following her appearance in mid-January 1908, when she sang selections—selections only, not the whole opera—from *Carmen* at the Ryman Auditorium, she extended her stay by three days to rest in the countryside.

The reviewer of that performance began by saying, "Once again has a Nashville audience bowed down in worship at the shrine of Emma Calvé, and in that audience were many ears untrained in musical technique, but these, and musically cultured folk as well, were pleased, delighted, satisfied. The size of the audience alone was a mute tribute to Madame's splendid art." The audience called for an encore on every rendition and a third on some. The reviewer added, "Taken as a whole, the programme was decidedly artistic, and Calvé has gained an even deeper hold upon Nashville's music-loving public."

A Union for Musicians

The union is the glue that holds the music industry together in Nashville.

—HAROLD BRADLEY

THE NASHVILLE Association of Musicians, Local 257 of the American Federation of Musicians (AFM) of the United States and Canada, founded in December 1902, is the second oldest musicians' union in Tennessee. Local 71 in Memphis, the oldest, was chartered in 1898. Local 257 had these charter members: Charles F. Davis, C.J. Schubert, Will R. Martin, Nick Melfi, Rudolph Moehl, Charles F. Hefferman, John Keech, and Jesse Martin. Joe Miles became the first president. The AFM was still a fairly new group, having been established in 1896, when Nashville's musicians playing in orchestras at the Tabernacle (the Ryman) and the Vendome and Grand Theatres (and later the Bijou and many other theaters) and dance bands joined up. One early group was Vito Pellettieri's Orchestra; Pellettieri eventually became WSM music librarian and stage manager for the Grand Ole Opry. If a traveling troupe needed musicians, Local 257 got a call. By 1917, there were 79 members of the local union. (In 1914, about 11,000 AFM members played in theater orchestras.)

From its founding, the union has had to adapt to changes—sometimes drastic or innovative ones—in the music business. As the introduction of talking movies and the demise of vaudeville reduced the need for live musicians, musicians were able to find jobs with radio stations. By 1925 there were several stations in Nashville: WEBX (Cain-Sloan), WDAD (Dad's Hardware Store), WBAW (Braid Electric), and WCBQ (First Baptist Church). WLAC started the next year. WSM's first broadcast in the fall of 1925 of the singers from Fisk University, Joseph Macpherson, the Knights of Columbus Vocal Quartet, Al Menah's Shrine Band, Francis Craig's Columbia Recording Orchestra, and Beasley Smith's Andrew Jackson Hotel Orchestra marked the beginning of a showcase for local talent.

To give some idea of the programming, here is the schedule for January 4–11, 1926 (all are evening times, except Sunday): *Monday*: 6:30, Beasley Smith and his orchestra from the Andrew Jackson Hotel; 7:00, WSM bedtime story interlude; 7:30, community program from First Presbyterian Church; and 10:00, Vito M. Pellettieri and his orchestra (one hour). *Wednesday:* 6:30, Francis Craig and his orchestra from the Hermitage Hotel; 7:00, bedtime story; 8:00, Mrs. Eva Thompson Jones and associates, classical music; and 9:00, program by Mrs. Mary Cornelia Malone, soprano, and Mrs. Daisy Hoffman, pianist (one hour). *Friday:* 6:30, Beasley Smith and his

orchestra; 7:00, bedtime story; 8:00, men's Bible class of Woodland Street Presbyterian Church; and 10:00, Dutch Erhardt and his orchestra (one hour). *Saturday*: 6:30, Francis Craig and his orchestra; 7:00, bedtime story; 8:00, Uncle Jimmy Thompson, champion barn-dance fiddler (he had first been heard on the station in November 1925); 9:00, Tennessee College Glee Club, Murfreesboro; and 10:00, Paul Sharpe's Orchestra (one hour). *Sunday*: 10:30, services from First Presbyterian Church, Dr. James I. Vance (one hour). Popular and classical music dominated the programming, the churches had a significant representation, but there was only one program of what was then considered old-time or hillbilly music. The impact of that one program on the city's future, however, could not have been foreseen by WSM's owner, National Life and Accident Insurance Company.

The radio station soon hired a staff band and also employed many other musicians and singers on an as-needed basis. Orin Gaston, WSM's first music director, was the son of G. B. Gaston, who had served twice as secretary-treasurer of Local 257. The continued popularity of the old-time music show brought in a live audience to the studio on Saturday evenings, and in 1927 announcer George D. Hay named it the *Grand Ole Opry* because it followed Walter Damrosch's program of grand opera on NBC. The *Grand Ole Opry* is now the longest-running radio show in the United States.

Harold Bradley is the current president of Local 257 and the first Nashville member to become an officer on the International Executive Board of AFM as vice president-U.S. He stated, "The *Grand Ole Opry* is the reason all the recording centers are here. We had the singers, the songwriters, the musicians, the engineers. All we needed was a studio." Castle Studios supplied that need in 1947— the same year that Francis Craig had a hit record with "Near You"—and Acuff-Rose, a publishing

In 1947 Francis Craig and his orchestra had a hit with "Near You," which became the first Nashville recording to sell more than a million copies. From the mid-1920s to the mid-1940s the band could be heard live at the Hermitage Hotel.

house organized in 1942 by Roy Acuff and Fred Rose, "was an outlet for the hillbilly songs because ASCAP didn't want the hillbilly songs," Harold added. Paul Cohen, working out of New York for Decca in 1947 as a record producer, was another vital part of the recording picture.

A member of the A Team of session musicians, Harold played for Elvis and Roy Orbison, Patsy Cline and Brenda Lee; sixteen people with whom he worked have been inducted into the Rock and Roll Hall of Fame. He had jobs at WSM radio while he was still in high school, and he has been a member of the union since he was sixteen—taking the advice of his older brother, Owen. He and Owen participated in the recording business as players as well as owners of a recording studio, Quonset Hut Studio, in the area now known as Music Row. (Music Row is a fairly recent name to identify that part of Nashville.)

George W. Cooper Jr. became the president of Local 257 in 1937 when it was not thriving. Of course not much was thriving during the Great Depression. He joined the union in 1916, at age nineteen, and in his career he played in silent movie theaters and at WSM, both radio and TV stations. During his tenure of thirty-six years as the union's president, musicians had more studio work and better working conditions. (Here is the roster of presidents of Local 257: Joe Miles, Charles F. Davis, H. J. Kilbourne, J. Able, E. J. Ignatz, Syd A. Groom, J. J. Caddy, Elmer Jones, G. B. Gaston, George W. Cooper, Johnny DeGeorge, Jay Collins, and Harold Bradley. Cooper had the longest tenure of anyone.) Although some unions were more than reluctant to admit hillbilly musicians because many of them could not read music, Local 257 was an exception and allowed them to join.

The Local did not have the same generous policy toward African-American musicians, however, sending them instead to the Birmingham, Alabama, Local. That error in judgment has been corrected, but the city's musical landscape lost talented people who could have added more diversity and styles of playing years ago. One loss was that of jazz musicians. Harold noted, "Jimmy Cleveland was a fantastic trombone player; he had to leave Nashville to make a living, as did all of the jazz players. I used to go down to Thirteenth and Broad to hear him play when I was in college."

Harold credited the union as a stabilizing force for Nashville's musicians: "When the recordings started coming here in 1947, George Cooper, my brother Owen Bradley, and Chet Atkins all were great union men. They never made us work for less than scale. Any record session I ever worked with Chet or Owen—they set the standard. Don Law of Columbia and Ken Nelson of Capitol—they knew this was a union town when they came here to record. The unions in some other southern towns—the musicians were on something like a salary, maybe $250 a week. They found out they could make $250 in three hours here in Nashville. It didn't take them long to pack their bags and move here."

In 1960, the Local had 710 members. When the seventy-fifth anniversary of the union arrived in 1977, Local 257 dedicated its own building on Music Row (11 Music Circle North). A peak of about 3,700 was reached in the mid-1990s, and the membership is closer to 3,500 now with country (Trace Adkins), bluegrass (Ricky Skaggs), rocking (Béla Fleck & the Flecktones), and Christian (Take Six) stars. Although applications are approved every month, existing members drop out of the business completely or become what Harold calls "weekend warriors," who play on weekends as nonunion musicians. He said, "Eighty percent of our membership are freelance musicians. They don't make records; they don't do jingles; they don't do television; they don't do radio. They play live gigs."

The venues for live musicians have changed over the decades and no longer include Opryland theme park or the Vendome Theatre. Sites such as the Ryman, TPAC, Gaylord Entertainment Center, the Coliseum, War Memorial Auditorium, and Ingram Hall at the Blair School of Music at Vanderbilt University are available, and the upcoming Schermerhorn Symphony Center will be a unique space for many events and performances. Cities such as Detroit and Memphis have less and less recording business. Although New York and LA are still recording centers, both places have such high costs of living and the quality of life in Nashville is so conducive to raising children that many people associated with the music business have moved to Nashville. Film and video production has added another dimension to the music business. Nashville is becoming known for all kinds of music so that when CD sales of one type (such as country) are down, the others (such as Christian) may remain stable or be on an upswing.

With technological changes in the business, everyone was—and is—learning on the job. Harold recalled that Don Law, who worked with Marty Robbins and Ray Price, among others, was the first to explain stereo to him: "He came to me at our studio one day and said, 'Harold, old chap—he was English—as you know, Marty has been recording in New York with Mitch Miller and I'm afraid of losing some of my artists up there. They have this new thing called stereo.' I said, 'What's that?' He said, 'It comes out of two speakers instead of one.' I said, 'Okay, I don't know what it is, but Owen and I will get it.' So we did. We got a two-track system. Now you can cut all of the tracks you want. It changed the recording industry considerably. The A Team that I was very proud to be a member of all those years— that was the reason we were around so long: we could play the song from beginning to end without making a mistake. That is why we were first call for so many years. Technology has changed so much. We didn't foresee CDs or DVDs or DATs. We certainly didn't anticipate the Internet."

The virtual reality orchestra, like having music in a box, to accompany Broadway shows is a looming problem. Harold observed, "If somebody brings it here [to Nashville], there will be quite a massive demonstration because we have all of these wonderful musicians in town, and they are used to supplementing their income [by playing with Broadway shows]. To take that away from them like that is unfair." Piracy of CDs means a loss for record companies, artists, songwriters, and musicians. Harold added, "In Japan they don't sell CDs; they rent them. One of our representatives negotiated with Geidankyo so that they would make some payments into a fund called the Special Payments that the recording musicians share, depending on their scale wages."

Harold explained his position on the need for Local 257 and its services: "It's simple. My motto is, 'United we stand, divided we beg.' The union is the glue that holds the music industry together in Nashville. For instance, on the recording—if we didn't make an agreement with the five big record companies that everybody else has to follow, then all of the record companies—even the small ones—would have to negotiate independently with every musician that played on a session. What a nightmare! And the paperwork. And you'd have different scales. Then they wouldn't give them any benefits. Why include pensions? Why include health and welfare? Why give them a taste of special payments? It would be a disaster." The same idea applies to radio and television.

The course of last resort for Harold is a strike: "We'd much rather negotiate. My theory is 'play and talk.' If there is a dispute, go on and play, and we'll talk about it with the employer and work it out. I don't think anybody wins in a strike. It takes too long to rebuild and regain what is lost. While I'm president I don't want to have to do that. I don't know that I can say that it will never happen, but I don't want it to. During a negotiation with a cable network, we did threaten to withhold services. It was a sticky situation." The specter of the strike called by AFM President James Petrillo that shut down the recording industry from 1942 to 1944 still hovers over musicians.

Tennessee is a right-to-work state, and under collective bargaining rules, union and nonunion can work together. Everyone in the Nashville Symphony is a union member. Harold said, "We just did a new six-year contract with the Nashville Symphony, which I think is a win-win for everybody. We are thrilled over that. I'm looking at some of the other symphonies in the country that are going through hard times."

For the one hundredth anniversary of Local 257 a special event was held at the Opry House, October 7, 2002, dedicated to George W. Cooper. All monies raised went to the Emergency Relief Fund and Opry Trust Fund. More than three thousand people attended *The Music of Music City: Celebrating a Century of Musicians,* and they heard Brenda Lee, Willie Nelson, Ray Stevens, the Jordanaires, and Kitty Wells, among others. Eddy Arnold was the recipient of country's Artist of the Century Award.

Everyone gave high marks to the event, but rave reviews went to the Nashville Symphony. Harold summed up the evening: "The people come here and their perception of us is still *Hee-Haw.* I fight that perception at times, but I don't think I will have to fight it again after the people saw the show because of the Symphony. The first thing in the review that is going in the *International Musician:* It calls the Nashville Symphony *the* superstar of the event. And it was. We had all of these acts in all kinds of genres, and if we had hired a regular country band to play behind them, we would have been another show like you've seen before. It would have been good. But to have the Symphony and to hear them play, it was incredible. They played 'The Tennessee Waltz'—the Ron Huff arrangement—just orchestrally it was fantastic. Then they went into 'Near

You' and sounded like a big band. Then they played 'Lucky Old Sun' with a harp and orchestra. It was so classy."

With leaders like Harold Bradley and George W. Cooper, the Nashville Association of Musicians can look forward to another one hundred years of work on behalf of its members and the further strengthening of this glue that holds together Nashville's music industry.

Outdoor Splendor

The public is cordially invited
to these high-class attractions.

—Nashville Globe, July 31, 1908,
advertisement for Greenwood Park

FOR THE FOURTH OF JULY, 1903, many activities were scheduled in the private and public parks of Nashville, and the performing arts were included in the celebration.

At Glendale Park Manager Y. C. Alley had arranged for a concert at the Casino by Professor Feustel's orchestra in addition to dancing in the pavilion, baseball games, fireworks, and barbecue. Local groups as early as 1894 had produced summer opera at the park's pavilion, led by Minnie Vesey and Mrs. Becky Levy Jacobus. The sixty-four-acre park, owned by the Nashville Railway and Light Company, was located in the area near what is now the intersection of Caldwell and Lealand Lanes. Patrons had to pay a small entrance fee, and the streetcar fare was an additional expense. Although it might not seem a great distance to us today, being seven miles from the city's center was a long way out. The park, which had added a zoo in 1912, closed in 1932. (In 1892 Glendale was one of four private parks; the others were Richland, Cherokee, and Maplewood.)

Thus, the public parks were even more important for citizens with the least means.

At Centennial Park the Mexican Building had been transformed into a theater, and the Orpheus Opera Company, organized locally, hoped to make summer opera a "permanent amusement feature." The company's season of *Pinafore, The Mikado*, and other Gilbert and Sullivan works was the first cultural recreation program of the Parks Board. Justin Thatcher, a vocalist with a studio on Woodland Street, seems to have been the driving force. Perhaps the April 1890 performance of *Pinafore* at the Vendome Theatre was his inspiration because he was in the cast featuring Lottie McCreary and Wallace McCreary, and John Ashford (husband of hymn writer Emma Ashford) conducted the orchestra. For *Pinafore* in Centennial Park on that hot July day in 1903, Charles Washburn, Marie Oakland, and Corinne Tabler joined Thatcher on the stage. There was a fee of 25 cents (about $5 today) for the single performance or 35 cents for a season ticket. (In later years the Parks Board tried to provide the performing arts at no cost.) Thatcher's inspired idea for opera in the park was not profitable, and he did not renew the contract with the city for 1904. In fact, he left the city by 1905, headed for New York City. Once again a proposed permanent performing arts endeavor died.

The parks have been the scenes of ongoing springtime and summertime arts fare and sometimes remarkable events. Only rarely have the parks been inactive, but at least one year nothing happened due to the threat of polio. Because of Nashville's moderate climate and its often sweltering summers, people's love of the outdoors, and the costs associated with building and maintaining a performing arts hall, the parks long filled a void for a performing arts venue.

Nashville's municipal park system had its beginning with an act passed by the Tennessee General Assembly, March 27, 1901, that amended

Theatre Parthenos was a local effort to present Greek dramas, in English, on the steps of the Parthenon. They were held on August weekends throughout most of the 1980s *(top left).* An unusual, but delightful, outdoor venue on April 27, 2003, was the Dyer Observatory for "Music on the Mountain." The first of the series featured Blair School of Music faculty members Bobby Taylor (oboe), David Schnaufer (dulcimer), Butch Baldassari (mandolin), G. R. Davis (bass), and friends from the Nashville music community performing Appalachian music *(top right).* Riverfront Park in downtown Nashville is often the site of celebrations, and the Fourth of July is always special—with a Nashville Symphony performance and fireworks. In the summer of 2003 the Symphony and several performers were broadcast nationally on the Arts and Entertainment Network *(bottom).*

the city's charter and authorized the establishment of public parks and a Board of Park Commissioners. By 1915 there were 18 parks covering 450 acres that served fewer than 160,000 people. Today, the 100 parks covering about 10,200 acres serve nearly 570,000 people. Metro's Board of Parks and Recreation manages baseball fields, swimming pools, golf courses, community centers, playgrounds, ice-skating rinks, soccer fields, greenways, and tennis courts. Riverfront Park is often the site of Fourth of July celebrations, complete with fireworks, the Nashville Symphony, and other musicians or groups. In 2003 the concert was broadcast nationally on the Arts and Entertainment Network. In a recent year, more than 5,000 children and adults studied music, dance, theater, and visual arts in classes taught by Metro Park instructors through the Arts Division.

Particularly for the private parks, advertisements highlighted the uplifting nature of the performances. Jake Wells, a baseball star who had gotten into the theatrical business and managed a circuit of theaters, leased Glendale Park in 1904. He enlarged the stage for vaudeville, melodrama, and musical comedies, and all were "high class."

Greenwood Park was owned by Preston Taylor, son of slave parents who became a businessman, religious leader, and husband of Georgia Gordon, an original Fisk Jubilee Singer. The private park at Lebanon and Spence Roads was for African-Americans. In the summer of 1908, W. W. Mishaw of Cincinnati, Ohio, the manager and a "show man of wide experience," scheduled vaudeville, comedy, and minstrel shows of "good character." The plays changed weekly, admission was 10 cents (about $2 today), and there was a guarantee not to present "Plantation shows."

From 1904 to 1910 a German brass band played at Centennial Park, and Percy Warner and the Nashville Railway and Light Company paid the musicians directly. Beginning in 1911, the City Council set aside funds to have concerts in Morgan, Watkins, Richland, and Meridian Street Parks. In that year, 1911, the First Tennessee Regiment Band provided concerts with drills of the local militias. G. L. Valdes and his City Parks Band played after World War I.

A history-making event occurred in 1912 when the city purchased thirty-four acres of land in an area that was once the John L. Hadley plantation. Hadley Park was dedicated on the Fourth of July, and it is considered the first public park in the United States for African-Americans. Some forty years earlier Frederick Douglass had spoken on that plantation, on that site. African-Americans were allowed in other city parks, but segregation was the norm—although not the law. Musical events were scheduled there, as in other city parks. Eventually the talented Don Q. Pullen, a TSU graduate, a jazz pianist who studied at Juilliard, and a band director at Washington Junior High, scheduled concerts for Hadley Park.

A sizable addition to the parks system resulted from a gift. In 1927 Luke Lea, lawyer, politician, founder of the *Tennessean,* and land owner, donated 868 acres of his Belle Meade property and requested that the section be named for his father-in-law, Percy Warner, who had been chairman of the Park Board until his recent death. Edwin Warner succeeded his brother as Park Board chairman and acquired more land for the parks system. The Warner Parks bearing the names of both brothers occupy more than 2,600 acres. It is significant that a prosperous man such as Lea was donating land for a park in Nashville just about the same time John Long Severance, and his wife, Elisabeth, were contributing the major portion of funds for a hall designed specifically for the Cleveland Orchestra. Perhaps the difference reflects something about each city—its climate and its appetite for the arts at that moment in time.

An outdoor concert on the evening of June 13, 1941, has to be memorable for anyone who attended it. It was sponsored by the Metropolitan Opera Guild for the benefit of General Hospital's tumor clinic. First, it was held at Sulphur Dell, site of more baseball games than classical concerts. Second, Leopold Stokowski was conducting the All American Youth Orchestra; by showcasing young artists of the free world, the conductor was responding to the Nazi glorification of the Hitler youth movement. Stokowski said of the young people with whom he worked, "These young people are phenomenal. Technically they are the equals of any musicians. And they have the enthusiasm of youth. They are so sensitive, so quick. With them the playing of music is not just a job. They have a love for it." Third, a noisy train managed to ruin the special evening's great performance by the college- and high-school-age musicians. Stokowski had programmed "Nocturne" by Debussy, D Minor Symphony by Franck, "Guaracho," a symphonietta by Morton Gould, and selections from Wagner's *Tristan and Isolde*. The reviewer Sydney Dalton could not resist writing, "It is regrettable that with all its advancement in musical and artistic affairs, Nashville still lacks adequate facilities for staging performances of this kind." With a proper venue, the embarrassment of the offending train could have been averted. During Franck's piece, Stokowski had to pause so that the locomotive could let off steam—literally. At the end of the program, during an encore of Weber's "Invitation to the Dance," Stokowski gave up and stopped the performers completely because the same locomotive repeatedly blew its whistle.

The Nashville Symphony has appeared regularly in city parks, and at the end of May 1976 the Symphony opened the park season with a concert in Centennial Park's bandshell. It was a special concert for the guest conductor, Kay George Roberts, then age twenty-six, because it was her conducting debut. Her father, S. Oliver Roberts, was chairman of Fisk University's Department of Psychology, and she had graduated from Fisk with a music major. Growing up in Nashville, Roberts had played violin in the Cremona Strings, a group organized for African-American youngsters by Robert Holmes; the Nashville Youth Symphony; and the Nashville Symphony. By the summer of 1976 Roberts had earned her Master of Musical Arts from Yale University School of Music (and she would later become the first woman to earn the Doctor of Musical Arts in orchestral conducting from Yale). The program featured music of eight countries and included Copland's "Fanfare for the Common Man," Shostakovich's "Festival Overture," "Solvejg's Song" from Peer Gynt Suite by Grieg, and Sibelius's "Finlandia." The audience's favorite was Joaquin Rodrigo's *Concierto de Aranjuez*, featuring guitarist Jorge Morel. All in all, it was a triumphant appearance for Roberts, who is now on the music faculty of the University of Massachusetts Lowell.

Dramatic productions have been less frequent in the parks than musical ones, but several deserve to be mentioned. A few years before the city's presentation of the extravagant pageants *The Fire Regained* and the *Mysteries of Thanatos* (see "Greatest Musical Treat Ever Presented to Nashville"), Pauline Townsend, director of expression at Belmont College, staged *Elektra* on the north terrace of the Parthenon with her students. It began at 4:30 P.M. on October 14, 1908. The Nashville Art Club, with Mrs. Katherine P. Wright as president, was the sponsor. The players performed with the "grace and the dignity demanded by the tragic plot," and "especially beautiful were the tableau effects when oblations had been poured in the pedestal urns and streams of rosy flames illuminated the encircling figures." Belle Warnock was Elektra, Juanita Evans was Orestes, and Avalyn Fleming "gave a spirited rendition" of Clytemnestra. Others in leading roles were Louise Brown, Leroy Smotherman, and Virginia Enochs. Fifty chorus members wearing white and attendants carrying shields with touches of gold completed the scene.

On weekends in August throughout most of the 1980s, ancient Greek plays returned to the Parthenon, thanks to Theatre Parthenos. The idea sprang from a discussion between Teresa Choate, now with the Communications and Theatre Department of Kean University, New Jersey, and Wesley Paine, director of the Parthenon. The goal was to educate people about these ancient plays and provide them free of charge, just as in ancient Athens. The plays, produced in English, were *Oedipus, Medea, Antigone, The Oresteia, Trojan Women,* and *Thesmophoriazusae; The Bacchae* was translated for the group by a local professor. The Metro Board of Parks and Recreation funded the effort for two years, and then they formed a 501(c)(3) organization. Most of the actors were local or had a Nashville connection and returned for the productions.

Shakespeare in the Park is the work of the Nashville Shakespeare Festival (NSF), which was founded in 1988. In August of that year the NSF offered its production of *As You Like It,* free of charge in Centennial Park. Other plays have been *The Tempest, Twelfth Night,* and *The Taming of the Shrew,* and in 2000 *As You Like It* was set in the American Old West, a creative, nontraditional production.

An unlikely participant in NSF's *Othello* was John Seigenthaler, then editor and publisher of the *Tennessean.* He was a spear carrier and had the grand total of two lines. Nashville's parks, especially Centennial Park, have been important in his life—he grew up in the West End area—and his work as a young reporter in the 1950s led him to cover the Sunday concerts sponsored by the newspaper. He met his future wife, Dolores Watson, who was a vocalist one Sunday afternoon. As he said, "Some people get more out of visiting parks than others."

Nashvillians—musicians, actors, and audiences—have accepted and made good use of these natural venues for the performing arts.

Extravagant Entertainment

I felt like shouting.

—A WOMAN VIEWING BEN HUR, 1904

TWO EXTRAVAGANZAS reached low and high points for Nashville audiences, and a third, a local production, stirred hometown pride. All were staged at the Vendome.

First, the low point. The *Twelve Temptations* was advertised to have nothing that would "shock the modesty of the most refined" for its one-week stay, beginning October 29, 1889. Charles H. Yale was bringing seventy people and twenty-six tons of scenery, guaranteed to entertain with "a great variety of features." In addition to comedians, there was a corps de ballet featuring Marie Bonfanti. (Born in 1847, she had danced at the Grand Opera in Paris and Covent Garden in London, but she was perhaps better known for having been in the original cast of *The Black Crook* in 1866 at Niblo's Garden in New York City, a groundbreaking event in U.S. musical theater. By the time she appeared in Nashville, she was pushing past the prime age for a dancer.)

Basically the "never-ending continuation of novelties of a humorous and amusing character" and scenic effects were the attractions. When Bonfanti danced a ballet that "the gay Parisian or the luxurious and veteran Viennese would have taken delight in," she and the corps were met with "freezing silence." Nevertheless, the reviewer felt that the ballet was "quite the finest ever danced in the South outside of New Orleans." As promised, no part of the performance was shocking to the refined.

The same could not be said of the audience's behavior. The reviewer grumbled about the crowd: "Applause and approbation is one thing and an intolerable, merciless, howling pandemonium is something else. . . . The Seven Points never, in its palmiest days, furnished such a horrible and intolerable contribution as was imposed upon the decent portions of the audience at the Vendome." Every woman there was reported to have gone home with a

Maude Adams delivered a "top notch" performance of *Peter Pan* in November 1907 at the Vendome for three nights and a matinee. Tickets cost 50 cents to $2 (about $10 to $39 today), which were worth the price to see J. M. Barrie's "masterpiece" and Adams's art as "merely the living expression of the fancy . . . as you would like to think it is at its very best."

headache. The reviewer urged Manager Milsom to put twenty or thirty "determined policemen" in the gallery to restore order before his theater sank to the Bowery's level.

The high point was Klaw & Erlanger's production of *Ben Hur*, scheduled for February 8–12, 1904. (The event was so popular that more showings had to be added.) Edgar Stillman Kelley, with the Conservatory of Music at Stuttgart, Germany, led the special orchestra augmented by the local theater orchestra. The score contained vocal and orchestral segments.

On the first night more than two thousand men, women, and children, who were "not frequenters of such a place of amusement," witnessed the play of six acts and fourteen scenes. Playwright William Young had so successfully dramatized Lew Wallace's book that the action was easy to follow. Despite the large cast, it was the spectacle, not the acting, that transfixed the audience. The crew of stagehands frantically maneuvered the mechanical devices to keep the action flowing seamlessly. A ballet in the Grove of Daphne was pleasing. The scene with the galley ship in the second act used a painted canvas to depict the sea, and the setting sun was a red lantern filled with electric lights.

Before the curtain went up on the chariot scene, the audience could hear horses' hooves pounding, whips cracking, and people cheering. Then the curtain was raised to reveal two chariots, each with three real horses. Ben Hur and Messala were racing, and the arena seemed to fly by. It was all over in less than a minute.

In the scene in which Ben Hur's sister and mother were healed of leprosy by Jesus, a white light—not a person—depicted the Son of God. At the end of the play when the chorus sang "Hosannah to the Highest," one woman who had not been in a theater for thirty years said, "I felt like shouting." Klaw & Erlanger gave the town something to shout about.

More than five hundred local musicians and performers participated in the musical extravaganza *Professor Napoleon*, which opened April 20, 1906, and was sponsored by the Nashville Grays, a local militia group. There really was no plot in the two-act play, just a succession of scenes and songs "of the most catchy variety."

Yateman Alley had the title role, and Horace Blankenship played the senator's son. Nannie Brooks Jordan had the female lead as a college student, and Agnes Lee was the stern preceptress. Dora Marie Raesfield rated a special mention for her singing of the "Grandpa" song with a chorus of witches and for her acting. Sixteen men of the Nashville Grays, commanded by Captain A. T. Levine, presented a fancy drill that lasted more than twenty minutes. The songs and choruses included "We're Sailors of Iowa," "My Chosen Chief" by Minnie Halperin and the chorus, and the "Banjo Girls' Serenade" led by Angela Grady. "A smoother, prettier or more meritorius amateur performance has not been witnessed in this city for some time," wrote the reviewer. The audience agreed and applauded almost continuously, adding cheers for good measure.

~

Shall I Book It?

*The booking people in New York
say they cannot book "split weeks,"
and imagine Nashville supporting one play for a WEEK!*

—LULA NAFF, 1954

LULA NAFF was a young widow when she began managing the Ryman Auditorium in the early 1900s. By the time of her retirement in 1955, many Nashvillians regarded her as slightly eccentric at best, but she was a savvy manager, who learned how to work with the townspeople, the artists and their managers, and the auditorium itself. Preachers made less frequent appearances as she booked the big names of opera, theater, and music. Caruso to Rosa Ponselle, Helen Hayes to John Barrymore, Paderewski to Yehudi Menuhin—all performed at the Ryman before the Grand Ole Opry made its home there. Local performers and productions showed up on the roster, too. Based upon Mrs. Naff's correspondence with Francis Robinson, reports in the newspapers, and items from her collection in the Nashville Room at the downtown public library, we can gain an understanding of why some things happened as they did—or did not—in the cultural world of Nashville.

Her reputation. For someone who admitted that she was no press agent, Mrs. Naff did pretty well, and she gained a solid reputation with the New York agents—eventually. Brock Pemberton described her as "America's most picturesque manageress" in the *New York Times Magazine,* discussing American theater's comeback on the road in 1939. Many other successful female managers were in Omaha, Toledo, Little Rock, and Des Moines. Pemberton explained, "Their success seems to lie in bringing a personal, social touch to a business which deals in human beings." During the Great Depression, many playhouses were boarded up and fell into such disrepair that they had to be demolished, or they were turned into movie theaters, but the Ryman averted either fate. The depression years were lean ones despite appearances of Lily Pons, Maude Adams, and Walter Huston, but at least some business was ongoing.

In a 1939 letter to Charlie Moss, managing editor of the *Banner,* Mrs. Naff took issue with misrepresentations of her that had appeared in the newspaper. She stated that the facts were all wrong: she did not carry a shoe box and sell tickets on the street; tickets were on sale at the music store in the Arcade. She made it clear that booking agents had told her that she ranked at the top as a woman manager. Artists were more than happy to perform at the Ryman and do business with her. She had letters to prove it, and she was still attracting class acts—all true comments. Stars also sent her birthday and Christmas greetings.

On her annual booking trip to New York in 1941, she met with anyone she wanted, no matter whether she had an appointment. Sol Hurok left a conference to talk with her, Mrs. Naff went backstage to see Ethel Barrymore after her appearance in *The Corn Is Green,* and she visited a different theater to talk with Gertrude Lawrence.

The artists. Some artists returned again and again: Paderewski, Anna Pavlova, Ted Shawn,

Ruth St. Denis, the Lunts, Helen Hayes, Marian Anderson, Fritz Kreisler, Lily Pons, Ethel Barrymore, and Maurice Evans.

Mrs. Naff had to take care of the back office during performances and rarely saw any of them. Even rarer were the times she gave visiting artists the courtesy of meeting with them. She had her reasons: they had to sell out the house before she was willing to gush over them. In November 1940 when Jeanette MacDonald was a sellout, MacDonald sent Mrs. Naff orchids, and Mrs. Naff could not recall an audience like hers since the days of Galli-Curci. MacDonald enjoyed Nashville quite a bit by going to the Hermitage and by having dinner with Governor Prentice Cooper and his family. Other stars did not have the opportunity or were unwilling to stay long enough to see the local sights.

The Lunts brought in a whopping $4,560 for the house in 1941 (about $55,800 today), more than the $2,800 (about $36,000 today) from their 1940 appearance in *The Taming of the Shrew.* People were wild about their performance in *There Shall Be No Night,* which was about Russia's invasion of Finland. In addition to Nashvillians' love of the couple, the war in Europe and sentiment toward it might have had something to do with the play's appeal. Since Mrs. Naff was so busy, the Lunts came by to see her.

The Ryman's faults. An anonymous typescript in Mrs. Naff's files described the Ryman as a fire trap, and the writer refused to set foot in it, saying, "I gnash my teeth when Stars [sic] like Helen Hayes and Walter Huston are here and I cannot go." Historically the threat of fire in theaters has not been an idle fear, but Mrs. Naff always had two firemen in the auditorium during performances. They inspected the auditorium before the event and stayed until everyone left. The fear of fire was the reason cited by many supporters of the Nashville Symphony for demanding that the Symphony's performances be held at the War Memorial Auditorium.

Miss Hayes

When Helen Hayes stepped off the train with her Yorkie under her arm on March 30, 1938, high school girls with flowers and boys with cameras greeted her. She had come to Nashville to present *Victoria Regina* at the Ryman Auditorium. Most of the young people were drama students, and some might have remembered her from a previous visit, in 1934, when she appeared in *Mary of Scotland* at the Ryman. Others might have been too young to attend that performance, but they knew of her theatrical reputation and star status.

Raymond Johnson, a graduate of Hume-Fogg High School, was in her company. Earlier he had played in *The Merchant of Venice* with her in Chicago. She complimented him by saying, "I call this part of my trip the Ray Johnson tour," and added, "I have no doubts as to his success on the stage." In fact he would perform with Laurence Olivier in England and return to Nashville during World War II and became active in community theater—even directing for a while.

Miss Hayes spoke to Mrs. Naff and asked, "You really will let us dress in the pews?" Mrs. Naff reassured Miss Hayes that there were real dressing rooms for the stars, but most of the cast would have to change and apply their makeup between the pews. Miss Hayes should have asked about a few other basics in the Ryman, too, as she was to discover.

Sydney Dalton's review of the event included a comment on Nashvillians: "If Nashville theatergoers have been neglectful in their attitude toward several worthwhile offerings of the spoken drama this season, they made up for it handsomely on Wednesday evening by packing Ryman Auditorium to see Helen Hayes and her company in Laurence Housman's 'Victoria Regina.'" He proceeded to praise Miss Hayes's talent and performance: "Of course, it was no secret that Miss Hayes had again made a notable contribution to the considerable achievements of the American stage; and that, having left New York—for no apparent reason, save that she may have grown tired of playing in the same theater—and gone out on the road, to repeat her triumphs at every stop, she is threatened with the appalling prospect of playing Victoria for the rest of her life in order to satisfy popular demand."

Edward Tarpley, M.D., was an usher that night, as he had been for many years, and Walter Sharp, another usher, was sitting with him. Dr. Tarpley said recently that he will never forget what happened: "They had that old curtain with the dust of ages in it. They were at the end of the second act, and Helen Hayes was standing there with her hand on Albert's shoulder. He was at the harpsichord or piano, and the thing fell. Dust flew everywhere. Bless her heart, she didn't move a muscle. She just said, 'I guess we better go.' We were sitting on the first row, so we got the dust, too!" Despite her near death experience, the diminutive Miss Hayes later wrote to Mrs. Naff that she would be happy to play in Nashville again—the healthy receipts were certainly a significant reason. She returned to Nashville for the premiere of *Hamlet*, presented by the Community Playhouse, in 1946.

At the Ryman, performers had to change in rest rooms or behind trunks, and dressing rooms were pipe dreams for many years. For some reason keeping the auditorium in spick-and-span shape was not among Mrs. Naff's interests. Even board members of the auditorium complained about the grime. There was no air-conditioning, of course, and opening the windows meant that street noises just poured in. The boiler did not always work well, and the "Solemn Old Judge," George Hay, was irritated that the six o'clock Opry show one evening was too cold. There was "not enough coal in Ky. to

Lula Naff, manager of the Ryman Auditorium, scheduled Helen Hayes in *Victoria Regina*, March 30, 1938.

heat it," according to Mrs. Naff. Drunken patrons were constantly going in and out of the doors on that snowy, icy night buffeted by cold winds.

A topic that recurs in her correspondence is the talk around town about building a new hall for the performing arts. As early as the spring of 1929, Mrs. Naff had written Mayor Hilary Howse to apply for the job of manager of a newly proposed auditorium. The Municipal Auditorium—completed in 1962—was the belated response to all of that discussion.

Problems with booking. In 1939 Mrs. Naff scheduled six performances without a booking office, but she was concerned that the dates were too close together. She learned over the years that she had to space events to attract a decent crowd. Holding two events in the same week could spell disaster. An exception was the week in April 1919 when Galli-Curci followed Caruso, and both sang to packed houses.

Despite her eye for talent and the ability to book solid acts, sometimes Mrs. Naff misjudged an opportunity. She turned down Leopold Stokowski and the Philharmonic Orchestra on the first transcontinental tour (1936) because she regarded Stokowski as an untried talent.

Early in Mrs. Naff's career, transportation problems sometimes prevented a performer from getting to town on time—or at all. Later on, in 1950, the booking people were having trouble routing performers, and she had to cut three of her most promising shows for the upcoming season.

Splitting weeks was a problem, too, for some agents, and planning to have players for a whole week in Nashville during these years was unrealistic (although it had been the norm during most of the nineteenth century). It seems that the farther the timeline moved Nashvillians from a vibrant pre–Civil War artistic environment, the less the interest of the citizens. In the 1950s, fewer and fewer attractions were offered, and Mrs. Naff refused to take a show just because it was available. She flatly stated, "I am not going to just present things to furnish the newspapers some place to go and take their friends."

Even in the thirties, before she took a chance on booking Billy Rose's *Crazy Quilt*, Mrs. Naff posed the following question in the newspaper (December 20, 1931) and awaited the public's response:

SHALL I BOOK IT?
An Open Letter to the Theatregoers
of Nashville and Environs

Billy Rose, producer of CRAZY QUILT, is now arranging a Transcontinental Tour for that Attraction. Between the larger cities where extended engagements will be played, a few less-than-week-stands will be booked. It is possible that I can secure a date for Nashville. To do so I will be obliged to post a large guarantee to insure the company against loss. While I believe there is no question that local amusement devotees will be liberal in their patronage, I do not feel justified in taking the large hazard until I have an expression from the public as to the interest there is in what I have

no hesitancy in declaring THE MOST COSTLY THEATRICAL ATTRACTION EVER SENT ON TOUR OUTSIDE THE LARGE KEY CITIES OF THE NORTH AND EAST.

SHALL I BOOK IT?

If CRAZY QUILT does come to Nashville you have My Personal Assurance that it will be headed by FANNIE BRICE, PHIL BAKER and TED HEALY and that the entire personnel and production will be PRECISELY the same as seen during the long runs of the show at the APOLLO THEATRE, CHICAGO, and FORTY-FOURTH STREET THEATRE, NEW YORK CITY. I cannot be too emphatic on this score. This will be part of an iron-clad contact with Producer Rose.

SHALL I BOOK IT?

If you wish to see this extraordinary attraction please write me immediately as to the number of tickets I can assign to your account. Other cities are bidding for the few available dates and I must exercise my option within the next few days. If the replies to the advertisement warrant, FANNIE BRICE, PHIL BAKER, TED HEALY and a company of over 100 will POSITIVELY be seen at the Ryman Auditorium in Billy Rose's CRAZY QUILT.

I AWAIT YOUR ANSWERS to Know Whether I SHALL BOOK IT.

Sincerely yours,
Mrs. L. C. Naff,
Manager

NOTE—Should CRAZY QUILT appear here you may rest assured that the scale of prices will NOT be in excess of the tariff in the larger cities, despite the large additional expense entailed in exhibiting in less-than-week-stands.

The response had to be positive because she presented the show on Friday, January 8, 1932. Nashville, Louisville, and Memphis were the only cities in the South to have it. The prices were $3.00 (about $40 today), $2.50, $2.00, and $1.00 for the lower floor; $3.00, $2.50, and $2.00 for balcony seats.

Scheduling conflicts with other events in the city. A dance at Vanderbilt University could mean a small crowd at the Ryman on the same weekend. Radio (and then TV) affected the size of Mrs. Naff's audiences. A major movie release could hurt sales: *Gone with the Wind* almost killed the box office in early 1940. In the fall of 1946, a Strauss Festival with Oscar Strauss faced the competition of football games, and people were tightening their purse strings anyway. As the Nashville Symphony was preparing its first season, Walter Sharp called on Mrs. Naff weeks ahead of time, and they carefully checked each other's dates to avoid conflicts. Community Concerts' upcoming Sadler's Wells Ballet hurt her ticket sales for the Ballet Theatre (now American Ballet Theatre), and as a rule, dance had the smallest audiences in town—even with no competition.

Threats of disease and weather. In January 1941, Katharine Hepburn was scheduled for the *Philadelphia Story.* Mrs. Naff was constantly answering the phone and taking orders, although a flu epidemic concerned her. As it turned out, Hepburn drove herself safely to town, did the show and had a big-enough crowd to sell $5,150 (about $63,000 today) in tickets, had an after-show supper with Mrs. Frank Berry, and then left. A bitingly cold night, January 22, 1948, however, prevented the audience from attending *A Night in Old Vienna.* Then frigid temperatures and a major ice storm in January and February 1951 brought life to a standstill, and Mae West had to be rescheduled.

Opera as a hard sell. Long memories of patrons involving several operatic events seem to have been a cause of poor ticket sales, although opera patrons' negative attitude toward the Ryman itself was a secondary cause. Because Nashville's

A native of Alabama, Tallulah Bankhead first appeared in Nashville in *Reflected Glory,* April 29, 1937. Later she was in *Antony and Cleopatra,* and in mid-January 1950, near the end of her stage career, she headlined *Private Lives.* All were at the Ryman. This daughter of William Bankhead, one-time Speaker of the House, was at her "rollicking best" on stage and off in that winter of 1950. At a small party after the performance, she turned the garden hose in the house's conservatory on attendees.

social elite took over operatic events in the early years (before the Great Depression), less affluent citizens seem to have been reluctant to attend.

February 21, 1929, was the only visit of the Chicago Civic Opera. Getting the opera company to Nashville had been a major coup. Usually Chattanooga booked the opera company for *several days* but relinquished the dates for that year. Nashville was able to arrange for *one night,* and if the event was a success, the company was willing to consider another date the next year. Mary Garden, Cesare Formichi, and Jose Mojica were to sing in *Thais,* conducted by Robert Moranzoni.

B. Kirk Rankin was the president of the Nashville Grand Opera Association, a newly organized group, and Mrs. Robert Fenner Jackson was the chairman general of the reception and entertainment for visitors. Civic and social organizations cooperated to plan the details, generate interest, and encourage ticket sales; they also appointed many chairmen—from Shelbyville to Springfield—so that out-of-towners

The Bijou Theater was built in 1904 following a fire that destroyed most of the Grand Opera House (formerly the Adelphi Theatre)—the arched entry was somewhat preserved. Later it became a movie and vaudeville house and a site for concerts for the African-American community. It was torn down in the late 1950s when the city began construction of the Municipal Auditorium.

would participate. The list of patronesses in the newspaper required almost three full columns—Mrs. Victor Abeles to Mrs. Lee Zibart. Dr. George Pullen Jackson had spent the previous summer, a hot one, securing the guarantors.

The Ryman Auditorium underwent renovations and beautification under the direction of Dr. Jackson. The stage was enlarged, better lighting was provided, a deep red velvet curtain was installed, new sets were built, and "crimson-lined" boxes were added to the gallery's front row. The workmen did their best to make it look like a real opera house. A reporter summed it up: "Big, utilitarian and sometimes gloomy Ryman has been glorified . . . and audience space has been made into a fitting setting for Nashville's leaders of society and public life." The newspapers repeatedly made the point that the opera festival was to be the "high peak" of the social season.

The bringing of culture was once again tied to the monetary outlay when Castner-Knott published a half-page ad urging patrons to attend:

Nashville takes another step into the metropolitan class. There's no doubt about this opera being a great thing for Nashville. It will certainly further the already flattering reputation of Nashville as a cultural center and enhance Nashville's prestige in our own section. But a great civic project of this magnitude has its practical as well as its aesthetic side. Naturally, the expense involved is considerable and the best evidence of Nashville's support will be a full house Thursday night.

People from across Tennessee, Kentucky, and Alabama, and "scores" of Middle Tennesseans had purchased tickets. Two social events were planned for out-of-town guests: a breakfast after the company's 12:30 P.M. arrival, which was to be held at the Centennial Club's auditorium, and a tea at Belle Meade Country Club. The third event, after the opera, was a supper dance at the Hermitage Hotel for members of the Nashville Grand Opera Association, and the entertainment was to include Francis Craig's orchestra, cellist Hugo Reindl from the opera company, and solos by members of the company's ballet. A newspaper reporter stated, "Musically, socially, civically Nashville is putting her best foot forward today, stepping perhaps into new musical advancement."

The only problem was that everyone's best foot stepped into fifteen inches of snow, and twelve of those inches had fallen in six hours. The temperature never reached the freezing mark, and ice had preceded the snow, which was the worst storm since 1917. The city was littered with abandoned cars, people were slipping and sliding, and accidents were common, despite the efforts of city workers to clear the roads. The special train bringing the opera company of 250 was three hours late.

Unwilling to be intimidated by the wintry conditions, almost three thousand people attended. "The flower of Nashville's society" was bedecked in jewels and evening dresses, for example, Mrs. Charles Nelson in a chartreuse chiffon gown, Mrs. Benton McMillin (wife of the governor) in orchid pink satin embroidered in silver and an opera coat of black velvet, Mrs. E. B. Stahlman in black velvet trimmed with gold (several others were in black velvet, too), and Miss Anne Leslie Nichol in red chenille lace with a black velvet wrap trimmed in ermine.

Notwithstanding the brilliance of the affair, it failed to achieve financial success. Then, too, the effects of the Great Depression hit Nashville the next year, so finances were affected throughout the city. In 1952 Mrs. Naff noted that some leading citizens were "still brooding over their loss on Mary Garden and the Chicago Opera." She was leery of staging opera after that failure because her business sense would not permit her to knowingly set up a loss for the auditorium. Later she

Lula Naff and Francis Robinson had a long-lasting friendship that began when Francis was an usher at Ryman Auditorium, managed by Mrs. Naff for several decades until her retirement in 1955.

did try again on a limited scale with not much better results.

When Lily Pons sang in late April of 1941, hers was a far less successful appearance than that of Jeanette MacDonald (more than $5,000) just a few months earlier. Mrs. Naff had printed five thousand programs—high hopes of attendance that were dashed. The gross was only $2,795.68, and the sponsors lost money.

Charles Wagner's *Mikado* had a small attendance, November 27, 1952, even though Mrs. Naff gave out her "usual passes and dressed up the Orchestra Circle." The Opera Guild bought only a few tickets but entertained the company at Richland Country Club.

Surprises. In the spring of 1948 *Harvey* grossed $4,297 on Monday and $4,621 on Tuesday (about $32,228 and $34,650 today). Mrs. Naff had "never heard people laugh as much at any show in all these years." When she staged *Macbeth* in January 1949, high school students came from southern Kentucky to Alabama and spent $3,500. The next year, however, school children from Mount Pleasant to Murfeesboro were saving their money to buy tickets to see Tallulah Bankhead in *Private Lives*. An unhappy Mrs. Naff declared, "I tried to get them to bring groups to Shakespeare [*Julius Caesar* was coming up], but Culture is not what they want."

Well-known artists such as Harpo Marx, Victor Borge, and Jose Greco did not have widespread appeal to the citizens, and sometimes Mrs. Naff guessed wrong in her engagements. A 1951 production of *Mr. Roberts* drew good crowds—except the matinee—because people were not used to it. Mrs. Naff commented, "Only folks like Mrs. A. B. Benedict, Fermine Pride, Jessie Green and the like, come. Thirty-five years ago, a good crowd would have come." Things change as times change and new audiences develop.

Madame Bernhardt

Nashville and Middle Tennessee are all suppressed excitement over the prospect of seeing Bernhardt.

—BANNER, MARCH 8, 1906

SARAH BERNHARDT took command of Nashville's stages in 1881 and 1906, and each time the French actress played to huge audiences for one night only. At least two things are remarkable about her appearances in Nashville—the first, that the audiences were entranced by a performer who spoke only French, and the second, that she could have as much, or more, appeal to audiences twenty-five years apart in the same role in *Camille*.

Her first appearance was at the Masonic Theater, Thursday, February 17, 1881, with Henry E. Abbey's French Company. Tickets cost $3 and

$2 (about $56 and $37 today). The reviewer revealed something about the atmosphere in the theater itself with the comment that "the filling of the boxes caused the audience much merriment and doubtless caused our French visitors to wonder if we always made that much noise filling a couple of boxes."

The reviewer credited Madame Bernhardt with relieving "the piece of all that realism and suggestiveness from which it is rarely entirely freed on the American stage. . . . It is not to be denied that we have a wicked way of dealing with naughty things, and the French impart a certain decency to wickedness." Her acting was "inimitable," and she had a "calm consciousness of power." The intense death scene and her excellent supporting cast rated special mention. Her costumes were elegant and costly, her diamond necklace (valued at $1,000 [about $18,600 today]) dazzled the "gallery gods," and her jewels appeared like "flowers of light when seen in a gas-illuminated room."

The railway car hired for Madame Bernhardt brought 28 people in the company, her 20 dresses for her stage wardrobe, and 106 pieces of luggage. She had come from Chattanooga. After the performance in Nashville, she stayed at the Maxwell House Hotel and then went to Memphis the next day.

For her Thursday, March 8, 1906, appearance, the stage and front part of the Ryman Auditorium were practically rebuilt, with J. Gordon Edwards supervising the renovations. Madame Bernhardt's special train, with equipment from tack hammers to a dressing room, brought her and the sixty people in her company for her farewell engagement. She had come to tour the United States from the Theatre Sarah Bernhardt in Paris, and she was under the direction of S. S. and Lee Shubert and W. F. Connor.

Regular seat sales began on Monday, March 5, at 9:00 A.M., and mailed orders were sent to

Sarah Bernhardt appeared as Camille in Nashville, 1881 and 1906. Each time the French-speaking actress held her audience in "rapt attention."

Mrs. J. T. Boyle, c/o Jesse French Piano and Organ. To guard against "speculators," mail orders were filled in the order in which they arrived. Ticket prices were $3, $2, $1.50, and $1 (about $60, $40, $30, and $20 today). The interest was at a "fever heat" because Madame Bernhardt was considered the greatest actress in the world and because she was the last of the Rachel school who would ever appear in the United States. (For Nashvillians who could not afford those prices, other entertainment that week included skating at the Hippodrome Skating Rink for 10 cents and seeing the *Wizard of Oz* at the Vendome for 50 cents.)

The three-hour-long play began at 8:00 P.M. The "brilliant audience" of "splendid proportions" saw Bernhardt's "matchless presentation," but the supporting cast needed improvement. The reviewer noted, "When it is considered that the play throughout was in French, that many in the vast audience were not familiar with the

story, that most of them knew not a line of French, the remarkable and rapt attention accorded every word and speech of the great actress is eloquent testimony of her talent, her magnetism, her dramatic and histrionic ability." The sixty-one-year-old Madame Bernhardt might have been too old in looks to be Camille, but she was Camille in her portrayal. She had a "voice of liquid sweetness" and did a "faultless reading. . . . When the curtain rang down for the last time there was many an eye tear-bedimmed—many a life that had been touched." She really must have been divine.

~

Greater Nashville
As a Musical Center

What Athens was to Greece, Nashville is to the South.

—Frederick Jerome Work, 1908

IN 1907 FREDERICK JEROME WORK and his brother John W. Work II published *Folk Songs of the American Negro* in Nashville. The next year Frederick wrote this eloquent summary about Nashville's place in the musical world:

Nashville has been styled the "Athens of the South" because of the great number and variety of its schools. Athens was the leader of all the cities of Greece not only in the opportunities it afforded for the study of the academic branches, but also as the fountain from which flowed a steady stream of musical culture. Before her ascendency, music had been cultivated to some extent in Egypt and Assyria, but no effort had been made to systematize it as a study. It remained for Pythagoras to make of it a science by the invention of the scale. Then it was that Athens became music mad and gave harmony its beginning. The musicians scattered throughout Greece and by their devotion to the art, created a strong love for melody and caused Athens to be a Mecca for those who wished to perfect themselves in this the loveliest and most divine branch of art. What Athens was to Greece, Nashville is to the South.

When Fisk University sent from her midst the "Jubilee Singers," who were to tour the world, and Central Tennessee College started the "Tennesseans" on a successful tour of our own country, they were laying the foundation of a musical culture which was to cause their native city to be regarded as the greatest musical center of the South. These two schools, by consistent work, have created such a broad musical culture that the normal Nashvillian who does not attempt to make music is an exception.

MUSIC IN OUR SCHOOLS

We have within our city four colleges and seminaries, and each one makes a specialty of music. They employ about twenty teachers of this branch each one of which uses the latest and most improved methods. About five hundred students coming from nearly all of our states and territories, and some from foreign countries, are pursuing this branch of art. There are two choral societies, which are preeminent; one orchestra to which city musicians are eligible; one glee club of male voices, which has no superior; and several fine quartettes. The ensemble work of these school organizations is unequaled by any similar organization in the South. They render only the masterpieces of the masters, and nothing bordering on charlatinism is ever heard. The soloists who serve these societies are selected from their own ranks, and are always equal to the occasion.

IN THE CHURCHES

In our churches the brand of music one hears on Sunday is of the very best. Instead of the bizarre so-called anthems of Excell [E. O. Excell, a writer and publisher of hymns and anthems] they use compositions that contain real merit and assist in worship; instead of using as they did some time ago to a great extent, the Moody [Dwight Moody, evangelist and founder of Moody Bible Institute] songs, which are weak to insipidity, they sing the old standard hymns, famous for their power to encourage religious thought. One of the best signs of our growing music culture is the constant series of sacred concerts which one hears on Sunday nights. Each church seems to vie with the other as to the quality of these concerts, and music is heard such as is seldom heard in any other Southern city.

TEACHERS

A city is judged musically not by the number and quality of its conservatories and colleges, but by the quality and number of its private teachers. Nashville now has a brand of private teachers that is superior to anything found in the other Southern cities. They come to us from different schools and teachers and the work that they are doing is creating an atmosphere that is fast spreading to all the remote parts of our city. When I say that we have in Greater Nashville, a city of one hundred and twenty-five thousand inhabitants, five stores doing an exclusive instrument business, you can better understand what a healthy atmosphere we have. A short while ago the writer was in a certain Southern city, claiming a larger population than Nashville, and had the pleasure of hearing one of the Negro's most famous singers in a recital. He sang the best things known for a singer, but he was unable to produce any kind of applause until, by a substitution, he sang "Teasing." The audience went wild with the delight. If the same singer had done the same thing in Nashville, his popularity would have been seriously impaired as a singer. The "Athens of the South" requires the best always.

FACILITIES FOR HEARING GOOD MUSIC

On account of its location Greater Nashville is in easy access of the Northern centers, and there is a steady influx of artists of all nationalities. Each year, from the galaxy of modern stars, we gather enough of them to keep our souls somewhat satiated.

~

Sacred Drama
at Spruce Street Baptist Church

*[It was a] society event as well as
a high-class church entertainment.*

—Nashville Globe, September 18, 1908

THE GREATER NASHVILLE edition of the *Nashville Globe* was distributed to South, Central, and West Coast Africa, the Philippines, Cuba, the West Indies, and across the United States. Those out-of-towners could only read about the production of *Out in the Streets* at Spruce Street Baptist Church, Monday, September 14, 1908, at 8:00 P.M. The drama is one example of the church's importance in the cultural life of African-Americans in the city.

The tickets—1,200 of them—had been on sale for more than a week beforehand, and there was a contest between Luther A. Lyon of Nashville (green tickets) and John T. Shelby of East Nashville (red tickets). East Nashvillians, who were known for patronizing each other's businesses and taking care of each other, helped Shelby win the $25 prize for selling the most tickets. Ticket sales amounted to $124.10, and sales of refreshments were $14.10, for a total of $138.20 (about $2,700 today).

Beautiful scenery had been set up in the church's auditorium, and almost seven hundred people saw the temperance drama written by S. N. Cook and produced by the Dramatic Club of East Nashville. Members of the club included A. N. Johnson, director; Mrs. A. M. Townsend, manager; Mrs. John T. Shelby; Floy Darrell; Laura Carter; Will Davis; Ernest Alexander; William Stockell; George Darden; Thomas Allison; and John H. Overton. The church's pastor was T. J. Townsend. Geneva Bender played the music during the drama.

Another part of the evening was devoted to a program of music and dramatic readings. Following a chorus by the choir, there were vocal solos by Mrs. Lula Woolforks and Madame Tartt, a reading by Lizzie Stockell, and a piano solo by Madaline Carter. Ending the program were a vocal solo by Mrs. J. E. Henderson, a duet by Miss M. E. V. Reed and Mrs. Henderson, and a piano solo by Helena Lowe.

~

"Greatest Musical Treat
Ever Presented to Nashville"

First man: *Great? Why, it's magnificent.*

Second man: *Glad to see you interested in the Greek drama.*

First man: *Drama hell. I'm talking about the crowd. I'm on the guarantee fund of this thing.*

THE MUSICAL TREAT was *The Fire Regained*, a Greek pageant held in Centennial Park with the Parthenon as a focal point. The word *spectacle* was probably a more apt description, however, with its "orgy of flaming torches." There was a chariot race, there was drama, and there was music with a chorus of five hundred—all carried out by hometown people. The performance dates were May 5 to 8, 1913, but the activity relating to the pageant began long before then.

The Nashville Art Association planned everything. Backers were from the Nashville Retail Merchants' Association of the Board of Trade and included B. W. Landstreet, L. A. Bauman, James Frank, Leland Hume, G. H. Baskette, J. H. Bransford, and Charles Mitchell, among others. Leland Hume was the director general, Sidney Mttron Hirsch wrote the play (which Putnam published in the same year), F. Arthur Henkel composed

Sidney, the Playwright

Sidney Mttron Hirsch is known to us today for his association with the Fugitives, but in May 1913, all eyes were on him as the author of *The Fire Regained*. Miss Annie M. Garfinkle wrote a biographical article about this "idealist in a materialistic age; a thorough student at a time when superfluity abounds." Hirsch, born in Nashville in 1884, had attended local grammar schools and spent a year in a local high school before attending Joseph W. Allen College in Carthage, Tennessee. He ran off to sea and eventually joined the U.S. Navy, where he put in some time in the brig for "breach" of discipline. On the gunboat *Wilmington*, he went six hundred miles into the interior of China, and Ernest Brooks, another Tennessean, was on board with him. Later Hirsch lived in a Buddhist monastery in China so that he could study religion, philosophy, and art, and in Europe, he pursued further study in art and mysticism. He learned Chinese and could decipher Egyptian hieroglyphics. Miss Garfinkle pointed out that Hirsch had investigated all religions and faiths but remained a staunch Jew. Back in the United States he wrote art criticism and short stories for eastern magazines. The directors of the Metropolitan Opera House had accepted at first reading his play *Potiphar's Wife*, based on the life of the biblical character Joseph, but a dispute over the proposed composer of the music between Hirsch and the directors had put the production on hold. Miss Garfinkle's praise of him was so high that he hardly seemed less than one of the gods of Olympus; he was a "genius" who would add to the "splendor of Tennessee's achievements."

Hirsch read his *Potiphar's Wife* to actor Lark Taylor, and Taylor thought that it was very similar to the play *Joseph and His Brethren* produced on Broadway in 1913 with Pauline Frederick starring in the title role. (The date of the reading is unclear in Taylor's autobiography.) Hirsch also wrote a one-act play, *The Madonna of Washington Square*, especially for Taylor, and Hirsch was certain that he could get booking for it on the Keith circuit. Taylor could not find an actress suitable for Hirsch's standards, however, and by the time Hirsch found an actress to fit the part, Taylor was on the road elsewhere. Copies of both *Potiphar's Wife* and *The Madonna of Washington Square* seem to be lost; I have been unable to find a copy of either one.

---

the music, and Pauline Townsend was pageant director.

Nashville's women made the required one thousand costumes, and therein lies a story in itself. Consultants from the northern and eastern United States told organizers that the costumes would have to be bought or rented from sources outside the city; the estimated rental cost was $3,000, certainly lower than a purchase price. When someone suggested that the costumes could be made in Nashville, the consultants laughed and said, "Why, of course Nashville couldn't even be expected to make them." Enter the board of the Florence Crittenden Home, which consisted of about thirty women who worked for "the good of wayward, friendless girls." Mrs. J. H. Stevenson was the board president, and Mrs. James Palmer was chairman of the executive committee. Mrs. Palmer took the response of the consultants as a challenge and said, "Look here, here's a chance for us to put a big feather in Nashville's cap, save the pageant some money, and at the same time make a few hundreds for the home. We can do anything New York or Chicago can do. Well?" They went to work and accomplished the so-called impossible for a cost of $1,800, using goods purchased from Nashville stores. It was a win-win-win situation for the home, the pageant, and the city.

A special amphitheater that would accommodate five thousand folding chairs was constructed on the south side of the Parthenon, complete with provisions for electrical lighting effects. Other preparations involved the schools and the newspapers. Boy Scouts were recruited to help out, primarily with ushering ticket holders. Children had been taught about Greek mythology to increase their understanding of what was happening. The papers educated readers concerning the plot as well as advertised the pageant. The railroads offered special half-fare rates, and department stores paid the railroad fare for any visitors who bought more than $25 in merchandise. People from Kentucky, Alabama, and other parts of Tennessee took them up on the deal. Culture and commerce were closely tied in this event to showcase Nashville's talents and its wares.

Anyone could reserve seats ahead of time by sending a check to the box office of the Vendome Theatre. General admission was 50 cents; reserved seats were 75 cents and $1; a private box of four seats was $8 ($1 in 1913, about $18.20 now; $1 in 1914, about $17.96 now). African-Americans were permitted to sit on the east end of the amphitheater.

Briefly the plot focused on one of the thirty virgins who guarded the sacred flame of the temple of Hestia and was falsely accused of being unchaste. Wood nymphs, the Muses, Athena, a shepherd youth, a priest, the god Hermes, and other characters graced the production. The maiden was to face the wrath of the gods, and she had to undergo trial by three ordeals: the first with doves; the second with a ceremony involving a lamb and a ram; and the third, a chariot race. She was condemned to death, but to please the audience, the story had a happy ending and the maiden survived.

Professor Charles C. Washburn was the high priest, Louis Sperry was the shepherd, and Burton Barr as Hermes appeared on the roof of the Parthenon (one has to believe he was not afraid of heights). Lucille McMillin was Athena, the leading lady; she had been a leading lady before in state government as the wife of the former governor, Benton McMillin (1899–1903). Eleanor McMillin, her daughter, was one of three solo dancers. Lucy Tillman was a Muse.

Procuring the animals and the birds had to be a major chore. The doves were, in fact, pigeons—one thousand of them—and some fell to the ground when they were released. Breathless females paid more attention to the doves wandering along the ground than to the action and were in fear of their being run over by the chariots. After the first night, the Boy Scouts had an additional job of rescuing birds before the chariot race could begin. Apparently quite an equestrienne, Florence Bogie was chosen to be the woman who "rode" the sixteen-hundred-pound bull in the "sacrifice" scene. The shepherd youth at one point mounted Pegasus, and the white

Professor Washburn

Professor Charles C. Washburn provided continuity in music education and local music events. In 1886 Washburn came to Nashville as a student at Vanderbilt University. He then went on to the College of Music in Cincinnati, and upon completion of his degree, he toured with Theodore Thomas's orchestra and Victor Herbert's orchestra as a baritone soloist. He returned to Nashville and opened a studio. He also directed the Vanderbilt Glee Club, and in 1907, he and Guy McCullum, a pianist, took a quartet from the Glee Club to Europe. Professor Washburn was hired to be a teacher of singing at Belmont College, and he remained after the merger with Ward Seminary. He responded to World War I by going to work in England, and Gaetano S. de Luca succeeded him at Ward-Belmont in 1918. Following the war, Professor Washburn was professor of sacred music at Scarritt College for Christian Workers.

horse with white wings was ready and waiting for him. The competitors in the chariot race were a priest in a black robe, driving a black chariot with four black horses, and the maiden in white, driving a white chariot with four white horses. The chariot driven by Charles Cayce overturned one night, and one bay horse was slightly injured, but amazingly no other injuries occurred in the entire event.

The weather was good, and 3,000 attended on the opening night, May 5. On the second day, a Tuesday, a threat of rain kept some people away and came close to canceling the event, but the show did go on. On the third night 6,000 pushed the capacity of the amphitheater.

People throughout the country heard about the event, and some saw it on the film made by International Feature Film Company. *Vogue* published pictures of the costumes, and *Collier's* carried a story about the endeavor. The pageant was such a success that Hirsch was commissioned to write another Greek pageant the next year.

The Greek pageant *The Fire Regained*, written by Nashvillian Sidney Hirsch and produced in May 1913, used the Parthenon in Centennial Park as a backdrop.

The chariot race was an integral—and exciting—part of *The Fire Regained*. During one performance a chariot overturned, but fortunately the driver was uninjured.

In 1914 the citizens produced *Mysteries of Thanatos*. Leland Hume was again director general, but Edwin T. Emery did the staging (Emery had the job by special arrangement with the Shubert Theatrical Company; the previous year he had directed the musical *The Geisha* in New York City). The Commercial Club, the Industrial Bureau, and other organizations were behind what was billed as the "most brilliant and thrilling spectacle ever attempted in the South." Harry Anderson was the business manager for the 1914 Greek Pageant Committee. The libretto, which cost 15 cents, was printed by Brandon Printing Co., and the pageant was dedicated to Dr. Charles E. Little.

The pageant was held for four days in early May. It had everything from wood nymphs dancing to characters hailing gods and having visions. Again, there was a chariot race, and again, one thousand doves (pigeons) were released. The cast included Aphrodite: Mrs. Harry Anderson; the shepherd: Marion G. Denton; the maiden: Marie Trebing; Athena: Mrs. Joseph B. Deeds; Eros:

Richard Franks; and the head demon: Charles Cayce.

A young shepherd, seeking a bride, sought help from Aphrodite, and she found one for him among the wood nymphs. The goddess Athena appeared to him and his bride, and Athena was livid because the young couple paid too much attention to Aphrodite. Demons tied up the shepherd and carried off the maiden. Then Aphrodite came to life and told the youth that his bride was taken to the netherworld to be the bride of the Being of Darkness—but he could rescue her by passing tests. At one point the activity between the shepherd and the demons took place at the top of the Parthenon. This story, too, had a happy ending.

Unfortunately the first night had to be canceled because of rain, but the other nights were nice. A forty-piece orchestra supplied the music, and the dance of the three graces was a big hit. The merchants had placed advertisements in the newspaper for Greek Pageant Week. The pattern seemed to be established of having an event in May to combine a Greek pageant with retail sales, and everyone had high hopes for annual events in the future. It was May 1914, however, and dire events were on the horizon.

The make-believe world of gods and goddesses, dancing wood nymphs, and menacing demons gave way to the real demon of war. Archduke Franz Ferdinand was assassinated in June 1914, and world war broke out in August of the same year. Foreign affairs suddenly changed the lives of Nashvillians, even though the United States did not enter the war until April 1917. An additional harsh reality was the influenza epidemic that would exact a heavy toll on soldiers and citizens (1918–19). Greek Pageant Week never occurred again.

The Bozart

The arts, save in the lower reaches of the gospel hymn,
the phonograph and the political harangue,
are all held in suspicion [in the South].

—H. L. MENCKEN

H. L. MENCKEN'S "The Sahara of the Bozart" condemned the South for a total lack of culture following the Civil War to the time of his essay (the first printing, November 13, 1917, appeared in the New York *Evening Mail,* and a more developed version appeared in *Prejudices: Second Series,* in 1920). Even his use of *bozart* for *beaux arts* took a jab at southerners. Too many people would agree with him and go so far as to extend his point to more recent years. In his typical overstated fashion Mencken blasted the South for being "almost as sterile, artistically, intellectually, culturally, as the Sahara Desert." He added that "it is as if the Civil War stamped out every last bearer of the torch."

Well, he was not totally incorrect: there have been deserts, sometimes expansive ones. There

have also been significant oases of the beaux arts to refresh the spirits of southerners, and Nashville has provided abundant examples. Many bearers of the torch continued to light the way through the deserts to help Nashvillians make it to the next oasis; they were not stamped out, but they were often discouraged. Occasionally the oasis was more like a mirage, just out of grasp, never fully materializing, tantalizing the thirsty citizenry.

Yet the beaux arts have survived into the twenty-first century and are flourishing in Nashville as never before. The oasis is blooming, and Nashvillians are pushing its borders farther and farther into the desert areas. All must continue to be vigilant and tend the fragile oasis, or the desert areas will encroach on it again. Nashvillians do not want an up-and-coming Mencken to be able to write the essay "The *New* Sahara of the Bozart" and use Nashville as a model.

A Stellar Year for Opera, 1919

In the past, Nashville has been rather too cool
in its reception of the great artists,
but the last few years have wrought a great change.

—ALVIN WIGGERS

AN OPERATIC DROUGHT was satisfied with four events in one year, 1919, held at the Ryman Auditorium.

The first, February 18, was Creatore's company in *Rigoletto.* Music lovers of the regular sort and from society's circles turned out en masse to hear the principal singers, orchestra, and chorus. Giorgio Puliti as Rigoletto "showed himself a singer of rich vocal powers and an operatic actor of resourcefulness." Lillian Gresham as Gilda "sang the rapturous soliloquy, 'Caro Nome,' with ease and fluency, executing the florid passages of the lovely air with grace and delicacy." Guiseppe

Amelita Galli-Curci drew a full house to the Ryman Auditorium on April 30, 1919, despite the appearance the previous evening by Caruso—who also packed the house. Opera lovers enjoyed a remarkable two consecutive days of the best in opera.

Corallo sang the part of the duke, and he was "warmly applauded for his 'La Donna e Mobile,' which he sang with ease and abandon and an infectious gaiety."

The second event had to be the pinnacle. Caruso's concert in April was to benefit the Florence Crittenden Home. Singing for philanthropic reasons had become almost routine for him because during World War I, he contributed his own money and his services in patriotic concerts to Liberty Loan bond drives and the Red Cross (the Third Liberty Loan resulted in sales of $3,060,000, and his appearances for the American and Italian Red Cross netted more than $40,000 [about $480,000 today]).

Caruso's one-evening performance was responsible for all of Nashville's hotels and probably many homes, too, overflowing with guests. He had his own suite of rooms at the Hermitage Hotel, which he filled with ten trunks, and he had brought along his new bride, the former Dorothy Benjamin, daughter of Park Benjamin of New York. Her brother, also named Park Benjamin, and his wife had been in Nashville from January to September of 1918, and Mrs. Albert H. Williams had befriended them. Mrs. Williams was to take both Carusos to lunch at the Belle Meade Country Club the day after the performance. The train was to transport the Carusos and their group to St. Louis that evening. They had come to Nashville from Atlanta, following his week there with the Metropolitan Opera Company, and the receipts in Atlanta had been $17,000 to $19,000 for *each* performance (about $177,480 to $198,360 today).

For the April 29 concert in Nashville, soprano Nina Morgana and violinist Elias Breeskin joined Caruso, and Salvatore Fucito was at the piano. Not only were all the seats taken at the Ryman, but there was no standing room left. Box seats went for $10 each, and other tickets sold for $2, $3.50, $5, and $6. The *Banner* reporter noted, "Some of the audience, doubtless a number of times, have heard the Neapolitan marvel in grand operatic roles, but to the rank and file this was a long-expected treat," and he added, "The great singer appeared to feel that here was an opportunity to feed music-hungry souls, for he rendered his famed numbers with a feeling that could not have been excelled had he been appearing in opera with scenic effects, stage settings, orchestra and all that go to inspire the artist to the best that is in him."

Caruso's program included "Celeste Aida" from Verdi's *Aida*, "A Furtive Tear" from Donizetti's *L'Elisir d'amore*, and the pathetic, weepy song from Leoncavallo's *Pagliacci*. He responded to the audience's enthusiasm with nine encores. Alvin Wiggers wrote in his review, "From the moment that Enrico Caruso stepped out upon the stage last evening to be greeted with a storm of applause, every one realized the sincerity of the artist, the humanness that has won him the warm friendship of all who have ever come in contact with him, from kings and his fellow artists down to the humblest attaches of the opera house."

Morgana sang arias from *Sonnambula* and *Dinorah,* and some English songs ("He Loves Me," "The Wee Butterfly," and "Summer"), which were better received than her other presentations. Breeskin was said to make the "so-called king of instruments talk, breathe, sigh, laugh, and simulate every emotion of the human heart. Faultless in technique, with a superb attack and handling the bow always as only a master can, he shared equal honors with the great star of the evening."

The townspeople hardly had time to take a breath before Amelita Galli-Curci's concert the next day, April 30. It was her second visit, and people lined up all day at Houck Piano Company for tickets. The soprano also stayed at the Hermitage Hotel and had come from Atlanta. She was not yet a member of the Metropolitan Opera Company, and according to Francis Robinson, "Her manager said when she heard she was following Caruso she nearly died." Luckily for Mrs. Naff, she did not, and Galli-Curci, too, had a packed house of music lovers. A few days before her appearance, a reporter for the *Banner* wrote that she was to "minister to our needs as does the perfume of the rose or the form of the lily, those things which are their own reason for existence, because of their beauty and their appeal to our instinctive sense of the beautiful."

The fourth event was the appearance of John McCormack on November 24, and not only were all seats sold but people stood in the aisles. A bit of folk legend surrounds this event because it was reported that Mrs. Naff took out a second mortgage on her house to meet the guarantee. She apparently never filed the papers, yet it was a powerful story that has been retold often.

A few weeks before the Irish-born tenor was to appear, an article in the *Tennessean* praised him:

You cannot force the public to appreciate art; you can only charm it into appreciation. What artist of the concert stage today has charged the public like John McCormack, or done so much to bring it to a true appreciation of the art of song?

He is unquestionably the chosen favorite of the great music loving public of America; and it is indeed as one of our ablest critics has so well expressed it: "Fortunate for the sake of artistry in music that a man of popularity so great as his, should be so great an artist."

As a singer he is a perfect artist. As an artist he is an inspiration and uplift. He deserves the wealth and fame his art has brought him, because it is such as he who make the world a better place to live in.

This "perfect artist" presented two pieces from Handel, Irish folk songs, and Harry T. Burleigh's spirituals. A reviewer observed, "Men and women come to hear McCormack sing who frankly disclaim a musical ear, and if his more classical numbers fail somewhat to strike the right chord within their hearts, they wait patiently for one of his matchless ballads sure to be given as an encore." To the accompaniment of Edwin Schneider at the piano, McCormack sang "Dear Old Pal of Mine," which drew a "deafening roar" from the audience as one encore number.

Mrs. Naff outdid herself with the operatic bookings for this exceptional year.

Seeking an Orchestra

It is surprising there was not greater curiosity to hear this orchestra at its best.

—Newspaper reviewer, 1891

THE DESIRE to have a permanent orchestra in Nashville was almost accomplished in the 1880s.

The newly organized Nashville Symphony Orchestra, conducted by F. Arthur Henkel, performed at the Princess Theater, April 25, 1920.

In those days an orchestra was associated with visiting artists, a notion dating back to 1830. On June 14 of that year Mme Feron began a three-night engagement in Nashville. Known in the theaters of Italy, Paris, and London, she had just come from New Orleans and was on her way north. An orchestra, led by Mr. Noke, a local music teacher, accompanied her as she sang "The Arab Steed," "I've Been Roaming," and "The Soldier Tired of War's Alarms," in addition to other pieces. (After her concert, Herr Cline performed "graceful Dances and astonishing feats" on an elastic cord.)

In September 1830 Mr. and Mrs. William Pearman, who had appeared at the Theatre Royale, Covent Garden, Drury Lane, and English Opera House in London and in various operas staged in Philadelphia and elsewhere in the United States, presented concerts at Nashville's Masonic Hall. The next month, October 18, they gave a "Grand Oratorio" (in other words, a sacred concert) with an orchestra of local musicians, and they sang selections from the *Messiah* and Haydn's "Creation." In November at the Nashville Theatre they, Signor Mondelli, and

other artists presented *The Bride of Abydos*, for which the music had been composed by Mrs. Noke, the wife of the orchestra conductor.

The successful orchestras for the theaters were the bases for later attempts to create a permanent symphony for the city. In January 1888, there was a report that conductors and members of the Vendome Theatre and Masonic Hall orchestras were trying to consolidate into "one permanent organization . . . for the purpose of giving Nashville such orchestral advantages as cities of lesser size and importance already possess." Eighteen "first-class musicians" were available, but they were missing a violoncello, a second horn, and timpani. They needed $1,500 (about $30,000 today) to get started, and they were certain that the orchestra could "be made self-supporting in the course of a few months." The plan was to hold monthly concerts during the regular season, with the proceeds going to a general fund, and summer night concerts. That plan did not make much headway.

A reviewer of the September 1890 benefit for the Vendome's orchestra thought that it was the best orchestra in Nashville at any time and that

Music Teachers, 1921

Music teachers (and other musicians) were so prevalent in Nashville in 1921 that J. C. Phillips compiled *Who's Who in Music: A Directory of Nashville Musicians.* I. Milton Cook, supervisor of music of the public schools, held various positions that were probably a record number—although having multiple jobs was fairly typical for musicians and teachers of music. He was the music supervisor of vocal work at Tennessee School for the Blind, bass soloist and director of the First Presbyterian choir, leader of the Scottish Rite Masonic Choir, director and bass of the Nashville Men's Quartet, director of the Nashville Choral Club, and director of the music department of the University of Tennessee Summer School. He had studied in Berlin, Paris, and London and was a graduate of the Conservatory of Music in Ypsilanti, Michigan. He first came to Nashville to teach at Peabody College in 1908, left briefly, and came back as assistant supervisor of music for the public schools.

Lessons for piano, voice, and violin seemed to be the primary instruction offered, but an aspiring student could learn music theory and history, too. Eighth Avenue and the surrounding area appeared to be the place for lessons. One could go to the Camerata College of Music, with Miss Frances Sullivan, at 118 Eighth Avenue South. She had been a pupil of Carl Seibert of Leipzig and had studied in Berlin and London. At the Browne Martin Studio, 178 Eighth Avenue North, one could learn musical science and violin from Martin, who had spent two years at the Royal Conservatory, Leipzig, and seven years at Ward-Belmont. At the Winkler Music Studios, also at 178 Eighth Avenue North, piano, theory, harmony, and music history were available from the following teachers: Mrs. Winkler, Ellene Brackin, Rose McGregor, Mrs. Iva Crabtree Pierce, Mary Sue Nolen, and Marguerite Meiers. Mrs. Emma Louise Ashford, a composer, had a studio at 1914 Eighteenth Avenue South.

Other piano teachers were Mrs. George Colyar, Mrs. Will C. Hoffman, Marie Hayes (former pupil of Godowsky and Edouard Dethier), and Idah Lee Kirkpatrick. Elizabeth F. Price had expertise in piano, musical history, and opera scores; she featured the Fletcher Method. (Miss Price's name was well known, for her father, the Reverend George W. F. Price, had established the Nashville College for Young Ladies on the corner of Ninth Avenue and Broad, where the federal courthouse stands in 2004. Later it became the Vauxhall Apartments, and Miss Price kept her studio there for many years.) Amy Alberta Sandefur, a soprano who studied with William Zerffi in New York City, taught voice and piano. Lucie Van Valkenburgh taught violin, and Josephine M. Evans, a contralto who sang at Christ Episcopal and Vine Street Churches, taught voice.

Some teachers shared space and had complementary skills. Frances E. Southgate taught voice and Carrie Schwarz taught piano at 206 Capitol Boulevard. Miss Frank Hollowell, who taught the Danning system on the piano, teamed up with Martha Carroll, who taught violin (and was a pupil of Edouard Dethier and Leopold Auer), at 191 1/2 Eighth Avenue North. Margaret and Mary Strobel taught piano and violin at 138 Eighth Avenue North; Annie B. Rowen, piano, and Lucy Jocelyn Bushnell, vocal, could be found at that same address.

Mrs. Aline Reese Blondner was the organist at McKendree Church for many years. By 1921, her skills were diminishing—after all, she was born in 1841—but she kept going (she died in 1931). This native of Georgia had studied in Germany with Franz Liszt, and she had known Richard Wagner personally. After the death of her husband, a German music teacher, she became a teacher at Ward Seminary and later opened her own studio. In 1902 and 1903, with the assistance of her pupils, she gave lecture-recitals on Wagnerian music. Because of her acquaintance with Wagner, Nashvillians considered her a primary source.

the individual and collective talent was of "a high order." Conductor Gustav Fischer was commended for his conducting skills as well as his violin playing; other soloists, notably Mr. Schreger and his xylophone, and the string quartet were "well received"; and two vocalists, Miss Shoellenberger and Mrs. McVitty, were a part of the evening that was "decidedly an event." Despite having all of this talent, the orchestra must not have developed a following.

We get a glimpse of some problems at a benefit concert for the orchestra in the fall of 1891. Allen Hall, "the well-known wit," facetiously called the audience the most refined, intelligent, and brilliant he had ever faced. Of course, he was facing many, many empty seats. The reviewer of the concert stated, "A stone pitched at random from the stage could by only a remote possibility have hit a man or woman." He regarded the event as being "richly worthy of a crowded house, and it is surprising there was not greater curiosity to hear this orchestra at its best." As a group and as individuals, the musicians were a credit to the city. Soloists included Minnie Vesey, Mrs. Stewart, Miss Wessel, Charles Sawrie, Mr. Schmidt, Gustav Fischer, E. O. Risley, and Franz Strahm. (Many of these people had integral roles in the development of music in the city and in major events, such as the Centennial Exposition.) The Nashville Mandolin, Banjo, and Guitar Club also made an appearance.

The Vendome had a succession of music directors. In 1892, it was Gustav Fischer, who eventually became music director of the New Masonic. Gary (Garibaldi) B. Gaston, J. Hough Guest, and then his wife, Maja Muse Guest, had the job before the Vendome became a movie theater in 1919.

By April 1899 the whole topic of an orchestra had become a sore spot with music lovers. They could not understand why Nashville was unable to create momentum to maintain a symphony.

More discussion centered on having an orchestra that would advertise and glorify the city. Again, discussion was about as far as it went.

Another ray of hope flickered in the fall of 1904. The initial concert of the Nashville Symphony, directed by J. Hough Guest, took place at the Vendome in the afternoon and evening of November 18. (Guest was then teaching at Ward Seminary.) There were thirty-eight musicians, and of those, seven had to be imported from out of town. The soloists were local: Minnie Vesey, contralto, and Professor Emil Winkler, violinist. The words *permanent fixture* were often said in the same breath as *orchestra*. Yet again, a group thought the ingredients for a successful orchestra were in place.

The next day, the *Banner* reviewer summed up the situation: "The establishment of a permanent symphony orchestra in Nashville would constitute a very great source of pleasure for the music-loving public and would be a decided step toward the advancement of musical culture and education," but "the liberal patronage of Nashville's many music-lovers" would be required. The program included "Pique Dame" by Suppé, Concerto for Piano in G Minor by Mendelssohn, Symphony in B Minor, First Movement, by Schubert, "Cavatina" from *Queen of Sheba* by Gounod, "An Arabian Scout" by DeMouleneux, "Concert Waltz" by Franz Strahm (a local musician), and "Coronation March" from the opera *Folkunger* by Kretschner. Even with great praise for the concert, the orchestra failed to become a permanent fixture.

A much more formal organization with the backing of many enthusiastic supporters swung into action in 1920. The Nashville Symphony Society, Inc., had the following officers: Mrs. I. Milton Cook, vice president; Miss Sara Hitchcock, secretary; and A. Maurice Loveman, treasurer. Board members included T. Graham Hall, W. E. von Otto, Sydney A. Groom, Mrs. A. B.

Anderson, Mrs. Weaver Harris, Vernon Tupper, and Daisy Sartain. The two men behind this Nashville Symphony were George Pullen Jackson and F. Arthur Henkel. (Orchestra members are listed in appendix B.)

Jackson was a professor of German at Vanderbilt University. Born in Maine, he attended the Royal Conservatory in Dresden, Vanderbilt University, and the University of Chicago, and he also studied in Bonn and Munich. Before his position at Vanderbilt, he taught at the University of Chicago and Oberlin College. He had been in Nashville only two years when he became the founder of the Nashville Symphony. Jackson was its first president and manager, and he also played trumpet.

Henkel was born in Cincinnati to a father who was a clarinetist and came to the United States after the Franco-Prussian Wars as assistant director of a German military band. Henkel took piano lessons with Frederick Werner Steinbrecher, a former pupil of Chopin and a friend of the Henkel family. He came to Nashville in 1906, just after graduating from the Metropolitan Conservatory. He taught first at the Tennessee School for the Blind and then, as a teacher of pipe organ and piano, at Belmont (beginning 1908), where he spent most of his time (until 1951), except for two years with the Nashville Conservatory of Music. He also became organist and choirmaster at Christ Church Episcopal. He was the conductor of the Nashville Symphony (1920–30).

Each season the orchestra held five or six concerts (October to April), and a visiting group gave two additional concerts, for example, orchestras of Cleveland and Minneapolis. The first concert was held at the Princess Theater, 511 Church, and the orchestra opened with "March and Procession of Bacchus" (Delibes), then played an overture from *Sakuntala* (Goldmark); Myrna Sharlow, soprano of Chicago Opera Company, sang selections that ranged from an aria in *Pagliacci* to "My

Love Is a Muleteer" and "Floods of Spring"; and Henkel at the piano performed Victor Herbert's "American Fantasie." Notable people appeared with the orchestra during its existence, and one of them was John Erskine, the first president of Juilliard School of Music, who was a pianist.

Beethoven Week

The commemoration of the death of Beethoven—one hundred years after the fact (he died March 26, 1827)—was cause for a series of events throughout the United States. In 1927 the Beethoven National Advisory Board in New York City coordinated the nationwide efforts, and the Columbia Phonograph Company made Beethoven records available. The Chicago Orchestra, the Detroit Symphony, the Metropolitan Opera Company, and the Cincinnati Orchestra had special plans.

Nashville was not to be left out of the opportunity to be perceived as "critical in the pursuit of cultural music," according to George Pullen Jackson. A committee of people from schools, churches, clubs, and music circles, including Charles Mitchell, president of the Nashville Symphony, E. J. Gatwood of Peabody College, and Mrs. T. Graham Hall of the Centennial Club, met at the Andrew Jackson Hotel; I. Milton Cook was the chairman. A representative of the Beethoven National Advisory Board, A. Frederick Carter, visited principal cities of the South to assist them with their plans, and he saw "lively response and eagerness" in Nashville citizens for the celebration, which was to be held March 20 to 26, 1927.

There must have been more than an adequate supply of observances for George Pullen Jackson because he commented, "Beethoven week is over, thank goodness! All 'weeks' have come to have a commercial smell. And the smell is offensive in matters of art."

The first guest conductor engaged by the Nashville Symphony Society was Enrico Leide, who was the organizer of the Atlanta Symphony in 1923 and also its conductor. A native of Italy, a graduate of the Milan Conservatory of Music, and a cellist, he had played in the orchestra of the Metropolitan Opera House. His Nashville appearance was March 14, 1926, after the close of Atlanta's season of eight concerts.

Edward Tarpley, musician and medical doctor, attended concerts of the first Nashville Symphony from 1920 to 1930 when he was a youngster, and he said recently, "They would give us student passes, and we would go to the War Memorial and sit in the balcony. They moved down to Loew's Theater [the Vendome] for two or three years, and we sat in that top balcony. For a while they charged us twenty-five or fifty cents, but then they gave us complimentary tickets because nobody was sitting up there anyway; it was fun. There were not too many activities on Sunday afternoons when the Symphony played. Henkel had certain programs that he would repeat year after year."

Audience attendance was not consistent or overwhelming, and musicians' attendance at rehearsals was equally sporadic, a problem related to having an orchestra of volunteers who had two or more other jobs. The crash of 1929 killed the U.S. economy and also the Nashville Symphony. During the years of the Great Depression, the Symphony tried to re-form twice. In 1932 there were three programs: in January, late February, and March. By then Dr. Tarpley had become a performer: "Dr. Eric Sorantin conducted the first one; I played in all three because they were looking for anybody that could read music and play. He did a pretty good job. But they had the worst ice storm ever seen, and half the people couldn't get into town. The next one was directed by Arthur Henkel, and the third by a man from Kentucky, whose name escapes me.

The people who belonged to the union were paid a minimum wage, whatever that was. The rest of us—like myself—they were just glad to have us."

During Iris Week 1935, the Nashville Symphony, conducted by H. Arthur Brown, presented a concert on April 30 at the War Memorial Auditorium with Sonja Yergin as the soloist. Brown was conductor of the El Paso Symphony and the University of Louisville orchestra. A Nashville native, Yergin had achieved fame at Berlin's State Opera since her performance eight years earlier with the Nashville Symphony. Sixty local musicians performed Schubert's Symphony No. 1 in B Minor, the overture of *Ruy Blas*, and Strauss's "Blue Danube." Yergin sang an aria from Verdi with the orchestra accompanying her, and three songs with Robert Tucker at the piano. Charles Mitchell, president of the Nashville Symphony Society, was hopeful that the concert would spark a renewal of interest so that the orchestra could be reorganized by the next season. Poor Charles and other music lovers were to be disappointed. The community could not support the orchestra, and there would be no more Nashville Symphony concerts until the end of World War II.

"What Is It Worth to You, Mr. Business Man?"

*We of the Society have faith . . .
in the farsightedness of the business men of Nashville.*

—GEORGE PULLEN JACKSON, 1921

GEORGE PULLEN JACKSON asked this question concerning the newly established Nashville Symphony in the October 15, 1921, edition of the *Nashville Review*, published by the Chamber of Commerce. He wrote,

The musically cultured people of the United States and those of other lands who are reached by the American musical journals know all about the Nashville Symphony Orchestra. They have heard, through these musical and theatrical journals and through the metropolitan press, which has given much space to our orchestral venture, that we have a permanent organization which supports a Symphony Orchestra of sixty people and gives an extended series of concerts each season. They know that this Orchestra is, in its management, musical conducting and personnel, "100 per cent Nashville"; that it is capable, young as it is, of playing all but the most exacting of orchestral compositions in a manner which pleases our own discriminating concert-goers and greatly surprises visitors from other and older music centers. They "didn't think it was possible" to develop such an orchestra here. They thought symphony aggregations had to be imported at a great outlay of money from other states and from foreign countries, as used to be the only way possible. That is why they look upon the "Nashville Plan," as they called it in one journal, as a thing unique in the history of American music.

But "unique" things have to struggle hard for existence. A traditional institution always manages to peg along, but an innovation, no matter how worth while, has to go through a long "starvation period" before the public wakes up to the necessity of giving its approval and steady support.

Realizing this, the Nashville Symphony Society resolved that Nashville people should first learn to know Nashville's Symphony. Then Nashville could take it or leave it, and with good reason either way. Accordingly, it gave, in its first year of existence, two entirely free concerts at Ryman Auditorium, one at the Chamber of Commerce, and three at Hume Fogg High School. And it gave complimentary tickets to its five regular membership concerts for every seat in Ryman Auditorium that was not used by a "Patron" or other members of the Society. (These last named used over 2400 seats at each of the five

concerts.) So there were between twenty five and thirty thousand Nashville people who heard their Symphony Orchestra in its "trial year"—more people than ever attended orchestra concerts in any other fifteen years of Nashville's history.

Now the Nashville Symphony Orchestra . . . awaits that public's verdict. Shall it continue to validate Nashville's claim to cultural eminence? Shall it continue to say to the best people of the land, "Nashville is a good place for you and your family to live"? Shall we keep on bringing big conventions here? It has brought one, and was the main reason for the decision of the Music Supervisors—450 of them—to hold their national convention in Nashville next March.

Shall we continue to keep $10,000.00 [about $100,000 today] of Nashville people's annual "amusement allowance" right here at home in the hands of our own people instead of allowing it to be spent elsewhere or spent here and taken elsewhere?

This is not the first time these questions have been asked. And they are being answered in the affirmative. The membership list of the Society is growing apace. Their dues are coming in, and it looks as though the 1921–1922 season (six concerts) of the Nashville Orchestra should easily eclipse all its previous efforts.

There is just one thing which is giving the Symphony Society a bit of a concern. The business men who were the financial backbone of last season's series and who were so "hard hit" by the depression of last winter and spring, have not yet "come back" in their subscriptions as heavily as the Society had hoped, and until they do, the Nashville Symphony Orchestra will have to subsist solely on its membership dues.

We of the Society have faith, however, in the farsightedness of the business men of Nashville and that they will do their indispensable part in patronizing this "Nashville Industry," in "buying these Nashville Made Goods," and in helping the Nashville Symphony Orchestra continue to advertise Nashville in the most effective way.

The Metropolitan Opera Company
and the
Russian Grand Opera Company

My suggestion is, whenever an opera is given in Nashville in a foreign language, most of all in Russian, that an ad or two be sacrificed on the program and a little synopsis take up their space.

—GEORGE PULLEN JACKSON, 1922

TWO OPERA COMPANIES, one performing in German and the other in Russian less than twenty years apart, had totally different experiences with Nashville's audiences. The warm embrace of the one can be readily explained, but the almost total rebuff of the other is somewhat puzzling.

The Metropolitan Opera Company performed Wagner's *Parsifal* on Saturday, April 29, 1905, at the Vendome. That was the second visit of the company to Nashville; the first was in October 1901 at the Ryman Auditorium (then still known as the Tabernacle). A reporter writing in the newspaper three days before the 1905 performance warned, "It is safe to say that no similar opportunity to hear the great Metropolitan Company in such a masterpiece as 'Parsifal' will ever come again to the people in this city and vicinity." The writer was prophetic because the company never returned to Nashville, only the occasional singer from the Met who gave a concert.

Parsifal, Wagner's last opera, had been the cause of serious controversy. Cosima Wagner, widow of Richard Wagner, was adamant that *Parsifal* was to be performed only at Bayreuth, but Heinrich Conried of the Met was even more adamant about staging the opera in New York City. Copyright and performing rights were not on Mrs. Wagner's side—there was no agreement between the United States and Germany then—and she could not legally prevent Conried from carrying out his plan. Germans who held Wagner in reverent awe were livid about the whole incident. In 1903 the Met first produced *Parsifal* with great success, and two of the original participants, Alois Burgstaller and Alfred Hertz, were banned from further performances in Bayreuth for having disregarded Wagner's wishes. Burgstaller and Hertz were in the group that came to Nashville.

The same stars, orchestra, and conductor who had been in Boston, Chicago, Pittsburgh, Kansas City, San Francisco, and Los Angeles—more than two hundred people in all—brought special scenery that had cost $40,000. Tickets for seats on the Vendome's first floor cost $8 and $7; for the balcony, $6, $5, and $3; for the gallery, $3 and $2 ($8 then, about $160 today). Since the opera itself lasted six hours, the curtain rose at 5:00 P.M., and there was a two-hour intermission in the middle for a dinner break.

Alfred Hertz conducted the orchestra of almost sixty musicians with "masterful domination and guidance," and the instruments seemed "to unite in one grand volume of typifying sound, the triumphs, the anguish, the anger, the scorn, the praise, exultation and benediction of the lines." The cast included Alois Burgstaller as Parsifal and Olive Fremstad as Kundry.

Kenneth Schermerhorn, current maestro of the Nashville Symphony, commented recently on the audience attending a more contemporary production of *Parsifal* at the Metropolitan Opera House: "It's glorious, but it's pretty static. It's always done around Eastertime, and Eastertime is when everyone goes to New York. 'What do we do? We have to go to the Met. We absolutely have to go to the Met.' The house was packed, but I managed to get a seat. After the first intermission—the first act lasts about an hour—maybe sixty percent of the people came back. The second intermission, there were forty percent returning. At the last act I looked up and down the row, and there were about ten of us."

Those visitors had been to the Met, but in the spring of 1905 the Met came to Nashville. The simple explanation for the enthusiastic audience made up of "cultured, discriminating theater-goers" from the city, the midstate, and adjoining states is this: the reputation and allure of the Met. The reviewer wrote, "The production was a distinct triumph and will live for many a day as the most profound, the most pretentious and the worthiest musical offering ever given in Nashville." Having the opera sung in the original language of German did not seem to cause a twitter of discontent.

Years later, the Russian Grand Opera Company had an unremarkable reception in mid-March 1922. Over the course of three nights at the Orpheum (managed by Tony Sudekum), the company staged *Carmen,* the *Tsar's Bride,* and *Eugen Onegin,* all in Russian. Only a few hundred people were willing to go, however; there were 300 empty seats and 400 occupied ones for *Carmen,* which was conducted by Eugene Fuerst. Although *Carmen* in Russian might have been unusual, people did know the story line, and *Carmen* had been a traditional favorite in Nashville. Russian music in general was popular among Americans, and Rimsky-Korsakov's "Song of India" was then being played frequently across the country by orchestras and on recordings. What should have been the "artistic sensation" of the year turned out to be a financial disaster.

The credentials of the one hundred people in the company were impeccable. All had been members of the czar's imperial theaters, and after they escaped from the Bolsheviks in 1917 with little more than their talent, they formed the company, which presented opera exactly as in Russia: same principals, orchestra, conductors, chorus, ballet, scenic artists, and technicians. The costumes were designed by Mme Ferder, formerly the wardrobe mistress of the St. Petersburg Opera. One conductor had been a pupil of Rimsky-Korsakov. The company had been all over the world before coming to the United States and had met receptive audiences.

After reviewing the *Tsar's Bride,* especially the work of Misses Burskaya and Kasanskaya, in glowing terms, commenting on the need for explanation of the action for those unfamiliar with the opera, and noting that the company was bringing a more lyrical Rimsky-Korsakov to the States, a frustrated George Pullen Jackson asked, "I wish someone who has heard the first two operas of this excellent troupe of artists would tell me why Nashville has given them such slim support. Was it the weather alone? Or what?"

There had been heavy rains earlier in the week, and the forecast for the upcoming evening

Another Performance of *Parsifal*

A large audience attended a performance of *Parsifal* by Walter Damrosch and the New York Symphony Orchestra at the Tabernacle (the Ryman) on April 26, 1904. To give the listeners a richer experience, Damrosch explained the opera story. The orchestra played Wagner's overture from *Tannhäuser,* then began act 1: the processional march of the knights of the Holy Grail and the invisible chorus, which was followed by Amfortas's lament of the divine prophecy, sung by Archambault, basso. In act 2, Parsifal and the Flower Maidens in Klingsor's Magic Garden was sung by Mmes Savage, Harmon, Wheeler, Crawford, Bloomfield, and Kennedy, and Mr. Bleno; and Harmon performed Kundry's song. In act 3, David Mannes played a violin solo of "Good Friday Spell." Although it was not exactly the complete opera, Nashvillians had another taste of Wagner. Aline Blondner's efforts to familiarize citizens with Wagnerian music seem to have paid off.

performance of *Eugen Onegin* was light rain, with temperatures from 40 to 50 degrees, so the weather might have been a factor for the slim attendance. The language was admittedly a problem. The political situation of the troupe and attitudes toward any Russian in 1922—exile or otherwise—cannot be underestimated. Even considering all this, we join Jackson in asking why there was so little support for a group with such outstanding credentials.

The Sheik and Jimmy Stahlman

Many in the audience [suspected]
that they were being toyed with by the famous "sheik."

—Review, Banner, June 14, 1923

IMAGINE turning the page in the *Banner* one afternoon and seeing this advertisement:

VALENTINO
The Incomparable "Sheik of Sheiks"
and His Beautiful Wife
Winifred Hudnut
In Feature Dance Program
In Person—Not a Movie
Positively Only One Appearance

You only had to pay the price of a ticket ($3, $2.50, $2, or $1.50, plus war tax; $1.50 then, about $16 today), make your way to the Ryman Auditorium, and you could see the hottest film star in the country. There would also be a dance contest (the fox-trot), and twelve young women were to compete in a beauty contest. What could be better than that?

Apparently many Nashvillians could not think of anything better than that. Tickets sold quickly. Everyone wanted to see the duo dance and hear their ten-piece Argentine orchestra. (By the way,

Mrs. Valentino's stage name was Natasha [sometimes spelled Natacha] Rambova, but she used her maiden name, Winifred Hudnut, for the Nashville appearance.)

Special arrangements were made to accommodate a request for tickets by the African-American community. More than five hundred university students and citizens wanted tickets, but the customary reserved section in the Ryman was too small to meet the demand. A performance for African-Americans was to follow the show originally scheduled.

The Valentinos were to arrive on their private railroad car the *Colonial-Mayflower*. They declined all invitations for luncheons and any other engagements because they were unsure of their precise arrival time. They could not have anticipated how wise they had been to make that decision.

Three thousand people filed into the Ryman on Wednesday evening, June 13, 1923, to await the sheik. But they waited . . . and waited . . . and waited—no sheik. As the minutes dragged on and on, the mood of the audience turned from anticipation to hostility. The people began surmising that he was not going to come, that he was trying to pull a fast one on them. Or if he did show up, he would not dance very long; he would probably spend most of his time advertising a beauty clay. (The purpose of the seventeen-week tour in more than eighty cities was to advertise Mineralava Beauty Clay. Because of a dispute with his studio, Valentino was forbidden to make films in 1923, and the tour provided him with an income, $7,000 per week [about $74,000 today], to tide him over until the dispute was resolved. He was, after all, a movie star with extravagant spending habits.)

It was a long time from the anticipated 8:15 opening until 9:50 when Valentino and his wife appeared, for the audience was thinking dark thoughts. Remember it was June, and the temperature in the auditorium must have matched the tempers of the people. Yet they chose to stay. Many would not have been there in the first place if the appearance had been just about dance; they stayed to see a movie star in person.

To his credit, Valentino won them over almost instantly. His train was late. What could he do? He turned on every ounce of his charm, and it worked; the audience sat entranced. He talked to them about films and the need for the American public to take more interest in the production of high-class movies, and he did not say a word about the products he was supposed to be advertising. Then the man with the magnetic personality and his beautiful wife danced beautifully his interpretation of the tango, as seen in *The Four Horsemen of the Apocalypse,* as well as other dances.

The silver fox-trot trophy, which had been on display at O. K. Houck Piano Company for a week, went to Tom Woolwine Jr. and his sister-in-law, Mrs. Sam Woolwine Jr. The woman chosen in the beauty contest, who would go to New York and compete against winners from other cities, was Mrs. Christine Ashley of Franklin.

Thirty-year-old Jimmy Stahlman (who later in life as publisher of the *Banner* was known as Mr. James Stahlman) was personally responsible for getting Nashville on the tour schedule. After he paid the expenses, including auditorium rental, fees to the musicians and stagehands, and advertising in the *Banner,* Stahlman had enough money left to buy his first car—a four-door Ford.

There was another brief Valentino appearance later in June. On the twenty-fifth he and his wife had a dance hall engagement at the Cumberland Park hall where they danced the tango before judging Nashville dancers in a dance contest. The admission charge was $1.50. Contest winners were Eugene Harris and Frances Hampton (later Mrs. Brownlee Currey, grandmother of my daughter-in-law Stephanie Ingram).

Lark Taylor

At last Nashville, Athens of the South, leader in things artistic, but long neglectful of the drama, is to have an active Little Theater.

—Tennessean, February 28, 1926

JOHN LARK TAYLOR was a cousin of Governors Alf and Bob Taylor, but his interests lay in the theater and in music, not in politics. He seems to have been bitten at an early age by the acting bug. The first play that young Taylor saw was *Romeo and Juliet* starring Mary Anderson at the Masonic Theater. He was only four years old then, and he was overjoyed at the sounds of the orchestra tuning up, the sights of the scenery and the costumes, illumined by gas lights.

At age twelve his first appearance was in what he called "Payne's Great Spectacle"—the *Last Days of Pompeii*—at Sulphur Dell Park, and the participants marched through the streets to the sounds of Verdi's *Aida.* He attended Tarbox School, where he was in the Tarbox Dramatic Club, and he sang in the boys' choir of the Church of the Advent.

The Vendome was the best theater in town, with the most first-class events, and Taylor recalled the theater's "warm, subdued tones" with crystal chandeliers. Adelina Patti's first farewell in Nashville occurred at the Vendome on the same evening (January 8, 1894) of the annual Jackson Ball at the Nicholson House Hotel. Taylor remembered more about the men and women "in evening dress, the gay silks, satins, laces and jewels" who drifted into the theater to listen to Patti. Top tickets went for $5, and even though there was an economic downturn, people were fighting over tickets for her appearance. The willingness of Nashvillians to pay about

$5,000 (about $100,000 today) to see her did not deter her from saying that the audience members sat there "like stone bottles." A contemporary Nashvillian noted that local audiences were always either "politely bored or else mildly [enjoyed] the performance in a high-bred, languid way." Mr. and Mrs. Stewart with Walter Damrosch's Opera Company performed in *Tannhäuser* and *Die Meistersinger* (December 1895), and Taylor even as a youngster could tell that the Vendome stage was too small for opera.

As a young man, he took classes at Fall's Business College in addition to studying voice with Minnie Crudup Vesey in her studio just downstairs from the college. She had studied with August Rotoli, an Italian composer and teacher, in Boston. (Miss Vesey was director of the Vanderbilt University Glee Club in 1895, a position that Taylor held decades later.) Taylor gave serious thought to becoming an opera singer, which he did not do, but he occasionally ran into Hugh Martin, another Vesey pupil, who achieved outstanding success as a tenor. Martin went to France and Italy for further training and then managed to come back to the States and sing at the Metropolitan Opera House—as Riccardo Martin. A native of Hopkinsville, Kentucky, Martin had roles at the Met from 1907 to 1915, and some critics have stated that he would have been much better known today but for his primary competitor, Caruso—the darling of his time.

After finishing the business course, Taylor sold music and instruments for Henry French on Summer Street (Fifth Avenue). That position held little interest for him, however, and he joined various theater companies. Seventeen-year-old Taylor had his first professional job in vaudeville while in St. Louis. By the time he was eighteen he was in New York in Augustin Daly's company. He started singing in the musical company but begged to move to the dramatic company. His Broadway debut was in Daly's production of *Taming of the Shrew* with Tyrone Power Sr., and Taylor was cast as a page. Following Daly's death in 1899, Taylor came back to Nashville and worked with Mrs. Pauline Boyle's stock company.

Later, Taylor joined Lillian Russell's company for a run of *Lady Teazle,* and while he was with her he had a fortuitous meeting with Julia Marlowe and E. H. Sothern (son of E. A. Sothern). He went to London with them, and he spent several years in their Shakespeare company touring England and the United States. Taylor played Polonius to

Lark Taylor, a native Nashvillian, performed with notable stars of the stage including E. H. Sothern, Julia Marlowe, Tyrone Power Sr., and John Barrymore.

A member of Sothern and Marlowe's Shakespeare Company, Lark Taylor toured with them in England and the U.S. Among other roles, he appeared with E. H. Sothern in *Our American Cousin* and *Hamlet*. (E. H. is pictured here.) E. H.'s father, E. A. Sothern, appeared in his signature role of Dundreary in *Our American Cousin* in Nashville, December 1876, at the Grand Opera House.

E. H. Sothern's Hamlet and Julia Marlowe's Ophelia at the Manhattan Opera House in 1913. He and E. H. appeared in a revival of *Our American Cousin* two years later on Broadway. By 1918 he worked in a succession of theater companies, including the company of Georgia native Charles Coburn (notably in a production of *Better 'Ole*) and the Chicago Great Northern Stock Company.

In 1922–23 Taylor had a season with John Barrymore in a widely and wildly acclaimed *Hamlet,* and he was cast as the First Player; Tyrone Power Sr. was Claudius. Many critics considered Barrymore's performance a groundbreaking interpretation of Hamlet's character. Although Taylor retained a pleasant memory of Barrymore's Hamlet, in his opinion it was "not as fine or as big as the Hamlet of E. H. Sothern."

Having been a member of the Actors Society of America (founded 1896) and Actors' Equity Association (founded 1913), Taylor had joined E. H. Sothern, Julia Marlowe, Otis Skinner, and others loyal to managers in forming the Actors Fidelity League with George M. Cohan as president in 1919. In that year Actors' Equity went on strike, shutting down theaters on Broadway and across the nation that were members of the Producers Association. The actors were protesting working conditions, unfair pay, and other perceived employment abuses. Meanwhile the Road (that is, taking theater companies on the road) was being killed by movies, which were taking audiences, and by unaffordable and unreasonable labor demands, which were destroying profits, according to Taylor. By 1925, troubles compounded for theatrical troupes because of high rail rates and hotel prices, big salaries for players, and costs of licenses. Taylor could see what was ahead, and he chose to return to Nashville with a grand plan.

That plan was to start a Little Theatre using local amateurs and bringing in stars "like the old stock-star system so popular after the Civil War," he said. Taylor was convinced that "the Little Theater came into being because people love the real theater, and even if the road should come back," it was a good training ground.

He rented a theater, which had been built by M. A. Lightman as a neighborhood movie house on Carlton Avenue (it is now the Belcourt Theatre but was then known as the Hillsboro Theatre). To make ends meet, he also directed the Vanderbilt Glee Club, taught girls public speaking at the YWCA, put on a play for the Vanderbilt Dramatic Club, and sang in choirs. He devoted his creative energies to the Little Theatre.

On February 28, 1926, a *Tennessean* reporter declared, "At last Nashville, Athens of the South, leader in things artistic, but long neglectful of the drama, is to have an active Little Theater." Lark Taylor was the director, and Jane Douglas Crawford, the associate director. (Crawford was known for going East occasionally to keep up with drama, and she was also associated with Little Theatre in Cleveland.) They planned to have an April 15–16 production of Moliere's *Imaginary Invalid,* sponsored by the Nashville Center of the Drama League, with Mrs. J. Barthell Joseph, Crawford, and Dr. H. B. Schermerhorn in the cast. That would be followed in May by a one-act play written by Taylor, called *Long, Long Ago*, and the actors were to include Taylor, Rebecca Jones, and Jennie Mai McQuiddy. The reporter stated with hope, "With these two competent actors and directors at the head of the organization, it is expected that it will not be long before the Little Theater of Nashville will take its place beside the Nashville Symphony Orchestra, oldest and best-known organization in the South, as an active expression of Nashville's culture."

By October of the same year, the players were ready to open the season with *Captain Applejack.* The theater was leased for eight plays to be given during the winter and spring. The reviewer remarked upon the "energy and persistence of the players and management" and added "if 'Captain Applejack' is any criterion of what is to follow this year, Nashville is fortunate in being saved by its own artists from a dramatic sahara [*sic*]." The players were Mrs. J. B. Joseph, Sara Catherine Chambers, Rebecca Jones, Neal Rutland, Dr. H. B. Schermerhorn, Sam Tarpley, Clara Haddox, William S. Howland, Charles Hunt, and Viola Engler. E. Ambrose Matthews was the scenic artist, and Rogers McCauley was in charge of the lighting.

Things failed to work out as Taylor hoped, and he was replaced as director in 1927. He meanwhile had felt a lack of resolve and thought people were unwilling to devote the necessary time or work to accomplish the results he desired from the group.

Furthermore, Taylor and the Little Theatre Guild officers could not agree on monetary terms.

He left town briefly for a position with the Boston Repertory Theater. Then he became a staff member at WSM in Nashville, doing dramatic works and working as a radio announcer, from 1933 until his retirement in 1942. Lark Taylor died in Nashville in 1946 at age sixty-five, having acted in many kinds of plays throughout his career, including forty roles in eleven Shakespearean plays.

Jeter and Smith

No city gave the dance more generous support than Nashville.

—Sarah Jeter and Louise Smith

THE DYNAMIC DUO of Sarah Jeter and Louise Smith came together at Ward-Belmont. These two invigorated the city for more than a decade and brought a new understanding of the dance to the citizens. Sarah Jeter had received training in ballet under Miss Emma I. Sisson at Ward-Belmont, and was later an instructor in the physical education department as dance director. Louise Smith had attended Nashville public schools and then entered Ward-Belmont. She received a diploma in physical education from there in 1924, but after a year of postgraduate work, polio struck, forcing a career change for her. She elected to pursue music and become a piano accompanist.

Jeter was the dance instructor for Signor de Luca's spectacular *Cavalleria Rusticana* in May 1927. In his review George Pullen Jackson wrote that the event was "nothing short of a revelation. Pupils' performances are not usually revelations." He continued, "The dancing forces of our operatic visitors [San Carlos and Scotti Opera Companies] have been weak indeed as contrasted to the half dozen comely and graceful sylphs of last night's performance who had been instructed by Sarah Jeter."

In October 1927 Jeter and Smith started holding classes at the Studio of Dancing, which they opened at 1812 Hillsboro Road. Their brochure explained why dance was important, emphasizing the benefits of health, poise, and pleasure: "The modern dance teacher is as interested in teaching the pupil to stand, to walk, to run and jump and skip correctly, as in teaching a dance step. Good posture, poise of body, sense of rhythm and grace of movement are the results of expert modern dance instruction."

Ruth St. Denis oversaw Nashville Conservatory of Music students dancing at the Parthenon: St. Denis, Virginia Criddle, and Marian Curell *(left side)*; Sally Rhea Askew, Margaret Winkler, and Jane Bagley *(center trio)*; Sarah Jeter *(standing)*; Claudia Whitson *(sitting)*; and Mai Delle Tarkington *(lying)*.

They held a children's class for three- to six-year-olds for 45 minutes on Saturday ($25 for 24 lessons); a special conditioning class for women (12 lessons, $15); tap (2 per week, 24 lessons, $32); ballet (24 lessons, 2 per week, $35); toe and ballroom dancing by request. They wisely added this disclaimer: "The privilege is reserved to place in public performances only those pupils who have done creditable work." Their pupils' recitals always drew large crowds and rousing rounds of applause.

In addition to being the accompanist, Smith planned and directed dances in the community for civic clubs, fraternities, and sororities. She was known for novel ideas for dances and entertainment, and she had studied scenery design and lighting effects in the Northeast.

Jeter had studied with various instructors: Greek classic dancing in Chicago with Nicholas Tsoukalas; ballet with Andreas Pavley, Serge Oukrainsky, and Alexis Kosloff (ballet master of the Metropolitan Opera); a special course in children's dance with Sonia Serova at the Vestoff-Serova School in New York; tap with Eddie Russell, who spent ten years at the New York Hippodrome; and ballroom dance at the Ned Wayburn Studios. (In fact the Pavley-Oukrainsky Ballet had appeared at the Ryman in 1925 and 1926.) Jeter shared her experience with her students, and she continued to further her own studies for many years.

After Signor de Luca founded the Nashville Conservatory of Music, Jeter and Smith joined the faculty as codirectors of the dance department. They remained there four years before returning to Ward-Belmont.

Vanderbilt University's Caps and Bells Club was an all-male student group formed to produce musicals, and Jeter and Smith directed the dance for the group's first show *There You Are,* staged May 1–4, 1929. Francis Craig and his orchestra supplied the music. Reber Boult sang a solo, and other participants were Vernon Berbetts, Joe Campbell, Carl Nicholson, and Tom Fuqua as "Ladies of the Ensemble," and Larry Corson, Guilford Dudley, Walter Sharp, and Charles Trabue as "Gentlemen." Dean Madison Sarratt was so appreciative of their help that he wrote a thank-you note to Jeter and Smith.

On October 29, 1929, the *Banner* reported a reception for the dancers Ruth St. Denis and Ted Shawn, which was held at the Nashville Conservatory of Music and drew four hundred attendees. Both Jeter and Smith knew the famous dancers because they had been pupils at the Denishawn school. (See more about St. Denis and Shawn in Nashville, "St. Denis, Shawn, and Modern Dance.") That day of the stock market crash would have dark overtones for the conservatory that were in sharp contrast to the celebratory event.

The first quarter of 1930 was busy for the duo. In January the Nashville Conservatory of Music held its dance recital at the Scottish Rite Temple. (The Scottish Rite Temple, built in 1925, is now the Masonic Grand Lodge on the corner of Seventh Avenue North and Broadway. The building, Greek in design, has an auditorium on the second floor that seats 1,455 people.) Among the offerings were tap, toe, and Mexican hat dances. In March the Ninth Annual Gridiron Dinner of the Lions Club of Nashville was held at the Noel Hotel. It was similar to gridiron dinners at the National Press Club in Washington, and Jeter and Smith helped plan the activities.

Their yearly schedule evolved to include work in Nashville during the greater part of the year, with summers in New York City or another city in the East to further their education, to meet old friends, and to learn firsthand what was happening in the world of the performing arts. They would have had little or no work in the summertime in Nashville. In February 1931 there was a dance recital staged at the Scottish Rite Temple, and the proceeds went to the Drought Relief Fund of the American Red Cross. In May of that year the Department of Dancing, Nashville Conservatory of Music, had an event at the Scottish Rite Temple: Dolly Dearman and Margaret Street were featured dancers, and Jeter waltzed with Fletcher Harvey (the portrait photographer). In the summer months of 1931, Jeter and Smith studied lighting in New York City, and the next summer Jeter studied dance with Fokine, the Russian ballet master.

Some people still remember the revue *Why Not?*, directed by Jeter and Smith for the Junior League and the Scottish Rite Club and held at the Scottish Rite Temple. The proceeds went to Shriners Burn Centers. The first one was so successful, they were recruited to help with the fund-raiser three more years.

October 17, 1932, was the opening night for the musical skits. The papers had been filled with publicity, and handbills were posted across town, declaring "100 of Nashville's best known artists are presented to you a galaxy of stars"—all for the cost of a $1 ticket. Beasley Smith and his orchestra also were participants. Junior League President Martha Keeble must have been pleased with the crowds because the show was so popular that they had to repeat it the next night—an unanticipated performance.

"Nurturing the Arts" was the headline for a *Tennessean* article on Tuesday morning, April 4, 1933. The lead was about the recital the previous Friday evening of the dance department of Ward-Belmont. The auditorium of the Scottish Rite Temple was packed, and the crowd was so enthusiastic that it prolonged the applause for each number. The most notable number was the waltz of Jeter with Fletcher Harvey. Jeter and Smith apparently left no detail of costuming and lighting effects to chance.

The writer of the article used the occasion to discuss the overall picture of the arts in Nashville:

Nashvillians have given plenty of evidence that they are interested in the creative work of Nashville artists in various lines. In proportion to the interest shown in its own creative artists does a city develop along artistic lines. John Erskine brought this idea out very forcibly in a brief talk before an audience two years ago which attended a concert of the Nashville Symphony Orchestra with which Dr. Erskine appeared as soloist. Dr. Erskine urged those at the concert to take a personal and a vital interest in those, both students and artists, who are working here at home. Without deprecating the value which a community receives from the visit of a great orchestra or virtuoso, Dr. Erskine placed emphasis upon the development by a community of the talent which exists within it.

And Nashville does not ignore the talent of its sons and daughters. The attendance at the recitals and exhibitions which are given by local groups shows plainly that the local singers, musicians, dancers, painters and artists in other lines find encouragement at home. Evidence is lacking, however, that the Nashville audiences are willing to give adequate financial support to those ventures which must depend upon public financing. But it is hoped that in time financial support will be forthcoming too and that we shall have a civic theater suitable for the presentation of such local theatricals as now look about in vain for a non-commercial house, an art gallery in which the artists of the city will find a suitable place to house their exhibitions and in which their work may be kept on display for sale, and every form of art will have the physical property it needs in order that it may develop to the full extent of the ability of its exponents and that it may the better serve the interests of its community.

In the meantime Nashvillians can remember that their mere presence encourages those who are working in the various fields of art, and the artists can hope that in the end that interest will result in some tangible help along the lines mentioned.

The lack of financing for the arts is not at all surprising during the depression years of the 1930s, but it took several decades more for "tangible help" to materialize and even then the "mere presence" of Nashvillians was not to be assumed at arts-related events.

A renovated fire hall opposite the old Tarbox School on Broadway became the studio of Jeter and Smith in 1936. In May they gave a recital after overcoming the obstacles of having no place to perform and problems with musicians and their union. The duo threw a memorable party on November 20, 1936, for Jack Manning, a top instructor in New York. As part of the festivities for Manning, there was to be a dance program, which had a most unusual start as the dancers drove right into the hall in a red car, with siren screaming, and stopped a few feet in front of the audience. It is doubtful that anyone there had ever been introduced to the dance in that way!

In May of 1937 Jeter and Smith arranged two events: the Dance Center Concert Group on the first at the Community Playhouse (a ticket cost 65 cents) and a recital on the twenty-eighth at the Scottish Rite Auditorium. That summer found Jeter and Smith in Stockbridge, Massachusetts, where they taught dancing and body training at the Berkshire Playhouse Drama School, and Jeter also studied at Ted Shawn's camp, Jacob's Pillow, in nearby Lee, Massachusetts.

That fall they were back at the Dance Center, 1712 Broadway, and teaching classes by the end of September 1937 in preparation for special performances with Ted Shawn in the spring of 1938. Shawn had visited the Dance Center and seen the Concert Group dancing "Song of the Bayou." The Concert Group included Ann Brodsky, Frances Carter, Dolly Dearman, Mary Alene Edwards, Sarah Goodpasture, Ann Loveman,

Some of the Junior Leaguers who were waiting to rehearse for the October 1932 production of *Why Not?* were Helen Cheek, Peggy Alexander, and Lulu Owen *(seated at left)*; Frances Hunt, Mrs. Stanlee Hampton, Frances Duke, Anne Wallace, Estelle Dickerson, and Frances Currey *(standing, left to right)*; Helen Philips and Susanne Warner *(seated on piano)*; Argie Neil *(seated at piano)*; and Cornelia Stevens *(standing at right)*.

Mary McComas, and Adelaide Roberts. When Jeter was at Jacob's Pillow that summer, Shawn invited the group to be guest artists for concerts in Nashville and Murfreesboro. It was a rare honor for a girls' group to have a part with Ted Shawn and His Men Dancers. In seven years of tours, Shawn permitted only one other female group (from Louisville). All of their hard work, training, and recitals paid off in showing that the Concert Group could dance with professionals.

It is unclear if Smith was becoming as restless as Jeter was, but Francis Robinson, who had just gotten a job at WSM in Nashville, wrote a letter to someone in Hollywood—addressed simply as Hermes, with no further identification—in May 1938. He recommended Jeter for a behind-the-scenes job as a coach for drill routines. He

A Disdain of Dance

Jeter and Smith stated that Nashville had been generous in support of the dance, but that certainly did not apply to Professor R. A. Lapsley of the Nashville Female Academy who left the staff in 1852 in opposition to the introduction of dancing. His next post was that of the principal of the Nashville Ladies College. The Civil War—not its position on dancing—caused the college's demise. In October 1857 C. D. Elliott explained his position on dancing, which he believed was in accord with the trustees, stockholders, and patrons of the Nashville Female Academy: "I found [the students] going out into the city, and taught Dancing as a fashionable accomplishment, to fit them for the Ball Room and similar places of sinful amusement. I took the Dancing to the Academy, divested it of its characteristics as an accomplishment, and had it taught and practiced only as a recreation, for the sake of health and cheerfulness, and in a manner consistent with Piety and Devotion." Almost a century later, in 1937, Fred Russell discussed Ted Shawn and His Men Dancers and their athleticism before they made an appearance in town. One was a pole vaulter, another a swimmer, still another a fencer. Two or three were wrestlers. Russell worked hard to convey the idea that dance is not "feminine"— a point that Shawn was determined to make. Dancers are still trying to emphasize their athleticism. As late as the 1970s when we were working to create the Tennessee Performing Arts Center, Athens Clay Pullias had to overcome objections to the idea of the dance from members of the Church of Christ; to them, he clarified the distinction between dancing (as personal entertainment) and the dance (as an art form). Historically the dance has been the least supported performing art in Nashville, although Nashville Ballet's impressive growth—artistically and financially— is at last changing this pattern.

acknowledged, though, that she was pretty good at choreography. He explained that Agnes Boone asked her to teach in New York, but Jeter wanted to go to Hollywood. The essential point of the letter was this: "She has gone as far as she can here. She is ready for the big things." We simply cannot overlook that point as it applies to other gifted performing artists in Nashville—past, present, and future. Nor can we overlook that Francis had contacts in Hollywood even then and he was ever helpful to people with a desire to pursue the performing arts there or in New York.

Jeter did not go to Hollywood, and I cannot find a follow-up source to see whether she had an offer. I have to believe that she would have been in California as quickly as the train would get her there if she had received even an inkling of a job offer. As it was, she remained in Nashville until early summer of 1940. A letter dated June 15, from the Dance Center and signed by Sarah Jeter, reported to their students: she and Smith were going to take a sabbatical year; they would be at the Berkshire Playhouse Drama School in Stockbridge, Massachusetts, from June to September and then on to New York.

The two women had help from various sources in Nashville while they were in the Big Apple. Mrs. Naff of the Ryman prepared a letter of introduction for Jeter and Smith to Sol Hurok, dated March 4, 1941. Jeter wrote the column "Localights Shine on Broadway" for the *Banner,* in which she reported on people with a Nashville or Tennessee connection. For example, in April 1941 Bobby Tucker played accompaniment for a party given by Count Lanfranco Rasponi on behalf of Jamila Novotna of the Metropolitan

Opera, and Jeter pointed out that the count's mother was Caroline Montague of Chattanooga. In early April, Francis Robinson had gone with Jeter and Smith to a Ted Shawn party in New York City, and by the end of that month, Jeter reported that William Fields had offered Francis a position on his staff; Fields was then representing Helen Hayes in *Victoria Regina.*

The declaration of World War II dictated changes in everyone's life. If Jeter and Smith had given thought to returning to Nashville at the end of their sabbatical, the war effort put a halt to that line of thinking. Smith received instruction and then taught international code to enlisted personnel at the Army Air Corps Technical Command in Chicago. She later transferred to the Navy Department in Washington as an expediter with the Bureau of Ships. In 1948 she left government service and settled in Delray Beach, Florida, with her mother, Mrs. Nancy Lee Lindsey. She became a freelance photographer for a while and then went back to the Bureau of Ships until her retirement in 1968, when she returned to Nashville. She did volunteer work at Cheekwood and gave a gift to the Tennessee Performing Arts Foundation in memory of Ted Shawn. When she died in 1983, the headline for her obituary referred to her as a "dancing activist."

Jeter worked with the American Red Cross, then went overseas with the Red Cross to Africa, Japan, Australia, and Israel. In 1948, she left the Red Cross and moved to Florida. Years later, she served briefly as publicity director for Ted Shawn at Jacob's Pillow Dance Festival. Of that experience she wrote: "It was wonderful to be in the world of dance again—surrounded by dancers and seeing different top-flight artists in performance each week." She, too, moved back to Nashville, where she died in 1985.

Jeter and Smith had given their scrapbook, covering events from 1926 to 1940, to the Nashville Public Library in May 1978, and in a letter to Marshall Stewart, the library's director, they said that the materials in the collection reflected "an exciting period throughout America of growth and recognition of Dance as an Art, and the blossoming of modern dance whose seeds had been sown earlier by Duncan, St. Denis and Shawn. The old clogging and buck-and-wing were replaced by the sophisticated tap dancing of Astaire and others; and American dancers were coming into their own in previously Russian-dominated ballet." Jeter and Smith introduced a level of professionalism to amateur productions, and at least for a little while they made the dance blossom in Nashville.

Signor de Luca's Grand Expectations

Who knows but that this opera . . .
may lead to a co-operation between Nashville people
in musical endeavor that finally
will give Nashville a municipal opera?

—GAETANO DE LUCA, 1927

A CENTRAL FIGURE in trying to lead Nashville to a greater appreciation of opera (and music in general) in the 1920s and 1930s was Gaetano Salvatore de Luca. A native of Italy, de Luca was the director of the Ward-Belmont School of Music Voice Department. Among the credentials he cited were three years of study with Chevalier Edouardo Carrado in Italy, and two years with Chevalier Alfredo Sermiento, Caruso's coach. He had been a pupil of Commendatore B. Carelli, director of Naples Conservatory; of Lombardi in Florence, Italy; of Buzzi Peccia and Carbone in New York City; and of Signor Baraldi in London.

De Luca had come to Nashville with a letter of introduction to banker Andrew Benedict (then on the board of Ward-Belmont) from a gentleman in Mount Vernon, New York, where he had been living. J. D. Blanton, president of Ward-Belmont, gave de Luca a job beginning with the 1918–19 school year. With de Luca's guidance, young John H. DeWitt Jr. set up the city's first radio station, WDAA, on the Ward-Belmont campus in 1922 and broadcast Caruso's recordings to the opening of the River and Rail Terminal on the river at Broad. In 1923, de Luca married Nancy Belle Rice, a pianist and music teacher, of Mount Juliet. Louis Nicholas, now in his nineties, former voice teacher and critic for the *Tennessean,* knew some of the people who had studied with de Luca, and he said, "They were united in saying that he wasn't much of a musician, but a great promoter." There is no question that he proved his skills as a promoter when he produced an opera and a music conservatory with and for local people. Beyond that, he deserves recognition for his teaching of notable students in voice (see "Students of Signor de Luca").

The opera was *Cavalleria Rusticana,* and most of the eighty singers and dancers were local people. After several months of planning and training, the big event was to be held Thursday, May 12, 1927. There was no charge, but everyone had to have a ticket, available at Claude P. Street's piano dealership. Ward-Belmont considered it a gift to the "music-loving public," and President J. D. Blanton garnered praise for the school's contribution. Ryman Auditorium was decked out with the set, which was patterned after the Met's hangings for this opera, painted by E. Ambrose Matthews of Nashville.

The Emma Juch Opera Company had brought *Cavalleria Rusticana,* written by Pietro Mascagni, for the first time to Nashville just a few years after its premier performance in Rome, 1890. (It was subsequently performed in Nashville on these dates: December 1899; February 1904; March 1912; February 1914; January 1915; March 1916; and December 1920.) The reviewer for the *Tennessean,* Alvin Wiggers, had heard it in 1902 under the direction of Mascagni and at other times in Berlin, New York, and Chicago, so he had ample previous experiences of the production.

Five thousand people were turned away at the door, and the opera had to be scheduled for the next night to accommodate them, bumping the old fiddlers' contest to Saturday and Monday nights. Wiggers noted, "The success of the performance itself is not so surprising as the amazing and unsuspected interest Nashville took in grand opera, a form of art to which this city has always been particularly apathetic, as many visiting companies can sorrowfully testify. This sudden interest was caused doubtless by the fact that it was a home-made production and that the scale of prices was so low."

F. Arthur Henkel was in charge of the thirty-piece orchestra. Franca Golda (Mrs. M. H. Goldschein), who was from New York and studying with de Luca, sang the role of Santuzza. Dr. Arthur Wright played Turiddu; Blanche Campbell was the "vampish" Lola; Louise Tanksley had the role of Mama Lucia; and John Lewis was "a splendid and vigorous Alfio." But Wiggers referred to de Luca as "the guiding genius of it all."

Instead of having an empty stage between the two scenes, a ballet was given with Misses Margaret Carthew, Jane Everson, Ellen Robinson, Dorothy Vessy, and Edna Earl Halbert. Sarah Jeter of Ward-Belmont had worked with the dancers.

Perhaps the citizenry's warm reception of the opera convinced de Luca that the time was right for his new venture: the organization of the Nashville Conservatory of Music, which he wanted to be independent of other academic institutions. He needed help with financing, though, and he found it in Joel O. Cheek, who became president of the board, and other businessmen:

In September 1928 the faculty of the Nashville Conservatory of Music *(top photo)*, 2122 West End Avenue, included Wanda Labunski, Verna Brackinreed, Eric Sorantin, Gaetano de Luca, Wiktor Labunski, and Louise Smith *(front row, left to right)*; Eduard Loessel, Evalyne MacNevin, Marguerite Shannon, Sarah Jeter, C. P. Bartolini, and May Herbert Dalton *(second row)*; and F. Arthur Henkel, Sydney Dalton, and Browne Martin *(third row)*. When Signor de Luca staged a production with mostly local talent of *Cavalleria Rusticana* in 1927 at the Ryman Auditorium *(bottom photo)*, F. Arthur Henkel directed the orchestra (he autographed this photo for Francis Robinson). From left to right on the front row of the stage were John Lewis, Louise Tanksley, Franca Golda, de Luca (director), Blanche Campbell, Arthur Wright, and an unidentified woman.

A. M. Burton, C. R. Clements, T. J. Tyne, E. W. Craig, Rogers Caldwell, P. D. Houston, Horace G. Hill, Luke Lea, and James Stahlman. Henry Colton became the corporate counsel. With those men in his financial corner, de Luca seemed to be on solid footing with his enterprise.

The foreword in the conservatory's catalog noted, "The Nashville Conservatory of Music was founded by a group of distinguished business and professional men who were actuated by a desire to make Nashville the musical center of the South." They regarded it a "great civic enterprise" with similar high standards found in American and European conservatories.

The Nashville Conservatory of Music was incorporated on October 24, 1927 (2,500 shares of 7 percent cumulative preferred stock were offered at $100 per share, and 5,000 unvalued common stock shares were offered to the public; $250,000 in 1927, about $2,600,000 today). When the conservatory opened in the fall of 1928 at 2122 West

The Nashville Conservatory of Music (opened in the fall of 1928) held its concerts and recitals at the Joel O. Cheek Auditorium. Signor Gaetano de Luca was the director.

End Avenue, de Luca was its president and the leader of the voice department. An auditorium, practice rooms, and a dance studio were provided for the students, and recitals by students and faculty, open to the public, would be held frequently.

Faculty members included Wiktor Labunski, Eduard Loessel, and Verna Brackinreed in the piano department; Eric Sorantin headed the violin department and conducted the school orchestra; Sydney Dalton was in the voice department; Dr. Browne Martin was selected to direct the Department of Musical Sciences. (Note: Labunski's assistant was his wife, Wanda, and she was the daughter of a Polish conductor.) F. Arthur Henkel taught organ until he returned to Ward-Belmont, then Leslie Grow and Frederick S. Andrews followed him. Sarah Jeter and Louise Smith began the Department of Dancing and were succeeded by Polly Gerts. May Herbert Dalton taught dramatic art. Other faculty members came and went over the school's lifetime, but quality staff always filled the roster.

Advanced degrees were available only in piano, voice, violin, and organ; after four years of fulfilling curriculum and performance requirements, a student could earn a diploma or a Bachelor of Music degree. After two years, a student would receive a certificate. Tuition depended on the student and the teacher, but for $375 a year an advanced student in voice would receive two, thirty-minute lessons per week from de Luca.

Good and bad news befell the school in the academic year of 1930–31. First the good news: the class was the largest enrolled, students came from several states, and the National Association of Schools of Music certified it (there were only five in the South with certification). Next the bad news: the Great Depression was slow to affect Nashville, *but* the collapse of Rogers Caldwell's empire and Luke Lea's financial woes overburdened the generally depressed economic situation and left de Luca and the conservatory on sinking

Dance Department students in 1929 from the Nashville Conservatory of Music, posing in Centennial Park, were Marian Hussey, Mary Louise Aymard, Marian Curell, Jane Bagley, and Claudia Whitson *(left to right)*.

sand. It managed to stay afloat a few more years, and students continued to receive degrees.

In his article on de Luca and the conservatory, Robert Ikard stated that de Luca "bemoaned a drift away from grand opera in the United States and said the conservatory was adjusting by training for radio, musical comedy, teaching, and 'general culture.' Compromise was necessary for survival." De Luca's hopes about the opera in Nashville that he brought to the citizens' attention in his staging of *Cavalleria Rusticana* and his opening of the conservatory seemed farther away than ever, and in many ways they died when Joel Cheek, a generous supporter, died in 1935. The conservatory could not make it financially. The final blow came when de Luca, who was diagnosed with a pituitary tumor in 1930 that gradually incapacitated him, died on June 19, 1936.

The same year, 1936, the Nashville Conservatory of Music was placed in the hands of a receiver. Although a professional organization for opera in Nashville had not materialized by then, de Luca should have been proud of the accomplishments in the various disciplines at the conservatory and the cultural contributions to the city of Nashville. Signor de Luca showed what could happen when enough money, an interested board, gifted faculty, and talented students came together under the leadership of a visionary leader.

Students of Signor de Luca

Study with Gaetano de Luca;
he's the best teacher in the South today.

—Attributed to Chauncey Olcott,
songwriter and balladeer

AS A VOICE TEACHER, Gaetano de Luca trained pupils at both Ward-Belmont and the Nashville Conservatory of Music who gained fame on the stage of the Metropolitan Opera House and elsewhere.

Joseph T. Macpherson, a baritone, was from Amqui, Tennessee (born 1899, died 1991). He gave concerts in Nashville in 1925 and 1927. In between, he debuted at the Metropolitan Opera House in *Aida* in 1926 and had subsequent roles in other operas. He returned to Nashville after the 1931–32 season and later sang at WSM radio station and in choirs.

Another pupil, born in Moultrie, Georgia, in 1904, James Melton had a long history with Nashville. The story was reported in a 1941 newspaper article about how he came to town. He had wandered into what he thought was an empty ballroom in a hotel in Columbia, South Carolina, played the piano, and sang "Mighty Lak a Rose." A man, who had been listening to him without his knowledge, approached him and said, "Young man, you will some day be a great singer, if you work, and study. You have a very beautiful and unusual voice [he was a tenor]. Go to Nashville, and study with Gaetano de Luca; he's the best teacher in the South today. And if ever you're in New York, look me up for I shall be interested in knowing what you do with this God-given talent of yours." The man was said to be Chauncey Olcott. The more reliable story is the one reported by Robert Ikard: when Francis Craig and his orchestra appeared at Melton's school prom, Melton asked for a job and got it as a tenor and a saxophone player.

In 1923, Melton transferred from the University of Georgia, where he was a junior, to Vanderbilt, and he also studied with de Luca, then at Ward-Belmont. He worked with Francis Craig and his orchestra and made a concert tour of the South in 1926. He set out for New York City in 1927.

Melton managed to get a job on *Roxy's Gang*, which was a variety show broadcast on the NBC-Blue network. (Roxy was Samuel L. Rothafel, a theater impresario who eventually worked with the Rockefellers, building Radio City Music Hall.) Melton made several pictures in Hollywood for Warner Brothers, and *Melody for Two* was created specifically as a vehicle for him. He entered the wide world of classical music when he debuted in 1938 with the Cincinnati Grand Opera Association and then sang with the Chicago Opera Company. He had roles in *La Traviata, Manon, Mignon, Martha, Madame Butterfly,* and *Lucia* (opposite Lily Pons).

In May 1941, Melton appeared in concert at the War Memorial Auditorium under the auspices of the Women's Division of Belmont Methodist Church. In a letter to Francis Robinson, Lula Naff reported that although the women worked hard, there had been poor publicity. Melton's performance was good and there was a full house, although Mrs. Naff referred to the people in the audience as a "motley bunch": church members, Belmont Methodists, shop and YW girls, and very few musicians. Mrs. Naff was on hand when Melton returned in September 1945, and he sang "I Hear You Calling Me." She said, "How well I remember standing in the aisle next to Sec. A, and hearing him sing that on his first visit here. Never shall I hear anything so fine!"

Melton had roles at the Metropolitan Opera beginning in the early 1940s and remained on the roster until 1950. He appeared on the *Texaco Star Theater, The Telephone Hour,* and NBC TV's *Ford Festival* (1951, 1952). He died in 1961. Of the films and CDs available for fans, one CD features him on the *Texaco Star Theater* with Grace Moore (about whom you will find more in this book) and Norman Cordon. The original recording was done in January 1945.

Norman Cordon was hired by the Met in 1935, and he debuted in *Rigoletto* the next year. He retired from the Met in 1946, and when he left New York City, he and his wife settled in Chapel Hill, North Carolina, where he had a radio program on WUNC called *Let's Listen to Opera*.

In April 1928, there was a civic pride concert in Nashville to help raise money for Ablee Stewart and John Allen Lewis so that they could get more training to become opera singers. Stewart joined *Roxy's Gang* in 1930. Lewis was a gifted baritone, who was to direct the West End Methodist choir and four or five other choruses, including the Southern Belles (employees of Southern Bell) and a chorus at a Masonic lodge. If he needed to fill a slot in one chorus, he could call on people from another group with which he worked. For a while, he also had a part in organizing the Sunday afternoon concerts at Centennial Park. At some point Lewis produced *Cavalleria Rusticana* on an outdoor stage at his home. Perhaps he chose that production because of his having appeared in de Luca's production for the city.

Louis Nicholas participated in a chorus at WSM for a couple of years in the mid-1940s, and he said, "They had a group that broadcast on Friday nights. It was a professional group of sixteen singers that John conducted. We got $15 each week. We met early and practiced and then did the broadcast."

Christine Johnson (Smith) worked at WSM a while, went to New York, and sang one year, 1944, with the Metropolitan Opera; her first role was in *das Rheingold*. Johnson next landed a role in the original cast of *Carousel* (1945).

Other students of de Luca who should be mentioned are Blanche Campbell, Aleda Waggoner, Tom Fletcher, Katherine Kirkham, Helen Todd Sloan, and Eugene Bugg.

~

St. Denis, Shawn, and Modern Dance

The religion of the future will be expressed by the dance.

—RUTH ST. DENIS, 1929

RUTH ST. DENIS (1879?–1968) and Ted Shawn (1891–1972) founded the Denishawn school in 1915. They became a leading couple of dance, and their pupils included Martha Graham, Charles Weidman, and Doris Humphrey, among others. Nashville's Jeter and Smith were also their pupils, and even though they did not achieve worldwide fame, they had a significant impact on Nashville. Both St. Denis and Shawn danced and taught in the city. The relationship of the four was long-lasting, although the bond of Jeter and Smith was perhaps stronger with Shawn.

Shawn was an unlikely man to have become so influential in dance. He set out to become a minister, but at college he was stricken with diphtheria. He recovered only partially—he was unable to walk—and he decided against the ministry because he was determined to overcome his disability and become a dancer. It required some time and a lot of physical and dance training, but he did it.

St. Denis had danced in Nashville at least twice in the 1920s (January 1921 and December 1922) before an engagement on October 29, 1929. A reporter for the *Banner*, Eleanor Hall, interviewed her while she was staying at the Andrew Jackson Hotel, and St. Denis expressed her strong opinions about the future of the dance: "The spiritual consciousness of the people will be released through the rhythm, tone, and color of the dance. Through this means, the thousand shades of each emotion expresses itself." She could not bear to discuss jazz, "a folk dance," but expounded that "the dance is the act of synthesizing art and religion, a place for focusing those elements of beauty to be found in the world."

Her words were a bit ethereal, but she and Shawn showed what she meant at the Ryman. The critic George Pullen Jackson glowingly stated, "The more one sees of Ted Shawn's and Ruth St. Denis' work, the more one is convinced that the art of bodily rythmic [sic] movement, for centuries neglected in favor of its sister arts, is being carried to new heights of attainment." Each costume of St. Denis "was such a treat for the eye and the imagination that it was hard to pick out the most beautiful." Shawn, on the other hand, gained attention for his lack of costumes, "for there was so little of them. He is an Apollo. And such gods use no clothing. His apollonic nature was best shown perhaps in the Cosmic Dance of Siva, in which he exhibited plastic posing and story-telling dancing to the nth degree of perfection." Jackson concluded, "It was quite evident that this leader among artistic dancers and dance creators [St. Denis] is still perfectly able in all the angles of the arts that are worth while. It is only in the matter of what dancers call 'elevation' and what ordinary folks call 'high jumping' where she defers to her more youthful partner."

St. Denis returned to Nashville in June 1930 to teach at the Nashville Conservatory of Music and to take voice lessons with Signor de Luca for three weeks. (Francis Robinson believed that her friendship with Jeter and Smith was directly responsible for her agreement to take on the teaching assignment.) She swore Jeter and Smith to secrecy on the voice lessons, however; as far as most people knew, she was in town as a teacher, not a student. She had thirty advanced students and teachers from Nashville and other cities.

Jeter and Smith were struck by what happened during one session:

> One humid day with temperature soaring to almost 100 degrees, Miss Ruth led us through a lovely Schubert waltz with vigorous leaps as well as lyrical movements. Hot and dripping, we went through the steps rather languidly. As the dance ended Miss Ruth turned on us with snapping blue eyes and said, "You move like fifty-year-old women! I *am* fifty" (actually about 54) "but you will *never* see me dancing like that. Sit down on the floor and watch this." We watched as she gave an electrifying performance that brought the class to its feet in a standing ovation.

She must have enjoyed her stay because she wrote the pair from her studio at Steinway Hall in New York, thanking them and noting that her memories were happy ones.

St. Denis and Shawn separated shortly afterward, and Shawn began in 1933 to work with the group that became his Men Dancers. They trained at Jacob's Pillow, the summer camp in Massachusetts. They came to the Ryman on Tuesday, February 5, 1935, and then on Wednesday, February 10, 1937, they appeared at the Orpheum Theater, with the latter appearance sponsored by Jeter and Smith's Dance Center.

The large audience, including many girls and many dance students, could choose tickets of $1.10, $1.65, or $2.20 ($2.20 then, about $28 today). Reviewer Sydney Dalton observed, "One is impressed . . . with the fact that a man may be quite as graceful and beautiful in bodily movement as a woman and still be a man. Of course, the Greeks knew this centuries ago, and it is well that we are reminded of it today." The program had four parts: "Primitive Rhythms," "Kinetic Molpai," "Folk and Art Themes," and "Religious Dances." Jess Meeker at the piano furnished all the music, and he composed much of it.

Shawn and His Men Dancers appeared at the Ryman Auditorium on the evening of April 25, 1938, with Sarah Jeter and her Dance Center Concert Group as guest artists. Jeter's group had four numbers; two were Shawn's compositions, and Jeter choreographed two. One of Shawn's was "Extase," danced to music of the same name by Louis Ganne and inspired by William Blake's illustrations for the biblical book of Job. Jeter's "Song of the Bayou" had attracted Shawn's attention in the first place, and she danced with the group. Louise Smith accompanied them.

Shawn's part of the program was "O, Libertad!"—created by Shawn and Jess Meeker. It was in three acts, representing past, present, and future. In the course of the evening he and his men danced as characters in the drama between Moctezuma, the Aztecs, and the Spaniards;

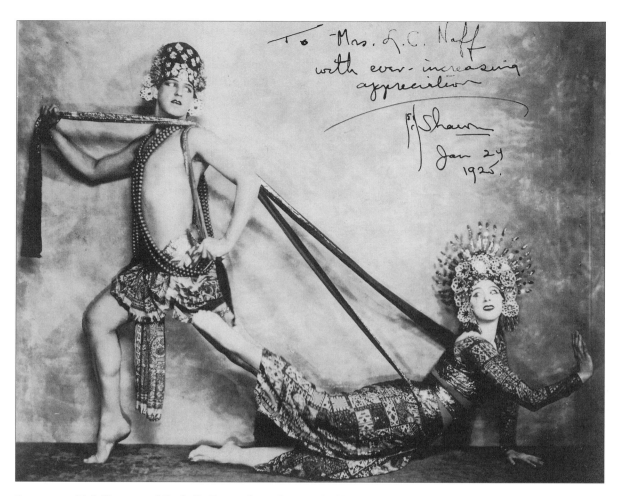

Innovators Ted Shawn and Ruth St. Denis danced in Nashville several times in the first half of the twentieth century; Shawn autographed this to Lula Naff, January 24, 1925.

Olympic athletes; basketball players; and "empty-headed youths" of the Jazz Age.

From June 13 to July 2, 1938, Shawn gave special courses in the dance at George Peabody College for Teachers. His assistants were dancer Barton Mumaw and accompanist Jess Meeker. Shawn's first teaching assignment in town had come the year before, in June, when he spent just one week in the Department of Physical and Health Education. No other institution in the South had offered a similar program. The person chiefly responsible was Clara Haddox, assistant professor of physical education and a student of Shawn. She had talked President Bruce R. Payne into making Shawn the offer. With much trepidation he did because no one knew really knew whether anybody would choose to take the course.

Peabody's summer bulletin announced it, and wham! Reservations poured in. The women's group and the men's group were full. Even Shawn was surprised at the numbers of men who were interested. A special bus from Texas brought some fans of Shawn who wanted to study with him. In addition to his course Shawn spoke several times at the college chapel. School authorities were so impressed with him and his work in 1937 that they made arrangements with him for the three weeks in 1938.

Shawn, Jeter, and Smith saw each other often when the latter two went to the Northeast in their dancing days. Later in life, long after the war, Jeter not only worked briefly for him at Jacob's Pillow but also recorded ten hours of tape with Shawn in the last summer of his life (1971). These personal relationships created artistic opportunities for Nashvillians that might not have been possible otherwise.

John Wesley Work III

He was a musician, and it was his life—like breathing.

—Mrs. John W. Work III

THE WHOLE WORK FAMILY felt the importance of music in their lives, and Fisk University was the base for many of their endeavors, enabling them to invigorate the lives of students and faculty. (Work III here refers to the main focus of this study; his grandfather was John Wesley Work, and his father, John Wesley Work II or Jr.)

John Wesley Work was born a slave, and when he was quite young, he learned French and an appreciation of music in New Orleans. In that city he attended opera rehearsals whenever he could. After the Civil War, Work directed the choir in the church in Nashville that became First Baptist Church, Capitol Hill, and members of the original Fisk Jubilee Singers sang with his choir.

John Wesley Work II attended Fisk (B.A. 1894; M.A. 1898), where he later taught Latin and Greek and eventually served as chairman of the Latin and history departments. He lent his talents to the Fisk Jubilee Quartet in 1909, joined by Alfred G. King, N. W. Ryder, and James A.

Myers. Beginning in 1913, Work II directed the Fisk students in Jubilee concerts at the Ryman. His wife, Agnes Haynes Work, later helped train the Fisk group. (For some periods there was no official group of Fisk Jubilee Singers, made up of male and female voices, sponsored by Fisk University.) Work II was also dedicated to preserving African-American folk music. *New Jubilee Songs as Sung by the Fisk Jubilee Singers* and *Folk Songs of the American Negro* are results of this interest, and he collaborated with Frederick Jerome Work (brother of Work II and uncle of Work III) on those titles. In addition to collecting folk songs, Frederick was a composer, and his F Major String Quartet was played in May 1934 at the Philadelphia Art Alliance's Annual Concert of Manuscript Music.

Other children of Work II had musical careers. Julian Cassander Work was a professional musician and composer, who moved away from Nashville and spent his adult years in New England. Following in the steps of her grandfather, Helen Elizabeth Work was minister of music at First Baptist Church, Capitol Hill, from 1952 to 1968, and she taught history and also served as a librarian in Nashville's public school system. Frances Work Alston, a music major at Fisk, was a vocal music teacher in Nashville's public schools.

John Wesley Work III (1901–67) became an educator, choral director, and composer at Fisk, even though his degree from that university was in history (B.A. 1923). He had training in music and music theory, and he loved music so much that he desired to become a professional singer. Yet he loved athletics, too. Music majors at Fisk had to attend too many rehearsals and play in too many concerts that would have interfered with his participation in football and basketball. He married Edith McFall, daughter of John A. McFall and a native of Charleston, South Carolina. She, too, was a Fisk graduate.

Work III studied at the Institute of Musical Art in New York City (now the Juilliard School of Music), but family obligations brought him back to Fisk to teach. He eventually received his master's degree from Columbia University, and with the assistance of two Julius Rosenwald Foundation Fellowships (1931–33), he took a leave of absence from Fisk to obtain his B.Mus. degree from Yale.

The positions he held at Fisk included teacher, director of the Fisk Jubilee Singers (1947–56), and chairman of the Department of Music. Upon his appointment as chairman, a writer for the *Nashville Globe* stated, "It is more than probable Prof. Work could have been serving as director in some of the other great colleges of the country for a long time had he chosen to leave Nashville. But he has remained steadfast and loyal" to Fisk, which he and his "father did so much to keep famous for its vocal music." As director of the Singers, he rebuilt the group as an ensemble of male and female voices. Matthew Kennedy succeeded Work III as director of the Singers, and he noted, "The repertoire was more varied with Mr. Work and me; he had classical works *and* spirituals, and I continued with that." (The emphasis had often been solely on spirituals.)

Work III wrote "Mandy Lou" as a teen, and after that he became a prolific composer, finishing more than one hundred compositions. He composed for orchestra, piano, violin, and organ, but his largest body of compositions was for choral groups (such as *A Child This Day Is Born, Isaac Watts Contemplates the Cross*, and *The Singers* [a cantata based on a poem by Henry Wadsworth Longfellow]). He also arranged spirituals. Many of his works were performed in Nashville beyond the Fisk campus. For example, on November 13, 1955, Fisk faculty and students gave a concert of his vocal and instrumental compositions at First Baptist Church, Capitol

The three generations of the Work family, who were so important to the musical life of Fisk University and of Nashville, about 1920: John Wesley Work II, John Wesley Work, and John Wesley Work III *(left to right)*.

Hill, where a similar concert had been held in 1938.

A book and recordings preserve the research efforts of Work III. In 1940 he published *American Negro Songs and Spirituals*, which he edited; it is a collection of religious and secular folk songs. He and his colleagues gained support from the Library of Congress's Archive of the American Folk Song for two projects. The first was *"Now What a Time": Blues, Gospel, and the Fort Valley Music Festivals, 1938–1943*, which Work III, Lewis Jones (a sociology professor at Fisk), and Willis Laurence James (a summer faculty member at Fort Valley State College) documented. The second was carried out by Lewis Jones, Charles S. Johnson (head of Fisk's sociology department), Work III, and Alan Lomax of the

Library of Congress in the summers of 1941 and 1942 in the Mississippi Delta. It is cited as Library of Congress/Fisk University Mississippi Delta Collection (AFC 1941/002). The CD *Negro Blues and Hollers,* now available from Rounder Records, features recordings gathered by Work III, Jones, and Lomax. The Center for Popular Music at Middle Tennessee State University has in its collection some instantaneous discs of recordings by Work III. Fisk awarded him an honorary doctorate of music in 1963, and the citation read: "As an interpreter and arranger of the Negro spiritual, you have no peer, for you have understood so deeply the heart which gave it birth."

Following his death in 1967, a *Banner* editorial observed, "As composer, arranger, and teacher, his professional skills matched the devotion and scholarship of a life dedicated to high standards in the total range of good citizenship. Death does not silence the song." Beyond his compositions that have survived his death, the John W. Work III Memorial Foundation Scholarship is offered through the Community Foundation of Middle Tennessee, and recipients are to be "undergraduate juniors, seniors, or graduate students, especially African American, pursuing a degree in music at an accredited university, college or institute." They must have demonstrated a "potential for excellence in music." John W. Work III, whose life was music, would have expected no less from the students.

Nashville Children's Theatre

Nashville Children's Theatre is an ensemble of professional artists who bring unique vision and compelling voice to the creation of meaningful theatre for young audiences. At NCT, we strive to make live theatre a vital part of the childhood experience for young people throughout Nashville and Middle Tennessee.

—MISSION STATEMENT OF NCT

A SERVICE PROJECT begun in 1931 by Nashville's Junior League has blossomed into the oldest surviving children's theater in the country: Nashville Children's Theatre (NCT), now located at 724 Second Avenue South. Junior Leagues in cities such as Lexington, Birmingham, and Charlotte followed Nashville's lead and formed their own children's theaters, so the influence of a determined group of women has been felt throughout the South. In her master's thesis about the NCT, Frances E. Daniel summarized the reasons behind its long-lasting success:

(1) sound leadership, determined volunteers, and capable directors, (2) financial stability, (3) community support, (4) local press interest, and (5) a board with a clearly defined plan.

The first season included productions of *Aladdin and His Wonderful Lamp* and *Alice in Wonderland*. In the early days actors were adults from the Junior League, and the plays were held at the Hillsboro Theatre, which had to be shared with the Little Theatre Guild. The first year that children were in the casts was 1937. One child actor was Claude Jarman Jr., who had appeared in a production of *The Garden Circus*. When Clarence Brown, a producer/director, was seeking a young actor for the movie *The Yearling,* he selected Claude. Claude was the recipient of a special Academy Award for outstanding child actor of 1946.

Eventually chartered as a nonprofit educational community organization, NCT needed its own space to better serve the community's children. A theater was built after the City Council passed an addition to a major bond issue, which included funds for the NCT, in 1959. The funds were for the building only, however, and the NCT board of directors oversaw the raising of $10,000 in individual contributions from the public to equip it. A comment that appeared in the *Southern Theatre News* has a familiar refrain about the city fathers: "This is the realization of a dream and the result of three years' hard work convincing politicians and city fathers of its worth to the community." Having its own building has been a boon for NCT, and it is a very busy place.

The NCT season lasts thirty weeks, and about 65,000 schoolchildren attend the School Performance Series. Other NCT efforts include an after-school workshop, afternoon drama programs at schools, weekend workshops at NCT, and summer drama camps.

Both traditional plays and new works are presented. In the traditional category children have enjoyed *Tom Sawyer, Cinderella, Reynard the Fox,* and *Treasure Island.* New plays and adaptations have included *Trickster Tales, Devon's Hurt,* and *Selkie.* NCT also produces works that have premiered across the country, such as *Sing Down the Moon* and *And Then They Came for Me: Remembering the World of Anne Frank.* The 2002–3 season scheduled *House at Pooh Corner, Sir Gawain and the Green Knight, Charlotte's Web, Bridge to Terabithia,* and *Lilly's Purple Plastic Purse.* The managing director is Allison L. Dillon, and the producing director is Scot E. Copeland.

What Others Were Saying About Nashville

Like every southern city, [Nashville] lives on inconsistencies.

—EDD WINFIELD PARKS

CULTURE IN THE SOUTH, edited by W. T. Couch and published in 1935, presented essays by various authors who offered their appraisals of the South generally—and of Nashville and other cities specifically—in the early years of the Great Depression.

Ula Milner Gregory surveyed the nation's musicians and said, "The majority of musicians in the South are obliged to teach most of the time, opportunities for concert appearances being almost entirely limited to programs at club meetings. The radio is affording some further outlet but as jazz programs are still most in demand, it is not a very ample one. Symphony orchestras are not widely or adequately supported in the South." Yet she named eight southern orchestras in the second tier (meaning they were of "less certain" financial status)—Mobile, Atlanta, Rome (Georgia), New Orleans, Charleston, Nashville, Dallas,

and a state orchestra in North Carolina. She added, "They are giving their communities each year the opportunity of hearing musical compositions that could be heard in no other way. . . . It is unfortunate, however, that more do not exist and that several of those that give promise of achievement are not established on a firm financial basis, without which it seems practically impossible for them to come to full fruition."

Dance was not doing as well as music, Gregory pointed out. "Dancing has perhaps had more place in the life of the South in the past than in that of any other part of the country. It has long been one of the widely enjoyed southern social diversions. But here, as elsewhere, the conception of it has been limited to its social or professional aspects. Now the South is also alive to the growing consciousness of the dance as an art." She did not list Nashville as one of the cities—Dallas, Atlanta, Birmingham, and Richmond—with this consciousness. She conceded that some cities were adding dance companies, such as the one led by Ted Shawn, to concert series, and that was as far as they were willing to go in their support of dance.

Acknowledging the decline of touring companies that brought drama to southern cities, she had high hopes for the Little Theatre movement to satisfy the dramatic thirst: "There is no reason why the South can not have as good little theatres as any other section of the country. . . . All that is required for success is local talent, intellect, and pride."

From Charleston, South Carolina, Josephine Pinckney's subject was change, and she wrote, "The stoutest bulwark against the forces of change is undoubtedly the natural conservatism of the southern mind." She observed that Nashville "resembles the new South in its outward conformation though its tempo is of the old and its propensities are toward conversation in the best sense, as opposed to mere talk—chiefly, one suspects, because of the presence there of the strongest and most original literary group in the South."

Edd Winfield Parks had more to say about Nashville:

Compared with Atlanta, Nashville seems an overgrown small town, with narrow and out-moded streets, grimy old buildings, and the settled placidity of middle age. This, however, is only a half-picture. Once it was a frontier town, but those days are completely past, and long since forgotten; today it is "the Athens of the South," boasting of fine educational institutions and of grand old days, yet reaching somewhat reluctantly for new commercial projects. It has Vanderbilt, Peabody, Ward-Belmont, and Fisk: the four extremes in modern education. For Vanderbilt represents the old-line classical college that has branched out into a large university; Peabody, the modernized institution that believes men can be transformed into teachers if they are taught the correct methods; Ward-Belmont remains an outstanding boarding school for well-to-do young ladies; and Fisk is preeminent in the field of cultural education for Negroes. Here are four radically different schools, in a city that rebuilds the Greek Parthenon, and now puts on, through its Chamber of Commerce, a five-year plan to lure new industries from the North. A divided city, that prizes on the one side, Friendly Five shoes [the name came from the sale price of $5 (about $65 today); Jarman Shoe Company (which eventually became Genesco) of Nashville manufactured them, beginning in 1924]—and, on the other, the Hermitage. Like every southern city, it lives on inconsistencies: allows baseball on Sundays, yet forbids movies; prides itself on culture, but has no decent theatre and is shunned even by road shows [Parks obviously was commenting on the Ryman, but we know that road shows were stopping at least briefly in Nashville]; points with pride to historical tradition while it seeks the very things that, inevitably, must destroy the value and the validity of those traditions.

Two Young Men and *Julius Caesar*

*There is something electric
about Nashville's creative atmosphere,
and two young men at the top of the TV industry
are striking evidence of it.*

—Louise Davis

THE TWO YOUNG MEN were Fred Coe and Delbert Mann, and the friendship that began in Nashville lasted forty years and took them through critically acclaimed work in TV, theater, and movies. They had first worked together on Nashville Community Playhouse's production of *Julius Caesar* in August 1939. It was not a typical staging of the play, either. Coe, then at Yale University School of Drama where he had been for a year, had cut and adapted the Shakespearean play and decided to use modern dress. The clothing of the women suggested the flowing draperies of Rome, and the men wore green shirts and military pants. The setting, lighting, and casting were good, but it was hard to hear some of the dialogue, said the reviewer, who enjoyed the production but added, "Whether the classic doesn't lose perhaps too much in being adapted to a revelation of modern Fascist thought is not a fit subject for debate here."

An unplanned part of the evening literally cost Julius Caesar, played by Thomas Donner, his blood. No one was sure how it happened, but Donner was wounded in the famous scene and the line "Then fall, Caesar!" was vividly accurate. Soldiering on, Donner was patched up between scenes and made his appearance as the ghostly Caesar. After the show he was taken to Vanderbilt Hospital where he received five stitches in his side. Ever the trouper he returned the next night, but the swords were taped to avoid another accident.

In addition to Mann and Donner, the players were Putt Reynolds, John Wands, Leslie Stern, Henry Clay Evans, Ed Hussey, Robert Booth, Hamilton Douglas, Richard Dunn, Billy Burroughs, Walter Ferguson, Sam Gooch, Scott Haddox, Opal Thompson, Felice Petrucelli, Rebecca Rice Lunn, Bill Keyser, H. G. Fentress, and Charles Edwards. The stage manager was James Bailey.

Both Coe and Mann attended schools in Nashville, although neither was born in Tennessee. At Peabody Demonstration School, Coe made evident his interest in drama. He was a member of Hillsboro Presbyterian Church that had dramatic activities for its young people, and when Fritz Kleibacker arrived in 1936 to work at the Community Playhouse, the young people jumped at the chance to participate in the happenings there. At George Peabody College for Teachers as a student, Coe was president of the Peabody Players, a dramatic club. When William Inge, who would later write *Picnic* and other Broadway hits, was at Peabody pursuing his master's degree in 1938, he and Coe worked briefly together on plays. Coe was the man behind some radio dramas broadcast on WSM, but he really made his name in television after he left Nashville. His TV credits include *Philco TV Playhouse/Goodyear TV Playhouse* and *Playhouse 90,* and he won an Emmy Award in 1955. He produced plays for Broadway (*The Miracle Worker, Two for the Seesaw, A Trip to Bountiful, All the Way Home,* and *Wait Until Dark*), and he produced the films *The Miracle Worker* and *A Thousand Clowns.* He died in 1979, and his longtime friend Mann established the Fred Coe Artist in Residence Series at Vanderbilt University in the late 1980s. Vanderbilt Theatre students have had an opportunity since then to attend a master seminar taught by guest artists, such as Olympia Dukakis, Fiona Shaw, and Karl Malden.

Mann's father brought the family to Nashville when he secured a teaching position at Scarritt College. Young Delbert went to Tarbox School, Hume-Fogg High School, and Vanderbilt University. Mann was the head of the Hume-Fogg Dramatic Club and learned from Inez Barrett Alder, the teacher of dramatic art in the city schools. Mann spent much of the summers of 1938 to 1940 laboring in the Nashville Community Playhouse. He, too, attended Yale's School of Drama. In a 1955 interview with Louise Davis, he said of the Community Playhouse days: "The whole atmosphere in Nashville was stimulating." With help and encouragement from Coe, Mann stepped into the world of live television, and his work on the *Goodyear TV Playhouse* production of *Marty* (1953) led him to the film world, where he won an Oscar for directing the film version in 1955. For television he directed *Jane Eyre, The Man Without a Country, All Quiet on the Western Front, All the Way Home,* and *April Morning;* a few of his films are *Desire Under the Elms, Separate Tables,* and *That Touch of Mink.* Despite his absence from Nashville for many years, Mann has generously donated his papers to the Special Collections of the Jean and Alexander Heard Library of Vanderbilt University, and he is a valued emeritus member of Vanderbilt's Board of Trust. Delbert and his late wife, Ann, have brought their own brand of Hollywood glamour back to Nashville for decades—gentle charms and irresistible twinkles.

~

Our Man at the Met

The public educated by the broadcasts from the Met is needy now for opera as it has never been before.

—Francis Robinson, 1943

AT THE METROPOLITAN Opera House, February 20, 1982, Verdi's *Requiem* was the

Francis Robinson was "our man at the Met" (the Metropolitan Opera House), and he had a speaking role in Mozart's *Impresario* there in 1974.

Saturday afternoon radio broadcast with Leontyne Price, Marilyn Horne, Placido Domingo, and John Cheek. It was a special event in memory of Francis Robinson, who had been Nashville's man at the Met for years until his death on May 14, 1980. As a little boy of seven, Francis had first heard Caruso when a saleswoman selling the Victor Talking Machine played a record for him. He created the book *Caruso: His Life in Pictures* after years of actually working at the Metropolitan Opera House with the greatest talents in the world of opera. In fact, he became known as "Mr. Metropolitan."

The path from Mount Pleasant, Tennessee, where he and his family had moved in 1917, to New York City took Francis through Nashville. He attended Vanderbilt University with the help of a scholarship. He tried out in December 1927

for the Vanderbilt Singers, and Arthur W. Wright gave him excellent overall ratings and a place in the group. Francis sang in the second annual concert of the Vanderbilt Singers in Alumni Hall, May 13, 1928, and as a senior in 1932, he participated in an April production of *Faust.*

In October 1923 at the Ryman Auditorium, he had seen *La Traviata* (a Friday matinee) for the first time. While he was a student at Vanderbilt, Francis was the head usher at the Ryman, which proved to be a fortuitous connection for him and for Nashville. Not only was he able to enjoy any production that came to the auditorium, but he formed a lifelong friendship with Lula Naff, manager of the Ryman. As Francis moved out into the world of theater and opera, he maintained his ties to Nashville and promoted the city to performers. He also returned occasionally to give a talk on things theatrical from an insider's point of view.

Other jobs that Francis held in Nashville included being the theater reporter for the *Banner* and working at WSM radio station. He left in 1938 to work for William Fields, a theatrical press agent, and before his press agent days were over, he could count Cornelia Otis Skinner, Alexander Woollcott, Walter Huston, Raymond Massey, and Katharine Cornell as his clients.

An episode that occurred during World War II reveals something about culture in Nashville then. Francis heard about an army officer and his wife stationed in Nashville who repeatedly and loudly deplored the lack of culture in the city. The officer happened to be a sixth-generation New Yorker. At a party Edwin Keeble had to respond to the officer in the midst of one of these diatribes. Referring to Edwin as "one of the best minds I have ever come up against," Francis reported that Edwin "silenced them [the man and his wife from New York] for a time anyway with this information. . . . When anything good ever comes to Nashville, he said, about five thousand people attend. That, he pointed out, is about three per cent of the population. Now can New York show a similar percentage supporting the arts?" At that point, 3 percent of New York City would have meant 240,000 at the Metropolitan Opera House.

After WWII Francis got a break with Sol Hurok, who managed the Metropolitan Opera's annual tours, and Francis became tour manager. As much as he would have liked it, he could not schedule Nashville because there was no appropriate venue for a complete opera. Atlanta and Memphis were opera-loving cities and became regular stops on the tour. Some Nashvillians made the pilgrimages each year to these two cities but apparently never worked to see that Nashville had a theater suitable for opera. Francis subsequently held other jobs at the Met, including assistant manager and host of *Live from the Met* television broadcasts. His "Musical Biography of Grace Moore," a native Tennessean, was one of the first in that series. Although he had other job offers, from the San Francisco Symphony and from Lee and J. J. Shubert, owners of New York theaters, Francis remained loyal to the Met. He also wrote the book *Celebration: The Metropolitan Opera*, which appeared in 1979.

A few points he made about the Met in his book are relevant for the discussion of the performing arts odyssey in Nashville. Francis felt that private philanthropy should be the basis of the Metropolitan's financial support, and it had a track record of that support. Some people assume that the Metropolitan Opera House has had a magical history, untouched by hard times, but that is far from the case.

The Metropolitan Opera House came into existence because old money would not allow new money into the Academy of Music. The newly wealthy Vanderbilts and Goulds, led by Alva Vanderbilt, built their own opera house, the Met, which opened in 1883. The first season lost $300,000 because of poor attendance, yet the Met

outlived the elitist Academy of Music. In essence the new philanthropists had created a real estate company, just leasing the building. This became quite apparent after a fire destroyed the auditorium (1892), and the Metropolitan Opera-house Company sold the building to satisfy judgments after the fire. The Metropolitan Opera and Real Estate Company, which had thirty-five shareholders—the Vanderbilts, J. P. Morgan, and A. D. Juilliard at the top of the list—purchased the property and began reconstruction in 1893.

When he was at Bayreuth, Germany (the shrine for Wagnerian opera), in 1891, Mark Twain had written an essay about the opera there. He pointed out the difference between German and American audiences, using the Met as an example:

Here the Wagner audience dress as they please, and sit in the dark and worship in silence. At the Metropolitan in New York they sit in a glare, and wear their showiest harness; they hum airs, they squeak fans, they titter, and they gabble all the time. In some of the boxes the conversation and laughter are so loud as to divide the attention of the house with the stage. In large measure the Metropolitan is a show-case for rich fashionables who are not trained in Wagnerian music and have no reverence for it, but who like to promote art and show their clothes.

Comments about Nashville audiences by theater critics and actors of the period may not sound so negative in comparison.

For some years Otto Kahn, banker and patron of the arts, made up any deficits at the Metropolitan Opera, but he died in 1934 and the Great Depression did not spare any group. Faced with the Opera's serious financial crunch in 1935, Mrs. August Belmont organized the first campaign for funds, which was a success, and she was also responsible for forming the Metropolitan Opera Guild. The next major crisis occurred in

Our Other Man at the Met

When the Metropolitan Opera Company was having problems making ends meet, three times George A. Sloan, a Nashville native, stepped in as a leader. On the Opera board since 1936, Sloan was integral in the 1940 campaign to raise more than $1 million to purchase the opera house.

Sloan knew firsthand about the costs associated with the Opera. There were only a set number of seats in the opera house and therefore only a maximum number of tickets that could be sold per performance; the most expensive tickets cost $7.50 (about $51 today) and the market could not bear a higher price. Building a larger opera house was out of the question—there was no money and a much-larger house was not conducive to the greatest experience for the audience (Sloan felt that the Opera was at its best in a smaller hall, not in one seating almost ten thousand, as in Cleveland). The expense to build new sets for older operas was prohibitive. In 1949, there were 105 artists, a chorus of 78, an orchestra of 92, a ballet of 36, stagehands, maintenance crew, and other employees to a maximum payroll of 580 persons. Opposed to the government subsidy of music as found in Europe, the board of the Metropolitan Opera sought relief from the tax that amounted to $400,000 in 1948.

Sloan became president and then chairman of the board (1946), and he was in that position when the Opera was facing a critical shortfall in the early 1950s. As part of the campaign, he asked Nashvillians for $1,000. (The operating deficit in 1950–51 was almost $463,000.) He beseeched Congress to repeal the tax on nonprofit musical organizations, which was hurting not just the Opera, and was successful in having it repealed in time for the opening of the 1951–52 season. As a result, the Met was able to reap 20 percent more (the previous amount of the tax) from ticket sales without a change in ticket prices and keep its financial head above water.

Nevertheless, by 1953, Sloan was leading the appeal for $1.5 million (about $10.25 million today). He died at the age of sixty-one in 1955, within months of his resignation from the Opera board, which had been precipitated by his extensive business commitments.

Sloan was the eldest son of Paul Lowe and Anne Joy Sloan. A graduate of Montgomery Bell Academy and Vanderbilt University Law School, he devoted more of his energies to sports than to music in his school days. He said that as a youngster, he "gave up the piano lessons of Professor Will Haury for the lure of baseball, football, and the old swimming hole," and he did not make it into Vanderbilt's Glee Club. After his tour of duty in Europe during World War I, he held positions in the American National Red Cross, Copper and Brass Research Institute, and Cotton Textile Institute—these are just a few of his jobs—so his work life kept him in businesses unrelated to music or opera. He did love music and started attending the Metropolitan Opera in 1922 when he moved to New York City. He was a fellow of the American Academy of Arts and Sciences, and in 1940 he received an award from the National Committee for Music Appreciation for his work at the Met, and in 1948 a plaque from the National Music League for efforts on behalf of young American musicians. Sloan married Florence Lincoln Rockefeller in 1929.

1940 when the Metropolitan Opera Association needed to buy the opera house and the land from the real estate company. The Met has had an impact on people nationwide, not just through seeing live performances but through hearing opera on the radio (and later viewing TV broadcasts), and they did their share. One-third of the funds came from purchase of bonds, one-third from the radio audience, and one-third from the guild. In the early 1950s another threat almost brought down the curtain—a tax on nonprofit musical organizations.

When he left Nashville in the late 1930s, Francis was technically on leave of absence from WSM; his position was never canceled. As late as the spring of 1951, Jack DeWitt asked him if he would be interested in coming back to WSM. Francis was by then committed to the Met, which was having to fight for its survival. He wrote to Mrs. Naff: "Mr. Sloan has said that if we don't get the twenty percent tax taken off we will have to close after next year. However, I think we will always somehow be a Metropolitan." The tax was repealed, but not without help from George Sloan and others. (See "Our Other Man at the Met.") The Met has had numerous ups and downs since then.

In a 1958 speech given at Vanderbilt University's Neely Memorial Auditorium, Francis told the audience, "We can't begin to supply the demand for opera in this country. . . . We haven't the houses for it. But opera houses are coming, one of these days." He thought that a sign of "democratization" of opera was a planned new opera house for New York City, which had not had a new theater since 1928. He also noted that there were seven hundred community operas in the United States. (Nashville was not one of them then; Francis did not state that to the group, but it was a fact.) He quoted a fellow who said, "There are millions of people in this world, hungry for music, who don't know what's wrong with them." On the subject of opera's appeal, he referred to the sextet in *Lucia di Lammermoor* and explained, "Think of six persons on the stage, all pouring out divergent emotions—and all in one beautiful sound. . . . All you have to do to get to like opera is to get to know it." In July 1974 Francis realized a dream of being on the stage in the title role of Mozart's *Impresario*; Julius Rudel cast him in the nonsinging role, but he did have several lines.

Nashvillians could count on Francis to make their visits to New York City memorable. One who benefited was Louise LeQuire, and she recently said, "Whenever I went to New York, it seems that Francis Robinson would get me tickets." Louis Nicholas, an old friend, met with Francis often when he went to New York to attend the opera, and Francis introduced him to everybody from Lotte Lehman to Rudolf Bing. Mr. Nicholas said, "Rudolf Bing tried to get Francis to write his biography. When he told Francis the kind of book he wanted—frank about everybody and everything—Francis refused. He didn't want anybody mad at him." Arts reviewer John Bridges never had the opportunity to meet Francis, but he had spoken to him a couple of times on the telephone. John summed up Francis's attitude: "He was so excited to be doing what he was doing, and he understood the privilege of what he was doing."

Some have said that the Met is not the same without Francis and his gentlemanly way of handling difficult artists. Nashville certainly misses the rare connection that was in place for so long.

TSU's Track Record . . . in Dramatic Art

My biggest reward has been in sending out worthwhile students to work in the field of dramatic art and stimulate interest in it among black people.

—THOMAS E. POAG

TENNESSEE STATE UNIVERSITY has had many athletes with outstanding records, such as Wilma Rudolph and Ralph Boston, who have achieved national and international recognition. Over in the Department of Speech and Drama (now Department of Communications) Thomas Edward Poag (1907–74) was setting records of a different kind in an endurance race toward excellence. Although he had played football at

Dr. Thomas E. Poag of Tennessee State University received the Theta Alphi Phi Medallion for excellence in educational theater *(right)*.   Faculty members in the Department of Speech and Drama congratulated him on the honor: Mrs. Rosa Dunning, Mrs. Carol Barach, and Miss Bertha Smith *(left to right)*.   *A Raisin in the Sun* was a featured production for the semicentennial of Tennessee State University, November 6–8, 1961 *(below)*.

Morgan State College, he came to the TSU campus (then Tennessee A & I State College) in 1939 with a master's degree in speech therapy (and a minor in speech) from Ohio State University and a Ph.D. in drama, theater, and speech from Cornell University. He was the first African-American to receive a Ph.D. in drama and theater. Following an interview with Poag at the time of his retirement (1973), Clara Hieronymus wrote that he was "a walking, talking landmark, a historical site in human form whose personal history has many parallels in theater history."

TSU's Department of English offered a minor in speech beginning in 1939, and two of the required courses were community theater and stagecraft. Four years later, Poag organized the Department of Speech and Drama, and he remained department chairman until he retired thirty years later. He also served as the dean of the School of Arts and Sciences.

Poag brought practical experience as well as academic qualifications to the campus. He had a role in the movie *The Emperor Jones,* starring Paul Robeson, in 1933. At Ohio State he founded the Civic Theater Guild in Columbus and directed and produced there. He founded the Tennessee State Players Guild and directed their productions including *The Emperor Jones, Inherit the Wind* (with Moses Gunn, Joan Bell Pryor, Bill Pryor, and Madelyn Houston), and *The Tragedy of Martin Luther King Jr.* (The group is now known as the T. E. Poag Players Guild.) Poag accompanied his actors on three international tours of military installations (1960, 1965, and 1970), sponsored by the American Educational Theater Association, the USO, and the U.S. Department of Defense.

Poag's talents extended to writing plays and giving speeches. His plays, *The Golden Heritage (The TSU Story), The Z. Alexander Looby Story,* and *The Clark Memorial United Methodist Church Heritage,* had local themes. He presented speeches at colleges, churches, and theaters, and the titles of two of his addresses—"The Negro in Drama from the Greeks to the Present" and "Better Human Relations Through the Medium of Dramatic Art"—indicate where his passions lay.

His attempts to provide quality programs and productions were not without hurdles, specifically the low budgets allocated to his department in some fiscal years. He was discouraged, too, that it was so hard to convince people of the necessity of paying to attend the theater. He said, "People must learn that art must be paid for. It costs money to create art, it is needed, and people must be willing to pay for it by buying tickets. . . . Dramatic art can touch lives—and change them, too."

Not all of the students whose lives were touched through their work in Poag's department went on to achieve the phenomenal success of Oprah Winfrey—today recognized simply by her first name–as talk-show host, actress in film and television, entrepreneur, and philanthropist. Not many people in the *world* have attained the prominence of Oprah! Moses Gunn was a founder of the Negro Ensemble Company, he had roles in TV, movies, and off-Broadway plays, and he was the winner of Obie Awards (for off-Broadway work). Helen Martin and Ellwoodson Williams were two other students who pursued acting careers. Yet Poag was equally thrilled when his former students achieved success in the business world, in science, or in education.

Of the many awards that he received, perhaps the one of which he was most proud was the 1973 Distinguished Service Award from the American Speech-Language-Hearing Association. In 1971 he was named an Outstanding Educator of America, based on his community service, professional achievement, and leadership in education.

Poag described his dream: "I want to have good theater in Nashville. I want plays so good people will be eager to pay to see them. And, someday, I hope, we'll have a professional company right here in our own community, a resident company well supported." His dream had not been realized by the time of his death in 1974, but it is becoming reality now.

The $9 million TSU Performing Arts Center was completed in the spring of 2003, and the first performance was *In the Blood*. Written by Suzan-Lori Parks, the adaptation of Nathaniel Hawthorne's *The Scarlet Letter* was produced by the Resident Professional Theatre Training Program. The director was Barry Scott, and the assistant director was Kimberley LaMarque, director of forensics and assistant professor of theater. The 40,000-square-foot structure encompasses spaces for teaching and performing; the theater itself seats 360 and has state-of-the-art lighting and sound equipment. TSU students may pursue a B.A. or a B.S. in speech communications and theater. Scott founded the training program, which is not included in the school's curriculum and, thus, is not mandatory. It provides students with hands-on experiences to get them to the next step in their education—whether graduate school or the dramatic world. He also gives them the benefit of what he has learned in that world.

Scott is a native of Nashville and an alumnus of TSU, who graduated with a bachelor's degree in speech communications and theater. Although he studied with William Dury Cox, not Poag, in TSU's theater program, he is a prime mover in fulfilling the dream shared by both teachers. After graduation, Scott left the city and spent time in LA—he has had roles in film (*Ernest Goes to Jail* with Jim Varney) and television (*In the Heat of the Night* where he had a recurring role as a minister)—but he chose to return to Nashville and develop his craft in his hometown. He writes, produces, and directs as well as acts now. He has worked with the Tennessee Repertory Theatre, and he is on the staff of TSU as the theater manager. As the founder and producing artistic director of the American Negro Playwright Theatre, he seeks out works such as August Wilson's *Fences,* directed by John Henry Redwood in the fall of 2001 (still in Thomas

Edward Poag Auditorium). He travels the country each year delivering his tribute to Martin Luther King Jr. through Dr. King's speeches; his is the voice heard on commercials for the Nashville Predators and other organizations and companies; and he narrated *Oh, Freedom!,* a musical history of the African-American experience written by Scott, in January 2003 for TPAC.

More than sixty years after Poag began to teach at TSU and exert his influence in the dramatic arts, the scene is set for a new race to be run with even higher expectations.

~

Not Banned in Nashville

Attorneys for Mrs. Naff contended
that the matter of controlling theatrical productions
should be [determined] by law rather than by
the will, the whim, or caprice of the Board of Censors.

—BANNER, NOVEMBER 21, 1939

LULA NAFF was uneasy about the Board of Censors. She was concerned that they would try to halt the showing of *Tobacco Road,* scheduled for November 23, 1939, at the Ryman, and she needed every event to be a success to bolster the auditorium's bottom line. A week before the play was to be given, what she feared did happen: the board imposed a ban. Furious that they had waited until virtually the last minute and had left her no time to schedule another performance, Mrs. Naff contacted her lawyers, Fyke Farmer and Raymond Denney.

Jack Kirkland had turned Erskine Caldwell's steamy, violent, controversial novel into a play that opened on Broadway in December 1933. It had run since that time in New York City, but the play had encountered bans elsewhere around the country. *Tobacco Road* had played before in Nashville

"Real Opera"

In the latter years of her management of the Ryman, Lula Naff was increasingly reluctant to book operas because of the poor turnout. She just could not afford to have a loss. Yet townspeople continued to go to Chattanooga, Memphis, or Atlanta to enjoy operas. The city really had no suitable venue for a complete production of opera, no matter how much Francis Robinson would have liked to book the Metropolitan Opera in Nashville. In 1940 Mrs. Naff reported to Francis that opera-lover Annie Mae Kennedy wanted to bring the opera to town and build a place to hold it, but the ever practical Mrs. Naff explained why that would not happen: the federal government would not lend money for it because no one—and certainly not the city—was willing to keep up the building.

If we go back to 1895, we hear complaints about the city's attitude toward opera that kept repeating themselves:

> Is it really the case that a good opera company must shun Nashville, or lose money? Certainly this must be, or else the enterprising managers of our theaters would, ere this, have had at least one such company before this much of the season had passed. And yet this is the "Athens of the South," with its schools and colleges, its academies and universities; we have musicians by the score, and hardly a home in which some one does not profess to be musically inclined. Hundreds of so called musicians spend hours in trying to persuade an amiable piano to give forth the strains of Beethoven's Moonlight Sonata, the weird harmonies of Chopin's Nocturnes, the soothing notes of Mendelssohn's Songs without Words, the scholarly compositions of Bach, and the grand overtures and choruses from Wagner. And yet operas come and languish for audiences. Is our love of music a sham? Do we profess it because it is "the thing in Paris?" We speak for an opera, a real opera. Something should be done by those who control our theaters to cultivate a love for such music, and the people in town who love music, should encourage such an effort by attendance.

(December 1938), and although Mrs. Naff had been apprehensive about the play's reception then, there were no unsold seats in the auditorium and there was no threat of censorship. She seemed to have her answer. She was steamed, however, about comments in the *Banner* in regard to the "dirty money" she made from presenting the play.

Why in the world did the Board of Censors wait to object until the play's second time in town? Mrs. Naff must have had some inkling of what was to come, or she would not have felt uneasy. She responded to the action in a way that must have caught the board—and the city attorney—by surprise. She made the issue the validity of the Board of Censors, not the play's obscenity or immorality.

Mrs. Naff filed an application for an injunction in circuit court and named the city of Nashville and the members of the board as defendants in her suit challenging the authority of the board itself. Board members named as defendants were E. C. Faircloth, B. F. Burrell, Sam Garfinkle, Hugh F. Smith Jr., Sam Davis Bell, Mrs. Alice Starnes, and Mrs. B. K. Marshall. The case was to go before Special Chancellor John J. Hooker Sr.

City Attorney W. C. Cherry used sections of the city charter as grounds for the authority of the Nashville Board of Censors in the banning of *Tobacco Road*. Section 12 dealt with the power of the mayor and the City Council to regulate theatrical and other forms of amusement. The specific Board of Censors involved in the case was named on February 21, 1939, but the board's action was based on authority "presumed to have been conferred upon it" by an ordinance passed on April 21, 1914, and amended June 9, 1914. Mrs. Naff's bill contended that when the legislature abolished the commission form of Nashville's government in 1923, the mayor no longer had power to appoint a Board of Censors. The city attorney referred to portions of the charter basically stating that ordinances, resolutions, and bylaws from the previous form of city government should continue in the current form unless they had been repealed, modified, or amended, and Section 81 concerned the continuation of duties of individuals employed by the previous city government.

Cherry also declared that "the play was profane and obscene in violation of both state laws and city ordinances." He continued, "It is true that 'Tobacco Road' has shown in New York City for a long time, but that is no test or yardstick by which its right to be shown in the City of Nashville is to be determined. . . . The administration has purged the newsstands of lascivious literature and it will not exact less decency from the theatrical stage." Mrs. Naff made no public comment, but let her attorneys do their work.

A front-page headline, November 22, proclaimed Hooker's decision: "Court Clears Way for 'Tobacco Road.'" He ruled that the city ordinance creating the Nashville Board of Censors was invalid, and he granted an injunction against the individual members of the board so that they could not interfere with the showing of the play.

Chancellor Hooker's ruling was based on the fact that Ordinance No. 186, as amended by Ordinance No. 210, is invalid because enacted in pursuance "of an invalid, unauthorized, and illegal delegation of municipal power and authority."

In his opinion, the special chancellor explained that the question of the impropriety, immorality, or obscenity of "Tobacco Road" was not the question before the court but that the sole question presented for the court's determination was the validity of Ordinance No. 186 of the City of Nashville, approved May 21, 1914, "empowering the Mayor to appoint a Board of Censors."

The ordinance was ruled invalid principally upon the ground that no statute or charter provision has been enacted by the State Legislature providing for a Board of Censorship for the City of Nashville and no authority has been conferred upon the Mayor and City Council to delegate any of the power conferred upon them to such a board or committee.

City Attorney Cherry responded by praying for an appeal to the Supreme Court. He said, "Ordinarily I wouldn't pray for an appeal on the same day that a decision is rendered but in this case the necessity of time causes me to take this action."

On the *Banner*'s editorial page the day of the play, James Stahlman strongly stated his opinion that he was totally against the showing of the play, and he urged strengthening the laws in regard to the Board of Censors. A modest ad on the entertainment page noted that John Barton was the star of *Tobacco Road* and cited admission prices of $1.10, $1.65, $2.20, and $2.75 (tax included; $2.75 then, about $36 today)—there was "no free list."

The next day, the *Banner*'s review ran under the headline "TR Filth Diluted for Nashville" and briefly commented on the play and the acting. The language had been toned down, and the reviewer regarded the play as entertaining but insignificant.

Mrs. Naff had her victory over the Board of Censors and also made a healthy $2,060 (about $26,780 today) on the play. She decided, however, to cancel an upcoming engagement of the *Night on the Moulin Rouge* and replace it with the Lunts in *The Taming of the Shrew*.

The arts are a vital part
in making the whole person.

—CAROL CRITTENDEN

Bold Steps: 1946-present

ALMOST IMMEDIATELY after World War II, Apollo had his answer. The citizens began a symphony orchestra—not without perilous twists and turns along the way—and it has now gained worldwide attention. Music recording was added to music publishing and education, and Nashville has become known as Music City USA. The booming health care industry has added another dimension to the diversity of the city's economy. The makeup of the population has been changing as people from around the world, not just across the South, move to Nashville.

A performing arts center was constructed (opening in 1980), and now professional theater companies, both local and imported, have a suitable place to stage their works. In addition local opera and ballet companies have achieved professional status and perform regularly. All have gained loyal audiences and are building new audiences—men, women, and children—through their good work and their outreach. Young people who aspire to be actors, ballet dancers, or opera singers are able to make a living in the city.

The boldest step of all is the building of the world-class Schermerhorn Symphony Center, and Apollo is charting an ever-more ambitious course for Nashvillians. With hard work, know-how, and funds the community will be able to follow that course and sustain the performing arts. ❖

Walter Sharp's "Creature"

The symphony is always there—
always avaricious of time and money,
ever on the verge of disaster and eternally hopeful.
A harassing, hand-to-mouth sort of creature
which manages, however, to keep most of its promises.
I doubt that the Met is either so troublesome
or so rewarding.

—WALTER SHARP TO FRANCIS ROBINSON,
NOVEMBER 22, 1949

WHEN WALTER SHARP penned this letter to his old friend Francis Robinson in late 1949, telling him about the progress of the Nashville Symphony and other local news, the Symphony had already been through its startup phase. Sharp had taken it upon himself to see that an orchestra was established in the city in 1946, and he was still much involved with its well-being three years later. Until his death in 1970, he was a leader in cultural undertakings within Nashville.

A native Nashvillian, a graduate of Vanderbilt University, and a lover of all of the arts (in addition to being a pretty good pianist and singer), Sharp returned from a stint in the U.S. Army during World War II determined to see that Nashville would have an orchestra of its own with an exceptional conductor. Years afterward, he stated in an interview, "I think it began as far back as my student days in Vanderbilt. It seemed to be part of our social tradition that most people of ability left Nashville to pursue careers and make a name. I determined to stay here. . . . I never wanted a 'messianic' role, but I suppose what I've tried to do is to dislodge to some extent what seems to be my home town's commitment to the second rate." Sharp's niece, the artist Ann Street, said that he referred to the city as a "cultural desert," and perhaps that compelled him to

try even harder to make the desert bloom. (As you know, an earlier Nashville Symphony was not able to survive the Great Depression.)

At the end of World War II, Nashville was like other U.S. cities trying to absorb returning servicemen who needed jobs and housing for themselves and, often, their young and growing families. In June 1946 getting sixty people to sign the charter of the Nashville Civic Music Association, which was "to encourage the musical development of Nashville and the State of Tennessee . . . and to provide opportunities for professional and amateur musicians of the State to appear in public performances," was a positive sign that the citizens would embrace cultural enterprises as well as industry and commerce. Raising funds was another matter.

Albert Werthan recalled that Sharp came to his home to ask him and his wife, Mary Jane, for a hefty $1,000 contribution to become charter members of the Symphony. (Asking for $1,000 then would be like asking for about $9,200 today. Here is an idea of the economic picture: the per capita income in Tennessee for 1946 was $872, would not exceed $1,000 until 1950, and reached $26,758 in 2001.) The initial response from Albert was along the lines of "What! Are you crazy?"—a refrain that became familiar to Sharp as he spoke to others—but the Werthans contributed that amount and were always generous givers to the Nashville Symphony. Since his wife's death, Albert has continued to be a member of the Stradivarius Society (the group of donors who give $5,000 or more annually to the Symphony).

Harold Bradley was present at a meeting in 1946 when Sharp asked the local musicians' union for a donation. Harold said, "The union donated $1,000. It was a lot of money then. I think it was incredible foresight on George Cooper's part [Cooper was the president of the union]; George was a French horn player and worked in orchestras around town before he became a bass player. He was classically trained, so he understood that. He saw that having a symphony would be good for the town. That was visionary, and he was going out on a limb. We didn't know that all of the recording business was going to happen and that the union would really have some money."

Even a cursory glance at the Symphony's bank records shows that the majority of contributions were in smaller amounts of $25 and $50; $100 contributions were sparse, and most were from individuals, not businesses. WLAC was one exception. Yet Sharp and other true believers were able to raise enough funds to make the Symphony

William Strickland was the first music director of the newly formed Nashville Symphony, beginning in 1946.

viable, and they formed a board of directors. The officers were Sharp, president; Mary Ragland, first vice president; Ovid Collins Jr., second vice president; Reber Boult, secretary; and Edwin Keeble, treasurer. Marjorie Cooney was the Symphony's first manager, and its first "office" was the mezzanine at the Hermitage Hotel.

Sharp had met William Strickland while both were in the army, and he seemed the right man for the job of music director, although many others sent applications because so few positions were available then. Strickland, born in Ohio, had a connection to Nashville through a relative bearing his name who had been the architect of the pre–Civil War Tennessee State Capitol and whose remains now rest in a niche there. Strickland was a gifted organist, having played at New York's Calvary Episcopal Church at age seventeen. After fellowships at Columbia University and at Trinity College of Music in London, he was assistant to the music director at St. Bartholomew's Church. He also had been associate conductor of the National Youth Administration Orchestra of New York and founder and conductor of the New York NYA Sinfonietta. His job in the army was to train band leaders at the Army Music School in Washington, D.C., and he also conducted the Cathedral Choral Society.

Hired in the fall of 1946 (the salary for 1946–47 was almost $6,000), Strickland immediately held auditions. Professional and amateur musicians responded to the call, and the first concert was scheduled for December 10, 1946, at the War Memorial Auditorium. (See appendix B for members.)

Dr. Edward Tarpley was a musician playing in that concert. A Nashville native, he had been taking violin lessons since the age of eight when his grandmother, a musician, bought him a half-sized violin. Dr. Tarpley said, "My mother sold eggs, butter, and milk to pay for my music lessons," and he studied first with Browne Martin and then

The Nashville Symphony with Strickland practiced and performed at the War Memorial Auditorium.

with Eric Sorantin in studios on Eighth Avenue. (Martin played viola in Henkel's Nashville Symphony and in Sharp's Nashville Symphony. Sorantin was a Viennese violinist who had played a Beethoven Concerto with the Vienna Symphony at age sixteen and had come to Nashville from the Cincinnati Conservatory.) Dr. Tarpley said of Strickland, "He was not a great conductor as far as technique was concerned. But . . . he established a certain quality for the orchestra. We had to be on time; if we were one minute late, we had to sit out. We had to be tuned and ready five minutes before the hour. He was very strict in every way. He did it because he felt it was necessary for a beginning orchestra."

On the program for the first concert were soloist Helen Jepson of the Metropolitan Opera singing the Gavotte from Massenet's *Manon*, the tone poem "Tennessee Variations" composed for the Nashville Symphony by Cecil Effinger, Beethoven's Seventh Symphony, and other pieces. Dr. Tarpley recalled the moment as the last notes of Beethoven's symphony faded away: "Tears were streaming down Strickland's face when we ended the concert, and most of the

Orchestra had joined him. It was such an accomplishment for us, and we all had worked hard to get to that point. It was an emotional high point in the musical life of Nashville." The audience responded with multiple curtain calls, and the triumphant evening ended with a reception at Cheekwood, Sharp's home that he shared with his wife, the former Huldah Cheek.

In 1949, George Sloan was quoted as saying, "[With] Nashville, which is still my first love, enjoying a sort of renaissance in the music field," through development of its own Symphony, "nothing could contribute more to the cultural life of a community which stands so high in the general field of education. And to this end community participation is vitally important."

Strickland included an American composition for each program, and he sometimes selected less frequently performed works by composers of other nationalities, as he did for the opening concert of the 1949–50 season. Dr. Hans Kindler, a friend of Strickland and founder of the National Symphony, had arranged three tunes—one was the Netherlands Song of Thanksgiving—by the seventeenth-century

Dutch composer Adrianus Valerius. Another selection was "Serenade for Wind Instruments" by Richard Strauss, composed when he was only twelve years old. The real feature of that evening was the Bach Concerto in C Major for Three Pianos with three Nashville pianists: Lawrence Goodman, Margaret Seely, and Mary Douthit Bold. A stretch for the Orchestra and the audience occurred in the fourth season when the Symphony expanded the usual six concerts to nine, and Strickland scheduled one of Beethoven's nine symphonies for each concert. Robert Bays, a former director of music at Peabody College, said, "The Orchestra received a lot of attention; the critics loved it. But the audiences seemed to consider that there was too much Beethoven—he often had other Beethoven works on the programs with symphonies. It was not a financial success."

Despite income from subscriptions and ticket sales over the years, deficits mounted. Sharp made personal loans, and eventually the Nashville Symphony obtained a note from Third National Bank. There were more problems that exacerbated the financial ones. Audiences were less enthusiastic and less numerous by 1950. As of June 1950, another war was in progress, this time in Korea, and it, too, seemed to have an effect on Nashvillians and their attendance habits. A direct blow to the Symphony was a serious falling out between Sharp and Strickland that caused Strickland to leave by the spring of 1951. To their credit, the young conductor and the energetic Sharp had managed to accomplish what they set out to do by forming an orchestra and more—the Nashville Choral Society and the Nashville Youth Orchestra (directed by Andrew Ponder) had started in 1947. Nevertheless, the talk around the city was that the Nashville Symphony could not survive; it would be finished before another year had passed.

"Southern-Nourished Minds"

Thinking, like cotton, thrives in the South,
judging by the thoughtful writing
that keeps pouring out of Southern-nourished minds;
but thinking, like cotton,
also finds its best market in the North.

—LOUISE DAVIS, 1949

THE OPENING STATEMENT by Louise Davis has writing as its focus, yet the same notion applies to the performing arts. Although she was specifically discussing men like the Fugitives and Agrarians, some points that she, they, and their critics offered about them pertain to this odyssey of the performing arts.

A few of the literary men had aspirations toward or strong sympathies for the performing arts, but chose to write and teach instead. Andrew Lytle attended Yale School of Drama for two years and then had acting roles in New York City before he returned to the South. John Crowe Ransom as a Rhodes Scholar made

William Strickland and Walter Sharp had happier days before a serious disagreement between the two caused Strickland to leave the Symphony in 1951.

the most of his educational experience by attending the opera and concerts in England and Germany, and later he helped his sister Annie study piano in New York City by providing funds for a four-month stay at the von Ende School. Annie had the position of director of music at the School of Fine Arts of Greenbrier College, Lewisburg, West Virginia, in 1929. Donald Davidson's mother was a piano teacher, and she shared with him her love of classical music. He played the piano, and he wrote the text for the opera *Singin' Billy*, which was a collaborative effort with Charles F. Bryan.

In an interview with Allen Tate in 1949, Louise asked him why most of the Agrarians went North. He said, "It just happened, without any plan on anybody's part." He noted the lure of publishing houses and the universities of the North that were "more interested in creative work." The upshot was that it was just hard to make a living as a writer in the South, and we cannot forget this quotation from John Crowe Ransom's preface to the first issue of *The Fugitive*: "*The Fugitive* flees from nothing faster than from the high-caste Brahmins of the Old South."

In his essay "You Can't Eat Magnolias," H. Brandt Ayers wrote of the Agrarians and *I'll Take My Stand*: "We were asked to believe that the agrarian way of life would nourish the arts in the South. The scrabbling existence of South Georgia tenant farmers provided neither the leisure nor the spacious means to organize a symphony or a ballet company." Not just tenant farmers but southern professors, too, had to struggle. In a letter to Allen Tate in 1932, Donald Davidson expressed the tenuous nature of everyone's financial security, which affected their "crusading spirit," and they had little more time than money after dealing with family and work responsibilities. He said that Andrew Lytle was the only one of them who came close to being a crusader—because he was single.

Robert Penn Warren explained his dilemma that has been shared by too many artistic people: "I wanted to live in the South . . . I'm a refugee from the South, driven out as it were. The place I wanted to live, the place I thought was heaven to me, after my years of wandering, was middle Tennessee, which is a beautiful country, or *was* a beautiful country—it's rapidly being ruined. But I couldn't make it work. . . . [I] didn't make a choice of living outside the South. I always felt myself somehow squeezed out of the South."

The editor of some of Warren's letters, William Bedford Clark, expanded on this issue by writing,

> Though Warren entered upon his new life in the North with characteristic energy and enthusiasm, he did so out of a sense of compulsion. . . . Though Warren did not recognize it at the time, his departure from Baton Rouge was in effect an act of final expatriation. He lived outside the South for the rest of his life; whenever he returned to the region that had shaped him (whether the Border South of his boyhood and youth or the Deep South of his *Southern Review* years) it would be as a visitor, an estranged observer. As Lewis P. Simpson suggests, Warren left Baton Rouge to pursue "a vocation to exile," and it is the voice of the exile that registers most compellingly in his mature work. To recast the matter in terms loosely appropriated from the "new theory," Warren's "absence" from the South came to be an abiding "presence" in his finest fiction, poetry, and social commentary.

My hope is that artistic individuals with "Southern-nourished minds" will not have to go into a similar exile but may remain in the South to pursue their craft; they will not have to seek a market in another part of the country or abroad.

Music Making at Peabody

Peabody was the *music school.*

—HAROLD BRADLEY

GEORGE PEABODY College for Teachers was the cultural center of Nashville for years when little else was happening in the performing arts, particularly in the summer, and a high point of activity was the decade following the end of World War II. Limited venues on campus meant that everything moved outdoors. A wonderful plan for a Department of Music building with an auditorium and plenty of rehearsal space had never gotten beyond the drafting stage because of the Great Depression. Once more, economics affected the availability of a proper performing venue, but the professors did a remarkable job with what they had.

The growth of the Department of Music, too, was remarkable. For some time Dr. D. R. Gebhart, the chairman of the department, was the only full-time faculty member, joined by one or two part-timers. Then more and more talented people came to the school, such as Charles F. Bryan, Werner Zeppernick, Walter Ihrke, and Dr. Irving Wolfe. During Dr. Wolfe's tenure, the department became a Division of Music and soared to preeminence. Later under C. B. Hunt's chairmanship, it became a School of Music. (Chairmen or directors of music at Peabody were D. R. Gebhart, E. J. Gatwood, Irving W. Wolfe, C. B. Hunt Jr., Robert Bays, Charles H. Ball, H. Gilbert Trythall, Billy Jon Woods, and Larry W. Peterson.)

Robert Bays explained why Peabody's Department of Music was so important:

> First, there was no major competition in the area in the forties and fifties. Nothing was happening at Vanderbilt except the Glee Club.

Cyrus Daniel had the Glee Club; he taught courses, played the organ, and had a choir. There was a football band, but eventually Peabody assumed the responsibility for that. (Henry Romersa was the band director at Peabody and a trombonist, who later became involved in the professional commercial world of music in Nashville.) Even UT [the University of Tennessee] didn't have a lot in music then. Not much was happening then at Memphis [State] or Murfreesboro [Middle Tennessee State] or Austin Peay. People had to go to Florida State, which wasn't coed until after WWII, for grad study in music.

> Second, Irving Wolfe had a vision of what the school could be. He built a fine doctoral program.

> Third, the name of the school was George Peabody College for *Teachers.* The emphasis was on music education. People who came were more interested in that than in performance, especially graduate students. There were a performance degree and a Ph.D. in musicology, however. By nature more of the people were more interested in being educators or administrators. Yet the faculty and some students were important in being able to provide performers *within* the town; the graduates of the school were important *outside* the city, across the U.S., as educators.

With the GI Bill's assistance, students swelled the school's rolls, and Harold Bradley was among them. Dr. Ihrke was one of his teachers, and Harold said, "We had big band guys coming back, thirty-five years old, and I was only twenty. There was no music school at Vanderbilt. Peabody was *the* music school. They were really good teachers."

Unfortunately after he severely hurt his little finger, Harold could no longer play bass—his major instrument—so he did not graduate. He stated, "I saw that Peabody couldn't train me for what I was going to do. I was playing in the big

Singin' Billy and the
Dolly Pond Church of the Living God with Signs Following

The unlikely combination of spirituals, singing schools, and snake handlers came together on the stage of Vanderbilt University in the work of Charles F. Bryan. Born in 1911 near McMinnville, Tennessee, Bryan was a 1934 graduate of the Nashville Conservatory of Music (his Bachelor of Music degree certified him in voice, piano, and public school music). While serving as director of the music department of Tennessee Polytechnic Institute, he studied folk music, the themes of which he would weave into his compositions. Pursuing his M.A. at George Peabody College for Teachers, he submitted his White Spiritual Symphony as his thesis.

After the war (1945–46), Bryan went to Yale University to study composition with Paul Hindemith, and a Guggenheim Fellowship enabled him to compose *The Bell Witch*, a folk cantata that premiered in April 1947 at Carnegie Hall with Robert Shaw conducting. In the course of his years in Nashville, Bryan had exposure to the world of radio as an arranger and vocalist on the WSM staff. While teaching at Peabody (1947–52), Bryan collaborated on two projects that resulted in world premieres at Vanderbilt University Theatre in the same year, and although the actors were amateurs, it was said that they carried off their roles with professionalism.

The first was produced February 6–9, 1952. *Strangers in This World* was written by Brainard Cheney, former newspaperman, friend of the Fugitives, and author of short stories and novels. Bryan composed and directed the music, which was somewhat like a series of religious chants and was referred to as "haunting."

The focus of the story was a mountain, snake-handling religious cult known as the Dolly Pond Church of the Living God with Signs Following. Not to leave too much to the audience's imagination on this point, real snakes were part of the cast,

and Jim Hodge was their handler. One reviewer considered it a sympathetic look at this group of mountain folk, and the play was "put together with equal parts of shock and sensitivity and skill."

Joseph E. Wright was the director, Robert M. Cothran Jr. took care of the sets, Robert E. Jones was the technical director, and Joy Zibart provided the dancers. Primary actors were Mary Ann Hodge, John Caldwell (from the drama department of the University of the South at Sewanee), and Bill Fisher; Barbara Bryant and Rosalyn Kennedy had minor roles. The play received "an unusually enthusiastic reception" at the theater.

The second collaborative effort was *Singin' Billy* with Donald Davidson, and it premiered on April 23, 1952, at Vanderbilt University Theatre. Davidson, a member of the Fugitives, had taught in the Department of English at Vanderbilt since 1920. He had chosen a teaching and writing career over music, although he still played piano and composed music.

Walk into virtually any house of worship in Nashville today and you will experience fine, if not glorious, singing by choir and congregation. That was not always the case in Nashville or American churches in general. In the early days everyone sang in his or her own way, at his or her own pace, so you can imagine how discordant was the result. To solve this problem, itinerant singing masters held singing schools in communities. Singin' Billy, about whom the folk opera revolved, was a real man named William Walker. He taught in southern singing schools and edited *Southern Harmony* (1835), filled with tunes, hymns, psalms, odes, and anthems written in shape-note notation, and he supplemented this with rules for beginning singers.

The setting for *Singin' Billy* was a South Carolina town in the 1830s. John O'Neal Culley, a bass baritone, was Singin' Billy, and other cast members included Fay Jennings, Robert Strobel, Helen Hudson, George Mayfield, Ruth Ray, and Jim Ware. Joy Zibart and Claude Chadwick staged the dances. Sets were created by Robert M. Cothran Jr., and the direction was by Robert E. Jones and Joseph E. Wright.

Reviewing the folk opera, Sydney Dalton wrote that all of the music was drawn from folk songs, but Bryan added modern harmonies: "Had he used the simple tunes in their original form with, perhaps, a few elementary chords, as some purists demand, even such lovely tunes as 'The Hawthorn Tree' and 'Wondrous Love' would become monotonous with repetition." Yet Bryan gave "interest and variety to the orchestra." The libretto contained poetry, dialogue, and some humor, and Dalton credited it as "an art piece" that would probably not become part of the popular repertory. He regarded it as "not primarily 'theater,'" but "a noteworthy achievement by two imaginative, talented and skillful craftsmen."

In his review Louis Nicholas complimented Davidson's book: "Much of the talk was appropriately homespun, and most of it was so near to the experience of a Tennessee audience that there was a warm and ready response." He thought that "The Hawthorn Tree," "The Quilt Song," and "The Low Country" were beautiful tunes that "matched the loveliness of Davidson's poetry"; however, he believed that the orchestra almost overpowered the actors.

Robert Bays recalled that Peabody College also produced *Singin' Billy* as part of the outdoor summer series, and he said, "It had lovely poetry, but it was not dramatic. Charlie worked white spirituals into the music. The weakest part was the dramatic element."

We can only wonder what other musical accomplishments lay ahead of Bryan. He died of a heart attack at the age of forty-three.

band at WSM when I was sixteen. I was playing in dance bands from sixteen on. I was not going to be a classical musician. It was great experience, though; I would not take anything for it." His history is now part of Nashville's musical history.

Peabody faculty contributed substantially to the Nashville Symphony, and many people played for several years: Don Cassel, principal oboe; C. B. Hunt, principal clarinet; Robert Bays, principal French horn; Andrew Ponder, viola; Kees Kooper, violin, concertmaster; Michael Semanitzky, violin, concertmaster; Vernon Taylor, viola; and Egan Kenton, viola. Spouses of faculty members were also in the Orchestra: Cleis Bays, violin; Jean Slates, oboe; and C. B. Hunt's first wife, Lillian, violin.

The Symphony was responsible for the Bays family coming to town. Bays had taught at Wichita University and had played with the Wichita Symphony. He and his wife auditioned for William Strickland and got their respective positions with the Symphony, and Bays also was to teach at Peabody. They arrived in the summer of 1949 and were immediately introduced to the summertime fare.

Charles F. Bryan was in charge of the summer opera, which was *Faust* that year. An outdoor stage, built in front of the SR (Social Religious) Building, now Wyatt Center, accommodated faculty performers, guests who were pianists or singers, chamber ensembles, and sometimes the Nashville Symphony. Clara Haddox directed the Peabody Dance Group. After 1949 Robert Bays conducted the summer musicals and operas (for example, *Merry Wives of Windsor, Carousel, Die Fledermaus,* and *South Pacific*). From the mid-1940s until 1960, Nashville's population grew substantially each summer because of the number of educators pursuing advanced degrees at Peabody. Thousands of people attended the free performances over the course of three nights, Thursday, Friday, and Saturday, usually around the first of August.

The long-lasting effects of these events cannot be overemphasized, and they made strong impressions on old and young. One attendee was Keel Hunt, who has been a participant in strengthening the arts community. He said, "I grew up in a middle-class, blue-collar working family. My mom was a teacher. If there were things to be exposed to [in Nashville], I think my brothers and I would have been exposed to them. I just think there weren't many. My mom and dad took me when I was a little kid to an outdoor performance of *South Pacific* on the campus at Peabody College, where my mom had gone."

Roy Harris, internationally known composer and student of Nadia Boulanger in Paris, and his wife, Johana, a distinguished pianist, joined the Peabody faculty in 1949. Before he came to Nashville, Roy had composed several pieces, including Symphony 1933, Symphony No. 3, and Folksong Symphony, and he finished *Kentucky Spring* in 1949. He and Johana were at Peabody two years, and Roy organized the Cumberland Forest Festival during his stay.

There was an annual symposium and concert with a major composer on the campus, sponsored by Peabody. Howard Hanson, William Schuman (of Juilliard), Randall Thompson, Aaron Copland, and Wallingford Riegger were some of the composers. These concerts were popular with the public, but the annual symposium of the Southeast Composers League held more appeal for league members and teachers. Phil Slates, theorist, composer, and Peabody faculty member, chaired these symposia; composers submitted scores of chamber music and choral music, and a program was given of that music and lectures. At one point there was interest in electronic music, and Louis Nicholas reviewed one program for the *Tennessean*: "The first man was from Canada, Udo Kasemets. I said in my review that it was like steam escaping from a radiator. The next one was a member of the Peabody faculty, and I said that it wasn't much better."

An annual event that drew full houses at War Memorial Auditorium was the singing of the *Messiah*. Dr. Wolfe and then Louis Nicholas directed the event, which was free of charge. In the spring the Peabody College Choir worked with the Nashville Symphony.

Many faculty members participated in other aspects of the community's musical life. Some directed church choirs: Charles Bryan at First Baptist, Louis Nicholas at West End Methodist, Robert Bays at another Methodist church, and Irving Wolfe at First Lutheran. The Peabody faculty was not key in the recording business but did have a role. When record producers occasionally wanted to add French horn and oboe to get an "uptown sound," they called upon Robert Bays and Don Cassel, while the string faculty more often participated in recording sessions.

Peabody's outreach extended around the world. The Madrigalians, composed of twelve members, faculty and students, sang folk music, madrigals, and some contemporary music. Irving Wolfe, founder and director, applied to the U.S. State Department for the group to go to the Orient, but health problems prevented him from making the trip, and Robert Bays took the group in the spring of 1964 for a three-month swing through Japan, Korea, Taiwan, and Hong Kong. Bays said, "We had a wonderful reception. There were enormous crowds of college students. We sang with the Tokyo Madrigal Society. And this wasn't that long after the end of WWII." It was a State Department program to present college students who were musicians to other college students, and the government paid all expenses.

In the mid-1970s, when Peabody College was restructured, a casualty was the School of Music, which became a department within a division called Educational Support Personnel. A former Peabody student and the first director of the Blair Academy, Del Sawyer, said, "As a result, the School of Music lost its identity and its historical mission of training both music teachers and performers." At the end of the 1970s, Peabody College itself was in dire financial straits and was preparing to become a part of Vanderbilt University.

Four Conductors

We all are very appreciative of them [conductors and musicians] because they helped build the Nashville Symphony.

—BOBBY TAYLOR, OBOIST

THE ANNOUNCEMENT that William Strickland was leaving the Nashville Symphony in the spring of 1951 led to grim predictions about the Symphony's future. The organization managed to survive—admittedly some years healthier than others—and a series of conductors served from 1951 to 1982. Here is a bit about them and the Orchestra's accomplishments during their tenures.

Guy Taylor (1951–59). An Alabama native, the thirty-one-year-old Taylor was conductor of the Springfield, Ohio, Symphony when he was appointed to succeed Strickland. Taylor was recommended by Thor Johnson, then the conductor of the Cincinnati Symphony and a former instructor of Taylor at Juilliard. The young man, who was a violinist, had also studied with Ottokar Cadek at the Birmingham Conservatory of Music and with Dimitri Mitropoulos of the Minneapolis Symphony. He had experience conducting a youth symphony organized by Fred Waring and, during World War II, the 87th Infantry Division Band.

Compared to Strickland, Taylor had a more easygoing style. Like Strickland, Taylor included American composers on the programs, and some of the notable guests in the Taylor years included Benny Goodman, Roberta Peters, Blanche Thebom, Guiomar Novaes, and Sylvia Stahlman.

The Symphony came very close to a shutdown in the 1951–52 season because of revenue shortfalls, but according to Grace Gardner, she and Mary Jane Werthan asked the executive committee, "Would you let us have one try at raising the money before you close up?" Hearing an affirmative response, the two persuasive women set to work raising funds and saved the day.

Although a committee of women had had an informal role with the Symphony at that point, the Nashville Symphony Guild came into being in 1952. One of the most successful fund-raisers in the city for many years was the Guild's Italian Street Fair, and Betty Gwinn and Sally Parker (a harpist in the Symphony) led that project at its beginning. (The Sally Parker Education Award is now given through the American Symphony Orchestra League. A dedicated volunteer, Sally shared with her father, George Pullen Jackson, a strong interest in music and the Symphony. Jackson's name appears repeatedly in this book.) The fair is no longer held because of our changing world. There was too much competition from other events, getting volunteers for a long-term project was hard, and it was no longer the best use of volunteer time. Instead in November the Guild has a Holiday House as the major fund-raising event. The Guild has strong leadership with an active board, and it provides scholarships to students in Middle Tennessee for summer music camp. (See appendix B for a list of Guild presidents.)

Attendance had made steady gains by the Symphony's tenth season, and for Taylor's last two years the Symphony scheduled six pairs of concerts (Monday and Tuesday). Educational outreach efforts included children's concerts at the War Memorial Auditorium and concerts and clinics at schools. Concerts broadcast on TV and radio reached audiences who might not otherwise have heard the Symphony.

The Symphony was able to make the most of its relationship with Peabody College by inviting composers who were visiting the campus to conduct and/or have their works performed, and some of the men in this category were Roy Harris, Howard Hanson, Aaron Copland, and Norman Dello Joio. The Nashville Symphony presented *The Bell Witch* cantata, written by Peabody's Charles F. Bryan. "Guy Taylor was a quiet, dignified man with good taste in music. Every spring we did a vocal-orchestral work. The Peabody College Choir participated with the Orchestra," said Robert Bays, who directed the choir. They performed concert versions of at least two operas, *Carmen* and *Tales of Hoffman,* and major choral-orchestral works, such as *Carmina Burana.* The Nashville Symphony also presented works by regional composers Gilbert Trythall,

Irving Kane, Tupper Saussy, and Conrad Susa.

Taylor oversaw the performance of excerpts from ballets as well as collaborations with country music stars. Sarah Cannon (Minnie Pearl) was the narrator for the "Carnival of the Animals" in 1952, and Tex Ritter sang with the Nashville Youth Orchestra. The first country artist to sing with the Nashville Symphony was Eddy Arnold (1956), which was fitting, given his contributions to what became known as the Nashville Sound.

Willis Page (1959–67). Although Page was from Rochester, New York, he had roots in Middle Tennessee because his father was a native of Donelson. A double bass player, he had studied at the Eastman School of Music and had worked with the Boston Symphony and Boston Pops. Page

Guy Taylor, conductor of the Nashville Symphony (1951–59), talked with members of Nashville's music clubs as they planned pre-concert discussions for the upcoming Symphony season: Evelyn Messmore, Mrs. Perkins Trousdale, Mary Agnes Morris, Mrs. Guy Taylor, Mrs. Joseph Van Sickle, Mrs. Kenneth Rose, Guy Taylor, and Mrs. A. A. Coult *(left to right).* Participating clubs were Musical Alumnae Club, Women's Musicale, Vendredi, Eastland Music Club, Sigma Alpha Iota music sorority, Piano Study Club, and the music department of the Woman's Club.

In the fall of 1951, the Nashville Civic Music Association (NCMA) held a reception at the Hermitage Hotel. Attending were Mrs. and Mr. Alfred Starr, Mrs. and Mr. Guy Taylor, and Mrs. and Dr. Rudolph A. Light (he was the president then of the NCMA).

came to Nashville from the Buffalo Philharmonic where he was the assistant conductor. *Volatile, fiery,* and *dynamic* were adjectives used to describe him.

Continuing a trend set by Strickland and Taylor, Page included contemporary and American composers in his programming. Under his direction, the Symphony cut its first recording on March 27, 1960, at the Ryman; it was for Dot Records. Notable guests during the Page years included Isaac Stern and Andrés Segovia. During a leave of absence in 1962 while Page conducted the Yomiuri Nippon Symphony in Japan, Harry Newstone assumed the baton for the Nashville Symphony.

Page wrote a substantive article for the Sunday *Tennessean* on December 13, 1964, titled "What Is Music State Here?" and he described a healthy state. The Nashville Symphony series of six pairs of concerts was sold out to 4,400 subscribers (students and faculty of Vanderbilt University purchased more than 700 season tickets). About 25,000 attended the Young People's Concerts each year at the War Memorial Auditorium, the

Symphony gave at least nine concerts in high schools, the Nashville Youth Orchestra was in full swing, and the Nashville Symphony String Quartet played for 250 educational concerts in schools. Financial support from individuals and businesses was up. The Symphony had good press and received help from the musicians' union. Page referred to a "possible Joint University–Civic Performing Arts Center. The need is apparent. Let us hope that this Center will become a reality." He doubted that the Symphony could have existed twenty years without university support in the form of players from Peabody College and other schools (faculty and students).

He also mentioned the state of music throughout the city. The churches and church-affiliated schools were giving more and better concerts. Music publishing was on an upswing. The Grand Ole Opry continued its popularity. The music department of the combined school system (after the formation of Metro Government) was in place, although a lack of string teachers and instruments was a problem. Faculty members of local colleges gave excellent concerts; Blair Academy was a new and "encouraging venture"; the Community Concert series was sold out.

Page's wish list for the Nashville Symphony's future is intriguing: he hoped that by 1985 the Symphony would give at least one concert each year in every high school in the county, that every child in grades five to eight would hear the Symphony at least once, and that the Symphony would be doing a variety of things throughout the year, from pops to festivals, opera to ballet.

A significant achievement while Page led the Symphony was the funding of the Nashville Concert Orchestra, which had sixteen members, and would be a step toward making the Nashville Symphony a full-time, professional orchestra.

Thor Johnson (1967–75). Johnson had degrees from the University of North Carolina and the University of Michigan. He had studied in Europe with Felix Weingartner, Bruno Walter, and Nicolai Malko. He had been choral director of the University of Michigan's Ann Arbor May Festival, and he had been guest conductor in New York, Philadelphia, Boston, Tokyo, and Milan. When he became conductor of the Cincinnati Symphony in 1947, his age (thirty-four) and his American heritage and American training made that a unique accomplishment in the history of major U.S. symphonies.

With the Nashville Symphony Johnson became known for his temper and his generosity. Louis Nicholas, who wrote the biography *Thor Johnson: American Conductor,* said of him, "Thor Johnson was generally stern in rehearsal," and toward the end of his life even more so. His conducting was always rather sweeping, and he loved to work with big groups, for example, in Mahler's Tenth Symphony.

In the fall of 1968 Johnson took the Nashville Little Symphony (the name then for the core group of musicians) on a tour of the East and played New York's Town Hall. Back at home the Little Symphony played in school concerts, accompanied the Nashville Ballet Society's Les Ballets Intimes, and gave concerts throughout Middle Tennessee.

The Symphony's twenty-fifth anniversary season had a low point—problems with the heating at the War Memorial Auditorium, which affected the schedule—and a high point—recognizing the musicians who had been with the Symphony for those twenty-five years (Dr. Edward Tarpley, Malinda Jones, Ovid Collins Jr., Jo Lennon Parker, and Walter Summers). Johnson's strength was more in the classical vein than pops fare, and notable guests who appeared with the Nashville Symphony during his tenure were Isaac Stern, Van Cliburn, Marilyn Horn, Leontyne Price, and Jessye Norman.

On the financial front Pat Wilson used his fund-raising skills to great effect and led a campaign to eliminate the Symphony's deficit. A benefit for the Symphony in October 1973, called The Outing and chaired by Pat's wife, Anne Wilson, featured Jack Benny as the violin soloist.

Johnson died in 1975, following surgery on a brain tumor, leaving an unexpected vacancy in the conductor's position.

Michael Charry (1976–82). Until a replacement for Johnson could be found, a process that took a year, John Nelson served as music advisor and principal guest conductor. The replacement, Michael Charry, had studied piano since he was a youngster, and he attended the Bronx High School of Science and Oberlin Conservatory. He trained at Pierre Monteux's school for conductors, Juilliard, and the Hochschule für Musik in Hamburg. He was the assistant conductor for the Cleveland Orchestra when he accepted the position with the Nashville Symphony.

The Symphony expanded the concerts from doubles to triples (and changed from Monday and Tuesday to Thursday, Friday, and Saturday nights), successfully completed a major subscription drive, and had a budget that exceeded $1 million by the 1978–79 season. Guest soloists

Willis Page, a native of Rochester, New York, conducted the Nashville Symphony from 1959 to 1967. Unlike the other Symphony conductors, he had roots in Middle Tennessee: his father was from Donelson *(above)*.   Thor Johnson was the conductor of the Nashville Symphony from 1967 until his death in 1975 *(lower right)*.   While Michael Charry was conductor of the Nashville Symphony (1976–82), the Orchestra made a major move from the War Memorial Auditorium to the new Tennessee Performing Arts Center in 1980 *(lower left)*.

Harmony Award

The Nashville Symphony Association was formed in 1946 when a group of prominent citizens led by Walter Sharp recognized the need for an organized effort to specifically maintain a symphony and to generally promote the arts.

In recognition of the important benefits music has brought to the culture and economy of Nashville, the Nashville Symphony Association established in 1986 the Harmony Award that would be given each year at the Symphony Ball. This award symbolizes the special relationship that exists in the many facets of the Nashville music industry.

The Harmony Award is given to the person who most exemplifies the unique synergy of Nashville music and who has contributed significantly to the development and appreciation of our music culture.

Recipients

1986: Barbara Mandrell
1987: Crystal Gayle
1988: Bud Wendell
1989: Chet Atkins
1990: Amy Grant
1991: Steve Winwood
1992: Wynonna and Naomi Judd
1993: Vince Gill
1994: Martha Rivers Ingram
      Kenneth Schermerhorn
1995: Emmylou Harris
1996: Dolly Parton
1997: Owen Bradley
1998: Trisha Yearwood
1999: Pam Tillis
2000: Lyle Lovett
2001: Michael W. Smith
2002: Mark O'Connor
2003: Linda and Mike Curb

included Isaac Stern, Eugene Fodor, and Rudolf Serkin, and some guest conductors were Robert Shaw and Leonard Slatkin. Pops concerts, included in the subscription season in 1979, featured Barbara Mandrell, Dizzy Gillespie, and Governor Lamar Alexander.

The biggest step forward for the Nashville Symphony was the move from the War Memorial Auditorium to TPAC in the fall of 1980. The Symphony finally had a place to call home, albeit not a perfect home, and a challenge was to attract enough people to fill Jackson Hall for the performances.

W. O. Smith

Music was my key to a good life.
Time after time, it opened doors for me—
to school, to work, to friendships
and professional associations.
I give thanks to Nashville,
a warm, loving, and concerned community,
for making my dream a reality.

—W. O. SMITH

HE CAME TO NASHVILLE in 1952 to teach at Tennessee A & I (Tennessee State University now, so TSU is used here to identify the school). The man whose grandmother was born in slavery was the first in his immediate family to graduate from college, and he spent more than thirty years as a teacher at TSU. W. O. Smith left behind his legacy as a musician, teacher, and dreamer.

The musician. As a youngster in Philadelphia, Smith played in a children's band and a Baptist church's Sunday school orchestra. After he graduated from high school (during the years of the Great Depression), he enrolled in music classes at Mastbaum Vocational School where his instruments were violin, viola, bass viol, and tuba. He was assigned briefly to the 1922 SCU Post Band in the army during World War II. Smith eventually played gigs with then famous or about-to-be famous names in music—Bessie Smith, Dizzy Gillespie, Fats Waller, and Thelonius Monk—and he was a part of the jazz scene in New York City.

Smith was passionate about classical music, too, and his father bought him tickets to the Philadelphia Orchestra, with Stokowski conducting. At TSU, one of Smith's jobs was to play viola in a new string quartet, which Smith said was "the only string quartet associated with a black college" then. The other members of the quartet were Brenton Banks, first violin; Maureen Stovall, second violin; and Dave Kimbrell, cello. The quartet's purpose was to promote classical music to students and other African-Americans through concerts at TSU, Fisk University, and African-American churches.

The Nashville Quartet was another string quartet in which Smith participated, filled out by Brenton Banks (violin), Byron Bach (cello), and Cecil Brower (second violin), and most performances were on the TSU campus. Brower sometimes played a tenor violin, and Smith wrote arrangements to take advantage of the sound.

Conductor Willis Page asked Smith to audition for the Nashville Symphony playing the bass. He passed the audition and became the second African-American member, joining Booker T. Rowe, a violinist. In the 1970s three members of the bass section of the Nashville Symphony were students at TSU: Charles Dungey, Joe Phea, and Ed Moon. Smith worked to garner African-American support for the Symphony, but black audience attendance remained small.

Smith had better luck incorporating works by African-Americans into the Symphony's programming. When Thor Johnson was conductor, Smith obtained a few compositions by John W. Work III, which the Symphony performed. Through his friendship with Mercer Ellington, Smith followed up on a symphonic composition by the late Duke Ellington. A performance of the "The Three Wise Men" would have been a world premiere, but the death of Johnson halted the project. Smith remained with the Orchestra until 1979.

Writing in 1991, Smith asserted, "Black symphony musicians are a rare breed. They are usually without honor or prestige in their own black community. I am hopeful that the day will come when they get the recognition they deserve from their own and also that the day will come when young black musicians will aspire to careers in symphonic music." His hopes are now being realized across the country.

The teacher. Dr. Herbert F. Mells, head of the TSU Music Department, hired Smith to be director of graduate studies in music education, and he would also teach music methods. Later he taught more undergraduate classes. Others in the Music Department were John Sharpe, university organist; Marie Brooks Strange, music history; Wilhelmina Taylor, music appreciation; and Jasper Patton, piano. Chick Chavis directed the Tennessee State Collegians, a group that played in Carnegie Hall.

Following Dr. Mells was Edward C. Lewis as the department head. Another addition to the department was Esther Cook, teaching music theory. She had graduated from Eastman School of Music and had been a trombonist with Sweethearts of Rhythm, an all-female jazz band. In the early sixties the piano staff included Don Barrett, Carol Stone, Charlene Harb McDonald, and Patsy Dugan. Smith observed, "I'd say we could compete favorably with any other college piano staff in the state. The community and the general public didn't know this because we were more or less confined to the campus, not traveling as solo recitalists." Composer and pianist Bill Pursell was an adjunct professor for a while. During the 1960s, TSU's Music Department was admitted to the National Association of Schools of Music.

The biggest concert at TSU featured Thor Johnson as guest conductor of musicians from the campus, supplemented by extra players from the Nashville Symphony, and the nearly one-hundred-member university choir. The program was Mendelssohn's Second Symphony.

At one point Smith served on the TSU lyceum committee, which brought cultural events to the campus. Although the students wanted only the Supremes or the Temptations, Smith made the case for the Nashville Symphony or classical performers. He was relentless in his efforts to expand the students' "cultural horizons," and the committee managed to provide four performances per year.

Reaching out to the community to expand horizons, Smith developed two radio programs. The first was a classical music program on WVOL when Noble Blackwell was the station manager in the 1960s. Called *Symphony Hall,* it was broadcast on Sunday afternoons, and WVOL, a rhythm-and-blues station, kept the program for eight years. The second program was a thirteen-week series focusing on African-American composers and their music for WPLN, the public radio station. Smith included John W. Work III of Fisk, T. J. Anderson of TSU, and Duke Ellington, among others.

The dreamer. Smith had a dream of helping low-income youngsters pursue an interest in music. What grew out of that dream was the nonprofit W. O. Smith/Nashville Community Music School. With help from people across the city—Buddy Killen (Tree Publishing Co.), Frank Sutherland (the *Tennessean),* Del Sawyer (Blair School of Music), the Reverend Fred Cloud, the local musicians' union, and many more—the

school got its start in a house on Edgehill Avenue in 1984 and added a second building ten years later.

Ken Wendrich was the first director, and following his death in an automobile accident, Jonah Rabinowitz became the second director. Rabinowitz, a graduate of the New England Conservatory, played trumpet for the Atlanta Ballet, the Atlanta Opera, and the Atlanta Symphony, and he had been in charge of the Georgia Academy of Music before he came to Nashville.

The W. O. Smith School now serves about four hundred students, who are charged 50 cents per lesson per half hour. They range in age from seven to eighteen, and they receive instruments and music at no additional cost. Most of the instruments are donated. Eligibility is determined by students' participation in Metro schools' reduced or free-lunch program, and there are always students waiting for admission.

The three staff members are musicians. They and a few volunteers teach a preliminary program for students before they are allowed to take private instrument lessons. During this time the students learn to read music and to understand basic music terminology. By being so involved, the staff get to know every child and most—if not all—of their family members. "Coming to W. O. Smith is a family thing," said Rabinowitz. That is only one difference that makes this a unique school.

The teachers are dedicated volunteers who have been Symphony members, public school or college teachers, Music Row musicians, church musicians, and retired music teachers. Rabinowitz said, "To come here even for an hour a week over thirty-two or thirty-three weeks is a lot of time. We have twenty-five or thirty who have been teaching longer than seven years. We have ten or fifteen who have been teaching longer than ten. I have about five who have been teaching here since the school opened. A couple of

William Oscar Smith *(left)* accepted a coat-hanger sculpture of himself in 1990 from Kenneth Wendrich, the first director of the W. O. Smith/Nashville Community Music School (1984–94). The sculpture, known as a "Smitty," was one of ten created by folk artist Vanoy Streeter and awarded to people who did great service for the school.

them give as much as three or four hours a week."

Rabinowitz is as passionate about the school's mission as Smith was. He explained, "Exposure to the arts is not the same thing as participating in the arts. The arts should be studied like mathematics or science or social studies because it is a subject that is as worthy as any of them and to exclude it is to belittle it." He added, "We live in a world right now—I don't think it is just the United States; I think it's the world in general—where quick-and-easy fixes are demanded. When something becomes difficult or hard or looks as if it is going to take a lot of work, we typically throw it to the side and go to the next thing. In music it just doesn't work that way. You have to sit down and you have to work at it. Some people have to

work harder than others, but even great musicians know there is no substitute for putting in hours and hours of work."

Students must work diligently, for twice a year a panel of teachers evaluates their playing; students may be removed from the school if they consistently fail to measure up. The school is not focused on producing music educators or music performers, although some students have gone to college and pursued music as a career. Others have attended college and selected various other careers, but certainly not all aspire to higher learning. Nevertheless, all students benefit from maintaining the self-discipline required for playing an instrument.

Most donations come from local individuals. The Metro Arts Commission and the Tennessee Arts Commission are the only governmental agencies from which the school accepts funds; there is no federal funding. Local foundations and corporations such as Sony Music Nashville, Gaylord, and the William Morris Agency have been sponsors. Rabinowitz noted, "They are giving funds to us simply because they believe in the mission of the school. They know that our students and their families are not going to be impressed or purchase things from them because of it."

What does the future hold for the school? A capital campaign is under way, and when the financial goals are met, work will begin on a building with enough space for teaching, a rehearsal hall large enough for a full symphony, and a library. Board members, staff members, faculty, parents, and students had input into the design, and the plans are already drawn. Rabinowitz and the board of directors do not intend to proceed until the funds are in hand. W. O. Smith had a dream, and others are now working to see that youngsters in the school bearing his name have access to his "key to a good life" and pursue their own ambitions in music or elsewhere.

The Nashville Sound

There is a real relationship between "both sides,"
for lack of a better term—
this commercial art form and the classical art form.

—KYLE YOUNG

"THERE HAS BEEN an interesting relationship between classical players and what has gone on here [in Nashville]—if you look, for example, at what people would say is the first golden age here with Chet Atkins and Owen Bradley and their very calculated approach to the music at that time. Rock and roll was cutting heavily into country sales figures and its market share. They intentionally went about to try to sweeten the sound, make it more accessible, make it more popular in tone. If you go back and look at the session sheets—and we have all of these—from that time period, you will see lots of classical players on those sessions. I think it has been a relationship that has worked both ways. Without that level of expertise in town perhaps Owen and Chet would not have been able to create what we all now refer to as the Nashville Sound," said Kyle Young, director of the Country Music Foundation, Inc. (The Country Music Hall of Fame and Museum is a division of that foundation.) He continued, "If you move forward and if you look at the scene today, I think you'll see the same relationship. You'll see people who are Symphony players who moonlight—I don't know which one is moonlighting—and support the vernacular music by coming in and doing sessions."

Bill Ivey, a former director of the Country Music Foundation and a former chairman of the National Endowment for the Arts, offered his definition of the *Nashville Sound*: it is "a phrase that denotes a style of country music and an era in which that style was especially influential. The term has also been more generally applied in descriptions of the relaxed, improvisational feel of any recording produced within the informal, good-humored atmosphere that pervades Nashville recording studios. The phrase has been employed to convey the notion of a special mystique surrounding record-making in Nashville." In other words, it is hard to explain in words; you know it when you hear it, though. The term first appeared in *Music Reporter* in 1958, and in November 1960 *Time* ran a lengthy article on Jim Reeves with "Nashville Sound" as a subhead.

The man who started the movement toward that sound was Eddy Arnold. Michael Streissguth wrote the book *Eddy Arnold: Pioneer of the Nashville Sound* in which he stated, "Eddy's mature voice, Chet's production, the Nashville rhythm sections, and—more and more often—the strings produced some of the finest music of Eddy's career."

At a special ceremony on March 6, 2003, at the Country Music Hall of Fame and Museum in which Eddy Arnold donated his memorabilia, he was recognized for his contributions to country music and to the evolution of Nashville as Music City. WSM broadcast the proceedings. Mr. Arnold's career spanned six decades, and he has sold 85 million records—and they are still selling. He was the headliner at Carnegie Hall in 1966 to a standing-room-only crowd, and when performing—whether on TV or before a live audience—he frequently wore a tuxedo. A native Tennessean who has lived in the Nashville area for decades, Mr. Arnold is an astute businessman and good citizen in addition to being a fine artist.

Kyle told the audience gathered for the ceremony that day: "Along with his 1954 hit 'I Really Don't Want to Know,' which he recorded with background vocals and *without* steel guitar, his 1955 rendition of 'Cattle Call' marked Mr. Arnold's experimentation with what would later be known as the Nashville Sound. It underscored his transition from rural, traditional, folk music to more polished and more widely accessible pop-influenced sounds. His diamond dream was shining far beyond the limits of Nashville and country music and would ultimately cut a trail for the likes of Patsy Cline, Jim Reeves, Elvis Presley, and many others."

The A Team studio musicians who played in untold numbers of sessions were Buddy Harman (drum); Ray Edenton, Grady Martin, Hank Garland, and Harold Bradley (guitar); Bob Moore and Henry Strzelecki (bass); Floyd Cramer and Hargus "Pig" Robbins (piano); and Pete Drake (steel guitar). On the sessions with artists such as Mr. Arnold, Patsy Cline, Elvis, and Jim Reeves, some of the same names appear repeatedly—many who were then members of the Nashville Symphony or had been. Here are just a few examples: on August 17, 1961, when Patsy Cline cut "True Love," "San Antonio Rose," "The Wayward Wind," and "A Poor Man's Roses," she had assistance from Byron Bach (cello); Brenton Banks, Lillian Hunt, Suzanne Parker, and George Binkley III (violin); Harold Bradley (bass); and John Bright and Cecil Brower (viola). The next year, September 5, she was working on "Why Can't He Be You," "Your Kinda Love," "When You Need a Laugh," and "Leavin' on Your Mind" with Byron Bach, Cecil Brower, Howard Carpenter, Solie Fott, Nancy Hearn, Lillian Hunt, and Verne Richardson (violin); Harold Bradley (electric bass); and Randy Hughes (acoustic guitar). When Chet Atkins was producing Eddy Arnold's "The Last Word in Lonesome Is Me" and Bill Walker was conducting it in October 1965, these musicians were on hand: Brenton Banks, Kenneth Goldsmith, Lillian Hunt, Sheldon Kurland, and Howard Carpenter (violin); Floyd Cramer (piano); Ray Edenton (guitar); Jerry Kennedy and Harold Bradley (electric guitar); Henry Strzelecki (bass); Murrey Harman (drums); Harvey Wolfe (cello); and Pamela Goldsmith and Martin

Katahn (viola). Some players for one of Elvis's gospel albums were Brenton Banks, George Binkley III, Lillian Hunt, and Solie Fott (violin) and Byron Bach (cello). Chet Atkins produced a little-known album released in 1967 called *Nashville Sound String Quartet: Country Songs by a String Quartet,* and some session players were participants: Roddy Bristol (leader and violin); William C. Sanders (bass); Brenton Banks (violin); Gary Van Osdale (viola); and Martha McCrory (cello).

A new generation is bringing expertise to the city, with Mark O'Connor, Edgar Meyer, and Béla Fleck prominent among them. Kyle noted that "Mark as a kid won a bunch of fiddling contests and moved to Nashville because he realized there was real potential here. There was opportunity here doing session work, and he did very well at that. But he is a virtuoso and he spins off and he is now doing things that are performed here and elsewhere. . . . We also have people who have come up through, certainly in Mark's case, a traditional musical background but who are so doggone good that they can cross the fence. Not only are there opportunities to play, but there are people going to those things who can discover new talent. There is this infrastructure: the publishing companies are here, a lot of recording is being done here, all of the major labels are here.

"In a sense Nashville is maturing musically, which does happen over time. And it is really a very short period of time for all of this to have happened. . . . This music goes through cycles. There are intensely creative cycles with innovators, and when that happens, the music gets bigger. Then it is human nature to be safe and get in to duplicating for a while. Then once that starts to go down, there is a big creative surge of energy, and it goes up. If you look at the history of this music from 1923 to now, you'll see these ebbs and flows and cycles. . . .When it is all said and done, it is art; it is music. That is its core; that is what it will always be, although market conditions will have an effect on how much is done."

An editorial that appeared in the *Nashville Union and American* on May 28, 1854, raised an issue with which Nashville has wrestled ever since it was written: "Nashville is greatly lauded for the fondness which its citizens display for music. Now a taste for music may consist in a fondness for reels and jigs, and for negro [*sic*] melodies; or it may be more cultivated and create a real enjoyment in the more celebrated works of the great masters. We shall see, for now is the test in which line the taste of Nashville runs."

More than one hundred years later, where is the taste of Nashville running? Kyle offered his opinion on this subject: "To me, a couple of things separate Nashville from most any other city in the country: one is the creative community, which is really vast and deep and varied, lots of different musics represented. And there is a sense of community within the creative community. The other thing is what is happening here is generally authentic in nature." Perhaps that is the *new* Nashville Sound—an eclectic offering of music, recorded by professional artists, with professional equipment.

Kyle summed up what he sees happening in the city: "We have a rich history and culture here. Outsiders come into Nashville and can be blown away by a performance at the Ramada Inn because the level of professionalism is so high. We are just used to that; we're spoiled in a certain way. There is so much expertise and the proficiency level is so high that you have to be fantastic to make an impression. . . . If you look at a great recital at Blair or a great line-up at the Opry or a great show at the Ryman or something here [at the Country Music Hall of Fame], this goes back to the depth of the creative community in this town.

"All you have to do is to travel around the country to understand how many musical offerings there are in this town. Part of it comes from the fact that a lot of people live here and are playing. Part of it has to do with people coming in to town. They are finally good enough to come, and they hope something will happen for them. It is an incredibly competitive marketplace. There are so many great choices literally on any given night. And some things don't even charge. That is part of the psyche of the city; that is part of the texture of the city. . . . Nashville is a music capital. Period."

~

An Opera Singer's Story

For as long as I can remember,
everyone assumed I was going to be a singer.

—JERRY JENNINGS

JERRY JENNINGS, a native of Paducah, Kentucky, came to Nashville in the 1950s to attend Peabody College, where his voice teacher and major professor was Louis Nicholas. Jerry said, "Singing (and music) was my ticket. For some kids, it's athletics; for others, grades. For me, it was my voice and music. In addition to the voice, I had a good ear and in later years learned that I was naturally very musical. It is a unique and generous gift, which I began using at a very early age. I began leading songs in my church when I was five years old. For as long as I can remember, everyone assumed I was going to be a singer. No one ever even suggested I do anything else with my life. In fact, I was told more than once that 'with a gift like that, you would be a fool not to use it.'"

During the summers of his sophomore through his senior years at Peabody College, he sang at the Municipal Opera in St. Louis. After college, he became a member of the U.S. Army Band and Chorus, often as a featured soloist. In late 1959, a former Peabody classmate, Bob Binkley (who had assumed the job of music director of Theater Nashville), asked him to sing the role of Rudolfo in a January 1960 production of Puccini's *La Bohème*. During the rehearsals, he met Nancy Wyckoff, who had performed several leading roles with Theater Nashville, and they were married by June of that year. Extending his enlistment in the army, Jerry received grants from the Rockefeller Foundation to study voice with Todd Duncan, the original Porgy of Gershwin's *Porgy and Bess,* and German with Professor Heinrich von Ihring at Georgetown University.

All of his hard work paid off when he successfully auditioned for a position at the Städtische Bühnen (Municipal Opera) in Bielefeld, a town in Westphalia, Germany. There he learned and performed the basic tenor repertoire for more than twenty-five leading roles, and he became one of the most widely used Mozart tenors in Germany. He was featured in *Opernwelt*, a monthly opera magazine, in which one writer observed, "There is hardly a house that would seriously consider mounting a new Mozart production without the services of this outstanding artist."

Although based in Bielefeld, Jerry sang regularly at the Deutsche Oper in Berlin as well as other theaters in Germany, Switzerland, and Belgium. He recorded Handel's *The Brockes Passion* and *Samson* with DGG (Deutsche Grammophon Gesellschaft). He performed the role of Camille Rosillon in a Eurodisc complete recording of *The Merry Widow* under the direction of Robert Stoltz, who had directed the premiere of this work in Vienna at Theater-an-der-Wein on December 30, 1905. In 1967 Jerry had the role of Lt. B. F. Pinkerton in a complete film version of Puccini's *Madama Butterfly* with the soprano Anneliese Rothenberger. Produced by the Zweites Deutsche Fernsehen (Germany's national Channel 2), it was broadcast by EuropaVision across Europe.

In 1967 Jerry accepted an invitation to join the Staatsoper (State Opera) in Hamburg, which at the time was considered one of the leading European houses. In December 1968 he sang the leading role of Tamino in a new production of Mozart's *Magic Flute* with stage direction by the actor Peter Ustinov and music direction by Sir Georg Solti. He was on the path to greater success in the opera world when he made a life-changing decision that shocked everyone. On a day after rehearsal of a new production of Tchaikovsky's *Eugen Onegin* he told his wife that he thought they (and by then two children) needed to go back home.

Jerry said, "There was something that I couldn't quite identify that was telling me we needed to get back to the States. I had just signed a very lucrative five-year contract that gave me first rights to sing the roles that were in my repertoire. It guaranteed me the opportunity to add some of the roles I had not had the chance to perform. It also gave me plenty of opportunity to accept guest engagements in other theaters. When a fellow American artist heard I had decided to return to the States, he put it this way: 'You've got to be out of your mind to leave this. Why, there is not a singer around who wouldn't give most anything to have the deal you have.' Perhaps I was, but time would prove otherwise.

"I set up a meeting with Rolf Lieberman, the general intendant of the Staatsoper at that time, and simply told him that I felt I needed to go home, back to my roots. He said that had I given him any other reason, he would not have let me out of my contract. But he understood. I later learned that it cost the theater more than $65,000 to cover my roles with other artists until they could sign a replacement."

Jerry finished the season, returned to Nashville in June 1969, and worked toward completing a master's degree at Peabody College because he thought he might teach. He said, "During that year I got word that New York City Opera was looking for someone to perform some of the roles I had performed in Germany. I went to New York and auditioned for Julius Rudel and was immediately engaged, making my debut with Beverly Sills in Mozart's *Die Entführung aus dem Serail*. While there, I also sang for Columbia Artists Management, and they signed me to a management contract. . . .

"It was a tough year [his wife underwent surgery to remove a malignant tumor of the thyroid, and he is convinced that already being at home with the extended family somewhat eased the situation for all of them as they could provide even more support for her]. I finished my degree and began preparing vocally to sing again. In the following four years, I sang widely in this country, in Canada, and back in Europe." Highlights were three seasons at City Opera; three seasons with the New York Philharmonic under Pierre Boulez; three seasons with Solti and the Chicago Symphony (Bach's St. Matthew Passion; a concert version of Strauss's *Salome* with Birgitt Nilsson in the title role, two performances in Chicago and one in Carnegie Hall; and the Haydn Mass in G); the Boston Symphony at Tanglewood with Seiji Ozawa; the role of Ferrando in Mozart's *Così fan tutte* at the Glyndebourne Festival and subsequently in Royal Albert Hall in England; and three seasons with the opera companies in Edmondson, Winnipeg, and Calgary, Canada.

"As my career continued to keep me busier and busier, I became an absentee father and husband," Jerry said. "Had I continued with that work and lifestyle, I would have lost my wife, my children, and my soul. It was too high a price. So I decided it was time to call it quits and try to find a way to support my family and not have to be away so much. That is when I made the decision to start my real estate career in Nashville."

Jerry's experiences in Germany gave him a perspective on the arts that otherwise he would not have had. Following World War II, the opera houses were among the first structures the Europeans rebuilt. He said, "I know of people who told of missing meals so they could afford to go to a performance of Beethoven's *Fidelio*. I recall an old Italian telling me of the significance of Verdi's *Nabucco* for the Italians after WWII."

He perceived two reasons to explain the difference with which the arts are valued in the States versus in Europe. "One reason is ignorance," Jerry stated. "Not in the dumb, stupid sense but simply in the sense of not knowing . . . not knowing the value of a really good symphony orchestra, not knowing how music feeds the soul, how beauty in art, music, ballet refreshes and uplifts one's inner self, how a beautiful Mozart melody or a chorus from Handel's *Messiah* or the Agnus Dei from Verdi's Requiem Mass can connect you to something far greater than yourself; a knowledge of the transcendent nature of something that is able to lift you up to where you are not, out of the ordinariness of life, and puts you in a place you don't want to leave. Humans don't tend to support something, the benefits or value of which they have little or no knowledge.

"Of course in any discussion of a topic such as this, you are inevitably faced with the chicken or the egg question. Is ignorance the result of history, or is history the result of ignorance? In a macro sense, the extent to which an emphasis upon and broad-based financial support for the arts [in the U.S.] have lagged behind Europe for the past one hundred years is, at least in my opinion, largely due to events that have made it virtually impossible for the vast majority of individuals and governments to focus their energies on anything beyond survival. Except for a few years in the early part of the twentieth century, from the middle of the nineteenth century on through WWII, the primary focus of the majority of our citizens and thus our governments in this country has been either reconstruction or survival.

The Europeans have had four hundred years of experience with the arts and learning the role the arts play in the enrichment of the soul. In Germany, Austria, and Italy after the war, their cultural institutions were a priority because they knew the role that arts and culture would play in the process of reconstruction. They needed these things to get them through the tough times. They knew the importance of things that fed their souls and lifted them above the drabness and ordinariness of their circumstances. [A report issued in the spring of 2003 by the Performing Arts Research Coalition indicated that Americans may be learning more about the importance of the arts. Although tourism was down after the terrorist attacks of September 11, 2001, more people who were surveyed by the Coalition went to a live professional performing arts event than to a live professional sporting event.]

"The other reason is the lack of sustained, significant financial support, either from governments or from private patrons. There is, without question, an exponential relationship between the vitality, quality, and availability of the arts and those who are willing to support them. Some of the more prominent patrons of the arts in earlier times were the Medicis, the Esterhazys, Emperor Franz Josef, and the Catholic Church. In more recent times, especially in Germany, the various governing entities have been willing to generously subsidize their cultural institutions. In our own country the National Endowment of the Arts has sort of put its toe in the water, as it were, and attempted to assume the role of public patron of the arts." He cited individual Americans who have had an impact on the arts: Adelaide Cooley in Peoria, Katie Westby in Tulsa, Lillian Disney and Dorothy Chandler in Los Angeles, Anna Rodale in Allentown, Pennsylvania, and Sue Shepherd in St. Louis—all women.

The city of Bielefeld, a city of 172,000 in 1966, paid Jerry a salary of a certain amount per month to sing in four or five productions for a total of twenty or twenty-five performances in the North Rhine–Westphalia area. He recalled reading about that time that LA—a city of several million—had just made a commitment to contribute $1 million to the arts. "That year in Bielefeld the city's portion to the arts was the equivalent of $750,000," he said.

Germany is having trouble now funding the arts, and one reason has been the cost of reconstructing East Germany. "But the *last* thing cut in East Germany was the arts, even though most things within the country were in such dreadful shape," Jerry said. He believes the country will catch up and the arts will receive more funds.

Jerry may not be singing on the operatic stage any longer, but he has not lost his passion for the performing arts. He is convinced that "music is the most direct channel to the heart of a human being and its impact upon it is enormous." His story is one shining example of how that may occur.

Public Radio and Television

It's an easy way to get an arts fix or a symphonic fix. It's not the same as being there, no question about that.

—BEN RECHTER

PUBLIC RADIO AND TELEVISION have provided access to the performing arts at regularly scheduled times throughout the United States, and Nashville is no exception. The need for public stations became evident when commercial radio and television generally neglected the arts. As Ben Rechter, an ardent arts supporter, pointed out, hearing the radio or watching television is not the same as actually attending a performance, but at the touch of a button it may introduce people to works they may not otherwise experience, provide old standards that may be new to younger audiences, and educate theatergoers and nontheatergoers alike. Beginning in the 1960s, the city sponsored both radio and television, although the stations have now achieved independent status.

The public radio station WPLN-FM was licensed to Nashville's Metro Government as part of the public library system. In December 1962 broadcasts began on a limited basis, Monday through Friday; it was 1989 before the station broadcast twenty-four hours a day, each day. The Public Broadcasting Act of 1967 authorized the creation of the Corporation for Public Broadcasting (CPB), which was to encourage "the growth and development of noncommercial radio." The next year WPLN was a charter member of National Public Radio, and in 1970 the CPB provided financial help to WPLN and other stations.

The downtown public library served as WPLN's home for most of its life until the station built a new facility in Metro Center at 630 Mainstream Drive and started broadcasting from there in May 1998. Having its own freestanding site was only part of the process associated with becoming independent of Metro. In 1996 Nashville Public Radio was chartered, Mayor Phil Bredesen and the Metro Council approved the transfer of the license and assets of WPLN to Nashville Public Radio, the FCC permitted the change, and the assets were actually transferred. As of the spring of 2003, WPLN was reaching 11 percent of its market, which meant it was in the top five public radio stations in the fifty biggest markets.

Broadcasts of classical music and many other kinds of music have filled most of the airtime, and sometimes local groups have been the performers, live (for example, on "Live on Studio C") and recorded. The Nashville Symphony has been presented in delayed broadcasts. The Metropolitan Opera has been a regular program. Interviews with people in various artistic disciplines have been recurring features. Lin Folk was an early employee as producer, interviewer, and narrator, and for many years she listed the cultural "Happenings" in the area. You can still hear about the "Happenings" on the radio, or you can log on to the station's Web site (www.wpln.org), launched in 2000, that allows you to access programming on a computer.

Since the birth of the television, technology has stepped on radio's toes and reduced radio audiences. As a Utah teenager, Philo T. Farnsworth envisioned the electronic television, and within a few years he transmitted an image (1927). The Great Depression and World War II hampered the development of TV and TV stations, but after the war, the TV industry exploded with talented people in front of and behind the cameras. The audiences grew as more people could afford to purchase a set, and in the early days they could view dramas along with comedies, westerns, game shows, and variety shows. Shows that became household names included *Texaco Star Theatre, Playhouse 90, Philco TV Playhouse, Goodyear TV Playhouse, Armstrong Circle Theatre, Studio One, Summer Playhouse, Ford Theatre, Kraft TV Theatre,* and the *Alcoa Hour.* Only occasionally were orchestral, ballet, and operatic performances broadcast.

In 1952 the FCC set aside channels for noncommercial public broadcasting systems, and in that year people throughout Davidson County endeavored—without success—to start an educational TV station. The "$2 for Channel 2" campaign had a goal of $100,000, and although the goal was not reached, the FCC reserved Channel 2 for Nashville. It was September 1962 before WDCN-Channel 2 was licensed to the Metropolitan Board of Public Education, and in 1973 WDCN moved to Channel 8, the first channel move in the nation. Since the mid-1970s, WDCN has broadcast from 161 Rains Avenue. As of July 1999, WDCN gained its independence from government ownership. The next year the call letters were changed to WNPT (Nashville Public Television).

More than 400,000 households tune in every week in Middle Tennessee and southern Kentucky; that figure was closer to 270,000 households in the early 1990s, so there has been growth. Ben Rechter, then chairman of the Board of Directors of NPT, said, "It has gotten to be one of the better stations in the country in terms of viewership. In percentage of population for one three-month period we were the highest in the nation, and we stand to be one of the better markets. You would think that would translate into more arts kinds of things, too."

Ben addressed the problems of trying to produce shows locally: "Let's say that we want to present our Symphony on public television and take it to PBS. To do that is very expensive to produce the quality that is needed. We have to have heavy sponsorship here [in Nashville]. Just for that one thing, you can suck up half of the dollars for everything else that you want to do." Knowing all of this, we were able to present "An Evening with the Nashville Symphony," produced by NPT and broadcast nationally on PBS in January 2002. In addition to performances of Beethoven's Prometheus Overture and Charles Ives's Symphony No. 2, there were interviews with Maestro Kenneth Schermerhorn and segments about the Orchestra. The cost was substantial because the musicians' performance fees of $20,000 had to be paid, but it was worth the effort and the cost to gain exposure for Nashville's fine orchestra.

Masterpiece Theatre and *Great Performances* are two of the longest-running series for the performing arts. NPT has worked with PBS in producing *A Death in the Family* for *Masterpiece Theatre* and a documentary on the Fisk Jubilee Singers. Another program with Nashville ties that had national exposure was the gospel opera *Make a Joyful Noise,* written by Bobby Jones.

Cable television was unheard of when Nashville's public station went on the air. The Arts and Entertainment Network and Bravo! are relatively new competitors for public television for viewing the performing arts. These networks now vie for programming and for viewers that public television for some years had all to itself, and A&E had become one of the top twenty cable TV networks by 2002. Americans in 2001 viewed an average of thirty hours per week of television, and cable television garnered the lion's share of viewers (49) compared to public television (3). (Share figures refer to a percentage of the viewing audience for all television viewing, twenty-four hours a day.)

Both public radio and television have their work cut out for them to keep pace with audiences' tastes, technological challenges, and the viewers' choices of how to spend discretionary time.

The Performing Arts and Metro Government

I believe that Metro Government was the single smartest thing that Nashville ever did.

—BILL PURCELL, MAYOR OF NASHVILLE

"THE PROCESS actually began in the 1950s, which is very much in advance of the rest of the country, thinking about the notion that we had too many layers of government and too much shared responsibility," said Mayor Bill Purcell of the move to create the Metropolitan Government of Nashville and Davidson County. The suggestion to form a metropolitan government was made as early as 1915, and over the years the idea reappeared only to fade away. But, explained Mayor Purcell, "they passed legislation that would authorize it, and then in 1963 they actually pulled it off. It took an incredible amount of sustained effort, and it became the model in the years that followed for Metro Government in Indianapolis, Jacksonville, and most recently and interestingly Louisville." The mayor cited two basic benefits of creating a metropolitan system of government: "One was greater efficiency of government. . . . It also provided us with a critical mass of people and resources for our city to advance."

Some attention was given to the performing arts in the Metro charter, and the relevant section appropriated "a sum not in excess of fifteen thousand dollars ($15,000.00) [an amount that was unchanging until recent years] for any year for the use of the Nashville Symphony Association of Nashville, Tennessee." Mayor Purcell pointed out, "I don't think there is any argument that cities that had greater wealth earlier and greater development earlier moved more quickly to develop a broad arts community that incorporated a larger amount of both visual and performing arts. But the government role in almost every city or the government's collaboration really is visible only in the last fifty years."

Mayor Purcell, the fifth mayor of Metro Nashville, took office in 1999; he followed Beverly Briley, Richard Fulton, Bill Boner, and Phil Bredesen (now governor of the state of Tennessee). I noted earlier Mayor Briley's reluctance to support the arts, saying he was too occupied with building sewers and roads. Mayor Fulton gave lip service to the arts, but funding never materialized. Mayor Boner, for all his leadership flaws, did help the Symphony get out of the ditch in 1988 (after nine months in bankruptcy) by budgeting $500,000. The next year the Symphony offered to share this amount with the other arts groups if the grant continued. It did, and all shared.

When Phil Bredesen was running for mayor in 1991, I spoke with him about making a stronger commitment to local public funding for the arts through the Metropolitan Nashville Arts

Bill Purcell, the fifth mayor of the Metropolitan Government of Nashville and Davidson County, took office in 1999 and was the first mayor to appoint a director of cultural affairs for the city.

Commission, which was a very small agency. The amount in the fund each year that was available for grants was very small, too. He understood that having thriving cultural institutions was important to the life of the city, and he understood that the arts are an important economic development tool when recruiting new businesses. (When I found myself chair of a bankrupt Symphony in 1988, Phil Bredesen and a few others helped me rebuild the devastated institution.) After Phil's mayoral election, he recognized that he could not expand funding for the arts commission without the cooperation of the Metro Council. Arts enthusiasts needed to raise the council's awareness of the significance of including a larger figure in the budget for the arts.

Keel Hunt of the Strategy Group and Lewis Lavine worked toward that end. Keel said, "We did a lot of talking to individual organization executives and some of their board members. We began to evolve a notion that, when grant application time came, it could be 'every man for himself'—but that we all needed to join hands in a positive spirit to raise awareness and grow the fund itself, in the first place. Our advocacy program eventually took the form of what we now call the Nashville Arts Coalition, and the fund has now grown to more than $2 million. Mayor Purcell has continued that growth since he became our mayor." Jane Fabian, formerly executive director of the Nashville Ballet, has long seen the wisdom of cooperation among arts organizations: "I am such an advocate for collaboration. I know it's critical to the long-term success and future of the arts in this city."

Keel noted, "Mayor Bredesen believed that some of the organizations are important beyond their specific program—the Nashville Symphony, the Ballet, the Opera, the Repertory Theatre, the Nashville Children's Theatre, and maybe two or three others—and are more broadly important to the welfare of the city and its growth. He referred to those organizations as being part of the 'civic furniture' of the community. I mention that because it's an ongoing policy discussion, one that has not been settled. It will probably never be settled because there will be competition for those dollars. We in our office continue to support the work of the Nashville Arts Coalition, and that takes the form of a year-long educational program—inviting policy makers to events, helping to give them current information as to the public being served, directly and indirectly, by the arts organizations."

What is the role of Metro Government in the development of the arts? Mayor Purcell had this answer: "We ought to be one of the preeminent supporters of the existing arts organizations in the city. We ought to be a part of the public discussion about the arts needs of the city. And then ultimately I think we need to be encouragers of the arts generally as part of our basic commitment to quality of life for all of our citizens. In there obviously is a combination of roles, from cheerleader to funder. I think it varies, depending upon the area of the arts that you're talking about.

"Quality of life requires that we do all of these things well in this city. It will not do any longer to say that we're going to have a great school system and at the same time suggest that we're not going to include music or art or the arts generally. That we're going to build great buildings, but we're not going to respect the importance of them being inspired and inspiring buildings that provide spaces for people to be inspired not simply by the great successes of the sports teams within but also of the world that still remains outside. That notion is clear in this administration from its start. John Bridges and I arrived in this courthouse together. I understood clearly that we had to have people who got up every day and thought about how that balance is created and maintained."

In his career John Bridges has worked with the Tennessee Arts Commission and has covered the arts as a reporter for the *Tennessean* and the *Nashville Scene*, but he now has the title of Director of Cultural Affairs for Nashville. He said, "I'm the first person to have a job like this in Metro Government. There had never been a mayor who had a person to deal with cultural affairs. There had not heretofore been the presence of the arts that necessitated the need for such an office. Things had begun to happen at a level in town so that this mayor realized he had to keep an eye on what was happening and the city had to be involved."

Even though the city's governmental structure has been organized for greater efficiency under the umbrella of Metro Nashville, it seems to be taking longer for some individual citizens, especially older citizens, to embrace that idea. Those individuals had for so much of their lives identified with their segment of the city, whether it was

Madison, Berry Hill, Oak Hill, or Bellevue, and trips to the city's center were few and far between.

Kelly Bainbridge has heard from her parents about this issue: "My parents both grew up in the northern part of Nashville in the 1950s and 1960s—my mom in Madison and my dad in Goodlettsville. Both of them have told me stories about how far away downtown seemed to them when they were growing up. Their lives were pretty much contained within Madison and Goodlettsville—for school, church, and other activities. My dad remembered riding the train to town on weekends to go to the movies, but that seemed to be the extent of his memories of downtown. They didn't dislike downtown so much as they didn't have a reason to go downtown."

The younger generation, including Kelly, has developed a different perspective on the city. She said, "I have a deep appreciation for the neighborhoods where I grew up as well as a love for the city. My church, St. Ann's Episcopal, is downtown, and I attended Meigs and Hume-Fogg. I think the fact that my circle of friends were geographically scattered across the county gave me a wider sense of my hometown. I had the best of both worlds—I lived in the 'country' in Whites Creek, but I went to school in the heart of the city. As a Hume-Fogg student, I definitely attended my share of arts events, mostly at TPAC, which I truly enjoyed. I think I identify more with the city itself because no matter where we happened to live (Madison, Joelton, or Whites Creek), the city was always my main neighborhood."

Perhaps it will not be long before all Nashvillians—older and younger generations, more established and new-to-the-block residents—regard the city in that way, no matter where they live within its boundaries. Many people have moved to Nashville because they value the city's quality of life, and they should not be disappointed by what they find after making that move. (According to the 2000 census, Nashville had 569,891 people compared to Atlanta's 416,474; the Metropolitan Statistical Areas, however, included about 4.1 million in Atlanta and more than 1.2 million in Nashville.) Coming to the heart of Nashville to attend events at TPAC and other venues, such as the Ryman, the War Memorial Auditorium, and the upcoming Schermerhorn Symphony Center, may be a means of strengthening this feeling.

Mayor Purcell addressed the challenges facing the arts: "What I think has changed over the last fifty years is the notion that quality of life really requires broad access to the broadest range of artistic inspiration. What that has meant and what presents a challenge now is that having greater expectations shared more broadly across the community, how do you meet more of those expectations? It's meeting those higher expectations in the arts that presents the greatest challenge and that probably will remain the greatest challenge across time.

"One of the great strengths here now is a committed group of arts advocates with great breadth and great interest in a variety of arts, people who also in the private sector get up every day and think about how we can do more and better. I do think there is a consensus within the city about this being a need, but I'm really looking forward to the day, which I don't think is too far off, that people have a greater understanding of just exactly what we have done together. I think they'll be surprised, and I think that will be a very pleasant surprise."

Keel echoed the mayor's statements: "I think part of what creates the environment now that is so positive is that local arts organizations, and especially performing arts organizations, have developed successful programs that have been popular among the publics they serve." He continued, "In Nashville it's easy now to look back and say, 'Gee, a lot of things happened fast.' People cite the Frist [Center for the Visual Arts], the library [the new downtown branch], the Country Music Hall of Fame. But what that masks is that each one of those had its own development track that required years of planning and also a different leadership matrix for each one. They just came to fruition at the same time. That was a glorious thing, but it is important to realize how those developed. The totality of those projects is a great testimony to Nashville and how it may have been ahead of any other city in the South."

Nashvillians have learned that we can work together on major projects and overcome obstacles to the benefit of all, and we have proven that again and again throughout the city's history. Now the question is this: Can we sustain all of these splendid, ambitious arts organizations?

Blair School of Music

Our history as a learning institution is one of good fortune and inspired guidance.

—MARK WAIT

BLAIR SCHOOL OF MUSIC became the tenth school of Vanderbilt University in 1981, and the name of Blair has become synonymous with high-quality music education and music. That achievement has come about in a relatively short period of time since the school's founding, but Nashville would never have had such a fine school without the foresight, dedication, and generosity of one family who wanted to honor the memory of Myra Jackson Blair. Love of family and love of music came together in this unique school bearing the name of this woman who had studied at the Boston Conservatory of Music and then taught piano and the theory of music in the Nashville Conservatory of Music in 1897–98. Her daughter, Valere Blair Potter, had the idea of doing something special

musically for Nashville, and through the guidance of C. B. Hunt, director of the School of Music at George Peabody College for Teachers, the Blair Academy of Music was begun as a pre-college division of the School of Music in 1964. For years Blair relied on the funding of the Justin and Valere Potter Foundation, and Mrs. Potter and her daughters and their husbands—Anne and Pat Wilson and Valere and Albert Menefee—were active supporters of the school.

A national search was conducted for a director, and the young man who was selected for that job was John Friedel (Del) Sawyer, a trumpet player with a master's degree in music from Peabody College. He was then a teaching fellow at Peabody College but had been an instructor in trumpet at the University of Houston and Northeast Louisiana State College, and he had performance experience in Nashville's studios and with the Houston Symphony and the Nashville Symphony. (He would also work with the American Ballet Theatre Orchestra, the Montavani Orchestra, and the Benny Strong Orchestra.)

With a grant of $25,000 (about $145,000 today) for each of the first three years from the Potter Foundation, Del set to work to establish a school, and that included renovating a home for it. There were other music preparatory schools in the nation, but having Blair as a pre-college division within a School of Music was a bit different. Del read all he could about the subject, particularly the preparatory programs at Peabody Conservatory of Music in Baltimore, Maryland, and Eastman School of Music in Rochester, New York, and he visited the Peabody Conservatory. During the summer of 1964, the house in Nashville at 1208 Eighteenth Avenue South (where Ann Carolyn Mann grew up) was transformed from a fraternity house to a music school, complete with wall-to-wall carpeting and air-conditioning. It had fourteen studios, two offices, and a waiting room.

In the school's first catalog, Felix C. Robb, president of Peabody College, called the school's opening a "landmark event in the musical history of Nashville," and how prophetic he was! Del wrote, "Through private and class instruction from outstanding specialists, Blair Academy has been designed to give training necessary for a career in music." It had further goals: "1) to enhance and support the musical instruction now available in the elementary and secondary schools and 2) to direct students toward a more effective contribution in the performance of music in church, school, and civic groups in the community."

The first faculty members were Roland Schneller (piano), Barbara Hofer* (flute), Ralph Strobel* (oboe; bassoon), Stephen Sefsik* (clarinet; saxophone), Donald Sheffield* (trumpet), Jerry Haynie (French horn), Gene Mullins* (trombone; baritone; tuba), Kenneth Goldsmith* (violin), Wilda Tinsley* (violin), Pamela Goldsmith* (viola), Harvey Wolfe* (violoncello), George Hofer* (double bass), Farrell Morris* (percussion; timpani), Sarah Croom Morris (piano), Peter Fyfe (organ), Diane Sheffield (accordion), Shirley Nonhof Cortner (voice), Bryan Lindsay (theory; ear training), Elizabeth Nohe Colson (history and literature of music), and Jerry O. Williams (recorder). (The asterisk indicates membership in the Nashville Symphony.) Schneller was the only full-time faculty member; the rest were part-time. Some taught at Peabody College, too, or in the public school system. Many had a master's degree in music.

The school opened in September 1964 and had a student enrollment the first year of 135. Music theory, ear training, and the history and literature of music were required or optional according to the program that a student followed, but all students had performance and class exams. Scholarships were available: twenty from the Potter Foundation for high school students planning to make music a career, and two from Owen Bradley for youngsters whose limited resources would not permit them to attend. The fee per quarter for private instruction (one thirty-minute private lesson and one fifty-minute class in music theory and ear training per week) was $45; there were other categories of private instruction and also class

Blair Academy of Music began in 1964 as a pre-college division of the School of Music of George Peabody College for Teachers, and for years Blair relied on the funding of the Justin and Valere Potter Foundation. It was one of the first schools in the country to use the Suzuki method to teach youngsters the violin.

instruction. Classes were held after school and on Saturday during the school year, and youngsters came from the city, the surrounding area, and Kentucky and Alabama.

Each year or so, Blair reached another milestone. It was one of the first schools in the nation to offer training on the violin, based on the Suzuki Talent Education Program, for children ages three to five. More and more students enrolled so that two converted buildings were in use on Eighteenth Avenue South. Del continued to insist on quality instructors and quality instruction. Out of his growing concern about having quality stringed instrument teachers in Nashville, he submitted a proposal in 1967 to the Potter Foundation to fund a resident string quartet to be a full-time string faculty as well as performers, and the Blair String Quartet was the result. Four years later (1971) the Blair Woodwind Quintet was established. Classical music at Blair was the emphasis and remains so to this day, although some instructors and concerts may adopt a different musical style.

The faculty took music to the community through solo recitals or ensembles (that community also included other cities and states). Beginning in 1969, Blair Academy of Music presented the Cheekwood Chamber Music Series. The Blair Chamber Players in 1972–73, for example, played on four Sunday afternoons (November 12, January 28, February 25, and March 25) at two o'clock. The program on November 12, with Jane Kirchner (flute), Cynthia Estill (bassoon), Enid Katahn (harpsichord; piano), Christian Teal (violin), Jean Dane (viola), and David Vanderkooi (cello), consisted of Telemann's Quartet in D Minor, Haydn's Quartet in G Major, Op. 77, No. 1, and Brahms's Quartet No. 1 in G Minor, Op. 25.

In 1972 Blair became cosponsor with the Nashville Symphony Association of the Nashville Youth Symphony, and the Junior Symphony was organized. In the summer of 1973 the first Youth Symphony summer camp was held. In 1973, the school had an enrollment of 421 pre-college students, and 185 college students received private instruction.

An article in the *Tennessean* on May 22, 1977, announced a major change for Blair Academy of Music. As of September 1, 1977, it would no longer be affiliated with Peabody College, and the name would become Blair School of Music, an independent, privately endowed entity. Anne Wilson was quoted as saying, "Our concentration has always been on the training of performing musicians rather than of teaching musicians." Three men had studied Blair and offered recommendations about its future: C. B. Hunt, then dean of fine arts at the University of Illinois at Carbondale; Samuel Hope, executive director of the National Association of Schools of Music (NASM); and Robert Freeman, director of the Eastman School of Music. Freeman said, "Nashville is the logical place for a major music center to develop, partly because of the new Performing Arts Center now going up, partly because of 16th Avenue, South (Music Row), partly because of the appointment of Michael Charry as director of the Nashville Symphony, and partly because of the musical leadership of Del Sawyer. That's an unusual combination of factors to find in one city." He also referred to the importance of the support from the Potter Foundation and the families behind it.

Another significant event in 1977 was Blair School's accreditation as a non-degree-granting institution by NASM. The school became affiliated with Vanderbilt University, and students who took courses at Blair received credit through the College of Arts and Science.

Blair School continued to rent the houses from Peabody College, but the school needed a larger, more up-to-date space. In 1978 the Potter Foundation agreed to fund a new building to be constructed on 3.5 acres of the Vanderbilt campus.

In 1967 when the Blair String Quartet was formed, its members were a full-time string faculty as well as performers. Current members are Christian Teal (violin), Cornelia (Connie) Heard (violin), Felix Wang (cello), and John Kochanowski (viola).

Faculty members contributed ideas to be incorporated in the new building while Del, architect Robert Street, and Justin Potter Wilson (chair of Blair's Board of Trust and grandson of Valere Potter) studied other structures to provide the best possible environment for the students and faculty.

To further enrich students, Del arranged to have visiting faculty. For example in the 1978–79 academic year, they were Dorothy DeLay of Juilliard with expertise in violin (that is an understatement); Elden Gatwood, the principal oboe of the Pittsburgh Symphony Orchestra; Menahem Pressler, a concert pianist; and the Fine Arts Quartet.

When the school moved in 1980, the more than 36,000 feet of space with soundproofed studios and a hall with a Holtkamp organ seemed too good to be true. Eventually the music library from the then defunct Peabody School of Music was moved to this building, and it is now the Anne Potter Wilson Music Library.

In 1981 Blair School of Music merged with Vanderbilt University, yet another remarkable event in the school's history. That year there were 1,059 students (425 pre-college, 426 from Vanderbilt, 17 from other colleges, and 191 adults). Of the forty-one faculty members, thirteen were full-time.

At the time of the merger Del said, "Historically, most music schools have an attitude that merely tolerates those students who do not wish to pursue music as a profession. This attitude has managed to reduce significantly the public support system essential to a healthy musical climate. At Blair we wish to share our love of music with others and involve the entire University community in music. Making music is entirely too much fun to be left only to professionals."

Jane Kirchner, currently associate dean and associate professor of flute, said, "You won't find many university music schools that started as a pre-college program." Blair is unique for another reason in that few schools granting music degrees emphasize musical training *and* liberal arts (two others are Oberlin and Rice).

Jane's experience with Blair goes back to its beginnings when she was a freshman in college and received instruction there because she could have a specialist teaching her instrument, the flute. She said, "I got a flute for my birthday, a big surprise [when she was a youngster]. I had wanted to play the violin because my friend was going to play the violin, but I got the flute instead. Then the involvement takes over your life real fast."

Although not a native Nashvillian, she played in the Nashville Youth Orchestra, the All-Star Band, sponsored by the *Tennessean*, and the Nashville Symphony (as a college student). Now she plays in the Blair Woodwind Quintet in addition to teaching and carrying out her administrative duties. Jane said, "The Blair Quintet is a fine performing group, and we work congenially together. I think we represent to the students what good chamber music playing can be. It is a real good training experience for your ears and your mind. You have to know who is on first. What are you supposed to be listening for? How does *this* fit? You practice your part and you all come together and wonder why it is like that." She continued, "If I didn't teach, you wouldn't see me here. Teaching is what I do for fun. I don't have many flute students, but it is energizing, the joy of my work."

The next step in Blair's development was authorization from the Vanderbilt Board of Trust to become a degree-granting school of the university. In 1984 the NASM approved a plan for a Bachelor of Music in Performance, and the next year the Vanderbilt Board of Trust approved the offering of a Bachelor of Music (B.Mus.) degree beginning in the fall of 1986. Thirteen students were in that first class seeking a Bachelor of Music, and nine graduated in 1990. Subsequently a B.Mus. in Composition/Theory and a B.Mus. in Musical Arts were approved. The newest degree program, developed with Peabody College, is the five-year Master of Education degree; a student becomes a solid musician through Blair training and in the fifth year, at Peabody, completes requirements for teacher licensure and does student teaching.

Del Sawyer was named dean of Blair in 1984 after a nationwide, two-year search. He remained in that position until 1993—two years after he announced his retirement—because he agreed to stay at the helm of the school in which he had invested so many years of his life until a replacement was found. The new dean and professor of music was Mark Wait, who had been at the University of Colorado; he has a Master of Music from Kansas State University and the Doctor of Musical Arts degree from the Peabody Conservatory of Music. Mark has presented piano concerts throughout the United States, he was a featured pianist in the recordings of the complete works of Igor Stravinsky (MusicMasters label) with Robert Craft, conducting, and he has performed Aaron Copland's *Piano Concerto* (January 2000) and Elliott Carter's *Piano Concerto* (October 2002) with the Nashville Symphony. He has brought energy and vision to Blair School of Music, and he is continuing to emphasize the professionalism so essential in developing young musicians.

Blair students come from states across the nation, although most are Tennesseans. Mark said, "We decided that about 180 music majors at the collegiate level is what we want. We could with these wonderful facilities let the enrollment even double if we needed to. Well, maybe not quite double, but certainly be much bigger. But I think we would lose the intensive interaction that there is between the student and the faculty member. We don't have any graduate programs here either. That is by choice.

"We want students studying with faculty members, not with graduate teaching assistants, from the very beginning. Parents and prospective students tell us that is very attractive; it is something they like about us. We want to be small; we want to be good. My statement to the faculty some years ago was that it is fine to be elite but never elitist.

"Thanks to Del Sawyer and Pat Wilson, we have a wonderful pre-collegiate program—about six hundred students in it. [Students may work toward a pre-collegiate Certificate of Achievement and College Preparatory Certificate.] Of those about 10 percent are adults and the rest are kids. I think it does enjoy a good grassroots support."

Jane made an interesting point: "Not everybody who comes through this school really wants to be a performing musician. Those who do usually go to grad school, and they usually go to pretty good grad schools, not necessarily in the Northeast. There is also Michigan, which is a fine school, Indiana, Texas at Austin, Colorado, and some great schools in California. We have sent them all around. New York, of course, but it's not the only place.

"Other of our graduates are headed to law school or to med school. Many eighteen-year-olds don't know for sure what they want to do. Some families of eighteen-year-olds know that music is a risk as a career. Vanderbilt has a fine reputation as a university, and some students say, 'Well, I know that I'm really going to be a doctor, but I'm not giving up my music. And I can do that at VU.'

"The string students are more likely to want to play in an orchestra and not teach public school. Our wind students typically come from a band program where they were turned on and they want to do that."

The school had been so successful that once again it was running out of room, and a major expansion was planned, quadrupling the size of the physical plant. When it was completed in the

Mark Wait is dean of the Blair School of Music.

fall of 2001, the school covered almost 131,000 square feet and gained classrooms, studios, practice rooms, rehearsal performance space, and the Martha Rivers Ingram Center for the Performing Arts. In Ingram Hall (seating 618) or the Steve and Judy Turner Recital Hall (seating 286), there is now a place for events such as the Blair Concert Series, faculty recitals, and Blair Ensemble concerts for Nashvillians as well as Vanderbilt students, and groups outside the university—whether opera, ballet, choruses, or orchestras—are invited to use Blair's facilities. The Nashville Symphony recorded three of its most recent CDs at Blair: the works of Elliott Carter, including the piano concerto performed by Dean Mark Wait; the virtuoso piano concerto and the Gaelic Symphony of American composer Amy Beach; and the Missa Solemnis of Beethoven.

Here are some of the programs provided by Blair School of Music: Nashville Youth Orchestra

Program (organized by degree of experience from the Suzuki Reading Orchestra to the Youth String Orchestra to the Repertory Orchestra to the Youth Symphony); Nashville Children's Chorus Program (Apprentice Boychoir, Boychoir of Nashville, Young Singers of Blair, Blair Choristers, and Concert Choir); pre-collegiate ensembles (Blair Suzuki Players, Flute Ensemble, Chamber Music, and Guitar Ensemble); and collegiate ensembles (Vanderbilt Orchestra, Vanderbilt Symphonic Wind Ensemble, Vanderbilt Symphonic Choir, Vanderbilt Opera Theatre, Vanderbilt Concert Choir [cosponsor, Student Services], Woodwind Choir, Brass Choir, Flute Choir, Saxophone Ensemble, Percussion Ensemble, Tuba Ensemble, Blair Bonz, and Chamber Music).

Sometimes a Blair faculty member develops a program or an event that is dear to his or her heart. For Bobby Taylor, that was "An Appalachian Celebration" presented in April 2003 with Butch Baldassari (on mandolin) and others as part of the Blair Concert Series. Bobby has been on the Blair faculty and has held the principal oboe position with the Nashville Symphony since 1969. He is also in the Blair Woodwind Quintet and often does studio work around town. He said, "I believe that the best results for a teacher come when someone is primarily a performer who also teaches rather than someone who teaches and also performs. In the course of a year I get to play every kind of music there is—opera, country, Christmas music, the great symphony literature, chamber music at Blair." But his roots are in the mountains, and he said, "My grandfather was a mountain banjo player; he and his brother used to play for weddings and gatherings like that. His brother played fiddle and actually made fiddles."

For a period in the 1980s, Blair had among its faculty a man with a special talent. William Moennig & Son, founded in the early twentieth century in Philadelphia, is famous as a violin maker and restorer and appraiser of rare violins, violas, and cellos. William H. Moennig Jr., who was the twelfth generation of his family (originally from Markneukirchen, Germany) to be a violin maker, became an artist teacher of stringed instrument repair. He was married to Wilda Tinsley, who was on the first faculty of Blair Academy.

Blair now has forty-eight full-time and sixty adjunct faculty members. The faculty members have studied at Indiana University, Peabody Conservatory, Vienna Academy of Music and Performing Arts, Juilliard, Eastman, and many more fine institutions, and they have performed at TPAC with the Nashville Symphony, the Kennedy Center, the Aspen Music Festival, Carnegie Hall, Concertgebouw, The Hague, and Paris Opera, just to name a few places. A new program for them, instituted in July 2003, allows them to be eligible for tenure; it was implemented to help recruit additional top-quality faculty members.

Mark Wait addressed what has been happening in music in Nashville: "There are some similarities between what the Symphony has been experiencing lately and what we [at Blair] have been. The Symphony has expanded its schedule; we have grown our enrollment. The Symphony has improved its quality; we have improved the quality of the students coming in.

"It's interesting—we have a number of faculty members who are in the Symphony, almost twenty. And several of them have principal positions. These people who started in the Symphony perhaps thirty years ago and started teaching at the Blair Academy thirty years ago—those two jobs then constituted one full-time job. [Some students from Blair's early days are in the Symphony, such as Roger Wiesmeyer, who was a pre-college student of Bobby Taylor.] Now they are two full-time jobs—or more. The Symphony by itself can do that, and Blair School by itself can do that. There is an inherent tension, but both have acquired greater independent status.

Serendipity at Work

Serendipity had to be at work to weave together education, love of music, and family connections and land three talented musicians in Nashville.

Jean Heard moved to Nashville from Chapel Hill, North Carolina, when her husband, Alexander Heard, became chancellor of Vanderbilt University in 1963. A violinist, she played with the Nashville Symphony for several seasons. She had studied at the University of Alabama with Ottokar Cadek, a Czech-born violinist, who was a noted chamber musician and had been first violinist with the New York String Quartet in the 1920s. Following graduation, she attended Juilliard for two years of further study.

Coming to Nashville was not a new experience for Jean, who had been in the city with her family while her father, an educator, was at Peabody College. She recalled, "My mother used to take me to violin recitals at the Nashville Conservatory of Music. Musicians from the conservatory would play on the campus at Peabody. I fell in love with the violin at a very early age." As a youngster, she studied in Montgomery, Alabama, with a teacher named Fannie Mark Seibels. By the time Jean was in her early high school years, her father drove her to Nashville from Montgomery on Saturdays to take lessons with Martha Carroll in her Eighth Avenue studio.

Jean and Alex had a daughter named Connie. She, too, loved the violin at an early age, and she took lessons from Wilda Tinsley. Later on, she attended Blair School of Music (then still Blair Academy), and she was a member of the Blair Student String Quartet. She, too, studied at Juilliard, from which she received her master's degree in music. She has performed chamber music with groups in famous halls and at summer festivals. She has been soloist with the North Carolina Symphony, the Nashville Symphony, the Municipal Chamber Orchestra (New York City), and the Aspen Brandenburg Ensemble. She was away from

Nashville for some years but returned and is now an associate professor of violin at Blair School and is a member of the Blair String Quartet. She is married to a most remarkable musician, Edgar Meyer.

Edgar's father, Edgar Meyer Sr., grew up in Chattanooga. He became a jazz bass player and traveled, but after his marriage he came back to Tennessee and taught strings in Oak Ridge's school system. He also taught Edgar, who said, "He gave me a violin at age five, and I wasn't that interested. I really wanted to play the bass, so my parents let me do it at five." He has not stopped playing since then. Although he started out as a math major in college, his degree is in music from Indiana University.

Edgar moved to Nashville at the beginning of 1984 for three reasons: Connie, Béla Fleck, and the musical opportunities. He had met Connie at the Aspen Chamber Symphony, and they performed together there for two years, 1982 and 1983. He had become very good friends with Béla. And he had become intrigued by the community of musicians in Nashville, particularly the instrumentalists.

"I wasn't likely to be playing in a bluegrass band, which is a lot about singing," explained Edgar. "It had really become clear to me that . . . this particular community, in addition to the fact that I loved the talent base, was happening right in my generation. That was screamingly obvious, although it didn't become obvious to the rest of the world until fifteen years later. . . .

"I would sit down with someone with a guitar and someone with a mandolin or a banjo and I could do everything I do and they could do everything they do and nobody had to play soft or loud for anybody. We all played naturally; it was a very natural dialogue in terms of how the instruments interacted sonically, so I knew that was a good fit for what I did. In addition to the fact that there was an innate interest in old-timey, traditional music, which came relatively late in life—i.e., fifteen or sixteen years old—as opposed to growing up with it since birth. I knew it was a place that I wanted to invest in heavily, and I did. . . . It was very clear that there was a vibrant scene of which I could be an active part and the opportunities would come with it."

The list of musicians and groups with which Edgar has played ranges from Reba McEntire to James Taylor to Hank Williams Jr., the Chamber Music Society of Lincoln Center to orchestras across the United States to Strength in Numbers (with Mark O'Connor, Jerry Douglas, Sam Bush, and Béla Fleck). A recording done by Edgar (double bass), Mark O'Connor (violin), and Yo-Yo Ma (cello), *Appalachian Journey*, won a Grammy Award in 2001 for the Best Classical Crossover Album.

Ask Edgar what type of musician he is, and he will respond, "I am a musician. If I was going to make a list of humans who influenced me deeply and musically, it would be more than five hundred people long; it might be a thousand people long, ranging from all kinds of composers and performers and from different eras. But I do have the ability at this point in my life to know that Bach was a bigger influence than anybody else on that list, and I could throw Mozart and Beethoven in there right behind him." His recent classical recordings, especially his *Bach: Unaccompanied Cello Suites Performed on a Double Bass*, have earned him widespread acclaim. He is also a composer and a teacher, some classes at Blair School but most are master classes around the world. He makes a yearly trip to the Banff Center for the Arts.

Edgar admitted, "I'm not bored. Overwhelmed on occasion, but not bored. It is true that I like being home, and when I leave town, then I go to work. I come home and that's nice. That's a transformation over twenty years. It used to be that most of what I was doing was in town. I do actually prefer it this way." At his rare appearances in Nashville these days the venues are always crowded.

In the fall of 2002 Edgar was named a MacArthur Fellow, an annual award made by the John D. and Catherine T. MacArthur Foundation, and the Foundation called attention to his music that "is a complex, intricate amalgam, creating a unique musical voice that broadens the technical potential of the bass and stretches the instrument's stylistic possibilities." The handsome five-year sum he receives—with no strings or demands attached—will give him the freedom to pursue projects of his own choosing. Whatever he does, it is certain to reflect his passion for music and for his instrument.

"We have expanded what we do because of the presence of some outstanding musicians in nonclassical areas. It is an expansion that would not have occurred if those musicians weren't here. Right after I arrived, I heard Mark O'Connor at the Station Inn, and I thought, *Boy, this guy has an incredible technique. He is a remarkable personality and artist. We need to make this available to our students.* So we now have a folk music program—fiddling and dulcimer and mandolin—simply because we have some of the finest artists on those instruments living and working right here in Nashville. Some of them have a modest enrollment; some have a pretty healthy enrollment. But it is part of being in the community.

"It's conventional wisdom: you shouldn't try to be all things to all people, but in education you can come closer to doing that and should try to come closer than in other fields. That is something we have tried here, and it has brought in new audiences to the Blair School. I like to think that it has brought in people who would never have walked through the doors of Blair before.

"Do we mix these on the same programs? No, we don't. I think a classical program is a classical program. I wouldn't want to mix genres. I think that would confuse different parts of the audience and require a disjointed level of concentration throughout the evening. I want people to know that yes, we are primarily a school of classical music, but we also do this. After all it is music and an expression of the human spirit."

Nashvillians can look forward with anticipation to the next milestone for Blair School of Music. Mark Wait's vision and drive are taking Blair to new heights, and both Vanderbilt and the Nashville community are the beneficiaries.

The Princely Players

I'm sometimes up and sometimes down,
Coming for to carry me home,
But still my soul feels heavenly bound,
Coming for to carry me home.

—From "Swing Low, Sweet Chariot"

THE PRINCELY PLAYERS epitomize the power that can come through the performing arts. Formed at a time in the city's—and the nation's—history when angry, violent speeches and demonstrations were more the norm, this group chose to tell the story of the African-American experience through music and literature. Even the name was selected to be positive.

Led by H. German Wilson, a graduate of Fisk University and a former Jubilee Singer, these young people and others had participated in the drama *Witness for the Prosecution* at Cameron High School in the spring of 1967. That summer Wilson and his small troupe reached out to the community through Drama in the Streets, a federally funded program based at Edgehill United Methodist Church.

Throughout the next school year, the Princely Players performed at Fisk University's arts festival, Vanderbilt University's Angry Arts Festival, and other venues in Nashville. They also had engagements around the country, notably at Yale University. The group disbanded following high school graduation and did not get back together for ten years. Then at their high school reunion in 1978, the Players decided to re-form the group. All live in Nashville, and more than twenty years later, they are still performing—in addition to working in their chosen occupations, which include the law, education, and nursing.

Their program "On the Road to Glory" takes listeners on a journey from Africa to America, through slavery, the Civil War, and the civil rights movement; the destination is freedom. Songs such as "Steal Away," "Swing Low, Sweet Chariot," "Oh Freedom," and "Glory, Glory, Hallelujah, Since I Laid My Burden Down" are interspersed with Langston Hughes's "Song for a Dark Girl," Richard Wright's "Between the World and Me," Paul Laurence Dunbar's "The

In Her Father's Footsteps

She was born into a household of music, so it was perhaps inevitable that she would start singing before groups of people at the age of four. Odessa Settles, the contralto member of the Princely Players, is the daughter of the late Walter J. Settles Sr. A tenor, Mr. Settles sang with the Golden Harp Jubilee Singers, the Spiritual All-Stars, the Olive Branch Singers, and the Fairfield Four (a group founded in 1921 at Nashville's Fairfield Baptist Church). Through his influence and his association with musicians in the city, through church and school, Odessa had constant exposure to music. She knew Roscoe Shelton and Little Richard; her oldest brother's first trombone had belonged to James Brown; she often saw Jimi Hendrix walking up and down Jefferson Street with a guitar slung over his shoulder. Jacqueline Smith (daughter of W. O. Smith, jazz man and teacher) and Ann McCrary (daughter of Rev. Samuel McCrary, first tenor with the Fairfield Four) were original Princely Players.

The Princely Players, through song and story, relate the African-American struggle for freedom: Gloria Ransom, Jacqueline Campbell-Elston, Nita Modley Smith, and Odessa Settles *(first row, left to right)*; Kevin C. Carroll, Roderick Kelley, James Albert Brown, and Robert Smith *(second row, left to right)*.

Along the way, Mr. Settles taught his daughter and his sons about the value of a life well lived, and his children learned their lessons well. Following her graduation from high school, Odessa chose to go to the University of Tennessee to study nursing, and now she is a registered nurse in Vanderbilt University's Department of Pediatrics, working closely with Dr. Mildred Stahlman, who has achieved international recognition for her work in neonatal intensive care (and is a cousin of opera singer Sylvia Stahlman).

Music and medicine have enriched Odessa's life in ways beyond what she could have imagined when she was a youngster. Commenting on the work of the Princely Players and the South of her youth, Odessa stated, "To effect change in a not-so-great world, we decided to live and personify what we wanted the world to be like. In the midst of adversity, it's a thin line that separates enemy and foe. If you become what you're fighting against, then you become the enemy. Because we were blessed with the gift of artistic expression in music and theater, we were able to tell it like it was and rechannel the negative feelings into something positive and meaningful. We grew up during Dr. Martin Luther King Jr.'s era. Dr. King was peaceful and unrelentingly optimistic. The group remained positive because our lives, the quality of life, our integrity, and the integrity of our future dreams were at stake.

"I'm glad I grew up in the South despite the fact that racial disparity was quite blatant. Living here proved to be the most influential and social educational experience for me. I do believe that it's not where you live, but how you live that makes the difference. Fortunately, during those days of segregation, I had strong family ties, neighbors, churches, and schoolteachers who prepared me to face the world as it is . . . not run away from it, but see what I could do to make it different . . . better. A lot of us didn't make it, but some of us did. Even today, as much as I travel, I still love coming home to the South. Moving away may have brought some respite but it wouldn't change history, and I never assumed that the North, East, and West were the promised lands."

Antebellum Sermon," and Gwendolyn Brooks's "A Song in the Front Yard."

The Princely Players have performed on NPR's Wade in the Water series and Time-Life Civil War series, they have collaborated with Ladysmith Black Mambazo and the Nashville Symphony, and they have recorded with Randy Travis, Danny O'Keefe, and Kathy Mattea. The group received a scholarship in 1999 to the Southern Arts Federation's American Traditions Training Institute and Southern Arts Exchange. Workshops on American history, African-American studies, sociology, women's studies, and choral studies have called upon the group. One special workshop with Nashville ties was held at Cheekwood: its focus was local sculptor William Edmondson, and the Princely Players selected songs typical of the era in which Edmondson was working (1931–51). In addition they have given a dramatic performance of "The Life and Times of William Edmondson" at Cheekwood.

Two of the group's stated purposes are "to interest and unite young men and women in the performing arts to the end that the sleeping talents which they possess may be awakened," and "to bring forth, by creative expression, a nobler manhood and womanhood and more perfect love of themselves."

The remaining original members are James Albert Brown, Roderick Kelley, Gloria Ransom, Odessa Settles, and Robert Smith, and they have added Kevin C. Carroll, Jacqueline Campbell-Elston, and Nita Modley Smith to the troupe, which is a nonprofit organization. Still reaching out as they did in that summer of 1967, they always reserve some of their earnings to help the community, most recently contributing funds to Cameron Middle School's music program. They emphasize education in all that they do, such as presenting diverse artists in a five-week program at Fisk University. The Princely Players are continuing to illustrate how to educate through the performing arts.

TPAC: An Arts Catalyst

*TPAC has truly become
a lively and valuable statewide resource,
and we will continue to find new and imaginative ways
to ensure the growth of the arts in Tennessee.*

—STEVEN GREIL

AFTER THE OPENING of the Tennessee Performing Arts Center in 1980, Nashville finally had a venue for the classical performing arts, but in the first season (1980–81) 119 performances attracted only 84,000 people. There have been bumps in the road—sometimes small and sometimes huge—in the past two decades, but the good news is that the performing arts keep moving along the road. Nashville Opera, Tennessee Repertory Theatre, and Nashville Ballet have become resident companies in addition to the Nashville Symphony and Circle Players. (TPAC itself does not *produce* productions; it *presents* events.) A Broadway Series has become a mainstay of programming, and educational outreach efforts have enabled thousands of Tennessee youngsters and adults to enjoy and learn about the performing arts.

The success of resident and visiting companies is reflected in the numbers for 2002 when almost 500,000 people attended 500 events at TPAC. TPAC is the largest arts organization in the state (with a $11.6 million budget), and its endowment has grown from $4 million (in 1980) to $21 million. The public-private partnership with the state of Tennessee continues: the state sees to the major building maintenance, and TPAC pays for its own staff, equipment, administration, marketing, box office, housekeeping, and ushers.

Audiences have come to TPAC to see classics such as *The King and I, Fiddler on the Roof,* and

Hello, Dolly!; new classics such as *Cats, Phantom of the Opera,* and *Les Misérables;* children's classics such as *Paddington Bear, Peter Pan,* and *Babes in Toyland;* Shakespearean plays such as *The Taming of the Shrew* and *Julius Caesar;* dance with artists from the Alvin Ailey Dance Theater, American Ballet Theatre, and American Indian Dance Theater or those in *A Chorus Line, Stomp, 42nd Street,* and *Riverdance;* individual artists such as Lena Horne, Tony Bennett, Hal Holbrook, and Joan Baez; and groups such as Manhattan Transfer, Vienna Choir Boys, Tokyo String Quartet, and the Chieftains. This is just a partial list.

Jane Fabian, native Nashvillian and supporter of Nashville Ballet, spoke about the significance of TPAC: "TPAC made it easier to deal with that quality-of-life issue: Do we want Nashville to be a city of some substance, or do we want the *Hee Haw* image for the rest of our natural days? I think they can coexist. Country music is where we made our name; we need to respect that. With

the establishment of TPAC it became a little easier to emphasize the cultural viability that was missing in the community. As Nashville began to attract more companies and/or executives from out of town, that helped to sell the arts as a major part of the city."

In 1981 Bob Fosse's *Dancin'* was the first Broadway touring show to appear at TPAC, and it packed the house, a heartening development after the failure to attract an audience for Pennsylvania Ballet, Martha Graham, and Twyla Tharp when TPAC opened, just a year earlier. We learned that people wanted more Opryland-type dancing or what they had seen in a movie such as *South Pacific* and not modern dance, not

The successful Broadway touring show of *The Phantom of the Opera* was a milestone for TPAC in the 1993–94 season *(top).* Hal Holbrook, who portrayed Mark Twain at TPAC, has a Tennessee connection through his wife, Dixie Carter. Her childhood home is McLemoresville, and she, too, has appeared at TPAC, in "An Evening with Dixie Carter" *(left).*

ballet. (That attitude would change, though, with the progress of TPAC's educational programs.)

The next year the first official Broadway Series began, and it has since become an essential revenue stream for TPAC operations. Yul Brynner got the series off to a royal start in September 1982 with *The King and I.* (TPAC staff were amazed that his contract stipulated that a limousine drive him from the Hermitage Hotel, where he was staying, to the stage door—a distance of perhaps one-half block. His dressing room at TPAC had to be painted brown, and a fresh fruit bowl had to be at-the-ready for him at every performance.)

A landmark event for 1983 was the live telecast of *The Member of the Wedding* with Pearl Bailey, directed by Delbert Mann. NBC broadcast it from the stage of Polk Theater in December. The next year, TPAC sold out for the appearance of Mikhail Baryshnikov, proving once again the power of a star in Nashville. Audiences were finally developing for the classical arts.

The first play at TPAC with more than 10,000 in attendance (during its stay of several days) was *CanCan* in October 1988, and in that 1988–89 season three other events in the Broadway Series played to more than 10,000 (*Nunsense, Me and My*

Circle Players

The Nashville Center of the Drama League of America was established in September 1921 with Dr. H. B. Schermerhorn as president, and the other officers included Miss Theo Scruggs, Miss Pauline Townsend, Charles Mitchell, Mrs. B. Kirk Rankin, and Morton Howell. A newspaper account explained the purpose: "The idea of the league is to crowd out vicious plays by attending and commending good plays, and building up audiences for them through study courses, reading circles and lectures to aid in the restoration of the drama to its honorable place as the most intimate, most comprehensive, most democratic medium of self-expression of the people both in and out of the theater." There have been active, not-so-active, and hanging-by-a-thread community theater groups in Nashville for decades. The quality has waxed and waned, but the intent—whether explicitly stated or implicitly understood—was to produce works that would have been satisfactory to the league.

The progression of local groups in the first half of the twentieth century was Stagecrafters, Nashville Little Theatre Guild, Nashville Little Theatre (the *Guild* had to be dropped for legal reasons), Nashville Experimental Theater, and Nashville Community Playhouse. Circle Players

was organized in 1949, and its first production was *Home of the Brave,* which premiered in the Assembly Room of the Hermitage Hotel on March 27, 1950. In 1958 it briefly merged with Nashville Community Playhouse to become Theater Nashville, but by 1959 Circle Players was reestablished as a separate entity.

The Players were ambitious. WLAC-TV aired the group's *Candida* in 1955 and *See No Evil* in 1960. An unprecedented and risky move was to sponsor an appearance by Dame Judith Anderson on February 2, 1962, at the War Memorial Auditorium. The highest-priced ticket was $4.50 (about $27 today), and the auditorium was almost filled. Anderson brought George Gordon, William Roderick, and Carmalita Scott with her, and they did Anderson's adaptations of scenes of Lady Macbeth and Medea, with her in the starring roles, of course. The group's 200th production, staged in January 1973, was *Cat on a Hot Tin Roof.*

As mentioned earlier, Circle Players was a resident company at TPAC when it opened in 1980, and the company is still there. For the company's fifty-fourth season, 2003–4, some plays included *To Kill a Mockingbird, Smokey Joe's Cafe,* and *Joseph and the Amazing Technicolor Dreamcoat.*

Girl, and *Les Misérables*). Each of the next two seasons, 1989–90 and 1990–91, had four events with more than 10,000 audience members. In 1991 Isaac Stern had a sold-out crowd in Jackson Hall as he performed with the Nashville Symphony.

TPAC had an economic impact on the city of $35 to $40 million in 1990, the tenth anniversary year in which it hosted four hundred public events. That record far exceeded what many had predicted earlier would be the dire failure of the Tennessee Performing Arts Center.

A climax for TPAC occurred with the smash hit *The Phantom of the Opera* for the 1993–94 season. Many new subscribers signed up for the Broadway Series, people from more than thirty-five states attended, and Broadway tours finally began to take notice of Nashville as a major market.

Steven Greil became president and CEO of TPAC in 1994 after five and one-half years as executive director of the Nashville Symphony. Steven's thirtieth year in Nashville was 2002, and he has worked in the music, entertainment, and arts businesses. He came to Vanderbilt University to get a degree in civil engineering, and he became involved with entertainment on campus. He has not stopped since, and he acknowledged, "My passion is for organizing and promoting. The job I now have with TPAC brought together all of my experience as a concert promoter and artist manager and in symphony management."

The 1995–96 season saw the beginning of the New Directions Series, and some events were co-presented with Great Performances at Vanderbilt University. In the third season of that series audiences were treated to Philip Glass's *Les Enfants Terribles,* the Kalichstein-Laredo-Robinson Trio, and Hal Holbrook presenting *Mark Twain Tonight!*

Computers received attention in 1996, and though they are not seen by the audience, they make jobs easier for TPAC staff to serve the public. TPAC had owned the Middle Tennessee license of Ticketmaster since 1980 but returned

Steven Greil, president and CEO of TPAC since 1994, delivered a progress report to TPAC's Board of Directors.

the license to Ticketmaster Corp. in exchange for improvements to the computerized ticket system and a cash payment. TPAC computer systems were updated, and this and a flourishing economy were some of the reasons the subscriber base for the Broadway Series reached more than 8,500.

Milestones for the 1997–98 season included returns of the *Phantom* and *Les Mis*—each nearly sellouts—and almost 200,000 enjoyed the Broadway Series. Faye Dunaway was in town, October 21–26, 1997, to star in *Master Class,* but she almost missed one of her "classes" at TPAC when she was late returning from a Rolling Stones concert at Vanderbilt. Two unusual events for resident companies occurred that season; Nashville Opera used an elephant named Kamba in the sold-out production of *Aida* in October 1997, and what was to be a grand *Swan Lake* for Nashville Ballet had to be rescheduled for the next season when on April 16, 1998, a tornado did about $1 million damage to the windows and roof of the TPAC building.

Steven Greil was named CEO of the Year by the Association for Nonprofit Executives for 2003. Among his accomplishments at TPAC

TPAC gained an electronic marquee in the fall of 2003 to announce upcoming events *(top)*. Susan Ross, as the character Dorothy Brock, won the hearts of Nashvillians in April 2003 in *42nd Street* at TPAC. She already had the heart of her uncle, State Architect Mike Fitts, who oversaw the building of TPAC. After graduating from Vassar, she was a singing waitress at Chaffin's Barn Dinner Theatre before moving on to New York's stages *(bottom right)*. Interior renovations of TPAC, completed in the fall of 2003, included windows, more lights, more rest rooms, a water feature, and more user-friendly space for concessions *(bottom left)*.

have been increased revenue, the assumption of the management of War Memorial Auditorium (1999), the development of long-range plans for the facility, and the consolidation of operations of Tennessee Rep and TPAC.

Education and outreach. The H.O.T. (Humanities Outreach in Tennessee) program started as a way to fill the empty theaters in 1983 when TPAC was getting established. Many students in Tennessee had not seen a live performance, trained actors could not find professional work, and TPAC's middle-sized Polk Theater (1,000 seats) had few users. I made a plea to Governor Lamar Alexander: "Would you be willing to give TPAC $25,000 for a pilot program so that we can turn all of these negatives into positives?" Lamar said, "I have in my discretionary fund $25,000," and he gave TPAC that amount to produce Tennessee Williams's *Glass Menagerie.* Out of that idea grew Tennessee Repertory Theatre, which I cofounded with Mac Pirkle. The Rep could not have come into being without the H.O.T. program because it underwrote tickets for students who saw the same play at 10:00 A.M. that adults saw in the evening. Mac is now using his creative talents in other directions, and David Grapes became the Rep's artistic director and producer from 1999 to the spring of 2004. (See details under the heading "Tennessee Repertory Theatre.")

As the director of the HCA Foundation, Ida Cooney was a supporter of the H.O.T. program in particular and arts education in general. After her death, a plaque at TPAC was dedicated in her memory, "in celebration of her life and in hope that it will inspire the young people who pass by it each day to remember that it was, in part, Ida Cooney's efforts that made possible the performance that they are about to see."

Jane Ann McCullough worked with the H.O.T. program in its early years, beginning in 1983. She had held a position with the Tennessee Arts Commission and knew the state and its schools. She said, "We went that first year from about 60,000 to a couple of years later to 600,000. It worked because it tied in to the curriculum. Theater was the mainstay then." Then the Symphony, Opera, and Ballet programming was added. Jane Ann observed, "Those students, very few had been to Nashville. They might have been to the Parthenon or to the Hermitage. I think it is clear that those students are still coming in from across the state to see art. And they may do another activity besides that. If the funds had been available for busing, I can assure you that if there could have been a way to get the students here—the buses were and are so expensive—the numbers would be much higher. Many years American General underwrote the busing with travel grants. They said, 'If you build it, we'll bring the kids in,' and that does work. But the transportation has to be there. Even with the local schools, the buses have to take the students and pick up the next one and the next one. If they are out of sync a little bit, it won't happen. We used to be able to use church buses, but with insurance costs we can't do that anymore. Transportation is an issue that has a direct impact on getting the kids to see the arts—whether the Opera, the Rep, the Ballet, or the Symphony."

Resources for teachers include performance guidebooks (with suggestions for lesson plans and information about each performance) and a workshop introducing the upcoming season. Reservations have to be made in the fall, and there is usually a waiting list for events. Students from throughout the state have participated in the H.O.T. program, and in November 1999 the one millionth child attended a performance, *The Gift of the Magi* staged by Tennessee Rep. Enough time has passed that now many of those young students who attended H.O.T. programs are coming back as adults buying tickets for performing arts events. Arts education does work.

There are other educational programs. In 1999 TPAC merged with the Nashville Institute for the Arts (NIA) and added ArtSmart and Wolf-Trap (WolfTrap Early Learning Through the Arts provides teachers with curriculum for three- to five-year-olds) programs. Basically the H.O.T. program brings youngsters to TPAC and the NIA programs send artists into schools. Adults are not overlooked, either, because TPAC Inside-Out is for people age eighteen and over to help them expand their understanding of the arts.

TPAC Friends was organized in 1985 to raise funds and provide volunteers. Special events sponsored by this group support TPAC's educational programs so that more children can participate in the arts. Although admission prices are low for young people in the H.O.T. program, some students need scholarships.

What's next? A $7.9 million renovation project completed in the fall of 2003 was the first extensive work that had been done on the TPAC facility since it opened in 1980. A new orchestra shell ceiling and seats in Jackson Hall, new seats and a new lobby for Polk Theater, and improved rigging in Jackson and Polk had been the only improvements. The changes did not include everything that architects had in the original plans for TPAC, but the addition of elevators, lobby windows, more lights, more rest rooms, a water feature, more user-friendly space for concessions and customer service, and an electronic marquee will make the experience of coming to TPAC more exciting for patrons.

Steven Greil said recently, "I'd personally love to take more risks, to present more eclectic artistic offerings, but supplying the demand for Broadway in Nashville is the most responsible way for us to earn the money we need to take care of TPAC." He continued, "Programming is cyclical, and it has been very difficult the last few years for TPAC. I'm proud of every show we've ever done, but we're just holding our own against all of the other options: Predators [hockey], Titans [football], Country Music Hall of Fame,

free activities at the new downtown library and all of the branch libraries, Opry Mills [mega-shopping center], the parks system. We're like a sponge. We've absorbed about as much as this market wants to. We need to get the sponge bigger, and doing that may take some time. The participation in the arts needs to be deepened."

Programming can be tricky in the best of times, and unanticipated national or international events—not just local ones—can affect what happens on the stage of TPAC. Since the schedule has to be made far in advance, who could have known that *Blast!*—a Broadway touring show—would be in Nashville a week after the events of September 11, 2001? Hardly appropriate after that tragic time! In the spring of 2003, with the war in Iraq filling every hour of television airtime, the Broadway musical *tick, tick . . . BOOM!* had to be canceled.

Bennett Tarleton, executive vice president for institutional advancement for TPAC, said that his job was rougher in 2003 than in 2002. There were not necessarily fewer givers—and some gave increased amounts—but some people's giving was tied to reduced portfolios hammered by international economics. In addition, he said, "Some people were buying last-minute tickets instead of season subscriptions because they were reluctant to commit to something six months in advance."

Yet TPAC has been at capacity since 1994 and needs more time slots to satisfy the groups wanting to perform there. With the building of Schermerhorn Symphony Center, the Nashville Symphony's dates at TPAC will be free as the Symphony will have its own home beginning September 2006. At that time, expanded seasons for the Nashville Opera, Nashville Ballet, and Tennessee Rep are expected, and of course, more Broadway productions may be scheduled.

Steven and his staff have taken to heart the mission of TPAC and each year endeavor to fulfill it:

The mission of the Tennessee Performing Arts Center is to provide facilities, services, and programs of the highest quality for the greatest benefit of the people, institutions, and communities of the State, and to take a leadership role in fostering the performing arts, arts education, resident arts groups, and other organizations.

Tennessee Repertory Theatre

*I told people around me
that if the guys I went to high school with
ever started coming to the theater,
we would be a success.*

—MAC PIRKLE

A PRODUCTION of *The Glass Menagerie* at TPAC in 1983 marked the beginning of the H.O.T. (Humanities Outreach in Tennessee) program and also led to the formation of the Tennessee Repertory Theatre, which is now the largest professional theater company in the state and a resident company of TPAC.

To understand the story of the formation of Tennessee Rep, however, you have to understand a bit about Nashville's acting pool in the 1980s and Mac Pirkle, a Nashville native with a degree in marketing and a passion for theater. In the early 1970s he and a few others had established the Play Group, an alternative professional theater group, in Knoxville because he was determined to earn his living as an actor and do it in Tennessee. Unlike many other aspiring young actors, Mac did *not* want to go to New York, LA, or Chicago, and he said, "We were committed to doing what we were doing. It literally had nothing to do with money—other than the fact that we wanted to survive. It had to do with our commitment to our art." Yet after a while he outgrew that organization, and he was

exploring his next professional step—still not wanting to leave Tennessee, but fearing that he might have to in order to find work.

He returned to his hometown of Nashville and was inspired by the possibilities. Mac explained, "The Play Group was one of the companies performing at the opening of TPAC [*If I Live to See Next Fall*]. When I got here, what began to work on me was the fact that the performing arts center was downtown. I knew in my heart and soul that if somebody brought a man or woman in from New York or Chicago or LA to start a theater company to go in that theater, I would regret it for the rest of my life."

He started Southern Stage Productions as a profit-making organization in 1982, and the first play produced was a version of *If I Live to See Next Fall* in Johnson Theater. Then TPAC contracted Southern Stage Productions to do the pilot program for what became H.O.T., and the cast in that March 1983 production of *The Glass Menagerie* consisted of local talent, except for the character of the mother.

Mac said, "The community of artists at that time—although it was bohemian, it was also very entrepreneurial. . . . It was made up of people who were working in studio productions, small video companies, Dennis Ewing and the Poverty Playhouse down on Second Avenue, which later burned and he later moved into a place across from Vanderbilt. We had the work that Southern Stage was doing.

"Then there were a bunch of actors. The reason there were a bunch of actors was that many of them were holdovers from Opryland. Some were the result of academic theater who didn't want to go to New York. I'm not sure they felt that theater was a way to make a living. We had a theater on West End; none of it is there now. C. B. Anderson—he had a little theater down on West End, and we created an event called Theater Sports, which was an improvisational

Tennessee Rep, a resident company of TPAC, gave a rousing presentation of *Cyrano de Bergerac*.

production. There was just a lot of energy, and a lot of us had dreams.

"There was this energy where we were just young enough not to know how difficult the task was that lay ahead of us or not to understand the barriers that lay ahead of us in a town like Nashville. It was an exciting time to be around. . . . There was an ensemble atmosphere [within Southern Stage Productions] because we all knew each other socially and professionally. By the time we were on stage with each other there were bonds that were different than if we just brought in a bunch of people to do a play together. . . .

"It had some of the greatest traditions of the community theater with the bar raised high enough to be really professional theater. Southern Stage had not become a successful fiscal model. But we had done what we set out to do, and we had created a very, very solid theater."

In essence Southern Stage provided the productions for Tennessee Rep for a period of about three years, and over time that relationship was severed, but in the interim "Tennessee Rep as a nonprofit institution could immediately be guaranteed a certain level of expertise, experience, and quality on stage and production values," said Mac.

Mac and I signed the papers to create the Tennessee Repertory Theatre in February of 1985, and by September of that year the first production was staged. Mac declared, "Our first season was unbelievable. We did *Macbeth, Amadeus, Man of La Mancha, Of Mice and Men,* a lot of *M*'s. Our first budget—this is the phenomenal thing to me, I still don't know how we did it—was $600,000. . . . The actors were known by audiences, the audiences that Southern Stage had built through the H.O.T. program and public performances. So when we actually started, people were saying, 'Yeah! Way to go!' There was a palpable sense of that." He added, "We were as successful, in the beginning, as any performing arts group in this state has ever been at getting sponsorships. Tennessee Rep for a long time was the leader in trying to establish aggressive, fun marketing."

Some of the success was tied to personal relationships. Mac said, "I told people around me that if the guys I went to high school with ever started coming to the theater, we would be a success. A friend told me this summer, 'I would never have gone to the theater had it not been for you.' I told him, 'You were our litmus test for success. You needed to be in the theater to make it work.'" And it did. Tennessee Rep created new musical theater productions while performing classic musical theater and classic American and world theater works as part of the H.O.T. program.

Changes in the theater world affected the fortunes of Tennessee Rep. Mac described the situation: "By 1992 or 1993 there were performing arts centers all over the country with empty stages, because like TPAC, they didn't have resident groups. Suddenly there was a commercial touring boom, a virtual gold mine for Broadway producers that never existed before. Nashville became a PACE city [PACE presented touring Broadway shows]. . . .

"Once there was a Broadway Series and it took off, everything changed. Nashville had huge theater audiences coming to the Broadway Series. Now we were in competition for sponsorship dollars and for ticket sales with another theater product. . . .

"The local acting pool had diminished. No more Opryland [which had closed its doors]. No more incubator for people who had tremendous ambition as performers—to be on Broadway, to be country music stars, to be singers, to be dancers, to be actors. It's why we became known for musicals. We had incredible singers, incredible musicians. The pit in our musicals was unbelievable because the musician community here is stunning."

Mac resigned from Tennessee Rep to take a position with Earnhardt and Company, but he emphasized this point: "One of the things that changed since 1980 and since I was a young man in the late 1960s and early 1970s, you can now make your living in the state of Tennessee in the city of Nashville as an artist. You can do that. It is

The Tennessee Repertory Theatre collaborated with the Nashville Symphony on a production of *West Side Story*; this is the segment "Dance at the Gym." A CD recorded for Naxos of America is having unprecedented sales.

David Grapes was artistic director and producer of Tennessee Rep from 1999 to the spring of 2004.

going to be a struggle. But people who were actors who worked with Tennessee Rep bought houses. This was beyond their wildest dreams. It was beyond my wildest dream. That alone says that a transition has occurred; never in the history of Nashville did that happen before."

David Grapes assumed the position of artistic director and producer of Tennessee Rep in 1999, which he held until the spring of 2004 when he left to pursue other endeavors. At this printing a search for a new director was under way, and David Alford was interim director. About 60 percent of the actors are local and 40 percent from out of town, although many—if not most—have Nashville connections. They have moved out of town to have enough work to survive. David Grapes said, "Part of the artistic mission of the Rep is to nurture and support Tennessee artists, but they have to be the best, and they have to be talented."

A unique collaboration started in 2002 with the consolidation of administrative operations of TPAC and the Rep; it is *not* a merger because each maintains its independent identity and mission. This collaboration is blazing a new trail for the two organizations—there are no similar models in the U.S.—but trying something unprecedented is nothing new for either TPAC or the Rep.

Some offerings of the 2003–4 season were *Crimes of the Heart* and *God's Man in Texas* for the Main Stage Series and *Who's Afraid of Virginia Woolf?* and *A Life in the Theatre* for the Off-Broadway Series. The Rep's motto is that it is "your ticket to the good stuff," and a goal is to continue to provide the good stuff.

Nashville Opera

The rest of the opera world is looking at Nashville Opera as being one of the premier regional companies in the country.

—CAROL PENTERMAN

THREE HUNDRED subscribers signed up to hear *Lucia di Lammermoor* in 1854, the first production of a complete opera in Nashville. Signor Luigi Arditi's Italian Opera Company would not come to the city unless there was a guaranteed list of at least 300 (about 3 percent of the population, then slightly more than 10,000 individuals), and for a while it seemed doubtful that the required number would come forth. One reason cited for the slow sign-up was that too many Nashvillians preferred minstrel shows to opera; the cost of $2 (about $40 today) for the dress circle and parquette may have been another. Nevertheless, the terms were met, and the company of forty performed on May 26 at the Adelphi Theatre; they remained in town long enough to do a total of five operas, including *Lucretia Borgia, Norma, Barber of Seville,* and *Sonnambula,* one every other evening. Following that company, other opera companies stayed for varying lengths of time on their tours around the South, as discussed earlier in this book.

By 1916, however, sixty-two years after that performance of *Lucia*, visits by opera companies were rare in Nashville. Many local opera lovers traveled to cities such as Atlanta, Chicago, and New York, a practice that persists in the early part of the twenty-first century. (Until the Met tour to Memphis stopped in 1984, Nashvillians could be counted upon to be in the audience there.) Yet a hard-core group strongly desired to have a local opera company, and in February 1916 J. F. Sullivan

Mary Ragland has been given justly deserved credit for being the founder of Nashville Opera.

won second prize in a contest for his essay "Benefits Accruing from Grand Opera" in which he listed five benefits. The first was "invaluable prestige—since the very fact of a city's wanting grand opera marks its development into a metropolis, thereby advertising it as such, as no other form of advertising could do." The second was the financial because performances brought in visitors who did business with merchants, jewelers, dressmakers, florists, hotels, and so on. The third was the educational: "For while grand opera entertains and diverts, it does so by means of the most beautiful in legend, poetry, mythology and religion, combining these with the best in music and the ballet, thereby acquainting and impressing these upon the minds of the general populace of a city, and reaching many who before have had no opportunity of their acquaintance, or by reason of their presentation as other than entertainment would make an opportunity of acquaintance. Then, too, if other cities of the South support grand opera, surely Nashville should, advertising herself as the Athens of the South and boasting of her many colleges and institutions of learning, annually inviting and expecting students to come here for superior educational advantages, leaving cities of less magnitude as educational centers, but who annually support a season of grand opera." The fourth benefit was the artistic. Sullivan wrote, "Inferior productions would in the future so suffer by comparison [to excellent productions] that [the city] would demand and support only the best. Then the great stimulus which such an event means to the student and even professional artists within her midst, broadening their conceptions, increasing enthusiasm, thereby stimulating endeavor, and by increased demand and facilities for art, eventually bringing to the city as residents numbers of professionals and students shortly, gaining for the city recognition as an art center." A final benefit—and hope—was that the nation would become a more "art-loving country" if more cities had opera companies.

More than sixty years after Sullivan wrote his essay, many of these benefits are being realized through the Nashville Opera. The company, I believe, has rearranged the list of his benefits and placed the educational and the artistic at the top, and that is why Nashville Opera has become so successful in such a short period of time.

The 1980s. Mary Cortner Ragland was the driving force behind the effort to establish a local opera company. She had an undergraduate degree from the Newcomb School of Music and a master's degree from Juilliard. She taught music at Centre College in Kentucky and had sung in operatic roles and in concerts. A soprano, she was a winner in the National Atwater Kent Radio Contest in 1931 and had an audition scheduled at the Metropolitan Opera. She declined to pursue the Met audition, however, and instead married Charles Ragland and moved to Nashville. She served on the board of the Met, was elected to the Met National Council in 1954, and chaired the Metropolitan Opera District auditions in Middle Tennessee. She was a cofounder of the Nashville Symphony. In 1994 the Opera Guild International presented her with a Partners in Excellence award, and the Opus Award from the Nashville Opera, created in her honor, recognizes an individual who promotes opera. Even though Mary died in 1999, she continues to assist the Opera through a Memorial Endowment and also the Mary Cortner Ragland Fund for the Nashville Opera Association at the Community Foundation.

Dr. William O. Whetsell Jr. knew Mary well, and they worked together on the Opera board. He said, "Mary Ragland was a lovely, charming lady; she was good at raising money for the arts, and she developed a lot of loyal supporters to start Nashville Opera. I know of a couple of people who were very pleased to say, 'Oh, sure I'll give you ten thousand dollars.' She was *so* determined to do it."

The first production with which Mary was involved was *Madama Butterfly* at TPAC in 1981, just after the performing arts center opened. The opera company was not a separate entity then, but operated in conjunction with the Nashville Symphony. Following the great success of *Madama Butterfly*, Mary single-handedly produced an opera in May for the next several years. Dr. Whetsell said, "She hired the singers; she hired the orchestra; she hired the conductor; she got the sets; she did everything. She hired a stage director. She literally produced it all herself, and she loved it. She brought some very good singers here. They were not just local singers. Of course the choruses and small parts were local, but generally the leading roles were professionals from various places. Mary would go to New York to audition them." John Bridges commented on the quality of the productions: "She wouldn't put up with 'this is all we can afford.' She would say, 'Let's spend that money better. Let's find somebody else who can sing this better'"—and then she found the money!

Mary had help with the fund-raising and business side of the operation. Dr. Whetsell explained, "In addition to Mary Ragland, there was another Nashville woman, a good friend of Mary, who was instrumental in getting the Nashville Opera started. She was Ellen Hofstead. Ellen was quite a persuasive fund-raiser, and she loved opera. She was very practical in the ways of handling money, and I think she and Mary Ragland made a really effective team for the job to be done. Mary was the artistic, idea person who could bring together the singers, orchestra, sets, and costumes and actually produce the operas in those early days. Ellen Hofstead, the practical one, could manage the funds and keep Mary's feet on the ground, so to speak. Ellen deserves a lot of credit for her dedication in the early days."

Nashville Opera was not a separate organization until 1988, and Mary became the executive director—at no salary—with a small office on the campus of Belmont University and a part-time secretary. Dr. Whetsell said, "Thanks to Mary's careful guidance and professional support, the Opera grew. We were able to hire a full-time paid executive director."

The Opera started doing two performances each year. For one season, the first was *Carmen*, and the second was *Carousel*, which was a cooperative venture with four other companies (from Cleveland, Fort Worth, Los Angeles, and Portland, Oregon). Dr. Whetsell stated, "We were going to buy the scenery and costumes and share the costs. We thought it was going to be a huge success because everybody would love to see *Carousel*. We scheduled five performances; never had we done anything like that before. Well, it was a total flop, and partly it was because the Sunday matinee was the afternoon of the Final Four in basketball. It was at TPAC in Jackson Hall, and we just couldn't fill it for five performances.

"We lost an incredible amount of money. It was very expensive to produce, and that really set us way back. That was a bad decision, but we didn't know that. What we learned from that is that people who like opera are not interested in seeing a Broadway play. And people who knew about it were older people; *Carousel* was such a period piece that younger people just weren't interested in it. Mary had shepherded this wonderful reserve amount of money, and that production blew practically the whole amount. We lost 90 percent of the reserve funds. We learned a lesson: we are not going to do any more Broadway plays."

The "opera man." For the next season Donizetti's *The Daughter of the Regiment* was scheduled, and Dr. Whetsell had just become president of the Nashville Opera Board. He was on vacation in August 1992 when the executive director called him to say that the opera would have to be canceled because of the cost. Dr. Whetsell said, "It became a public announcement in the newspaper; we weren't broke, but we didn't have enough to pay for the production. It would cost another $100,000 or so that we just didn't have. But it was a wise decision. We got good press because of it; they said that we were being fiscally responsible. Then we had to start to build all over again from the ground up." (As part of the rebuilding, the executive director's contract was not renewed, and the search began for a new executive director.)

Dr. Whetsell was the one who led that buildup. He is professor of pathology and psychiatry, director of the Division of Neuropathology at Vanderbilt University Medical Center, and a John F. Kennedy Center Senior Fellow. He readily confessed, "People know how crazy I am about the opera, and they'll say, 'Oh, God, here comes the opera man!'" Seeing a professional performance of *Die Fledermaus*, his first opera, when he was eight years old got him hooked on the art form. In high school in Orangeburg, South Carolina, he was fortunate enough to have a teacher, Frederick Ulmer, who inspired students and brought out the best music in them.

Having a father who was a physician and a mother who was a professional-level pianist was influential in Dr. Whetsell's future. In college he minored in music and majored in premedical sciences. In medical school he continued to study music and audition for roles, and after medical school, in the mid-1960s, he divided his time between the Metropolitan Studio, studying to be an opera singer, and medical centers, learning about neurobiology. He said, "Kind of schizophrenic, but it was fun to try to maintain both at the time. I thought I would keep doing it until I had to make a decision. After two years with the studio and multiple auditions, studying roles, doing some recital work at various places, finally I decided, having the experience that I had and seeing the climate, that I was not going to become Sherrill Milnes, as much as I wanted to, that was not very practical. I did my residency then, but did not pursue a professional opera career any farther. Since I don't have much opportunity to perform, I really enjoy working with the Opera to help it develop. And even if I were performing, I would still work with it. I love seeing it. I like to foster it. It is one of my major interests in the community."

Die Fledermaus was the opera chosen to get the company back on its feet, and since there was no executive director in place, Dr. Whetsell filled that role temporarily. He said, "I would go over two or three mornings a week to Belmont and try to manage things: to write letters, to get out mailings, to do fund-raising. [He had only a part-time secretary to help him.] I practically handcuffed the executive committee, and we went to the bank. We managed to persuade them to let us have a line of credit. We all had to sign for it, and we all met—the executive committee included the president, vice president, secretary, and so on, about six people—and everybody was feeling a little uneasy about being there. We all signed the promissory note. I think it was for $35,000.

"It was a real learning experience for me. I called and worked out the deals with the singers and the Orchestra. Kenneth Schermerhorn was the conductor, and he and I met in August to work on the plans. He was quite reassuring about how the thing would go. He had done the opera before. The production was successful and fun because of the great cast." To Dr. Whetsell's great relief, a new executive director and a new artistic director were hired and began work in January 1995.

An emerging success story. Dr. Whetsell said, "We were very fortunate to find Carol Penterman and John Hoomes. It's a unique combination. I was president of the board at that time, and I thought—and I think the board thought—that having a woman as the executive director would be a unique approach. She has everything in hand. She is a wonderful organizer and efficient, and John is a very talented opera producer and director."

Nashville Opera produced *La Traviata* in the spring of 1995, and Dr. Whetsell called it "a smashing success." Word got around town after the Saturday night performance, and more than 1,800 people were in TPAC for the Tuesday night performance. Some attendees were not regular operagoers, either.

Carol explained the reasons for that success: "We said when we first came here, the first thing we had to work on was the product. If you don't have a good product to sell, it doesn't matter. So that is one reason you'll see in our budgeting that all our money is going to production. And we said that every show has to be special. Our artistic director says that if we entice someone into the hall to finally see one of our operas and he or she leaves, thinking, *What was the big deal?* then we have failed.

"*La Traviata* and every production after that we have tried to make impressive. And we're still doing that. As our budget has grown [about $1.7 million now], the money is going into the productions [expenses for productions (49 percent), production-related costs (3 percent), and production staff (17 percent)]. We get higher quality singers; we are using bigger sets and scenery; we are using better quality costumes. We want every show to be a turning point so that people will go away saying, 'This is really great. This is as good as what I could see anywhere else in the country.'"

Carol and John recognized the need to have a subscription series, but with only one or two events a year, that was not possible. The merger in September 1997 of Nashville Opera with Tennessee Opera Theatre and the Nashville Opera Guild to become the Nashville Opera Association made possible the progression to four operas a year.

John Hoomes is artistic director and Carol Penterman is executive director of Nashville Opera.

"We are one of the fastest-growing opera companies in the country," said Carol. "The only one that is growing faster than Nashville Opera is the Boston Lyric Opera. It's interesting seeing the recognition that we're getting; the rest of the opera world is looking at Nashville Opera as being one of the premier regional companies in the country. There has been a learning curve because when we [Carol and John] first got here, we were calling agents about singers, New York agents who deal with bigger singers, and literally the agents would say, 'Oh, are you sure you should be doing that piece?' We'd say, 'Well, yes, we are. And obviously you're not interested in having your people sing in it.' So we'd go on to the next agent."

An agent from Columbia Artists, which is one of the largest agencies, came to see two of its singers who were cast in *Rigoletto*. The quality of the production and the size of the hall impressed him. That agency—barely returning Carol's phone calls five years or so ago—now has an agent saying, "You know, this would be a great tryout place for the Met."

Nashville Opera and Opera Memphis collaborated on *Turandot*. Carol addressed some differences between the cities and their opera companies: "Executives and businesses are coming to Nashville for a number of reasons, and I credit that to the community leaders who are attracting them here. The executives are well educated and that is our core audience—highly educated people are the ones with more of an interest in classical music. I think Memphis's difficulty is that they are not attracting as many of those individuals. And the attitudes of the communities are entirely different. Memphis is an Old South town with a 'we don't want to change' attitude. Nashville is a real can-do, up-and-coming, cosmopolitan, let's-keep-up-with-the-times, vibrant city."

The Opera has a local ensemble of about twenty people who sing in all of its productions. Other performers are hired as needed, depending on the production; for example, *Aida* required seventy-two. Singers who make a living professionally in opera, singing with the Metropolitan Opera or other American opera

Nashville Opera, a resident company of TPAC, produced Richard Strauss's *Der Rosenkavalier* in 1999. In the pit Maestro Kenneth Schermerhorn conducted the Nashville Symphony.

companies and in Europe in the bigger houses, fill the principal, leading roles. Carol said, "Nashville is very much a 'star' town, but that is one thing that *doesn't* always work for us. Unless you are going to bring in a star the level of Pavarotti or Domingo, it doesn't seem to matter that much. There are only a handful of opera 'stars' that really draw an audience, and to the world at large, they are far lesser known than some of the 'stars' that are seen on the streets of Nashville every day. Denyce Graves was here in recital, and she sang to a half-filled house. She's one of the hottest commodities right now."

Some roles are filled by local singers who are not in the company. Carol said, "The teaching has improved tremendously. In the old days, a young singer usually had to go to Europe to get recognition or to get experience. Now there are some wonderful Young Artist programs in the United States. We have a Young Artist program here at Nashville Opera for just that purpose. Young singers no longer have to go to Europe to get their experience, so we now have a better crop of young people who are here in the States."

Most singers are traveling vagabonds. They come to town, stay three or four weeks, long enough to rehearse and complete the performance requirements, and then go to their next job. There is no job security; there are no benefits. The singers are independent contractors who have to pay their own taxes and health insurance.

As for sets, Nashville Opera rents them from other opera companies because they are so expensive. That is a limiting factor sometimes in what can be produced, so one future desire is to start building sets in Nashville. The costumes often come from a professional opera costume house in Canada, called Malabar.

Challenges and opportunities. Carol observed, "Nashville, I think, is quite unique in its community. One reason is that, by and large, Nashville is not presented as a classical arts town. One challenge this gives us is the fact that if we produce an opera considered very popular in most cities or if it's an opera with a composer of name recognition, it often doesn't matter as far as attendance. But that same challenge also gives us the opportunity to do some of the works that would be considered nonmainstream and riskier. Because audiences here have not had the chance to see the lesser known works, they often attend out of curiosity. We can do a Benjamin Britten opera such as *Turn of the Screw,* and we'll get almost the same audience numbers that we would get for *La Bohème.* This is unheard of in most cities, but audiences here have not had the chance to experience enough different and diverse operas, and so their minds are still open to challenging works.

"Our core audience—we have a core here of about one thousand people—will attend the opera because they know and love opera. Interestingly they are often the ones that choose *not* to come to the nonmainstream works. But with the lesser-known works, we are able to pull in all those other new people that are just experiencing it for the first time. Or perhaps they're new to the art form and come because they want to experience every opera we produce. The difficulty comes when we program Mozart's *Don Giovanni,* assuming it's going to sell out (as it would in most cities) and it underperforms at the box office. *Don Giovanni* is one of the most popular operas ever written, and our core people all attended, but it didn't draw many of the other people, for whatever reason.

"We now sometimes try to sell the spectacle or the drama of the opera versus selling the composer or the name of the piece. That has worked fairly well for us. Obviously there is an audience for opera here; our audience has grown by 350 percent in the last five years.

"Opera has changed radically in recent years, and now it's seen as more of a theater piece as well as a musical piece," said Carol. "Our goal is to present opera as intense, music theater and not as a stuffy, museum piece."

Another challenge in Nashville is scheduling. Carol noted, "There is a black-tie event almost every night. People just don't seem to stay at home." Because TPAC is so much in demand, the Opera has to schedule performances years in advance. One year an opera was scheduled on the weekend of Vanderbilt graduation and the Iroquois Steeplechase, and the audience numbers were much lower than expected. Nevertheless, one person who was in town for the Steeplechase also made it a point to go to the production of *Rigoletto.* Princess Michael of Kent wrote me a note basically saying that the opera was as good as anything she had seen in Covent Garden.

Funds. Carol is determined to have a balanced budget: "We have no deficit, and we're going to keep it that way. We are very cautious. We have grown hugely, but it has been a managed growth. We didn't grow without having the financial backing to do so. We know of a lot of companies that didn't match their bottom lines." The Opera pays on a per-performance basis—singers, stagehands, and others involved who are not on staff. Carol said, "If we add a show, we're also adding probably $50,000 to $100,000 in expense. I can't justify that unless I know I'm going to have a sellout crowd."

Subscriptions have hovered close to 1,500 since the year 2000, sometimes slightly above and sometimes slightly below. Out of Nashville's population of more than 560,000, that number is less than 1 percent. (Nashville's Metropolitan Statistical Area [MSA] totals more than 1.2 million.) Yet the dollars collected for subscriptions have had a healthy, steady increase, and the subscriptions for fiscal year 2003 were 15 percent of the annual revenues (slightly less than the single ticket revenues of 16 percent). There are two fund-raisers each year: Ballo del'Opera and La Bella Notte. The Opera Guild has a membership of about five hundred, and they contribute more than $100,000 annually. Carol considers it "literally one of the top guilds in the country."

The makeup of the board has been changing. Carol explained, "We have a fabulous board. We have successfully made a transition in the board from being a social organization because the opera company started as a guild. It was more of a social thing than it was a business thing. We have slowly but surely transformed it, and the board is attracting top business leaders.

"We also demand of our board that they be active; we don't have any board members in name only. Everybody must participate. We try to make it fun and informative and targeted to what they want to do. Obviously their main goal is to fund-raise. But when we speak to our board, we ask members, 'What are we not doing for you? What would you like to get out of this board you are not getting now?' We have restructured a lot of the board committees to answer those desires, and that has helped us a great deal as far as keeping our board active.

"One of the challenges of the board was that nobody wanted to leave it, so we had to put in term limits and we created an advisory board so they can rotate off the main board onto that advisory board and then back on if they want to three years later."

Education and outreach. To Carol, "the classical arts' survival is dependent on the educational

Nashville Opera featured lead soprano Lori Phillips and tenor Randolph Locke in the 2001 production of Puccini's *Turandot*. Nashville Opera is one of the fastest-growing opera companies in the country.

process. We have to educate people that this is not something to be frightened of and that it is something that mainstream folks can enjoy as much as turning on a radio and hearing pop music. And that it is special—it doesn't just happen; it takes a great deal of preparation, it takes a great deal of dedication, and it is unique."

Dr. Whetsell has personal and professional experience with the effects of the arts on youngsters. He said, "In a young brain where not so much learning has taken place, it is just a fertile field waiting for stimulation. The point is that positive stimuli are very good, but negative stimuli also can be influential. A child who grows up in an environment of violence and poverty and those kinds of things can be imprinted by negative stimuli just as much as a child who grows up in an enriched environment and has exposure to music or computers or reading, for example. It is so critical that these young children get the right stimulus, and it is important in terms of the arts that they get exposed very early. I think my experience is an example. I had come up in an environment where I was exposed a lot to music, but the fact that I still remember the opera from when I was eight years old so vividly and it was positively enforced and reinforced immediately, my brain was receptive. I was just waiting for that to happen in my brain, and I didn't know it." With its outreach efforts Nashville Opera hopes to make that happen in the brains of other youngsters.

Through the OperaNET tour, the company visits Metro Park's after-school program and schools in ten Tennessee counties. The fully staged productions with sets and costumes use talented young artists who have been chosen from national auditions. Study guides are provided to teachers to prepare students for what they will see and hear in an operatic performance, and students are encouraged to ask questions of the performers.

The first year that Carol tried it was 1995, and the tour had a tough beginning. She said, "I sent out the mailing to all the schools. *No* response. I started making calls, and the response from the teachers and the principals was, 'Well, it's opera. It's going to be so boring. I don't think the kids will enjoy it.' I literally had to beg that first season to get them to let us come: 'Let us show you that this is not the case.' Since that year we have been booked solid, and we have added two additional weeks. We now have a waiting list of schools that want us to come. Word has gotten around that this is a great program and the kids are going to love it. Students are more open minded until they hit the high school years. We don't tour to high schools for exactly that reason. By that time they often seem to have made up their minds on a lot of things. Their minds will reopen again later.

"We have the youngest audience of all the art forms. Opera is the fastest growing art form for eighteen- to twenty-five-year-olds. I think it's because of Broadway. Broadway is now mimicking opera, with *Rent* and *Miss Saigon* and *Aida* and *Phantom of the Opera.*"

It's Not What You Think. Nashville Opera produced the publication *It's Not What You Think* to dispel myths about opera and answer basic questions about it so that potential audience members will become more comfortable with the art form. Carol said, "We spend most of our time trying to alleviate the fear factor that is associated with opera to get people to give it a try." No, operas are not boring—unless you are bored by "passion, murder, true love, comedy, magic, and suspense." Story lines are diverse, and not even opera fans like *all* operas. The use of supertitles, which are English translations projected above the stage, has been significant in improving understanding of the action on the stage as it is happening. The fat lady probably will not be on stage, much to the surprise of some audience members. The guide informs readers: "Just try running, wrestling or sword-fighting, all while singing—*beautifully!* Opera is athletic!" Carol said, "What we have found is that once you prove that your product is a good product and that it really is an event people will enjoy, they're going to come."

Collaboration. Nashville Opera would like to collaborate or share programs with the music schools in the area. "But because of schedules and other conflicts," said Carol, "we have not been as successful as we would like. In many cities, local music students get their first taste of the professional world while singing in the chorus for the local opera company. We think that singing in our ensemble would be an incredible experience for a voice student."

Carol commented on the cooperation and collaborative attitude among the arts groups themselves and the staffs: "My experience in other cities has often been that there is a lot of close-to-the-vest behavior, back-stabbing, and infighting because the groups think there is only one pot of money out there and each wants the bigger portion. . . . That is *not* the attitude here [in Nashville]. It's a wonderful cooperative attitude. We're all looking for ways to work together. When we need a ballet, we go right to the Nashville Ballet, and they can't wait to join in and be in one of the operas. And the Symphony plays for us. The Rep and the Chamber Orchestra use our rehearsal studio."

The future. For the 2003–4 season the performances included *Tosca, Pagliacci, The Pirates of Penzance,* and *Salome.* One notable singer in *Pagliacci,* tenor Clifton Forbis, a Belmont University alumnus and resident of nearby Goodlettsville, has sung at La Scala, Vienna's Staatsoper, Paris Opera, and the Juilliard Opera Center. He debuted with the Metropolitan Opera in 1996 in *Othello* with Placido Domingo.

Carol offered this invitation: "If you have one night to go out for classical music, come to an opera. You'll get choral music, you'll get solo singing, you'll get symphony, quite often you'll get ballet, and you'll get theater. In what other art form can you do that? You'll understand every word of it because it's translated for you above the stage, you can wear whatever you want to wear, you can applaud whenever you feel like it, you can boo the bad guy. . . .We want you to misbehave. We're the fun art form."

Opera Singers with Nashville Connections

It is highly gratifying
and touches the state pride of every patriotic Tennessean
to witness this recognition of talent
from our own commonwealth and from our own South.

—Tennessean, February 9, 1928

GRACE MOORE. Her biographer Rowena Rutherford Farrar wrote, "With opera always her first love, Grace dreamed of singing the leading role in a complete opera on film. By making more and more operas available to everyone, she argued, Hollywood would become the artistic center of the Western world." Grace Moore became well known for her work in opera, movies, and recordings, and her first movie, *A Lady's Morals* (1930), which was about the life of Jenny Lind, had "the first complete operatic scenes ever filmed." I will leave it to others to decide whether Hollywood achieved the lofty status that Moore desired for it, but subsequent films were made with opera stars.

Moore, born in Slabtown and reared in Jellico, Tennessee, came to Nashville in 1916 to attend Ward-Belmont. In addition to English and French, her courses included piano, voice, history of music, and ear training. Professor Charles C. Washburn must have heard something special from her because he provided more musical instruction for her, but he did not have Moore as a pupil very long. According to Farrar, Moore was expelled in January 1917 for "bad" conduct, which included sneaking out to dances at Vanderbilt University and failing French.

A determined Moore pursued voice training in Washington, D.C., and New York, and by 1920 she had a role on Broadway in *Hitchy Koo*; she later performed in *Music Box Revue* (1923). With more determination and more training she made it to the Metropolitan Opera, and for her debut February 7, 1928, many Tennesseans and both U.S. senators from the state were in attendance. The editorial page of the *Tennessean*, February 9, 1928, labeled her "Our New Prima Donna" and proclaimed, "It is highly gratifying and touches the state pride of every patriotic Tennessean to witness this recognition of talent from our own commonwealth and from our own South. There is nothing sectional in music." Moore was the second singer with a local connection to appear at the Met in 1928, the first being Joseph Macpherson: "It is worthy of note and a source of pride to the people of Nashville that both Mr. Macpherson and Miss Moore are former students of Ward-Belmont college. They are both in part the products of our own educational institution." The irony is that when Moore came to Nashville a few weeks later to perform at the Ryman Auditorium in a personal appearance sponsored by the Lions Club, the club lost money because the numbers of people in the audience did not come close to what was expected. It was probably small comfort to Moore to be staying with her parents as house guests of Governor Henry Horton in the executive mansion.

Moore had two more recitals in Nashville, the last in October 1945 at the War Memorial Auditorium. She was killed in a plane crash in January 1947, but because of her interest in promoting

Grace Moore had a role in Irving Berlin's *Music Box Revue*, beginning in 1923, on Broadway, and this photo was taken during that period. A native Tennessean who briefly attended Ward-Belmont in Nashville, she achieved fame for her roles in opera and movies and for her recordings.

music, there are now Grace Moore Scholarships in Voice at the University of Tennessee in Knoxville.

Mme Charles Cahier. Sarah Jane Layton Walker was born in Nashville in 1870 (died in 1951) but moved to Indianapolis; her father was General I. N. Walker. She studied voice in Paris, Vienna, and Berlin. Gustav Mahler, then the artistic director at the Vienna Court Opera, hired the contralto to sing there, and they worked together over a period of years (not only in Vienna). She also performed at the Met and did several recordings. As a voice teacher on the faculty of Curtis Institute in Philadelphia, she taught Marian Anderson everything she had learned from Mahler, according to Peter G. Davis in his book *The American Opera Singer.* Davis wrote, "It was Mme. Cahier who passed on Arturo Toscanini's famous 'voice of the century' comment to Anderson after the black contralto's breakthrough recital in Salzburg in 1935, an assessment that would soon be known and repeated the world over."

Sylvia Stahlman. The only child of George W. and Josephine Gaskill Stahlman, Sylvia was born in Nashville in 1929. She attended Hillsboro High School (a 1946 graduate), Vanderbilt University (1947), and Ward-Belmont (as a voice student in 1948); she also studied at Juilliard.

She had a role in the Broadway musical comedy *Love Life* (1949–50) with lyrics by Alan Lerner and music by Kurt Weill, but the extensive list of her accomplishments had opera at its core: leading soprano at the Brussels Royal Opera House (1951–53); soloist at New York City Opera, Lyric Opera of Chicago, San Francisco Opera, and Santa Fe Opera; guest appearances throughout the United States and Europe, such as the Bayreuth Opera Festival and the Handel Opera Society. Among her recordings was Mahler's Fourth Symphony with Georg Solti and the Amsterdam Concertgebouw

Orchestra (1961). She occasionally performed in Nashville, and in April 1957, she participated with the Cathedral Singers in a tribute to Marguerite Shannon, a pianist, and also sang with the Nashville Symphony. Sylvia Stahlman was a leading soprano at the Frankfurt Opera (1958–71) until her retirement, and she settled in St. Petersburg, Florida. She died there in 1998, but she is buried in Mount Olivet Cemetery in Nashville.

Alice Nielsen. This soprano was born in Nashville (1876?–1943) but reared elsewhere, and she trained in the United States and Italy. For her European debut in Naples she had the role of Marguerite in *Faust;* she sang several times at Covent Garden, and she eventually formed her own company, the Alice Nielsen Comic Opera Company. Victor Herbert wrote *The Fortune Teller* (1898) for her.

Kitty Cheatham. She was the daughter of Richard Boone and Frances Anna Bugge Cheatham. Born in Nashville and educated in the city's public and private schools, Kitty Cheatham left Nashville as a young girl "to seek her fortune on the stage," according to her obituary (she died on January 5, 1946, in New York City but is buried in Nashville's Mount Olivet Cemetery). The Duchess of Somerset arranged her first formal concert, with Mme Nordica and the violinist Kubelik, in England. A mezzo-soprano, Cheatham became known worldwide for her interpretations of children's songs. She had more than one thousand songs in nine languages in her repertoire, although she seems to have favored American composers, and she also wrote several books (*Early Voyages of the Norseman, Spiritual Music, A Nursery Garland*). In December 1905 she participated in a benefit held in New York City to raise funds for Jews who were suffering in Russia; other participants were Mark Twain, Sarah Bernhardt, cellist Auguste Van Biene, and Margaret Anglin and her company. Cheatham was an early presenter of children's concerts for the New York Philharmonic and the Philadelphia Symphony, and she sang before many crowned heads of Europe and their children.

Elizabeth Carter and Dawn Upshaw. These two up-and-coming singers with Nashville connections have performed in the city. Carter sang as the Queen of the Night in Nashville Opera's 1996 production of *The Magic Flute.* Upshaw performed at Ingram Hall in September 2003 and also led a master class at Blair School of Music.

Nashville Ballet

I think of ballet as visual music or musical painting. There is nothing to "get" about it. It's a visceral experience.

—PAUL VASTERLING

WHEN ANNA PAVLOVA danced on the stage of the Ryman Auditorium on March 12, 1914, the reviewer said that she "interpreted music and art and literature and expressed it in all of its beauty and color and tone and expression infinitely more perfect than it could have been painted by an artist, or written or played by an author, poet or composer." He also emphasized that Pavlova's dancing was not for "the exclusive enjoyment of 'highbrows.' . . . It was not a series of intricate, puzzling dances to be understood by only those who had read books and poems and dramas and operas. . . . It was a marvelous interpretation of beauty and nature." To enjoy the thirty-three-year-old Pavlova, one needed only "two eyes and a love of music and things beautiful." Even then she was recognized as one of the world's great ballerinas.

Most members of her company had been ballet masters or mistresses; Laurent Novikoff, a graduate of the Imperial Ballet, would become ballet master of the Chicago Opera and the Metropolitan Opera. The program was diverse, reflecting the company's versatility: a comedy-drama dance to the "Magic Flute"; "Invitation to the Dance," set in an 1830s ballroom; the "Gavotte Pavlova," a modern dance with Pavlova and M. Berge; a Russian dance; and "Autumn Bacchanale," a pastoral dance. She brought an orchestra with her for the one-evening engagement. There was no mention of the size of the audience—just "many people" at the auditorium.

Two years later Pavlova and her company returned, accompanied by the Boston Grand Opera Company, for a two-evening engagement, February 11–12, 1916, at the Vendome Theatre. The costs were $2, $4, and $5 ($2 then, about $33 today). On Friday the program was *Pagliacci* (with Thomas Chalmers, Felice Lyne, Giovanni Zenatello, Romeo Boscacci, and conductor Roberto Moranzoni) followed by *Coppelia,* and the next morning two reviewers reviewed Nashvillians more than they did the programming—although they spoke highly of the excellent work. It was a "miserable crowd" in numbers, not enthusiasm, that greeted the "splendid galaxy of artists" who had come so far to appear in the Athens of the South; the lower part of the theater and the first gallery were not even half filled. A clearly exasperated Charles Washburn wrote, "With the long years of musical training Nashville has enjoyed, through more than one generation, it was a surprise and a disappointment that so small a house should greet an organization superb in personnel and training; one that has won instant and enthusiastic recognition in all the musical centers of America." Add the fact that the city was full of students, the poor showing was even more a negative reflection on Nashville, which claimed to represent the "aesthetic culture of the South." (Despite the turnout, Pavlova returned at least twice more to dance at the Ryman, February 1922 and 1924.)

One of the world's great ballerinas, Anna Pavlova danced at the Ryman Auditorium in March 1914, and her performance was "a marvelous interpretation of beauty and nature."

The next evening, Saturday, the ballet company performed a program of Spanish dances following *La Bohème*. That programming choice meant that the dancers were still in motion past midnight, well into Sunday morning, and many attendees were uncomfortable at having a dance program on the Sabbath.

The small audience for that special performing arts event was in great contrast to the sizable crowd for a commercial event two days later, beginning on Monday morning. Despite cold weather and some snow that had fallen on Sunday, hundreds of people thronged the Hippodrome to see $250,000 worth of cars and accessories in the city's first auto show, which was to run February 14 to 19. Attendees were treated to singing that week by Marcella Hamilton and music provided by the Nashville Symphony Band directed by Mme von Stechow.

Perhaps the cost of the tickets restricted the size of the audience. Perhaps the opera lovers were not willing to sit through a ballet, no matter how famous the ballerina. Perhaps the idea that such entertainment was only for "highbrows" or the ladies or the "learned" kept them at home. Perhaps others thought that all dance was like that in vaudeville halls. Perhaps there was a problem with seeing men in tights. Perhaps there was a fear that something shocking would appear on stage, as had happened in Paris with the introduction of *The Rite of Spring* in 1913. Whatever the reason, the recognition of ballet as an art form was slow to develop in Nashville, a familiar situation in other southern cities. To this day audiences for the ballet—though increasing—are not yet growing by leaps and bounds, and the complaints expressed by Charles Washburn almost ninety years ago still reverberate.

Throughout the United States, few professional ballet companies were in operation early in the twentieth century—most were in New York City—and there were not many civic (amateur) companies, either. In the late 1920s Ward-Belmont, the Nashville Conservatory of Music, Peabody College, and a very few private studios offered ballet classes to young girls and adult women, and they occasionally had recitals. It took the passion of a woman, Albertine Maxwell, who moved to Nashville from Chicago and opened a dance studio in 1936, to lay the groundwork for professional ballet and to provide the continuity that has finally enabled Nashville to have its own professional ballet company, one that is gaining an outstanding reputation.

Albertine and her legacy. Jane Fabian began taking classes with Albertine when she was four years old, and she once wrote, "Albertine, a woman small in stature—whose love of ballet knew no bounds, who believed ballet should be central to the cultural life of our city—will forever seem larger than life. . . . Time in the studio taught grace, courtesy, teamwork, musicality, and self-discipline, as well as wondrous joy in viewing performances and the exhilaration of being a performer." She and many others, such as Janet Clough, who studied with Albertine are active in the arts today. Jane said, "Albertine's first priority was good training and a commitment to that."

Before she came to Nashville, Ellen Albertine Chaiser Maxwell had danced with the company at the Chicago Opera, the Adolf Baum Dance Company in Los Angeles, and the Ruth St. Denis Dance Company in New York City. She set up the Albertine School of Dance in the living room of the red brick two-story home on West End Avenue at the corner of Orleans (a bank is there now) that she shared with her son, Frank, and her husband, Boyd. She ran the school until 1980—*forty-four years*. She also held the Albertine Summer Dance Workshop in Bar Harbor, Maine

(1952–89), and she was the founder and director of Les Ballets Intimes with the Nashville Ballet Society (1945–80). (Albertine registered the name Nashville Ballet Society with the secretary of state, and she called her performances Les Ballets Intimes. When she relinquished the name Nashville Ballet Society, the present company assumed that legal name, having been the Nashville City Ballet.) Albertine died in 1996 at the age of ninety-four.

Jane Fabian attended Harpeth Hall, Hollins College, and Vanderbilt University. After her marriage she was away briefly from Nashville, but she has never been away from ballet. While she was rearing two sons, she did volunteer work with Albertine's Nashville Ballet Society, doing everything from handing out programs at performances to selling ads to raising money. Then with the current company Jane became president of the board, company manager, school administrator, and executive director until her retirement. She remains on the board of directors and is an advocate for *all* of the arts in the city—from the Ballet to the Grand Ole Opry—and for a lot of other things, too.

"I have all of this natural conversation: it is as natural as breathing to talk about professional football or baseball. I can bait a hook, shoot a gun, play golf. I was not my father's son, but I did do a lot of that type of thing," said Jane. "It's a plus when you're out there in the community talking about ballet that you can love ballet and be passionate about it but have a real appreciation for other types of entertainment, if you will."

Jane recalled, "My first time on stage I was a doll in Dr. Coppelius's toy shop in the ballet *Coppelia*. The gal who had the lead is still living in Nashville: Jody Bowers Slaymaker. You didn't do anything. You had been threatened not to move or blink. It was an alarming first experience. Albertine had recitals and/or performances, and she performed in many of the programs that I was involved with and that would have been in the 1950s. . . .

"We actually performed in front of the Symphony on a makeshift half-moon build-out at the War Memorial Auditorium. We had maybe three feet of space, and it curved to conform to the stage itself." The performance was excerpts from the *Nutcracker.*

Albertine sought out high-caliber teachers and special experiences for her students. Nashville Symphony conductor Guy Taylor's wife, Renee, was Albertine's pianist at one time. When Jane was a teenager, she often went to Albertine's summer workshop in Bar Harbor, Maine. Renee

Albertine Maxwell directed the Albertine School of Dance in her home on West End Avenue for forty-four years, and she instructed many youngsters who as adults have led the way for the establishment of the professional company, Nashville Ballet.

and Guy also were there, and Jane said, "We had the benefit of musical theory sessions and so forth with one and/or both of those artists." Albertine brought in teachers from the School of American Ballet, and Jane learned from "'the white Russians,' who worked with Balanchine at New York City Ballet—Pierre Vladimirov and Felia Doubrouska, who were husband and wife. . . . The Hindu dance instructors, Edna Dieman and Julia Bennett, were from Cedar Rapids, Iowa." Twenty or thirty students attended the camp. Jane was privileged to go to New York City with Albertine a couple of years and take classes at the School of American Ballet.

When the Sadler's Wells second company came to Nashville to perform *Coppelia* at the Ryman, they needed extra people on the stage for the last act, and Jane was one of the five performers from Albertine's. She will never forget the experience: "The Ryman backstage then was something. We changed in a little hallway that led to the men's room. Whoever decided to put five teenage girls there! The principal ballerina was Elaine Fifield. . . . The orchestra conductor was very British and very loud. He had to change into his tails behind an open wardrobe trunk. He said, 'As God is my witness, I will never come back to this blankety-blank city.' Of course, he didn't say blankety-blank. And they didn't."

Anytime a ballet company visited, Albertine insisted that her students be there. On March 13, 1950, for example, when the Ballet Theatre (now American Ballet Theatre) with Nora Kaye and Igor Youskevitch performed at the Ryman, most of the audience was from her school. Mrs. Naff reported that the company expected ticket sales to reach the $5,000 mark (ticket prices were $3.60, $3, $2.40, $1.80, $1.20; $1.20 then, about $9 today), but they did not reach half of that—and it was the Ballet Theatre's tenth anniversary season.

The first time that Jane saw Nashville Symphony conductor Kenneth Schermerhorn, he was then conducting for the American Ballet Theatre (ABT) in the Ryman. She said, "Albertine bought the center balcony at the Ryman, perhaps three rows, and you were expected to go. Your parents had to pay for your ticket, but it was part of your education, from her perspective. Whenever ABT or Ballets Russes came, I have been to many a performance there because Albertine said you had to do it, so you did it."

When the first regional ballet festival was held in Atlanta in 1956 (it was the first regional festival anywhere in the United States, not just in the Southeast), Albertine took her students. Jane noted, "From that gathering of people like Albertine came eventually the Louisville Ballet, the Atlanta Ballet, and others in the Southeast. She was really in on the beginnings of some exciting times in the world of dance in this country. Then in the seventies we moved forward and the regional companies were coming into their own. There were more regional festivals established nationwide. In the seventies the Ford Foundation monies for the arts, particularly for dance, were a big boost." The Southeastern Regional Ballet Festival was held in Nashville in 1970 and was well attended, bringing in exceptional dignitaries from the greater ballet world, yet little notice was taken in the city except by those directly involved.

Despite what she achieved in terms of bringing good dance and good training to Nashville, Albertine's need to maintain her autonomy and her unwillingness to collaborate with other groups were serious hindrances to the development of a professional ballet company for the city. It would take the diligent work of her former students and some others to attain that goal.

History. Jane said, "My dream has always been for Nashville to have a professional ballet company and a school that is worthy of a ballet company. When I went to New York the first time, I was fifteen. I'm a linear thinker and a realist. I did not know that there were that many girls in the world who thought they were going to be ballerinas, much less concentrated in one place where they were getting exceptional training. At fifteen I saw the light that there was nowhere in Nashville for those of us who might have dreamed about a career [in ballet] to go. If we couldn't go to New York or Chicago or the West Coast, it was over." But she did not give up the idea of having a professional company and a ballet school in Nashville.

Jane began teaching at the Dancers Studio in 1976, and "from the Dancers Studio came the nucleus of Nashville Ballet as it is today," she said. A small group of volunteers started the Young Dancers' Concert Group in 1981. "We did exactly what Albertine did: we had a group of strong high school students and started with them. We did the same types of things—at just different places—with those youngsters that some of us had done with Albertine. We took them to the Lawn and Garden Fair. Ingram Industries had a reception for a Degas exhibit at Cheekwood, and we had a little performance there with our students [reflective of the Cheekwood partnership].

"We moved from having a group of exceptional teenage dancers to having that group augmented by a guest artist from Cincinnati Ballet and his partner to using the artistic leadership here on stage with a couple of dancers who were teachers. Eventually we moved away from the Dancers Studio, which was a commercial dance school, to try to establish ourselves as an independent entity [Nashville City Ballet in 1984]." In this period Jane spoke with Warren Sumners, the director at TPAC then, and asked for permission to have the civic dance group work in the rehearsal hall at TPAC until the group could find a space. He agreed.

"From 1982 to 1985 we had some relative success," Jane continued. "We had a small board, and that grew. And before we moved ahead the two people I personally talked with were you

[Martha] and Ida Cooney [at the HCA Foundation]. . . . I was asking, 'Where do we go from here? Do you think we can make it?'" The professional company, the Nashville Ballet Society, actually began in the fall of 1986.

Ingram Industries provided the first executive on loan, who served as the board finance person and treasurer. The makeup of the board had been developed carefully to include business and corporate members. Jane noted, "I had spent a lot of years as a volunteer in this community, so I had a sense of what a board should look like. We had an executive from AVCO, from the United Methodist Publishing House. A representative from SunTrust [it was Third National Bank at that time], and he was the uncle of one of the teenagers who was in the original civic company. He is a music person and will tell you so to this day, a longtime subscriber to the Symphony. We wanted to have a discriminating and diverse board." The board now has more than fifty members, and there is a ten-member advisory council.

Stewardship of funds has been another significant element of the success of the Nashville Ballet. Jane said, "There is all of this verbal homage: if you can't run a nonprofit like a business, you are going to go out of business. Sometimes I think the nonprofits are run more efficiently than some businesses because you are basically shepherding public funds and private funds; you are under the gun in terms of good management of those dollars."

The Company. Paul Vasterling became the artistic director in 1998. (Previous artistic directors were Peggy Burks, Dane LaFontsee, Edward Myers, Janek Schergen, and Benjamin Houk.) Other staff members include a ballet master, a ballet mistress, a school director, and a music director. The company's home is now located at 3630 Redmon Street, the Martin Center for Nashville Ballet. In what used to be an

Paul Vasterling has been the artistic director of Nashville Ballet since 1998.

indoor tennis center with three courts, there are now four dance studios, a costume shop, costume and prop storage, and administrative offices. Paul addressed the Martin Center's importance to the company: "Having the right space for us is like having good instruments for musicians to play or good acoustics in a hall. For me it makes the dancers work harder, work better, and in turn they look better on stage, and in turn the audience likes them better. It all blossoms from there. We're very lucky to have this building."

Paul came to Nashville to be a dancer in the company in 1989. A native of Louisiana, he had never been exposed to ballet in his youth and never dreamed of becoming a ballet dancer. Through his piano playing for a community theater production, he met a choreographer who offered to give him ballet lessons. He said, "It was like a revelation. I realized that I should have been doing this. I was always the only young man who would dance at any of our dances. I would dance every dance. But I didn't make the connection." Paul has a theater degree with an emphasis in dance from Loyola.

The company holds two open auditions, one in New York and one in Nashville. The eighteen company dancers have come from as far away as the Philippines and Soviet Georgia, and as close as the Nashville area. Paul stated recently, "Dancers from all over the country will come here, and they're lining up to get into the company. I have people on a list waiting to come in. That says something about us." Jane added, "In a small repertory company the dancers are afforded the opportunity to do more; the work is very diversified. They do *Swan Lake* one year and something with Hal Ketchum and Nanci Griffith the next year. You can't beat that. That is a good thing. In the dance world Nashville Ballet is gaining a strong reputation."

There are three categories of dancers in the Ballet: company dancers, apprentices, and trainees. The company dancers work a thirty-week season, Monday through Friday, from 9:15 to 6:00. It is their *real* job. Apprentices are paid less, but they work the same schedule. The trainees usually have parents helping them, or they work part-time jobs to make ends meet—

Anna Djouloukhadze-Srb and Alexander Srb of the Nashville Ballet danced in the classic *Swan Lake.*

they are, after all, being trained. The trainees do most of the children's ballet performances.

One story illustrates how far Nashville Ballet has come in a short period. Jane received a call from Ed Benson, the executive director of the Country Music Association. He told her that the CMA Awards show was looking for dancers for a segment with the song "I Hope You Dance" (which won CMA Song of the Year), and the producers had planned on flying to New York City to find them. Jane explained what happened: "Ed said, 'I'm trying to get them to take a look at what is here.' I said, 'I'll write you a million thank-you notes.' They did in fact meet Paul [Vasterling] and spent a whole lot more time in the studio with the company than they had said they were going to. And they wound up using our dancers. For us that was a big breakthrough: first of all, that the executive director of the Country Music Association would say to the CBS producer in Los Angeles, 'Why don't you take a look at the hometown folks instead of flying to New York?' It had to save them money, but that was okay. He agreed to look, and when he did, he was excited about what he saw. We've experienced a lot of that in recent years, which is good for us and, I hope, good over the long haul."

The School of Nashville Ballet takes students as young as age three, and more than thirty-six weeks of classes are offered each year. In a recent Summer Intensive Program the school had 84 students, most from out of town. There may be 240 to 250 during the school year. It is getting harder, however, to enlist male dancers. Ballet dancers have to face the reality of having a short-lived career as actual dancers because of their aging muscles and joints. Then they have to make the transition to other careers that put less stress on their bodies. Their artistic lives are much different in this regard from, say, violinists in the Symphony or actors at the Rep.

Paul Kaine became the executive director of Nashville Ballet in January 2002.

Individual success stories. Cathy Sharp grew up in Nashville and now has her own professional dance company in Basel, Switzerland, called Tanz Ensemble Cathy Sharp. Her brother still lives in Nashville, so she returns for visits. She invited Nashville Ballet to be a part of her twenty-fifth anniversary in Switzerland in 1999, and the next year Tanz Ensemble Cathy Sharp performed at the Polk Theater on the program of the Nashville Ballet. Despite the apparent achievements of both companies, Jane expressed her disappointment at the lack of hometown enthusiasm: "Nobody cared that Nashville Ballet went to Switzerland; the press in Switzerland was extraordinary. Nor did many people care that Cathy is the hometown girl who made good and comes home with her own dance company to a town that really doesn't give a flip. Over the last eight or nine years that was one of the most discouraging situations that I experienced. Yet when Cathy took her bow onstage at TPAC, I don't think it made a bit of difference to her that it was not a full house or that there hadn't been a lot of press coverage. The look on her face—she was so happy and so proud to be there. I wish I had that moment on video.

"No matter who we talked to or what we did, we could not generate any excitement at the Chamber of Commerce, the newspapers, or the TV stations that Nashville Ballet had been invited to perform and we did what some have called our signature piece—I'm not sure I agree with that—but we did the down-home country Nanci Griffith piece: 'This Heart.' Not only did we go, but we represented Music City USA, we felt."

Adelaide Vienneau works at the Frist Center for the Visual Arts now. Her last performance with Les Ballets Intimes was in the spring of 1980, and she went to New York and danced with Dance Theater of Harlem from 1983 to 1988, but had to quit because of an injury. She came back to Nashville and taught at the School of Nashville Ballet for a while and also attended Vanderbilt University.

Innovation and collaboration. Paul addressed the Ballet's programming: "People are a lot less patient about what they see. It's all about relevance in what you present without selling out. That's the fine line we walk. We don't want to do MTV because it's not about that. It's about people telling stories or expressing something that is inexpressible, like painting or abstract art. It's not about shake, rattle, and roll.

"I have eclectic taste—my taste runs from pop music and pop movement all the way to classical ballet. The classical form is the scariest for people to approach, so the idea is to bring them in and slowly teach them using popular elements, just as the Symphony does a pops series, and then bring them into other kinds of forms."

He has choreographed *Dracula* and *Robin Hood*, for example, and he has staged his works

Nashville Ballet's production of *Robin Hood*, choreographed by Artistic Director Paul Vasterling, was full of energy in April 2003.

Modern Dance

Joy Zibart was a teacher of modern dance in her studio on Clifton Lane, and her students included all age groups: youngsters, teens, and adults. She could be counted upon to present programs at public events; for the week-long arts festival held in mid-May 1961 at Centennial Park, the feature was her "Bell Witch" dance. She choreographed numbers for the Nashville Children's Theatre and other local groups. Her death in June 1966 left a vacuum in the modern dance field in Nashville, a city that had been her home since 1946. An editorial in the *Tennessean* noted, "Few have contributed so much to the cultural life of a community in so brief a time." Puryear Mims created a sculpture to memorialize Joy Zibart's work in dance, and in 1969 he placed it in the lobby of Nashville Children's Theatre.

Tennessee Dance Theatre (TDT), founded in 1985 by Donna Rizzo and Andrew Krichels, did innovative and professional works in modern dance, and the company with its fifteen-year history of existence seemed destined to survive. The Tennessee Arts Commission and the Metropolitan Nashville Arts Commission were very supportive of TDT, which had a three-pronged mission—re-create dance classics, create artistic works with southern themes, and provide education about dance—and the company fulfilled that mission.

TDT used live music, often collaborating with local musicians such as Chet Atkins, Mark O'Connor, Riders in the Sky, and faculty members of the Blair School of Music. Many of the company's works—*Quilts, Front Porch, Signs* (about snake handling), and *Ghosts of the Civil War*—incorporated southern themes. The dancers worked with the late Otha Turner and the Rising Star Fife and Drum Band, and the company received a National Endowment for the Arts grant to go to schools in the Delta and introduce the dance piece with Turner's music. The dancers presented H.O.T. programs at TPAC and had a part in the Tennessee Bicentennial. They performed at Festival de Lille (Lille, France) and at the Spoleto Festival; they made appearances in the states of Pennsylvania, Kansas, New York, Massachusetts, and Maine. For two seasons TDT performed in New York City, and critics such as Anna Kisselgoff of the *New York Times* gave the company outstanding reviews. Some of the dancers trained by Donna and Andrew wanted to come back to Nashville, but there was not enough work to support them.

In August 2000 the dream of sustaining TDT vanished. Andrew cited the attitude of "If it's art, what is it doing here? If it's fun, it can't be art." Nashville audiences were hesitant to accept much of the material with southern themes, although French and New York City audiences loved the works. TDT had a good core audience, but it was not enough. There was too much competition for dollars. TDT had created a presence in the community, but that was not enough, either.

Linda Mason was president of the board four years and executive director three years. She said, "The hardest part was raising money. It was a terrible ordeal. It was an uphill battle. But I loved working with TDT. I had a passion for it because I was working with people of passion.

"The years that TDT was in existence were exciting years. TPAC was new. People were willing to see what there was to see. People were willing to stretch themselves. But now there are so many entertainment offerings. It's an entertainment overload of a diversity of things. Before, people loved to go to TPAC to see Broadway shows; now, they get on a plane and go to Broadway. Or they go to football games.

"Whenever I feel really stagnant or overloaded, watching a live performance can lift my spirits. You take people who haven't been to a performance of the arts, whether it's dance or music, and they will be surprised at how uplifting it is. We can't allow creativity to die, and the arts keep it alive."

in other states and even in the Philippines. Paul and the Nashville Ballet worked with Hal Ketchum on *Awaiting Redemption,* each segment about a life passage.

In the spring of 2003 a program with the title *Emergence* was a collaborative effort of the Ballet and Blair School of Music faculty, and it featured new choreography, stories, and music. For one segment Paul choreographed *The Night of the Iguana,* based on the work by Tennessee Williams, and Michael Rose wrote the music for it. For another segment, *LAPse DANCE,* Stan Link was the composer and Robert Philander, the choreographer. Paul said, "We did it to appeal to a whole set of people who may not normally come to TPAC. Maybe Vanderbilt audiences. Part of our mission is a broad approach and presence in the community."

The Ballet has performed with the Nashville Chamber Orchestra, the Nashville Symphony accompanies the Ballet for many performances, and the Nashville Opera uses some of the company's dancers in productions when ballet is required. Nashville Children's Theatre called upon the Ballet to do *Dracula* for the middle school opening performance one year. Jane commented, "There had never been a collaboration between the ballet company and Children's Theatre. I don't know that they have collaborated with other arts groups in town. They took a huge risk to put us on their season as their middle school opening show." For the 2003–4 season of Nashville Ballet world premieres included *The Bell Witch, Romeo and Juliet,* and a collaboration with the Bluebird Cafe to present *Bluebird Cafe at the Ballet.*

Community outreach. Everyone at the Ballet is devoted to community outreach. Paul observed, "People say that they don't know what is going on in the ballet, and they feel that they should know what is going on. At the symphony you may not know what is going on, but you don't feel that you *have* to know—you can still enjoy it at some level. People feel as if it should be a theatrical experience when they see something on the stage as opposed to visual music. Ballet and dance are more related to a symphony performance or an art museum visit as opposed to a theatrical experience, depending on the work. That is not just in Nashville; that is a pervasive idea. I think most of it has to do with that whole tradition of going to the performing arts and understanding them. In all of the performing arts we have to find our audience and make the art relevant to the people who live in the community that we're in. That's what we try to do here."

To Paul, outreach is as important as regular performances: "If we can get them younger, before the fear develops, they can start to understand. We see it as investment in our future." The auditorium of the downtown Nashville Public Library is the site of ballet performances for children on several Saturdays each year. Trainees go to the library story hour, dress in costumes, read *Angelina Ballerina* or a similar story, and talk to the children. Ballet 101 is like an illustrated lecture to explain what ballet is all about, and it is usually for adults. It took a while for the idea to catch on—maybe three people would show up—but now more and more people attend. Members of the Ballet visit local schools, too.

The Nashville Ballet is an advocate for arts careers. Very few people can be performing artists, but more can be photographers, set designers, critics, or costume managers. The Ballet and other arts organizations need administrators, board members, ticket buyers, and most of all, volunteers.

The future. "As far as what it's like now to have a ballet company, I believe that we are leading the pack in terms of a model. Ballet companies, even the big ones, are trying to figure out their place and what they need to offer people and how the art form is relevant to the audience of today," said Paul.

"The old models—the models that existed from the 1950s to the 1970s or so—have expired. That whole idea of using popular music—I did a ballet to Nanci Griffith in 1996. I am just reading on-line now that all of these companies across the country are using vocal music—like it's a big, new thing. My friends are the directors of these companies—it's not surprising to me that they are starting to use local talent, local music, in their ballet companies and trying to develop new audiences that way.

"I don't believe that the classic forms are ever going to go away. Ideally we can use these new forms to get people in and feel comfortable with the art form and then ease them into the classic forms. It's all about comfort level and the experience.

"We've had some hard times and had to struggle. That is true for any performing arts group. It's almost like you raise the bar but have to watch that you don't raise it too high. The trick is to raise it just incrementally enough that you can go up and that your public goes with you and your donors and your supporters. That is the fine line we're walking now. There is a momentum about the art and getting people excited about what you're doing."

Paul emphasized this point: "My artistic development is in and of Nashville. I came here as a dancer; I had choreographed one ballet when I was a student in college. I never really thought I could be a choreographer, and this organization and this community have allowed me to do that. I have established myself as a choreographer in this art form. That is pretty remarkable." All of the accomplishments of Nashville Ballet are pretty remarkable, especially given the company's short life span, and the company is regularly creating for Nashvillians the kind of visual music that they could have in earlier days only when guest artists such as Pavlova and her Russian company presented it.

The Maestro and the Maelstrom

When you conduct opera or ballet, you have the benefit of all of the makeup, the gold curtain, the lights, and the drama of the whole occasion.
When you conduct a symphony orchestra, there is no makeup, no lights. Everything is black and white. All of the drama has to be provided by the conductor and by the musicians themselves.

—Maestro Kenneth Schermerhorn

FOLLOWING Michael Charry's departure, the Nashville Symphony arranged to have guest conductors for a season until a new leader could be found. One of them was Kenneth Schermerhorn, who was also to be the interim music advisor and help in the search.

I have been very much involved with the Nashville Symphony since my family and I moved back to the city from New Orleans in 1961, and I was on the selection committee in 1983 to choose the next conductor. Kenneth had done an exceptional job of conducting during the interim period, and he really brought excitement to the Orchestra and to the audience. He seemed to be the perfect choice for the Nashville Symphony and the city, so I asked him, "Why don't we hire *you* for the job?" He replied, "You're not offering enough money to hire a seasoned conductor. That is the reason we have auditioned only younger conductors." Then I said, "Well, what would it take?" The board managed to work out terms favorable to the Symphony and to Kenneth—doubling the salary that had been offered—and his appointment was announced in June 1983.

A native of Schenectady, New York, Kenneth has been dancing to music since he was a youngster. He said, "As early as I can remember, I would dance wildly when the music came on, leaping up and down on the furniture and be punished for it. That was the magic of the time—the radio." Every network—NBC, ABC, and CBS—had its own orchestra, and companies sponsored weekly programs of classical music. He recalled, "Longine's watch sponsored a symphonette that played every Sunday afternoon. The NBC Symphony played every Saturday at six o'clock. The Bell Telephone Company sponsored a program every week that featured all of the greatest artists in the world. I mean everybody sang and performed. Jascha Heifetz performed on *The Bell Telephone Hour*. I ultimately did, too, when it was on television, when I was music director of American Ballet Theatre." As soon as he was old enough, he took the train into Manhattan to hear Toscanini and the NBC Symphony at Studio 8H.

It was only natural then that Kenneth would want to study an instrument or two in school. He credited the Works Progress Administration (WPA) with providing music teachers and instruments: "It was really quite dramatic. It fashioned a lot of my youth just because of the availability of free instruction." He had lessons on the trumpet, the clarinet, and the violin. Of course everybody sang in school, in choruses, in church choirs. He wanted to learn to play the piano, but his father, who as a former football player was "not inclined to support my musical habit anyhow," was unwilling to crowd a piano into the Schermerhorn home.

Kenneth noted his early experiences in dance bands: "We had a dance band as soon as I got to junior high school. Just friends from the neighborhood. By the time I got to high school there was a real curriculum for the orchestra and the band and the chorus. When I was fourteen years old, I played in a dance band—not the same one in junior high school. This was much more professional."

World War II was in progress, and the band played at the Friends Lake Inn in the Adirondacks during the summer, six nights a week, from 8:30 P.M. to 1:30 A.M. Fourteen-year-old Kenneth received $13 a week and room and board—and experience. The pianist in the band went on to write "Chances Are" and other big hits; he was the late Bobby Allen (known as Bobby Deutcher then).

After graduating from high school, Kenneth said, "I just generally used the trumpet to support my other habits, to get through the Conservatory." He applied to several music schools, but the numbers of ex-servicemen using the GI Bill in 1946 meant that scholarships were scarce. Nevertheless, he did obtain a small scholarship from the New England Conservatory of Music, from which he graduated with high honors.

Drafted in 1950, Kenneth spent six miserable months in the infantry while many of his friends had joined military bands. One who was at West Point in the U.S. Military Academy Band persuaded him that coming to West Point was a wiser move than being sent to Korea. Kenneth said, "In order to do that I had to enlist for four years as opposed to the allotted two years of the Selective Service. It was a much more civilized life at West Point. The surroundings were so beautiful, and it was a very fine band in those days because it attracted so many graduates from music conservatories and music schools.

"I was deliriously happy for about six months. I was also a bit of a malcontent. The disciplines got to me: shining your shoes and shining your forehead and shining everything. I didn't last that long. I shortly got transferred . . . I got orders to leave. Fortunately I didn't go west to Korea. I went east to Europe.

"I was in the Sixth Army Cavalry, but that was rather brief. An orchestra was formed in the Seventh Army Special Services, and I became a member of it and then its conductor. That changed my whole life. We had some fine musicians. Some of them are still active, playing in symphony orchestras in the United States, even at this late date."

When he was released from his military obligations in 1955, Kenneth studied conducting with Leonard Bernstein at Tanglewood, and he also studied Italian lyric theater at La Scala in Milan. From his early dancing to the sounds emanating from the radio, he danced on the podium as he conducted—and his first professional conducting job was with a dance company, American Ballet Theatre. He said, "I also was guest conducting here and there—in Mexico, the summer series of the Philadelphia Orchestra, St. Louis. I had some pretty good dates, but my main job was music director of the American Ballet Theatre. Then simultaneously I got the New Jersey Symphony and stayed there for five years."

Daniel Morganstern, principal cellist for Lyric Opera of Chicago and the American Ballet Theatre at the Met for more than thirty years, met Kenneth at American Ballet Theatre during his first year there. Morganstern said, "Over the years Kenny came back to American Ballet Theatre. He was just fabulous; he could take a trite piece and make it sound elegant. He is a sincere musician whose interest is in making music. And isn't that what it's all about—making music? Nashville is lucky to have such a great conductor who is doing a phenomenal job. I hope the people there realize that. I have worked with many, many conductors, and nobody came up to Kenny's level of ability."

Kenneth was offered the job of music director of the Milwaukee Orchestra, and he moved to Milwaukee. He said, "I kept my hand in Ballet Theatre off and on. Then I rejoined it at the behest of Mikhail Baryshnikov in 1982, I think it was. From 1982 to 1984. By that time I had other obligations. It didn't last that long. I didn't intend it to."

As for Milwaukee, Kenneth noted, "When I went there, it was with the obligation that I was going to build them a symphony orchestra. They already had a good foundation for an orchestra. And they had quite a good subscription series. They had ten programs a year; they played them once. By the time I left we had twenty programs a year, and we played them three times each. The orchestra grew from sixty-five to ninety or ninety-five." He spent twelve years (1968–80) building up that orchestra before he left for other projects.

"I wanted something fresh to do," explained Kenneth. "I had a sponsor who subsidized my becoming a visiting professor of the faculty at Yale, where I went one day a week. Then I had quite a few guest engagements during that time in Southeast Asia, in Hong Kong, in Europe, in the United States." When he accepted the position with the Nashville Symphony (1983), the orchestra had to share him for a while with the Hong Kong Philharmonic because he had also become the music director there.

Relying on Kenneth's expertise and the musicians' talent, the board of directors had a goal of building the Nashville Symphony into a major orchestra. Kenneth stated that the Symphony then was "vastly different from what it is now because it was a nighttime orchestra. It was not a bad orchestra. It was quite a good orchestra, but it rehearsed in the evenings so that people could have day jobs. The salaries were pretty low. There were some fine and gifted musicians, and there were some who were barely adequate. By moving it into a daytime orchestra, one that rehearses during the day, you automatically eliminate some of those people who are more amateur than they are professional. Also you can make more demands on the orchestra. It is very difficult to make demands on a musician who has been working all day teaching school or something like that [and some commuted from nearby towns such as Murfreesboro and Clarksville].”

Most of the musicians wanted to become a daytime orchestra, full-time employees with benefits and higher salaries. The problem, as usual, was tied to the budget. In 1981 the musicians and the Symphony board had to call in a federal mediator because the musicians three times rejected the board's contractual offer. The result was a three-year contract that had a modest pay raise and stipulated that twenty-four players were members of the core orchestra. That contract was to expire in May 1984, and the musicians had even higher expectations for the Symphony's future with Kenneth as the new conductor.

The next proposed contract did not meet the expectations of the musicians, and many were reluctant to accept it. Eventually, in February 1985, the musicians voted to strike until two months later when they accepted a new contract. The terms included almost doubling salaries over four years, from a minimum of $9,200 to $17,500, and most of the raise was to come in the fourth year. By August of the 1987–88 season there were seventy full-time musicians, compared to forty-seven in the 1986–87 season.

The Symphony had deficits every year, however, and a study was undertaken to evaluate the problem and to develop a long-range plan. One finding was that there was a need for a substantial endowment. Denny Bottorff, a board member,

Maestro Kenneth Schermerhorn celebrated his twentieth year with the Nashville Symphony in 2003; the Schermerhorn Symphony Center is named in his honor.

said, "In studying the finances of many different arts organizations, a rough rule of thumb is about half of your income comes from gifts, from contributed income. That holds all across the United States. Then you say, 'Does that come in annual gifts? From earnings on endowment?' To secure the future, you must have a big-enough endowment to overcome changes in annual giving that fluctuate with the economy. Endowment is essential." The plan indicated that if we could raise $7 million for an endowment and get the union to slow the pace of the big salary increase, we could make the Symphony fiscally sound.

Denny explained the dynamics of what led to the shutdown of the Nashville Symphony in early 1988: "We went to the union ahead of time and said, 'Would you be willing to work with us if we can raise this money?' I wasn't the chairman of the Symphony at that time, and I did not want to be unless we could achieve a fiscally sound operation. They said yes. You [Martha] and I cochaired the campaign and raised that endowment. When we went back to the union, they wouldn't work with us. They said no, they would not adjust the contract.

"I then became chairman of the board. You [Martha] and I had made a commitment to the donors. We had promised people that if they gave this money, the Orchestra would be fiscally sound. Now we were in a situation where the basis under which we had raised the money was no longer accurate. We still had a structural deficit. The Symphony was not in a fiscally sound position.

"We looked around the country at that time, and symphonies were failing left and right. I can't remember all of them—New Orleans, Denver, Long Beach—they had enormous losses. We did an analysis and found that in Nashville at that time, our mix of contributed income versus earned income was very solid. We were doing a fine job as a community in support of the Symphony. It wasn't a problem with the level of philanthropy; it was an issue of not having enough attendance.

"We said [to the union leaders], 'If you won't work with us on smoothing the salary increases, we have to go back to the donors and tell them that the deal has changed and give them an opportunity to change their minds.' It was a real conflict. It was a moral issue."

Compounding the bleak financial picture of the Symphony was the stock market plunge in October 1987, led off by Black Monday (the nineteenth) when the Dow Jones Industrial Average lost 508 points, or 22.6 percent of its value. Never mind that the year ended with a small gain (as of January 2, the close was 1927, and as of December 31, the close was 1938; it was certainly not up to the 2722 level it had been on August 25); the aftershock lasted well into the next year as far as corporate and private willingness to contribute funds.

It was as if we on the executive committee were stuck in a maelstrom: we could not cover the Symphony's debt, and we could not renegotiate with the musicians. Denny stated, "It was a hard thing to do. I was a young kid, and I went into the board meeting and said, 'Here is where we are. I see no way except for us to take this position. If we don't take this position, we are going to be running structural deficits for a long period of time. We have just raised all of this money. We have raised a lot more than other orchestras, and they're all having problems. We've got to build an audience over time. We can't think, *Gee, we can go on and do this, and we'll just raise more money.*'"

The union remained unconvinced of this dire situation, and the announcement was made in February 1988 that the entire operation would have to shut down. The musicians and the staff were released, the Symphony office was closed, and the board disbanded. Kenneth was out of the country, conducting the Slovak Philharmonic, so Denny called him there to deliver the news. It was a nightmare for everyone involved. The selection committee and I had convinced Kenneth in 1983 to accept the job as conductor of what was expected to become a major orchestra, and in 1988 the Symphony was shut down. What a blow to all of us! The organization filed Chapter 11 bankruptcy in June 1988.

Denny had been transferred out of state to Virginia Beach, Virginia, by his employer, Sovran (now Bank of America), so as the former vice chairman, I stepped in as chairman of the board of the now defunct Symphony in May. I did not like the idea of living in a city with no symphony, and furthermore, I felt a responsibility to Kenneth and to the musicians—many of whom had rearranged their lives because they were counting on being full-time Symphony employees and they now had no job and bills to pay. I had enlisted the help of Phil Bredesen (now governor of Tennessee but then a health care entrepreneur), Ben Rechter, Lewis Lavine, Martin Simmons, Dave Sampsell (who worked with me at Ingram Industries as a strategic planner), and a few others to develop a viable economic model for the Symphony. We had thought we had a chance to avert the bankruptcy if the musicians went along with the figures projected by the model, but the union representing the musicians did not accept the proposal. It was a horrible time.

A few years later, in 1991, Denny came back to Nashville as CEO of First American Bank (recently sold to AmSouth) and is involved again with the Symphony. He said recently, "As difficult as bankruptcy was, I believe it helped us. The Orchestra shut down without the enormous burden of accumulated debts over a long period of time that other orchestras had . . . it had some debts, but they weren't so insurmountable that they couldn't be worked out through a reorganization. It built a commitment to financial discipline as well as artistic achievement.

"Looking back: we didn't have the audience participation in those days that was needed. Why didn't we have that? I think part of it is that people in the South didn't grow up with the arts. As a matter of fact in later years, at First American the money we gave to the Symphony was to underwrite tickets for youth. We said, 'If you grow youth participation, we'll give more money. The money we give is for audience development purposes.' As I now think about it, the reason we structured it that way related back to my 1985 experience. When I came back to Nashville in 1991, I knew that it was not enough to sponsor performances; what we really needed—for the long-term success of the Orchestra—was to build an audience. It starts with the youth."

Harold Bradley was not leading the musicians' union at the time, so he was not a participant in any of the negotiations. He became union president in 1991 and offered his perspective on the series of events: "The secretary-treasurer was Vic Willis, and he kept saying that the union spent $55,000 to get the Orchestra back up and running. I never tried hard to document it, but it seemed that some of the people who came after Vic could document $35,000 for sure that we spent to try to get it put back together.

"I don't know what the problem was then. I do know one of the things was that we had people come in from the national level and try to negotiate. Sometimes that is not a good thing. We here know the dynamics, and we know the people better than they do. And everybody responds better to each other if they can sit down, knowing that they're going to live with each other after the meeting. But they were able to get the Symphony back up and running.

"There have been some times when we had to take cuts. I know of one particular time that the average in the Orchestra was going to go down from $17,000 a year to $15,000 a year [in 1988 after the bankruptcy]. But the Symphony also took cuts in its staff. That was one of the things that was negotiated. Hard times for both of us.

The Heritage Symphony

Victor S. Johnson Jr., chairman emeritus of Aladdin Industries, commissioned Bill Pursell to write a symphony in celebration of the various elements of music in Nashville. The result was Symphony No. 2: "The Heritage," which was a gift from Aladdin to the city that had been its home for forty years.

The world premiere of the symphony opened the 1989–90 season of the Nashville Symphony on September 15–16, 1989, in the War Memorial Auditorium, and it was part of the *Tennessean* and *Nashville Banner* Classical Concert Series. Also on the program that evening was James Galway, the flutist, who played Flute Concerto No. 1 in G Major by Mozart and Carmen Fantasy, Op. 25, by Bizet/Sarasate.

Each movement of Pursell's symphony was tied to the city's history. The first movement was "United Electric Railway—1890" (allegro energico), and it was inspired by a photograph of an electric trolley car on West End Avenue in the late 1800s. Pursell said, "I wanted an energy feel, a sense that anything could happen within this system of conveyance."

The second movement was "Centennial—1897" (waltz), which was inspired by pictures of young girls on a horse-drawn wagon for the Floral Parade during the Centennial Exposition. Pursell noted, "The oboe solo, complemented by the harp, carries the main theme of this movement creating a light and airy interpretation of this time in Nashville's history."

A totally different mood came with the third movement "Aftermath—December 18, 1864" (adagio grave). December 18 was two days after the Battle of Nashville, and Pursell spoke to the loss and despair of that time through the use of the English horn.

The fourth movement "The Ryman" (allegro vivace) paid homage to the Ryman Auditorium from its early days as a performance hall for Sousa, Caruso, Bernhardt, and other musical and dramatic greats to the glory days of the Opry. "The Ryman was the liveliest thing going in this town for a long time," observed the composer.

Pursell, currently associate professor of music at Belmont University, has been a faculty member since 1980. He received his Doctorate of Musical Arts, Master of Music, and Bachelor of Music from the Eastman School of Music, and at Eastman, he worked with Howard Hanson. Not only a composer and arranger, Pursell has played the piano in recording sessions with Eddy Arnold, Boots Randolph, Patsy Cline, and Jim Reeves, among many others. Born in California, the versatile musician has been in Nashville since 1960.

But we worked out of that, and we did the contract we had to do to keep it going during that period of time. Not happy for the union, not happy for the Symphony players, and not happy for management. We have endured that and we seem to be on a lucky roll right now. I'm sure that they have had good management before. I don't really have any complaints against any of them because basically they were doing their job based on the amount of money that they had to spend. And we were trying to do our job, seeing that the musicians could make some kind of salary." The most recently negotiated contract gradually escalates for six years; the rank and file in 2003 made about $35,000, including benefits.

Oboist Bobby Taylor was in the Symphony then and now. He stated, "Now in perspective, it seems like it was growing pains. The other side of the story is that a lot of orchestras were running into trouble about that time and a lot of them didn't do nearly as well as we've done. Kansas City and Denver and New Orleans and San Antonio and San Diego. A lot of them have come back—the musicians managed them for a while to try to get them going again. Birmingham had a major orchestra, as did New Orleans. Both of them went down the tubes and are trying to come back. I don't think they're nearly what they once were.

"It was a thing that maybe almost had to happen for both sides so that the management of the Orchestra could get the idea that things are different now; this is a group of professional musicians who are trying their best to make a go of this and to make a life for themselves. They need this to make a living. You can't be a schoolteacher all day long and then expect to come out at night, when there is nothing left of your energy, and perform on a high level. You do the best you can, but it has to have an effect. And the conductor is up there, having no sympathy. You produce or don't.

"The Orchestra had to become full time, and the salaries had to get much better. It was a way to get management's attention that we were serious about this. Then they closed us down. Luckily we survived it all and lived to tell about it, and it looks like things are going to be good in the future.

"The reorganization included some things that were good, for example, including more musicians on the board of directors. There are always musicians on the board of directors—and not that we know all that much about management and the business world, but we have their ear and they have our ear. The communication has really been important." Now there are ten union members on the Symphony board, so there are good relationships, and we got rid of the "us" versus "them" mentality. One union member is on every subcommittee, and two are on the larger subcommittees, including the executive committee.

It was not many months after the declaration of bankruptcy (1988) that the union leaders were more willing to talk, and we were able to negotiate terms to get the Symphony under way again. The start of the season was delayed, but at least there was a season that began with a pops concert in early November 1988. An interim executive director, Steven Greil, was hired just before the new year began. The city government and the citizens realized how close they had come to losing a valuable asset permanently. The city pledged $250,000 to underwrite free concerts for schoolchildren and other groups, and citizens bought tickets. Things were looking brighter, and many became hopeful that the Symphony was headed toward a more stable future. Much hard work by musicians, Maestro, Symphony staff, volunteers, and Guild members over the next decade brought about a success story that is still unfolding.

"Passion for the Music"

*I want the whole community to believe
that every time something important happens here—
whether it's a celebration or a catastrophe,
anything that requires music—
the Orchestra is somehow always right in the middle of it.*

—ALAN VALENTINE

"THE LAST THING you want on your watch was what was then the biggest budgeted arts organization going down the tubes. It sends all the wrong signals about arts and artists," said Bennett Tarleton, who was the executive director of the Tennessee Arts Commission at the time the Symphony shut down and declared bankruptcy. Some subscribers took more than one season to return, and new ones were reluctant to sign up. A period of rebuilding trust within the community was necessary.

In the wake of the bankruptcy a major boost to the reinvigoration of the Symphony came from the Symphony Guild. It had continued to function because the Symphony and the Guild have separate charters, and the Guild was able to give the Orchestra a one-time $90,000 gift.

Bennett credited Steven Greil, especially his business skills, his instincts, and his ability to work with musicians, as a primary ingredient in the success of the reestablished Nashville Symphony.

Steven spent five and a half years with the Symphony as executive director (the *interim* was soon dropped), and he admitted, "They were some of the hardest but most fulfilling years of my life. . . . It's really important to have an economic model that keeps up with the community and is not too far out in front of it; successful groups are able to do that. But you need the passion for the music to make it grow and not just stabilize it. . . . As for the bankruptcy of the Symphony, I think it was a good thing in the end. At first the Symphony hurt itself, but it came back and did a better job of reaching out to the community."

The first of Amy Grant's Tennessee Christmas concerts took place in 1993 at the Opry House, and almost $250,000 was raised for the Symphony, which accompanied her. Those proceeds and gifts from individuals and businesses retired the bankruptcy debt. In several subsequent years in addition to having a Christmas concert in Nashville, Amy took the show on the road with the Nashville Symphony to as many as twenty-two cities, and usually ten thousand or more filled the arena at each stop. She again donated some of the proceeds from the Nashville concert to the Symphony and paid the musicians the equivalent of double scale for the whole tour. Amy's 1996 concert marked the opening of the new Nashville Arena (now called the Gaylord Entertainment Center). Alan Valentine noted, "People across the country who might not have attended a classical performance had the opportunity to hear the Symphony, which always was a special feature, and the Symphony's reputation was enhanced by being in such a high-profile show."

By 1994, the dark financial cloud had lifted, although the Symphony board remains ever vigilant to make sure that a similar cloud does not descend once again on the Symphony. The Symphony now has a balanced budget—twelve years without a deficit and no debt—a situation in which many orchestras across the country would like to find themselves.

World-famous pianist Van Cliburn opened the fiftieth anniversary season of the Nashville Symphony in 1996. With each season the Orchestra has become stronger and moved closer to becoming a major, world-class orchestra. In 1999 it became an eighty-six-member ensemble of full-time musicians.

"Kenneth Schermerhorn has a lot to do with the current stability," said Bobby Taylor. "He has never been afraid to think big. We haven't always had leaders like that. Somebody told me once that the best combination to make an orchestra work is to have a conductor who has the biggest, most grand ideas for that orchestra and is always just push, push, push to make it happen and a manager who can think big but not let it happen too fast. Or you can have a manager doing the pushing and the conductor is more conservative. But I think it works best if the conductor has the ideas and the manager lets the ideas happen with control and not go too far too fast. I think we have had that for a while now."

In June 1998 Alan Valentine became executive director of the Nashville Symphony Association, succeeding Stephen Vann, who had assumed the job in 1994. (Vann left to take a position in New York with the Eos Orchestra.) Alan came to Nashville from the executive director position of the Oklahoma Philharmonic Society. Before that, he had been manager of Mid-Columbia Symphony Society in Richland, Washington, general manager of the Greensboro (North Carolina) Symphony, orchestra manager of the San Antonio Symphony, and managing director of the Chattanooga Symphony and Opera Association.

Alan commented on his experiences in the music world: "What I've learned in my years of managing orchestras is that there is no such thing as status quo. An institution is either on its way up or on its way down. If you make it try to maintain status quo, it will eventually turn down. You have to continually push and stretch, and that is dangerous because that puts you on thin ice in terms of finances and everything else. You run the risk of getting ahead of the community's *willingness* to pay. People talk about the community's ability to pay, but any community has the ability to pay for the best orchestra in the world. The question is, How *willing* is it to pay for it?"

The community's growing willingness became evident after the Symphony launched a $20 million endowment campaign in 1998. Within two years that goal was exceeded, and the Symphony undertook an East Coast tour that ended with an engagement in Carnegie Hall on September 25, 2000, to celebrate its success. Hundreds of Nashvillians flew to New York to support the Symphony; one-third of the audience that night was made up of Nashvillians, and the excitement was palpable.

"Kenneth, man, he hit a home run with that one," observed Bobby Taylor. "I remember having some meetings about what program we should play. He was very concerned; you don't go up there and play a Brahms symphony or a Beethoven symphony because two nights before the Philadelphia Orchestra or the Berlin Philharmonic probably played the same piece. That doesn't make any sense. What can we do that would bring some uniqueness to our concert and yet still get a good audience?

"We got Mark O'Connor, who has an international reputation and a following, and Nadja Salerno-Sonnenberg. She is really popular in New York. It was a brilliant program. It really worked. Some of us were leery of it, not so much me but some in the Orchestra. They were afraid it would contribute to our hillbilly image, going up there with Mark O'Connor. But it worked. It was brilliant to put the two of them together."

Alan Valentine is the current executive director of the Nashville Symphony Association, having held that position since June 1998.

The program began with Beethoven's Overture to *The Creatures of Prometheus* and Charles Ives's Second Symphony with so many exposed French horn passages, I was tense, wondering how our musicians' nerves would react. They were all perfect. After intermission, I began to relax and really enjoy Mark O'Connor's Double Violin Concerto and Richard Strauss's *Der Rosenkavalier* Suite, which was then and will always be one of my favorites. Reviewer Allan Kozinn of the *New York Times* called it "a knockout," and it was.

It is almost as if there is finally a convergence of positive circumstances for the Orchestra—again, not without huge efforts by dedicated people. Michael Buckland, the Symphony's director of marketing and communications, said, "I worked in the ad agency for the Philadelphia Orchestra. I was close to four years with the LA Philharmonic and the Hollywood Bowl. Then two and a half years with Toronto. I can tell you that coming here from Toronto, I feel that I have come to an exuberant place led by energetic board members and a brilliant executive director. The thing [the Symphony] is on an accelerated climb and probably climbing as optimistically, if not more optimistically, than the best around the country. The Volunteer State is very real compared with the whole of Canada, for example."

Alan offered his perspective: "Carnegie Hall and the endowment campaign and the effort for the symphony hall [see "A Time for Greatness"] and the recordings [for Naxos] that are out there all around the world now, which are getting rave reviews in every language on the face of the earth—those things are all contributing to a growing sense in the music community out there that the Nashville Symphony is a force to be reckoned with. It's a growing, viable artistic concern that will bring great credit to Nashville."

One sign of this recognition is the number and caliber of musicians who audition now when there is an opening with the Symphony. (Having higher, more competitive salaries helps, too; the base salaries exceed $35,000 with benefits.) Alan said, "The whole thing is not about money, particularly if you talk to the youngest players. Obviously, ultimately they want to earn a good living. But they say, 'You know what really matters? It's that we know that somebody is going to bring the standard of our colleagues up.' That is, ease the dead wood out and bring in more people who are at the right level. We're going to be constantly striving for a higher standard of quality. The community is somehow willing to put resources

The Nashville Symphony Chorus, directed by George Mabry, joins the Orchestra in such works as Handel's *Messiah*.

behind making that happen—the symphony hall, the endowment. That excites the young players. They see in that a future whereas they could leave here and go to an orchestra that is struggling and the salaries might be higher, but they would be on shaky ground. They'd like to see us build not a house of cards but a house of concrete and steel."

Alan continued, "The goal for an orchestra is to get 50 percent of its income from earned income sources—ticket sales, fees. We're considerably far from that now. We are at about 28 percent from earned income. . . . The growth of our contributed income has been so rapid that it has pushed that number down. . . . Most orchestras in our size range are in the 35 to 45 percent range. The other 50 percent: you want an amount equal to about 30 percent of the total budget from contributed income, that is annual fund drive and that sort of thing; something in the neighborhood of 15 percent coming from endowment; and as much as 15 percent coming from government sources. That is a difference in the Northeast and the South—in New York State, for example, the state gives the Buffalo Philharmonic, which is our peer, almost $1 million a year. We get $500,000 from the city Arts Commission [fiscal year 2003–4], which is terrific, but our percentage of grant money from other public sources is way low. I'm not sure I want government money. Don't get me wrong. I'd rather do without it if we can. But it is a factor.

"When you're having a lot of money problems, it also causes everything about the artistic development of the orchestra to be stunted. If you talk to a citizen who is not a die-hard classical lover, he will tell you intuitively, 'I can't tell the difference if your budget was $15 million and you had all full-time musicians or if it was $2 million and you had a bunch of good part-time musicians.' But if he sits down in the hall and listens, he can tell the difference. He knows deep down inside; he can tell the difference between really great and mediocre or good enough. 'Good enough' doesn't get people excited, but greatness in anything does."

Nashville audiences are discerning ones, according to Alan and Michael. Alan noted, "We can bring a big-name artist in, and what I've learned determines whether or not it will sell: Is it generally regarded in the wider music community as good? . . . And is it somebody I haven't seen before? Show me something I haven't seen. One of our big successes was the Irish tenor John McDermott. Who had heard of John McDermott? He was one of the three Irish tenors. We brought him to town and we sold tickets like you wouldn't believe." Michael observed, "When we put on a mediocre to good show, they don't come—even if we've marketed it like hell and it has a great name, but maybe a fading name. They know. In other cities of our size people wouldn't know. People here in Nashville are exposed to a lot of music."

Bobby Taylor stated, "Nashville had a more conservative audience, but it's getting more sophisticated. As the Orchestra has gotten better, I think we have built a feeling of trust. For a long time if they saw a program that had a composer that they didn't recognize and they might be a little bit afraid of it, they might not come. Now with Kenneth Schermerhorn here and the Orchestra has gotten to the point that it is good enough that they can trust us not to do something that they are going to absolutely hate, we are going to expand people's horizons a little bit, but make it a good performance and program stuff that is interesting. . . . I feel that I can communicate better playing the oboe than I can with speech, especially the great emotions of life. If music is not communicating something to people, I think it has failed."

Kenneth quoted the legendary impresario Sol Hurok on audiences: "He was famous for several crazy statements. One of the best is: 'If the peoples don't want to come to concerts, there is absolutely nothing you can do to stop them.' When you program for a season, you tend to choose pieces that have not been played in the last five years or that deserve to be played. Quite a bit of repertoire has never been played here at all. Now we are trying to build a chorus. [George Mabry is the choral director.] Some of the greatest musical thrills are the choral masterpieces, pieces for chorus and orchestra. We're trying to work the chorus into at least two programs a year and to balance the soloists with pianos and violins, cellos, and others. To choose works that will tend to accentuate the building of the Orchestra, works that are demanding for the woodwinds or certain sections of the Orchestra, or just demanding for the whole ensemble.

"There is always an obligation just for the future, for posterity, to perform works of our time, contemporary music. This has to be done with great care because somewhere around the turn of the twentieth century, audiences and composers moved farther and farther apart. By the middle of the last century the composers were writing music only for other composers more often than not, with a kind of disdain for the audience. 'If I can't shock them, then I'm not going to bother to entertain them'—that kind of attitude. Or 'I won't take my level of thought down to their level of appreciation.' The future of all the performing arts depends ultimately more on what we contribute to the whole literature, more on that than how many times we perform and how many houses we fill with the Tchaikovsky Fourth Symphony. The obligation has to be tempered because you don't want to break the bank. You want to sell tickets, too.

"There is a new wave of composers all over the world. It's very noticeable in the United States. They are really reaching out to the audience. They are not just repeating the formulas from the famous nineteenth-century works. There were, as described in certain circles, lamentable compositional efforts throughout the twentieth century that became more minimal and more unlistenable, unreadable, unapproachable by audiences. This new wave of composers is writing music that is much more approachable, more melodic. It's a different compositional venture."

As for the programming in the years that Kenneth has been the maestro, the Nashville Symphony has performed works from Adams to Zwilich. The classical repertoire has included Beethoven and Brahms, Schubert and Strauss, and Verdi and Vivaldi. There have been contemporary works by Bernstein and Gershwin, and works by hometowners Mark O'Connor, Edgar Meyer, and Kenneth himself ("Jubilee, a Tennessee Quilting Party" for orchestra, "An Invitation to Dance" for orchestra, "Two Lullabys" for mezzosoprano and string quartet, "Grand March of the Titans," fanfare for the new Nashville Library, and fanfare for the opening of the Frist Center).

Guest artists over the past twenty years have included the world's best: violinists Itzhak Perlman, Isaac Stern, and Joshua Bell; pianists Emanuel Ax, Andre Watts, Peter Serkin, and Alicia deLarrocha; vocalists Kathleen Battle, Charlotte Church, Jessye Norman, and Robert Merrill; cellist Mstislav Rostropovich; flutist Jean-Pierre Rampal; guitarist Christopher Parkening; and the groups Canadian Brass and Eroica Trio. This is only a selected list.

The Symphony began an indoor Beethoven concert festival series at War Memorial Auditorium in the summer of 2002. Seats were taken out of the flat main floor, and tables and chairs were set up so that people could enjoy their picnic baskets before the concerts and have the luxury of being in an air-conditioned, no-bugs, no-rain environment. The series made more money that first year, twice as much in three concerts, than it ever made when it was outdoors. The heat and the bugs and the unpredictability—all were factors that affected people's willingness to come. If the

Symphony was rained out, it lost all of the revenue, and people were reluctant to buy tickets because they did not want to have to tear them up or come on a Tuesday rain date. That series has made a difference in lengthening the season and enhancing the Orchestra's earning power. In 2003 concerts were held on Sunday afternoons as well as Saturday evenings. That event gives management an idea of how much hot weather—and unpredictable weather—people are willing to tolerate for their musical pleasure.

Maestro Schermerhorn's twentieth anniversary was technically a few months later, but the Symphony elected to celebrate a bit early because the March 28-29, 2003, program was all Sibelius (*Valse Triste*, Op. 44, No. 1; Violin Concerto in D Minor, Op. 47; Symphony No. 2 in D Major, Op. 43) with guest artist Aaron Rosand, a longtime friend and colleague of Kenneth. One of the Maestro's specialties is Sibelius, and he was awarded the Sibelius Medal in 1979 from the Finnish government. Phil Bredesen, governor of Tennessee, referred to Kenneth as "a true cultural ambassador for the residents of our state" with an "ongoing commitment to the advancement of the arts and quality of life in Tennessee," and Bill Purcell, mayor of Nashville, noted, "Through the depth and creativity of your programming, which has often crossed over traditional barriers, you have helped spread the word that Nashville is a place where every kind of work is nurtured." Others sent their congratulations, including Senators Bill Frist and Lamar Alexander. Perhaps the tribute in the program summed it up best: "Today we honor Maestro Schermerhorn for his artistry, and for the countless performances he has rehearsed and conducted that have absolutely thrilled us. For his sense of musical adventure, which has opened our ears to a world of new repertoire. We will treasure the place he has carved for The Orchestra, through recording, and through nurturing its players both young and old, until it can now stand proud on the world stage."

In his position on the Symphony's staff Michael Buckland talks to his counterparts in other orchestras and other people in the music industry, and he said, "What I hear now is that 'there's a lot going on in Nashville.' For instance, I hear, 'You guys are doing great stuff.' I'm not even sure if people know what it is specifically, but there's a buzz about what's going on. And in truth, immodestly, since I arrived [in 2001] we have gotten vastly improved renewal figures, which is partly marketing and partly good programming. Even here within Nashville there is some positive movement."

Kenneth spoke of the Symphony's future: "The story remains the same: How best to reach the young people? How to make the perfect program? How to build the subscription series? How to serve the living composers? How best to treat personnel? The performing arts are finally not that dissimilar to performing sports. If one year you have a great team and the next year somebody is dropping the ball or somebody is limping, you have to do something about it. It's where the buck stops. That is really cruel and very hard—the constant appraisal of personnel is a necessary part of all of the performing arts."

One of the biggest difficulties that the Symphony has to deal with is the fact that the recording studios pay a much higher hourly rate than the Symphony does. The music is much less challenging and, for serious musicians, less satisfying, but they can make so much more money doing that. If they have children in school, they are tempted to leave the Orchestra. There was a time when they could simply supplement their wages doing studio work, but now the Symphony is a full-time job. The ones who are really devoted to classical music really do not want to go and play whole notes or play background for singers and advertisements, although some of them may do that as they can work it around the Symphony's schedule.

The Nashville Symphony gives more than two hundred performances in its classical and pops series, and it also plays for the Nashville Opera, for the Nashville Ballet, and occasionally for the Tennessee Repertory Theatre, as it did for *West Side Story*, which also resulted in a sales-record-breaking CD. To those performances can be added special events at TPAC, the Ryman Auditorium, and the Grand Ole Opry House. The Fourth of July is always special in Nashville, and the summer of 2003 was a milestone for the Nashville Symphony as it was broadcast nationally on the Arts and Entertainment Network as part of the city's celebration. As Alan pointed out in his opening statement about the Symphony, the intention is for it to be a visible, essential part of the community, and Schermerhorn Symphony Center will allow the Symphony to continue its artistic growth while educating—every child, every grade, every year—entertaining, and uplifting its audiences.

A World-Class Relationship

[We have a] world-class team here.

—JIM STURGEON

"ARE YOU CRAZY? A classical label in Tennessee?" people kept asking Klaus Heymann when he moved Naxos of America to Cool Springs, just down the road from Nashville, in 1998. He replied that it would be a good move, and so it has proven to be for the community, for the company, and for the Nashville Symphony. For years classical CDs have had minimal sales compared to sales of pop, rock, or country CDs (in 2001, 15.8 million classical CDs were sold out of 762.8 million total CDs), but Naxos has developed a winning strategy. The company offers "quality at an affordable price," according to Jim Sturgeon, president of Naxos of America, and it is now the number one independent label in the United States for classical music. Another part of the company's success is that it does not offer duplicates of its repertoire, and at this writing it has 2,400 recordings in its catalog. In April 2002 the worldwide parent company (HNH International) celebrated its fifteenth anniversary (HNH International, H for Heymann, N for his wife, Takako Nishizaki, who is a violinist, and H for Henryk, their son, who graduated recently from Belmont University).

The American headquarters had been in New Jersey, but things were not working out well there. When Jim, who had been with Warner in Nashville before taking the Naxos job, realized that they needed to rebuild the company, he suggested the move to Tennessee, and Klaus agreed. The company has found that there are "educated people in the area who are passionate about classical music," said Jim, and he has been able to build a "world-class team here."

A welcoming event for the label was held in June 1998 at the Parthenon, and leaders from businesses, the music industry, and government attended. The setting was an inspired one for an idea that developed between Jim and then governor Don Sundquist. In 1999 the state and Naxos cooperated in giving to every Tennessee newborn a CD called *Listen, Learn and Grow*, which featured selections from composers such as Mozart, Bach, Handel, and Vivaldi. Unlike European youngsters who grow up with classical music as part of their culture, American youngsters often have little exposure to it. The CD gives them a head start in their musical education, and the music also stimulates their young brains (the Mozart Effect). It has been so successful, so many people want to buy a copy, that the company has created several volumes in the series to satisfy demand.

Klaus had met Maestro Kenneth Schermerhorn when he was music director for the Hong Kong Philharmonic, and the orchestra made several recordings for Marco Polo (another label of HNH International). Kenneth and Klaus renewed their friendship and their working relationship, and the Nashville Symphony was the first American orchestra to perform for the Naxos American Classic series, recording Howard Hanson's Symphony No. 1 in 1999. "This exceptional new recording accomplishes many things at once: it brings a fine American orchestra to disc for the first time on a major label; it offers CD premieres of some excellent unknown music; and most important of all, it imbues Howard Hanson's work with a stature and significance that previous performances, including the composer's own, barely suggest," noted reviewer David Hurwitz.

There will be more than two hundred recordings in the American Classics series, for which an advisory board of musicologists determines which American composers are most significant and need to be recorded. In addition to Hanson's Symphony No. 1, the Nashville Symphony has recorded Charles Ives's Symphony No. 2/Robert Browning Overture (a world premiere recording of the Charles Ives Society critical editions by Jonathan Elkus) and George Whitefield Chadwick's Symphonic Poems. The sales of the Symphony's CDs have been impressive: Ives, 22,745; Hanson, 18,521; and Chadwick, 11,541 (as of this writing). Kenneth and pianist Alan Feinberg received a Grammy nomination for the Amy Beach CD; the category was best instrumental soloist performance with orchestra. Two CDs released in March 2004 were Beethoven's Missa Solemnis and Elliott Carter's Piano Concerto (Mark Wait, pianist) and Symphony No. 1.

Critic David Hurwitz has called the partnership between Naxos and the Nashville Symphony "the American music happening of the new millennium." Through the CDs, the Symphony has received exposure around the world. Alan Valentine, executive director of the Symphony, received an e-mail from a woman in Sao Paulo, Brazil, requesting information about how to start a privately funded philharmonic society. She said, "I'm

The Nashville Symphony has a world-class relationship with Naxos of America, the recording company founded by Klaus Heymann, pictured here with his wife, Takako Nishizaki.

contacting several world-renowned orchestras, and the Nashville Symphony is one of them. Can you help?" Of course he agreed. She had learned about the Nashville Symphony from the CDs.

A joint effort by the Symphony and the Rep was released in October 2002; *West Side Story* featured the Symphony with singers coming from the Tennessee Repertory Theatre. A historical music story must be told about this recording. As a young conducting student, Kenneth studied with Leonard Bernstein, and this CD uses Bernstein's original score instead of ones adapted later for use in the play and the film. A youthful Kenneth was

Passion for Educating Students

The Nashville Symphony takes great pride in providing educational opportunities for students, and there are various components of the educational program in addition to the H.O.T. program at TPAC.

Curb Records Young Musicians Concerto Competition. Curb Records sponsors this instrumental competition that is open to ninth- through twelfth-grade students in five categories (woodwind, brass, string, piano, and percussion). The winner in March 2003 was a junior at Martin Luther King Magnet School, Paula Cheng, who played Ravel's Piano Concerto in G Major. She competed against thirty-one other students, and the first runner-up was a cellist, Hamilton Berry, a senior at Montgomery Bell Academy. Cash prizes, tickets to the Symphony, and gift certificates went to the winners, and Cheng also played with the Symphony at the annual Donor Appreciation Concert in June 2003.

The Ann & Monroe Carell Family Trust Pied Piper Series. Held on Saturday mornings three times each year, the programs are geared for three- to eight-year-olds and their families.

Ensembles in the Schools. Musicians from the Symphony visit elementary schools throughout Middle Tennessee and present brass, woodwind, and string ensemble programs. It is a good way for youngsters to learn about the instruments up close.

Dress Rehearsals. Third- through twelfth-grade students in limited numbers (150 each time) may attend the Symphony's dress rehearsals featuring classical guest artists. They are held in the mornings at Jackson Hall, and most guest artists are willing to answer students' questions after the rehearsal.

AmSouth Classroom Classics. Because of AmSouth Bank's underwriting, free tickets to selected classical concerts are available for middle school music students and high school students, their families, and teachers.

Young People's Concerts at the Ryman (underwritten in part by the Memorial Foundation). Students from the third through the eighth grades may attend free daytime Symphony performances at historic Ryman Auditorium.

"I, Too, Have a Dream"—Martin Luther King Jr. Essay Contest. At the annual "Let Freedom Sing!" celebration concert honoring Dr. King in January, the winning student (grades five through twelve) reads an essay explaining how he or she would participate in Dr. Martin Luther King's efforts, were he alive today. The grand prize winner in 2003, the tenth year of the contest, was Brianca Eileen Williams, a sixth grader at Northeast Middle School in Clarksville, Tennessee. Her essay was selected from more than five hundred, and she received a cash prize and a gift certificate. The contest is open to students in private and public schools in Middle Tennessee.

Liberty! The American Revolution. The Nashville Symphony is featured on the soundtrack for this PBS miniseries, which teaches American history in a powerful way. Videos, a teaching manual, and visual aid materials are part of the package available from the Symphony's Education Department.

Nashville's students participated in the "Let Freedom Sing!" celebration concert honoring Dr. Martin Luther King Jr. at TPAC, January 2001.

considered as the conductor for the premiere of *West Side Story* in 1957; he was not given the opportunity then, but he has gloriously taken on the job for this CD. Reviewer Victor Carr Jr. stated, "The Nashville Symphony plays with an ideal blend of symphonic elegance and jazzy swagger that shows why this work is such a wonderful classic . . . this production faithfully recreates the magical and enthralling world that is *West Side Story*, and anyone coming to this piece afresh is in for a rare and special experience." The sales of the CD were 57,061 as of February 2004. A total sales figure of 5,000 copies of a classical CD is considered good, so Naxos and the Nashville Symphony are very happy with the relationship.

Naxos has relied on other groups in Nashville, too; the Nashville Chamber Orchestra, with Paul Gambill conducting, recorded Aaron Copland's "Appalachian Spring," Clarinet Concerto, and "Quiet City." As Jim remarked, having Naxos in the neighborhood is "a win-win situation for all."

Mockingbird Theatre

We have to make the experience better and richer. Otherwise there is no reason for people to come.

—DAVID ALFORD

THE STORY of Mockingbird Theatre conveys some of the drama that professional theater groups have experienced on and off the stage over the last few years in Nashville. The artistic director, David Alford, grew up in Adams, Tennessee, on a farm that has been in his family since 1884, and it is where he now lives. The town's current population is up to 550; it was even smaller in David's youth! His father is a retired Methodist minister, and the first time that David performed before a group of people he was singing in the church. As a youngster, he wrote a play based on the poem "The Courtship of Miles Standish." In high school, he started acting. It was a small public school and everyone was involved in the theater, but there was no official theater club or group. David said, "We had football players and people in the chorus and the geeks and the freaks and everybody all putting on the play—there was really no division. I benefited from that. I always felt that the performing arts are for everybody. It didn't matter what segment of society or school or economic strata you were from—it was for everybody. That's the benefit of growing up in a small town. I got an education later in how it all *really* works. At the time it was just fun."

He was a music major until his fourth year in college at Austin Peay State University, although he acted in a couple of productions. He came very close to dropping out of school and playing with a country band, but after he was granted a theater scholarship, he changed to a drama major. At Austin Peay he met Arthur Kopit, who was visiting in the Center of Excellence in the Arts. Kopit encouraged him to pursue a career in acting.

David's life took a course he had never expected it to take. He went to Juilliard to audition and competed against fifteen hundred people; only twenty were accepted, and he was one of them. He dreamed of one day starting a theater company back in Tennessee, but he knew he needed to punch the proverbial tickets before he could do that. After he finished his schooling at Juilliard, he picked an agent who helped him get work—mostly out of New York City—and he lived in Swarthmore, Pennsylvania. It was the life of a vagabond, and David stated, "There is no sense that you are going to have a job next week or next month. You are living month to month, and you're always on the verge of filing for unemployment. You're hoping that you don't have to get a 'day job' or a 'real job,' as we call it in the business."

He was able to support himself with his acting jobs, so when he announced he was leaving the Northeast to start a theater company in Nashville, his classmates and friends in New York were stunned by his decision. He had gotten married in 1992, and David started thinking more seriously about his long-term future: "Here is the way the system works: you go through casting agents before you get to read for the director. If they don't know you, you read for the casting agent's assistant first—a twenty-two-year-old college graduate, basically a receptionist, who is giving you notes about a play you may have studied for three years at school. That didn't sit well with me then or now. I don't know how my friends continue to do it. It is an absolutely brutal business.

"A successful actor, and I put myself in that category, even though I wasn't getting rich—I was making a living, and that is a successful actor in New York—still is told 'no' 95 percent of the time. That is a lot of rejection. . . . I felt that I could handle that because I believed what I was called to do. This is where the bulk of my talents lie, and this is where I could best use them. But I was not able to do work I wanted to do. I was relying on other people to tell me whether or not I could do it, even if I did respect them. The absurdity of that began to gradually dawn on me, and I realized that what I was going to have to do if I were going to continue down the path of my discipline, if I were going to maintain any happiness and have any control over my life, I'd have to leave New York. . . .

"I wanted to have kids and . . . I didn't want to have them in New York or LA. So I decided to move home for all those personal reasons and also because I was looking at Nashville at that time. What I saw in 1992–93 was a town with one Equity company—the Rep—and I was a member of Actors' Equity. The Rep was, as far as I could tell, focusing strongly on developing new musicals. . . . And I saw great children's theater. I saw dinner theater. I saw a Shakespeare Festival. Darkhorse [Theater] at that time was doing cutting-edge work. What no one was doing at that time was presenting standard regional theater work—you do one classic every year, you develop a new play every year, you have a festival of some kind every year, and you do something contemporary that you really want to do, preferably with a regional focus or twist, and you try to promote local artists. That became my rallying cry."

With friends Tucker McCrady and Paul Valley, David founded Mockingbird Theatre, named for the state's bird. He renewed a working relationship with René Copeland, wife of Scot, who is the artistic director for the Nashville Children's Theatre. René became the co-artistic director of Mockingbird. Funds received through a Fox Fellowship from the Lincoln Center and the book *How to Form a Not-for-Profit Corporation* were other components in getting the company up and running. The first show, in May 1994, was a production of *Becket* at Scarritt-Bennett Center.

The second production was *The Glass Menagerie* that fall, and David recalled, "We had one performance where only four people showed up, and they were my friends. They tried to leave because they didn't want to make us do the show. I pleaded with them: 'Don't go. We're going to do the show because we need the rehearsal.' They gave us a standing ovation." Since then, many productions have sold out, and the company routinely receives outstanding critical reviews.

Raising and earning enough funds have been constant challenges, but the company started paying actors with its second show. One time David painted a house for $3,000 and put the money into a production. He admitted, "When I think about the outrageous nature of what I had attempted to do, I'm still baffled by my own moxie—with really no community ties at all, no community support. Just the fact that I was from this area. . . . We were going to focus on doing the best work we could possibly do, and if that was enough, then great. If it wasn't enough, we didn't want to do it anyway."

A breakthrough came in 1997 with a production of *Hamlet* for the H.O.T. program at TPAC. It was so well received that the company produced the same show the next year. In 1997 the company was able to seek state and local grant money, and since that time, the budget has grown, except for a brief downturn related to the decision to become an Actors' Equity company.

David has strong feelings about his craft and professionalism: "The idea that you're not successful unless you're famous is irritating to me. It puts the onus on the actor, and there is nothing any actor can do about becoming famous. You can't become famous unless you shoot people or rob banks. Other people make you famous. They decide whether you're right for their movie or play. You can suck up to those people and live a life of that. But at what cost! Or you can just do the work. I consider myself to be successful in that I make a salary. I have worked hard and made a lot of sacrifices, but I'm in a place now where I can make a living doing what I love to do. I would like to make it easier for other people. . . . Equity for us was the idea that everybody should be able to have health insurance. If you're a professional actor, you need health insurance. That is the primary reason. Equity offers health insurance if you work ten weeks out of the year. It is not great, but it's something. You should not have to be bankrupted if you have to go to the hospital." Mockingbird was the second Equity company in Nashville.

As of this writing, Mockingbird Theatre was doing three projects a year and spending more on each project to achieve the highest quality production. One recent special project was a play about the Bell Witch in Adams, *Spirit: The Authentic Story of the Bell Witch of Tennessee,* and the little town responded with enthusiasm to help put it

together and to attend. It was also produced in Nashville. David wrote and directed the play, the first original theater work for Mockingbird Theatre, and he was able to enlist Carney Bell to play John Bell, an ancestor who is a major character in the play. As part of its community outreach, the theater company presented a check for $14,000 to the Adams Museum.

The climate for theater companies in Nashville is changing, and the sources of funds are more grassroots related than the traditional sources in the city. David said, "The money is coming from people who know somebody who knows somebody: 'You need to meet my uncle. He has a car dealership. You need to meet so and so; he is willing to help. He'll give you five hundred dollars. He loves theater; he has been to New York.' It has become about networking and people knowing where the 'new money' is. It is certainly not the old money. It is people who want to see it happening in Nashville who are interested in it." According to David, the proliferation of theater companies is making these changes possible.

The real bottom line for David is this: "We [the theater companies] all want to see more actors live in Nashville. We want to see actors make a living in Nashville. That is what we're after. And we want to see our audiences grow. We want to see that they can discern the difference between professional theater and community theater. . . .

"We are very sensitive about our money, our sense of stewardship of public money. But if you define your company by the amount of money that comes in and goes out, then you are going to do *Annie* repeatedly or *A Christmas Carol* over and over again because you're worried about the bottom line. The accountant gains control of the artistic not-for-profit.

"[In other cities] the cultural elite, for lack of a better term, the people who can most afford and are most interested in culture, that community has made a proactive decision that 'we want this to happen here and we think it is good for our city.' They all have that in common and they work hard. They all get the idea and they let artists do what artists are supposed to do. They trust the artists and they let them go. . . . The support of the artists has yet to happen in Nashville. . . .

"We make more out of less than any businessman ever dreamed. When we get businesspeople on our board, they look at what we accomplish with the funding we have, and they just shake their heads. They say, 'We don't know how you do this.' Well, we do it because we have to."

David's cultural concerns go beyond Nashville and the South: "We have a huge artistic and cultural drain out of the middle part of the country; artists are going to the coasts. Our culture is becoming homogenized and Wal-Martized and sanitized. I'm all for people respecting and tolerating each other. But what makes the world great is that there is difference, there are different regions.

"By all accounts theater should be dead by now. It can't compete with television; it can't compete with movies; it can't compete with video games; it can't compete with the Internet; it can't compete with sports. On a strictly entertainment level we can't compete; theater doesn't have the same uncertainty and excitement. Why is it alive? It has to be—and this applies to the performing arts in general—because there is something about an audience being in a space with artists and the synergy and the dynamic that that creates. It has to be that. There is no other real reason. It has to be about that communion. I hope that the theater artists in this country—all of the performing artists—can recognize that that is the thing. The marketplace has drawn us away from spirituality, which is how all of these disciplines got started in the first place. . . . The only reason that people should come to the performing arts is to be fed spiritually. If we're not doing that for them, they are going to go someplace else.

"The church is theater. Modern worship services are more like Greek theater than theater is like Greek theater. You go in, you sit down, there are parts where the entire audience responds, you have a chorus of people saying things, and you have a leader who comes out and gives the central message. Everyone has a spiritual experience and then goes home. There is plenty of music, and there is even dance in some churches. That is where they are going to get it, and the church has responded by doing it. All that said, I think the performing arts survive because people need that."

Metropolitan Nashville Arts Commission

One of the things that we learned that really surprised me was that the organizations in Nashville— 60 to 65 percent of the organizations— were less than fifteen years old. I know that the arts have been in existence in Tennessee, but the current groups— there has not been continuity.

—TOM TURK

THE METROPOLITAN NASHVILLE Arts Commission (MNAC) awarded $2.4 million in grants to local arts organizations in 2003, and the individual grants ranged in size from $1,000 to $500,000. For a commission that had its beginnings in 1978 with no grant-making ability and virtually no funds, the growth is significant. In fiscal year 1988–89, the first year that there was money available for grants, the MNAC had a total of $500,000. The numbers dropped to a low of $251,532 in fiscal year 1991–92, but since then they have marched steadily upward with support from the mayor and the Metro Council. More significant than the numbers is the impetus to "create a vibrant, vigorous, healthy community where all the arts flourish and grow," as the MNAC is charged to do.

In addition to making grants, the MNAC presents workshops, holds forums, and conducts research—all dealing with arts issues—and it produces publications such as *Nashville Arts Alert!*, the *Metro Nashville Arts Directory*, *The Arts in Nashville* marketing studies, and the *Arts and the Economy* study. (See appendix B for the performing arts groups listed in the *Arts Directory*.) The commission also serves as Nashville's liaison with state and national arts groups.

Tom Turk became the executive director of the MNAC in March 1993. He arrived from Texarkana, Texas, with experience as a fine arts TV producer, the director of a performing arts center, and the managing director of the Perot Theatre, but he had no firsthand knowledge of how Nashvillians viewed the arts. One of the first things with which he became involved was a study of the visual and performing arts called *The Arts in Nashville*, released in October 1994, conducted by Perdue Research Group, and funded by the HCA Foundation. Several conclusions emerged:

1. *Nashville has a high level of interest and participation in the arts.* (Ninety-two percent of the population participated at a level 22 percent higher than national levels of participation.)

2. *There is a high level of crossover participation among different arts groups.*

3. *The clearest way to differentiate among arts participants is by their level of participation* (dedicated patrons, frequent attenders, regular attenders, and infrequent attenders).

4. *Women play the key role in arts participation in Nashville.* (They make up two-thirds to three-fourths of participants, supporters, and contributors of all arts organizations. A "typical" arts supporter and participant is a married white female, aged thirty-five to fifty-four, with a college degree or higher education and a household income over $75,000; she has lived in Nashville more than twenty years.)

5. *Minorities participate in the arts to the same degree as the total population, but their level of participation is not identified by most arts organizations.* (They may not be listed as patrons because they are not using credit cards, or they participate in arts organizations out of the mainstream.)

6. *Children play a major role in arts participation.*

7. *Subscribers and contributors are a small part of the population but contribute at a high average level.*

8. *Internal benefits of arts participation and psychological barriers to participation play major roles.* ("People who participate in the arts are different from me" was a major psychological barrier. Lack of time was a recurring, serious problem for supporters or participants; farther down the list of problems were cost, travel time, and convenience.)

9. *Current facilities are adequate, but there is a clear desire for a new art museum.* (This point has changed considerably: Nashville now has the Frist Center for the Visual Arts, although current facilities are inadequate for the Symphony and for smaller, newer theater groups.)

10. *Arts organizations take a passive approach to communicating with their market.* (Arts organizations have addressed this point and have been taking a more aggressive approach, described elsewhere in discussions of various organizations.)

The study identified groups and their numbers: dedicated patrons (about 60,000), frequent attenders (about 80,000), regular attenders (about 130,000), and infrequent attenders (about 400,000). According to Tom, "the real gold mine" is the regular attenders "who go to a modest amount of events and have the opportunity of increasing their attendance." He believes that group deserves more attention from arts organizations.

A similar study done in 1998 found that participation had increased and broadened to include more kinds of arts activities; Nashvillians were participating in the arts at a level 33 percent higher than national averages; women were increasingly patrons of the arts. Lack of time remained a factor as a barrier to participation, parking was emerging as a negative factor, and newcomers to the city were unlikely to become patrons.

Another of Tom's tasks was to make sure that the grant-awarding process was fair. Keel Hunt observed that "the leaders of the Arts Commission began to do important work about how to make their program more formal and more objective. That contributed to an increase in the confidence level: if the city leaders were going to put more money in the fund, there should be no question but that those funds would be responsibly managed. It shouldn't be a buddy system or a crony system. It needed to be an objective system. That strategy proved very effective with the Metro Council members."

Tom and others at the MNAC—the commissioners and the citizens on the grants panel—worked diligently on the grants program, and that work paid off. Tom recalled, "One councilman told me, 'Tom, you have done three things. You have done what you said you were going to do, you have kept us informed, and you have created a high level of trust in the department and what you do with the grants.'"

The growing grants program had another impact on arts organizations besides providing funds. Jane Ann McCullough, development coordinator for the MNAC, stated recently, "I think it's very important to note that the Metro Arts Commission was not an arts council—an umbrella agency for all of these existing arts organizations. There had never been one of those here in Nashville. The Symphony was growing up here; Cheekwood growing up there. Everybody

was going in their own direction. I think the grants program—unfortunately it came along at the time of the demise of the Symphony [the Symphony shut down in 1988 for several months]—was the first time these organizations had to come together for a common cause. . . . They came together, even though the Symphony was going to get the bulk of the money and might have gotten all of the money if the groups had not come together in a good way. It was successful for all of them. Some of them wanted to whine and nag that 'we're not getting as much money as the Symphony,' but everyone kept saying, 'As long as the Symphony grows, the pot of funds will grow, too, and everyone will benefit.' Now you look at some of the same groups that are still around—they've grown into medium-sized groups. And some of those are growing into the large category. The funding has grown all of the arts groups. But it was the first time that all of the arts groups came together. They had a common focus. And to this day, this is the major reason that they are working together."

An arts organization requesting a grant must meet certain criteria: excellence; need in the community; inclusive planning; community outreach and impact; educational merit; innovation; and administration, development, and financial management. Specifically an organization must "a. Be a not-for-profit organization chartered in the State of Tennessee with 501(c)(3) IRS tax-exempt status; b. Serve Nashville/Davidson County citizens and be headquartered in and have a substantial portion of its programming within Nashville/Davidson County; c. Produce, present and/or directly support programs, projects and/or works in the arts that enrich the artistic experience of Nashville citizens in a significant way; d. Have, or be in the process of creating, a diverse board of directors; e. Show a demonstrated and continuing ability to build a base of financial support through earned income plus public and private support as needed." The Metro Council approves the total amount of grant funds available as part of the annual Metro budget process. The process, from submitting an application to being approved and receiving a check, requires seven months, and each proposal has to be reviewed by the grants panel.

The citizens who sit on the grants panel assist the community while they gain something personally from the experience that they can take to other arts groups and thus strengthen them. Jane Ann said, "We have about forty members a year, and it is exciting for us to see that these panelists move on from being panelists. They get so involved and become so knowledgeable—they may not be the leading funders for a board, but they certainly are going into the boards [of arts organizations]. They are interested. The grant panels are made up of people from diverse backgrounds—they have a strong commitment to the arts."

There are several categories of grants: basic operating support I and II, program, initiative, and creation. Tom was particularly pleased with the results of the creation grants for new works of art, and he referred to Paul Gambill's work with the Nashville Chamber Orchestra in that category: "He came to us when we created a creation grant category and got the idea of trying to have a new work of music on each one of his programs. He has been very successful in doing that. The grant was $2,000 for that. We have increased the category—because there were other organizations in that peer group—to $5,000, and this year [2002] to $10,000 [the amount that one group receives, not the total fund for that category]. When the history of this commission is written, the one thing that is going to be more important than all of the other dollars is the new works that have been commissioned."

Based on the MNAC research and his tenure, Tom offered these comments about the local arts organizations: "The organizations are doing a pretty good job on their level of earned income. It has been close to 50 percent. Seven years ago it was over 50 percent; it has dropped a little bit as public funding has grown. There is the view in the community that the arts always have their hand out, but that really isn't true. The arts have done a good job of having high enough earned income. The arts traditionally have to sit on that three-legged stool with public, private, and corporate funding. If any of those get shorted, it is going to wobble. The arts organizations have tried to do too much; they need to do less and do it better."

Both Jane Ann and Tom have witnessed changes in the staffing of the arts groups. Jane Ann said, "Historically the staffing changes within the groups that have been around for a long time, such as the Shakespeare Festival, the Circle Players, the same people just sort of shifted. But now we are seeing new people come into the staffs of these groups." Tom added, "I've never really studied it, but I have a feeling about this: probably about fifteen years ago, there began to be a leadership shift in the community. A lot of the home-grown leaders, directors, professionals in the organizations, as they left or retired or went on in some form or fashion, the organizations began to hire people from outside. They brought in a lot of different ideas and different backgrounds."

In 2001 Nashville ranked twenty-second in population among the fifty largest U.S. cities, and it ranked twenty-third in the amount of city government support of the arts. The *Arts and the Economy 2001* study, a result of research by Middle Tennessee State University, the Nashville Area Chamber of Commerce, and the MNAC, revealed that the arts contributed $65.25 million to the city's economy in 2001. That was slightly more than a 9 percent increase from the previous year. The fragile nature of the arts industry was made apparent, however, with a net loss of

$1.44 million; total revenues increased, but operating expenses rose even more. Individual, business, and government contributions were reduced 3.97 percent, 25 percent, and 47.36 percent, respectively. Yet gifts from guilds and auxiliaries increased 201.55 percent. (All of the reporting for this period did not include the impact of September 11 and subsequent events of 2001. The 2002 study indicated that, even though arts activity stalled a bit in the fall of 2001, there was modest growth in the economic impact of the arts.)

The 2001 study also reported that "arts venue capacity was reached six years ago. If arts organizations are to grow in the face of increased competition for entertainment dollars, they will need additional rehearsal, performance, and exhibition spaces. The recent opening of the Martha Rivers Ingram Hall at the Blair School of Music [at Vanderbilt University], current modifications being made to the Tennessee Performing Arts Center, and the proposed new symphony hall downtown [Schermerhorn Symphony Center] are first steps to address these needs."

The Metro Nashville Arts Commission received a special award—the Arts Leadership Award—from the Tennessee Arts Commission in March 2003. The MNAC was honored for its "outstanding work in bringing financial stability to local arts organizations, fostering quality, proliferation and diversity of the arts, assisting in the development of individual artists, increasing the value placed on the arts in both the public and private sectors of the local economy, and implementing ways of bringing the arts into the mainstream of life in Middle Tennessee." Tom Turk resigned as executive director in the spring of 2003, and we can hope that the new director will continue the good work that has characterized the agency since 1993.

Performing Arts in Metro's Public Schools

The arts are a vital part in making the whole person.

—CAROL CRITTENDEN

FIVE HUNDRED female students, ages four to seventeen, dressed in white and "festooned with flowers in profusion" performed in the cantata *The Flower Queen, or Coronation of the Rose* on

June 21, 1855, at the Adelphi Theatre. The purpose—besides entertaining their parents and many other citizens—was to raise money for a piano for Hume School. The school, Nashville's first public one, had been open only since February, yet in that brief period the impetus to teach music to the students and their willingness to learn evolved into a full-fledged performance.

Leaders of the enterprise were J. F. Pearl, the principal, and Mr. Dorman (his first name was not given, but it was more than likely Roderic). Tickets were sold at bookstores and at the door for the eight o'clock performance about flowers meeting in a dell to choose their queen. While there they found a recluse and convinced him, by speaking of love and duty, to return to the greater society. Dorman played the recluse, and Miss Eastman played Rose; other students with major parts were Misses Cannon, Bang, Dyer, Wise, Dashiell, Sayers, Gregory, and Erwin. There were solos and choruses, which gave "evidence of thorough training," according to the reviewer. Not to be left out, an unspecified number of male students in the gallery "gave additional zest to the entertainment" during an interlude. So many people had to be turned away at the door that a second performance was scheduled for June 26. From the charge of 50 cents per ticket, $410 (about $7,900 today) was raised from the first evening, enough to purchase the piano.

The public schools were closed during the Civil War, and it was not until 1873, eight years after the end of the war, that the first music administrator, John E. Bailey, was hired (he was called the vocal music principal). Singing was the extent of music education for many years because of economic conditions; later instrumental music was added—orchestras and then bands. Today the public school system has formal programs with well-trained, certified professionals to teach not only music, but also dance and drama. More than 69,000 students are enrolled in Metro's 129 public schools, K-12, and two of those schools have a performing arts emphasis. For the 2002–3 academic year 579 students attended Nashville School of the Arts, a high school, and 436 attended Wharton School for the Arts, a middle school. (There are approximately 20,500 students in Davidson County private schools; the focus here is on public schools because of the greater number of students, but many private schools, such as Montgomery Bell Academy, University School of Nashville, Ensworth, and Harpeth Hall, have increasingly offered classes in the performing arts.)

Carol Crittenden, coordinator of visual and performing arts, brought to the job experience as a choral music teacher and as an instrumental music teacher in Metro schools. More than two hundred music teachers direct students in the following divisions: elementary, fifth through eighth grade general choir and high school choir, middle school band and high school band, middle school and high school strings, guitar, piano, and music theory (an optional high school course). Then there are the dance and drama teachers. Carol strongly believed that teaching—not performing—should be the primary line of work for teachers, but she said, "I want all of my teachers to perform in some way. They need to keep the personal part alive to be able to carry the passion to the classroom. They are passionate about music in general and what it does. Some of my teachers are doing CDs, participating in small groups. They are choir directors or in church choirs." The teachers play everything from folk to rock to jazz to classical music.

The greatest change Carol has seen in recent years occurred in 1997 with the addition of elementary music specialists. The core curriculum drove the impetus for elementary arts and music, and there has been an increase in participation in band and string programs, which is "directly due to children getting comfortable with it," she said.

"An arts-based education gets the child engaged. Building self-confidence and self-esteem helps the students achieve more, and the arts foster that. The arts open up the creative mind and emotions."

The core curriculum has also been at the heart of other changes. Dr. Pedro Garcia, the director of schools, and Dr. Sandra Johnson, chief instructional officer, are *for* the arts, but they have placed the spotlight on language arts, math, science, and reading. They are hiring reading teachers so that students will be reading at the kindergarten level. Test scores have been improving in the schools, yet more improvement is needed because literacy rates in the city have not reached 100 percent. Slightly more than 81 percent of Nashvillians over age twenty-five (more than 307,000 people) are high school graduates (or have a GED). The remaining percentage, which includes more than 69,000 adults, have insufficient literacy skills (reading, writing, and computing). (In 1870 Davidson County had a population of 62,896, and of those, 19,431 [or about 30 percent] over age ten could not read.)

Principals have a certain number of staff members allotted for their schools to fill out a master schedule, and there are now fewer staff members. Some middle school band and string programs have been affected by the tightening of staff; some have been eliminated. If one studies the history of the arts in Nashville's schools, this is nothing new. Virtually every time there is a tightening of the economic belt and renewed emphasis is placed on the core curriculum, arts programs are reduced or eliminated entirely. (A notable nineteenth-century exception occurred in February 1879 when the board of education needed to cut expenses, and it was suggested that vocal music be dropped. J. L. Weakley, who was a champion of music in schools, persuaded the board members to retain the program, and they did.)

Another challenge has been the recruitment of string teachers because there has been a nationwide shortage. The string programs have been harder to develop than band programs because teachers have not stayed in one school long enough to build the programs. Just about the time a program starts to flourish, the teacher is moved or has left for some reason. The existing program wanes and then has to be rebuilt. Once a program falls apart, Carol explained, it usually takes twenty to thirty years to repair, so continuity of teachers is a critical factor in a program's success. Despite these difficulties, Carol declared, "My goal is to have a full orchestra in every middle and high school before I retire."

Another goal is to have international choirs and help children who speak the eighty-four languages in Metro schools become comfortable as they share the music of both old and new countries. Children sing everything from Russian folk songs to the blues, and ESL (English as a second language) students can communicate in music classrooms. As they sing songs in Spanish or German—often learned from native speakers, whether students or parents of students—the experience helps them become a part of a group and integrated into the culture. Carol described the situation: "You could walk into Wright Middle School at the beginning of the school year and hear all kinds of languages. Go back at the end of the year and they are using English as their primary language."

Drama is strong in several Metro high schools, and there are dance classes at Antioch, Nashville School of the Arts, and Wharton. Dance generally receives less emphasis than the other performing arts in Tennessee schools, and one reason may be that there is no dance certification for teachers in the state's colleges or universities.

Students who attend the Nashville School of the Arts are serious about their classes. Carol reported, "The greatest statistic at the Nashville

School of the Arts [NSA] is that there were *no* fights in the past school year, and that is a high school. The students have better things to do with their time. And they don't want to wreck their hands. But that is an amazing statistic."

In addition to a guitar program at NSA, there are the Delta Blues Band and the Nashville Swing Thing. "The Nashville Swing Thing performed for the central office retirement lunch," said Carol. "There are five musicians and two vocalists, and they do music of the forties, fifties, and sixties. They are taught to be professional from day one, from the beginning to the end. They know that as a professional musician, if you are late or goof off, you will be fired. Those students had set up everything and were ready to go on time; then they took everything down and left while the rest of the events of the lunch were going on, but they did it quietly and professionally."

Carol noted, "Half of what we teach in music is life skills. Group effort, depending on each other for success, self-discipline. The goal is not to turn out professional musicians, although that is okay, too. We would like for them to be lifelong players of music, become a really good audience, and apply all of those skills in their jobs to make them productive citizens."

When she was still teaching in the classroom, she brought home the importance of music to her students by conducting an experiment: "I played Mendelssohn for my students before they were to play it. They all said they didn't like it. So I gave them this assignment: they were not to listen to *any* music—on the radio, on TV, on a CD, anywhere for the rest of the day—and they were to write a short essay on the experience. It was a tough assignment. The next day I could tell which students had done the assignment. Suddenly Mendelssohn didn't sound so bad to them. They felt starved for the music in just that short time, and I explained to them how fortunate they were to have music at the touch of a button. In Mendelssohn's time and other times in history people had to make a big effort to hear music."

Making music has become more and more difficult for some students, however, because they have no instruments or poorly maintained instruments. Carol said, "This may be Music City USA, but I have to deal with thirty- to fifty-year-old instruments." Chewing gum and duct tape have taken on new meaning in band rooms. The last big purchase of musical instruments occurred in 1972.

Carol praised one young man's stick-to-itiveness: "A child at West End, a tuba player, sat for a semester just air playing. We had no tubas to share. He finally got a baritone. He *may* get a tuba next year. But he loves what he does. He has character and spunk to stick it out. A lot of students would have said, 'Forget it.' It is hard to get parents to buy instruments for middle school students because they may not be serious about the instrument yet and the expense is great."

A good cornet costs $800 to $1,500, a flute, trombone, or saxophone costs $500 to $1,200, and instrument rental ranges from $5 to $35 a month. The system recently purchased fifty-two sousaphones, which cost quite a bit more than cornets, because the cost to repair the sousaphones in use was more than they were worth. Carol estimated that it will take $15 million to put the department on its feet.

At one point she was able to supply only two grade levels of music books and some CDs, and the schools had to furnish the players (PTOs are sources of much equipment). She credited the excellent teachers for doing so much with so little and then cited an example: "A teacher called in February and said, 'When am I going to get a boom box?' I said, 'What have you been doing for one?' 'I have been bringing one back and forth from home.' So I called the assistant principal and sent the bid papers, and the teacher got one within a week."

Organizations and businesses outside and inside the city have stepped up to support the school's music programs. VH1 Save the Music Foundation (separate from the cable music channel) is a nonprofit organization that began in 1997 and donates new musical instruments to public schools. The foundation gave the first two guitar labs in the country to Metro's schools. With the state-of-the-art equipment fourth to eighth graders can prepare to move on to the Nashville School of the Arts or other Metro guitar programs. In November 2002 Comcast and VH1 Save the Music Foundation donated more instruments to Metro, and Gibson Guitar has been generous to Wharton School for the Arts.

Individuals have also offered their assistance. Carol said, "I was so pleased after a newspaper article appeared about our programs and a man called. He said that he didn't have much money—he was on a fixed income—but he wanted to send something. His children went through Metro schools, and the music program meant a lot to them. He sent $25, but I would have been happy with the call."

The Nashville Symphony sends quintets and quartets into Metro classrooms. That is one advantage for Nashville's students, and after Schermerhorn Symphony Center is completed in 2006, even more students will have the opportunity to hear live music in a world-class facility.

Leon Miller, the head of the Musical Conservatory of Ward Seminary, presented a lecture on music in January 1908. In his opening comments he "deprecated the disparagement of art and art culture in our country," and he said, "We have been told that music is an accomplishment, which can only be properly studied by those having a gift for it. Music has usually been considered as merely an idle amusement, ministering to the gaiety of social evenings." His lecture was "a plea for the study of music, as a study, an incentive to the highest that human life can attain, an essential to the thorough beautifying of soul and body."

Almost one hundred years later, an editorial in the *Tennessean*, February 15, 2003, ran under the headline "Keep Music on Agenda." It began, "Ironically, music often has to sound off to be heard in school curriculum issues." A move from seven to six periods a day affected the elective classes, and "music, for some reason, frequently seems to get shortchanged." Music is often thought of as recreation, not a legitimate field of study, and whenever the budget comes up, "music becomes a target."

We could substitute *performing arts* here for *music* in Miller's lecture and the *Tennessean* editorial, and the point would remain. Yes, the performing arts in Nashville's public schools occupy a greater part of the curriculum than they have ever held, and for that we can be grateful. More and more children are receiving this important element in their education. Yet the fragile nature of the programming is reaffirmed almost every year. If we have to keep sounding off to be heard and to reinforce the legitimacy of the field, then that is what we will have to do. The city's children deserve no less.

Vanderbilt University

*I do not think that you can be
a world-class liberal arts university
without having a strong commitment to the arts.*

—Chancellor Gordon Gee

VANDERBILT UNIVERSITY, founded in 1873, has a long tradition of academic and professional excellence, and its leaders have steadily moved it toward its position as one of the finest educational institutions in the United States. A private university, it is home to more than ten thousand undergraduate, graduate, and professional students in its ten schools, and they come from across the country and around the world. Vanderbilt is the largest private employer in Nashville with more than seventeen thousand employees, about ten thousand of whom are associated with the Medical Center. Thus, the fortunes of the university and the city are interrelated on economic and cultural levels.

Gordon Gee became the university's seventh chancellor in the year 2000, and he brought passion, wisdom, and energy to his job, which includes expanding the university's commitment to the arts. He grew up in Vernal, Utah, a very small town in the Rocky Mountains with no movie theaters and no television. "I started listening on a Saturday afternoon, when other kids were listening to Roy Rogers or Gene Autry, to a clear channel radio station called KSL out of Salt Lake City, 50,000 watts, and they had the *Texaco Opera of the Air*. That is how I started. That was a major introduction to the arts for me, and I had none of these other diversions," he said. "I played the violin; I played the oboe; I played the bass drum. I was very heavily engaged in theater and enjoyed it a lot. I've always enjoyed the performing arts. I took piano lessons for many years. I have been very interested in music."

Chancellor Gee's personal and professional experiences have brought him to this conclusion: "I do not think that you can be a world-class liberal arts university without having a strong commitment to the arts. Otherwise you become a technical school—strong in the sciences, the social sciences—but the reason we talk about the liberal arts is that it is a balanced approach to the intellectual life.

"Historically we [at Vanderbilt] have not done as well in terms of emphasizing the arts as we should have done. I hope that one of the hallmarks of my own time here will be to make a strong commitment to the arts, and I'm talking

Gordon Gee has been the energetic chancellor of Vanderbilt University since 2000. Here he was part of the dedication ceremonies of Ingram Hall at Blair School of Music; a featured group for the event was the Fisk Jubilee Singers.

not simply about the performing arts. In the last twenty years Blair has grown into one of the fine conservatories in the country, and the fact that we have an undergraduate conservatory as part of a liberal arts university is quite unusual so that gives us great power. We have a very small, a very dedicated, and a very fine theater department that needs to grow. [Neely Auditorium is the venue for that department.] We do not do as much in terms of dance as we should be doing. And then in terms of the studio arts, we have a fine, small faculty, but we need to grow the studio arts program and we're just in the process of planning a brand-new studio arts building."

Chancellor Gee observed, "I think I've come to Nashville and to the South in a time of renaissance." Yet much remains to be done: "The arts represent the soul of a city in so many ways, and sports represent the play of a city. Schools represent the democracy, the values, of a city. . . . The city has a number of educational institutions, and I think the truth of the matter is that we have done a fairly poor job of using the power of the whole—by that I mean the University of Tennessee, Tennessee State, Middle Tennessee State, Fisk, Lipscomb, Belmont—I could go on.

"We have all developed these silos around ourselves, the worst of those probably being Vanderbilt, isolated, even arrogant, the Magnolia Curtain we have put around ourselves, not even acknowledging that we are in Nashville, sort of wishing that we were somewhere else sometimes. One does not build an Athens of the South by not being connected. So the opportunity for us to create a very strong intellectual infrastructure here is present. We just need to connect those dots. And that is one of the roles that Vanderbilt should play—an institution that can be a gathering place for that kind of conversation."

Another role is that of fostering arts education for students in kindergarten through high school: "I think the university needs to become more engaged in helping sustain a critical mass of well-trained arts teachers in our community and in

The Martha Rivers Ingram Center for the Performing Arts at Vanderbilt's Blair School of Music has seating for 618 and is a recently added venue for recording and performing. It opened officially on January 15, 2002.

Mike Curb and Bill Ivey *(left to right)* participated in the announcement, spring 2003, of the new Curb Center for Art, Enterprise and Public Policy at Vanderbilt, which was made possible by $2.5 million from the Mike Curb Family Foundation. Bill, Harvie Branscomb Distinguished Visiting Scholar at Vanderbilt, is the director of the innovative program.

our public education system. We have a lot of things that have to do with the arts but that are not on the direct stylistic side of it.

"I chaired the search for the new school director, and one of the things that I learned through that process is that Nashville is large enough to have all of the problems of urban America but small enough to be able to still have solutions. It's in that size and solution context in which we're talking about focusing on Nashville as a living, learning environment.

"Nashville in the last five years, particularly in the last two or three years, is becoming a hot city. I hear people saying that Nashville is the new Atlanta in the best sense of the word—we don't have all of the problems that Atlanta has, urban sprawl and so forth, but we have all of the possibilities.

"One cannot have a great university in a crumbling city. One cannot have a great university where there are not good public schools, good housing, good health care, low crime. We have a huge stake in terms of the quality of life here, but obviously with the kind of people we're trying to attract—Nobel laureates and medalists, the best and the brightest in the

world—that is the reason that a community that has a strong cultural base is very important for us." Through programs offered by the Community Relations Department and in other ways, Vanderbilt strives to be a good citizen in the community.

Vanderbilt@TPAC is a partnership established in the spring of 2003 between Vanderbilt and the Tennessee Performing Arts Center to develop programs to advance the performing arts in the city. The first program was a lunchtime learning series called "InsideOut of the (Lunch) Box," held at the War Memorial Auditorium, and the events included a panel discussion of African influences on contemporary American choreography and composition, a presentation by David Grapes of Tennessee Rep and Terryl Hallquist of the Vanderbilt University Theatre of "Shakespeare: In and Out of Love" (including scenes from *The Taming of the Shrew* performed by the Rep's actors), and a conversation with Bill Ivey about arts funding in the United States.

Bill Ivey, former chairman of the National Endowment for the Arts (1998–2001) and current Harvie Branscomb Distinguished Visiting

Scholar at Vanderbilt, is the director of a new program at Vanderbilt, announced in the spring of 2003. Chancellor Gee noted, "We're creating this program in the arts, private enterprise, and public policy, which we think will be unique in America. The reason we can do that is that it comes from the confluence of music in all of its forms in a unique American city—the performing arts in general make this a place that is quintessentially American. The notion of focusing on policy and the arts is a natural for a national university like Vanderbilt."

The official name is the Curb Center for Art, Enterprise and Public Policy, which was made possible by $2.5 million from the Mike Curb Family Foundation. Mike Curb, chairman and owner of Curb Records, is passionate about music of all kinds and about Nashville, and he emphasized, "I believe Nashville is Music City USA." His family includes two daughters who are Vanderbilt graduates.

Bill said that "it is the first university-based program to fully engage the American cultural policy system." His definition of *American cultural policy* is "the decisions, practices, regulations, and laws that nurture or constrain creative work, and that facilitate or restrict the availability of art and artistry." The Curb Center will "explore the five primary sources of cultural policy in the United States: the decisions of individual actors in the arts industries; corporate practice; trade agreements and regulatory agencies; the passions and objectives of private arts patrons and NGOs [nongovernmental organizations]; and intellectual property law," and it will operate under the umbrella of the College of Arts and Science. In the exploration of this significant topic, the Curb Center will work with the Owen Graduate School of Management, the Law School, the Blair School of Music, Peabody College, and the Divinity School, all part of Vanderbilt University.

Belmont University

*A great university shapes the future;
it doesn't just gin out more people as it always has.*

—PRESIDENT BOB FISHER

BELMONT UNIVERSITY is a private institution affiliated with the Tennessee Baptist Convention, and its fourth president is Bob Fisher, who has held that position since the year 2000. (Here are names and dates in what can be a confusing progression: the first Belmont College [1890–1913], Ward-Belmont [1913–51, a merger of Belmont College and Ward Seminary], Belmont College [1951–91, after the Tennessee Baptist Convention assumed the indebtedness of Ward-Belmont], and Belmont University [1991–present].) On the campus is the mansion that was the summer home of Adelicia Acklen, designed by the architect Adolphus Heiman, who also designed the Adelphi Theatre that was so important in the city's cultural life in the nineteenth century. Music has been a hallmark of the institutions occupying this lovely site.

"Fifteen years ago Belmont began this focus in the music business, and it has really grown to be our signature program," said President Fisher. "We have 3,400 students at Belmont and we have 750 music business majors and we have 500 music majors, so 1,250 students are either in music or in music business. And all of these music business majors are not performers, but at least half of them are."

He continued, "That program originated in this way—the story is that one of our former presidents, Dr. [Herbert C.] Gabhart, was traveling with a famous country music star of the day, and as they left the hotel, this person said, 'I need to go back to my room. I forgot something.' Gabhart went with him to the room, and the guy went over to the curtain and pulled it back. There was an envelope taped to the back side of the curtain. Gabhart said, 'What is that?' 'That's my money.' The lesson was, these folks need to know how to manage their money. The guy said, 'I gave my money one time to other people to manage, and they lost it all. I'm not going to do that again.' That is where the idea originated for the music business program.

"Artists and others need to understand the industry and how it works. They need to understand the economy, personal finance, and corporate finance so that they can make deals that are good for them and good for the industry as well. That is what really distinguishes Belmont's music business program from, for example, MTSU or the Berklee College of Music in Boston, which are great programs. Ours has this business core that requires you to take economics and accounting and finance and marketing so that you understand the business."

Although a fairly new program, "it has already had successful graduates such as Trisha Yearwood, Lee Ann Womack, and Brad Paisley." President Fisher explained, "They are music business graduates; they took all the music courses, the composition and the theory, but there are hundreds of people with talent. Talent is not the only thing in this city. There aren't opportunities for all the talented people.

"As we think about the range of what we do, I just mentioned country music artists, but I was at the Boston Symphony Hall when Mike Curb was being inducted into the National Junior Achievement Hall of Fame. The ceremony was elaborate—trumpeters up in the balcony. When it was over, this young lady came up to me and said, 'Are you Dr. Fisher from Belmont?' I said,

The annual President's Concert showcases Belmont University's musicians and ensembles, such as the Belmont Orchestra (shown here), and is a fund-raiser for music students.

Bob Fisher is president of Belmont University.

'Yes, how did you know that?' She said, 'I've seen your picture in alumni magazines. I'm Melissa Jenkins, and I graduated from Belmont two years ago. I'm the assistant events coordinator here at the Boston Symphony Hall. This was my event tonight.' I said, 'Good grief, Melissa. Wow!'

"The range of what our students do is from running the sound boards to running events at Boston's Symphony Hall, but ultimately our goal is for her to be the executive director. That is what we educate them for. And to own the studio, not run the sound boards. We want them to have the opportunity to be the leaders in the industry. Many students who are in our music business program aren't performers. They just love music or musical theater or theater. Period. They want to learn how to manage in that environment. They want to learn how to facilitate that. That is just as important as the person who takes the stage."

The music business program is in the College of Business. Within the College of Visual and Performing Arts are programs in painting, sculpting, and other visual expressions of art. "Music is the biggest piece by far in the performing arts," said President Fisher. "There is a whole range of possibilities in the music program. I believe what Belmont does very, very best is the vocal performance. We're good at instrumental as well and getting better and better. But we're most widely known for our vocal, and we claim to be the best in this whole region of the country. The other piece of the performing arts is theater. We have musical theater, which is a natural for us. We have opera, which is a natural for us. And we also have drama. We're in the process of a fundraising campaign to build a new theater. We're excited about the prospect of getting that done in the next two years."

Being in Nashville with its active theater environment was a plus for some Belmont undergraduates in the spring of 2003. The students, who were musical theater majors, worked with the professional actors in Tennessee Rep's production of *Evita*, which was presented at TPAC. That kind of synergy is good for the students, the Rep, and the audiences, and it is another indication that actors may be trained and find work in Nashville.

A new resident to the city, President Fisher is enthusiastic about it: "I cannot imagine a better place than Nashville with what Vanderbilt does, especially with the Blair School, Fisk and the Jubilee Singers. Belmont purchased Ocean Way Studio. [Students gain practical experience to go along with their classroom work.] *Billboard* said that it's the number one studio in Nashville. Yo-Yo Ma has recorded there. Bob Seeger. I got to meet him there. The Nashville Symphony has recorded one of its CDs there. I offer all of those as examples. I really do believe that Nashville is the Athens of the South and probably of the West until you get to California.

"Vince [Gill] and Amy [Grant] and Sarah Cannon have participated in the community; Sarah was a Ward-Belmont grad, and Amy has come to us by marriage. Vince is one of our very best friends at Belmont. Of course Vince has been so good to the whole community, and Amy, too."

Mike Curb's influence, philanthropic and otherwise, is evident on the Belmont campus with the Curb Events Center, which can accommodate up to five thousand people at concerts and other events, and the Mike Curb School of Music Business. He has been in Nashville about ten years now, having moved from LA, and he said, "I want to do all I can for the city. We take half of the profits from Curb Records and put it in the Mike Curb Family Foundation." The Curb Foundation also purchased the historic RCA Studio B and leased it to the Country Music Hall of Fame and Museum for $1 a year; the Museum and Belmont are partners in its management, and that is another partnership that is good for students and for the city.

"Mike Curb is our strongest supporter, and we are trying hard to diversify our music," said President Fisher. "In 2003 at our President's Concert we honored [Maestro] Kenneth Schermerhorn. Each year we focus on one honoree, but in the previous year it was Vince Gill and Amy Grant. We honored Chet Atkins while he was still alive. If you come to a President's Concert, you will hear vocal jazz and instrumental jazz, a show choir, percussion ensembles, rock and roll, contemporary Christian, country, symphonic, classical voice, pop voice. We want to prepare our students for all those genres of music.

"We do a Best of the Best Concert. There are ensemble competitions in different categories all year, and then in May we go to the Ryman and our students run the whole thing. I'll never forget my first semester here. There are country and rock and classical and songwriters categories. But in the 'other' category the group that won that year was a metallic rock Christian band. It just blew me away; it turned out to be really good. When they came on stage, six women stood up and cheered. I realized that was their mothers. But by their third number the whole place was on its feet. They were that good."

Music will continue to be a significant part of what is happening at Belmont, thanks to its president and faculty. President Fisher said, "When I arrived here, I looked at what Belmont had done. It is wonderful and remarkable. But a great university shapes the future; it doesn't just gin out more people as it always has. We have thought about what the future of music should be, and that means broadening what we do and not just what has been done in the past. We are trying to shape that future and give students opportunities in areas that Nashville has not traditionally been known for. The recording studios are underutilized right now because country music is down. Well, then, we need to fill that with more pop musicians and more classical musicians and R and B and, heaven help me, hip hop.

"Mike started with the Curb Congregation Singers. Sammy Davis Jr. had them on 'Candy Man.' His career has been all over the place. He signed Donny Osmond. But the thing about Mike is that he has the same vision that we do here, and that is why he is connected so closely with us. The Curb School—he wants music for everyone. He relishes the opportunity to promote the Fisk Jubilee Singers, and he would like to promote other genres of music. He would like to see that happening here in Music City. We are so proud of everybody who has come here and all that they've done. Our theme at Belmont is 'From Here to Anywhere.' Here is Melissa Jenkins in Boston just two years after graduation; that was a big deal. The place was full of people in tuxes, honoring several important men, and she ran that event. She is competing with folks right there in Boston at the Berklee College."

Many Belmont students have a famous musical heritage, and President Fisher offered examples: "This beautiful woman showed up in my office and had her son with her. She said, 'My name is Natalie and this is my son, Robbie. He is currently at the Berklee College of Music in Boston. We've done some thinking and talking, and we'd like for him to transfer here to Belmont.'

"I said, 'Natalie, is your last name Cole?'

"She said, 'Yes, it is. How did you know that?'

"I said, 'How did I know that? I'm one of your biggest fans.' It was a kind of groupie comment, but I said, 'Miss Cole, it's an honor to have your son here. But it's an equal honor to have Nat King Cole's grandson at Belmont.' What a wonderful privilege! If you go out on this campus and see who is here: there is Floyd Cramer's grandson; you just go down the list of some of the greatest artists, and they send their sons and daughters to Belmont. That is an honor, and it's a huge responsibility."

Musical Training at Ward-Belmont Conservatory

In the 1890–91 Belmont College Announcement and Prospectus, the founders Ida E. Hood and Susan L. Heron wrote, "We desire to acquaint our pupils with the finest expressions in art, music, and oratory, and the opportunities of the school will be constantly supplemented by visits to the city." In turn, the city was often invited to recitals or other musical events at the college, so the two women established a tradition that has been in place for more than one hundred years. They and subsequent directors of the musical departments of Belmont or Ward-Belmont hired the best-trained teachers possible, and eventually a visiting artist series was introduced.

In that first academic year the piano teachers included Katie McCandless (Vienna Royal Conservatory), Annie Wendel, and Martha G. Dismukes (Chicago Conservatory of Music; Vienna with Julius Epstein and Theodor Leschtizky; she was still on the faculty in 1908). Mamie E. Geary (New England Conservatory) taught violin, and Mrs. M. S. Clements taught guitar, banjo, and mandolin. College tuition was $30 or $35, boarding costs were $100, and piano lessons for five months were $40 extra (about $800 today).

The Belmont College School of Music hired Edouard Hesselberg as its director in 1905 (he remained until 1912, when he assumed a position at the Toronto Conservatory). Born in 1870, in Riga, Russia (now Latvia), Hesselberg had a famed great-uncle on his mother's side, the cellist Charles Davidoff. Hesselberg performed his first solo at a Philharmonique symphony concert in Moscow, and he graduated as laureate from the Philharmonique Conservatory of Music and Dramatic Art. He performed for Russian royalty, "concertized with Sembrich, Marconi, Nordica, de Reszke, Fritz Sheel, John Philip Sousa," and studied with Anton Rubinstein. By 1908 he had written almost one hundred original compositions for piano, violin, voice, or orchestra. Hesselberg came to Belmont from the Conservatory of Music at Wesleyan College, Macon, Georgia, where he and his family had been since 1900. Although he was at Belmont less than a decade, he was said to have "taken a first place in Nashville as a pianist" as well as a director. His young son Melvyn, born in Macon in 1901, did not follow in his father's footsteps as a pianist or teacher, but he gained fame as a Hollywood actor. You may know Melvyn Edouard Hesselberg as Melvyn Douglas. (Melvyn starred with Grace Moore in the 1937 move *I'll Take Romance*.)

By 1921, there was a remarkable talent pool at the Ward-Belmont Conservatory of Music overseen by President J. D. Blanton. The following

A Time for Greatness

One of the attractions [of going to hear the Symphony] is just not knowing when perfection is going to break out.

—STEVE TURNER

THE NASHVILLE SYMPHONY has scheduled its first concert in Schermerhorn Symphony Center for September 2006. Behind that single sentence lie years of planning and even more years of dreaming. The completion of this building is going to be in some ways a culmination of efforts by many people throughout Nashville's history to bring its citizens to a certain level of competence in the arts. Having this excellent Symphony play in its own hall—in addition to having opera and ballet and theater performances in TPAC and other venues—Nashvillians

---

is a selected list of staff members: Lawrence Goodman, director of the School of Piano (pupil of Ernest Hutcheson, Josef Lhevinne, and Segismund Stajowkski; student at Ferrucio Busoni's Master School for Pianists, Basel, Switzerland; scholarship pupil at Peabody Conservatory of Music, Baltimore); Buda Love Maxwell, piano (New England Conservatory of Music with Mme Hopekirk and George Proctor; pupil of Harold Bauer and Wager Swayne, Paris); Annie Phillips Ransom, piano (Von Ende School of Music; pupil of Lawrence Goodman); Amelie Throne, piano (she was encouraged to become a pianist when the violinist Camilla Urso heard her play; pupil of Mary Weber Farrar, Nashville; Maurice Aronson, Vienna; Josef Lhevinne, Berlin); Florence N. Boyer, voice (Oberlin; pupil of Signor Vananni, Italy; Mesdames de Sales and Bossetti, Munich; Oscare Seagle and de Rezke, Paris); Elise Graziani, voice (pupil of Stockhausen and Fraulein Lina Beck in Julius Stockhausen's Gesangschule, Germany; pupil of Signor Graziani, and she assisted in his Berlin studio); Helen Todd Sloan, voice (pupil of George Deane, Boston; Isidore Braggiotti, Florence, Italy; Gaetano de Luca, Nashville); and Kenneth D. Rose, violin (pupil of McGibeny, Indianapolis; Arthur Hartmann, Paris; George Lehmann, Berlin; Souky, Prague; teacher at Metropolitan School of Music, Indianapolis, and concertmaster of Indianapolis Symphony).

The catalog for 1929–30 noted that the Ward-Belmont Conservatory of Music consisted of the Belmont School of Music and Ward Conservatory of Music, and it stated the conservatory's purpose was "not simply to 'give lessons' in some special branch, but to give all the instruction the student can digest, all that is required to develop a broad and cultured musician." Students could earn certificates in piano, voice, violin, pipe organ, and harp, but if availability of equipment is any sign of popularity, the piano was the winner with ten grand pianos and ninety uprights.

The Ward-Belmont Orchestra, founded in 1908, had Kenneth Rose as its director since 1918. (Rose remained at the school from 1918 to 1952.) Many members of the Nashville Symphony (the one founded in 1920) were present or past members of the Ward-Belmont Orchestra, which gave at least one public performance yearly.

For the 1940–41 academic year Roy Underwood was dean of the Ward-Belmont Conservatory, and he also taught piano. Sydney Dalton was the head of the voice department, and Mary Elizabeth Delaney taught dance. There was still a Ward-Belmont Orchestra. For the 1950–51 academic year instructors were Ellen Jane Anderson (from the San Francisco Ballet School) for dance and Maribel Benton, Mary Douthit Bold, Allan Irwin, and Florence Irwin for piano.

are getting back to the high aspirations of the city's forebears, and this book has given multiple examples of those aspirations.

Many elements have come together to make the concert hall a reality, such as the Carnegie Hall performance, which permitted the musicians of the Symphony, Nashvillians, and everyone else in attendance to hear just how good the Symphony is today. This experience was a catalyst for serious discussion of the need for a dedicated concert hall. There was also the Chamber of Commerce visit to Benaroya Symphony Hall in Seattle. In addition the willingness of individuals and corporations to donate funds, the vision of city leaders, the enthusiastic support of the community, and the assembling of a world-class design team are contributing factors.

The Chamber of Commerce took a group from Nashville to Seattle, Washington, in April 2000 to determine whether any ideas that were working there would work back home. Alan Valentine was to go on that trip, and he arranged to have the city's new symphony hall as one of the stops. It was the Seattle Symphony's first home of its own, and as Alan said, "It is a miracle story. The orchestra was having all kinds of financial problems; it was in deep debt. Somebody gave them some money to get the project started, and it just took off. . . . At the same time the orchestra kind of got things settled down. They had some more deficits as they got ready to open the building because they grew so fast. But once the building opened, it solved all of that permanently. Their ticket sales income doubled." Benaroya Symphony Hall opened in 1998, the orchestra had a $20.1 million balanced budget for 2002–3, and more than 300,000 people attended more than 220 performances for the 2002–3 season.

Alan continued, "The Chamber group was stunned by how beautiful the building was. It was our last tour stop on the last day, so right from there we went to their equivalent of the City Club

downtown and had a facilitated discussion about what ideas we wanted to bring back to Nashville. We wanted to pick the top five for the Chamber to focus on. We listed all of the things we saw, and there were about forty things on sheets of paper torn off and stuck on the wall. Each of us was given five little green dot stickers and told to vote on the top five things. The symphony hall made number two on the list. I was stunned. I called you [Martha] immediately and said, 'Martha, you are not going to believe what happened.' That really helped when everybody said, 'Maybe we can do this.'"

Alan contacted a financial consultant to do a ten-year analysis of projections that would show what would happen to the Symphony's operation if we did not build a hall *or* if we did. The results indicated that building the concert hall would enable us to sustain a major orchestra for the long term with only a little more endowment.

It was already evident that TPAC was overbooked, and Steven Greil proposed a "2020 program," part of which involved getting the Nashville Symphony out of TPAC so that the Symphony's dates would be available for other performers. The outdated War Memorial Auditorium was suggested as a home for the Symphony, but a study revealed that it was not suitable and never would be, even if millions of dollars were expended. At a quarterly meeting of Nashville Agenda—a group that evaluates needs within the community and works with the Nashville Chamber and city government—one proposal was that a concert hall should be built from the ground up because the Symphony had earned a home of its own.

Cities that want to be considered successful places for both business and quality of life need to demonstrate that by providing an infrastructure that includes the arts. A symphony hall makes the point loud and clear, although fewer than a dozen halls have been built in the United States since the end of World War II. The Symphony's goal is to have one of the best halls in the country—and maybe the world—but the primary focus is to have the best acoustics and other features in the hall that will serve Nashville well. Schermerhorn Symphony Center is to be of neoclassical revivalist design with a limestone exterior, which complements other major buildings in the city (see appendix C for specifications). The Chamber of Commerce has conducted an economic impact study of the Center, and the results are pretty staggering: the economic impact by 2010 of the Symphony and the new Center, measured conservatively, will be more than $215 million.

The Symphony has undertaken a $145 million endowment and capital campaign to fund expanded operations and Schermerhorn Symphony Center itself. The fund-raising during a period in late 2002 and early 2003 was a challenge because of dips in the stock market, the impending war in Iraq, and then the actual war. Leaders of the effort had to be more patient, more creative, and more persistent. Such uncertainties present a good time to borrow money, however, because of low interest rates. The Center's construction ($125 million) will be funded by tax-exempt revenue bonds repaid by the Symphony's A Time for Greatness Campaign pledges. The additional $20 million will form a permanent endowment to generate monies to underwrite the cost of operating the facility.

The design team consists of architect David Schwarz (David M. Schwarz/Architectural Services of Washington, D.C.), Nashville architectural firms Earl Swensson Associates and Hastings Architecture Associates, acoustician Paul Scarbrough (Akustiks), and theater consultant Joshua Dachs (Fisher Dachs Associates). (See appendix C for a complete list of the design and construction team.) Here are a few notable projects for each, which may include new construction or renovations: *Schwarz*, Severance Hall in Cleveland, Nancy Lee and Perry R. Bass Performance Hall in Fort Worth, and the Dallas Arena; *Swensson*, Mayo Clinic Hospital in Phoenix, the Delta of Opryland Hotel, and BellSouth Tennessee Headquarters; *Hastings*, 315 Union Street, Park Center at Maryland Farms, and Pinnacle Bank in Green Hills; *Scarbrough*, Oklahoma City Civic Center Music Hall, Severance Hall, and the Concert Hall at the Kennedy Center; and *Dachs*, Broward Center for the Performing Arts in Fort Lauderdale, Hult Center for the Performing Arts in Eugene, Oregon, and an opera house in Taegu, Korea.

The design team accompanied several leaders from the concert hall project on a whirlwind tour of European halls in April 2002. Denny Bottorff, who chairs the Concert Hall Steering Committee, was on that trip, and he said, "We saw seven halls in five days, and listening to four concerts, we were able to do an in-depth look at each of these halls and draw on the knowledge of world-renowned experts. What I learned is that in Europe there is a different relationship between the orchestra and the audience than what I had been used to in the U.S. Here you listen to the orchestra; there the halls create an engagement with the orchestra—the halls are more intimate. You not only hear the music; you are visually engaged with the orchestra. . . . We have an opportunity here to build more audience participation by building a hall that will change people's experience, one that makes people say, 'Wow! I like this.' . . . Building the hall is just the beginning. The success will come from people attending."

Paul Scarbrough added, "I think the one that stood out for me and probably for everybody was the hall in Vienna, the Musikvereinsaal, which is the shrine to music and acoustics. It's the place where Brahms conducted, where Mahler conducted, where many of the pieces that we associate with the core of the symphonic repertoire today were first debuted. Many of Mahler's symphonies were first performed there, and many of Bruckner's, so that core repertoire finds its home in that room. . . .

"One of the other things that made a big impression, in addition to the acoustics of the space, was the natural light and the quality of natural light in the room. As it happened, we went to an afternoon concert, Dvořák's Requiem. The concert started around 3:30, and just as the concert was finishing up, it was about 5:15 or so, the sun began to come down in the west, which was the far end of the room behind the audience, and the sunlight just streamed into the room. It filled the room with this wonderful, gold light. That was the cap of the experience for everybody."

The Nashville Advisory Committee, which was formed early in 2002 with cochairmen Kevin Lavender and Howard Stringer, seeks input on the concert hall from more than fifteen committees that reflect diverse interests in the city, from Realtors to businessmen and women, educators to artists to pastors. More than 250 people on these committees are also the hall's ambassadors as they respond to questions about the project from the greater community.

Steve Turner chairs the Building Committee for Schermerhorn Symphony Center, and he has been generous with his time, his input, and his funds. He said, "One of the most pleasing things I've seen: when we announced the gift [of $15 million] that my brother [Cal] and I are going in together to make, it was a rainy Monday morning [in May 2002]. Very miserable weather for the time of year that it was. There were two hundred community leaders there at 7:30 in the morning. That in itself was a statement to me that *yes!* people want this."

The 1,900-seat performance hall will be named in honor of the late Laura Goad Turner, Steve and Cal's mother, who was from Kentucky. Steve said of his mother, "She tried her hardest to get us to pay attention to music," and she took them to the Community Concerts in Bowling Green at Western Kentucky University. Steve took voice lessons and still loves to sing, and Cal played the organ at his church and took organ and voice lessons.

Mrs. Turner was a blues singer and obviously had a good sense of humor along with a joie de vivre. Steve described a memorable event with her: "When I got out of high school, we went to the Bavarian Alps and to King Ludwig's castle. There was a piano in that castle where Wagner had composed a few of his operas; he was very much protected by King Ludwig. They asked if anybody wanted to play it, and my mother sat right down and played 'Five Foot Two.' I was over in the corner cringing."

Steve's passion for music is one reason that he has been so involved with the concert hall project. He said, "I think the one thing about music that I've always loved so much is it's the greatest way to escape and the greatest way to be involved I've ever seen in my life. It does something to your emotions, your personality, that nothing else does. . . . One of the things that has worried me about our society in general is that we are beginning not to come together and communicate with each other. You do that in the experience of sitting in a symphony hall, seeing other people, and then at intermission visiting with them. . . .

"Even just sitting and listening to music, even pieces you've heard all of your life and you know where the melody is supposed to go, there are still those wonderful experiences when somebody goes just a little farther than anybody else you've ever heard go with it. It's almost like you have a beeline straight to God. Boom! Here is the best that a human can do. And isn't that wonderful that a human can do it? Isn't it as wonderful that I happened to be there at that special moment when it happened?"

The Symphony board voted in February 2003 to name the building after Maestro Kenneth Schermerhorn, who has spent twenty years nurturing the Orchestra to its present professional status. He said, "It is cosmically flattering to have the building named after me." Marv Cermak of the *Times Union* (Albany, New York) said, "I recall Schermerhorn as a super band trumpet player and a capable high-hurdler on the Mont Pleasant

Schermerhorn Symphony Center is scheduled to open in the fall of 2006. This is the northwest perspective of the hall, facing Fourth Avenue South.

High track team more than a half-century ago." John Marcella, who was a clarinet player in the high school band with Kenneth in the late 1940s and also played in the West Point band with him, said, "Naming the concert hall after Ken is fitting. . . . He is an unbelievably talented musician and a great conductor."

Schermerhorn Symphony Center will be four stories tall with seven half-floors, and in Laura Turner Hall, there will be space for 115 musicians on stage plus 140 choral seats on the platform (a feature new to Nashville will be that the public may sit there when no chorus is used). It will be the only major concert hall in North America with natural light, provided by thirty soundproof windows. There will be two inches minimum acoustical isolation joints between the concert hall and the rest of the building to assure no transfer of vibration or noise. (For information about the site, see "The Site for Schermerhorn Symphony Center.")

How does an architect start his work on such a special building? David Schwarz said that he started with questions: "What are the appropriate symbols and what is the appropriate ritual for Nashville when it comes to classical music and pops? What are the kinds of things that symbolize this community's commitment to design? What are the kinds of things that symbolize this community's commitment to quality? What are the kinds of things that symbolize this community's commitment to the performing arts? What is the architectural heritage of Nashville? What are the expressions that people have chosen in the past to express Nashville's aspirations? How did those get carried into the future? What will be timeless here as opposed to somewhere else? And what sort of building will last and contribute to the richness of life in Nashville for the next three hundred years? . . .

"Nashville, like many cities in America, is coming of age in the twenty-first century. One of the things I find so interesting about the town is the questioning and thoughtfulness that is going into who do we want to be? How do we want to build? How do we want to represent ourselves?"

David continued, "I want people to come away from this building, those who only visit the outside, with a real sense of pride and a real sense of Nashville's commitment to music and classical music." For those who go inside, "I want people to have a sense of joy."

He added, "A building like this has to be designed to be flexible. It has to be able to grow and change as its community users grow and change. None of us has any idea of what music will be performed one hundred years from now. That is a challenge. Let the building grow with its public—whether it be a product of its environment as well as a statement about its environment. . . .

"We have to satisfy everybody. We can't have any unsatisfied constituency. I think that the intertwining of the architect and the acoustician on a project like this is hand in glove. We need to accomplish what Paul wants from an acoustic point of view, and he needs to accomplish what we want to accomplish from an artistic point of view."

Kenneth said of the architect and the acoustician: "They know exactly what my wishes are. My wishes are that they should get lucky and make the greatest concert hall in the world." He referred to another landmark building by saying, "Carnegie Hall wasn't always Carnegie Hall. It has been up and down. The Sixth Avenue subway ran under it, and especially on matinees on Friday the subway would run every fifteen minutes or so. In the evenings it wasn't nearly so bad and certainly not on Sunday when it didn't run much at all. It also had ambient sound problems."

In his job as acoustician Paul Scarbrough evaluates the effect of everything—windows, walls, seating, materials, ductwork, ventilation systems, mechanical systems, you name it—on

the sound quality. He said, "I can design you a concert hall that is completely made out of wood that sounds appalling and one that sounds fabulous; it all depends on how you detail the wood. If you make very thin wood panels and suspend them over an air space, they will tend to suck all the bass out of the room, so the double basses and the cellos will have no richness or body to them. But if you make them substantially thick wood panels, like the ceiling in the Musikvereinsaal, which is a couple of inches of wood decking and material on top of that, then you can reinforce and sustain the bass tones. You have to look at things in a very, very detailed way. Our work actually goes from the big picture to the increasingly minute picture as we go through the project."

Wallace Clement Sabine, a professor at Harvard University and a physicist, is considered the father of the modern science of acoustics, still a relatively new science. Paul explained how Sabine became involved: "When the university opened a new lecture auditorium in the late 1890s, it was a horrible room to speak in. They asked him to take a look at it, and that is where he did his first experiments, which yielded the first formulas for acoustics. Then when the Boston Symphony decided to replace its music hall with a new symphony hall, they engaged him to work with McKim, Mead and White, the design team."

Although acoustics is a science of formulas and equipment, the human element is essential. Paul said, "We do bring in a variety of test gear to see what's happening in the room and be able to quantify what we're hearing. But in the end it's our own ears we use as the judge for any tuning exercise to get the balance in a room. We depend on our ears much more so than measurements. Measurements are crude on a certain level because the ear is such a sophisticated mechanism."

Art enters the picture because, according to Paul, "There is no one perfect acoustic for a symphony hall or an opera house or a drama theater. There is a range for each one, and the trick is to get somewhere in the middle of the range where most people like to listen as opposed to going to the extreme edges where some people might be happy but the vast majority might be less happy. . . .

"The challenge has been to create a room that's resonant and yet has the impact of a wonderful, smaller room. We've been pushing both the architects and the theater consultants to really be efficient about the way they lay out the seats in the hall so that we minimize how much area is devoted to the seats without compromising the patron comfort."

The Martin Foundation has donated $2.5 million toward the cost of an organ to be built by Jack Bethards of Schoenstein and Co. Paul noted the importance of having this instrument: "There is practically no great concert hall in the world that is without an organ. What the organ does for us is to create a backdrop behind the orchestra that actually is very diffusive; it breaks up and scatters the sound; it blends it around the room very, very evenly. It's hard to find some other surface that does the same thing as well as an organ does it." There is no one-size-fits-all when it comes to putting together an organ and a concert hall. This organ will be designed specifically for Laura Turner Hall, and Paul will work directly with the builder on it.

Paul stated, "Alan Valentine and his colleagues in the Orchestra feel very strongly about this room being for many things. It is first and foremost the home of the Nashville Symphony, but they want it to be a place where all Nashvillians feel at home coming to and find some aspect of the programming relevant to their lives. The design that we're trying to evolve is very much oriented toward the idea of being able to accommodate these different things and to do them well—not just passably well."

When you enter Schermerhorn Symphony Center, you will be able to feel the effects of Josh Dachs's work, but you may not be able to explain *how* or *why*. Josh stated, "I'm as concerned about the audience's total experience of the building as I am about any one small technical consideration. They are going to walk into the room [Laura Turner Hall] and go, 'Wow! This is great! It feels really good.' For me that is one of the most important things. . . . While that is my field of endeavor—to make a room feel really good to an audience and to performers—unfortunately there is not a word to describe that and I have to resort to analogies and lengthy descriptions to get people to know what I'm talking about."

He has proposed three words to clarify his job. *Feelology* is one, "but nobody would take it seriously," he said. "Or we could combine a bunch of Greek roots with *Thespis*: call it *thespacionics*. Or we could go to the German and call it *Raumgeistology*—the study of the spirit of the room, which has the advantage of being difficult to pronounce."

On this project Josh will use everything he has learned from being a violinist to attaining an architecture degree to working in the theater. He said, "We make contemporary buildings that need to last for a long time, and yet we know that things are going to change over time. What do we do? We make sure that we put plenty of electrical power in the building, and we make it very easy to install temporary cabling between one point and another.

"When Lincoln Center was built, it was fully wired for black-and-white television, which was obsolete on the day it was opened and has never actually been used. It's there to this day. We certainly don't want to do something like that, so if we installed whatever the latest ethernet wiring or the latest optical whizbang, I can guarantee that we will have installed something that will be abandoned in relatively short order in the life of the building.

"Then the question becomes the next step: Is there a way to move temporary recording cables in and out of the room or temporary video equipment in and out of the room without tearing up the walls or taping stuff to the carpet? That's what we do. We make sure that there are good ways of doing these things.

"Then we work out all the backstage layouts. We make sure that all of the dressing rooms are in the right places and they can accommodate all of the equipment that needs to go in them and that you can roll pianos from this place to that place—all of the functional aspects of a performing arts building. We also are concerned about where the coat check is and where the bathrooms are and the quantity of toilets and where the box office is. We are concerned about how to operate this building as a performance space, too. And ultimately we also design all of the stage lighting systems and all of the related rigging systems and anything that moves. If Paul says, 'I need some drapery here for amplified events that needs to go away for other things,' we do that, too." A unique system will remove the tiered seats so that a flat floor may be used for various occasions.

How will Josh know when he and his firm and the rest of the team have achieved success? "Success is an interesting question," he said. "How do you measure it? On the one hand, you can say we'll be successful if the room is good acoustically. But if it's good acoustically and it's only open ten times a year, is it a success? The answer is probably no. When you talk about success, you also have to talk about an acceptable level of activity in the building. Alan [Valentine] and company are aiming very high in that they want to see a building that has a high level of activity: not just a high level of activity for concert events, but also for educational programming, for preconcert lectures, for preconcert dining opportunities, for social events—rentals for banquets and weddings and things like that—so that the building

is a lively and active place in the community. If it achieves that, it will have achieved a certain kind of success.

"If the backstage works out as we hope that it will and the building is extremely efficient and economical to operate, then it will contribute to its economic success. If the backstage is comfortable and extremely pleasant to be in, as opposed to feeling like you're in a basement somewhere, and if together with that, we have a room that is as fine acoustically as we all hope and expect that it will be, then the room will develop over time a reputation among the world's artists as being a really good place to perform. And that's a measure of success: when the musicians say, 'This is a really good place.'"

Josh added a historical perspective to the concert hall project: "Since the Second World War and since the beginnings of resuscitating these art forms [building concert halls], there have now been a few cycles, and people like Paul have lived through some of the experiences that have taught them a great deal. And the generation before Paul made a lot of mistakes, but everybody learned from those mistakes. I find that fascinating that we are at the start of a new century and it seems that we should be very advanced in all of this.

"So how come there are so many failures? Well, it's because in fact we're *not* so experienced at this. First of all, the building type is not that old, and second of all, the practitioners who have been trying to make these buildings—they aren't that many generations deep. I think we're better able to do this job than ever before, and we've all tried to learn from the past—not only in terms of the acoustics but in terms of the graciousness of the experience."

Denny Bottorff commented on other lessons learned from the past: "It is a great pleasure for me to be involved in the building of this new concert hall, having been involved in that very difficult time [when the Symphony had to close

Cellist Yo-Yo Ma, Maestro Kenneth Schermerhorn, and I were at a party in downtown Nashville in 1996 marking the release of the Sony CD *Appalachian Waltz*, featuring Yo-Yo Ma, Edgar Meyer, and Mark O'Connor.

and declare bankruptcy]. I believe that it is sort of like when you're learning to ride a bicycle: you fall down and have a little scrape and then you're more careful. That's better than at a later age just getting on a motorcycle and having a really serious accident. We stubbed our toes at an early enough age and in a small enough problem—even though it seemed like a big one at the time—that it enabled us to come out of it with lessons learned that have really helped the arts."

Alan Valentine addressed the need for the concert hall: "Even though TPAC is wonderful and has done exactly what it needed to do when it was built, and without it we wouldn't have the Opera, we wouldn't have the Ballet, we wouldn't have the Rep, and we wouldn't have had any touring shows, it has been fantastic and has spurred the growth of the Orchestra in a lot of ways, it is still not thought of as the home of the Orchestra. It is a place where everything happens. Because it's so busy, the Orchestra has a

leased truck. A lot of orchestras lease trucks when they need them to go out and do concerts and things, but we have a leased truck, and we practically live out of the back of it. We're always going to different places to rehearse and to perform. . . .

"It's hard to run a business—where in our case our product is music—unless you have a place that is suitable to call home. If we're limited by not just how many dates we can get but can we get on stage when the public wants to come and when we can get the artists that we want to present and put on the programs that we want to present, the answer to that is no." As just one example, Alan tried to sign up B. B. King one season, but King had only two dates available, and the Symphony could not get a venue. That concert could have meant $40,000 in the budget's plus column.

Bobby Taylor offered his perspective as a longtime member of the Symphony: "The Symphony absolutely does need a single-purpose hall, and here are the reasons why: we live in a world today where anybody can go to Radio Shack or Circuit City or Sears, for that matter, anywhere, and buy a nice CD player and put on a CD of the Berlin Philharmonic or the Philadelphia Orchestra or the Cleveland Orchestra or Boston Symphony and have incredible quality right there in their living room. That has not always been the case. When I first got involved listening to LPs, there was this sizzle and the crackles and the pops. The fidelity wasn't nearly as good. The technology involved in all of that has increased so much that I see that as what we're competing against.

"We can't compete with a multipurpose hall that lets us sound pretty good but distant because it is set up so that rock and roll groups can come in there and sound fantastic and they can do opera in there and they can do ballet in there. That is a wonderful thing, but it does not allow us to compete with a good CD player. When Nashville folks heard us in Carnegie Hall, that was when they really started talking in earnest about the new hall. Several people told me that on the plane back to Nashville, there was a definite buzz about having to get a new hall. If it is designed especially to allow the Symphony to sound at its absolute best and to make a sound that can completely envelop the audience, then I'm not afraid of the CD player.

"Right now I know people who say, 'Why should I go to TPAC and worry about parking and have to get dressed up? I can sit home in my skivvies and hear the Berlin Philharmonic.' I hope people understand that that is what we're up against. If we are going to keep doing this and growing and succeeding and building audiences, we can't hold anything back. We've got to give it everything we've got, and we've got to be able to present our sound in the ultimate fashion. I'm 1000 percent behind it."

Mayor Bill Purcell weighed in with the view from Metro Government: "The whole symphony hall project has the potential to be a model for the way in which we move forward in these kinds of projects in the future. I think it was much informed by what occurred with TPAC and later with the Frist Center. There was a very early recognition that a project of this size and quality was going to require private leadership. There had to be a critical mass of private interest as well as private support in order to move a project like this forward. But simultaneous with that understanding was the belief that the city needed to be not just informed but also a partner in the process. The project at this point has proceeded ideally, and I do not often say that things proceed ideally.

"Typically in the city that hasn't been our experience. In this case I really do think that there was very early communication, an honest effort to build consensus, not just among the constituencies most interested. There was an understanding that not only the government leaders but the broader government needed to be informed and engaged. And lastly an understanding that I think is new to us: that there was an obligation to inform the larger city about the purpose and intent as well as the process. At this point I honestly think it is among the best-positioned projects of its kind."

Michael Buckland spoke about the younger audiences: "We have to accept that although we are doing things like this [programming] to get young audiences, young audiences are an investment for the future. You get students and college kids, and they make the audience look younger and they put some energy in the room and then they go off to other cities and they travel and they get married and they haven't got any spare money and they're looking after the kids and they can't get a babysitter and you don't see them for fifteen or twenty years. But if you've invested in them there or if their parents have dragged them by the ear to the Symphony, fifteen or twenty years later they will come back. . . . We will grow audiences by bringing in younger people—no. We will invest in the future by bringing in younger people—yes.

"We currently play music, in one form or another, to 80,000 schoolchildren in Middle Tennessee. The language used for the new hall—'every child, every grade, every year'—is no idle boast and is embraced by Pedro Garcia. I believe the new hall will allow us to serve up to 120,000 schoolchildren."

As part of her job Joyce Searcy, president and CEO of Bethlehem Centers of Nashville and a lifelong lover and maker of music, helps children who walk through the doors of her agency to grow to self-reliance. The children learn about various instruments, and even the youngsters in day care listen to classical music as they take their naps. She said, "We may have some very talented musicians, but we won't know unless they have that choice. . . . Or they may not become musicians, but they will teach their kids about music. And we'll have a generation of kids who can buy a ticket, coupled with the training and the literacy that they get here. They can say, 'Now I have a job; now I can really buy a ticket.'" And their trips to Schermerhorn Symphony Center will give them continuing exposure to professional musicians and their music.

Kevin Lavender commented on the perception held by some that the new concert hall is just for the wealthy: "I have found that it is a hard sell to some people, for example, to ministers, who say, 'Help us understand how it's not just for them [the rich].' I explain that rich people can leave town and fly to New York to go to Carnegie Hall or fly to Italy to go to La Scala. I explain that one goal is to help school-age children enjoy the arts and learn about the arts because the hall will provide a place for more educational opportunities with the Symphony and other groups. Church choirs would be able to use the space to hold special events or to record CDs. Hearing that usually changes the ministers' minds. Getting those kids in the doors means that they are going to go home and talk about the experience. And then they may get their parents interested, too.

"Professional sports and performing arts attract different crowds. And the business community sees the need to balance the emphasis of entertainment venues for people. When I talk about the symphony hall, I focus first on the fact that it will help move the city forward. The city's moniker is Music City USA, and the hall will contribute to the continued maturation of the city. Then I focus on the educational benefits. And the talented musicians in the Orchestra ought to have a world-class facility. It will be a good addition to downtown and will emphasize that the city is progressive economically and culturally. The last thing we want is for the downtown area to be perceived as stagnant."

Chancellor Gordon Gee of Vanderbilt pointed out, "Having a great concert hall balances out having a great stadium and a great arena. . . . And we have a very fine orchestra. One cannot be Music City USA without having clarity and support for all the musical forms, not simply for the recorded forms such as the blues or country."

Kyle Young, director of the Country Music Foundation and a neighbor of Schermerhorn Symphony Center, said, "We're down here [in downtown Nashville] for several reasons, but I think one of the things that motivated Phil Bredesen, who was mayor at the time, was to stimulate economic growth here. We are situated at the south end of the Capitol Mall redevelopment district, and he wanted to reenergize downtown. He needed a downtown anchor with activities. That is one reason we came here. We were out of room. Our archives were just bulging at the seams. I think if you look at just that, I would like to think we have some part to play or have had some role in things happening down here. The concert hall is the key piece of the puzzle. From an educational point of view, we are committed to that and spend 18 percent of our budget on education and education outreach [total budget is $11.5 million, so 18 percent equals $2.07 million]. The Symphony does great things in that area, too.

"Alan and I have had some fun talking about what might happen there. There could be connections between what is going on in the outreach area at the Symphony and here. Then another reason is that it is going to be a spectacular building. From a purely business point of view, I know what it was like to open this building and all the excitement and the national press it generated. I can only believe that the same thing will happen when the concert hall opens. It is another feather in Nashville's cap. It is another symbol of the indisputable fact that this is one of the three music centers in the whole country." New York and Los Angeles are the other two.

Michael Buckland asked, "Wouldn't it be great if this was thought of as being *the place* where the major artists had to come and play? And our new concert hall will help that. But I think that's possible because there is talent here and brains here, all related to music."

It is very hard to resist splendid music; it is very hard to resist a compelling orchestra. It is going to be even harder to resist splendid music by a compelling orchestra in the new Schermerhorn Symphony Center. People with season tickets to the Symphony will have rights of first refusal by the time of the building's completion, and many plan to secure the best seats by getting ahead of the line and signing up—even as the first shovels dig in the ground.

The Site for Schermerhorn Symphony Center

Downtown can become a place to come to celebrate.

—RICK BERNHARDT

SCHERMERHORN Symphony Center will be situated on a city block between Third and Fourth Avenues, South, north of Demonbreun. Its neighbors will be the Country Music Hall of Fame and Museum, Gaylord Entertainment Center, and Hilton Suites Nashville Downtown. It will be adjacent to the landing of the Shelby Street Pedestrian Bridge and across from a park known as Gateway Commons.

The general area south of Broad Street was first called Black Bottom because when it flooded, the river brought in black silt and created soggy, unhealthful conditions, and then called Hay Market (sometimes spelled as one word, Haymarket), which was a place for farmers to sell hay and sell and/or swap horses. Irish immigrants settled there, beginning in the 1850s, and the structures they occupied were little more than shanties. Then saloons, brothels, and some legitimate businesses followed. As the Irish improved their financial situations and moved to other parts of the city, many African-Americans moved in—but with no improvement in the crowded housing and unsanitary conditions.

There was, however, more excitement in the neighborhood over the years than drunken brawls and hay sales. For example, on October 5, 1896, William Jennings Bryan, a champion of free silver and a presidential candidate running against William McKinley, gave three speeches that evening, and the first was held at the Hay Market at 9:15 P.M. Estimates were that 7,000 crowded around him there, then others heard him at the public square and at the Athletic Park, for a total of approximately 20,000 people and the requisite numbers of horses, buggies, and wagons. (If that estimate was even close, that was about three-fourths as many people in all of nearby Williamson County in 1890 [26,321].) Regular trains and excursion trains after noon had dropped off droves of people and the Louisville train brought some out-of-towners, but mostly merchants and businessmen from Nashville and smaller, outlying towns were in the audience.

At the end of July 1905, the writer Will Allen Dromgoole spent time with some of the people living in Black Bottom and did a story for the *Banner,* complete with pictures. According to her, Black Bottom extended from Broad to where the hills began to rise. She was appalled by what she found and spared no details for readers, from inadequate water and sewage facilities, to twelve families living in one tenement and paying $2 to $3 *per room* (about $40 to $60 today) per month. She hammered on the point that the rich who owned the tenements were making a profit off really desperate people.

A proposal to purchase Black Bottom, tear down the structures, and create a park had the support of women in civic clubs and Mayor Hilary Howse. In 1910 voters defeated a bond issue, which would have been necessary to purchase the land.

Mayor Howse and some citizens were unwilling to let the matter drop. Three years later, it became an issue again, as reported in the *Tennessean,* May 13, 1913:

The citizens of South Nashville are clamoring for a small park or parkway in the heart of Black Bottom. They have had many meetings, at some of which the park commissioners were present. At a mass meeting held at Dr. Lofton's church two years since committees were appointed and an advisory board to council [*sic*]

and act with the Women's Federation of South Nashville was selected, they have been active continually and in conjunction with the Women's Federation have worked both in the legislature and among the people, and have concentrated their efforts on eliminating Black Bottom by appealing to the park commission to establish a small park south of Molloy street and running south to Peabody street. In speaking of the move Oliver J. Timothy, a leading Nashville merchant [and original trustee of the Union Gospel Tabernacle (the Ryman)], says,

"This would, they claim, effect the objects they have in mind which, briefly stated, are: First, To clean up the approach to their homes, open up a decent driveway to the Hermitage, and the cemeteries, Mt. Calvary and Mt. Olivet.

"Second, The establishing of the Vanderbilt college on the Peabody campus with its 1,000 to 1,500 students, in the near future will be best served by having the debauching influence now existing in this bottom obliterated. The new Methodist hospital now being built demands such a change. The daily walk of the numerous students to and from the new high school will be more safe, and the effect of this movement will be beneficial to every home south of Broad street, and every citizen living on the Lebanon, Murfreesboro and Nolensville pike.

"The park commission has it in its power to give effect to this plan, and no easier or better way can be suggested to clean up black bottom [*sic*]. Memphis has such a park, and the property around it is the most valuable in that city.

"South Nashville people have been patient and persistent in their efforts to abolish black bottom [*sic*], and this simple demand of theirs will no doubt receive the practical support of the park commissioners.

"A large park in the suburbs would not effect one-tenth of the good this small park will produce, because its location upon the point chosen by the citizens' meeting and the federation removes the core or center of all the evil producing influence as it now exists."

Others protested that the job of cleaning up the "evil producing influence" belonged not to the Parks Commission but to other parts of city government, and they basically posed the questions: Where would the effort stop to wipe out such influences? Would the city buy up other tracts to try to accomplish similar goals?

The citizens of yesteryear who hoped to turn the neighborhood into an asset for Nashville would be delighted to see the progress made by the early years of the twenty-first century. Today, the city government and the citizens are working together in the area, which is undergoing a renaissance with new buildings, renovated buildings, and improved infrastructure. Rick Bernhardt, executive director of Metro's Planning Commission, offered his expertise for the Schermerhorn Symphony Center project: "I have two parameters when dealing with planning for the city and adding something like the symphony hall. The first is to have a balanced, sustainable city. Cultural opportunities and the performing arts are an important aspect of that. . . . The second is the specifics of the project. I have helped them look at how a symphony hall fits into the urban fabric and provided a site-specific examination of how it fits in relationship to the streets. . . .

"I was involved as they narrowed the process. They looked at the Rolling Mill Hill site, which would put the hall on a wonderful pedestal. But the final site choice is one that, in the long term, will add to the fabric of the community.

"American cities have gone through a long period of twenty or thirty years of suburbanization. The new concert halls being built now add more value than the events themselves. The football stadium and Gaylord have become the living room of the region. We need to look at the downtown of tomorrow not necessarily in terms of employment opportunities. Downtown can become a place to come to celebrate."

Metro Council members have given their enthusiastic support to the Schermerhorn Symphony Center project by speedily passing Ordinance No. BL2002-1050, cosponsored by Councilmen Ludye Wallace and Jim Shulman. The building will be in Councilman Wallace's district, and Councilman Shulman chaired the council's Budget and Finance Committee. The ordinance was introduced to the council for first reading on May 9, 2002, and it passed; subsequently it passed on second (May 21) and third (June 4) readings, and Mayor Bill Purcell approved it on June 6, 2002. (Fire Station No. 9 was already on the site when the Maintenance and Repair Shop for the Fire Department joined it in the early 1950s; the fire hall and shop will be moved to another part of Nashville.) The ordinance in essence conveys the property to the Nashville Symphony "for the purpose of promoting the good and proper public interest by developing a music hall."

Schermerhorn Symphony Center will be a part of the Rutledge Hill Redevelopment Plan, and I think I can see the spirit of Septima Sexta Middleton Rutledge—she of the gold Italian harp with her fine home on Rutledge Hill—looking down on this elegant building and smiling her approval.

The Next Steps on the Journey

You will ever remember that all the end of study is to make you a good man and a useful citizen.

—JOHN ADAMS, 1781, TO HIS SON JOHN QUINCY ADAMS, WHO WAS AT HARVARD

ALTHOUGH JOHN ADAMS was writing to his son specifically about his college education, we can create a similar statement about the performing arts: we should ever remember that in addition to enjoyment, attending performing arts events can help make us better-educated men and women and more useful citizens. Nashvillians are beginning to understand the significance of the arts as part of being a learned person. To know of these things is really quite important in being a complete individual with the chance to live a full, exciting, and balanced life. Many believe that one's education should never come to an end—whether it is discovering something new about a Verdi opera, hearing a Mahler symphony for the first time, seeing a ballet such as *Robin Hood,* or watching as professional actors bring a great play by Ibsen alive on stage.

It is implicit that money is not enough to sustain and stabilize the performing arts; there is also the need for educated leaders and audiences and well-trained performers. After almost two hundred years of struggle in moving toward this point, Nashvillians seem to have the elements working well together so that the classical performing arts—symphonic music, dance, opera, and theater—have achieved a healthy level of success, but Nashville's citizens must not let it slip away. Perhaps arts organizations can use the lessons from past successes *and* failures to map out a future that will keep them on the road and out of the ditch—even if they hit a few bumps or get stuck in the mud on occasion.

Jane Fabian noted that "culture and history are tied together, and you are a product of them." This book has presented just a sampling of the performing arts in Nashville throughout its history, past and present, and endeavors to assure that the city's future will have even richer artistic offerings. It is too costly in terms of wasted human potential to let the arts fall by the wayside.

Michael M. Kaiser, president of the Kennedy Center for the Performing Arts, wrote an editorial for the *Washington Post* at the end of 2002. He titled it "How to Save the Performing Arts" and stated, "The arts world needs leadership. It needs concerted action. And it needs them fast. There are five key issues that must be addressed if we are to solve the problems arts organizations face today. . . . If we can take all these necessary steps, we will create an arts ecology that can withstand the horrors of terrorism, economic decline and social unrest. If we don't, even a healthy economic and social climate will not save us." Listed here are the five issues he identified, and for each one I have cited steps being taken in Nashville.

"1. Such organizations must once again be willing to develop and implement large-scale, important projects that are risky and energizing."

Nashville is undertaking the building of Schermerhorn Symphony Center for the Nashville Symphony at a time when several orchestras in the nation are shutting down (Florida Philharmonic, Colorado Springs, Colorado [seventy-five years old], San Antonio, Texas, and Savannah, Georgia, orchestras). As noted earlier, the commitment to the project is strong throughout the city.

"2. If arts organizations, large and small, are going to take risks on meaningful projects and maximize their impact, they need entrepreneurial management better suited to the current climate in which they operate."

Two initiatives by Nashville universities address this need: Belmont's Mike Curb School of Music Business and Vanderbilt's Curb Center for Art, Enterprise and Public Policy.

"3. As we train arts managers, we must actively focus on the needs of all kinds of arts organizations."

In 2002 the city's nonprofit professional theaters established the Nashville Professional Theatre Consortium to explore ways to work together, strengthen their presence, and lay a firm foundation for the future of theater in Nashville. The consortium has prepared a position paper with action points, some of which deal with creativity, educational outreach, and variety of programming. The study revealed that attendance figures are better than the national average. Ben Cameron, executive director of Theatre Communications Group in New York City, is consulting with the consortium, and he said, "Nashville theatres stand at the brink of a wonderful chapter. . . . There's a sense of dynamic energy. It's a moment of growth and excitement—growth that will not only serve the artists and the arts groups, but that will serve Nashville as well, making it a vibrant center of creativity for generations to come."

"4. The need for diversity in performers and performing institutions is equally strong with respect to audiences."

Public and private schools are doing a better job of training students in the performing arts. All of the arts organizations have educational outreach programs, and the tickets for H.O.T. programs at TPAC are provided at low or no cost and the youngsters see live, *professional*

performances. The Symphony at the soon-to-be-constructed Schermerhorn Symphony Center has promised to bring in every student, every grade, every year in addition to continuing to send small ensembles to all the Metro schools. The city parks offer affordable programs in the performing arts: performances of music, theater, and dance that are regularly staged at the parks and other outdoor venues—many at no charge.

Ben Rechter pointed out, "We're going to have to identify younger people and newer people coming to town very quickly in terms of what their interests might be and try to nurture those interests. If they have any interest or inclination at all toward the arts, we are going to have to bring those people along." The various arts organizations are working on this.

"5. Finally, we must address the need to record the performances of merit that are mounted each day of the year."

Arts organizations within the city regularly produce performances of merit. The Symphony is recording with Naxos, Belmont and Fisk Universities collaborated on a new CD for the Fisk Jubilee Singers, and local public TV filmed the Symphony's pre–Carnegie Hall performance. Local public radio often presents broadcasts of local arts groups.

The leaders of city and state government—Mayor Purcell and the Metro Council, and Governor Bredesen and the state legislature—understand the need to support the performing arts. The Metropolitan Nashville Arts Commission extends grants and is a clearinghouse for information and assistance for performing arts groups. During Tennessee's budget crisis in 2003, the state proposed that the Tennessee Arts Commission (TAC) take a cut in its budget of almost 25 percent. (Tennessee was not alone in experiencing a financial crisis, and states such as Arizona and Missouri seriously considered eliminating their arts commissions completely.) Such a severe cut would have affected grants for H.O.T. and a matching grant from the National Endowment for the Arts. Governor Phil Bredesen spoke up on the TAC's behalf and reduced the proposed cut to 9 percent, a loss of about $400,000 instead of $1.3 million. (The 9 percent cut for the arts was the same as the cut for all state departments.)

Mark Wait, dean of Blair School of Music, stated, "There is a spirit within Nashville of support of the arts not only philanthropically—and that does exist certainly—but almost as a civic duty. For a city this size to have a professional ballet company, a thriving opera company, a symphony orchestra that is getting bigger and better practically by the day, plus several institutions of higher education, is simply astonishing. There does seem to be an element of civic pride that fuels that. I have found it very, very impressive from the beginning [of my tenure at Vanderbilt]. There is a broad, grassroots support of the arts here."

While Apollo, the god of art and music, has indeed struggled to become a sustainable part of the Nashville community, this odyssey has not been in vain in the Athens of the South.

APPENDIX A:
PERFORMING ARTS TIMELINE FOR NASHVILLE

1779   James Robertson leads settlers to the future site of Nashville.

1780   John Donelson arrives with a second group of settlers, many of whom are women and children, following an adventurous river voyage.

The Cumberland Compact sets forth rights of settlers.

1783   The Revolutionary War ends.

The North Carolina legislature creates Davidson County.

1784   The North Carolina legislature passes an act to establish the town of Nashville (named for General Francis Nash).

1785   The North Carolina legislature passes "An Act for the Promotion of Learning in Davidson County," and the Davidson Academy springs from that act.

1796   Tennessee, the sixteenth state, is admitted to the Union.

1806   Nashville is incorporated as a town.

1807   The first theatrical performances given in Nashville are the comedy *Child of Nature: or, Virtue Rewarded* and the farce *The Purse, or the Benevolent Tar*.

1812   War of 1812 begins.

1815   War of 1812 ends.

1816   The Nashville Female Academy is founded.

The Nashville Musical Society is established; it is a short-lived endeavor.

1817   A renovated salt house becomes the Market Street Theater.

1818   The first steamboat arrives in Nashville.

A group of amateur actors form the Dramatic Club of Nashville.

1819–20   Financial panic.

1820   A Frenchman living in Nashville, Mr. Terraas, builds a real theater, the Nashville Theatre.

1824   Music publishing begins in Nashville with the publication of *Western Harmony*, a book of hymns and instructions for singing.

1836   William Nash establishes the Nashville Academy of Music.

1837   Financial panic.

The Musical Fund Society of Nashville is formed.

1838   The earliest known piece of sheet music published in Nashville is C. F. Schultz's "Pas Redoublé," printed by G. H. Burrell.

1843	Nashville becomes the permanent capital of Tennessee.
1850	The first steam engine, ordered by the Nashville and Chattanooga Railroad, arrives in Nashville.
	The Adelphi Theatre opens. (It subsequently has the names of Nashville Theatre, the Gaiety, and the Grand Opera House.)
1851	Jenny Lind performs at the Adelphi Theatre.
1854	The first full production of an opera, *Lucia di Lammermoor,* is presented by Signor Luigi Arditi's Italian Opera Company.
1855	Nashville's first public school, Hume School, opens.
1857	Financial panic.
1859	The Tennessee State Capitol is completed at a cost that exceeded $800,000 (including furnishings; about $16 million today). Its architect, William Strickland, died before the building was finished.
1861	The Civil War begins.
1862	Federal troops occupy Nashville.
1865	The Civil War ends.
1866	Fisk opens, and it is chartered as Fisk University in 1867.
1871	The Jubilee Singers begin a series of tours to raise money for the struggling Fisk University.
1873	Financial panic.
	Vanderbilt University is founded.
	Anton Rubinstein holds two concerts.
1880	Nashville celebrates the centennial year of its founding.
1881	Sarah Bernhardt appears at the Masonic Theater.
1887	Emma Abbott and her opera company open the Vendome Theatre.
1892	The Union Gospel Tabernacle (now the Ryman Auditorium) is completed.
1893	August Schemmel founds the Nashville Conservatory of Music.
	Financial panic.
1895	The first opera in German presented in Nashville is *Tannhäuser.*
1897	The Tennessee Centennial Exposition opens, and a full-scale replica of the Parthenon houses the art exhibits.
1898	The Spanish-American War begins; the gunboat *Nashville,* with Knoxville native Washburn Maynard commanding, fires the first shot of the war.
1901	The Metropolitan Opera Company performs *Carmen* and *Barber of Seville* at the Union Gospel Tabernacle.
1902	The Nashville Association of Musicians, Local 257 of the American Federation of Musicians (AFM) of the United States and Canada, is founded.

1904   Adelina Patti holds a farewell concert.

Professor J. Hough Guest directs the initial concert of the Nashville Symphony.

1905   The Metropolitan Opera Company performs Wagner's *Parsifal* at the Vendome Theatre.

1906   Sarah Bernhardt appears at the Ryman Auditorium.

1909   Peabody Normal College becomes George Peabody College for Teachers.

1912   Tennessee Agricultural and Industrial State Normal School (which becomes Tennessee State University) opens.

1913   Citizens produce the Greek pageant *The Fire Regained* at the Parthenon.

1914   The National American Woman Suffrage Association meets in Nashville.

Anna Pavlova performs at the Ryman Auditorium.

1917   World War I begins.

1918   A Spanish flu epidemic strikes the nation.

1919   World War I ends.

The 18th Amendment of the U.S. Constitution is ratified and begins the era of Prohibition.

Enrico Caruso, Amelita Galli-Curci, and John McCormack perform operatic numbers at the Ryman Auditorium.

The Tennessee General Assembly passes a law permitting women to vote in municipal and presidential elections.

1920   Tennessee becomes the 36th and deciding state to vote for ratification of the 19th Amendment of the U.S. Constitution, granting suffrage to women.

The Nashville Symphony Society, Inc., is formed, and F. Arthur Henkel becomes conductor of the Nashville Symphony (1920–30).

1922   John H. DeWitt Jr. sets up the city's first radio station, WDAA, on the Ward-Belmont campus and broadcasts Caruso's recordings to the River and Rail Terminal.

1925   The Grand Ole Opry begins.

The War Memorial Building is constructed, and the Nashville Symphony plays there.

1927   Signor de Luca's Nashville Conservatory of Music is incorporated.

1929   The Chicago Civic Opera, starring Mary Garden, performs in Nashville for the first and only time.

The Great Depression begins.

1931   The Parthenon reopens in its permanent form.

Nashville's Junior League begins Nashville Children's Theatre.

1941   Leopold Stokowski conducts the All American Youth Orchestra at Sulphur Dell.

World War II begins.

1943   The Grand Ole Opry moves to the Ryman Auditorium.

1945	World War II ends.	1981	Blair School of Music merges with Vanderbilt University.
	Three WSM engineers open Castle Studio, the first recording studio, in the Tulane Hotel.		Nashville Opera (operating with the Nashville Symphony) presents *Madama Butterfly*.
1946	Walter Sharp leads the founding of the Nashville Symphony, William Strickland conducting.	1985	Tennessee Repertory Theatre is chartered and stages its first production.
1949	Circle Players is organized.	1986	The Nashville Ballet Society begins.
1951	Belmont College opens.		Tennessee celebrates its bicentennial.
1962	Public radio WPLN-FM, licensed to Nashville's Metro Government as part of the public library system, begins to broadcast.	1997	Nashville Opera merges with Tennessee Opera Theatre and the Nashville Opera Guild to become the Nashville Opera Association.
	Public television WDCN-Channel 2 is licensed to the Metropolitan Board of Public Education.	1998	Naxos of America moves to Cool Springs, not far from Nashville.
1963	Metropolitan Government of Nashville and Davidson County with Beverly Briley as the first mayor swings into action.	1999	The Nashville Symphony is the first American orchestra to perform for the Naxos American Classic series by recording Howard Hanson's Symphony No. 1.
1964	Blair Academy of Music opens.	2000	The Nashville Symphony plays in Carnegie Hall.
1977	Blair Academy separates from Peabody College and becomes Blair School of Music.	2002	The Nashville Association of Musicians, Local 257, celebrates its 100th anniversary.
1978	Metropolitan Nashville Arts Commission begins but has no grant-making ability until fiscal year 1988–89.	2003	TPAC renovations include addition of elevators, windows, more lights, more rest rooms, a water feature, and an electronic marquee.
1979	Nashville begins to celebrate its bicentennial year.		
1980	The Tennessee Performing Arts Center (TPAC) opens.	2006	The Schermerhorn Symphony Center opens.

APPENDIX B:
PERFORMING ARTS ORGANIZATIONS

BOARD OF DIRECTORS OF THE LITTLE THEATRE GUILD, INC., 1927

Mrs. Inez Bassett Alder, Mrs. J. C. Bradford Jr., Mrs. Rogers Caldwell, Mrs. Leslie Cheek, Mrs. J. Y. Crawford Sr., Miss Anne DeMoville, Miss Evalyn Douglas, Mrs. Byrd Douglas Jr., Miss Lucy Gage, Mrs. W. D. Haggard, Mrs. J. A. Hawkinson, Mrs. Morton B. Howell III, Mrs. Granberry Jackson, Mrs. J. B. Joseph, Miss Cornelia Keeble, Rumsey Lewis, Mrs. Benton McMillin, Charles Mitchell, Mrs. Ed Potter Jr., Mrs. John Reeves, Mrs. Canby Robinson, Miss Theo Scruggs, Mrs. E. B. Stahlman, and W. H. Wharton.

FISK JUBILEE SINGERS, 2002–3

Paul Kwami, *director.* The singers' names, hometowns, and majors are Darcie Chism, Memphis, TN, psychology; Brandon Colvin, Montgomery, AL, undecided; Demetrius Delancy, New Providence, Bahamas, music; Sarah-Vaughn Dottin, Orlando, FL, music education; Jermaine Dunn, Sandersvillle, GA, political science; Joslyn Keel, Denver, CO, music; Jeremy Kelsey, Gallatin, TN, business; Morio Konchellah, Belle Glade, FL, music; Olivia Mack, Houston, TX, music; Darwin Mason Jr., Hendersonville, TN, music; Donald Shipman, Birmingham, AL, business/finance; Brandon Singleton, Nashville, TN, music; Akua Taylor, Milwaukee, WI, drama/music; Kyle Twaites, Seattle, WA, psychology/music; Jantina Virgil, Macon, GA, music; and Stephanie Wise, Lima, OH, music.

METRO NASHVILLE ARTS COMMISSION LISTING FOR PERFORMING ARTS GROUPS, SPRING 2003

ACT I (Artists' Cooperative Theater 1, Inc.), Actors Bridge Ensemble, American Negro Playwright Theatre, Arts in the Airport Foundation, Belmont University Little Theatre, Belmont University School of Music, Blair School of Music, BroadAxe Theatre, Inc., Cheekwood Botanical Garden and Museum of Art, Circle Players, Community Concerts/GCPC, Darkhorse Theater, David Lipscomb University Music Department, David Lipscomb University Theater, Dramaturgy Project, Epiphany Dance Company, Friends of Music, Lakewood Theater Company, LifeWork Productions, Metro Nashville Chorus, Metropolitan Board of Parks and Recreation, Mockingbird Public Theatre, Music City Blues Society, Music City Chorus, Nashville Ballet, Nashville Chamber Orchestra, Nashville Children's Theatre, Nashville Country Dancers, Nashville Jazz Orchestra, Nashville Old Time String Band Association, Nashville Opera Association, Nashville Pro-Musica, Nashville Public Theatre, Nashville Shakespeare Festival, Nashville Symphony, Nashville Theatre Works, Native American Indian Association of Tennessee, One Hand Clapping Comedy Improv Troupe, Parthenon, People's Branch Theatre, RUBY GREEN, Sarratt Performing Arts, Scarritt-Bennett Center, Scattin' in the Schools, Shalom Theater, Tennessee Performing Arts Center (TPAC), Tennessee Players, Inc., Tennessee Repertory Theatre, TSU—Aristocrat of Bands, TSU—Meistersingers and Choir, TSU—Showstoppers, TSU—Theater Groups, TuneTown Show Chorus, Vanderbilt Dance Group, Vanderbilt University Office of Cultural Enrichment, Village Cultural Arts Center, Inc., and VSA arts Tennessee.

NASHVILLE SYMPHONY, 1921–22

F. Arthur Henkel, *conductor. First violins:* William E. von Otto, Mrs. N. G. Erwin, Mrs. I. Milton Cook, Mrs. A. B. Anderson, Miss Lucie Van Valkenburg, Mrs. Weaver Harris, Miss Elizabeth Johnson, Mrs. I. B. Dilzer, A. Petrucelli, L. F. Coleman, and C. Roland Flick. *Second violins:* Jesse Martin, William Keshner, Miss M. E. King, Miss Gertrude Nenon, Miss Jennie Schwartz, Miss Margaret Strobel, Mrs. J. A. Wands, Nick Melfi, John Rook, Perkins Sexton, and William Cailluoette. *Violas:* Browne Martin, Miss Sara Hitchcock, M. R. Sansom, F. J. Virgeant, and Fritz Hahn. *Cellos:* Orin H. Gaston, Pierre Briquet, and Charles F. Davis. *Bass viols:* G. B. Gaston, George W. Cooper, and John C. Krech. *Oboes:* Oscar Henkel and John Parmelee. *Flutes:* J. J. Scull, James Hudson, and A. Maurice Loveman. *Clarinets:* G. L. Valdes and Will A. Hudson. *Bassoon:* R. T. Payne. *Trumpets:*

George Pullen Jackson, James J. Cady, R. Kilvington, and J. Q. Owsley Jr. *Horns:* W. D. Scott, J. Simmonds, and T. A. Gabriel. *Trombones:* Syd A. Groom, Thomas Carter, and F. E. White. *Tuba:* Ben H. Gray. *Timpani:* S. C. Willis. *Drums:* O. S. Bomar and G. E. Trowbridge.

NASHVILLE SYMPHONY, 1946–47

William Strickland, *musical director. Violins:* Harold Johnson, Ovid Collins Jr., Arvo Aho, Mary Laura Cannon, Martha Carroll, Harry Draper, O. D. Hawn, Lillian V. Hunt, Malinda Jones, Dorothy Lassiter, E. B. McDowell, Louis Mertens, James Punaro, Kenneth Rose, Edwin Stover, Edward Tarpley, Wilda Tinsley, and Jo Lennon Williams. *Violas:* Andrew Ponder, Cyrus Daniel, C. L. Gorton, Browne Martin, Henri Minsky, and Emily Schoettle. *Cellos:* Oscar Eiler, Martha Blackman, Mary Louise Hager, Vivienne Olson, Barbara Gatwood Thompson, and Virginia Wolf. *Basses:* Samuel Hollingsworth, Frank Ray, and Dan E. Rice. *Flutes:* Edwin Stein and Patricia Teter. *Oboes:* Shirley Medcalf and Carl Genovese. *Clarinets:* C. B. Hunt Jr. and Elmer Jones. *Bass clarinet:* Jack Gregory. *Bassoons:* Grace Schneck and James Pritchett. *Horns:* William De Turk, George Cooper Jr., James Lancaster, William Scott Sr., and Dudley Howe. *Trumpets:* Sammy Swor, Henry Cunningham, and Bill McElhiney. *Trombones:* Frank Cofield, Irene Beavers, and Beverly Le Croy. *Percussion:* Edward Cleino and Martha Anne Earhart. *Harp:* Frances Helen Parker.

NASHVILLE SYMPHONY, FALL 2003

Kenneth Schermerhorn, *music director and conductor;* Byung-Hyun Rhee, *associate conductor;* Emelyne Bingham, *assistant conductor;* and George L. Mabry, *chorus director. First violins:* Mary Kathryn Van Osdale, concertmaster, Gerald C. Greer, Erin Hall, Denise Baker, Deidre Fominaya Bacco, Isabel Bartles, Beverly Drukker, Alison Gooding, Anna Lisa Hoepfinger, Erin Long, John Maple, Kirsten Mitchell, Kristi Seehafer, and Paul Tobias. *Second violins:* Carolyn Bailey, Zeneba Bowers, Kenneth Barnd, Rebecca Cole, Joann Cruthirds, Rebecca Dorcy, Radu Georgescu, Benjamin Lloyd, Laura Ross, Lisa Thrall, and Jeremy Williams. *Violas:* Daniel Reinker, Shu-Zheng Yang, Judith Ablon, Mary Helen Law, Bruce Christensen, Christopher Farrell, Michelle Lackey, Rebecca O'Boyle,

Clare Yang, and Melinda Bootz. *Cellos:* Anthony LaMarchina, Julia Tanner, Stephen Drake, Bradley Mansell, Keith Nicholas, Lynn Marie Peithman, Michael Samis, Christopher Stenstrom, Matthew Walker, and Xiao-Fan Zhang. *Basses:* Gary Lawrence, Glenn Wanner, Jack Phelps, Elizabeth Stewart, Yuching Mark Huang, Ryan Kamm, and Joel Reist. *Flutes:* Erik Gratton, Ann Richards, and Norma Grobman Rogers. *Piccolo:* Norma Grobman Rogers. *Oboes:* Bobby Taylor, Ellen Menking, and Roger Wiesmeyer. *English horn:* Roger Wiesmeyer. *Clarinets:* Lee Carroll Levine, Cassandra Lee, and Daniel Lochrie. *E-flat clarinet:* Cassandra Lee. *Bass clarinet:* Daniel Lochrie. *Bassoons:* Cynthia Estill, Dawn Bradley Hartley, and Gil Perel. *Contra bassoon:* Gil Perel. *Horns:* Leslie Norton, Kathyrin Hagen, Joy Worland, Beth Beeson, and Radu V. Rusu. *Trumpets:* Patrick Kunkee, Jeffrey Bailey, and Gary Armstrong. *Trombones:* Lawrence L. Borden and Susan K. Smith. *Bass trombone:* Steven Brown. *Tuba:* Gilbert Long. *Timpani:* William G. Wiggins. *Percussion:* Samuel D. Bacco and Joseph Rasmussen. *Harp:* Licia Jaskunas. *Keyboard:* Charlene Harb. Address: 2000 Glen Echo Road, Suite 204, Nashville, TN 37215; www.nashvillesymphony.org.

NASHVILLE SYMPHONY GUILD PRESIDENTS

Grace Gardner (1952–54), Sally Parker (1954–56), Betty Gwinn (1956–57), Elizabeth Kirkpatrick (1957–58), Peggy Jones (1958–60), Susan White Perry (1960–62), Laura Knox (1962–64), Adele Hinton (1964–66), Julia Stifler (1966–68), Ellen Lawson (1968–70), Patricia McPherson (1970–72), Marion P. Couch (1972–74), Helen Rosenfeld (1974–75), Sally Levine (1975–76), Mary Enoch (1976–77), Anita Woodcock (1977–78), Toni Foglesong (1978–80), Carole Sergent (1980–81), Katherine Linebaugh (1981–82), Ann W. Thomason (1982–83), Jane Entrekin (1983–84), Eleanor L. Willis (1984–85), Ruth Sinquefield (1985–86), Delores Sorey (1986–87), Jeannie Hastings (1987–88), Cathey Fuqua (1988–89), Judith Humphreys (1989–90), Barbara Barton (1990–91), Linda Guthrie (1991–92), Pam Pfeffer (1992–93), Barbara Barton (1993–94), Joyce Redden (1994–96), Lee Anne Parham (1996–97), Ceil Chapman (1997–98), Lisa H. McDonald (1998–99), Marsha Blackburn (1999–2001), Rose Miller Grindstaff (2001–2), Caren Shaffer (2002–3), Kimberly Cooper (2003–4), and president-elect Penny Kiel (2004–5).

APPENDIX C:
SCHERMERHORN SYMPHONY CENTER

STEERING COMMITTEE

Denny Bottorff, chair; Martha Ingram, vice chair; Steve Turner, vice chair; Howard Stringer, cochair, Nashville Advisory Committee; Kevin Lavender, cochair, Nashville Advisory Committee. *Committee members:* John Bridges, Monroe Carell, Douglas Cruickshanks, Gregory Daily, Marty G. Dickens, Thomas Frist, Gordon Gee, Jeannie Hastings, Ellen Martin, Charles Martin, Beth Mooney, Richard Ragsdale, Carolynn Reid-Wallace, and Cal Turner.

BUILDING COMMITTEE

Steve Turner, chair. *Members:* Carolyn Bailey, Rick Bernhardt, Monroe Carrell Jr., Mike Dye, Martha Ingram, Ellen Martin, Gerald Nicely, Ken Roberts, Mark M. Schimmenti, Carolyn Baldwin Tucker, Bill Wiggins, and Tim Wipperman.

FACTS

Exterior: 301 x 274 feet; 180-foot colonnade facing Gateway Park; 4 main public entry points; 4 box office windows; 3 loading bays; platform space for 115 musicians and 140 choral members; seating for 1,900; 3 elevators and 1 freight elevator; education classroom; Green Room; Donor Room; Banquet Room. Total building square footage is 197,000: office space, 16,500; public amenities, 9,000; concert hall, 30,000 for performance space, and 19,000 for backstage /support; education classroom, 3,000; front of house, public space, 48,000; and back of house and circulation, 22,000. Design and Construction Team: *Architects:* David M. Schwarz /Architectural Services, design architect; Earl Swensson Associates, architect of record; Hastings Architecture Associates, consulting architect. *Acoustician:* Akustiks, Inc. *Theater planner:* Fisher Dachs Associates. *Organ builder:* Schoenstein & Co. *Owner's representative/project manager:* Mercedes Jones. *Construction manager:* American Constructors. *Cost consultant:* Donell Consultants, Inc. *Structural engineer:* KSi/Structural Engineers. *MPE engineer /information technology consultant:* I. C. Thomasson & Associates. *Lighting design:* Susan Brady Lighting Design, Inc. *Landscape architect:* Hawkins Partners, Inc. *Civil engineer:* Barge Waggoner Summer & Cannon. *Code consultant:* Code Consultants, Inc. *Local code consultant:* Doug MacKenzie-Teasley Design Services. *Food service design:* Inman Associates, Inc. *Graphics/signage:* Two Twelve Harakawa. *ADA consultant:* Evan Terry Associates, P.C. *Curtainwall consultant:* CDC. *Fire protection consultant:* Code Consultants, Inc. *Commissioning agent:* Smith Seckman Reid, Inc. *Geotechnical engineer:* GeoSciences Design Group, LLC. *Structural peer review engineer:* Structural Design Group, Inc.

Abbreviations

FRC: Francis Robinson Collection of Theatre, Music, and Dance, Special Collections, Vanderbilt University.

SC: Special Collections, Vanderbilt University.

THQ: *Tennessee Historical Quarterly.*

TSLA: Tennessee State Library andArchives.

The Nashville Room, Nashville Public Library, has an extensive collection of programs, photos, and more from Lula C. Naff's years at the Ryman Auditorium.

Preface: epigraph from H. W. Crew's *History of Nashville, Tenn.*, ed. J. Wooldridge (Nashville: Publishing House of the Methodist Episcopal Church, South, 1890).

The Tennessee Performing Arts Center: interviews with Victor Johnson, Alyne Massey, Annette Eskind, and John Bridges; Nashville Area Chamber of Commerce Directory, 1978–79; House Bill 1519, Senate Bill 1380 in Public Acts 1974, passed by the Eighty-eighth General Assembly, vol. 2; *Tennessean* reports; Federal Reserve: prime interest rate figures.

War Memorial Auditorium: *Tennessean*, Feb. 4, 1949; *Nashville This Week,* Jan. 1926, March 18, 1926; *Banner*, Feb. 7, 1926.

The Long-Awaited Municipal Auditorium: various *Banner* and *Tennessean* articles, FRC.

Early Aspirations: Address to Alumni Society of the University of Nashville, "Tennessee; and the Duty of Her Educated Sons," William H. Stephens of Memphis, June 15, 1871, 8–9, 15, SC; J. G. M. Ramsey, *The Annals of Tennessee to the End of the Eighteenth Century* (Philadelphia: Lippincott, Grambo, and Co., 1853), 197–202: John Donelson's journal; "Cumberland Compact," in *Tennessee Encyclopedia of History and Culture*, ed. Carroll Van West (Nashville: Tennessee Historical Society/Rutledge Hill Press, 1998); *History of Tennessee* (Nashville: Goodspeed Publishing, 1887), 415: Davidson Academy; Aug. 22, 1823, unidentified newspaper clipping, Hickman Vertical File, TSLA: Nashville improvements; Miss Jane Thomas, *Old Days in Nashville* (Nashville: Charles Elder, 196–[?]), 115: Belmont Domestic Academy; Kenneth Rose, "A Nashville Musical Decade, 1830–1840,"

THQ 2 (1943): 219, Female Academy; Marsha A. Mullin, chief curator/director of Museum Services, The Hermitage; WPA Project, *Tennessee: A Guide to the State* (New York: Viking Press, 1939): free African-Americans in Tennessee; *Nashville Whig*, April 9, May 1, 1816.

City on a Hill: W. W. Clayton, *History of Davidson, County, Tennessee* (Nashville: Charles Elder, 1971), 209.

The Early Temples of the Muses: E. C. Faircloth Sr., *Tennessean,* April 5, 1925; Ida Erckman Abernethy, *Tennessean,* July 11, 1926: Jane Placide and 1826 theater opening; Francis Robinson, "Theater's Great Visited Nashville in 130 Seasons of Successful Performances," *Banner*, April 12, 1936; Mr. Caldwell's Theatre, 182–, "Devil to Pay," broadside, TSLA; Noah Ludlow, *Dramatic Life As I Found It* (St. Louis: G. I. Jones, Co. 1880), 107, 113, 114 (italics Ludlow's about first season), 108, 115, 118, 167–70, 178, 201, 205, 206, 240, 256, 270, 291, 314, 377, Ludlow's quotes and salt house theater, other two theaters, Sam Houston anecdotes, Julia Drake; http://www.new deal.feri.org/guides/tnguide/ch17.htm: *Tennessee: A Guide to the State*, compiled and written by the Federal Writers' Project of the Work Projects Administration for the State of Tennessee: William Jones, number of plays from 1830 to 1839; Ida Clyde Clarke, *All About Nashville* (Nashville: Marshall & Bruce Co., 1912): 1820 thespians in theater; Henry McRaven, *Nashville: Athens of the South* (Chapel Hill, N.C.: Published for the Tennessee Book Co. by Scheer & Jervis, 1949), 65–66: 1830 theater; http://www.saengeramusements.com/theatres/nawlins/stcharle/stcharle.htm: Signor Mondelli and New Orleans theaters; Lewis Maiden Smith, *Highlights of the Nashville Theater, 1876–1890* (New York: Vantage Press, 1979): Ludlow and 1831 appearance; 1819 Acts of 13th General Assembly, 73–74, approved Nov. 26, 1819; M. Liston Lewis, "Caldwell Is Bright Name in Nashville Theater Annals," *Banner*, Oct. 15, 1930: banned cigar smoking; M. Liston Lewis, *Banner*, Oct. 22, 1933: Caldwell in multiple roles.

A New Orleans Connection: http://www.bestofneworleans.com/dispatch/2002-05-07/blake.html; Crew's *History of Nashville, Tenn.*, 302, 305, 311: travel between New Orleans and Nashville.

The Rutledges: Mary Bray Wheeler and Genon Hickerson Neblett, *Chosen Exile: The Life and Times of Septima Sexta Middleton Rutledge, American Cultural Pioneer* (Nashville: Rutledge Hill Press, 1980); interview with Mary Bray Wheeler.

The Piano: U.S. Census Bureau; Crew's *History of Nashville, Tenn.*, 215: on 1820; *Daily Republican Banner,* June 1838; Nashville City Directories; McRaven, *Nashville: Athens of the South,* 109: Maxwell House; *Nashville Union and American,* Jan. 11, 1872: McClure's ad for Steinways; Nashville Blue Book of 1896; Kay Beasley, "French Family's Music Plays a Century Later," *Banner,* Sept. 18, 1991; *Banner,* Nov. 1905, May 9, 1908; Baldwin Web site: www.baldwin piano.com/what/baldnews.html; interview with Robert B. Street, Claude P. Street Pianos; *Banner,* May 6, 1941: Steinway interview; U.S. sales figures: www.bluebookof pianos.com/uspiano.htm; www.cantos.org: numbers of pianos built.

Music in the Newspaper: Rose, "A Nashville Musical Decade, 1830–1840," 225; the statement about the first music printed in the newspaper is based on the best available knowledge.

Francis Joseph Campbell: Louis R. Harlan, ed., *Booker T. Washington Papers,* vol. 5, 1899–1900 (Urbana: University of Illinois Press, 1982), 149–50, letter dated July 5, 1899; historical marker in Franklin County, Tenn.; "Francis Joseph Campbell," in *Tennessee Encyclopedia of History and Culture*; Aletha M. Bonner, *Music and Musicians of Tennessee* (Nashville: Lellyett and Rogers, 1942), 6; Francis Sinclair, "Sir Francis Campbell, Noted Educator of Blind, Was Tennessean," *Tennessee Historical Magazine,* series 2, vol. 3, no. 3 (April 1935): 188.

Years of Promise: Rose, "A Nashville Musical Decade, 1830–1840," opening quote on 224, quote from Schultz on 226, quote from Rose about early sheet music on 230, anonymous person's description of Masonic Hall on 231; U.S. Census Bureau; Crew's *History of Nashville, Tenn.,* 245–46: prices of goods and number of grocery stores and taverns; *Nashville Republican and State Gazette,* Jan. 13, 1831: editorial; *National Banner and Nashville Whig,* June 12, 1837: "Nashville Academy of Music"; *National Banner and Nashville Whig,* June 16, 1837: Mrs. King's Academy; *Daily Republican Banner,* June 21, 1838: Nash and music education; W. Nash as arranger of music: www.lib.unc.edu; 1865 Nashville City Directory, 39: financial revulsion; *National Banner and Nashville Whig,* May 1, 1837: wording about credit by Hicks, Ewing; Houston *Morning Star,* October 1840: Heerbruger's concert in May 1840, Houston, Texas; *Appleton's Cyclopedia of American Biography,* 1887–89, and Horn Family Page: www.users.totalise.co.uk: Charles Edward Horn; *National*

Banner and Nashville Whig, April 15, 1837: Horn's visit; *Nashville Republican,* April 1837: Horn's soiree; *National Banner and Nashville Whig,* Aug. 2, 1837: Pucci's visit; Masonic Hall: historical marker on Church Street.

Henri C. Weber: Nashville City Directories; Bonner, *Music and Musicians of Tennessee,* 13; card file, TSLA.

Licensing Drama: *National Banner and Nashville Whig,* June 30, July 10, 17, Aug. 2, 1837; County Court Clerk, Davidson County, Tenn., Oct. 31, 1879.

Immigrants: epigraph from Alfred Leland Crabb, *Nashville: Personality of a City* (New York: Bobbs-Merrill, 1960), 29; "Emigration," *Nashville Republican,* Jan. 17, 1837: the anti-immigration position; article signed "Emigrant," *National Banner and Nashville Whig,* Jan. 23, 1837: pro-immigration position; "Emigration," signed W. H. H., *National Banner and Nashville Whig,* Jan. 23, 1837: pro-immigration and Irish and Scottish contributions; Anita Shaefer Goodstein, *Nashville, 1780–1860: From Frontier to City* (Gainesville: University of Florida Press, 1989), 131: percentage of foreign-born in 1850 and 1860; U.S. Census Bureau; Clyde L. Ball, "The Public Career of Colonel A. S. Colyar," *THQ* (June 1953): 112–16; Ridley Wills, "The Monteagle Sunday School Assembly," *THQ* (spring 1985): 3, 4: Colyar; William G. McLoughlin Jr., *Modern Revivalism: Charles Grandison Finney to Billy Graham* (New York: Ronald Press, 1959), 298: continental Sunday; 1890 City of Nashville Annual Reports: police report; 1905 City of Nashville Reports; *New York Times,* May 1, 1907, dispatch from London on April 30; "Schiff Would Turn the Jewish Tide: Says in Speech the Great Inrush to the Cities Should Be Diverted South," *New York Times,* May 27, 1907; Don Doyle on immigrants treated as slaves: e-mail; Steven A. Camarota and John Keeley, Center for Immigration Studies, "'The New Ellis Islands': Examining Non-Traditional Areas of Immigrant Settlement in the 1990s," Sept. 2001.

"Longing for Amusements": Ludlow, *Dramatic Life As I Found It,* 711: Julia Dean; Crabb, *Nashville: Personality of a City,* 211, 212; M. Liston Lewis, "Grand Theater, First Known as Adelphi, Opened in 1850," *Banner,* Nov. 19, 1933: cholera and musicians, Julia Dean, Eliza Logan, all in 1850; F. Garvin Davenport, *Cultural Life in Nashville: On the Eve of the Civil War* (Chapel Hill: University of North Carolina Press, 1941), chap. 5: "The Nashville Theater: Drama and Opera, 1850–1860," 117–44, for dates, performers, and performances; U.S. Census Bureau: population 1860; Robinson, *Banner,* April 12, 1936; *Nashville Republican Banner,* May 23, 1858: travel time by train to Washington; *Nashville Republican Banner,* Sept. 5, 1859: redecorated Gaiety.

Arias in the Air: Clayton, *History of Davidson County*, 209.

The Glory of the Adelphi: *Daily American*, July 2, 1850; act to establish Adelphi Theatre, Tennessee Acts 1849–1850, pp. 447–48; *Nashville Daily Union*, June 21, 1850; Linda Carter, "Chancery Court, the Adelphi, and Adolphus Heiman," *Nashville Historical Newsletter*, July–Aug. 1998; *Daily Evening Reporter*, Sept. 20, 1850.

Jenny Lind: Now Singing at the Adelphi: Ridley Wills II, unpublished manuscript, "Jenny Lind Takes Nashville By Storm!"; *Daily Nashville Union*, March 29, 30, 1851; Davenport, *Cultural Life in Nashville*, 1, 146; McRaven, *Nashville: Athens of the South*, 88; Lewis, *Banner*, Nov. 19, 1933; Peter G. Davis, *The American Opera Singer* (New York: Double-day, 1997); Charles Robert Crain, "Music Performance and Pedagogy in Nashville, Tennessee, 1818–1900" (thesis, George Peabody College, 1975); J. H. Ingraham, *Life and Experiences of a Southern Governess in the Sunny South* (New York: G. W. Carlton, 1880); http://www.jsonline.com/dd/destmid /mar01/mccacol11030801.asp, Milwaukee *Journal Sentinel*, online; *Penguin Biographical Dictionary of Women:* about her later life; Robinson, *Banner*, April 12, 1936: "Lind" piano.

Opera Firsts in Nashville: Louis Nicholas's notebooks, and Crain, "Music Performance and Pedagogy in Nashville," 100.

Camilla Urso: Crain, "Music Performance and Pedagogy in Nashville," 112: her mother working at Female Academy; Nashville City Directories; Marriage Record, 1856, Davidson County, p. 213, #2545, Metropolitan Nashville Archives; 1860 U.S. Census; *Nashville Daily Gazette*, May 4, 7, 1856; Kenneth Rose, "Pioneer Music in Nashville," 100–101, TSLA; *Notable American Women*, ed. Edward T. James, vol. 3 (Cambridge, Mass.: Belknap Press, 1971), 502–3; *Nashville American*, Dec. 13, 15, 1900; Doak Papers, "Nashville Amusements," 2, TSLA: Blondner memory; Kenneth Rose sheet music collection, TSLA; Randal W. McGavock, *Pen and Sword: The Life and Journals of Randal W. McGavock* (Nashville: Tennessee Historical Commission, 1957), 365.

Health at the Academy: Clayton, *History of Davidson County*, 268: 1860 profitability.

Drama in Real Life: interview with Ann Street; *Chat*, March 2, 1895: Kate Kirkman's remembrances; Jesse C. Burt, *Nashville: Its Life and Times* (Nashville: Tennessee Book Co., 1959), 60, 68; *Nashville Union and American*, Oct. 9, 12, Nov. 13, 1861, and *Nashville Patriot*, Oct. 15, 1861: Walter Keeble and Nashville Theatre; Claude Ahmed Arnold, "The Development of the Stage in Nashville, Tennessee, 1807–1870" (thesis, State University of Iowa, 1933), listed many theatrical events, which are summarized here; Walter Durham, *Reluctant Partners* (Nashville: Tennessee Historical Society, n.d.), esp. 147, 208, 232, 266–67, and *Nashville: The Occupied City* (Nashville: Tennessee Historical Society, 1985), 182—these sources are particularly useful because of the way they are broken down by date and because Durham captures the impact of the occupation on all elements of society; Richard N. Current, ed., *Encyclopedia of the Confederacy* (New York: Simon and Schuster, 1993), 337–39: Losses and Numbers section of Civil War for casualty figures and percentages: Union total casualties: 680,850; killed in action 67,000; William J. Cooper Jr. and Thomas E. Terrill, *The American South: A History* (New York: Knopf, 1990), 385: costs; Fedora Small Frank, *Beginnings on Market Street: Nashville and Her Jewry 1861–1901* (Nashville: Jewish Community of Nashville and Middle Tennessee, 1976), 70: Davidson County dollar losses in the war.

Pauline Cushman, Actress Turned Spy: Smithsonian Web site: http://www.civilwar.si.edu/leaders_cushman. html; Hartnett T. Kane, *Spies for the Blue and Gray* (Garden City, New York: Hanover House, 1954), 182–91; Arnold, "The Development of the Stage in Nashville, Tennessee, 1807–1870."

Adelina's Brother: "Hither and Yon: The Best of the Writings of Jill K. Garrett," Maury County, Tennessee Homecoming '86 Committee—no page numbers; "Historic Maury," *Maury County Historical Society Quarterly* 6 (1970): 79: Mrs. Margaret McLean Dale, Columbia Female Institute class of 1861, a speech delivered at the annual school banquet, May 30, 1930; Richmond *Dispatch*, March 19, 1893: "Dixie"; Rose Music Collection, "'Twas But a Dream," TSLA.

"Pure, Elevated Drama": *Republican Banner*, Oct. 13, 14, 15, 1867: *Black Crook*; Polly Braswell, "From Fifties to Early Part of This Century Stage Here Drew Famous Players," *Tennessean*, March 24, 1935: New Nashville as skating rink.

Fisk University and the Performing Arts: Special Collections, Fisk University Library; *Fisk University News*, 1871–1911, vol. 2, no. 5; *Fisk News*, Nov.–Dec. 1933; *Banner*, April 28, May 3, 1966: Fisk Centennial Arts Festival; interviews with Dr. Carolynn Reid-Wallace, Dr. Lucius Outlaw, Joyce Searcy, Dr. Jessie Carney Smith, and Matthew Kennedy; *Tennessean*, cited in "Professor Work Called to Presidency of Roger Williams University," *Fisk University News*, Oct. 1923, 8: "civic asset"; Andrew Ward, *Dark Midnight When I Rise: The Story of the Fisk Jubilee Singers* (New York: Farrar, Straus and Giroux, 2000), 83 (1867 concert pieces), 155 and 157 (reviews); *Fisk University News*, Oct. 1911: Ella Sheppard on slave songs; *The Story of Music at Fisk*

University, Special Collections, Fisk University Library; *Nashville Globe*, May 16, 1913; *Tennessean*, May 13, 1913: "Jubilee Concert a Notable Event"; Ralph Ellison, "Going to the Territory," in *Going to the Territory* (New York: Vintage Books, 1987), 139–41; various programs of the Singers, Special Collections, Fisk University Library.

Two Noteworthy Programs: programs, Special Collections, Fisk University Library.

Herr Rubinstein: *Republican Banner*, Feb. 14, 1873.

A German Peace Festival: *Nashville Union and American*, March 9, 10, 1871.

Going for the Gold: *Daily American*, Oct. 5, 1885.

Emma Abbbott and the Reverend: Smith, *Highlights of the Nashville Theater, 1876–1890*; Sadie E. Martin, *The Life and Professional Career of Emma Abbott* (Minneapolis: L. Kimball Printing Co., 1891), 71, 73; *Daily American*, Oct. 4, 1887; "Nashville's Old Vendome Flourished in Golden Age," *Banner*, June 22, 1930; William Waller, *Nashville in the 1890s* (Nashville: Vanderbilt University Press, 1970), 17: Malone's story.

There's No Place Like Home: James M. Trotter, *Music and Some Highly Musical People* (Boston: Lee and Shepherd, 1878); the book focuses on African-Americans.

"Shall We All Go to the Theater?": sermon, 48-page booklet, published in 1888 by Cumberland Presbyterian Publishing House; Robinson, *Banner*, April 12, 1936; W. C. Cherry, "Can Any Good Come Out of Nazareth?" *Vanderbilt Observer*, Feb. 1888, 5–13: a pro-theater position; "The By-Laws," *Vanderbilt Observer*, Feb. 1888, 15–17; Edwin Mims, *History of Vanderbilt University* (Nashville: Vanderbilt University Press, 1946), 126–28: Vendome attendance and Minutes of Board meeting; U.S. Census Bureau; "Faith and Values," *Tennessean*, Sept. 21, 2002: denominational totals in Davidson County.

"A Blow to Patriotism": *Chat*, Dec. 9, 1894, 9–10.

The Prodigy and the Diva: Blind Tom and Black Patti: to view sheet music of the "Battle of Manassas," go to http://scriptorium.lib.duke.edu/sheetmusic; *Nashville Patriot*, Oct. 10, 1861: Tom performing at Masonic; Barbara Schmidt, "Archangels Unaware: The Story of Thomas Bethune Also Known as Thomas Wiggins Also Known as 'Blind Tom,'" http://twainquotes.com/archangels.html; *Chat*, May 11, 1895; *Daily American*, July 21, 1891; *Nashville Globe*, July 10, 1908; Geneva Handy Southall, *Blind Tom, The Black Pianist-Composer: Continually Enslaved* (Lanham, Md.: Scarecrow Press, 1999), 1, 2, 98; Rosalyn M. Story, *And So I Sing: African-American Divas of Opera and Concert* (New York: Warner Books, 1990), 3, 7; *Banner*, March 29, 1893; http://www.afrovoices.com/burleigh.html; *Chat*, Jan. 14, 1895.

Ryman Auditorium: http://www.ryman.com: for chronology of events; "Ryman Auditorium," in *Tennessee Encyclopedia of History and Culture*.

Professor Schemmel and His Conservatory: "Nashville Conservatory of Music," *Chat*, March 2, 1895, 11; charter, Jan. 4, 1893, registered Jan. 7, and another charter, Sept. 1895 for Schemmel's conservatory, Metropolitan Nashville Archives; Crain, "Music Performance and Pedagogy in Nashville," 184–185, 247, 254; University of Nashville records, microfilm, Nashville Room: conservatory becoming part of university; Waller, *Nashville in the 1890s*, 35; Nashville City Directories; Charter of Tennessee Academy of Music, Metropolitan Nashville Archives; Alumni Directory of Peabody College, 1877–1909; John Lawrence Connelly, ed., *North Nashville and Germantown* (Nashville: North High Association, 1982), 17, 34: Franz Strahm and Germantown connection; Western Kentucky Library, Archives: latter years of Strahm; *Banner*, Nov. 24, 1909: Nashville Chorus and Florence Hinkle; McRaven, *Nashville: Athens of the South*, 173–74: Victor Herbert composing *Fortune Teller*; charter, Jan. 3, 1902, Schubert's conservatory, Metropolitan Nashville Archives; Handbook of Texas online: www.tsha.utexas.edu/handbook/online: August Schemmel as teacher of Lota May Spell, San Antonio, Texas, and Bristol, Virginia, connections; Xaver Scharwenka, *Klänge ans meinem Leben* (Leipzig: Koehler Verlag, 1922), 113–14, thanks to the assistance of Prof. Evelinde Trenkner in Germany; e-mail from Prof. Edward Eanes on Ferrata.

Monteagle: Wills, "The Monteagle Sunday School Assembly—A Brief Account of Its Origin and History," 3–26; Web site for Schumann-Heink http://www.sandiego history.org/bio/heink/heink.htm.

Music in Nashville: *Chat*, March 2, 1895.

The Tennessee Centennial and International Exposition: Douglas Anderson, "The Centennial Idea and the Centennial 'Dream,'" *Tennessee Historical Magazine*, series 2, vol. 3, no. 2 (Jan. 1935): 107–10, on Anderson and beginning of celebration, and on Tully Brown; Special Collections, Fisk University Library; Web site of Tulip Street United Methodist Church: http://www.lookupclear.org; Centennial bells; interview with Mayor Bill Purcell; "Tennessee Centennial Exposition," in *Tennessee Encyclopedia of History and Culture*; *Tennessee Blue Book*, 1995–96, 392: quote of Governor Taylor; Richard A. Couto, "Race Relations and Tennessee Centennials," *THQ* (summer 1996): 146–56; Bobby L. Lovett, *The African-American History of Nashville, Tennessee, 1780–1930* (Fayetteville: University of Arkansas Press, 1999), 235–37; Alyce K. Holden, "Secular Music in Nashville, 1800–1900" (thesis, Fisk University, 1940): musical events; *Banner*,

May 1, 18, 1897: events of Centennial; Waller, *Nashville in the 1890s*, 170, Charles S. Mitchell recalled Fred Thompson and Edward McDowell; Herman Justi, ed., *Official History of the Tennessee Centennial Exposition* (Nashville: Brandon Printing Co., 1898); Charlotte A. Williams, comp., *The Centennial Club of Nashville: A History from 1905–77* (Nashville: privately printed by the Centennial Club, 1978), 3; WPA, *Tennessee: A Guide to the State*, 185: funds for Centennial; Louise Littleton Davis, *Nashville Tales* (Gretna, La.: Pelican, 1981), 154, 170: profitability figures on Exposition; Robert E. Corlew, *Tennessee: A Short History*, 2d ed. (Knoxville: University of Tennessee Press, 1981), 411–13; *Banner*, June 14, 1898: amount disbursed, music and entertainment amounts.

Nashville's Centennial: McRaven, *Nashville: Athens of the South*, 136: lights; Crain, "Music Performance and Pedagogy in Nashville": theater information; various newspaper accounts; Clayton, *History of Davidson County*, 348–49.

Tennessee's Bicentennial Celebration: http://www.comptroller.state.tn.us/sa/reports/pa 96068.pdf; Sept. 1996 state audit.

Organized Women: Carole Stanford Bucy, "'The Thrill of History Making': Suffrage Memories of Abby Crawford Milton," *THQ* (fall 1996): 230; Anastatia Sims, "'Powers that Pray' and 'Powers that Prey': Tennessee and the Fight for Woman Suffrage," *THQ* (winter 1991): 206; "Horrid Plot of Suffragettes" (AP report out of London), *Tennessean*, May 13, 1913; Louise Grundy Lindsley letter to Alfred Leland Crabb, *Seven Women of Nashville* (Nashville Room, Nashville Public Library, 1974), 66; Fannie E. S. Heck, *In Royal Service: The Mission Work of Southern Baptist Women* (Richmond: Foreign Mission Board of the Southern Baptist Convention, 1913), 142; John A. Simpson, *Edith D. Pope and Her Nashville Friends* (Knoxville: University of Tennessee Press, 2003), 83, 134–35; Cora Sutton Castle, "A Statistical Study of Eminent Women," *Archives of Psychology* 4, no. 27 (Aug. 1913); *Tennessean*, April 27, 1919: Southern Baptists; http://www.fbcmb.com/Missions/lottie_moon.htm; Hickman Vertical File, TSLA.

The Home of the Philharmonic Society: *Nashville American*, Oct. 4, 6, 1899.

Musical Appetite at the Turn of the Century: *Nashville American*, Dec. 31, 1899.

The Trouble with the Diva: William Waller, *Nashville, 1900–1910* (Nashville: Vanderbilt University Press, 1972), 61–63; Ada Scott Rice, writing in the *Daily American*, Oct. 24, 25, 1901; Jerry Henderson, "History of the Ryman Auditorium in Nashville, Tennessee: 1892–1920" (Ph.D. diss., LSU, 1962), 133–34: details of debt situation and role of Stahlman et al.; *Banner*, Oct. 23, 1901: interview with Sembrich; "Calve Too Ill to Sing This Evening," *Banner*,

Oct. 23, 1901: legal plight and doctors' certificate; *Nashville American*, Oct. 25, 1901: quoting *Louisville Times*; *Nashville American*, Oct. 26, 1901: railroad and dog, and proceeds from the event in Nashville; *Banner*, Jan. 14, 1908: review of Calvé's appearance.

A Union for Musicians: interview with Harold Bradley; articles by Walt Trott in *The Nashville Musician* for the Centennial Anniversary; program *The Music of Music City*, Oct. 7, 2002; *Nashville This Week*, Jan. 4–11, 1926: WSM programming.

Outdoor Splendor: historical marker for Glendale Park; *Chat*, June 2, 16, 1894: summer opera at Glendale; Craig Allan Kaplowitz, "A Breath of Fresh Air: Segregation, Parks, and Progressivism in Nashville, Tennessee, 1900–1920," *THQ* (fall 1998): 136 on General Assembly act, 134 on Hadley Park; Connelly, *North Nashville and Germantown*, 129–30: city parks in 1915; *Nashville American*, July 4, 1903: Glendale and Orpheus Opera; Leland R. Johnson, *The Parks of Nashville: A History of the Board of Parks and Recreation* (Nashville: Metro Nashville and Davidson County Board of Parks and Recreation, 1986), 56 on Orpheus Opera, 87 on 1904–11 band at parks, 146 on Don Q. Pullen; *Daily American*, April 17, 1890: *Pinafore*; Metro Parks Web site: http://www.nashville.gov/parks/; statistics on parks; "More Theatres on Wells Circuit," *Banner*, Nov. 3, 1905: Jake Wells; *Nashville Globe*, July 31, 1908: Greenwood Park; Hadley Park historical marker; W. O. Smith, *Sideman: The Long Gig of W. O. Smith* (Nashville: Rutledge Hill Press, 1991), 205: Don Q. Pullen; *Banner*, Oct. 15, 1908, June 14, 1941; http://www.classicalnotes.net/columns/youthweb.html: All American Youth Orchestra; Werner Zepernick, "Nashville Symphony Opens Summer Park Season," *Banner*, May 31, 1976: Kay George Roberts; interview with Wesley Paine, director of the Parthenon, on Theatre Parthenos; *Tennessean*, Dec. 31, 2001: John Seigenthaler and the parks.

Extravagant Entertainment: *Nashville Daily American*, Oct. 28, 29, Nov. 2, 1889: *Twelve Temptations*; *Banner*, Feb. 1, 9, 1904: *Ben Hur*; *Banner*, April 21, 1906: *Professor Napoleon*.

Shall I Book It?: letters from Mrs. Naff, a clipping ("Theater Critic Compliments Mrs. L. C. Naff") attached to letter, Aug. 28, 1939, but source unknown, FRC; Gossip column section, *Banner*, Jan. 11, 1939: comments attributed to Katharine Cornell about Mrs. Naff; "Localights of Broadway," *Banner*, Oct. 1, 1941; Brock Pemberton, *New York Times*

Magazine, Aug. 20, 1939: comeback of the Road in American theater; *Tennessean,* Feb. 17, 1929: list of patronesses for Opera Festival; *Tennessean,* Feb. 21, 22, 1929: *Thais,* festival details, and weather; Robinson, *Banner,* April 12, 1936: Dr. Jackson securing guarantors for *Thais;* Walter Sharp to Francis Robinson, Nov. 22, 1949: Mrs. Naff and Stokowski, FRC.

Miss Hayes: *Banner,* March 30, 31, 1938; FRC; *Tennessean,* March 31, 1938, Oct. 31, 1944; interview with Dr. Edward Tarpley.

Madame Bernhardt: *Daily American,* Feb. 17, 18, 1881; *Banner,* March 6, 7, 8, 9, 1906.

Greater Nashville As a Musical Center: *Nashville Globe,* Sept. 4, 1908.

Sacred Drama at Spruce Street Baptist Church: *Nashville Globe,* Sept. 4, 11, 18, 1908.

"Greatest Musical Treat Ever Presented to Nashville": *Tennessean,* May 2, 4, 6, 7, 1913; May 8, 1914; Louise Davis, "Glory That Was Greece," *Tennessean Magazine,* July 6, 1952; Nashville Room program ephemera; *Banner,* April 20, 1914: staging by Emery; Johnson, *The Parks of Nashville,* 88: location of amphitheater.

Sidney, the Playwright: *Tennessean,* May 4, 1913; Lark Taylor, *With Hey Ho,* 244, SC.

Professor Washburn: Robinson, *Banner,* April 12, 1936; Waller, *Nashville, 1900–1910,* 189.

The Bozart: H. L. Mencken, "The Sahara of the Bozart," in *A Mencken Chrestomathy* (New York: Vintage Books, 1982), quotes from 184, 185, 194.

A Stellar Year for Opera, 1919: Robinson, *Banner,* April 12, 1936: Mrs. Naff guaranteeing McCormack and Galli-Curci's fears; "Creatore Wins Great Ovation in Grand Opera," *Tennessean,* Feb. 19, 1919; "Caruso Charms Vast Audience," *Banner,* April 30, 1919, report of Caruso's performance on April 29; "Caruso Here for Concert Tonight," *Tennessean,* April 29, 1919: prices of tickets and proceeds from Atlanta; "Caruso to Be Here Socially, Too," *Tennessean,* Feb. 23, 1919; "Packed House Will Hear Galli-Curci," *Tennessean,* April 30, 1919; *Banner,* April 20, 1919: Galli-Curci and the perfume imagery; "Famous Tenor Who Will Sing in Nashville Soon," *Tennessean and the Nashville American,* Oct. 26, 1919: McCormack; "John McCormack and Assisting Artists Give Nashvillians Pleasurable Evening," *Banner,* Nov. 25, 1919: details of McCormack's concert; William U. Eiland, *Nashville's Mother Church* (Nashville: Opryland USA, 1992), 36: mortgage rumor for Naff.

Seeking an Orchestra: *National Banner and Nashville Whig,* June 14, 1830: Mme Feron; Robinson, *Banner,* April 12, 1936: opera, Guests and Vendome orchestra;

Banner, April 28, 30, 1935: Sonja Yergin and 1935 NSO appearance; Rose, "A Nashville Musical Decade, 1830–1840," 223: Pearmans; Crain, "Music Performance and Pedagogy in Nashville," 36: Pearmans; *Daily American,* Jan. 12, 1888, Sept. 19, 20, 1890, Oct. 16, 1891; obituary of F. Arthur Henkel, July 8, 1958; interviews with Louis Nicholas and Dr. Edward Tarpley; George Pullen Jackson: biographical information, SC; *Banner,* Nov. 18, 19, 1904; J. C. Phillips, ed., *Who's Who in Music: A Directory of Nashville Musicians* (Nashville, Oct. 1921): officers and board of first NSO; McRaven, *Nashville: Athens of the South,* 228: first program for 1920–21 season; *Tennessean,* Feb. 28, 1926: Enrico Leide conducting.

Music Teachers, 1921: Phillips, *Who's Who in Music: A Directory of Nashville Musicians;* Robinson, *Banner,* April 12, 1936: Mrs. Blondner; Bonner, *Music and Musicians of Tennessee;* interview with Louis Nicholas.

Beethoven Week: undated articles by George Pullen Jackson, FRC.

"What Is It Worth to You, Mr. Business Man?": George Pullen Jackson, "What Is It Worth to You, Mr. Business Man?" *Nashville Review,* Oct. 15, 1921.

The Metropolitan Opera Company and the Russian Grand Opera Company: www.historicopera. com: banning of Hertz and Burgstaller from Bayreuth; *Banner,* April 29, 1905: ad for *Parsifal* at the Vendome cited prices; *Banner,* May 1, 1905; interview with Kenneth Schermerhorn; Alvin Wiggers, "Forty Years of Grand Opera in Nashville," *Tennessean,* Dec. 16, 1934: Tony Sudekum at Orpheum when the Russian troupe visited; "Russian Opera Company Open Engagement Monday," *Banner,* March 12, 1922; review of *Tsar's Bride* by George Pullen Jackson, *Banner,* March 15, 1922.

Another Performance of *Parsifal:* *Banner,* April 27, 1904.

The Sheik and Jimmy Stahlman: *Banner,* June, 13, 14, 22–25, 1923; J. G. Stahlman, letter to Roy Miles Jr., June 12, 1973, FRC.

Lark Taylor: quotes from Lark taken from *With Hey Ho* by John Lark Taylor, Feb. 7, 1944, and "My Season with John Barrymore in *Hamlet,*" SC; *Chat,* April 28, 1894, 9: Patti review of Nashville audience and editorial comments; *Tennessean,* Feb. 28, 1926: Little Theater; *Tennessean,* Oct. 28, 1926: *Captain Applejack; Nashville This Week,* Feb. 22–March 1, 1926; *The Metropolitan Opera Encyclopedia,* ed. David Hamilton (New York: Simon and Schuster, 1987), 214: details of Riccardo Martin; Bill Holder, "Memories of the Golden Age," *Tennessean Magazine,* Oct. 28, 1945, 7–8; *New York Times,* March 27, 1946: Lark Taylor obituary.

Somber Days: *Tennessean,* Oct. 25, 1931.

Jeter and Smith: letter from them, May 15, 1978, to Marshall Stewart, director of Public Library, giving collection to the Nashville Room; *Tennessean*, Feb. 25, 1983: rites for Louise Smith; *Tennessean*, March 1, 1985: death of Sarah Jeter; *Banner*, May 13, 1927, George Pullen Jackson review of *Cavalleria Rusticana*; catalogs, Jeter and Smith memorabilia, copy of letter from Francis Robinson to Hermes, May 12, 1938, Special Collections, Belmont University.

A Disdain of Dance: Crabb, *Nashville: Personality of a City*, 200; C. D. Elliott, "Nashville Female Academy—Dancing," October 16, 1857, broadside, TSLA; Fred Russell, "Dancing Athletes," *Banner*, 1937: Shawn.

Signor de Luca's Grand Expectations: Robert W. Ikard, "Signor de Luca and the Nashville Conservatory of Music," *THQ* (fall 2001): 176–94: specific details, names, and figures related to the conservatory; http://www.nashville.gov /mhc/markers1.htm: DeWitt and radio station; interview with Louis Nicholas; *Banner*, May 1927, and *Tennessean*, May 13, 1927: *Cavalleria* accounts; Phillips, *Who's Who in Music: A Directory of Nashville Musicians;* Robinson, *Banner*, April 12, 1936: teachers of the conservatory.

Students of Signor de Luca: http://www.angelfire. com/de3/viviandettbarn/radiodays.html: CDs now available; interview with Louis Nicholas; Ikard, "Signor de Luca and the Nashville Conservatory of Music"; Bonner, *Music and Musicians of Tennessee*; WPA Project, *Tennessee: A Guide to the State*: Melton; www.harrywarrenmusic.com /indimovies/melodyfortwo.html: *Melody for Two* movie and Melton; *Tennessean*, April 12, 1928: benefit concert for Stewart and Lewis; Naff to Robinson, May 9, 1941, Sept. 24, 1945, FRC: Melton; *Banner*, May 7, 1941; University of North Carolina Archives: history of Cordon; Robert W. Ikard, *Near You: Francis Craig, Dean of Southern Maestros* (Franklin, Tenn.: Hillsboro Press, 1991), 136–39.

St. Denis, Shawn, and Modern Dance: Russell, "Dancing Athletes," *Banner,* Feb. 1937; Jeter and Smith scrapbook, Nashville Room: St. Denis teaching at Nashville Conservatory; Eleanor Hall, *Banner*, Oct. 29, 1929; George Pullen Jackson, *Banner*, Oct. 30, 1929; Sydney Dalton, *Banner*, Feb. 11, 1937; Francis Robinson, *Banner,* March 19, 1938; Alvin Wiggers, *Tennessean,* Feb. 11, 1937.

A Matter of History: Howard W. Eskridge, "Forum of the People," *Banner,* April 18, 1914: reply to St. Denis.

John Wesley Work III: William Burres Garcia, "The Life and Choral Music of John Wesley Work (1901–1967)" (Ph.D. diss., University of Iowa, 1973); *Tennessean*, March 19, 1972: interview with Mrs. Work III; *Banner*, May 27, 1967: death of Work III; *Tennessean*, May 19, 1967: death of Work III; *Tennessean*, March 10, 1978, Sept. 13, 1986: Helen Work;

Community Foundation Web site: http://www.cfmt.org; scholarships through John W. Work III Foundation; "Fisk Praised for Promotion Given Prof. John W. Work," *Nashville Globe,* Sept. 1, 1951; interview with Matthew Kennedy; http://popmusic.mtsu.edu/research.html; http://memory.loc.gov.

Nashville Children's Theatre: Frances E. Daniel, "The History of the Nashville Children's Theatre, 1968– 1976" (thesis, LSU, 1979), 41: citing *Southern Theatre News* (spring 1959); Web site for Nashville Children's Theatre: http://www.net-dragonsite.org.

What Others Were Saying About Nashville: W. T. Couch, ed., *Culture in the South* (Chapel Hill: University of North Carolina Press, 1935): "The Fine Arts" by Ula Milner Gregory, 291, 292, 293, 298; "Bulwarks Against Change" by Josephine Pinckney, 44, 48; "Towns and Cities" by Edd Winfield Parks, 509–10.

Two Young Men and *Julius Caesar:* Louise Davis, "The Star Makers," *Tennessean Magazine*, Sept. 4, 1955: opening quotation and Nashville background on Coe; *Tennessean*, Aug. 16, 1939: stabbing of Caesar and play review; Margery Hollister Hargrove, "A History of the Community Theatre Movement in Nashville, Tennessee, 1926–1951" (thesis, Tennessee Tech, 1965), 53: Fred Coe; Louise Davis, "Big Man on the Set," *Tennessean Magazine*, Sept. 11, 1955: Delbert Mann interview; Internet database of Broadway shows.

Our Man at the Met: FRC; John Bridges, *Tennessean*, Feb. 20, 1982: performance of the Verdi *Requiem;* Francis Robinson, *Celebration: The Metropolitan Opera* (New York: Doubleday, 1979), 43, 258, 268; *Illustrated American*, Sept. 10, 1892: Metropolitan Opera-house Company; Mark Twain, "At the Shrine of St. Wagner," Bayreuth, Aug. 2, 1891; Ed Huddleston, *Banner*, Oct. 10, 1958: Robinson speech at Neely Auditorium.

Our Other Man at the Met: FRC; *Opera News,* Nov. 4, 1940; Louise Davis, "Music for the Firesides," *Tennessean Magazine*, Feb. 20, 1949; *Nashville Families and Homes* (Nashville Public Library, Nashville Room, 1983), Nashville History Lecture Series, 1979–81: "The Sloan Family," by John E. Sloan, March 10, 1980, 23; *New York Times*, May 21, 1955: Sloan obituary.

TSU's Track Record . . . in Dramatic Art: TSU Web site: http://www.tnstate.edu/library/digital/poagt.htm; Clara Hieronymus, "Poag's Ph.D. Pathway to Firsts," *Tennessee Magazine*, Dec. 9, 1973; *Tennessean*, Aug. 27, 1971: educator award.

Not Banned in Nashville: Naff to Robinson, Nov. 3, 25, 1939, Naff to James Stahlman, Nov. 1939, FRC; *Banner,*

Nov. 17, 1939: *Tobacco Road* ban; *Banner*, Nov. 22, 1939: court cleared way for *Tobacco Road*; *Banner*, Nov. 23, 1939: Cherry delayed action.

"Real Opera": Naff to Robinson, April 13, 1940, FRC; "Opera in Nashville," *Chat*, Jan. 19, 1895, 5.

Walter Sharp's "Creature": Walter Sharp to Robinson, Nov. 22, 1949, FRC; obituary for Walter Sharp, undated interview, Nashville Room personal files; *The Nashville Symphony Celebrates 50 Seasons, 1946–1996*; interviews with Albert Werthan, Ann Street, and Edward Tarpley; microfilm of NSO records, 1215, TSLA; Tennessee per capita income: Regional Economic Information System, Bureau of Economic Analysis; Davis, "Music for the Firesides"; *Tennessean*, Oct. 18, 1949: unusual works featured.

"Southern-Nourished Minds": Louise Davis, "Export Product," *Tennessean Magazine*, April 17, 1949, 24–25; *Selected Letters of John Crowe Ransom*, edited with an introduction by Thomas Daniel Young and George Core (Baton Rouge: LSU Press, 1985); Ransom Papers, clippings of Annie Phillips Ransom, 1929 program, TSLA; *Talking with Robert Penn Warren*, ed. Floyd C. Watkins, John T. Hiers, and Mary Louise Weaks (Athens: Univesity of Georgia Press, 1990): "The South: Distance and Change," Louis D. Rubin Jr., 272: refugee from the South; *Selected Letters of Robert Penn Warren*, vol. 2, ed. William Bedford Clark (Baton Rouge: LSU Press, 2001), 400–401; *You Can't Eat Magnolias*, ed. H. Brandt Ayers and Thomas H. Naylor, a publication of the L. Q. C. Lamar Society (New York: McGraw-Hill, 1972): "You Can't Eat Magnolias," by H. Brandt Ayers, 3–24; Donald Davidson to Allen Tate, Marshallville, Georgia, Oct. 29, 1932, in *The Literary Correspondence of Donald Davidson and Allen Tate*, ed. John Tyree Fain and Thomas Daniel Young (Athens: University of Georgia Press, 1974).

Music Making at Peabody: interviews with Harold Bradley, Louis Nicholas, Robert Bays, and Del Sawyer; Harry Eugene Williams, "Music at Peabody: A Personal and Factual History" (thesis, George Peabody College, 1979), 9, 37.

Singin' Billy and the Dolly Pond Church of the Living God with Signs Following: biographies of all three men, SC; Louise Davis, "He Clings to Enduring Values," *Tennessean Magazine*, Sept. 4, 1949: Donald Davidson's parents; Marshall Cox, *Tennessean*, Feb. 7, 1952, and Doug Fisher, *Banner*, Feb. 7, 1952: reviews of *Strangers in This World*; Sydney Dalton, *Banner,* April 24, 1952: *Singin' Billy*; Louis Nicholas, *Tennessean*, April 24, 1952: *Singin' Billy* premiere; *Tennessee Folklore Society Bulletin* 13, no. 2 (June 1947): 42, Bryan on WSM staff; interview with Robert Bays. The papers of Charles Faulkner Bryan,

including his music scores, are located at Tennessee Technological University.

Four Conductors: *The Nashville Symphony Celebrates 50 Seasons, 1946–1996*; interview with Louis Nicholas.

W. O. Smith: *Sideman*, 305, opening quote; 206, quote about quartet in a black college; 236, piano staff quote; 261, quote on black symphony musicians; interviews with Del Sawyer and Jonah Rabinowitz.

The Nashville Sound: interview with Kyle Young; *Encyclopedia of Country Music*, comp. Country Music Hall of Fame and Museum staff, ed. Paul Kingsbury (New York: Oxford University Press, 1998), 371–72: Bill Ivey's definition; Michael Streissguth, *Eddy Arnold: Pioneer of the Nashville Sound* (New York: Schirmer Books, 1997), 157; session sheets from Country Music Hall of Fame and Museum Archives.

An Opera Singer's Story: interview with Jerry Jennings; editorial in *Nashville City Paper*, May 6, 2003: Arts Coalition.

Public Radio and Television: Web sites for Nashville Public Radio, WPLN: www.wpln.org, and Nashville Public Television, WNPT: www.wnpt.org; interview with Ben Rechter; FCC governmental records; Paul C. Hancock, "A History of Music Education in Nashville and Davidson County Public Schools (1873–1975): Local Reflections of National Practices in Music Education" (Ph.D. diss., George Peabody College for Teachers, 1977), 203: educational TV in Nashville; *Cable TV Facts; Cable Television Developments;* Jeanne A. Naujeck, *Tennessean*, March 23, 2003: figures on WPLN listenership for 2003.

The Performing Arts and Metro Government: interviews with Mayor Bill Purcell, John Bridges, Keel Hunt, Jane Fabian, and Kelly Bainbridge; Article 18 of Miscellaneous Provisions, Charter of Metropolitan Government of Nashville and Davidson County, Tennessee: funding for the Symphony.

Blair School of Music: interviews with Del Sawyer, Mark Wait, Jane Kirchner, and Bobby Taylor; catalogs of Blair Academy and Blair School of Music; *Tennessean*, May 22, 1977.

Serendipity at Work: interviews with Jean Heard and Edgar Meyer; Blair School Web site; http://www.mac found.org/programs/fel/2002fellows/meyer_edgar.htm.

The Princely Players: interview with Odessa Settles; "History of the Princely Players," represented by Baylin Artists Management; program "On the Road to Glory."

In Her Father's Footsteps: interview with Odessa Settles.

TPAC: An Arts Catalyst: interviews with Steven Greil, Bennett Tarleton, and Jane Ann McCullough; TPAC brochures, records, and *Center Stage*.

Circle Players: Robinson, *Banner*, April 12, 1936; Hargove, "A History of the Community Theatre Movement in Nashville, Tennessee, 1926–1951"; *Tennessean*, Sept. 11, 1921, Feb. 3, 1962.

Tennessee Repertory Theatre: interviews with Mac Pirkle and David Grapes.

Nashville Opera: interviews with Dr. William Whetsell, John Bridges, and Carol Penterman; *Republican Banner*, May 24, 1854; Robinson, *Banner*, April 12, 1936; "Benefits Accruing from Grand Opera," *Tennessean*, Feb. 11, 1916.

Opera Singers with Nashville Connections: Rowena Rutherford Farrar, *Grace Moore and Her Many Worlds* (New York: Cornwall Books, 1982), 49, 51, 52, 117, 138, 165; *Tennessean*, Feb. 9, 1928, editorial page: Grace Moore; Alvin Wiggers, *Tennessean*, Oct. 21, 1945: review of Grace Moore; George Pullen Jackson, Southern Musician series in *Banner*, undated articles, SC: Mme Cahier, Kitty Cheatham; Wiggers, *Tennessean*, Dec. 16, 1934: Alice Nielsen; *Banner*, Sept. 12, 1958, April 11, 1961, Sept. 6, 1965, and *Tennessean*, Aug. 25, 1998: Sylvia Stahlman; *New York Times*, Dec. 19, 1905: Kitty Cheatham; Davis, *The American Opera Singer*, 285–86: Mme Cahier; Bonner, *Music and Musicians of Tennessee*, 6: Kitty Cheatham; unidentified newspaper article, Nashville Room, biographical file, Jan. 6, 1946: Kitty Cheatham obituary; *Tennessean*, Jan. 1, 1933.

Nashville Ballet: Wiggers, *Tennessean*, Dec. 12, 1934; *Tennessean*, March 13, 1914, Feb. 12, 1916, Nov. 21, 1996 (Albertine's obituary); interviews with Jane Fabian and Paul Vasterling; Naff to Robinson, March 14, 1950, FRC.

Modern Dance: *Tennessean*, May 14, 1961, *Tennessean* and *Banner*, June 24, 1966, *Banner*, May 20, 1969: Zibart; interviews with Andrew Krichels and Linda Mason.

The Maestro and the Maelstrom: interviews with Kenneth Schermerhorn, Denny Bottorff, Harold Bradley, and Bobby Taylor; Dow Jones information from Dow Jones Industrial Average Web site: http://www.djindexes.com.

The Heritage Symphony: program: *Tennessean* and *Nashville Banner* Classical Concert Series, NSO, Sept. 15, 16, 1989, basic information and Pursell's quotations; www.Belmont.edu: Pursell biography.

"Passion for the Music": interviews with Bennett Tarleton, Steven Greil, Alan Valentine, Kenneth Schermerhorn, Michael Buckland, and Bobby Taylor; *Program, Kenneth Schermerhorn: 20th Anniversary Tribute*, Jackson Hall, TPAC, March 28–29, 2003.

A World-Class Relationship: interview with Jim Sturgeon; SoundScan: CD sales in 2001; Naxos Press Release, Oct. 22, 2002: *West Side Story*; David Hurwitz, http://ClassicsToday.com, Aug. 2, 2000: Hanson review;

Rebecca Davis, manager of publicity and promotion for Naxos of America; Victor Carr Jr., review in http://Classics Today.com.

Passion for Educating Students: http://www.nashville symphony.org; Nashville Symphony records and brochures.

Mockingbird Theatre: interview with David Alford.

Metropolitan Nashville Arts Commission: interviews with Tom Turk, Jane Ann McCullough, and Keel Hunt; *Arts & the Economy 2001, 2002*, published by Metropolitan Nashville Arts Commission; grant history of MNAC; the MNAC's purpose is set forth in Metropolitan Code Section 2.112.030; *The Arts in Nashville*, Oct. 1994, Oct. 1998; *Nashville Arts Alert!* March 3, 2003; rules and regulations of the MNAC.

Nashville and the Arts, 1969: *Nashville and the Arts*, by Bolt, Beranek and Newman (1969), 143, 168, 170, found in the Nashville Room, Nashville Public Library.

Performing Arts in Metro's Public Schools: Hancock, "A History of Music Education in Nashville and Davidson County Public Schools (1873–1975)," i, 27, 33 n. 15, 60, 90; *Nashville True Whig*, June 21, 23, 1855; *Banner*, Jan. 18, 1908; *Tennessean*, Feb. 15, 2003: editorial; Metro Schools: http://www.mnps.org; interview with Carol Crittenden; U.S. Census 2000 for population and literacy; University of Virginia Geospatial and Statistical Data Center. *United States Historical Census Data Browser*. Online. 1998. University of Virginia. Available: http://fisher.lib.virginia.edu/census/. (26 May 2003).

Vanderbilt University: interviews with Gordon Gee, Bill Ivey, and Mike Curb.

Belmont University: interviews with Dr. Bob Fisher and Mike Curb.

Musical Training at Ward-Belmont Conservatory: 1890–91 Belmont College Announcement and Prospectus, 3; details of Hesselbergs: *Baker's Biographical Dictionary of Musicians*, 8th ed., revised by Nicholas Slonimsky (New York: Schirmer Books, 1992), 767; 1908–9 Catalog of Belmont College School of Music, 8–9; Helen Gahagan Douglas, *A Full Life* (Garden City, New York: Doubleday, 1982), 82; *American National Biography*, vol. 6 (New York: Oxford University Press, 1999); Phillips, *Who's Who in Music*: Ward-Belmont Conservatory of Music staff credentials; Belmont and Ward-Belmont catalogs: 1929–30 catalog for Urso and Throne, 31–32.

A Time for Greatness: interviews with Alan Valentine, Denny Bottorff, David Schwarz, Paul Scarbrough, Josh Dachs, Kenneth Schermerhorn, Gordon Gee, Bill Purcell, Michael Buckland, Steve Turner, Joyce Searcy, Kevin Lavender, Bobby Taylor, and Kyle Young; *Times Union*,

Albany, New York, March 2, 2003; http://www.seattle symphony.org.

The Site for Schermerhorn Symphony Center: interviews with Rick Bernhardt and Assistant Fire Chief Wayne Vick; James Summerville, "The City and the Slum: 'Black Bottom' in the Development of South Nashville," *THQ* (summer 1981): 182–92; *Banner,* Oct. 5, 6, 1896: Bryan speeches; Johnson, *The Parks of Nashville,* 74: *Banner,* July 29, 1905: Will Allen Dromgoole; *Banner,* Nov. 7, 1910: Central Park, south; *Tennessean,* May 13, 1913: parkway through the Bottom.

Next Steps on the Journey: David McCullough, *John Adams* (New York: Simon and Schuster, 2001), 260: end of May 1781; *Washington Post,* Dec. 29, 2002, posted at http://www.kennedy-center.org/about/kaiserhowtosave. html; *Tennessean,* March 16, 2003: Tennessee Arts Commission and Bredesen; "Nashville Professional Theatre Consortium Position Paper: An Overview and Action Plan for Nashville, 2003," cited with permission of the Nashville Professional Theatre Consortium; interviews with Mark Wait, Jane Fabian, and Ben Rechter.

Captions
Charlotte Cushman: *Nashville Union and American,* April 2, 1858.

Adelina Patti: Robinson, *Banner,* April 12, 1936; *Banner,* Feb. 2, 1904, "Queen of Song" at the Tabernacle; Waller, *Nashville in the 1890s,* chronology.

Edwin Booth: *Daily American,* Feb. 26, 29, 1876; *Edwin Booth* (Freeport, N.Y.: Books for Libraries Press, 1970), 45–46, letter from Nashville, Feb. 27, 1876.

Annie Pixley: *Daily American,* Feb. 5, 1880.

Christine Nilsson: *Daily American,* Jan. 19, 1883.

Emma Abbott: *Life and Professional Career of Emma Abbott,* 1891.

Lawrence Barrett: *Daily American,* Jan. 23, 24, 25, 1888.

August Schemmel: *Chat,* March 2, 1895.

Lillian Lewis: *Chat,* Dec. 29, 1894.

Lily Langtry: *Chat,* Feb. 6, 1895, appearance; Robinson, *Banner,* April 12, 1936.

Pi Kappa Alpha and Bellstedt: http://www.angel fire.com/music2/thecornetcompendium/well-known_ soloists_1.html; *Daily Sun* (Nashville), May 1, 1897.

Joseph Jefferson: *Banner,* June 22, 1930: "Nashville's Old Vendome Flourished in Golden Age"; Waller, *Nashville in the 1890s,* 112.

Maude Adams: *Tennessean,* Nov. 22, 1907.

Tallulah Bankhead: *Banner,* April 29, 30, 1937; *Tennessean,* Jan. 15, 18, 1950; FRC.

E. A. and E. H. Sothern: *Daily American,* Dec. 19, 1876.

SELECTED RESOURCES

Note: to compute the difference between dollars from previous years and 2004 dollars, the calculator is based on Handbook of Labor Statistics, U.S. Department of Labor, and Bureau of Labor Statistics. It is available at the Web site of the Federal Reserve Bank of Minneapolis: http://minneapolisfed.org/economy/calc/hist1800.html. The figures for current dollars are estimates only.

BOOKS

Clayton, W. W. *History of Davidson County, Tennessee.* Nashville: Charles Elder, 1971.

Crabb, Alfred Leland. *Nashville: Personality of a City.* New York: Bobbs-Merrill, 1960.

Crew, H. W. *History of Nashville, Tenn.* Ed. J. Wooldridge. Nashville: Publishing House of the Methodist Episcopal Church, South, 1890.

Davenport, F. Garvin. *Cultural Life in Nashville: On the Eve of the Civil War.* Chapel Hill: University of North Carolina Press, 1941.

McRaven, Henry. *Nashville: Athens of the South.* Chapel Hill, N.C.: Published for the Tennessee Book Co. by Scheer & Jervis, 1949.

Smith, Lewis Maiden. *Highlights of the Nashville Theater, 1876–1890.* New York: Vantage Press, 1979.

Tennessee Encyclopedia of History and Culture. Ed. Carroll Van West. Nashville: Tennessee Historical Society/ Rutledge Hill Press, 1998.

Thomas, Jane. *Old Days in Nashville.* Nashville: Charles Elder, 196–(?).

Waller, William. *Nashville in the 1890s.* Nashville: Vanderbilt University Press, 1970.

————. *Nashville, 1900–1910.* Nashville: Vanderbilt University Press, 1972.

Ward, Andrew. *Dark Midnight When I Rise: The Story of the Fisk Jubilee Singers.* New York: Farrar, Straus and Giroux, 2000.

WPA Project. *Tennessee: A Guide to the State.* New York: Viking Press, 1939.

SPECIAL COLLECTIONS

Naff Collection of photographs, programs, and more from Lula C. Naff's days at the Ryman Auditorium, Nashville Room, Nashville Public Library.

Francis Robinson Collection of Theatre, Music, and Dance, Special Collections, Vanderbilt University.

Special Collections, Fisk University Library.

Special Collections, Belmont University.

ARTICLES

Robinson, Francis. "Theater's Great Visited Nashville in 130 Seasons of Successful Performances." *Banner*, April 12, 1936.

Rose, Kenneth. "A Nashville Musical Decade, 1830–1840." *Tennessee Historical Quarterly* 2 (1943): 216–31. (The Tennessee State Library and Archives houses an extensive collection of sheet music and other materials related to music in the Kenneth Rose Collection.)

Wiggers, Alvin. "Forty Years of Grand Opera in Nashville." *Tennessean*, Dec. 16, 1934.

THESES

Arnold, Claude Ahmed. "The Development of the Stage in Nashville, Tennessee, 1807–1870." Thesis, State University of Iowa, 1933.

Crain, Charles Robert. "Music Performance and Pedagogy in Nashville, Tennessee, 1818–1900." Thesis, George Peabody College, 1975.

Holden, Alyce K. "Secular Music in Nashville, 1800–1900." Thesis, Fisk University, 1940.

PHOTO ACKNOWLEDGMENTS

Many thanks to the following groups and individuals for their gracious permission to use photos or illustrations in this work.

Banner, March 29, 1893: page 71.

Belmont University: pages 275, 276.

Harry Butler, Nashville: pages 99 (*bottom*), 245, 251, 252, 258.

Chat, March 2, 1895: page 74.

Fisk University: page 57; Special Collections: pages 46, 50, 51, 53, 55, 152.

David Grapes: pages 30, 44, 64 (*upper left; lower left and right*), 67 (*right*), 68, 69, 70, 103, 134.

Joe Hardwick: page xii.

D. B. Kellogg: page 72.

Joan Marcus: page 209 (*top*).

Sadie Martin, *The Life and Professional Career of Emma Abbott* (Minneapolis: L. Kimball Printing Co., 1891), page 62.

Metropolitan Government of Nashville and Davidson County: page 194.

Middleton Place Foundation, Charleston, South Carolina: page 10.

Nashville Association of Musicians, Local 257: page 123.

Nashville Ballet: pages 234; 236, 237, 238, and 239 (all by Marianne Leach).

Nashville Opera: pages 219; 223 (*both photos*); 224 and 226 (Marianne Leach).

Nashville Public Library, the Nashville Room: pages 66, 107, 109, 121, 136, 139, 143 (*top*), 145, 149.

Nashville Symphony Archives: pages 170, 178, 181 (*lower right; lower left*).

Naxos: page 257.

Wesley Paine: 99 (*top left*).

Parthenon, Nashville: pages 118, 119.

Herb Peck Collection: pages 33, 43.

Princely Players: page 207.

W. O. Smith School: page 185.

Earl Swensson Associates: page 283; back cover (artwork provided by Earl Swensson Associates; design by David M. Schwarz/Architectural Services, Inc.).

Tennessean: pages 169, 171 (Charles Cowden), 179, 181 (*top*), 211 (photo by Bill Steber, © February 17, 2002, reprinted by permission). All are copyrighted by the *Tennessean*.

Tennessee Performing Arts Center: pages xxii, xxvii, xxix, 209 (*left*), 212 (*all photos*).

Tennessee Repertory Theatre: pages 216, 217, 218.

Tennessee State Library and Archives: pages 6, 7, 18, 19, 37, 40, 60, 64 (*upper right*), 67 (*left*), 76, 79, 80, 81, 82.

Tennessee State Museum Collection: facing page 1, pages 35, 38.

Tennessee State University, Special Collections: page 161 (*both photos*).

Vanderbilt University: 271, 272, 273 (Daniel Dubois); Francis Robinson Collection, Special Collections: pages 111, 113 (Brown Brothers), 143 (*bottom*), 157 (Ken Howard), 229; Lark Taylor Collection, Special Collections: pages 133 (Covell Studio), 232 (Claude Harris, London); Blair School of Music: pages 99 (*top right;* Neal Brake), 166, 198, 200, 202 (Neal Brake).

Ridley Wills II: pages 95, 110, 144.

Numbers in **bold** indicate photos.